kiva, cross, and crown

12/16/87

KIVA, CROSS, and CROWN

the pecos indians
and
new mexico
1540-1840

john l. kessell

university of new mexico press
albuquerque

Library of Congress Cataloging-in-Publication Data
Kessell, John L.
    Kiva, cross, and crown.

    Originally published: Washington: National Park Service, U.S.
Dept. of Interior, 1979.
    Bibliography: p.
    Includes index.
    1. Pecos National Monument (N.M.)—History.
2. New Mexico—History—To 1848.   I. Title.
E99.P34K47   1987   978.9'55   87-6050
ISBN 0-8263-0968-2 (pbk.)

Cover: The three panels of the cover design symbolize the story of
    Pecos.

    At the top is Spain's royal coat of arms after a rendering by
    Pecos Alcalde mayor Bernardo De Miera y Pacheco. In the
    center stands a Pecos "captain" portrayed on pottery from the
    period of first contact between Spaniard and Pecos. And be-
    neath, the crossed arms of Christ and St. Francis personify two
    centuries of Franciscan presence at the pueblo.

contents

preface to second edition

Picture a busy, medium-sized man in starched shirt, bow tie, and dark suit. His firm mouth turns down at the corners. The natty derby hides his receding hairline. He is forty. Unsuited for management, worried that the Peabody Museum's refusal to publish any more of his endless footnotes has jeopardized a second career, he has to prove himself.

At Pecos, finally in the field—deliriously absorbed in collecting sherds, obsidian chips, and beetles, disapproving of amateurs who carried off specimens and littered the site with Anheuser-Busch beer bottles, pacing off crumbled walls, clambering up sandy-sided arroyos, noting fascinating bits the locals told him— between August 28 and September 6, 1880, Adolph Francis Alphonse Bandelier resolved his mid-life crisis. "I am dirty, ragged & sunburnt," he crowed, "but of best cheer. My life's work has at last begun."

For over a century now, scholars of every stripe have visited and written about Pecos, and for some of them the experience has been intensely personal. It was for Alfred Vincent Kidder, who embarked in 1915 on those ten heady field sessions at Pecos that revolutionized New World archaeology. Later, after a quarter-century among the Maya, Kidder returned to thinking and writing about Pecos, "a keenly nostalgic experience," as he put it. Lamenting that he had not devoted more study to the people who made the pots, he offered some astute observations. He dismissed Comanche hostility as the ultimate Pecos curse, and suggested, along with disease and emigration, "some inner defect." "Were internal rifts partly to blame?" He loved the story about Agustín Guichí impersonating the bishop. "I only wish," he wrote in the 1950s from Cambridge, Massachusetts, "I could return to that wonderful country," Eventually he did. A. V. and Madeleine Kidder are buried at Pecos, on a gentle hillside dotted by pinyon and juniper, not far from where the field shack stood.

The works of Bandelier and Kidder and of not a few others, bearing on Pecos and the Pueblo world, are listed in the bibliography of this book. Several more recent studies deserve mention. Two by Carroll L. Riley—"Pecos and Trade," in *Across the Chichimec Sea,* ed. Riley and Basil C. Hedrick (Carbondale, Southern Illinois University Press, 1978), and *The Frontier People: The Greater Southwest in the Protohistoric Period* (Albuquerque, University of New Mexico Press, 1987)—place Pecos, that teeming, frontier trade depot, processing plant, and redistribution center, in the broader "group of autonomous but interlocking regions" invaded by the Spaniards in 1540.

Historian Joe S. Sando, in his intimate *Nee Hemish: A History of Jemez Pueblo* (Albuquerque, University of New Mexico Press, 1982), picks up the Pecos story at the other end, in 1838, when the sad remnant (he lists twenty-one persons by name) abandoned their crumbling home at the eastern gateway and moved to Jemez. A native of Jemez, he questions the assumption that the refugees chose that pueblo because of linguistic similarity. Whatever the reason, today, says Sando, "Toya and Pecos are the only surnames at Jemez that signify Pecos ancestry, although most people at Jemez have equal amounts of Pecos blood." Of the Pecos and Jemez, and of the peoples they knew, there is much in the monumental *Handbook of North American Indians,* vols. 9 and 10, *Southwest,* ed. Alfonso Ortiz (Washington, Smithsonian Institution, 1979 and 1983).

Although the people and their land had parted company, it was never so simple. The intricacies of tradition and law continued to bind the Pecos, local Hispanos, and subsequent "owners" in a web of conflicting interests, the subject of G. Emlen Hall's exemplary case study *Four Leagues of Pecos: A Legal History of the Pecos Grant, 1800–1933* (Albuquerque, University of New Mexico Press, 1984). David J. Weber, in *The Mexican Frontier, 1821–1846: The American Southwest Under Mexico* (Albuquerque, University of New Mexico Press, 1982), describes the world beyond at this critical time for Pecos.

With a tip of his hat to Immanuel Wallerstein and Fernand Braudel, Timothy G. Baugh, "Southern Plains Societies and Eastern Frontier Pueblo Exchange during the Protohistoric Period," *Papers of the Archaeological Society of New Mexico,* vol. 9 (1984), proposes a Southern Plains macroeconomy with nucleus (Pecos and other eastern frontier pueblos), periphery (the Plains Apaches), and semiperiphery (the Plains Caddoan-speakers, or Teyas).

Since the summer of 1984, visitors to Pecos National Monument have been introduced to the Pecos story in a new visitors' center, long anticipated and at last hastened by the generosity of Mr. and Mrs. E. E. Fogelson whose Forked Lightning Ranch surrounds the monument. The handsome, low-profile, adobe structure, tucked unobtrusively behind the hill and unseen from the ruins, houses a fully bilingual museum. Not only are signs, exhibit texts, and talks by the staff offered in English and Spanish, but also the short documentary movie, narrated on one sound track by famed actress Greer Garson (Mrs. Fogelson) and on another by famed actor Ricardo Montalban.

I am gratified that the University of New Mexico Press has seen fit to reprint *Kiva, Cross, and Crown*. This is not a revision. Some of the typographical errors, misspelled words, and misplaced punctuation, as well as a few minor slips, have been fixed. I have not, however, brought Juan de Oñate's wife back to life on page 68 (we know now that she did not die for another quarter-century). Nor have I altered the year of the undated mission census cited on pages 169, 170, 176, and 489 (evidently 1656 instead of ca. 1641), or renamed the destructively resourceful Mr. Kozlowski on page 474 (Martin, not Andrew as Bandelier had it).

Since the book first appeared, I have taken some well-deserved teasing about the alliterative title. "So, what's a kiva?" asked a friend in Glendale, California. Good point. Beyond New Mexico and Arizona, one should not presume familiarity with a generic term for Pueblo Indian ceremonial chambers. The title came, I confess, after the exchange of some very bad alternatives with National Park Service editors, when, in a postscript, I conjured up the letterhead of Kiva & Crown, Ltd., Importers of Fine East Indian Chutney.

Were I to write this book today, I would probably do it differently. I might look more perceptively for structure, for connections, crises, patterns, and systems. Still, at the time, the narrative approach seemed right for the subject and right for me. To have followed Adolph Bandelier and A. V. Kidder, and so many others, to Pecos was my eminent good fortune.

John L. Kessell
July 1986

pReface

The ruins of Cicúique are still to be seen at the site where
[Hernando de] Alvarado visited it, close by the modern town of
Pecos. This is one of the most historic spots in the Southwest, for
in every era since it was first seen by Alvarado as the guest of
Bigotes, it has occupied a distinctive position in all the major
developments of the region. It was the gateway for Pueblo Indians
when they went buffalo hunting on the Plains; a two-way pass for
barter and war between Pueblos and Plains tribes; a portal through
the mountains for Spanish explorers, traders, and buffalo hunters;
for the St. Louis caravan traders with Santa Fe; for pioneer Anglo-
American settlers; for Spanish and Saxon Indian fighters; for Civil
War armies; and for a transcontinental railroad passing through
the Southwest. Pecos deserves an historian.

Herbert E. Bolton, *Coronado,*
Knight of Pueblos and Plains, 1949

Another project definitely planned was a study of the documentary history of Pecos and other Rio Grande Pueblos. This,
most unfortunately, was never done.

Alfred Vincent Kidder, *Pecos, New Mexico,* 1958

So wrote Bolton and Kidder, the twin war gods of Southwestern history and archaeology. Although neither of them produced such a study himself, they were agreed. Pecos, that evoca-
tive "mess of ruins" twenty-five miles southeast of Santa Fe,
was worthy.

Here then is a beginning, a historical documentary of the
eastern fortress-pueblo from earliest Spanish contact in 1540, to
abandonment three hundred years later. It is largely narrative,
written in the active rather than the passive, largely biographi-
cal, concerned more with people than with inert phenomena. I

have tried throughout to let the juices flow, the stuff of life that wells up in the documents, convinced that we historians too often squeeze them out in the interest of neat and dry, methodical monographs.

I have made every effort to get to the documents. In no case have I cited in the notes an archival source without having seen the Spanish myself, whether the original, a photographic copy, or a transcript. Such an approach would have been hopeless without the previous researches of France V. Scholes, Eleanor B. Adams, Fray Angelico Chavez, and a score of others who charted pertinent islands in the oceans of material. I have rechecked and revised others' translations—not because I mistrusted George P. Hammond and Agapito Rey, or Charles Wilson Hackett and Charmion Clair Shelby, or Alfred Barnaby Thomas—but rather because my closeness to Pecos gave me the advantage of historical continuity. Knowing from other sources, for example, that the Pecos had built a low, mud-plastered rock wall around the entire perimeter of their building site was reason enough to question the sudden appearance of a "stockade," even though that, in another context, might have been an accurate rendering of the Spanish word.

I have seasoned the text with quotations, with the words of eyewitnesses and participants, of protagonists and antagonists, recognizing at the same time that the Pecos Indians themselves, when they are allowed to speak at all, do so only in a foreign tongue. In that sense, the story is one-sided. Forewarned by anthropologists that the Pecos of 1540 or 1740 were likely very different from their linguistic cousins, or even their own descendants who live at Jémez pueblo today, I have attempted no reconstruction of Pecos social organization. For those who would do so, blending the data of artifacts and the written record full citation of sources will be found in the notes.

There are scenes that would delight a scriptwriter: the entrance of Alvarado in 1540, bold but wary, as two thousand Pecos watch from the rooftops; Gov. Diego de Peñalosa's vain bullying of the Franciscan superior he had come to arrest in the mission cloister one dark night in 1663; the devil-may-care, three-day burlesque of a bishop's visitation by a Pecos carpenter in 1760; and the solemn harangues of Comanche warriors gathered at the Pecos peace conference of 1786 to embrace Juan Bautista de Anza, to smoke, and to barter.

There are themes, too, that run through the story from beginning to end. None is more persistent than factionalism, the fatal flaw that festered to a head in 1696, when Felipe Chistoe, one Pecos, delivered to Diego de Vargas the severed head, hand, and foot of young Caripicado, another Pecos. Still, despite the unrelenting decline in population and the violent rift that made them their own worst enemies, the Pecos people never did succumb to cultural submergence. The Pecos bull still cavorts at Jémez.

This book is dedicated to Eleanor B. Adams, generous scholar and kind friend who first pointed out to me the historic trail to Pecos. I am much indebted to Em Hall of present-day Pecos for relating to me the story of the pueblo land grant from the time John Ward peddled it in 1872 to date. His lively study of the subject will soon be published.

Jerry L. Livingston drew many of the illustrations and the maps, and Gary G. Lister took many of the photographs. Together they restored the 1758 Miera map. To them, and to a score of others in the National Park Service, my wholehearted thanks for the opportunity to tell the Pecos story. It has been good fun.

John L. Kessell

February 1977

chapter 1

the invaders
1540-1542

Hernando de Alvarado states . . . that he came to New Spain nineteen years ago [in 1530] with the Marqués del Valle [Hernán Cortés] and that he has spent these years in the service of His Majesty in the first discovery of the South Sea, on the expedition that the marqués made, and on the expedition to Cíbola. Under the command of the general [Francisco Vázquez de Coronado] he discovered and conquered more than two hundred leagues in advance, where he discovered the buffalo. On all these expeditions he served with the rank of captain at his own cost, providing many horses and servants without receiving pay from His Majesty or any other person. He has not been remunerated and as a result lives in poverty.

Statement of Hernando de Alvarado, c. 1549

QUIVIRA

Hopi Pueblos

Río Colorado

Río Napestle (Arkansas R.)

Zuñi Pueblos

Tiguex Pueblos
Ácoma

•Taos
•Pecos

Río Gila

Río

Río Grande del Norte

Río Pecos

Río Sonora

Casas Grandes

Río Yaqui

Río

Río Mayo

Río Conchos

NUEVA VIZCAYA

NUEVO LEÓN

Río Grande

Río Fuerte

•Santa Bárbara   Almadén•

Río Sinaloa

Indé•

Culiacán•

Río Nazas

Saltillo•

Cuencamé•
•Avino
•Durango
•Nombre de Dios

NUEVA GALICIA

Zacatecas•

Northern New Spain

•Compostela

Guadalajara•

Río Pánuco

Not to Scale

Mexico City•   •Veracruz•

It was early fall, the time when the maize plants begin turning brown, 1540. Twenty-two summers had passed since the conqueror Hernán Cortés first stepped ashore on the mainland of Mexico, to trade, he said. Now, eighteen hundred miles northwest of that dank tropical coast, a small column of helmeted Spanish soldiers marched across high, semi-arid country through arroyos, chamisa, and piñon to receive homage from the fortress-pueblo of Cicuye.

Even though they numbered not many more than twenty, this medieval-looking detachment from the expedition of Gov. Francisco Vázquez de Coronado faithfully represented the conquering forces of Catholic Spain in America. The youthful captain, who wore a coat of mail and rode a horse covered with leather or quilted cotton armor, hailed his earthly Holy Caesarean Catholic Majesty in the same breath as his Heavenly Father. Having marveled firsthand at the incredible fruits of Cortés' success, he had willingly financed himself and his retainers for this venture of discovery. Several of the other horsemen had outfitted themselves and brought along black slaves. Behind them on foot marched four paid crossbowmen. Also on foot, in emulation of St. Francis, walked a gray-robed Spanish friar, a rigorous and visionary priest bent on conquest to the glory of God and the church militant.[1]

Capt. Hernando de Alvarado, from the northern mountain province of Santander, was probably light skinned with sandy hair and beard. In 1530, at age thirteen, he had crossed the Atlantic in the grand fleet that returned Cortés to México. He had served the conqueror, as he phrased it, "in the first discovery of the South Sea." Later, in the excitement of sensational reports from the far north, the well-born twenty-three-year-old Alvarado had signed on with Coronado as captain of artillery. During the battle for the Zuñi pueblo of Hawikuh, he and García López de Cárdenas shielded the fallen Coronado with their bodies and thereby saved the general's life. At least one chronicler later claimed that young don Hernando was kin to the more famous Pedro de Alvarado, hell-bent conquistador of Guatemala.[2]

At Alvarado's side rode Melchor Pérez. His father, Licenciado Diego Pérez de la Torre, had succeeded the notorious Nuño Beltrán de Guzmán as governor of Nueva Galicia. When the elder Pérez died in an Indian revolt, the viceroy appointed Coronado to the vacant governorship. The Pérez clan was from the villa of Feria in southern Extremadura just off the highroad between Zafra and Badajoz. Don Melchor had gambled a small fortune fitting out himself and his servants, more than two thousand gold castellanos, he calculated.[3]

Juan Troyano, from the market town of Medina de Río Seco, northwest of Valladolid, had fought as a youth in the armies of Emperor Charles V in Italy. He had come to New

First contact.
After Códice
Florentino, central
Mexico, 16th century

Spain in the fleet that brought over Coronado and his patron, don Antonio de Mendoza, first viceroy of New Spain and heaviest financial backer of the expedition. Evidently Troyano possessed a flair for languages. He had already begun picking up phrases in various Indian tongues. He also, now or later, picked up an Indian girl, not unusual for a Spanish soldier. But Troyano refused to give her up, married her, and spent the rest of his life with her.[4]

After Lienzo de Tlaxcala, central Mexico, 16th century

Unlike Troyano, Fray Juan de Padilla was profoundly disappointed in the Pueblo Indians, in all Indians for that matter. This belligerent Franciscan had joined Coronado for only one reason. He would, by the grace of God, find and reunite with Christendom the long-lost Seven Cities of Antillia. According to a popular romance of the time, seven Portuguese bishops fleeing the Moslem invasion of their homeland had embarked their congregations in the year 714 and sailed off to the west. They had founded seven immensely wealthy and utopian cities—cities that lay, Father Padilla was convinced, somewhere north from Mexico. Visits to both the Zuñi and Hopi pueblos had shattered his illusions that Cíbola or Tusayán might end his quest. Perhaps to the east, far to the east of Cicuye in the land of Quivira.

A son of the Franciscan province of Andalucía in southern Spain, Father Padilla likely had been among the twenty friars shepherded to Mexico in 1529 by Fray Antonio de Ciudad Rodrigo, one of New Spain's revered original twelve. Padilla turned out to be a fighter as well as a visionary. He had joined earnestly in the war of Franciscan Bishop Juan de Zumárraga against the tyrannical first *audiencia* of Mexico, the ruling tribunal dominated by Nuño de Guzmán. He had taken part in the ill-starred venture of Cortés to build ships at Tehuantepec for exploration of the South Sea. He was quick-tempered, obstinate, impatient, and as the soldiers found out, a holy terror when aroused by swearing or alleged immorality.[5]

After Códice Azcatitlán, central Mexico, 16th century

Alvarado, Pérez, Troyano, and Padilla—these then, along with a handful of unnamed horsemen, crossbowmen, and servants, were soon to become the European discoverers of the populous stone pueblo of Cicuye.

Although most of the chroniclers of the Coronado expedition used variant spellings—Acuique, Cicúique, Cicuic—this word as spoken by the initial delegation from there, which sounded to Spanish ears like Cicuye, was probably the natives' own name for their pueblo. The people of Jémez, the only other Towa-speakers among the Pueblos, called Cicuye something

The Names Cicuye and Pecos

After Códice Florentino, central Mexico, 16th century

like Paqulah or Pekush. That evidently became Peago, Peaku, or Peko among the Keres in between. From them, the Spaniards of don Gaspar Castaño de Sosa heard it forty years later. Hence the historic name Pecos.[6]

Nuño de Guzmán sets out to conquer Nueva Galicia, 1529. After Códice Telleriano Remensis, central Mexico, 16th century

Cicuye was expecting them. Located as it was at the portal between pueblos and plains, the community had served for a century as a center of trade. Along with shells, buffalo robes, slaves, chipped stone knives, and parrots came news. The people of Cicuye must have learned of the Spanish presence along the gulf coast, of the Aztecs' fall, and of Nuño de Guzmán's rapacious forays up the west coast corridor soon after these events took place. They surely had heard reports of the itinerant white medicine man and his black spokesman—Álvar Núñez Cabeza de Vaca and Estebanico—as they and two

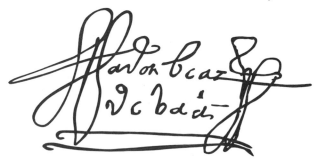

Álvar Núñez Cabeza de Vaca

companions made their tedious way from coast to coast across the whole of northern Mexico. The black had come north

again swaggering. He had made demands on the Zuñis, and they had killed him. Cicuye knew the details. [7]

Next, Spaniards with their awesome horses and firearms had appeared before Hawikuh and defeated the Zuñis, less than two hundred miles away. The headmen of Cicuye must have met in council. Should they stand against the invader or ally themselves with him for purposes of trade or war? It was a basic question that would later turn clan against clan and rend the social fabric of the pueblo. Initially, Cicuye sent a mission of peace.

At Hawikuh, Coronado had received them as foreign emissaries. They told the general that they had learned of the arrival of "strange people," in Coronado's words, "bold men who punished those who resisted them and gave good treatment to those who submitted." The inhabitants of Cicuye wished to be allies. Their spokesman, a large, well-built young man, evidently a war captain, was dubbed by the invaders Bigotes because, according to chronicler Pedro de Castañeda, he wore long mustaches. Such a display of individuality was unusual for a Pueblo Indian. Probably Bigotes was a trader, well traveled, experienced, and somewhat affected by his dealings with foreigners. He may even have spoken some Nahuatl, the lingua franca of central Mexico, which would have been readily understood in the Spanish camp. [8]

The embassy from Cicuye exchanged gifts with Coronado: buffalo robes, native shields, and headdresses, for artificial pearls, glass vessels of some sort, and little bells. The Spaniards were particularly intrigued by the large hides covered with tangled and woolly hair. The men of Cicuye described the

Zuñi pueblo, successor to Halona, one of the six Zuñi "cities" of Coronado's time. Photographed during the Shalako ceremonial, November 20, 1896, by Ben Wittick. Museum of New Mexico

Coronado Meets Bigotes

After Códice Florentino, central Mexico, 16th century

buffalo as best they could. They pointed to a painting on the body of a Plains Indian lad in their party, from which the Spaniards deduced that the animals were big cattle. To receive formal homage from Cicuye and to see these cattle, Coronado appointed the ready Captain Alvarado.

On the feast of the beheading of St. John the Baptist, August 29, 1540, Alvarado's squad had moved out from Zuñi, led by Bigotes and company. They had "discovered" invincible Ácoma set on a rock twice as tall as the Giralda of Sevilla, then proceeded east to the cultivated valley of the Rio Grande, which they christened the Río de Nuestra Señora because they saw it first on September 7, eve of the Nativity of the Blessed Virgin. They passed through the cluster of pueblos they called the province of Tiguex, and apparently traveled as far north as Taos, which Father Padilla thought might have had a population of fifteen thousand! Now in late September or early October, the first Europeans approached Cicuye.[9]

A Spaniard's Description of Cicuye

For an Indian pueblo, all agreed, it was impressive. "Cicuye," wrote chronicler Pedro de Castañeda,

is a pueblo of as many as five hundred warriors. It is feared throughout that land. In plan it is square, founded on a rock. In the center is a great patio or plaza with its kivas (*estufas*). The houses are all alike, of four stories. One can walk above over the entire pueblo without there being a street to prevent it. At the first two levels it is completely rimmed by corridors on which one can walk over the entire pueblo. They are like balconies which project out, and beneath them one can take shelter.

The houses have no doors at ground level. To climb to the corridors inside the pueblo they use ladders which can be drawn up; in this way they have access to the rooms. Since the doors of the houses open on the corridor on that floor the corridor serves as street. The houses facing open country are back to back with those inside the patio, and in time of war they are entered through the inside ones. The pueblo is surrounded by a low stone wall. Inside there is a spring from which they can draw water.

The people of this pueblo pride themselves that no one has been able to subdue them, while they subdue what pueblos they will.[10]

Southwest corner of Pecos plaza. Artist's restoration by S. P. Moorehead. Kidder, *Pecos, New Mexico*

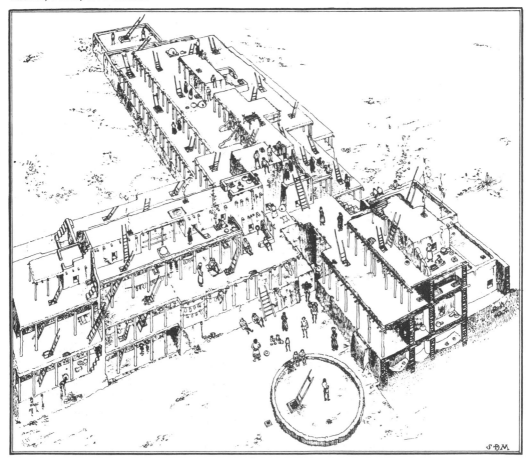

Bird forms from Forked Lightning-Pecos black-on-white pottery.
After Kidder, *Pottery,* I

Origin of Cicuye

Ever since at least the thirteenth century by Christian reckoning, the upper Pecos River Valley had been a frontier of the Pueblo Indian civilization that flowered in the cliffs and valley floors to the west. While Spaniards under the sainted Ferdinand III took the offensive against the Moors, recapturing Córdoba in 1236 and Sevilla in 1248, a sedentary, farming, pottery-making people was settling the banks of the Pecos. This cultural and human migration came mainly from the area of the San Juan drainage. It seems also to have absorbed increments from the plains to the east. Geographically, the upper Pecos lay between; culturally, it owed more to pueblos than to plains.

The immigrants had lived at first in haphazard collections of rectangular rooms built mostly of coursed adobe mud, easily added to or abandoned as need arose, sometimes more or less linear, sometimes enclosing small patios, "straggling affairs on flat land open to attack from any direction, sites chosen with no eye to defense." One such town, known to archaeologists as the Forked Lightning Ruin, lay on the west bank of the Arroyo del Pueblo, or Galisteo Creek, just half a mile below the site of the future Cicuye and a little over a mile above the arroyo's confluence with the Pecos. Its time of maximum occupancy, during which it must have housed hundreds of people, had run from about 1225 A.D. to 1300, when nomads from the plains, or other Pueblos, began sporadic raiding.

Forced for the first time to think in terms of defense, the people of Forked Lightning had made an orderly exodus up the arroyo and crossed over to where a steep-sided, flat-topped ridge afforded them an unobstructed view all round. To the north loomed the great gray-green mountains in whose ponderosa vastness the river rose. Clear and cold but shallow, really no more than "a small perennial stream," it flowed by their ridge a mile to the east. The valley here, four or five miles wide, was contained toward the sunrise by the gentler foothills of the

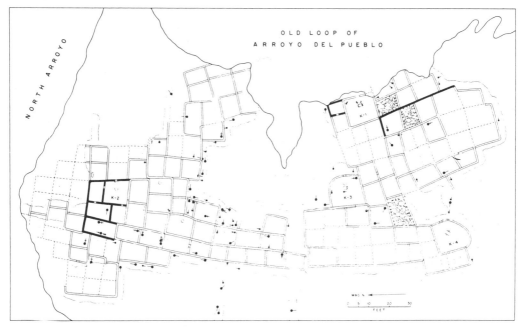

A. V. Kidder's excavations of the Forked Lightning Ruin, 1926–1929. Black walls are masonry, all others coursed earth; skeletons (flexed) shown as oriented, cross-lined buried above floor level, others below or in open.   Kidder, *Pecos, New Mexico*

Tecolote Range and toward the sunset by the towering reddish cliffs of Glorieta Mesa. Here, too, scattered piñon and juniper trees, chamisa bushes and cholla cactus gave way to open spaces of tall native grasses. If one followed the river southeastward around the end of the Tecolote foothills, he soon looked out upon the ocean-like expanse of the true plains.

For about a century and a half, from roughly 1300 to 1450, generations of the Forked Lightning people and others who joined them on their long narrow ridge, or *mesilla* (literally, little mesa), had moved about from one spot to another, building new clusters of one-storied dwellings rather than repairing the old ones. Because there was an abundance of sandstone at hand, they had become masons, laying up walls of "stones embedded between cushions of mud." Curiously, their earliest work was their best. Examining examples of later buildings, pioneer archaeologist Adolph Bandelier concluded that it was no better than "judicious piling," and sometimes worse.

Presumably because of pressure from enemies, everyone in the valley had gathered on the mesilla by about 1400. Around 1450, a year before Isabella of Castile was born in Spain, they had begun a monumental community project. Designed in advance and built as a unit, a single, defensible, multi-storied apartment building, it took the form of a giant rectangle around a spacious plaza. In all, it covered about two acres at the mesilla's north end. This was the fortress-pueblo of Cicuye, or Pecos.

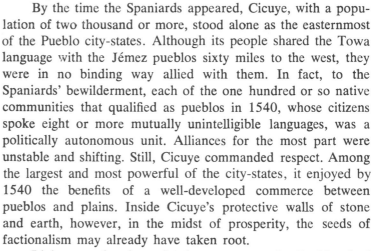

Factionalism at Cicuye

By the time the Spaniards appeared, Cicuye, with a population of two thousand or more, stood alone as the easternmost of the Pueblo city-states. Although its people shared the Towa language with the Jémez pueblos sixty miles to the west, they were in no binding way allied with them. In fact, to the Spaniards' bewilderment, each of the one hundred or so native communities that qualified as pueblos in 1540, whose citizens spoke eight or more mutually unintelligible languages, was a politically autonomous unit. Alliances for the most part were unstable and shifting. Still, Cicuye commanded respect. Among the largest and most powerful of the city-states, it enjoyed by 1540 the benefits of a well-developed commerce between pueblos and plains. Inside Cicuye's protective walls of stone and earth, however, in the midst of prosperity, the seeds of factionalism may already have taken root.

Living together in such close quarters, the Pueblos had long striven for conformity of behavior. Passive assent to the group will, suppression of individualism, and the pursuit of uniformity in all things characterized Pueblo tradition. There was no place in the rigidly controlled Pueblo community for the boastful self-assertiveness esteemed among some plains tribes. Yet at Cicuye, gateway to the plains, the danger of such "contamination" ran high. Plains Indians came regularly to trade at Cicuye. Slaves from the plains lived in the pueblo. And certain men of Cicuye, it would seem, in the interest of diplomacy and trade had become virtual plainsmen themselves, men like Bigotes.[11]

Pecos Glaze IV pottery. Kidder, *Pottery,* II

Reception of Spaniards

They all came out that day to gawk and to receive the Spaniards. "With drums and flageolets similar to fifes, of which they have many," they escorted their visitors into the pueblo. The mood was one of guarded festivity. As an offering, the Indians laid before Alvarado and his men quantities of native dry goods—cotton cloth, feather robes, and animal skins. They held out objects made of turquoise mined locally. As intently as any fortune seeker, Father Padilla studied these natives for just one ornament of gold, for some indication of trade with the rich Seven Cities he sought so passionately.

But they wore none. Their beads and pendants were of turquoise, shell, and non-precious stones. They prized eagle claws and grizzly bear teeth. Flageolets, whistles, and rasps they fashioned from bone, and jingles from shell. Despite his disappointment, the friar must have proceeded as in the other pueblos. [12]

Ever since the first twelve Franciscan apostles of New Spain had erected a great cross at Tlatelolco in 1524, members of the Order had been setting up crosses in Indian communities wherever they went. Father Padilla reported to Coronado from Tiguex that they had put up large crosses in the pueblos along the Río de Nuestra Señora. And they had "taught the natives to venerate them." Watching the Indians sprinkle sacred corn meal and tie prayer plumes to the crosses, the Spaniards assumed that they were venerating them. "They did it with such eagerness," Father Padilla observed,

that some climbed on the backs of others in order to reach the arms of the crosses to put plumes and roses [feather rosettes] on them. Others brought ladders, and while some held them others climbed up to tie strings in order to fasten the roses and feathers." [13]

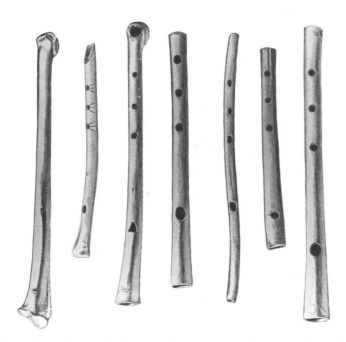

Pecos flageolets made from bird bones, up to 8″ long.
Kidder, *Artifacts*

At some point during the festivities, Alvarado was obliged to explain to assembled Cicuye what it meant to be vassals of the Spanish crown. Almost certainly he had the *requerimiento* read to them, as he had ordered it read to the Hopis. This remarkable manifesto, which had accompanied all Spanish conquerors in America since 1514, related how God the creator and lord of mankind had delegated His authority on earth to the pope, "as if to say Admirable Great Father and Governor of men," and the pope in turn had donated the Americas to Their Catholic Majesties, the kings of Spain. Therefore, Cicuye must acknowledge the sovereignty of "the Church as the ruler and superior of the whole world," the Pope, and in his name, Charles, king of Spain. They must also consent to have the Holy Catholic Faith preached to them. They would not be compelled to turn Christian unless they themselves, "when informed of the truth, should wish to be converted." If they did, there would be privileges, exemptions, and other benefits.

But should they refuse, the requerimiento continued, "we shall forcefully enter into your country and shall make war against you in all ways and manners that we can, and shall subject you to the yoke and obedience of the Church and of their highnesses." Their wives and children would be sold into slavery, their goods confiscated, and their disobedience punished with all the damage the Spaniards could inflict. "And we protest that the deaths and losses which shall accrue from this are your fault, and not that of their highnesses, or ours, or of these soldiers who come with us." [14]

If they understood any of it, which is unlikely, the people of Cicuye did not object, not initially.

The invaders stayed several days, camped outside nearby. One of them, after a look around, reported that the pueblo had "eight large patios each one with its own corridor." He must have been referring to patios on the upper levels of the house blocks, not to the great central plaza. [15] Even though made of rough sandstone and mud, some of the houses struck him as tolerably good. For the characteristic underground rooms they found in the pueblos, the Spaniards used the descriptive word *estufa,* in Spanish a heating stove, and by extension, an enclosed heated room for sweat baths. They assumed that these warm estufas with their fire pits served as quarters for the unmarried lads of the pueblo and as council rooms for the men, as baths in the Roman sense. On first contact, the invaders missed the kivas' religious function.

Pedro Cajete, a Pueblo Indian with bigotes, or mustaches. Photographed by F.A. Rinehart, 1898.   George Bird Grinnell, *The Indians of To-Day* (Chicago, 1900)

Buffalo as pictured in López de Gómara's history, 1554.

The People of Cicuye   The inhabitants of Cicuye, in the Spaniards' eyes, were no different from those of Tiguex. They looked the same. They showed the same respect for their old men, practiced the same division of labor between men and women, and raised the same crops—maize, beans, and squash—except for cotton and turkeys which they obtained in trade. They dressed the same, made similar pottery, and observed many of the same customs. As in the other pueblos, the Cicuye maidens, Castañeda noted later, "go naked until they take a husband, because the people say that if they do wrong it will soon be seen and therefore they will not do it." [16]

Alvarado and Father Padilla pressed their hosts about what lay to the east. The Indians obliged with two guides, captives from "the kingdom of Quivira" on the eastern plains. Because one of them looked to the Spaniards like a Turk, they called him El Turco. The other, known as Sopete, was the same lad who had sported the buffalo painting on his body. Despite language barriers, El Turco proved extremely apt at communicating. He soon grasped what the invaders were after.

With the loan of El Turco and Sopete, the Spanish column sallied forth from Cicuye. "After four days' march from this pueblo they came upon a land flat like the sea. On these plains," wrote an eyewitness, "is such a multitude of cattle that they are without number." Alvarado had discovered the buffalo plains. After his men had enjoyed some sport jousting with the beasts, the captain ordered an about-face. He had something more important than buffalo to report to his general.

El Turco, it seemed, under Father Padilla's withering questioning, had indicated by signs and a smattering of Nahuatl that Quivira, some days to the northeast, abounded in gold, silver, and rich textiles. This at last must be the Seven Cities. Furthermore, alleged El Turco, Bigotes of Cicuye could confirm it. Bigotes had in his possession a golden bracelet that had belonged to El Turco.

El Turco's Tales
of Quivira

Back at Cicuye, the anxious Alvarado confronted Bigotes and the elderly headman the Spaniards called Cacique. They denied that any such precious bracelet ever existed. When the two natives refused to go with him to see Coronado, the Spanish captain succeeded in getting them to his tent. There he had them put in collars and chains along with El Turco. That was too much for the people of the pueblo. "They came out to do battle, shooting arrows and reviling Hernando de Alvarado, saying that he was a man who broke his word and betrayed their friendship." Either they feared for the lives of the hostages and were trying only to bluff the invaders, or the pueblo with "as many as five hundred warriors" was badly divided, for the men of Cicuye inflicted no casualties.

The events of the next few days are jumbled in the accounts of the expedition. El Turco "escaped" twice. Both times Alvarado let Bigotes and Cacique go to retrieve him. Then, while relations between Spaniards and Cicuye seemed badly strained, the Spanish captain and his men purportedly joined forces with three hundred of the pueblo's warriors for a campaign against a people called Nanapagua. A few days later, the campaign was dropped, and the Spaniards withdrew to rejoin Coronado, taking with them Cacique, Bigotes, El Turco, and Sopete collared and chained. [17]

The first meeting of the invaders and Cicuye had ended in bad faith.

Snow had already fallen when Hernando de Alvarado reached the Tiguex pueblos with his prisoners. There he found García López de Cárdenas and an advanced detail setting up camp for the entire army. The invaders would winter among the Southern Tiwas as Alvarado and Fray Juan de Padilla had suggested, an experience none of them would ever forget.

Alvarado Takes
Captives to Tiguex

The night after Coronado arrived, Captain Alvarado reported to him with El Turco in tow. The Indian captive cooperated fully. What he related delighted the general. Across the plains to the east, he gestured,

there was a river two leagues wide where there were fish as big as horses and a great number of very large canoes with more than twenty oarsmen on each side and bearing sails. The nobility traveled in the stern seated beneath canopies and on the bow was a great eagle of gold. He said further that the lord of that land took his siesta under a large tree from which were hung numerous little bells of gold that played for him by themselves in the breeze. The common table service of everyone was wrought silver and the pitchers, plates, and bowls were of gold. . . . They believed him at the time because of the effectiveness with which he said it and because when they showed him trinkets of brass he smelled it and said that it was not gold, that he knew gold and silver very well and had little use for other metals.[18]

Visions of Riches to the East El Turco was probably describing the Mississippi where some rulers did indeed travel in ornate ceremonial barges and the garfish grew as long as horses. Father Padilla could see it all, and more. This heathen plainly had glimpsed the marvels of Antillia. To Coronado and his wearied adventurers, lodged in earth houses, El Turco's mirage must have sounded like another Mexico. But before they could see it themselves, they had to endure the pains of winter and a war against the people of Tiguex.

The invaders had simply taken over one entire pueblo, just above present-day Bernalillo. The natives had moved out grudgingly, seeking in other pueblos shelter from the biting cold. At first the Spaniards traded petty merchandise for blankets, turkeys, and maize, as the viceroy had ordered; then in dire need they resorted to forced levies. A soldier raped an Indian woman. Trying to get at the truth of the golden bracelet, someone sicced a dog on Bigotes. Even so, neither Captain Alvarado nor Father Padilla could shake the Indian's plea that El Turco was lying.

The rankled Tiwas began by stealing and killing Spanish horses. When Coronado sent captains to reprimand them, they holed up in their pueblos and shouted abuse. The invaders had no choice. They could not hope to set out for the golden land to the east with defiant Indians at their rear. Therefore the general, with the necessary if reluctant consent of the friars, resolved to wage the kind of war spelled out in the requerimiento. If the Indians refused to submit, he would show them no quarter. They refused.

After Proceso de Alvarado, central Mexico, 16th century

The first assault aborted. Inside the pueblo, called Arenal by the Spaniards, the defenders held out. Not until the attackers knocked holes in the walls and lighted smudge fires did the battle turn. Then as the choking Tiwas poured out, the Spaniards cut them down or burned them at the stake. As an object lesson, Cacique and Bigotes, leaders from the powerful Cicuye, along with El Turco and Sopete, were made to watch the Tiwas burn.

The Sieges of Arenal and Moho

The extreme penalty inflicted upon Arenal did not end the war. Fortifying several other pueblos, the unyielding Indians forced the Spaniards to maintain long winter sieges. As attack after attack failed, months passed. From early January to late March 1541, the defenders of a pueblo called Moho repulsed every onslaught and every appeal to surrender. When finally thirst forced them to flee one night in the dark, the invaders on horseback rode them down or took them captive. Another pueblo fell and was sacked. Dozens of Tiwa women and children found themselves slaves in the camp of the Spaniards, just as the requerimiento had warned.[19]

The Pueblos Divided

Coronado's rude thrust into the heartland of the pueblos upset the prevailing balance of power. While besieged Southern Tiwas fought for their lives, the Keres pueblo of Zía provided the invaders with blankets and foodstuffs and an offer of alliance. The Tiwas appealed to Cicuye, a pueblo with reason enough of its own to oppose the Spaniards. If the eastern

After Lienzo de
Tlaxcala, central
Mexico, 16th century

stronghold did send aid, it went unrecorded. On the contrary, claimed Coronado, the captives Cacique and Bigotes told him that Cicuye and the Tiwas were enemies. If the Spaniards would give them one of the Tiwa pueblos as spoils to settle and farm, the men of Cicuye would "come and help him in the war." Whether or not the two Indians really made that offer, and whatever their intent, Coronado knew that he must make his peace with their pueblo, the gateway to the east.

By all accounts, Cicuye was a power to be reckoned with. "Feared throughout that land," the eastern pueblo, because of its very location, had to maintain relations with people of both plains and pueblos. About 1525, according to Pedro de Castañeda, the fierce Teyas had tried to conquer Cicuye.

This plains people, likely Caddoan-speaking ancestors or relatives of the Wichita Indians, allegedly had destroyed some pueblos in the Galisteo Basin so thoroughly that Castañeda thought the attackers must have used war machines. They had assaulted Cicuye but failed to carry it. Now, in 1541, the Teyas were at peace with the Pueblos. "Although they receive them as friends and trade with them, at night the visitors do not stay in the pueblos but ouside under the eaves." [20]

Evidently the strength Cicuye had shown against the Teyas had brought the Tano pueblos of the Galisteo Basin under its sway. "There are along this road," wrote Castañeda, "toward the snowy mountains seven pueblos—one of them half destroyed by the above-mentioned people—which are under obedience to Cicuye."

Sometime during the course of the Tiguex war, Coronado resolved to go in person to cement an alliance with Cicuye. To show his good will, he released Cacique and escorted him home. Bigotes, "ill disposed and somewhat dishonest in his conduct," he refused to return just yet. Approaching the tiered gray-brown citadel, the personal emissary of the emperor's viceroy must have awed the natives in his suit of golden armor and his plumed helmet from which the dents of Zuñi had been hammered out. This was an occasion of state.

Coronado Seeks Aid of Cicuye

They welcomed him in their pueblo and accorded him a fine reception. He entered the pueblo accompanied only by don Lope de Urrea [a gentleman from Aragón] and Fray Juan de Padilla, although he did not stay in the pueblo overnight. They refused to grant him the favor he was asking of them, excusing themselves by saying that they were busy with their plantings, but that if he insisted they would abandon everything they were doing. As he saw that they did not volunteer willingly he did not try further to urge it on them. On the contrary, he told them he was grateful to them and that if he needed them he would let them know. [21]

In late April or early May 1541, the residents of Cicuye looked out to see Coronado's entire army encamped in the valley below: more than fifteen hundred persons counting Mexican Indian allies and Tiwa slaves—likely an exaggeration—with hundreds of horses, cattle, and sheep. Behind them the pueblos of Tiguex lay deserted. The general, against the counsel of some of his officers, had committed his whole force to the discovery of Quivira. As incentive, El Turco had embellished his description to the point "that had it been true, it would have to have been the richest thing in the Indies." [22]

En Route to Quivira

Cicuye now "rejoiced" at the restoration of Bigotes and the thought of the invaders' imminent departure for the plains. The inhabitants shared their provisions. Cacique and Bigotes gave Coronado another Quivira guide, a young lad named Xabe, who like Sopete agreed that gold and silver were to be found in his land, but not in the abundance El Turco had implied. "The army set out from Cicuye," observed Castañeda, "leaving the pueblo at peace and to all appearances content and bound to maintain friendship because their governor and captain had been restored to them." Later, hundreds of miles to the northeast, El Turco would implicate Cicuye in a plot to destroy the invaders. [23]

Francisco Vázquez de Coronado

Much as the Pueblo Indians might have wished it, the plains did not swallow up the Spaniards. Four days out the army built a bridge not far from today's Conchas Lake and crossed over the Canadian River. [24] Led on by El Turco, they came upon the buffalo, so numerous, said Coronado, that "there was not a single day until my return that I lost sight of them." They met and marveled at the Apaches called Querechos, with their portable skin tipis and dog travois, following the great, dark herds.

Some days southeast over the hauntingly flat Llano Estacado, the Spanish caravan encountered the people called Teyas. Although these tattooed and painted natives closely resembled the Querechos in appearance and style of life, at least while on the hunt, the two groups were enemies. The Teyas led the Spaniards down into a deep gorge. What they conveyed to Coronado, the abrupt change in terrain, and the expedition's southerly instead of northeasterly route finally convinced the general that El Turco was purposely leading them astray. Ordering the bulk of the army back to Tiguex, Coronado with thirty of his best mounted men, a dozen or so servants, and the pigheaded Fray Juan de Padilla struck north "by the needle" for Quivira about June 1, 1541. Sopete led the way. El Turco followed in chains.

By mid-summer the invaders beheld Quivira. They were in present-day Kansas, centuries before the first plow. The countryside appeared gloriously rich and verdant. The rivers and streams ran clear. But instead of the alabaster walls of Antillia or even a tree hung with golden bells that played in the breeze, there were only scattered settlements of grass lodges and one old chief with a copper ornament. The people of Quivira were the semisedentary Wichitas living along the great bend of the Arkansas River.[25] Several weeks of exploration failed to turn up anything but stories of wonders farther on. A council of officers agreed with the general: they should turn back to Tiguex and next year marshal a larger force to explore beyond Quivira. Nothing could shake Father Padilla's belief that the Seven Cities rose farther east, ever farther.

El Turco had become a liability. Because of his alleged scheming with the natives of Quivira, the Spaniards decided to eliminate him. Under interrogation he laid bare the plot of Cicuye as well. Why, the Spaniards demanded, had he lied and so maliciously misguided them? He answered

The Murder of El Turco

that his country was in the direction of that region. Furthermore, the people of Cicuye had asked him to lead the Spaniards astray on the plains because, lacking provisions, their horses would die and when they returned weak the people of Cicuye could kill them easily and avenge themselves for what they had done to them. For this reason he had misled them, believing that they would not know how to hunt or sustain themselves without maize. As for the matter of the gold, he said that he did not know where there was any.[26]

Melchor Pérez, one of Cicuye's discoverers, "from behind put a rope around El Turco's neck, twisted it with a garrote, and choked him to death."[27] Burying the body at night, the Spaniards broke camp in haste and rode west by a more direct route to rejoin the army at Tiguex. Coronado feared what Cicuye might already have done.

By their actions, the people of the eastern fortress-pueblo confirmed El Turco's story. When Capt. Tristán de Arellano, in command of the main army returning from the plains, had approached Cicuye, he found the pueblo hostile. The inhabi-

Cicuye Defies the Invaders

After Lienzo de
Tlaxcala, central
Mexico, 16th century

tants retired inside their walls, pulled up their ladders, and
offered no provisions to the Spaniards. The Tano pueblos, evidently prompted by Cicuye, did the same. The natives at
Tiguex, who had reoccupied some of their pueblos, fled again,
and the invaders moved back in.

Late that summer of 1541, Arellano, a relative of the
viceroy, took forty men and went back to Cicuye to meet
Coronado. He sensed that the general and his party might be
marching unawares into an ambush, which is precisely what the
warriors of Cicuye had in mind. Confident that they could deal
with Arellano's force first, they poured out of their fortress to
do battle. But the Spaniards, some wielding sword and lance
from horseback, others with feet firmly planted firing their
smoke and lead-belching arquebuses, turned the Indians back.

Early in the fight two of Cicuye's most touted warriors
fell dead. After that, said Castañeda, the Indians refused to
come out in the open, retiring instead to the refuge of their
stone pueblo. The Spaniards kept up the battle for four days
"to inflict some punishment on them, as was done, considering
that they killed some of their people with cannon fired at the
pueblo." These casualties, the first ones recorded at Cicuye
by the invaders, seemed to take the fight out of the pueblo.

To make certain they did not assault Coronado, Captain
Arellano camped nearby until the general arrived, sometime
in mid-September. News of what had happened at Cicuye
saddened Coronado, just as the Tiguex war and the execution
of El Turco had saddened him. He knew that sooner or later
he would be obliged to justify each and every Indian death
before the authorities of New Spain. He had discovered nothing to make the judges forget their duty. Before he rode on to
Tiguex, the general reportedly calmed Cicuye, "leaving the
pueblo more settled, for presently the people came out in peace
and spoke with him." [28]

Father Padilla
Persists
in the Quest

Talk of going back to explore beyond Quivira persisted
in the Spanish camp at Tiguex all through the winter, even
after the general suffered an apparent concussion in a fall
from his galloping horse. Fray Juan de Padilla would not let
it drop. He had vowed to return to Quivira—and return he
would. He even claimed to have permission from his superior,
Father Provincial Marcos de Niza, though it is doubtful that
Niza would have let him go back virtually alone.

By early spring the mood of the majority was against the
Franciscan. Most of the army wanted to abandon the quest and
go home. The melancholy, shaken Coronado, easily swayed

now by disenchanted officers, would hear of nothing but New Spain. He forbade any of the soldiers to remain behind with Father Padilla. If the other friars wanted to stay, he would not prevent it. That was their business.

Padilla did stay, and not entirely alone. A simple and prayerful old lay brother, Fray Luis de Úbeda, chose to end his days among the Pueblos rather than face the walk back to New Spain. Lucas and Sebastián, Tarascan Indian catechists and helpers trained by Father Padilla in his former convento of Zapotlán, would accompany their master wherever he wanted to go. They were *donados,* native lads "donated" to the friars, dressed in knee-length gray tunics and girded with the knotted cord of the Franciscans. In addition, Padilla talked Coronado into allowing him the services of a Portuguese soldier, one Andrés do Campo. Here was an interpreter for the Portuguese-speaking court of the Seven Cities. Several more servants and the half-dozen natives of Quivira who had guided the general back across the plains completed the roster of those left behind.

Coronado provided them with supplies and a mounted escort to Cicuye. Brother Luis intended to remain there while Father Padilla pursued his vision of the Seven Cities. Very soon, Padilla, Campo, Lucas and Sebastián, a black and a mestizo, along with the Quivira guides, sheep, mules, one horse, religious paraphernalia, and gifts, set out eastward, never to be seen in Cicuye again. The obsessed friar did reach the cross he had erected in Quivira the year before. A short way beyond, Indians killed him. The Portuguese, after nearly a year's captivity, escaped south to New Spain with news of Padilla's violent end. Lucas and Sebastián too trekked back by another route.[29]

The Death of Padilla

After sending to Cicuye another flock of sheep for Brother Luis, Coronado gave the order for the army to move out from Tiguex. They had forsaken their conquests. It was April 1542. Almost as suddenly as they had come, the invaders had gone.

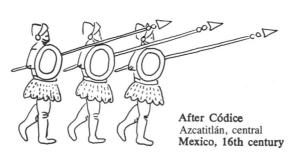

After Códice
Azcatitlán, central
Mexico, 16th century

The Spaniards
Depart

At Cicuye only the bitterness remained. The Spaniards had come in peace and provoked war. They had held certain of the pueblo's leaders captive and they had killed some of its people in battle. Yet nothing they had done, nothing they had brought, vitally affected life at Cicuye once they were gone. Their gifts— the beads, the glass and metal trinkets, the ribbons—wrought no revolutions among the people of Cicuye. Their sheep did not survive. The reading of the requerimiento and the symbolic planting of the cross meant nothing after Coronado and his army had vanished in the direction from which they had come.

If the invaders had aggravated a rift among the people of Cicuye—revealed perhaps in the pueblo's alternate "friendliness" and hostility—it did not drive them apart. Subsequent expeditions found them still living together in the closeness of their one fortress-pueblo.

A Missionary
Left Behind
at Cicuye

As for the aged Brother Luis de Úbeda, the first Christian missionary to the people of Cicuye, neither he nor the trials of his humble ministry moved them to make room in their hearts for a poor man nailed to a cross or His Blessed Mother. Describing his aspirations to Capt. Juan Jaramillo, the friar had said

> that with a chisel and adze which he still had he would erect crosses in those pueblos and would baptize the children he found on the verge of death and send them to heaven. For this purpose he desired no other company than a young slave of mine named Cristóbal for his solace. He said that Cristóbal would soon learn the local language if the natives would only help him. The friar did so much to obtain him that I could not refuse him, and thus no more has been heard of the boy.[30]

Much respected by Coronado's soldiers because he embraced poverty so completely and prayed continually, qualities they expected in a Franciscan, Fray Luis had come from Spain with the returning Bishop Zumárraga in 1533 and had served in the famous prelate's household. He was an artless soul, anything but an intellectual. Because he spent so much of his time in prayer, he preferred to be alone. Still, no matter how unobtrusive and gentle he was, apparently the people of Cicuye did not want him around. The last bit of reliable evidence about him, as recorded by Castañeda, leaves his fate in doubt.

> Before the army set out from Tiguex, the men who were taking him a certain number of sheep he had coming met him accom-

panied by people on the way to visit other pueblos which were fifteen or twenty leagues from Cicuye. This gave rise to no little hope that he was in the good graces of the pueblo and that his instruction would bear fruit, even though he complained that the old men were forsaking him and he believed that in the end they would kill him.

For my part I trust, because he was a man of good and saintly life, that Our Lord would watch over him and grant him grace that he might convert some of those people and leave at the end of his days someone to maintain them in the faith. There is no reason to believe otherwise, because the people of that region are merciful and in no way cruel.[31]

The details of Brother Luis's "ministry" at Cicuye supplied by the mid-seventeenth-century Franciscan chronicler Fray Antonio Tello may have some basis in fact or they may be pure fancy. According to Tello, the Indians promised the departing Spaniards that they would treat the old friar kindly. They gave him a tiny room and board. After Coronado's men last saw him being led away, Brother Luis returned to Cicuye, or so the story goes. Every morning the natives would bring him a portion of "atole and tortillas" without saying a word. As the scowling old men passed by, the friar would salute them, "May God convert you!" [32]

Whatever happened to Brother Luis, there is no reason to believe that anyone at Cicuye wanted to learn more about the Christian faith.

It was as if the invaders had never come.

After Códice
Florentino, central
Mexico, 16th century

chapter II

the new mexico:
preliminaries to conquest
1542-1595

I traveled throughout the whole of that new land on all the explorations made. I saw with my own eyes all that there is in it and I perceived with the utmost clarity . . . the particular malice that intervened to obstruct and prevent what was to the best interest of your royal service, namely, that it be settled.

Juan Troyano to the king, December 20, 1568

From this Río de Tibuex, which they say is four hundred paces wide, the army marched toward Cicuic, the best and most populous of the pueblos discovered by Coronado and Antonio de Espejo. It is congregated on a high and narrow hill and enclosed on both sides by two streams and many trees. The hill itself is cleared of trees. Half a league from the site is a heavy growth of cedars, pines, and oaks. Entrance is on the east and west sides. It has the greatest and best buildings of those provinces and is most thickly settled by *gente vestida* [clothed people]. They possess quantities of maize, cotton [?], beans, and squash. It is enclosed and protected by a wall and large houses, and by tiers of walkways which look out on the countryside. On these they keep their offensive and defensive arms, bows, arrows, shields, spears, and war clubs. On the shields are painted some red crosses like the Tau insignia [evidently a familiar phallic symbol among the Pueblos].

Baltazar de Obregón, *Historia,* 1584

Title page of Cabeza
de Vaca's book, first
edition published in
Spain, 1542, featuring
Spanish Hapsburg coat
of arms.
Wagner, *Spanish
Southwest,* I

Juan Troyano, veteran of Coronado's army, had not forgotten. More than a quarter-century had passed, yet he could still see the crowded plaza of Cicuye, the people's feather robes, and their turquoise. The haunting strain of their flageolets and the cadence of the chants came back to him. He recalled the incredible sight of a buffalo herd that blackened the horizon and the strength of an angry bull hoisting a horse on its horns. He could see the *tierra nueva,* the new land, in his wife's face. She was, he claimed, the only woman brought back from there.

Still, in all the years since his return from the north, Troyano had found only three government officials, or so he said, who would admit the truth—that Spain had knowingly turned its back on a countless multitude of heathen souls, and in so doing had denied them the saving water of baptism.

Troyano wrote to the king from prison. He had been put away five years before, in 1563, for, in his words, "speaking the truth and remaining faithful to your royal crown against those who exceed their authority." As a partisan of New Spain's jealous second generation, Troyano laid to venal, power-mad royal officials the corruption and confusion he saw around him. He begged Philip II to send honest judges and to restore military command to the second Marqués del Valle, son of Cortés. For himself, he sought a reprieve and the authority to implement reforms as protector general of Indians. And lastly, stressing the advantage of having a native wife, Juan Troyano wanted to join the Marqués del Valle in an expedition "to settle that new country which Francisco Vázquez de Coronado discovered and add to our Holy Catholic Faith and the majesty of your royal crown another new world." [1]

But Philip II, sobered by near civil war in New Spain, had no intention of allowing don Martín Cortés another chance.

If new expeditions to Quivira were to be, they would spring not from a junta of disgruntled conquerors' sons, but from the frontier society emerging to the north, a society based on silver, slaving, and stock raising.

Silver Strike at Zacatecas

The spectacular failure of Coronado set the conquest of the far north back a lifetime. Realized wealth closer at hand, in the form of an incredibly rich silver strike, soon captured the fancy of New Spain. Quivira was forgotten.

In September 1546, six months after Coronado was acquitted of all charges arising out of the Cíbola quest, a small party of mounted Spaniards with their ever-present Indian auxiliaries and four Franciscan friars camped at the foot of a distinctive hump-backed mountain a hundred and fifty miles north of Guadalajara. Capt. Juan de Tolosa was out pacifying Indians and prospecting. When he enticed some scared Zacatecos down the mountain, whose shape reminded someone of a hog bladder, the natives handed him chunks of silver ore. Within four years there had sprung up "a turbulent mining camp, full of prospectors from all parts of New Spain, who abandoned mines as quickly as they opened them up, jumped claims and neglected to register their workings." Fifty mine owners with mule-driven stamp mills and smelters and foundries, employing hundreds of Indians and black slaves, soon operated in the shadow of "La Bufa."

The mines of Zacatecas represented more than princely wealth for Tolosa and his Basque cronies. It represented a commitment to bring within the Spanish empire the vast and harsh Gran Chichimeca, a region twice the size of "civilized" Mexico. It meant conquest and pacification by sedentary New Spain of the nomadic peoples who inhabited the high deserts and jagged sierras, and who by their ferocity and oneness with the environment more than made up for the sparsity of their presence.

The Nomadic Chichimecas

They were the "Chichimecas," a generic term of contempt picked up by the Spaniards from the natives of central Mexico, meaning something like "dirty, uncivilized dogs." Far-ranging hunters and gatherers who planted maize only marginally, they presented the conquerors with a wholly different challenge. They refused to settle in pueblos. They refused to work voluntarily in stinking mines. The more the Spaniards learned of the Chicimecas, the more they despised them.

At first the nomads struck at stragglers on the lonely roads between mining camps and at isolated ranches. They favored ambush and surprise hit-and-run attack. Their deadly

After a 16th-century map in Powell, *Soldiers*

accuracy, penetration, and rapid fire with bow and arrow awed Spanish soldiers. No Spaniard who survived ever forgot an attack by the screaming, stark-naked Guachichiles, their bodies painted grotesquely, their long hair dyed red. Stories of the excruciating, slow mutilation practiced on captives, of frenzied Chichimecas drunk on fermented juices, and of ritual cannibalism deepened the Spaniard's disgust.

For a generation and more, from roughly 1550 to 1585, most Spanish frontiersmen so abhorred the Chichimecas that they could think of no alternative to enslavement or annihilation. Even in the face of intensified Chichimeca hostility, the mining-slaving-ranching frontier advanced hundreds of leagues, creating pockets of Spanish settlement in the vastness between the two great coastal sierras. Towns were fortified, travel was restricted to armed convoys, and military men preached all-out war, *guerra a fuego y a sangre,* by fire and blood! In response, the Chichimecas banded together, at times under the effective leadership of *indios ladinos,* natives who had lived with the Spaniards and had learned their ways. They began to use horses. Now they attacked towns and wagon trains.

War by Fire and Blood

While royal officials sought to impose peace on contentious Spaniards in central Mexico, they left the Chichimeca war pretty much in the hands of individual frontier captains. Not until the politically stable viceregency of Martín Enríquez, 1568-1580, did the government take the initiative. A general build-up, the founding of defensive towns, new regulations on slaving, plus unified command, financing, and supply—these measures, the hawks avowed, would rapidly bring the savages low.

After Códice Florentino, central Mexico, 16th century

A chain of frontier garrisons, or *presidios,* was set out along the major roads and manned by the first regularly paid and organized Spanish troops in New Spain. Still, jealous, self-serving captains more interested in profits than military advantage kept taking natives, peaceful as well as hostile, and

After Lienzo de
Tlaxcala, central
Mexico, 16th century

selling them as slaves. Despite the government's war effort, the Chichimecas struck at will. Mines lay idle, towns deserted. Not all the Spaniards in New Spain, wrote the disillusioned Enríquez to his successor, would be enough to conquer the wild men of the north.[2]

A Peaceful Alternative

There was an alternative to military conquest—peace by persuasion. The famous Fray Bartolomé de las Casas had spent a lifetime preaching its virtues. But not until Spaniards on the embattled northern frontier began to admit that they were losing the war against their detested enemies could such an idea influence general policy. Long before that, however, certain vocal individuals spoke out against the war.

One advocate of peaceful persuasion, a sort of frontier Las Casas, was Fray Jacinto "Cintos" de San Francisco, conqueror-turned-Franciscan lay brother. As Sindos de Portillo, soldier of Cortés, he had been rewarded with Indian tributaries, mines, and laborers. But he had renounced all that for the habit of St. Francis. Unlike many of his religious brethren, Fray Cintos refused to end his days at a comfortable convento among the sedentary Indians close to Mexico City. He looked instead to the pitifully neglected north and beyond to *el nuevo México,* the new Mexico, that mysterious land from which the

Aztecs and their civilization allegedly had sprung, a place Coronado had somehow failed to find.

In 1561, after he had been recalled temporarily from the *tierra de guerra,* the war zone, because of Zacateco hostility, the friar professed his commitment in a letter to Philip II written from Mexico City.

In the hope of seeing in my time another spiritual conquest like that of this land, I set out from this city in the company of two other religious, now more than two years ago, in search of the New Mexico, of which there has been word, although unverified, ever since we came to this land. . . . We traveled one hundred and fifty leagues from this city to where there is a great disimilarity in the people. They are at war with the Spaniards. I do not know if it is a just war. I do know that they came to see us and to beg that we go baptize their children. They appeared very content with us.

Had the viceroy provided a captain, fifty "good Christian" Spaniards, and a hundred peaceful Chichimeca auxiliaries, Fray Cintos believed, "without wars, killing, or taking slaves, the way might have been opened from here to Santa Elena and to the new land where Francisco Vázquez de Coronado went, and many leagues farther." This was a region so immense in the friar's mind that he envisioned a thousand or two thousand Franciscans engaged in the conversion of its inhabitants. The new Mexico would have been verified at last. But unfortunately the viceroy, occupied in launching Tristán de Luna y Arellano's ill-starred expedition to La Florida, could not spare the men.

Fray Cintos appealed to the king. Like Las Casas, he inveighed against Spanish greed and cruelty toward the natives. He wanted the Chichimeca war and the killing stopped. He urged a peaceful campaign completely under the management of the Franciscans with the assistance of a God-fearing captain and a hundred moral Spaniards.

In a related memorial to the king, Dr. Alonso de Zorita, justice (*oidor*) of the audiencia, or high court, of Mexico and the Franciscans' choice for the assignment, proposed to conquer the Chichimecas " by kindness, good works, and good example." If the Spaniards would but give these Indians the chance, asserted Zorita, they would settle down in towns, respond to the friars' gentle rule, and embrace the civilized agricultural way of life. In the long run, the expenses of such a policy would be less than the cost of waging war. But the Council of the Indies disagreed. Fray Cintos and Alonso de Zorita were a generation ahead of the times.[3]

Under the cloud of *guerra a fuego y a sangre,* war by fire and blood, condoned by a majority of their Order, the few Franciscans in the north did what they could to instruct the Chichimecas. Fray Cintos and a handful of his brothers worked in the early 1560s alongside the young Francisco de Ibarra, founding towns like Nombre de Dios and Durango and exploring the sprawling, ill-defined province of Nueva Vizcaya. Lucas, the donado who had been with Coronado and who had witnessed the death of Fray Juan de Padilla, assisted the missionaries as interpreter and catechist. He must have filled old Fray Cintos' head with grand stories of the buffalo plains and populous pueblos like Cicuye.

By 1566, the year Fray Cintos is supposed to have died from a scorpion's sting, Francisco de Ibarra had trekked back and forth across the rugged western Sierra Madre over much of Sinaloa and Sonora, the region that would later become the Jesuits' northwest missionary empire. Ibarra and Fray Pablo de Acevedo camped in the impressive Casas Grandes ruins in the northwestern corner of the present state of Chihuahua, just days short of the Pueblo Indians. Meanwhile east of the mountains, the mining frontier vaulted north up the "middle corridor" as Avino, Indé, and Santa Bárbara were staked out.

The first of a cluster of settlements in the rich Parral mining district, Santa Bárbara developed slowly. Founded about 1567 by Ibarra's able associate, Rodrigo del Río de Losa, the community in the mid-1570s had a population of only some thirty Spanish families and a few natives. A serious labor shortage at first retarded the mining operation. The nearby Concho Indians, whom the Spaniards described as naked, lazy, and unattractive, were little inclined to work for Spanish masters. So the slavers pushed farther, provoking hostilities and catching what hostiles they could. The mesquite and grasses of this entire foothill region proved ideal for grazing, and the valleys grew good wheat. The mining, stock-raising, slaving frontier had reached present-day southern Chihuahua.[4]

With a thousand arroyos leading north to the Río Conchos and then to the Rio Grande, it was now only a matter of time before Spaniards would appear anew to demand allegiance from the Pueblos.

After decades of dealing with naked Chichimecas, friar and slaver approached the Pueblo peoples with new respect. They gratefully distinguished these rumored city dwellers as *gente vestida,* clothed people. A captured native, who told of "very large settlements of Indians who had cotton and who made blankets for clothing, and who used maize, turkeys, beans, squash, and buffalo meat for food," fired their imaginations, for different reasons.

Renewed Interest in the Pueblos

By the late 1570s, such reports, which seemed to confirm the allusions to rich northern cities in Álvar Núñez Cabeza de Vaca's book, had emboldened a small company of veteran Indian fighters and prospectors. They had talked Fray Agustín Rodríguez, an overeager Franciscan lay brother, into petitioning the viceroy for a permit "to preach the holy gospel in the region beyond the Santa Bárbara mines." [5] Without the cover of evangelization, such an entrada would have been illegal.

A native of Niebla, not far from where Columbus sailed in 1492, Fray Agustín had made his profession in 1541 at the Franciscans' Convento Grande in Mexico City. He had traveled widely among the Chichimecas "with the zeal of converting those barbaric infidels." In the Santa Bárbara area, this simple Franciscan evangelist fell in with frontiersmen Francisco Sánchez Chamuscado, Pedro de Bustamante, and Hernán Gallegos, an ambitious young paisano from Andalucía. When he learned of their willingness to join him in exploration, Rodríguez trudged back to the capital where he appeared before the viceroy in November 1580 and won approval to travel as a missionary north from Santa Bárbara. Moreover, he might take with him other friars and up to twenty men as an escort. Before he set out again for the frontier, he recruited two priests from the Convento Grande, Fray Francisco López, another Andalusian who went as superior, and Fray Juan de Santa María, a native of Cataluña well versed in the science of astronomy.[6]

Before anyone had second thoughts, the little expedition trooped out of Santa Bárbara in the dry heat and dust of early June 1581.[7] Francisco Sánchez Chamuscado led the escort of mounted men-at-arms which, including him, numbered nine. Each had an Indian servant. The three friars took along half

Rodríguez-Chamuscado Foray

a dozen Indians and a mestizo. Driving several hundred head of stock, they followed the drainage of the Río Conchos northward to the Rio Grande, which they eventually called the Guadalquivir after the river that flows through Sevilla, birthplace of both Fray Francisco López and Hernán Gallegos. These were the first Spaniards of record to approach the pueblos up the great river.

Although some of the naked peoples first encountered fled—for fear they were slavers—the Spaniards, according to Gallegos' account, inspired both respect and friendship by firing their arquebuses, giving cheap trade goods, and setting up crosses. By August 21, they were camped beside the first inhabited pueblo, some thirty miles below today's Socorro. Here they took possession of the province for Spain, naming it San Felipe in honor of the king. Again they had to entice the natives back from the hills. Traveling on through the Piro pueblos of gente vestida, who lived in tiered houses "whitewashed inside and with well-squared windows," they exulted that surely they were being "guided by the hand of God."

For the next five months this daring party of nine armed Spaniards with servants, friars, and livestock toured the pueblos. Because they were constantly reminded of the sedentary Mexican Indians—and because they were quite naturally maximizing the importance of their exploration—the members of the expedition began calling the province of the Pueblo Indians "the new Mexico." This time the name stuck.[8]

Though the accounts are vague, evidently Sánchez Chamuscado and his men, who now threw off their guise of subordination to the Franciscans, proceeded eagerly up the Guadalquivir through the Tiwa pueblos. These Indians, so badly beaten by Coronado's army forty years before, received the Spaniards with cautious hospitality, as did the Keres farther north. From here, it would seem, the intruders were led on a quick "one-day" trip to see a pueblo which, with the possible exception of Ácoma, impressed them as more populous than any other. This probably was Coronado's Cicuye.

Nueva Tlaxcala

They did not say that they entered it, only that they saw and "discovered" it. It had, wrote Gallegos, "five hundred houses of from one to seven stories." In a later effort to ingratiate themselves with the king, the discoverers designated this prominent pueblo a royal town whose tribute, once New Mexico was pacified, would go directly to the crown. "Because of its size," they called it Nueva Tlaxcala after the capital city of Cortés' stalwart allies. The people of this new Tlaxcala indicated by signs that there were other pueblos farther on, but the Spaniards, short of horseshoes and gear, turned back. They made no demands of the inhabitants.[9]

The expedition had already begun to break up. Apparently just before or just after the discovery of Nueva Tlaxcala and a successful buffalo hunt, the astronomer Fray Juan de Santa María struck south from the Galisteo Basin with two native servants. He meant to report the soldiers' insubordination and to bring back more friars. The date was September 7, 1581. A few days later while he lay sleeping somewhere just east of the Manzano Mountains, the local natives dropped a big rock on him, crushing him in the manner they reserved for evil witches.[10]

The Death of Father Santa María

When the rest of the little band learned of Fray Juan's murder, they pretended not to understand. Instead, keeping up a bold front, the soldiers threatened to burn the pueblo of some Indians who had killed three horses and to execute the culprits. All that fall they explored the province, from the extensive salines of the Estancia Valley to the "great fortress" of Ácoma and the Zuñi pueblos beyond. Because of snow, they did not go to Hopi.

The surviving two friars meanwhile had begun evangelizing the southern Tiwas of the Rio Grande. On January 31, 1582, at Puaray, the escort bid the Franciscans and their servants farewell—reluctantly, says Gallegos—and made for Santa Bárbara with the news of their discoveries.

The ailing Francisco Sánchez Chamuscado, bled by his companions with a horseshoe nail, died en route. The others rode into Santa Bárbara and woke up the town with a volley from their arquebuses. It was Easter Sunday, April 15, 1582. Early next morning, the aspiring Hernán Gallegos, taking all the pertinent documents and two of his comrades, galloped out of Santa Bárbara hell-bent for Mexico City. He barely eluded the grasp of local officials who sought to secure for the Ibarras this "new discovery which they are calling the new Mexico." [11]

The Escape of Gallegos

The second expedition of rediscovery, another small-scale impromptu affair, resembled the first and grew out of the Franciscans' concern for their two brethren left defenseless among heathens two hundred leagues beyond Santa Bárbara. Again, an opportunistic frontier "captain" stepped forward to

Shalako, the Zuñi winter solstice ceremonial. *Century* (Feb. 1883)

offer the friars his services. Again, dissension split the expedition once it reached New Mexico. And again, a handful of haggard adventurers returned full of wonders they had seen or imagined.[12]

Antonio de Espejo, an enterprising Cordovan of some means, had spent a most active eleven years in New Spain. Lay officer of the Inquisition, cattle rancher and buyer, convicted accomplice in a murder case, don Antonio had removed to the frontier to avoid his sentence, a considerable fine. There he meant to recoup his fortune. As it happened, according to Espejo, one Fray Bernardino Beltrán of the Franciscan convento in Durango had volunteered to embark on a relief expedition to New Mexico. "As I was in that area at the time and had heard about the just and compassionate wishes of said friar and the entire Order, I made an offer—in the belief that by so doing I was serving Our Lord and His Majesty—to accompany the friar and spend a portion of my wealth in defraying his costs and in supplying a few soldiers both for his protection and for that of the friars he meant to succor and bring back." [13]

Espejo Offers His Services

Despite some confusion about who had authorized the entrada and which friars should go, they got off from the Santa Bárbara district on November 10, 1582. A month later, just before heading up the Rio Grande, the dozen or fourteen soldiers, outfitted by Espejo, "elected" don Antonio their captain. Because the religious superior, who was supposed to catch up, did not, Father Beltrán remained the only friar. The whole party, counting the wife and three small children of one of the soldiers, cannot have added up to many more than forty. And they had begun their venture just as winter set in.

Espejo cut a wider swath through the pueblos than Sánchez Chamuscado. By the end of February 1583, bluffing and cajoling, he had visited and "taken possession of" Piros, Tompiros, Southern Tiwas, and Keres. He had learned for sure that the Tiwas of Puaray had put to death Father Francisco López and Brother Agustín Rodríguez. Over the objections of Father Beltrán, who considered their mission accomplished, don Antonio resolved to see all the pueblos and potential mines he could.

After Lienzo de Tlaxcala, central Mexico, 16th century

Among the Zuñis, where he found four Mexican Indians left behind by Coronado in 1542, Espejo jettisoned his dissenting chaplain and a number of others, pressing on to the awed Hopi pueblos with only nine soldiers. From there with four of them, he rode southwest over a hundred miles in search of mines. By the time the entire party reassembled at one of the Zuñi pueblos in early June, the breach was irrevocable. A mutiny miscarried. Seizing the royal standard, Espejo and eight loyal soldiers allowed the mutineers, including Father Beltrán, to depart for Santa Bárbara. Unencumbered, the captain now led his diminished column back to the Tiwa pueblos.

The Ravage of Puaray

News of what happened at Puaray spread. In the words of Diego Pérez de Luján, the only eyewitness who recorded the event, "all the provinces trembled and received the Spaniards very well." The people of Puaray had taken to the hills, all but about thirty men on the rooftops who greeted Espejo's request for food with mocking. "In view of this," wrote Pérez de Luján,

the corners of the pueblo were taken by four men, and four others with two servants began to seize those natives who showed themselves. We put them in a kiva. Because the pueblo was large and the majority had hidden themselves in it, we set fire to the great pueblo of Puala [Puaray], where some we thought were burned to death because of the cries they uttered. At once we took out the prisoners, two at a time, and lined them up against some cottonwoods close to the pueblo of Puala where they were garroted and shot many times until they were dead. Sixteen were executed, not counting those who burned to death. Some who did not seem to belong to Puala were set free. This was a remarkable deed for so few people in the midst of so many enemies.[14]

Ten days later, in early July, the terrible invaders appeared before Cicuye, which Espejo wrote "Ciquique" and Pérez de Luján "Siqui." One of the soldiers, whose impressions were recorded the following year, considered this "the best and largest of all the towns discovered by Francisco Vázquez de Coronado. It is set down on rocks, a large part of it congregated between two arroyos. The houses, of from three to four stories, are whitewashed and painted [inside?] with very bright colors and paints [or paintings]. Its fine appearance can be seen from far off." [15]

Cicuye Intimidated

The Spaniards camped two arquebus shots away, perhaps three to four hundred yards. When they asked for food, the natives indicated that they had none to spare. They pulled up their ladders and refused to come down. Pérez de Luján thought the pueblo "must have contained about two thousand men armed with bows and arrows." Yet when Espejo and five soldiers, threatening to burn the place, entered and began firing their arquebuses "in the plaza and streets," nearly everyone hid.

Just then a Mexican Indian who had been with Coronado appeared, perhaps the "interpreter of these people" mentioned in one of the Sánchez Chamuscado accounts. He begged the Spaniards to desist. The people of Cicuye wished to be their friends and would give them food. "Thus a compromise was reached between the natives and the six Christians." After the Spaniards had withdrawn to their camp, the Indians brought them quantities of provisions, enough to last them all the way back to Santa Bárbara.

Before they left, Espejo's soldiers abducted two Cicuye men. Ideally these Indians would learn Spanish and then serve as guides and interpreters in the pacification of their land, a common practice of the conquerors. One got away. The other, closely guarded, had no choice but to accompany the Spaniards down the Río de las Vacas—the Pecos—and back to the mines of Santa Bárbara, which they reached on September 10, 1583.[16]

Bent on gaining for himself the royal contract to pacify New Mexico, don Antonio Espejo used his Indian captive from Cicuye to good advantage. He arranged in Mexico City that the native be placed under the tutelage of Fray Pedro Oroz, Franciscan commissary general for New Spain. A most compassionate teacher and scholar, Oroz was profoundly interested in the distant land where three fellow friars had so recently died martyrs. On April 22, 1584, the Franciscan wrote to the king urging that Espejo "be pardoned for a certain unfortunate episode" so that he might continue "to serve the Lord, disseminate Our Holy Catholic Faith, convert souls created in the image and likeness of God, and expand your royal domain." [17]

A Native of Cicuye in Mexico City

Later in 1584, Father Oroz commented on the progress of his New Mexico pupil.

In this city of Mexico there is an Indian whom they brought from that land, and he is a man of great intelligence, very friendly and conversant with everyone, and he is learning doctrine so that he may be baptized, and together with it he learns the Mexican tongue. Four Indians from here are learning the language of this Indian of the new Mexico (for thus they call the new country), so that after they have learned it they may go with the first religious who should enter that country for its conversion.[18]

NEW MEXICO.
Otherwife,
The Voiage of Anthony *of*
Espeio, who in the yeare 1583. with
his company, difcouered a Lande of 15.
Prouinces, replenished with Townes and villages, with houfes of 4. or 5. ftories height,
It lieth Northward, and fome fuppofe
that the fame way men may by places inhabited go to the Lande
tearmed De Labrador.

Tranflated out of the Spanifh copie printed firft at Madreol, 1586, and afterward
at Paris, in the fame yeare.

English translation of Espejo's narrative, published in 1587.   Wagner, *Spanish Southwest,* I

When he did receive the sacrament of baptism, this native of Cicuye took the name Pedro Oroz. Although Pedro died before the pacification of New Mexico finally got under way, one of the Mexican Indians he taught, Juan de Dios, came among the people of the great eastern pueblo in 1598 to preach the foreign gospel for the first time in their native language.

After 1583, when Philip II instructed his viceroy in New Spain to find a man to pacify and settle New Mexico, competition intensified. Hernán Gallegos went to Spain and was politely brushed off. Antonio de Espejo, on his way to the royal court, died at Havana. Then while courtiers and northern frontier magnates contended for the prize, gouging at one another, don Gaspar Castaño de Sosa, a desperate would-be Cortés, gambled everything on getting there first, illegally.

Castaño's Desperate Gamble

The law was explicit. The king had decreed in 1573 a whole set of ordinances designed to regulate expeditions of discovery and settlement. In part this represented the fruition at court of Las Casas' long advocacy of gentle persuasion. Use of the word *conquest* was banned in favor of *pacification*. Spaniards were to emphasize the wonderful advantages of Christianity, justice, and security that the natives might gain for themselves by peaceful submission. The horrible penalties of devastation and enslavement for those who refused—spelled out so graphically in the earlier requerimiento—found no place in the new legislation. Settlement was to be made without injury or prejudice to the Indians.[19]

The ordinances of 1573 also reflected the financial straits of the Spanish monarchy. To encourage pacification without expense to the crown, the king fell back on granting exorbitant privileges to rich men. The medieval office of *adelantado,* a sort of lord of the march, as well as great entailed estates, hereditary fortresses, and the right to grant lands and Indian tribute—all this the ordinances held out to the prospective pacifier. Accordingly, as Philip reiterated in 1583, the Spanish colonization of New Mexico must be undertaken "without a thing being expended from my treasury." [20]

The hope of such grand concessions—after the fact—must have filled the head of Gaspar Castaño de Sosa. An eager and resourceful frontier veteran, Portuguese by birth, Castaño had joined Luis de Carvajal in "pacifying" Nuevo León, that practically boundless region north of the Río Pánuco, east of Nueva Vizcaya, and extending "clear to La Florida." But it

Don Alonso Espino, a secular priest killed by Chichimecas in 1586.
D. Guillén de Lampart, *La Inquisición y la independencia en el siglo XVII*
(México, 1908)

had gone sour. Carvajal's prolonged trial before the Inquisition on charges of being a crypto-Jew tainted his endeavors and his associates. Try as they might, neither he nor his roving minions discovered paying mines. Instead they resorted to wholesale slaving, bringing the added wrath of the viceroy down on Carvajal.

As lieutenant governor of Nuevo León, Castaño de Sosa tried to carry on for his jailed chief. But he had a plan of his own, based, he claimed, on permission implicit in the king's concessions to Carvajal. He would colonize New Mexico himself.

To secure the viceroy's concurrence, Castaño dispatched agents to Mexico City. Viceroy Marqués de Villamanrique would have none of it. To the contrary, he cautioned his successor in 1590 to be wary of Castaño and his followers—"outlaws, criminals, and murderers—who practice neither justice nor piety and are raising a rebellion in defiance of God and king. These men invade the interior, seize peaceable Indians, and sell them in Mazapil, Saltillo, Sombrerete, and indeed everywhere in that region." [21]

In the heat of June 1590, Capt. Juan Morlete rode into the dusty, unprosperous settlement of Almadén, later Monclova. He handed Castaño orders from the new viceroy, don Luis de Velasco II. They specifically forbade the lieutenant governor to take slaves or to set out for New Mexico without authorization. But Castaño, like Cortés seventy years before, chose to gamble on a dramatic fait accompli and the mercy of a grateful king. He ignored the viceroy.

Taking matters wholly unto himself, Gaspar Castaño de Sosa resolved to move the entire settlement of Almadén to New Mexico—men, women, children, servants, dogs, oxen, goats, the lot. They were headed, he assured the nearly two hundred persons, for a land of mines and clothed, town-dwelling people. The king would reward them as he had rewarded the first colonists of New Spain. But they must make haste less some unscrupulous rival steal the march on them. The viceroy's blessings would overtake them en route.

On Friday, July 27, 1590, the ungainly caravan moved out. A train of cumbrous, creaking two-wheeled ox carts, *"una cuadrilla de carretas de Juan Pérez,"* imposed a crawling pace. These were to be the first wheeled vehicles seen in New Mexico. Strangely enough, the accounts of the expedition mention no friars, or even a secular priest. Perhaps the viceroy was right. Perhaps this lawless band of slavers had no use for missionaries. Castaño may have promised his colonists the

A Colony on the Move

benefit of clergy once they were settled in their new homes.
Still, it is difficult to imagine a Spanish colony on the move
without a priest.

Six weeks later, near today's Ciudad Acuña, they reached
the Rio Grande, which they knew as the Río Bravo. Here a
slaving party sent out earlier by Castaño rejoined the colony
with a catch of some sixty male and female Indians. The lieutenant governor took his share, distributed the others among
the soldiers, and made arrangements to ship the chattel south
for sale.[22] By late October, after weeks of extreme hardship
traversing the dry, broken terrain north of the Rio Grande,
the scouts finally found their way down to the brackish water
of the Pecos—Castaño's Río Salado—the river that would lead
them north to the pueblos.[23]

Just above present-day Carlsbad, Castaño convinced himself that he must be approaching the first settlements of clothed
Indians. On December 2, he sent out his second-in-command,
Maese de campo Cristóbal de Heredia, and at least eleven men-
at-arms. They were to capture one or two Indian informants,
but were not to enter any native town. Twice in the next two
weeks, members of the advance party returned to report and
to ask for provisions. Then on December 23, the lieutenant
governor spied from a hill a lone figure plodding toward camp
behind an exhausted horse without a saddle. Not long after,
the rest of Heredia's woebegone troop dragged in. Three were
wounded. They had found a pueblo.

To a man they described it as large and fortresslike. The
inhabitants wore clothes of cotton and animal skins. The
pueblo sat on a rocky ridge just west of the river the Spaniards
were following. Curiously the author of Castaño's "Memoria"
—probably secretary Andrés Pérez de Verlanga, if not the
lieutenant governor himself—did not give this prominent pueblo a name. It was without a doubt Cicuye. The next year, 1591,
after they had been among the Keres people, some of Castaño's
soldiers began referring to the big eastern pueblo by an approxi-
mation of its Keresan name, the name by which it has been
known to outsiders ever since—*el pueblo de los Pecos.*[24]

Accounts of what happened to Heredia and his worthies at Pecos varied according to who was telling the story. The author of the apologetic Memoria, who endeavored to make Castaño out the hero and faithful vassal of the king, told how the advance party, cold, wet, and hungry, had chanced upon and followed a trail leading up from the river to the pueblo. Numbed by the freezing weather and snow, they sought shelter inside, ignoring the lieutenant governor's order to the contrary.

Castaño's Advance
Guard Humiliated

The Indians of this pueblo received them well, fed them that day, and gave them a supply of eight or ten fanegas of maize. Next morning, wishing to return to camp, the maese de campo ordered some soldiers to go through the pueblo asking for more maize, which they proceeded to do. So as to reassure the Indians and not scare them, they went completely unarmed. In this way all of them, except Alonso Lucas and Domingo de Santiesteban, who were shelling a little maize the Indians had given them, were walking securely about the pueblo relying on the goodwill that had been shown them, when all of a sudden the Indians set up a great howl and let fly a hail of rocks and arrows.

In the face of this attack the Spaniards fell back as best they could to where their weapons were. But some of the Indians who were on the flat rooftops—for the houses are of three and four stories—had come down and carried off some of the weapons, so that the men had no more than five arquebuses. With these they retreated and got out of the plaza where they had been lodged, leaving in the Indians' possession five arquebuses, eleven swords, nineteen saddles, nine sets of horse armor, and lots of clothing and bedding.[25]

An ornate 16th-century style Spanish spur allegedly found at Pecos. Drawn by Jerry L. Livingston.

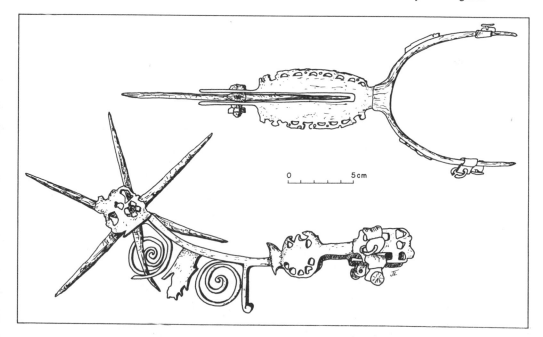

A clear case of Indian treachery worked on hungry but well-mannered Spaniards—thus the Memoria made it out. Cristóbal Martín, a member of Heredia's party who testified in proceedings against Castaño eight months later, saw the episode somewhat differently. He agreed that the Pecos had received them peacefully, "making the sign of the cross with their fingers," feeding them, and putting them up for the night. Next morning, however, when Heredia asked the Indians for maize "they brought so little that it was nothing. As a result, he ordered some of his men to enter the Indians' houses and remove some maize." At that, the Pecos "rebelled" and drove the Spaniards out of the pueblo.[26]

Whatever the circumstances, the Pecos affair put Gaspar Castaño to the test, just as the Tlaxcalans had tested the iron Cortés. If he failed to win the submission of the first pueblo he faced, how could he hope to pacify a kingdom? Without provisions his people would starve. The Memoria records his response. Taking Heredia, twenty able men, seventeen attendants, and a supply of freshly slaughtered ox meat, don Gaspar rode forth to humble the Pecos.

In the predawn cold and darkness, the lieutenant governor moved about camp reassuring his men. They must eat hearty and take courage. Because he intended to do the Indians no harm, he was confident that they would receive them well. No man was to make a move on his own. Everyone must obey orders. They were now only a short league from the pueblo. In hopes of finding an Indian who might carry word of the Spaniards peaceful intent, Castaño had Heredia send three men on ahead. Then on the last day of 1590 he and the others, "in formation with banner high," advanced on Pecos.

As they came in sight of the pueblo, he ordered the trumpets blown. Drawing near, he noted that all the people were armed and ready for battle, men as well as women, on the rooftops and down below. When he saw how matters stood, the lieutenant governor ordered the maese de campo to set up camp an arquebus shot from the pueblo on the side where it appeared strongest. This was done. Then he ordered Juan Rodríguez Nieto to position two bronze cannon and to stay with these small pieces with fuse lighted so that all might be ready in case they were necessary for defense against the Indians and their pueblo, or more precisely, in case of some shameless trick like the previous one.

The Pecos obviously meant to fight. Fearing reprisal from the invaders after the Heredia episode, they had thrown up earth parapets atop the pueblo's flat roofs. The other more permanent fortifications, "the low ramparts, earthworks, and barricades which the pueblo has at the places most vital for its defense," puzzled the Spaniards. Later the Indians explained that they were at war with other peoples.

The lieutenant governor tried sign language. When no one ventured out of the fortified pueblo, he approached with Heredia and three others. The Indians shouted their derision. The women continued carrying rocks to the rooftops. The five Spanish horsemen circled the massive, tiered pueblo holding up knives and other gifts. As the clamor increased, the Indians let loose a barrage of arrows and rocks. For five hours, records the Memoria, Castaño sought in vain to placate the Pecos.

Back in camp he put everyone on alert and had the horses rounded up. A group rode down and circled the pueblo trying to find out who the "captain" was. They claimed they saw him. Diego de Viruega dismounted and started to climb up a collapsed corner of the pueblo to give gifts to some seemingly less belligerent natives. But they would not let him. When the Pecos captain came over, the Spaniards gave him a knife and other goods, probably tossing them up to him. Still the Indians refused to parley.

Castaño was losing patience. Taking his secretary in good Spanish legal fashion, the lieutenant governor started for the pueblo again. This time when the Pecos spurned his peace overtures, he had a writ drawn and witnessed. Then in council he asked his men what course he should take "since these Indians have utterly refused to listen to reason. With one accord they responded, 'Why does Your Grace wait on these dogs?'" The pueblo should be carried by force of arms. But was it not too late in the day, suggested Castaño. "If it is God's will to grant us victory," they reasoned, "there is time to spare."

It was about two in the afternoon. On Castaño's orders, Heredia stationed two men on high ground north of the pueblo to report any Indians leaving. Once again the lieutenant governor appealed to the Pecos to lay down their arms. Just then a native woman came out on one of the overhanging corridors and threw ashes at him to the boisterous delight of the crowd. That did it. Castaño shouted orders. All the armed men mounted. Rodríguez Nieto fired a cannon shot over the pueblo and the others discharged a fearful volley from their arquebuses.

As the Spanish battleline advanced toward the walls, the Indians showered the horsemen with arrows and rocks, some hurled by hand and some with slings. Displaying fierce courage, the women kept on carrying rocks to the men on the roofs.

Pecos Spurn Castaño's Peace Offer

Spaniards Attack

Castaño, noting a house block on one side where there were no defenders, shouted at four soldiers to scale the wall and hoist up one of the little cannon. At the same time, he attacked some Pecos who were harassing the climbers from behind parapets. With the four firing their arquebuses from the elevation, the lieutenant governor galloped back around to where the main force was assaulting the most heavily defended section of the pueblo. Blasting away with their firearms, the Spaniards expected the Pecos to break and run. They did not. "Each defended the post assigned to him without giving ground—a most incredible thing, that barbarians should be so astute."

Ironically, a couple of Indian servants turned the tide in the Spaniards' favor. When Tomás and Miguel began shooting arrows at the Pecos, for some reason they panicked. The defenders began to fall back. While some of the invaders entered the rooms, others climbed up onto the roofs. Firing from the first high point taken by the Spaniards, Diego Díaz de Verlanga, with an incredible shot, felled a Pecos war leader who was bringing up reinforcements. The Indians withdrew. As Capt. Alonso Jáimez and his squad climbed from level to level, other soldiers covered them from below, bringing down at least three Pecos. The ascent was risky.

No one could go up except by ladder made of poles which only one person can climb at a time. There are no doors for going from room to room or up, only some hatchways just large enough for one person. As a result, our men to get through these hatchways and climb to the roofs had to do so without sword or shield, passing them from one to another.

Suddenly the battle was over. Like Cortés, Gaspar Castaño de Sosa, utilizing horses, fire power, and steel, had humbled a foe that greatly outnumbered him. He had suffered very few wounded and apparently no dead. "As a sign of rejoicing and victory" he sent his ensign and the buglers to the top of the strongest house block to blow their trumpets. "Now, as the lieutenant governor walked through the pueblo with some of his men, no Indian threw a stone or shot an arrow. On the contrary, all tried by signs to show that they wanted our friendship, making the sign of the cross with their hands and saying 'Amigos, Amigos, Amigos.'"

Not all the Pecos believed the fight had ended. One entire house block held out. The inhabitants who crowded the outside corridors of the other house blocks refused to come down. These corridors were "made of wood along all the streets, plazas, and house blocks. The natives get from one house to

After Códice
Florentino, central
Mexico, 16th century

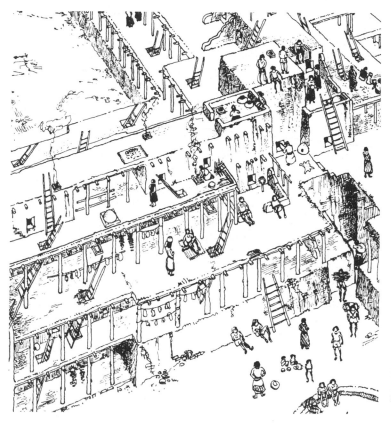

Artist's restoration of
Pecos pueblo by S. P.
Moorehead, detail.
Kidder, *Pecos, New Mexico*

another by means of them and some wooden bridges from
rooftop to rooftop where a street intervenes." When Diego de
Viruega climbed up to greet the captain face to face, the
natives ran from him, all but one old man. The Spaniard embraced him.

Viruega scrambled down and the captain and people reappeared. By signs Castaño tried to convince them that they
had nothing to be afraid of. In response some brought food
and threw it down. When one Indian started to descend, the
others restrained him.

The lieutenant governor made them understand that he
wanted the weapons, saddles, and clothing taken from Heredia
returned. That, the native captain replied, was impossible. The
clothing had been distributed among the people and everything
but a few sword blades had been destroyed. Castaño would
not be put off. He dispatched soldiers to apprehend, if they
could, some Indians from the unyielding house block. Back in
camp they might be made to reveal the truth about the missing
gear.

Then he returned to where he had left the captain of the pueblo, telling him that the Indians should not be afraid because no harm would come to them. They understood it clearly and gave signs of wanting our friendship. The Indian captain climbed up onto the rooftops and from there in a loud voice delivered a speech to his people and the pueblo. Immediately we saw many natives coming out onto all the corridors with signs of happiness and of good will. Still, with all this, not one wanted to come down to the plazas and the streets.

It was getting dark. Asked a second time for the weapons and clothing, the Pecos threw down from the corridors a couple of sword blades without guards, one piece of thigh armor, and a few worthless scraps. Castaño told the native captain to have a further search made. He then returned to his camp where he learned that the soldiers had failed in their attempt to catch an Indian or two of those holed up in the one house block. It was almost impossible, they claimed, because "there were in this house block so many trap doors and hatchways and underground passages and counterpassages that it was a real labyrinth." Castaño ordered the maese de campo to post guards on the rooftops of this house block and horsemen around the entire pueblo to prevent an exodus under cover of night. Then the new Cortés slept.

A Graphic Portrayal of Pecos

Next morning—New Year's Day, 1591—in full-dress regalia don Gaspar mounted his horse to inspect the pueblo he had won. The description preserved in his *Memoria*, taken with the details of the day before, is the best ever written of Pecos in its heyday.

The lieutenant governor proceeded to the pueblo, accompanied by some soldiers on horseback and afoot, in order to reassure the entire population as best he could and to see what was there. A great many people showed themselves and made signs of real friendship toward the Spaniards, who saw everything there was to see.

Most noteworthy were sixteen kivas—all underground, thoroughly whitewashed, and very large—constructed for protection against the cold, which in this country is very great. They do not light fires inside but bring from the outside numerous live coals banked with ashes in so neat a manner that I am at a loss to describe it. The door through which they enter is a tight hatchway large enough for only one person at a time. They go down by means of a ladder set through the hatchway for that purpose.

The houses of this pueblo are arranged in the form of house blocks. They have doors leading out all round and they are built back to back. They are four and five stories high. There are no doors opening on the streets on the floor just above the ground. They use light ladders which can be pulled up by hand. Every house has three or four rooms [per floor], so that the whole of each from top to bottom has fifteen or sixteen rooms, very neat and thoroughly whitewashed. For grinding, every house is equipped with three and four grindstones with handstone, each placed in its own little whitewashed bin. Their method of grinding is novel: they pass the flour they are grinding from one to the next, since they do not make tortilla dough. They do make from this flour their bread in many ways, as well as their atole and tamales.

There were five plazas in this pueblo. It had so great a supply of maize that everyone marveled. There were those who believed that there must have been thirty thousand fanegas, since every house had two or three rooms full. It is the best maize seen. There was a good supply of beans. Both maize and beans were of many colors. Apparently there was maize two or three years old. They store abundant herbs, greens, and squash in their houses. They have many things for working their fields.

The dress we saw there was for winter. Most if not all the men wore cotton blankets and on top of these a buffalo hide. Some covered their privy parts with small cloths, very elegant and finely worked. The women wore a blanket tied at the shoulder and open on one side and a sash a span wide around the waist. Over this they put on another blanket, very elegantly worked, or turkey-feather cloaks and many other novel things—all of which for barbarians is remarkable.

They have a great deal of pottery, red, varicolored, and black —plates, bowls, saltcellars, basins, cups—very elegant. Some of the pottery is glazed. They have an abundant supply of firewood as well as timber for building their houses so that, as they explained it to us, whenever anyone wanted to build a house he had the timber right there at hand.

There is plenty of land as well as two waterholes at the edges of the pueblo which they use for bathing since they get drinking water from other springs an arquebus shot away. At a quarter-league's distance flows the river [the Pecos] along which we had made our way, the Salado as we called it, although the brackish water is left many leagues back.

We spent the entire day looking at the things there are in the pueblo. Never once did an Indian come out of the houses.

Because the Pecos returned a few more worthless bits of the equipment lost by Heredia and his men, Castaño decided to remove most of the guard that night as the Indians had requested. At dawn the next day in the crystal cold air, the pueblo seemed unusually still. The Spaniards began a house-by-house search. Not a soul—man, woman, or child—could be found. The entire population had vanished.

Their tracks in the snow should have been easy to follow. Instead, Castaño waited for them to come back. They did not. A further search of the houses turned up more bits of Spanish gear, all of it smashed to pieces. Taking a portion of maize, beans, and flour from each house—in all, claims the Memoria,

Pecos Desert Homes

Interior of a pueblo room at Zuñi, showing grinding bins. *Century* (Feb. 1883)

no more than twenty-one fanegas—the lieutenant governor ordered eight soldiers and eight or ten attendants to transport these provisions to the half-famished main camp downriver. Four days later there was still no sign of the Pecos. "Therefore the lieutenant governor resolved to break camp so that the Indians might return to their pueblo. He felt very sorry for them because they had left their homes in the bitter cold of this season, with its winds and snows, so incredibly severe that even the rivers were completely frozen."

Because he could not hope to get the carretas through the narrows along the river south of Pecos, the lieutenant governor hoped to find other, more accessible pueblos where the entire expedition could wait out the winter. He was also prospecting. When he had shown the Pecos ore samples, they pointed west and north, perhaps intentionally in the direction of the Tewa pueblos.

On Epiphany, January 6, 1591, the Spaniards made ready to leave deserted Pecos. Castaño told Maese de campo Heredia to conceal four men with good horses inside the pueblo. If

Dress of the Indians of New Mexico, after a map illumination by Bernardo de Miera y Pacheco, 1758.

they could capture a few Indians, these might be convinced to bring back the others. But just then a couple of natives approached. They were grabbed and brought before Castaño, who plied them with gifts. In their presence, he had a tall cross erected "giving them to understand what it meant." He asked his secretary to draw up a proclamation of amnesty in the name of the king, handed it to one of the Indians, and told him to take it to the Pecos captain. Then, with the other Indian "contentedly" leading the way, Gaspar Castaño and company departed Pecos.

Two leagues later they came upon another Indian, reportedly a son of the Pecos cacique. Taking him as a second guide, the party fought through Glorieta Pass in a snowstorm. Probably these two Pecos led the invaders northwest toward the Tewa pueblos for good reason. Their own people had likely taken refuge among the Tanos in the Galisteo Basin, southwest of Pecos, motive enough to steer the Spaniards in another direction. Moreover, there was, it would seem, no love lost between Pecos and the Tewas.[27]

A sequence of Pecos pottery design,
from 1200s to 1800s.
After Hooton, *Indians of Pecos*

Castaño Tours
the Pueblos

As the conqueror of Pecos traveled first through Tewa country and then back by some of the Keres and Tano pueblos, no one dared oppose him. Only once, at a large northern pueblo, possibly Picurís, did the inhabitants show signs of resisting. But Castaño chose not to force entry, vowing instead to come back later. The Spaniards had it their way everywhere else. At each pueblo, they set up tall crosses to the sound of trumpets and arquebuses, whereupon the lieutenant governor, with all the pomp he could muster, took possession in the name of Philip II. As the awed natives rendered obedience in the manner shown them, he appointed a governor, a justice (*alcalde*), and a constable (*alguacil*).

Late in January after a month's absence, Castaño reappeared at the main encampment on the Pecos River. Remobilizing the benumbed colony, he now led it westward toward the closest of the Tano pueblos. More snow fell and carts broke down. Once among the Tanos, who shared of their stores like it or not, the colonists revived. Meanwhile their leader rode back to settle accounts with the Pecos.

Don Gaspar had taken Pecos in battle, but he had yet to receive the obedience of its people. Approaching again on March 2, he deployed Maese de campo Heredia on a commanding elevation to prevent a second exodus. This time he found the Pecos "confident and very much at ease." This time they made no show of war.

Many people turned out to receive him and also the maese de campo on the other side where he had gone. Not a person fled from the pueblo. When all of them assembled there was a very large number of Indians. To further reassure them and overcome their fear, all the Spaniards paraded through the pueblo on horseback, sounding their trumpets to the great entertainment of the Indians—men, women, and children.

With the crowd milling around them, the Spaniards made camp "next to the houses." This time the natives volunteered quantities of maize, flour, beans, and "some of their trifles." The invaders accepted.

Next day the lieutenant governor summoned them all and appointed a governor, an alcalde, and an alguacil. A cross was set up to the resounding of trumpets and volleys, which pleased the entire pueblo immensely. Despite what had passed, as related earlier, they were so at ease and content that it was a pleasure to behold them.

Many women and children came down to converse with us, and the lieutenant governor greeted them cordially. They brought him five sword blades intact and two others broken in half, as well as some shirts, capes, and a few pieces of coarse cloth. They did this with real earnestness, so that we took it for granted that if they had known of more they would have given it to us. And thus we saw that all were confident and obedient, showing real friendship toward us. They presented us with maize, flour, and beans, as much as we could carry. We spent three days here. [28]

While Gaspar Castaño de Sosa, the outlaw colonizer, boldly met the challenges of the trail, the weather, and the Pecos, the viceroy of New Spain moved against him. Within days of the colony's unauthorized departure for New Mexico, a courier had galloped south with a full report from Castaño's "old rival" Juan Morlete of Mazapil. Viceroy Velasco acted swiftly. On October 1, 1590, he instructed the eager Morlete

The Viceroy versus Castaño

to mount a military counter-expedition. "Since, as I have said, the primary purpose of this expedition is to stop Gaspar Castaño, it is important that you do not come back without him and his men, using all suitable care and taking every precaution." [29]

Juan Morlete

In the viceroy's mind, a great deal more was involved than the letter of the law. He and his predecessor had reversed the long-standing policy of war by fire and blood on the northern frontier. Through diplomacy, expanded missionary effort, placement of sedentary Indian colonies, and large-scale government subsidies, they had brought unprecedented peace to the Gran Chichimeca. The cost of supplying once-hostile wild men with maize and beef had proven far cheaper than war. Now, as Velasco sought to consummate the peace, an obstacle stood in his way—the unscrupulous, self-serving Indian slaver.[30]

After Lienzo de
Tlaxcala, central
Mexico, 16th century

Rightly or not, Velasco put Gaspar Castaño in that category. Moreover, when the accused Judaizer and slaver Luis de Carvajal died in Mexico City, the viceroy transferred his ire to Castaño, Carvajal's lieutenant. From his vantage point in the viceregal palace, he saw the members of Castaño's illegal entrada as "vagabonds who had joined him and indeed all the riffraff left over from the war against the Chichimecas. . . . And since I regarded as extremely improper and injurious the damage these men were doing in capturing and selling Indians, and was mindful of the danger involved, I decided to send Capt. Juan Morlete in pursuit of the malefactors." [31] Quashing Castaño, as the viceroy saw it, would put an end to the whole sordid business of Nuevo León.

Even as the unknowing Castaño celebrated his pacification of Pecos in early March 1591 with trumpets and volleys, Morlete, Fray Juan Gómez, and forty soldiers were closing on their prey. The confrontation occurred at Santo Domingo. Castaño had moved his colony to this Keres pueblo on March 9 and 10; then a couple of days later he had set out with twenty men "in search of some mines and a people he had not yet visited." Toward the end of the month, just hours before the lieutenant governor got back, Morlete reached Santo Domingo.

Castaño rode up at a gallop, dismounted, and embraced his rival. He asked what brought him to New Mexico. All of them, replied Morlete, were under arrest. His orders from the viceroy called for him to escort the entire colony to Mexico City. Castaño demanded proof. When he had seen and heard the orders for himself, he yielded without a struggle. Unlike Cortés, he had discovered nothing in this new Mexico with which to bribe his rival's force. A goodly number of his own people were sick of the venture and ready to desert him. Thus Gaspar Castaño de Sosa, the would-be master of New Mexico, commanded that his own banner be lowered. He then submitted to the leg irons.

Castaño Arrested

Readily conceding that he was a miserable sinner in the eyes of God, Castaño never would admit willful crimes against the king. He began his defense en route. "I insist," he pleaded in a letter to the viceroy, "as God is my witness, that if I have indeed erred I did so in sincere reliance upon authority granted by His Majesty's order to Luis de Carvajal as governor and captain general of the kingdom of Nuevo León." As for the reports of slaving among peaceful Indians, these, Castaño averred, were malicious lies told by envious and hateful rivals.

Tried before the audiencia of Mexico on charges of "invading lands inhabited by peaceful Indians, raising troops, entry into the province of New Mexico, and other acts," Gaspar Castaño was found guilty and sentenced to six years' military service in the Philippines. He sailed in 1593. Later, word was received in Mexico that the ill-starred don Gaspar had died at the hands of mutinous Chinese galley slaves on a voyage to the Moluccas. Only then did the results of his appeal to Spain arrive. He had been acquitted of all charges. [32]

By the closing decade of the sixteenth century, the precedents were set, not only in the heartlands of Mexico, but in the far north as well. A half-century of frontier experience—of first fighting then buying off the Chichimecas—had given shape to the familiar institutions of the next centuries: the mining-hacienda complex, the presidio, the frontier mission, and peace by purchase. Both the massive church Fray Andrés Juárez built at Pecos in the seventeenth century, and the peace with the Comanches signed there by Gov. Juan Bautista de Anza late in the eighteenth had their roots deep in the century of Fray Cintos de San Francisco and the Ibarras.

Men of great wealth, products of the silver frontier, vied for the New Mexico contract. Viceroy Velasco bided his time. "It is readily apparent," he advised the king, "that no one will care to enter into a contract for this venture without assurance of great advantages and profit, or without the aim and prospect of encomiendas and tribute from the Indians." Because he rightly presumed that the Pueblo Indians were New Mexico's greatest asset, he suggested that the king himself finance their conversion. [33] But prudent old Philip was in no mood. European wars cost mighty sums. The viceroy must seek a rich and suitable Christian gentleman.

Whether the king of Spain chose to call it conquest or pacification, New Mexico's time had come.

Philip II, king of Spain, 1556-1598.   Rivera Cambas, *Los gobernantes,* I

chapter III

oñate's disenchantment
1595-1617

For many years I have had reports of how important the discovery and pacification of the provinces of New Mexico would be to Your Majesty's service, and having made a careful study to find out all that could be learned about them . . . I offered myself and my estate.

Juan de Oñate to Philip II, December 16, 1595

Don Juan de Oñate, adelantado of New Mexico . . . asks Your Majesty to favor him by lifting the orders of banishment and suspension to which he was sentenced by the Council of the Indies. He makes this request in view of his many important services, because he has paid the fine of six thousand ducats, because he spent more than five hundred thousand pesos in said conquest, and because he is now eighty years old.

Consulta en favor de don Juan de Oñate, 1617

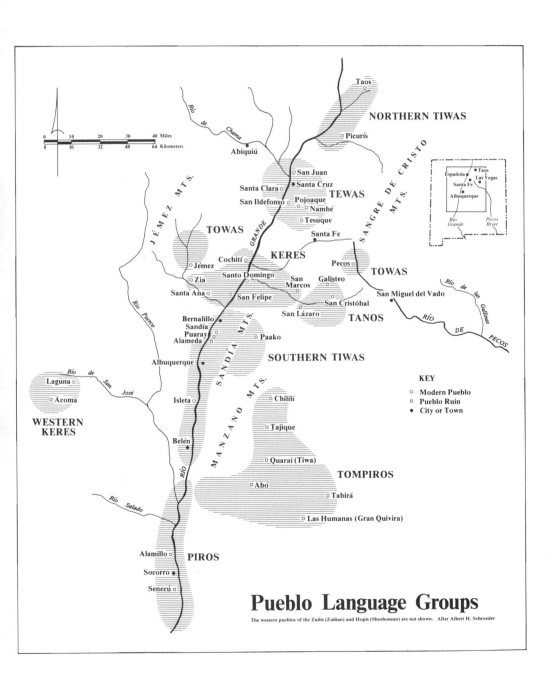

Pueblo Language Groups

The western pueblos of the Zuñis (Zuñian) and Hopis (Shoshonean) are not shown. After Albert H. Schroeder

Like Carolingian kings, attended by swarms of family, servants, and hangers-on, the rich and powerful moguls of New Spain's northern marches held court in their fortified adobe castles, dispensed justice like patriarchs, and welcomed travelers with prodigal hospitality. Because these *hombres ricos y poderosos* colonized, governed, and sustained vast reaches of the silver-rich north at their own expense, the king granted them notable, almost feudal independence. Not that he ever intended it to last. Always royal lawyers hovered about, eager to retract the privileges of an adelantado who defaulted. For their part, the frontier ricos kept agents at court, married their daughters to royal judges, and applied bribes and favors where they would do the most good.

Men of Wealth and Power

Juan Bautista de Lomas y Colmenares, master of Nieves north of Zacatecas, epitomized the medieval mentality of the northern barons. In 1589, one year before the Castaño de Sosa fiasco, don Juan Bautista had signed a contract for the pacification of New Mexico with Viceroy Marqués de Villamanrique, whose secretary happened to be Lomas' son-in-law. Not only did Lomas ask for the title and privileges of adelantado for his family in perpetuity, the office and authority of governor and captain general for six heirs in succession, and the noble rank of count or marqués, but also, among other things, forty thousand vassals in perpetuity and a private reserve of twenty-four square leagues, or 120,000 acres. That was too much. Philip II did not want New Mexico that badly.

Next, Viceroy Luis de Velasco entered into a contract with Francisco de Urdiñola, Lomas' archenemy. Its terms were more in keeping with the 1573 colonization laws, and for a time it appeared that the crown would accept Urdiñola's offer. Meanwhile Lomas fumed. By intrigue and influence, the lord of Nieves spun so tight a web of litigation, including the charge

After Lienzo de Tlaxcala, central Mexico, 16th century

Viceroy the Count of
Monterrey, 1595-1603.
Rivera Cambas,
Los gobernantes, I

that Urdiñola had poisoned his wife, that his rival could not move. Velasco looked for another candidate.[1]

For some time the viceroy had discussed the pacification of New Mexico with don Juan de Oñate y Salazar, a member of his intimate circle, a man whose "age, fortune, and talents" well qualified him to undertake the venture. Evidently this gentleman had excused himself previously from consideration because of his ailing wife. When she died, he found himself "free to negotiate." In September of 1595, Velasco signed a contract with him. The viceroy could hardly have done better.

Viceroy Luis de
Velasco II,
1590-1595,
1607-1611.
Rivera Cambas,
Los gobernantes, I

Forty-seven years old, experienced in frontier affairs, and rich, Juan de Oñate had been born with a Zacatecas silver spoon in his mouth. His Basque, conquistador father Cristóbal de Oñate and father-in-law Juan de Tolosa were half of the Zacatecas big four. Through his elite wife, Isabel de Tolosa y Cortés Moctezuma, don Juan could claim both the conqueror of Mexico and the Aztec emperors as relatives. "From the time he was old enough to bear arms" he had fought Chichimecas and developed mines. Now, for stakes he deemed high enough, Juan de Oñate would gamble his fortune on the chance that he could make New Mexico pay.[2]

Las capitulaciones que el Virrey Don Luys de Velasco hizo con Don Iuan de Oñate, Gouernador y Capitan general de las Prouincias de la Nueua Mexico, en conformidad de las ordenanças Reales para semejantes descubrimientos, con las dichas ordenanças, y las moderaciones del Virrey Conde de Monterrey, con las conuenencias que se siguen, de que se confirmen las capitulaciones del Virrey Don Luys, y los incouinietes que traen consigo las dichas moderaciones que hizo el dicho Conde de Monterrey.

1. Capitulacion.

Item que pueda leuantar gente en qualquiera parte de los Reynos de su Magestad, para la poblacion y pacificacion, nombrando para ello los Capitanes y officiales necessarios, arbolando vande ras y tocando ... jornada. Lo dispuesto en el capitulo. 73. delas ordenanças.

Ordenança. 73.

Den se cedulas para que pueda leuantar gente en qualquiera parte destos nuestros Reynos, dela Corona de Castilla, y de Leon, y para la poblacion y pacificacion, y nombrar Capitanes para ello, q̃ puedan enarbolar vanderas, y tocar atambores, y publicar la jorna da fin que à ellos, ni a los q̃ a ella vuieren de yr, se les pida alguna cosa.

Moderacion.

Que el poder leuãtar gente no sea generalmente y siempre, sino por esta vez: y que quando se acabe, ò fuere necessaria mas, pida licencia al Virrey, como se conce dia à Vrdinola.

Que el nombrar officiales de guerra, no sea siempre que quisiere, sino por esta vez, y con consulta como se concedia a Vrdinola: y que si vuiere de hazerse ... que esto para adelante desde agora se entienda por el tiempo que estuuiere subjecto al cargo de los Virreyes desta Nueua España, que no lo estando seria en desauthoridad suya venir Capitanes y officiales nombrados por otro, a leuantar gẽte en ella.

Conuenencias de la 1. capitulacion.

Para jornadas de tan grã de importancia es muy necessa rio el poder leuantar gente, todas las vezes que conuenga, assi por lo que toca al mayor seruicio de su Magestad, en cuyo nombre y authoridad conuiene que la tenga el Gouernador, para poder leuantarla a su eleccion y voluntad, y assi esta...

Oñate's agents appeal changes by the Count of Monterrey in the New Mexico contract, Madrid, 1599 or 1600. Wagner, *Spanish Southwest*, I

Francisco de Urdiñola

Velasco had already accepted Oñate's offer to arrest and bring back from New Mexico another party of illegal entrants. One Capt. Francisco Leyva de Bonilla, commissioned by the governor of Nueva Vizcaya to punish some cattle-thieving Indians east of Santa Bárbara, had thrown off the governor's authority and made for New Mexico. There was no telling what harm "such unrestrained and audacious men would cause the inhabitants of those provinces." Therefore on October 21, 1595, when Velasco in the name of Philip II appointed Oñate "governor, captain general, caudillo, discoverer, and pacifier" of New Mexico, he charged him with a twofold mission: proceed against the traitor Leyva and pacify the land.[3]

Under the contract, Oñate committed himself to provision and take to New Mexico at least two hundred men and to supply thousands of head of stock, tools, and necessities, twenty carts, and a large personal outfit. All of this he hoped to have assembled at Santa Bárbara by March of 1596. Besides the governorship for two lifetimes, with all the many powers that went with it, don Juan was to receive the title adelantado as soon as he took possession. He was to govern independently of the viceroy, answering instead directly to the Council of the Indies in Spain. Velasco had been scrupulous in adhering to the 1573 ordinances. Where Oñate had bid too high, the viceroy cut him down—Oñate requested his offices for four lives but Velasco confirmed them for two. Oñate asked for a loan of twenty thousand pesos while Velasco authorized six thousand. Oñate bid for an annual salary of eight thousand ducats and Velasco countered with six.

Even as recruiting lists were opened amid pageantry at the viceregal palace and to the beating of drums in Puebla, Zacatecas, and elsewhere, a new viceroy entered Mexico City. Luis de Velasco, Oñate's friend and patron, had been promoted to Peru. Instead of speeding don Juan on his way, as he might have done, the outgoing executive insisted that his successor study the contract and satisfy himself that all was in order. That cost Oñate two years.

The Count of Monterrey listened to Oñate's detractors as well as to his friends. The New Mexico grantee was not really so rich. His father had badly mismanaged the estate. There were debts. Even if relatives and friends contributed, Juan de Oñate would be hard pressed. Carefully, the new viceroy studied the contract, along with copies of the Lomas and Urdiñola documents. He then proceeded to strike or significantly limit at least seven major concessions to Oñate. The one that most offended him was the New Mexico governor's independence of the viceroy and audiencias of New Spain. If aggrieved Spaniards and Indians in New Mexico could appeal only to Spain, reasoned Monterrey, Oñate's authority would be virtually unchecked. Besides, some concessions should be withheld until don Juan proved himself. The king could always reward him and his people later for a job well done.[4]

Grudgingly, Oñate's agents accepted the changes. By late summer 1596, the governor had the bulk of the expedition on the road north from Zacatecas. Just as he was about to cross the difficult Río de las Nazas, a viceregal inspector, don Lope

Colonization Delayed

de Ulloa, overtook the lumbering train. He carried an urgent secret message. The king had suspended the expedition. Don Juan was to hold up the entire operation until further word from Spain.

Stung by the unreasonableness of the order, Juan de Oñate did the only thing he could, he "took the royal decree (*cédula*) in his hands, kissed it, placed it on his head, and rendered obedience with due respect." Then he protested. Such a delay, if prolonged, could ruin him and others who had mortgaged all but their souls to join the venture. Hungry colonists would consume the provisions on the spot. They would disband overnight if they ever found out why the expedition had halted at the mines of Casco ten days short of Santa Bárbara.

To prove that he had more than fulfilled his contract, as well as to reassure his impatient following, Oñate requested Ulloa to carry on with "the inspection, review, and inventory of the people, provisions, munitions, equipment, and other things he is taking." The livestock and stores already collected in the Santa Bárbara area could be tallied there and added to the inventory. When finally the count and appraisal of everything from laxative pills and horseshoe nails to jerked beef and colonist families was completed in February 1597, it was found that Oñate had indeed surpassed the requirements of the contract. Still he had to wait.[5]

By casting doubt upon the financial capability of Oñate, the Count of Monterrey had opened the door to a rival pretender, don Pedro Ponce de León, wealthy Spaniard of Bailén. Ponce proposed a contract to the Council of the Indies more favorable to the crown in every regard. For over a year Philip II played off the two contenders one against the other. Meanwhile Monterrey had taken up Oñate's cause, probably for no small consideration. Ponce's health and finances worsened. In the spring of 1597, the king, while keeping Ponce on the string, secretly instructed Monterrey to find out if Oñate was still in a position to proceed. If so, he was to be given the royal blessing.[6]

A second inspection of the Oñate expedition, finally pulled back together again by December 1597 and encamped in the Santa Bárbara district, lasted more than a month. This time only 129 men passed muster, 71 short of the two hundred Oñate had agreed to take. When a cousin of means gave bond for another eighty soldiers and for shortages of equipment and provisions, the last obstacle fell away. The inspector took his leave at the Río Conchos. Some twenty-five miles farther on, the caravan halted for a month while an advance party scouted ahead and the Franciscans caught up. Then in March 1598—two years behind schedule—the colonizing expedition of Juan de Oñate moved out.[7]

It was no coincidence that Franciscans accompanied Oñate. Viceroy Velasco's ill-advised suggestion that members of all the religious orders, especially the Jesuits, should join in the spiritual conquest of New Mexico ran counter to more than half a century of tradition.[8]

First on the scene in New Spain, the friars of St. Francis, beginning in 1524, had pre-empted whatever areas they chose —in the environs of Mexico City and Puebla, in the present states of Hidalgo, Morelos, and Michoacán, and in the vastness of Nueva Galicia and the Gran Chichimeca. The Dominicans who disembarked in 1526 found themselves already limited geographically by Franciscans. When the Augustinians arrived in 1533, they had to fit their apostolate into spaces left by the other two orders. Although the majority of Franciscans preferred to minister to the sedentary natives of central Mexico, other, more venturesome grayfriars, explorers, military chaplains, and itinerant missionaries to the Chichimecas, laid

their Order's claim to the north. Not until the last years of the sixteenth century did the energetic new Society of Jesus gain a foothold in the Sierra Madre Occidental and begin building a triumphal northwest missionary empire. Even then, the great arc stretching from Tampico on the Gulf of Mexico west to the foothills of the Sierra remained a Franciscan monopoly.

Franciscans converting the Tarascan Indians west of Mexico City despite the wiles of demons. After Pablo de la Purísima Concepción Beaumont

As early as July 1524, seventeen sons of St. Francis had met in chapter in or near the Mexican capital and organized themselves as a proper "custody," or dependent administrative district, of the Spanish Franciscan province of San Gabriel de Estremadura. As the Custodia del Santo Evangelio, they elec-

ted one of their number *custos,* superior for a triennium, and
designated four towns as sites for Franciscan houses, known
as *conventos,* with Mexico City as headquarters. At each
house, a designated friar acted as local superior, or *guardián.*
Several members, called individually definitors, and collectively
the definitory, made up a council to advise the Father Custos.
So rapidly did the Franciscan ministry grow in Mexico that
the order raised the custody of the Holy Gospel to full provincial status in 1535. The following year at their fourth
triennial chapter, the members elected a Minister Provincial.

To the west and north in Michoacán-Jalisco, where the
mother province of the Holy Gospel set out one of several
custodies, the process repeated itself. In 1565, that custody

Franciscan method of
teaching the Indians by
pictures (From an
engraving based on
Fray Diego Valadés,
O.F.M., in his
Rhetorica Christiana,
Rome, 1579.)

The Franciscan Convento Grande, Mexico City. After a 19th-century engraving adapted by Ross G. Montgomery. Montgomery, *Franciscan Awatovi*

came of age as an autonomous province, later splitting in two as the province of San Pedro y San Pablo de Michoacán and the province of Santiago de Jalisco. A 1573 shipment of twenty-three friars from Spain made possible the founding of the custody of San Francisco de Zacatecas in Chichimeca country. Despite the proliferation of custodies and provinces, Holy Gospel retained its primacy as the original Mexican province. Its principal house, which came to be called the *convento grande,* regularly served as the residence of the Franciscan commissary general of New Spain, overseer of the Order's entire Central and North American theater.[9]

Oñate's contract called for six Franciscans, five of them priests and one a lay brother. As provided in the 1573 ordinances, they were to be outfitted for the expedition at the crown's expense. Early in 1596, the Holy Gospel province made the appointments, at the same time requesting through the commissary general of New Spain that the number be doubled.

Just as the chosen six were about to set out "in keeping with Your Majesty's instructions that for the present only friars of this Order be sent," the bishop of Guadalajara hurled an unsuccessful challenge at them. Brandishing his episcopal dignity, he avowed that churches established in New Mexico "must belong to his diocese." At base this was more than

Friars versus Bishops

another round in the unending jurisdictional feud between Guadalajara and México. It was a typical confrontation between the secular, or diocesan, clergy of bishops and parish priests, on the one hand, and the regular clergy, or religious orders, on the other.

Because of the immensity of converting and ministering to the New World, the popes had granted members of the religious orders authority to administer the sacraments, not only to their native converts but to the faithful as well. When the Council of Trent in principle returned the faithful to the exclusive care of the parish priest, Pius V restated the friars' right to administer the sacraments to all in the absence of a secular, even without the bishop's authorization. Extremely jealous of their privileges, the regular clergy on occasion tried to throw off the bishops' authority entirely. The bishop of Guadalajara's bid to assert his jurisdiction in New Mexico before the Franciscans entrenched themselves was only the beginning. For two and a half centuries, Mexican bishops would claim authority over the distant colony, and for at least half that long, the Franciscans would defy them.[10]

Viceroy Monterrey had no intention of permitting shared jurisdiction in New Mexico. "This might give rise to dissension and clashes between friars and secular priests." While he awaited the confirmation of theologians and the audiencia, another dispute broke over the friars assigned to join Oñate. Without the viceroy's knowledge, one of them carried with him authority from the Inquisition to act as its agent on the expedition and in New Mexico. Almost immediately someone objected. The friar was a *criollo*, a Spaniard born in New Spain, as well as intimate friend of Oñate, "for which reasons he might in some way cover up whatever excesses don Juan and his people might commit." If, wielding the power of the Inquisition, he sided with Oñate against his superior and the other friars, he could retard missionary work among the Indians and scandalously split the church in the new colony. When the Holy Office refused to rescind the friar's commission, Monterrey prevailed upon the Franciscan commissary general to recall him. Not until the mid-1620s did the Inquisition formally extend its influence to New Mexico.[11]

Oñate En Route   At final count, Oñate's band of Franciscans numbered ten, two short of the apostolic twelve requested. Led by Comisario fray Alonso Martínez, their superior in the field, they and their escort caught up with the expedition on March 3, 1598, while it was encamped near the Conchos. One venerable religious, later identified as don Juan's confessor, had been with the enterprise from the start, through all the delays and frustrations. He was the almost seventy-year-old Fray Francisco de San Miguel, "a saintly old barefooted and naked-poor friar." Eight of the ten were priests and two were lay brothers. Three Mexican Indian donados attended them.

When the scouting party reported back, the whole train pointed north, stringing out in a narrow, dusty procession, miles long. Unlike previous entradas, which had detoured eastward down the Conchos, Oñate struck almost due north across the trackless Chihuahua desert. That way he gained the Río del Norte just south of present-day Ciudad Juárez. On its banks, the entire company from captains to oxherds assembled to see the resplendent adelantado take formal possession of New Mexico. It was Ascension Day, April 30. Personally nailing a cross to a living tree in the name of the Holy Trinity, the Blessed Mary, and St. Francis, Oñate prayed, "Open the door of heaven to these heathens, establish the church and altars where the body and blood of the son of God may be offered, open to us the way to security and peace for their preservation and ours, and give to our king, and to me in his royal name, peaceful possession of these kingdoms and provinces for His blessed glory. Amen." [12]

For weeks the Pecos knew they were coming. But not until July 25—feast day of Santiago, as the invaders reckoned it—did the latest army of Spaniards draw up before the impressive eastern pueblo. Leaving his cumbrous wagon train behind, Juan de Oñate had ridden ahead with some sixty armed and mounted men to receive the homage of his Pueblo subjects. He had encountered no resistance among Piros, Southern Tiwas, Keres, Northern Tiwas, and Tanos. Now he beheld "the great pueblo of Pecos," subdued eight years earlier by Gaspar Castaño de Sosa only after a fierce battle. "This is the province Espejo called Tamos, from which came a certain don Pedro Oroz, an Indian of this land who died at Tanepantla under the care and instruction of the Franciscan Fathers." [13]

Standing nearby in his abbreviated Franciscan habit was the Mexican Indian donado Juan de Dios. He had learned the language of this pueblo from the abducted Pedro Oroz. He interpreted for the governor and the two friars present, Comisario Alonso Martínez and Fray Cristóbal de Salazar, a cousin of don Juan. Two of Oñate's men, likely on hand this day, had fought in the battle of 1590—the medium-built, brown-bearded Ensign Juan de Victoria Carvajal and graying Juan

The Adelantado at Pecos

Rodríguez, a Portuguese who would soon desert the New Mexico colony "at full gallop."

A couple of weeks earlier at the Keres pueblo of Santo Domingo, where he had received in a large kiva the submission and vassalage of several native leaders, don Juan apprehended two of Castaño's Indians, Tomás and Cristóbal. They had been there since 1591 and spoke Keresan. They too stood with the Spaniards before Pecos. Even though he had Juan de Dios, interpreter in the language of this pueblo that called itself Cicuye, Oñate consistently used the Keresan name Pecos, as did the soldiers and Indians of Castaño, and everyone who came after them.

This day the Pecos chose not to fight. Apparently they permitted the Spaniards the usual ritual acts—the harangues and planting of the cross and volleys. In honor of the day, the friars assigned Santiago as patron saint of the Pecos. The governor and his party left the next day. Six weeks later, after the Spanish colony had settled in at San Juan pueblo among the Tewas, the "captains" of Pecos were summoned to present themselves there, along with principales from other pueblos who had not yet rendered obedience. Most likely Juan de Dios delivered the message. Whoever did, the Pecos responded.

Like Coronado, the bold Oñate had appropriated an entire native pueblo as his headquarters. Its name sounded to the Spaniards like Ohke. They had christened it San Juan Bautista. Here Oñate had set colonists and Indians to work building the first church in New Mexico, "large enough to accomodate all the people of the camp." By September 7, it was far enough along to dedicate. The following day, Tuesday, feast of the Nativity of the Blessed Virgin, the Spaniards crowded inside for solemn high Mass with all ten friars assisting. Father Commissary Martínez consecrated altar and chalices. Fray Cristóbal de Salazar delivered the sermon.

Oñate's Grant
to the Friars

When the Last Gospel had been sung, Oñate's secretary Juan Pérez de Donís, a man of medium build with gray beard and an old scar across his forehead, stepped to the front to read a proclamation from the governor. "In loud and intelligible voice" he began in the name of "don Juan de Oñate, governor, captain general, and adelantado of the kingdoms and provinces of New Mexico and those adjacent and bordering, their pacifier and colonizer for the king our lord, etc."

Having been in this land since May and having personally pacified more than one hundred leagues of it, the governor deemed that the time had come to realize the expedition's highest purpose—"the conversion of the souls of these Indians,

A Santo Domingo kiva photographed on October 1, 1880, by George C. Bennett. The figure is Adolph F. Bandelier.   Museum of New Mexico

the exaltation of the Holy Catholic Church, and the preaching of the Holy Gospel." He had therefore summoned the native captains and principal men "with an Indian messenger and a small book of mine as a memento," and they had come.

Fixing my eyes and my heart attentively upon the great merits that the most glorious Order of the Seraphic Father St. Francis displays in all the world and most particularly in this land of New Mexico, for Franciscan friars discovered it and already three have died for its spiritual well-being at the hands of these natives, and likewise on the hardships they have suffered for many days past on this expedition with me, in remuneration to them and in discharge of the royal conscience; recognizing their apostolic spirit and fervor for the conversion of souls and confident of their great virtue, of their willingness to dedicate themselves to the task as they always have, and of their great wisdom, ability, and goodness; and because at present they alone are the ministers and preachers of the Gospel who should cultivate this vineyard of the Lord; for all these reasons, in the name of the king our lord, by his royal authority which I enjoy for the purpose, and by virtue of the Royal Patronage and the special trust and obligation that the Apostolic See granted to and imposed upon the aforesaid king our lord and his successors of distributing curacies (*doctrinas*) in all the Indies and supplying them with suitable and capable spiritual ministers to proclaim the word of God in their temples and churches . . .

Juan Pérez de Donís caught his breath. He had reached the critical point—Oñate's concession of New Mexico to the Franciscans.

I do concede, grant, designate, and entrust, the Lord as my witness, from now for all time binding to the aforesaid sacred Order of St. Francis and its Friars Observant present and future and in its name and theirs, especially the Reverend Father fray Alonso Martínez, apostolic commissary, and the Franciscan religious of these kingdoms here present, the following provinces, pueblos, and Indian doctrinas with full faculty and license to build in each of them the churches and conventos they deem necessary for their residence and the better administration of Christian doctrine.

The secretary then intoned the list of provinces and pueblos, stretching from the Piros in the south to Taos in the north and from the Hopis in the west to "the province of the Pecos situated to the east of us, with the Querecho and Serrano Indians of its district." The proclamation concluded with an assurance to the friars that the king would sustain them with his royal alms in temporal matters while "they sustain their pueblos in spiritual matters."

Father Commissary Martínez accepted for himself, his brethren present, and all sons of St. Francis. In order that Oñate's laudable act might be of lasting record, the Franciscan

Juan de Oñate

superior requested a copy of the concession. When he had signed with the governor's principal officers, the formalities concluded. Don Juan de Oñate, broadly interpreting his instructions and his authority, had installed the friars "for all time." [14]

After they had consecrated their church and provided for the conversion of heathen souls, the Spaniards gave themselves over to "great celebrations," singing, dancing, jousting, gaming, and the like. As a climax, they treated the assembled Pueblo leaders to a thoroughly Iberian ceremonial, "a good sham battle between Moors and Christians, the latter on foot with arquebuses, the former on horseback with lances and shields." [15]

The next day, September 9, 1598, the governor bid the native leaders "of the Tiwas, Puaray, Keres, Zías, Tewas, Pecos, Picurís, and Taos," join him in the main kiva. There in the presence of his officers, the friars, and his secretary, don Juan explained "the purpose of his coming and what was best for them." He spoke through at least four interpreters, including "the beloved brother Juan de Dios, Franciscan donado, interpreter of the language of the Pecos." He used words suggested by the ordinances of 1573 and his instructions from the viceroy,

The Pueblos Render Homage

telling them how he had come to this land to bring them to the knowledge of God and the king our lord, in which lay the salvation of their souls and a safe and peaceful life in their republics, sustained in justice, secure in their properties, and protected from their enemies. He had not come to do them any harm.

Then, in the close atmosphere of the kiva, he gave them a lesson in elementary theology: one God, creator of the universe and judge of all men; good and evil; heaven and hell; God's servants on earth, the Roman pontiff and the Spanish king. He admonished them to obey and respect the representatives of pope and king. When the seated Pueblo principales "understood the meaning of this explanation, they replied through their interpreters that they of their own free will desired to render . . . obedience and vassalage to God and king." As a sign of their commitment Oñate instructed each of them in turn to rise, approach Father Commissary Martínez and him, kneel, and kiss their hands.

It would be very much to their advantage, the adelantado continued, if they would take the Franciscans to their pueblos so that these men of God could learn their languages, instruct them in the Christian faith, baptize them, and thereby save their souls from the fires of hell. The Indians agreed. Before dismissing them, the Spaniard cautioned that they must treat the padres well, support them, and obey them in everything. He repeated this three times. If they failed to heed their friars or harmed them in any way, "they and their cities and towns would be put to the sword or burned alive." They said they understood.

Missionaries
Assigned

Next Oñate and the Father Commissary, who had agreed beforehand, assigned the missionaries.

To Father fray Francisco de San Miguel, the province of the Pecos along with the seven pueblos of the marsh to the east and all of the Vaquero Indians of that range as far as the Sierra Nevada, and the pueblos of the great saline back of the Sierra de Puaray, and, in addition, the pueblos of Quauquiz, Hohota, Onalu, Xotre, Xaimela, Aggei, Cutzalitzontegi, Acoli, Abbo, Apona, Axauti, Amaxa, Cohuna, Chiu, Alle, Atuya, Machein, and also the three large pueblos of the Jumanas, or Rayados, called in their Atzigui [Piro] language, Genobey, Quellotezei, and Pataotzei, together with their subjects.[16]

Sketch of a buffalo found among the Oñate documents (AGI, Patronato, 22).

After all the priests and pueblos had been matched, the Indian principales in attendance were told to kiss the hand of the friar assigned to them "and to take charge of him." That concluded the rite.

A week later Sargento mayor Vicente de Zaldívar led a well-mounted and well-supplied Spanish column, some sixty strong, out of San Juan bound for the buffalo plains. Fray Francisco de San Miguel and donado Juan de Dios accompanied them as far as the teeming pueblo of Pecos, which they reached September 18, 1598. After two days, the expedition moved out, leaving the aged friar and his assistant to begin their ministry to the Pecos people. It lasted not three months.[17]

The Ministry of
Francisco
de San Miguel

Fray Francisco was old in years and poor in worldly goods, full of his God the Father, God the Son, Holy Poverty, and a Blessed Mother, none of which necessarily offended the Pecos. This elderly Franciscan already knew some words in their language, words he had learned from Juan de Dios. He wanted to know more. Three years later, when he was "seventy years old more or less," Fray Francisco testified that he had begun learning four native languages, "that he had worked very hard at it, and that he had labored with the Indians and native people to convert them and bring them to the holy gospel." But he admitted to "very great difficulty" in his ministry because other Spaniards abused the Pueblos.[18]

Despite his advanced age, Francisco de San Miguel had not been a friar as long as he might have been. Evidently he had entered the Order in 1570 relatively late in life, at the age of forty or so. After the year-long novitiate, he professed his religious vows on April 18, 1571, at the Holy Gospel province's convento in Puebla. A cumulative provincial roster compiled in the eighteenth century provided no further informa-

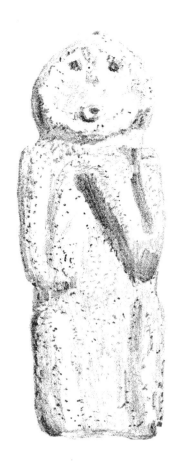

Humpbacked Pecos stone "idol,"
8¼″ tall.

tion about him, not even his place of birth. A decade after his profession—about the time of the Sánchez Chamuscado and Espejo entradas—Fray Francisco had set out for the frontier. Unfortunately he was not a theologian, an administrator, or a martyr, so the chroniclers ignored him. Only as a participant in the Oñate enterprise did he emerge again.[19]

Father San Miguel's apostolic labors at Pecos are as shadowy as the rest of his life. There is no record of his acceptance or rejection by the people: how many baptisms of Pecos Indians in danger of dying, if any, he performed; how many of his assigned Tiwas, Tompiros, Jumanos, Apaches, and others, if any, he visited. It is not known whether at this early stage Fray Francisco chose to confront the "idols" in Pecos kivas, as did a successor twenty years later.

The First Church
at Pecos

There is only one tangible clue to San Miguel's ministry, and even it is questionable. On a narrow, piñon-studded ridge, a thousand feet more north than east of the main Pecos pueblo, archaeologists uncovered the ruins of a simple, rectangular adobe church built, in their opinion, "not later than in the first two decades of the 1600's."

Near the trail the Pecos used going and coming from their fields along the river, the site afforded a dramatic vista of tiered pueblo set against massive, reddish cliffs of the mesa beyond. The church faced south, more or less in the direction of the pueblo, rested on a rather narrow but well-laid stone foundation, and measured inside roughly twenty-five by eighty feet. It had been roofed and mud-plastered inside and out. An unfinished sacristy, containing some two hundred and fifty stacked adobes, clung to the east wall. Because the level area was barely wide enough for the church alone, and the bedrock near the surface, the builder cannot have planned to adjoin either convento or cemetery. Just north of the church, however, where the ridge broadens out, he could have built either. If ever the structure was used, it must have been only briefly. The excavators found no trace of European artifacts.[20]

The distance of church from pueblo may be evidence of Pecos resistance. If in fact Father San Miguel and donado Juan de Dios were supervising construction of this first Pecos church during the fall of 1598, they left in a hurry. Early in December, chilling news reached them.

When he had received the vassalage of Pueblo leaders and distributed the Franciscans among them, don Juan de Oñate had set about exploring his huge domain in earnest. He had dispatched Vicente de Zaldívar to the buffalo plains to report all he saw, to contact the natives, and to find out if the "cows" could be domesticated. Oñate himself had ridden out in October to assess the value of the salines east of the Manzano Mountains and to receive homage from nearby pueblos. From there he headed westward for the sea. At the pueblos of Ácoma, Zuñi, and Hopi, he and his men had been received without incident and given water, maize, and turkeys. He had sent a captain to verify the Zuñi salt lake and some silver deposits the Hopis had described. Then, in mid-November, he turned back to the Zuñi pueblos to await the appearance of his elder nephew Maese de campo Juan de Zaldívar with reinforcements for the trek to the South Sea.

Zaldívar Murdered

Zaldívar never made it. He and his column had stopped at Ácoma to exact provisions. Invited up onto the peñol with a small party on December 4, the maese de campo had walked into a trap. He and a dozen of his men, fighting savagely hand-to-hand in the sudden onslaught, went down under swarms of Ácoma warriors. A few Spaniards escaped. Within days Oñate knew. As word spread, the governor led his men back to San Juan. The missionaries and their helpers hastened in from their posts on orders from Father Commissary Martínez. Father San Miguel and Juan de Dios abandoned Pecos. Evidently the people razed the church and used some of the beams and adobes to construct a kiva. No missionary would live at Pecos for another twenty years.

At San Juan, the hastily assembled colony prepared to meet the crisis. Oñate listened to survivors recount the tragedy. He established for the record two important facts: that the attack on Zaldívar's force had been deliberate, premeditated, and treacherous; and, that until the Spaniards laid waste the defiant fortress-pueblo of Ácoma, there could be no peace in the land. The governor next called upon Father Commissary Alonso Martínez for a definition of just war. The friar, dutifully citing scripture, church fathers, philosophers, and legalists, concluded, "Finally, if the cause of war is universal peace, or peace in his kingdom, he [i.e., the Christian prince] may justly wage war and destroy any obstacle in the way of peace until it is effectively achieved." The five Franciscan priests on hand, including Father San Miguel, affirmed their superior's "very

The pueblo and rock of Ácoma. Stylized engraving based on Lt. J. W. Abert's sketch, 1846. Abert, *Report*

Christian and learned" opinion. After Mass on January 10, 1599, the colonists resolved at a general meeting that Ácoma must be punished at once: any delay would see the entire kingdom in rebellion against the Spaniards.

The Harsh Punishment of Ácoma

Taking seventy soldiers—about half the colony's total force—the slain Zaldívar's younger brother Vicente set forth to humble the rebels of Ácoma. Incredibly enough, he did just that. In a bold and well-engineered two-day assault, he carried and sacked the "impregnable stronghold." According to Spanish

Vicente de Zaldívar, commander

sources, the Ácoma men, sensing defeat, began to kill one another and their families rather than surrender. The invaders took as many captives as they could, "upwards of five hundred men, women, and children."

At populous Santo Domingo, an elated Oñate met the returning heroes and dealt with the Ácoma prisoners. All the Pueblos watched. They did not understand the formalities of the trial the Spaniards recorded so diligently, but they saw the brutal results. Ácoma males, twenty-five and older, the governor sentenced to have one foot hacked off. Like the young men and the women, these defeated and mutilated warriors must in addition serve twenty years as slaves of the invaders. Two Hopis caught at Ácoma were to lose their right hands and "be set free in order that they may convey to their land the news of this punishment." [21]

After Códice Florentino,
central Mexico,
16th century

The next serious threat to Oñate's rule came not from rebellious Pueblo Indians, but from his own hungry, disillusioned
colonists. For two long years they prospected in all directions
for the rich lodes that would make New Mexico another Zacatecas, while all the time their families endured a mean
existence dependent on what tribute of maize and blankets they
could exact from sullen Indians. Oñate professed excitement
over meager assay reports. In hopes of further government
support, he wrote to viceroy and king describing the expanse
of the new land, its tens of thousands of town-dwelling vassals, the potentially rich silver mines and South Sea pearl
fisheries, the salines, and the fertile soil. On the plains to the
east were untold multitudes of Cíbola cattle and great settlements of natives. "It would be an endless story," he avowed,
"to attempt to describe in detail each one of the many things
that are found there. All I can say is that with God's help I am
going to see them all and give to His Majesty more pacified
worlds, new and conquered, greater than the good marqués
[i.e., Cortés] gave him . . . if your lordship but gives me the
succor, favor, and aid I expect from such a [generous]
hand." [22]

In the spring of 1599, Oñate sent this appeal to Mexico
City with Fathers Martínez and Salazar, recruiters, and an
escort. Among the supporting documentation they carried was
the testimony of one Jusepe Gutiérrez, Mexican Indian servant
and interpreter, who had entered New Mexico about 1594 with
Captain Leyva de Bonilla, the outlaw Oñate was commissioned
to apprehend. According to Jusepe, Leyva's party had spent
about a year among the Pueblos, most of the time at San
Ildefonso. From there they had gone "through the pueblos of
the Pecos and Vaquero Indians" far out onto the plains to
"the Great Settlement." Soon after, Jusepe's master, Antonio
Gutiérrez de Humaña, stabbed Leyva to death with a butcher
knife, whereupon half a dozen Indian servants including
Jusepe made their escape. He alone, after numerous adventures,
had made it back to New Mexico.[23]

The Ácoma troubles had sobered the friars. Now they
stuck closer to the Rio Grande. Father San Miguel did not
go back to Pecos. In the absence of Father Commissary Martínez, he functioned as vice-commissary at the colony's sorry
"capital." Perhaps to make room for their numerous Ácoma
slaves, the Spaniards moved across the river to the larger
west-bank Tewa pueblo of Yunqueyunque, renaming it San
Gabriel. All rejoiced on Christmas Eve 1600 when the caravan of reinforcements, supplies, and stock—for which Oñate's

Capt. Gaspar Pérez de Villagrá, author of an epic poem describing Oñate's conquest of New Mexico through the battle of Ácoma, 1599, from the first edition, Alcalá, Spain, 1610.

A drawing by Julian Scott, 1890. Thomas Donaldson, *Moqui Pueblo Indians of Arizona and Pueblo Indians of New Mexico* (Washington, D.C., 1893)

relative had earlier given bond—trudged into San Gabriel. With them came seven new friars ready and eager to expand the New Mexico apostolate. Still, none of them ventured to live among the Pecos.[24]

New Mexico's first superior, Fray Alonso Martínez, did not return with the new friars. Fray Juan de Escalona, his replacement as commissary, meant to consolidate missionary effort along the Rio Grande, and he assigned his men accordingly. The venerable Father San Miguel moved down to San Ildefonso only ten miles south of the capital. Testifying in October 1601, Capt. Bartolomé Romero told how he had seen "the Tewa Indians at San Ildefonso, where Fray Francisco de San Miguel was guardian and where they have built a church, come to prayers and to work on the convento." [25]

Still, the colony was bitterly unhappy in 1601. The new settlers may have provided security but they too had to be fed. Prospects of easy wealth faded daily. Oñate, grasping for truth in the reports of Jusepe Gutiérrez, took half the colony's armed men, Vicente de Zaldívar, a couple of friars, more than seven hundred horses and mules, eight carts, and four pieces of artillery, and embarked in late June via Galisteo for the great plains.

Desertion of the Colonists

With the governor gone, talk of desertion surfaced. Only Oñate's iron rule and harsh treatment of previous deserters had kept the majority of colonists from fleeing before this. The suffering of their women and children, the plagues of bedbugs and lice, the unbearable cold of winter, the sullen looks of the Indians—how they despised this place. They had a saying about New Mexico: *Ocho meses de invierno y cuatro de infierno!* Eight months of winter and four of hell! [26]

Even the friars—later accused by Oñate of fomenting mutiny—spoke gloomily of giving up, of leaving for "a place where His Majesty might be informed of the many legitimate causes for taking this step." Unlike Father Commissary Juan de Escalona, who stayed out of it, old Father Francisco de San Miguel, "vice commissary in these provinces with full powers," preached the abandonment of New Mexico. Testifying in the convento at San Gabriel before Lt. Gov. Francisco de Sosa Peñalosa, the disillusioned San Miguel and four of his fellow Franciscans described the grinding poverty and desolation of the colony. To extract every kernel of stored maize, desperate Spaniards had taken to torturing Indians. Drought had parched the milpas. "If we stay any longer, the natives and all of us here will perish of hunger, cold, and nakedness." [27]

When Governor Oñate and his explorers reappeared late in November no more than two dozen colonists turned out to greet them. The others had deserted. Treason, averred don Juan as he ordered Zaldívar after them. But they had too great a lead. They had made it to Santa Bárbara, beyond the adelantado's jurisdiction. They did not have to go back. Their bold protest had drawn the attention of the viceroy. The entire New Mexico endeavor would now be reevaluated. Don Juan's luck had not changed.

New Mexico
in the Balance

All the Franciscans, except Father Commissary Juan de Escalona and the two friars with Oñate, had gone. They had abandoned every mission in New Mexico. Even the governor's confessor, the "saintly old barefoot and naked-poor friar named Fray Francisco de San Miguel, over seventy-four years of age," had willingly joined the exodus. Father Escalona, who had given the others his blessing and had himself written damning indictments of Oñate's rule, remained at San Gabriel to make a point: the Franciscans did not want to give up New Mexico permanently. But because Oñate lacked resources, because he condoned the plunder of the Pueblos, because he oppressed the colony, "we cannot preach the Gospel now, for it is despised by these people on account of our great offenses and the harm we have done them." The friars begged the government to take over the colony.[28]

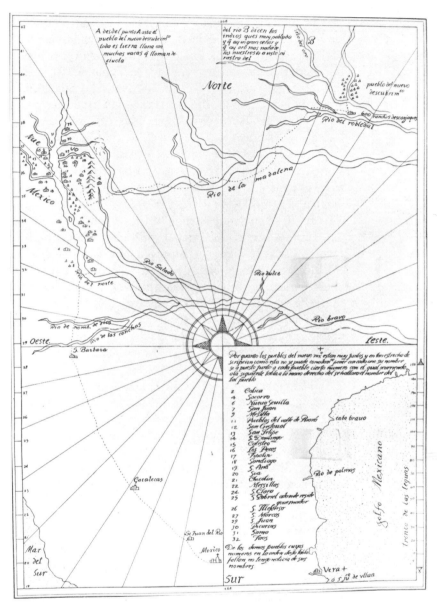

Enrique Martínez' sketch map of New Mexico, c. 1602, reflecting Oñate's exploration of the plains. The pueblo de los Pecos is no 16. AGI, Torres Lanzas, México, 49. Courtesy of the Archivo General de Indias, Sevilla, Spain

Baptism.
After Códice
Azcatitlán,
central Mexico,
16th century

Just how many persons they had baptized in New Mexico no one seemed to know. They had administered the sacrament to sick Indians in danger of death, and some no doubt had survived. They had baptized some Pueblo children. Because of the uncertainty of the colony's future and because a few baptized Indians ran away, they had confined themselves for the most part to natives in and around the Spaniards' camp. According to several witnesses who had stood as godparents, the friars, just before deserting, had celebrated two general baptisms. At the first, they had brought into the church "a large number of Indian children belonging to the women slaves from Ácoma and many natives in the service of the Spaniards from the pueblos where we reside;" at the second, a number of women servants, both slave and free.

In the conflicting welter of reports by Oñate's partisans and his detractors, the matter of Indian baptisms became a pivotal issue. If there were only a few Christians among the Pueblos, and these already in the Spaniards' employ, they could simply be brought along to New Spain. But if, on the other hand, many and diverse natives had received the saving water, how could the crown in conscience withdraw the colony? While government officials, jurists, and theologians debated New Mexico's fate, the Franciscans consigned another six workers to the vineyard.[29]

Oñate Resigns

The embattled Oñate sent Zaldívar to Spain to plead with the Council of the Indies. He himself led an expedition to the Gulf of California where he discovered, in his words, "a great harbor on the South Sea." But try as he might, the adelantado could not dispel the cloud of doubt that had settled over New Mexico. Finally, in a letter to the viceroy dated August 24, 1607, don Juan poured out his bitter cup and resigned.[30]

Baptisms
Save the Colony

Between 1601 and 1607, estimates of the number of baptized Indians in New Mexico ranged from five dozen to more than six hundred. Viceroy Marqués de Montesclaros, who succeeded Monterrey, had advised the king in 1605 that even "if there should be one lone Christian, Your Majesty would be obliged by justice, conscience, and reputation to preserve him, even at great cost to the royal treasury." Knowing that it would take more than one convert to loosen the royal purse strings, a Franciscan, just returned from New Mexico late in 1608, reported a figure so high that it could only have resulted from truly prodigious evangelical effort, or gross exaggeration— more than seven thousand!

But Fray Lázaro Jiménez knew what he was about. He

had first gone to New Mexico in 1603 or 1605 and returned late in 1607 "to beg in the name of all" that the crown either send men, clothing, and livestock, or permission to abandon the colony. If they received no orders to the contrary by June 1608, they would all leave. The king meantime decreed that exploration cease, that Oñate be replaced, but that the colonists stay on until a final decision had been reached. Viceroy Luis de Velasco, back in New Spain for a second term, favored abandonment and the withdrawal of Christian Indians. But he had used Father Jiménez, sent back again to New Mexico with escort and supplies, to advise Oñate and the settlers not to leave until further word from Spain, at least not before December 1609. Only when the friar reached the colony in 1608 had he found out, marvelous to relate, that a couple of his brethren in six months had baptized thousands.[31]

Whether fact or fiction, "the more than seven thousand" sudden Pueblo converts saved New Mexico for the friars. Obviously, wrote Velasco to the king, "we could not abandon the land without great offense to God and great risk of losing what has been gained." With unusual dispatch, the viceroy arranged for reinforcements, more supplies, more friars, and a royal governor to take over the colony's administration from the lord proprietor Oñate. By late 1609, the whole outfit was on the road north.[32]

Oñate waited impatiently at San Gabriel. By early February 1610, soon after he had received the officious new governor, one don Pedro de Peralta, the undone adelantado took his leave. After all his trouble, after all the past fifteen years of his life, after all the six hundred thousand pesos he and his associates had spent on the New Mexico venture, don Juan de Oñate braced himself not for a hero's welcome but for a trial on criminal charges. Another México, another Cortés, at this point nothing could have been farther from his mind.

New Mexico plainly was not an asset to anyone but the Franciscans. The decision to convert it from proprietary to royal colony rested not on economic potential, but on Christian obligation. A pious monarch, Philip III could not in conscience turn his back on thousands of baptized Indians. And no one challenged the friars' claim. Neither Luis de Velasco, the well-respected viceroy who had originally given Oñate the contract, nor don Juan himself looked as bad in the light of so rich a harvest of souls. They had made the best of a bad bargain.

A Royal
Missionary Colony

CANCIONES

LVGVBRES, Y

TRISTES, A LA MVERTE DE
DON CHRISTOVAL DE OÑATE-
Teniente de Gouernador, y Capitan General de las conquiſtas del nueuo Mexico.

COMPVESTAS POR FRANCISCO
Murcia de la Llana, profeſſor de letras humanas.

DIRIGIDAS A DON IVAN DE
Oñate, Adelantado, y Conquiſtador
del nueuo Mexico.

A book of poetry
dedicated to Juan de
Oñate commemorating
the alleged death
of his son
by New Mexican
Indians and bearing
the Oñate family
crest, Madrid,
1622.
Wagner, *Spanish
Southwest,* I

CON LICENCIA
EN MADRID, Por la Viuda de Fernando
Correa. Año M.DC.XXII.

As for the friars, they now enjoyed an advantage over everyone else in the colony. Because the government had pronounced New Mexico a vineyard of the Lord, they as the Lord's ordained workers were indispensable. Clearly, in their minds, the layman-colonist existed to aid and protect the missionary. The friars appeared to have it all their own way. No rival order competed with them. There was not a single diocesan priest anywhere in New Mexico, which meant that the faithful had no one else to turn to for the sacraments. No bishop exercised effective jurisdiction over the isolated colony. New Mexico had become an ecclesiastical monopoly of the Franciscans. They *were* the Church.

The only check on the friars was the royal governor. As the colony's chief executive, legislator, and judge, as well as commander of the meager military, he wielded a countervailing force as concentrated and as potentially tyrannical as theirs. He and his appointees *were* the State. The colonist, exhorted by both masters, had often to choose between the two.

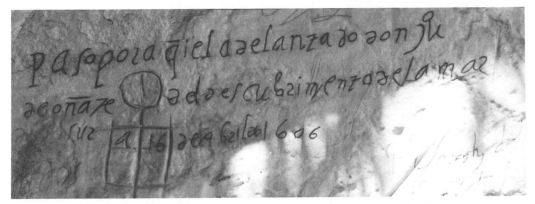

Adelantado don Juan de Oñate passed this way from the discovery of the South Sea, April 16, 1606 [1605]. The inscription on El Morro near Zuñi.

The Struggle of Church and State

Rarely in seventeeth-century New Mexico did the minions of church and state coexist in harmony. They fought, at times physically, over the poor colony's prime resource—the Pueblo Indians. The governors' belligerent exploitation of the natives for personal profit ran headon into the friars' jealous paternalism. Never did the viceroy define precisely the respective jurisdictions of church and state in New Mexico. Even if he had, appeal from the colony took so long that it was no deterrent to criminal acts. Thus, from the arrival of don Pedro de Peralta in early 1610 until the Pueblos revolted in 1680, the single most notorious feature of life in colonial New Mexico was the war between the governors and the Franciscans.[33]

If the viceroy intended his governor of New Mexico to be the friars' lackey, he did not say so. The instructions Velasco issued to Peralta, a royal bureaucrat trained in the law, stressed putting the foundering colony on a firm footing. First, he must lay out a new municipality for the colonists "so that they may begin to live in some order and decency." By peaceful means or by force, he must defend New Mexico and restore respect for Spanish rule. Where the Indians lived dispersed, Peralta was to consolidate them. He must not allow further exploration by colonists "since experience has shown that greed for what is out of reach has always led them to neglect what they already have." The viceroy's admonition to proceed in certain matters "in consultation with the friars and persons of practical experience" in no way implied subservience.[34]

Don Pedro de Peralta

Despite the alleged burst of evangelization in 1608, only two or three friars were left in New Mexico when Governor Peralta arrived. With him came Father Commissary Alonso Peinado, fifty-five-year-old native of Málaga, and eight others. In 1612, a second supply train lumbered up the valley of the Rio Grande bringing nine more.[35] This put the missions of New Mexico on a solid basis for the first time. It also set the stage for the scandalous first round of the church-state conflict.

Ordóñez versus Peralta

If later on, crude, heavy-handed governors deserved a greater share of the blame, this time it was a crude, heavy-handed Franciscan. Fray Isidro Ordóñez was everything a friar should not have been: personally ambitious, hot-headed, scheming. He had been in New Mexico twice before and had come back again as superior of the mission supply caravan of 1612. Perhaps he meant to establish the church's supremacy over the state once and for all, to set the precedent. Whatever his intent, the methods he used alienated some of his own brethren. Even before he reached Peralta's new villa of Santa Fe, he had begun his play for power.

At Sandía, southernmost of the mission pueblos, Ordóñez produced a patent allegedly making him the new Father Commissary. The "saintly" Fray Alonso Peinado yielded. Later, another friar pronounced the document a forgery. In Santa Fe, the overbearing Ordóñez insisted that Gov. Pedro de Peralta proclaim at once a viceregal order allowing any dissatisfied soldier-colonist to leave New Mexico at will. The governor protested. Ordóñez had it proclaimed anyway. Then he accused Peralta of underfeeding the natives working on public projects in Santa Fe. In May 1613, an even better chance to humble the royal governor presented itself.

Peralta had dispatched several soldiers to collect the spring tribute of maize and mantas from Taos. At Nambé the busy Ordóñez intercepted them and turned them back to Santa Fe to celebrate the Mass of Pentecost. Livid, the governor sent them out again. They could hear Mass at some pueblo along the way. At that, Father Ordóñez excommunicated don Pedro and posted the notice on the doors of the Santa Fe church.

A whole series of incidents followed as harried governor and overzealous friar sought to enlist partisans from among the colonists. During a lull, worried citizens prevailed upon the prelate to absolve the governor. Other disputes, one over a levy of Indian laborers from San Lázaro, erupted in rapid succession. Then on a Sunday in July, don Pedro found the chair he was accustomed to occupy at church thrown outside in the dirt. Holding his temper, he had it picked up and placed in the back near the baptismal font. There he sat down among the Indians. Shortly, a grim-faced Father Ordóñez mounted the pulpit.

Do not be deceived. Let no one persuade himself with vain words that I do not have the same power and authority that the pope in Rome has, or that if his holiness were here in New Mexico he could do more than I. Believe you that I can arrest, cast into irons, and punish as seems fitting to me any person without exception who is not obedient to the commandments of the church and mine. What I have told you, I say for the benefit of a certain person who is listening to me who perhaps raises his eyebrows.

Next day the prelate, expecting servile compliance, requested that the governor loan him several soldiers to collect the tithe. Peralta refused. The soldiers were in the king's employ. Besides, there were no tithes to collect. Furious over this rebuff, the Franciscan branded the governor a Lutheran, a heretic, and a Jew, and threatened to arrest him. That was too much for don Pedro. Taking several armed men, he marched across the plaza to the Franciscan convento and ordered the Father Commissary to leave town. A scuffle ensued. The governor's pistol discharged wounding a lay brother and a soldier. Ordóñez straight-away reexcommunicated his adversary, ordered the host consumed and the church locked, and then rode to Santo Domingo to address an urgent council of all the clergy.

With matters in the colony verging on civil war, don Pedro de Peralta resolved to take his case to Mexico City in person. Spies informed Father Ordóñez. In the middle of the night of August 12 near Isleta, the prelate and his gang descended on the governor's camp and arrested him. At Sandía, whose guardián Esteban de Perea disapproved, the governor was thrust in a cell in chains. For the next nine months, Fray Isidro Ordóñez ruled New Mexico unchallenged. "Excommunications were rained down," according to one horrified friar, ". . . and because of the terrors that walked abroad the people were not only scandalized but afraid . . . existence in the villa [Santa Fe] was a hell."

The Governor Imprisoned

Even when a new governor, don Bernardino de Ceballos, entered New Mexico in the spring of 1614, he was forced to acknowledge the strength of the Ordóñez faction and to proceed cautiously with his investigation of the previous administration. Ex-governor Peralta was not allowed to depart the colony until the following November, then only after Ceballos and Ordóñez had despoiled him of most of his possessions. For another two years, the stormy Father Ordóñez held on as prelate of New Mexico despite growing discontent among the friars. Evidently, at a council of the clergy, he and Father Peinado came to blows. He also fell out with the new governor, mainly over use and abuse of Pueblo Indians. Not until the next mission supply caravan reached the colony in the winter of 1616-1617 did the tumultuous reign of Fray Isidro Ordóñez come to an end. In just four years, he had indeed established the precedent—doubtless justified to some extent by outrages on the other side—for a malignant, divisive tradition of church-state discord.

And of course the Pueblo Indians, ordered in the name of the king to do one thing and in the name of the church to do another, took it all in and bided their time.[36]

After Lienzo de Tlaxcala, central Mexico, 16th century

Exacting Tribute from the Pueblos

During these years, the Spaniards did not often mention Pecos. Fray Francisco de Velasco, a missionary in New Mexico from 1600 to 1607, did report that the Pecos had joined an alliance against the Tewas and other Indians who were aiding and abetting the invaders. "Because those Indians have shown so much friendship for the Spaniards they have lost the good will of the Picurís, Taos, Pecos, Apaches, and Vaqueros, who have formed a league among themselves and with other barbarous nations to exterminate our friends." This would surely happen, Father Velasco told the king, if the Spaniards pulled out of New Mexico.[37]

As vassals of the Spanish crown, all the Pueblo peoples owed tribute. In the words of the 1573 colonization laws, Indians who rendered obedience "should be persuaded to pay moderate amounts of tribute in local products." The crown reserved the right to collect this revenue only "from principal towns and seaports," a hopeful clause that did not apply on the northern frontier. Tribute from all other native settlements was conceded by the crown to the colonizers themselves.[38]

By the terms of his contract, don Juan de Oñate could reward his followers by granting them so many Indian tributaries. The number, from several entire pueblos to a fraction of one, depended on the colonist's rank and the services he had rendered. In no legal sense did a grant of Indians in *encomienda* (literally, in trust), good for three lifetimes in succession, imply use of native land or labor; rather only the collection of tribute in kind as personal income, usually maize and mantas or animal skins.

In turn, the *encomendero,* recipient of an encomienda, swore to answer the governor's call to arms, providing his own horses and weapons, whenever the need arose. He was also required to maintain residence in Santa Fe. Since there were no regular troops in seventeenth-century New Mexico, the encomenderos, whose number was later set by the viceroy at thirty-five, became the core of the local military. As officers, customarily designated captain by the governor, they rode escort, served as guards, and commanded levies of lesser colonists and native auxiliaries in the colony's defense.[39]

To keep from starving, Oñate and his men had collected tribute from the beginning, sometimes by violent means. Just how many pueblos the adelantado committed to individual colonists is not clear. He did commit some.[40] In New Mexico, stark necessity evidently precluded the customary decade of exemption from tribute applied in some new missionary areas, although from time to time, the friars alluded to it. Governor Peralta's instructions contained the standard admonition that when granting encomiendas, he must not prejudice those awarded by his predecessor. And like Oñate, the perplexed Peralta tried to feed his colony by collecting the tribute from pueblos not yet held by individuals.

Pattern in a Pecos Glaze V bowl. After Kidder, *Pottery,* II

Potentially, Pecos was the richest encomienda in New Mexico. If Oñate himself did not grant it to some worthy colonist, one of his successors must soon have done so.[41] Abandonment of San Gabriel in favor of Santa Fe during the spring of 1610 brought the Spaniards much nearer to the teeming eastern pueblo. Both the lure of the pueblo-plains trade and the lure of souls aroused their interest. Within a year or two, the Franciscans had established a convento among the Tanos at Galisteo. The arrival of seven friars during the winter of 1616-1617 made possible even greater missionary outreach.

And one of their objectives was Pecos.

the "christianization" of pecos
1617-1659

To unburden his conscience the witness states that five years ago
more or less, he went to the pueblo of Pecos to collect certain
tribute payments that the encomendero of that place owed Gov.
don Juan de Eulate. He found me, the present notary [Fray Pedro
de Ortega], at the time guardian there, distraught because an Indian called by the evil name Mosoyo who lived there had spread
a perverse doctrine, persuading the Indians that they should not
go to church and that they should set up idols, many of which I
the present notary state that I ordered smashed.

Testimony of Francisco Pérez Granillo,
January 27, 1626

Seal of the Franciscan Custody of the Conversion
of St. Paul.

The Franciscans' expanding ministry to the Pueblo In- Franciscan
dians rested in 1616 on the fervor of sixteen friars. In addition New Mexico
to Santa Fe, they maintained "conventos," however tenuously,
among the Tewa at San Ildefonso and Nambé; among the
Keres at Santo Domingo, "ecclesiastical capital" of New Mexico, and at Zia; among the Tano at Galisteo and San Lázaro;
and among the Southern Tiwa at Sandía, Isleta, and across the
Manzanos at Chililí. Several other pueblos were designated
visitas, or preaching stations. Still, no missionary worker had
returned to the harvest at Pecos.[1]

At about this time, the Order's superiors in Mexico City—
galvanized, it would seem, by the Peralta-Ordóñez troubles—
decided that the New Mexico field should be elevated to
custody status. Previously, the local superior in the colony
had worn the title *comisario,* which implied delegated, temporary authority. By erecting the missions of New Mexico into a
semi-autonomous administrative unit with its own chapter, its
own definitors, and its own Father Custos, the Holy Gospel
Province was belatedly acknowledging the success and permanence of the enterprise. It was also girding up its loins.

Still, because of the great distance from Mexico City, the
mission's utter financial dependence on the crown, the example
of the violent, headstrong Isidro Ordóñez, and the precedent
for church-state conflict, the mother province did not surrender
to the new custody as much autonomy as she might have. The
New Mexico custodial chapter would not choose its own
superior, as was customary. Rather he would be elected by
the province.[2] The new entity would be known as the Custody
of the Conversion of St. Paul, in honor of that saint who, on
the feast of his conversion January 25, in the year 1599,
divinely aided the Spaniards at the battle of Ácoma, almost
certainly delivering the little Christian colony out of the
jaws of Satan.[3]

The long-awaited supply train of 1616 reached the missions in the dead of winter—before the end of January 1617—bringing among the baggage seven cold, trail-worn Franciscans and a patent from Mexico City naming as Father Custos of New Mexico the able and unbending Fray Esteban de Perea. Soon after, at his first chapter, Perea probably assigned one of the new friars to the populous pueblo of Pecos.

Fray Pedro Zambrano Ortiz, guardian of "the convento of Nuestra Señora de los Ángeles de los Pecos" at least as early as 1619, was born in the Canary Islands about 1586. At the age of twenty-three, he had received the Franciscan habit at the Convento Grande in Mexico City along with two other young Spaniards. As was customary, the service of investiture took place in the evening after compline—last of the seven canonical hours—on Tuesday, October 27, 1609. Exactly a year later, his novitiate behind him, Fray Pedro pronounced his simple religious vows. When the mission supply caravan bound for New Mexico had headed out in the autumn of 1616, Zambrano, already ordained a priest, and half a dozen of his brethren rode with it.[4]

Given the size of the pueblo de los Pecos—still reported at about two thousand souls—and its strategic location for pueblo-plains trade and intercourse, it is strange that the Franciscans delayed two decades in taking up their mission there. Certainly the harvest was potentially greater at Pecos than at Chililí. Perhaps the Pecos themselves, or a faction of them, had made it clear that they did not want a friar. Yet if that were the case, why did the veteran Esteban de Perea assign to Pecos an untried newcomer?

The first convento of Our Lady of the Angels at Pecos was doubtless a makeshift affair. St. Francis had originally bestowed that name on Our Lady of the Assumption at Portiuncola near Assisi, the Order's mother church. It may be that Fray Pedro Zambrano and some of his fellow missionaries dedicated the new convento on August 2, 1617 or 1618, the very Franciscan feast of Nuestra Señora de los Ángeles de Porciúncula.

Unwilling to move into the great pueblo itself—or forbidden to—the friar likely had living quarters built in or adjoining the southern end of a low, mostly unoccupied ruin, later expanded and peopled by the "Christian faction," the so-called South Pueblo. As for a church, Zambrano evidently asked some of the more favorably inclined Pecos to put up a temporary shelter where Mass could be said for them in some decency,

Our Lady of the Angels
painted on hide.
Museum of New Mexico

perhaps the "*jacal* in which not half the people will fit" described by a successor in 1622.[5]

Whatever Zambrano accomplished at Pecos, he did it in
spite of the governor at Santa Fe. Don Juan de Eulate, veteran
of Flanders and the Spain-to-Mexico fleet, has been characterized by France V. Scholes, the historian who knows him best,
as "a petulant, tactless, irreverent soldier whose actions were
inspired by open contempt for the Church and its ministers and
by an exaggerated conception of his own authority as the
representative of the Crown."[6] A saying frequently attributed
to Eulate summed up his allegiance: "The king is *my* patron!"
For obvious reasons, he idolized the Duke of Bourbon, that
French ally of Charles V whose troops had sacked Rome a
century before.[7] A particularly avaricious exploiter of Indians

Opposition of Eulate

in the friars' eyes, Eulate took office in December of 1618 and held it until 1625, precisely the years that Zambrano and his successors were trying to establish themselves at Pecos, to overturn the pueblo's "idols," and to raise up a monumental temple to the God of Abraham, Isaac, and Jacob.

In testimony heard by Custos Perea—which eventually found its way to the Tribunal of the Holy Office in Mexico City—the Franciscans and their allies damned Eulate on a variety of counts, making him out a blaspheming ogre, a mortal enemy of the church, the faithful, and the Indian. To ingratiate himself with mission Indians and loosen the friars' hold, the governor deliberately encouraged these natives to continue their pagan ways. At Pecos in 1619, Father Zambrano heard that interpreter Juan Gómez, encomendero of San Lázaro and minion of the governor, was going about proclaiming that newly converted Indians did not have to give up their idols or their concubinage, at least not for many years. As a result, the Tanos of Galisteo and San Lázaro wallowed in sin while their missionary, Fray Pedro de Ortega, grieved. Eulate protected and favored Pueblo ceremonial leaders, "idolaters and witches," alleged Zambrano, "because they trade him tanned skins." [8]

Zuñi sacred clowns, or mudheads, photographed by John K. Hillers, 1879. Museum of New Mexico

The governor paid no heed to Indian rights, charged the missionaries, only to Indian exploitation. He condoned forced labor, slavery, and even the kidnapping of "orphans." As a reward for loyalty to him, Eulate issued to his henchmen licenses on small slips of paper, *vales,* entitling them to seize one or more orphaned Indian children, a practice Zambrano witnessed at Pecos. "Like black slaves," these children, the friars averred, ended up perpetual servants in Spanish homes. The slips merely read: "Permit for Juan Fulano to take one orphan from wherever he finds him, provided that he treats him well and teaches him the Christian catechism." [9]

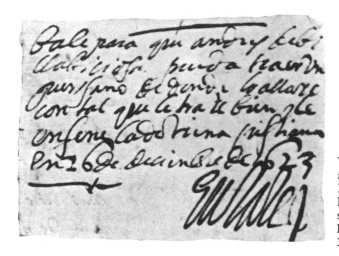

Vale, or permit to abduct an orphaned Pueblo child, December 16, 1623, signed by Governor Eulate (AGN, Inq., 356).

Sometime between mid-1619 and August of 1621, Fray Pedro Zambrano changed places with the missionary of Galisteo. During Zambrano's tenure at Pecos, he had built a temporary convento and dedicated it to Nuestra Señora de los Ángeles, but evidently no more of a church than the jacal. How much of the time the missionary was actually in residence at the pueblo is impossible to say. From his testimony, it would appear that he was often in Sante Fe. He may well have chosen to reintroduce the reluctant Pecos to Christianity by gentle stages. He hinted at resistance from an anti-Spanish element in the pueblo, a resistance that surfaced under his successor. Whatever else he managed, Pedro Zambrano did put Pecos on the missionary map.

At Galisteo, and especially at its visita of San Lázaro, the reassigned Father Zambrano found the Tanos practicing idolatry publicly. When he reprimanded a native catechist for the sin of concubinage, the Indian replied that interpreter Juan Gómez was at that very moment en route from Mexico City with permission for the Tanos "to live as before they were Christians." Behind this and every other woe in the land, Zambrano saw the malevolent figure of don Juan de Eulate, "a man," in his words, "more suited to a junk shop than to the office of governor he holds."

None of the friars, not even Custos Perea, was more constant or more zealous in his attack upon Eulate. In a scathing letter to the viceroy, setting forth the governor's venal acts, his defiant immorality, and his crass misuse of the natives, Zambrano characterized his adversary as "a bag of arrogance and vanity without love for God or zeal for divine honor or for the king our lord, a man of evil example in word and deed who does not deserve to be governor but rather a hawker and [a creature] of these vile pursuits." Years later, in 1636, Fray Pedro Zambrano Ortiz was still alive in New Mexico, still railing at a royal governor.[10]

Fray Pedro Zambrano Ortiz

Fray Pedro de Ortega

Ortega Confronts the "Idols"   Youthful Fray Pedro de Ortega cannot have been more than twenty-seven when he came to live with the Pecos. At Galisteo, native idolaters had made him doubt his calling. He would not give them the satisfaction at Pecos. He was determined also to build a church, a lasting structure large enough to hold all the Pecos. But his resolve was not enough. Both of his intentions fell short, not for any lack of zeal on his part, but rather because don Juan de Eulate prevailed against them.

Ortega was a Mexican, a criollo born in Mexico City about March of 1593. His parents, Pedro Mateos de Ortega and Catalina de Ortega, were "not only noble," said Fray Alonso de Benavides, "but so wealthy that, although there were numerous children, more than seventy thousand ducats fell to the share of Father fray Pedro de Ortega alone." His father, who wanted him to be a secular priest, thwarted the lad's early desire to become a Franciscan. But when the elder Ortega died, eighteen-year-old Pedro straight-away renounced his inheritance and sought the friar's habit, which he received in the Convento Grande at the hour of Compline, Sunday, May 8, 1611. He professed on the same date a year later.[11]

Soon after ordination to the priesthood, which he must have received at the canonical minimum age of twenty-four, Fray Pedro volunteered for the missions of New Mexico. He had just missed the supply caravan of 1616. The following year however, the viceroy dispatched a new governor. It was Eulate. In his train, escorted by Capt. Francisco Gómez and a detachment of soldiers, Father Ortega and Fray Jerónimo de Pedraza, a medically skilled lay brother returning to the missions, traveled the long road to New Mexico.

The young Franciscan and the crude governor quarreled en route. Somewhere along the camino real, while the party was camped, Eulate allegedly declared in front of everyone that marriage was the more perfect state than celibacy. Captain Gómez and Alonso Ramírez applauded. The others seemed to agree, which was too much for the boyish Fray Pedro who jumped up and tried to admonish the governor for saying such a thing. Eulate, smiling wryly as the friar recalled it, retorted in a most condescending manner "that religious didn't work, that all they did was sleep and eat, while married men always went about diligently working to earn their necessities." Fray Pedro was neither intimidated nor amused. "To that I replied that the sleep of John had been more acceptable to Christ Our Lord than the diligence of Judas." But his words were wasted on Eulate.[12]

Don Juan and Fray Pedro had entered Santa Fe together in December 1618. Not long after, Custos Perea placed the new missionary at Galisteo. During his ministry there, which probably lasted not much more than one year, Fray Pedro had found himself on the defensive. Try as he might, the young Franciscan could not break the pernicious hold of the governor's men, the likes of encomendero Juan Gómez, who emboldened

Flat-bodied human
effiges from Pecos,
taller 2½".
Kidder, *Artifacts*

the Tanos to flaunt their old religion in the missionary's face.
He apparently vowed to seize the initiative at his second mission.

At Pecos, where he likely took over from Pedro Zambrano
sometime in 1620, Ortega summarily launched a campaign to
break the back of pagan idolatry. In a bold frontal assault, he
rounded up and smashed "many idols," the clay, stone, and
wooden figurines and effigies, the curiously painted stone slabs,
and the other ceremonial paraphernalia they venerated. This
was the first direct all-out Christian attack on the native Pecos
religion. It would not be the last.

Why did the Pecos, still relatively unsubjugated, still two
thousand strong, stand by and watch? Given the irreverence of
Governor Eulate, it is unlikely that Father Ortega relied on a
large, heavily armed military escort to cow the pueblo. Obviously the Pecos were not agreed on resistance. A majority
of them passively suffered themselves to watch their idols
destroyed. Only a few ceremonial leaders objected. As a
community, the Pecos were unable to act decisively, either to
reject or to embrace the new order. Deep-seated internal dissension, unrelated to the Spaniards' presence, may have underlain
this paralysis. Perhaps, too, the Pecos remembered their humiliation thirty years before at the hands of Castaño de Sosa, or
Oñate's harsh punishment of the Ácoma survivors. Whatever
the reason, once they had admitted the utility of the invaders'
material culture, of horses and steel blades, the token acceptance
of their supernatural baggage was not so hard. Yet in their

hearts—as missionary after missionary lamented—the pagan Pecos changed little.

Three hundred years later, archaeologists digging in the ruined pueblo unearthed ceremonial caches containing numerous artifacts that had been smashed or otherwise "subjected to violent misuse." One greenish stone image about a foot tall, representing a squatting human figure with elbows resting on knees, like many of the other broken objects, had been reverently reassembled and laid in a specially prepared hiding place. At Pecos, as in central Mexico, idols hid behind altars, or beneath the earth of the plaza, and the people knew.[13]

Not all the Pecos bowed meekly before Fray Pedro. The case everyone remembered involved an Indian "called by the evil name Mosoyo." He and a brother had gone about the pueblo propagating, in the friar's words, "a perverse doctrine, persuading the Indians that they should not go to church and that they should set up idols, many of which . . . I ordered smashed." Mosoyo was telling the Pecos that Gov. Juan de Eulate did not want them to go to Mass or catechism, to attend prayers, to obey their minister. The governor was their friend, not the friar!

Ortega grew anxious. He could see Mosoyo's seductive message pervading the pueblo, undermining the gospel of Christ. He prayed and wept. When don Francisco Pérez Granillo, "a faithful and Catholic Christian," reined up at the pueblo to collect tribute, the Pecos encomendero—probably Capt.

Pecos "idols," 11¼ to 8″ tall. After Kidder, *Artifacts*

Resistance to Ortega's Ministry

Francisco Gómez[14]—owed Eulate, Fray Pedro unburdened himself. Pérez was moved. He would do what he could in the Franciscan's behalf.

Summoning together the entire pueblo in the presence of their missionary, the Spaniard ordered the agitator Mosoyo brought forward. There, in front of everyone, he rebuked the Indian. Even then, Mosoyo refused to admit that he had proclaimed his seditious lies in Governor Eulate's name. The interpreters, native captains, and the rest of the pueblo clamored that he had. At that, Pérez delivered an oration—which presumably lost something in translation—assuring the Pecos that the governor of New Mexico could not have meant any such thing. He exhorted them to obey the holy precepts of the church and its minister, "telling them that the doctrine the Fathers were teaching them they were also teaching the Spaniards and the latter obeyed it as they did their parents and teachers. Regarding this he gave them many sound reasons and examples, whereupon they all were satisfied." Having done this good Christian deed, Francisco Pérez Granillo stepped down rather pleased with himself.

Governor Eulate's
Wrath

It was night before he rode back into Santa Fe. He made straight for the governor's quarters to report on the tribute payment and on the situation he had found at Pecos. He related exactly how he had admonished the Indians, assuming that the governor would be grateful to him "for having defended his honor and the cause of God." Instead, Eulate exploded. By whose order, he demanded, had Pérez meddled in affairs at Pecos. That was none of his damn business! Stung by such "pharisaical words," Pérez Granillo made his exit, having, as he put it, formed a bad opinion of the governor.

As for Francisco Mosoyo, that "great idolater and witch about whom our Father Custos has compiled an extremely full report," Ortega tried to rehabilitate him and his like-minded brother, "assigning them no greater penance than placing them in the home of Christian and honorable Spaniards." When Eulate heard what the friar had done, he bellowed. The accused must be released at once and sent back to Pecos with a letter informing Fray Pedro that they were not to be harmed but favored. What more could the missionary do? [15]

A Proper Church
for Pecos

At the beginning of the 1620s, the friar at Pecos resided, it would seem, in a modest several-room adobe convento, abutting the "South Pueblo" ruin. He celebrated Mass in a nearby jacal too small for even half the people. Yet well before the end of the decade, his successor presided over "a convento and most splendid temple of singular construction and excellence," the largest in New Mexico. Fray Pedro de Ortega, who gets none of the credit from Benavides—probably at his own insistence—must have had a hand in this ambitious project, at least in its early stages.[16]

There is no doubt that Ortega planned to build a church at Pecos. Several contemporary witnesses testified that he had borrowed teams of oxen from certain Spaniards to haul rock and timber. He already had the animals at the building site in 1621, presumably on the job. Surely before arranging for draft animals, he must have chosen the site and staked out the foundations. That would at least confirm to the credit of Fray Pedro the location as well as the original plan and orientation of the new church.

The site lay a good six to seven hundred feet south of the pueblo proper at the opposite end of the same long mesilla, closer and less isolated than Father San Miguel's 1598 church, but hardly in the laps of the Pecos.[17] To picture the relationship in space of pueblo and projected church, with "neutral zone" between, it is worth pirating a few lines from seaborne ex-Army chaplain, historian, and poet Fray Angelico Chavez.

Let us imagine, first, a long, low mesa of red and buff stone rising above a medium-height forest of piñon and juniper, as also clearings here and there planted with corn. This mesa platform looks roughly like the hull of a massive modern battleship drawing deep water on a choppy sea of evergreens. It lies at anchor, of course.

Along the center of the great stone deck rises a reddish-brown superstructure of mud-plastered stone tenements in four receding tiers. This is the pueblo itself . . . . a low wall of mud-plastered flagstones forms the railing all along the edges of the deck.[18]

To carry Fray Angelico's naval analogy a little further, the grounded dreadnought rides with her broad, ill-shapen bow to the north, as if a norther had swung her around at anchor. Amidships aft she tapers noticeably, all the way back to the slender stern. Precisely there, athwart the poop deck, still within the ship's railing but as far aft of the main superstructure as possible, the friar meant to set his church.

It would face to starboard, to the east like most seventeenth-century New Mexico churches. Because the bedrock deck of the mesilla was not entirely level at its southern or stern end, but rather humped in the center, preparation of an area spacious enough to contain a large church with adjoining convento and cemetery required considerable fill. The massive foundations would rest entirely on the bedrock but they would be deeper at the two extremes than in the middle.[19] Father Ortega may have overseen the hauling of fill with his borrowed oxen, perhaps even laying up some of the stone-faced, rubble foundations, but that was about all. Once again Governor Eulate intervened.

Eulate Halts
Construction

At every turn, to hear the friars tell it, Eulate thwarted their missionary program. He abused or threatened mission Indians who worked for or cooperated with the Franciscans. He opposed mission expansion, denying escorts to friars who wished to carry the gospel to neighboring heathens, even though he exacted tribute and services from such people whenever he could. When certain encomenderos, like Capt. Francisco Gómez, volunteered as escorts, Eulate ordered them back. But perhaps most scandalous of all, the governor openly obstructed the building or repairing of churches and conventos, even threatening to hang the Indian laborers who refused to quit.

With his outrageous bullying, he brought work on the Santo Domingo and San Ildefonso churches to a standstill, but the one they were all talking about was Pecos. A number of Spaniards had lent Father Ortega their oxen, presumably in the off season, to help build his grand church. One such cooperative citizen was diminutive Canary Islander Juan Luján, a resident of New Mexico since 1600. Eulate accosted him. If he did not send immediately to Pecos for his oxen, he could count on a fine of forty fanegas of maize! Ensign Sebastián Rodríguez, who had traveled to New Mexico with his wife in the company of Eulate and Father Ortega back in 1618, also had oxen on the Pecos project, as did Ensign Juan de Tapia. With them, the governor was even more brutal. If they did not go at once and bring back their animals from Pecos, "he would dispose of them and the oxen." When they protested that they had no horses to ride, Eulate yelled at them "to go on foot and bring in the whips, the yoke straps, and the yokes on their own backs!" [20]

The governor had made his point. "In order to avoid disputes and strife," Father Custos Esteban de Perea reluctantly ordered his religious to stop all building.[21] At Pecos a frustrated Pedro de Ortega complied.

Perea, a fighter if ever there was one, cannot have meant the stoppage as more than a temporary measure calculated to buy time. He had petitioned his Father Provincial to allow him to come to Mexico City and present in person the friars' case against the governor. In August 1621, he appealed to the people of New Mexico to denounce anyone guilty of offenses against the church. At least seven friars responded—including Fathers Ortega and Zambrano—each verifying and expanding upon the list suggested by their superior. Eulate was reported to be in a rage, vowing to have two hundred lashes applied to anyone caught informing against him. To some New Mexicans, it must have seemed as though open warfare between the two factions was about to erupt again as it had less than a decade before. Just then, the supply caravan arrived.

Father Perea's term of office had ended. A new Father Custos, an appeaser, had been dispatched from Mexico City. Instructions from the viceroy to both the prelate and the governor urged restraint and mutual aid. For about a year, a welcome spirit of forbearance overlay the quarrel between church and state.²² At Pecos that meant a resumption of building, not under the eye of Fray Pedro de Ortega but of another Franciscan, unquestionably the most effective missionary ever to live among the Pecos.

By the time he moved in at Pecos late in 1621 or early in 1622, Fray Andrés Juárez was a scarred veteran. He had ridden muleback to New Mexico a decade earlier, in the train of Comisario Isidro Ordóñez, who later imprisoned him. While guardian at Santo Domingo, he had suffered the abuse of Governor Eulate's men. At Pecos he would endure the trials of thirteen years, longer than any other missionary in the pueblo's history.

Andrés Juárez of Fuenteovejuna

He was from Spain, from the pleasant oak-studded hill country northwest of Córdoba. His parents, Sebastián Rodríguez Galindo and María Juárez, were natives of Fuenteovejuna, where Andrés was born in 1582, six years before the Armada. All over Andalucía people knew the town for its hearty *vino de los guadiatos,* the product of vineyards that grew along the banks of the Río Guadiato, and for its rich honey, prized since Roman times. The variant spelling of Fuenteovejuna, which translates Sheep Well, is Fuenteabejuna, Bee Well. Still, it was history, and the incredibly restless pen of Lope de Vega, that conferred upon the town its enduring fame.²³

A Franciscan missionary. After Fray Diego Valadés, Rhetórica Christiana (1579)

Andrés Juárez and Lope de Vega were contemporaries. As a native son of Fuenteovejuna, Juárez, who chose to use his mother's surname instead of his father's, had heard the story told and retold even before Vega popularized it. He was reminded of it every time he entered the parish church of Nuestra Señora del Castillo. On this spot in the eighth century, the Moslems had built a fortress. The Christian knights who stormed back five hundred years later made it a castle. When the crusading military order of Calatrava received the town as a fief, the castle became the palace of the Order's knight commander, or *comendador*. The deeds of Comendador don Fernán Gómez de Guzmán, and Fuenteovejuna's shocking response, were recorded in the *Crónica de la Orden de Calatrava*. From its pages, the ebullient libertine Lope de Vega, "Nature's Wonder," mined the story and shaped it into one of the most intense dramas of Spanish classical literature.

It is a story of heroic community solidarity, of mutual action and loyalty in the face of cruel tyranny. The comendador, Fernán Gómez, personifies the jealous and unruly nobility. When not inciting his fellow knights against the Catholic Kings, he delights in seducing the women of Fuenteovejuna, virgin and married alike, sadistically beating the men who object. At last by force he deflowers the comely, high-spirited Laurencia. In her shame, she stands before the town elders and harangues them to vengeance. The people unite, storm the castle, and tear the evil Gómez limb from limb. An investigator dispatched by the king subjects men, women, and children to judicial torture, asking each the question *"Quién mató al comendador?"* No one breaks. Each replies *"Fuente Ovejuna, Señor. Y quién es Fuente Ovejuna? Todos á una!"* Throwing themselves on the mercy of Ferdinand and Isabella, the town as a whole is pardoned and royal justice prevails.

This drama, known so well by *fuenteovejunense* Andrés Juárez, was given to the world by Lope de Vega in 1619—while Juárez was guardian at Santo Domingo. The playwright called it simply "Fuente Ovejuna."[24]

Entry no. 554 in the Convento Grande's "Libro de entradas y profesiones" records the investiture on Thursday, December 4, 1608, of "Andrés Xuárez, native of Fuenteovejuna in the diocese of Córdoba." It gives no hint of when he sailed from Spain to America. He was old enough when he entered the Order, twenty-six, to have had all or most of his priestly training behind him. Concluding his novitiate, he professed his vows on December 5, 1609. Two years later, when recruiter Fray Isidro Ordóñez returned a second time from the missions of New Mexico, six priests and three lay brothers volunteered. Father Juárez was among them.[25]

Since Ordóñez' previous visit to the capital, Oñate's friend, two-term viceroy Luis de Velasco, had gone back to Spain and the archbishop of Mexico, the famed baroque Dominican García Guerra, had succeeded him, ruling as both primate of

Archbishop-viceroy fray García Guerra, 1611-1612.   Rivera Cambas, *Los gobernantes,* I

the Mexican church and chief of state. To unwashed crowds who
gathered, mouths agape, to glimpse the great man gesture from
his glittering carriage, and to finely attired dignitaries who
waited upon his every command, it seemed that Fray García,
despite earthquakes, floods, and physical distress, thoroughly
relished his awesome dual authority. Judging by the subsequent
actions of Isidro Ordóñez in New Mexico, that image was not
wasted on the Franciscan.[26]

The officious Ordóñez busied himself with details of sup-   The Supply Train
ply. By order of the archbishop-viceroy, dated October 1, 1611,   to New Mexico
he oversaw the purchase, stockpiling, and transportation of
goods for the missionaries in the field as well as for those he
would shepherd to New Mexico himself, everything from oil
paintings of saints in gilded frames, damask vestments, huge

illuminated choir books containing introits and antiphonies for
the saints' days to forty pairs of sandals, "twelve large latches
for church doors with their locks, keys, and ring staples, and
one hundred twenty Sevillan locks for cells with their keys,"
from two-hundred-pound bells to pins, from vintage wine,
raisins, almonds, and peach and quince preserves to olive oil
and vinegar. Early in 1612—about the time Viceroy don fray
García Guerra breathed his last—they set out, "giving thanks
to God," Ordóñez, Juárez, and eight other friars astride saddle
mules that had cost the crown 129 pesos 2 tomines each with
full trappings. Erect, dark-skinned Capt. Bartolomé Romero,
veteran of the Oñate conquest, commanded the armed escort.
Whip-cracking muleteers, high aboard the twenty heavy, groan-
ing wagons overloaded with the mission goods, cursed their
mule teams and their luck. Sundry servants, animals, and
hangers-on ate dust at the rear. [27]

The journey north from Zacatecas, which they must have
left late in March, was hell. But for a few poor settlements, the
country through which they rode for a hundred leagues was
"desolate . . . almost without any convenience or refuge." The
friars, "almost all raw recruits and hardly world travelers,"
found themselves forced to do without necessities, "things
we could have got in Mexico City." The temperature climbed.
They griped. To a man, said a harsh critic of Ordóñez, they laid
the blame to Fray Isidro "for having perversely misinformed
us about the road." One lay brother lost heart and deserted.
When the superior admonished the others at the Río Florido to
make do in the knowledge that they would appreciate the provisions even more in their isolated missions, they tightened their
cords. After all it was not material comfort that had moved
them to become missioners, rather the love of God. Therefore, "with confidence in His Divine Majesty and in accord
with what Father Ordóñez proposed and promised, we traveled
on and suffered en route what only Our Lord knows." [28]

Juárez Tested   Neither did the suffering cease when they reached New
Mexico. Father Ordóñez had allegedly tongue lashed several
of the friars on the road. He continued to do so in the missions. Juárez' turn came soon enough. Evidently assigned first to
the convento in Sante Fe where he witnessed the shooting incident involving Governor Peralta, Fray Andrés suffered
Ordóñez' wrath on several occasions in public. It mortified him.
The sin of vengeance welled within his breast. He had to get
out, to carry word of the local prelate's excesses to his superiors
in Mexico City. Juárez would gladly pay for his desertion with
whatever penance they prescribed.

The attempt of Andrés Juárez to flee New Mexico, like most everything else known about the regime of Comisario Ordóñez, was recorded by Fray Francisco Pérez Huerta, who considered Ordóñez a monster. Whatever the facts of the case, Pérez Huerta's interpretations were sure to be colored. According to him, Father Juárez hired a manservant for the journey and made secret plans to slip away. The servant informed Ordóñez. Rather than confront the scheming friar, the comisario gave him the rope to hang himself.

Unaware that his servant had betrayed him, Juárez headed for Galisteo to provision himself. There the Father Guardian gave him what he could, at the same time trying to talk him out of taking so rash a step. Juárez would not listen. It was in God's hands now. If he did not go, he knew he would "either hang himself or kill the Father Comisario." Pérez Huerta gave him the arquebus and horse armor he wanted.

Meanwhile, having sworn the other friars to silence under their vow of obedience and on pain of excommunication, Ordóñez laid a trap. Waiting undercover just far enough down the road to establish without a doubt Juárez' intention, he grabbed the startled friar, confiscated the letter of Pérez Huerta

Fray Andrés Juárez

he was carrying to Mexico City, and soundly rebuked him in front of a layman. "Straight-away they took him prisoner to the convento of Santo Domingo where he was absolved and actually put in the jail for a term of four months."

Confinement seemed to take the fire out of Fray Andrés, at least for a while. It was Ordóñez who left New Mexico. Juárez became guardian at Santo Domingo. Unlike Custos Perea and Father Zambrano, he did not attack Governor Eulate. He saw work on the Santo Domingo church stop because of the governor's threats. Still, when the opportunity to testify against Eulate presented itself, Juárez had little original to say. He did not even mention what allegedly happened on Sunday, August 1, 1621. He had gone in to say Mass for the Spaniards of Sante Fe, then returned to preach in Santo Domingo. After his sermon, Capt. Pedro Durán y Chávez, one of Eulate's closest supporters, was supposed to have quipped that what Father Juárez needed was a good punch in the nose.[29]

Respite in
Church-State
Conflict

The peacemaker arrived in October 1621. Sent out from the Convento Grande, Fray Miguel de Chavarría, newly appointed custos of New Mexico, made no pretense. He warmly embraced Governor Eulate. Ex-custos Perea blanched. Here once again was Christ in the embrace of Judas Iscariot. The two friars' exchange at chapter must have been tense. There was no common ground save their faith. Veteran Perea, mulish protector of the church, knew what the perfidious Eulate was capable of. Chavarría, the administrator from headquarters, had come to restore harmony. The viceroy had decreed it. Surely, as God's children, they could work things out. Perea did not think so. His one hope to save the church in New Mexico from the anti-christ Eulate was to present the facts in person in Mexico City. But Chavarría would not let him go.

There was a reason for Custos Chavarría's conciliatory attitude toward Eulate, beyond Perea's allegation that they were old buddies. The viceroy's instructions had plainly laid the onus on the Franciscans. With the contending parties' "letters, missives, memorials, depositions, and other documents" before them, the viceroy and his advisers had been more offended by the picture of a royal governor, excommunicate, shackled, doing humiliating public penance before omnipotent friars than by alleged crimes against the church and morality. The friars must cease their interference in secular affairs.

Getting down to specifics, the viceroy admonished both custos and governor not to meddle in the annual elections of native pueblo officials; he cautioned the friars not to obstruct the collection of tribute from pueblos like Pecos that had already been granted in encomienda, at the same time ordering that no tributes be exacted from unconverted pueblos like those of Zuñi and Hopi. He instructed the governor to provide escorts for the friars and forbade him to let Spaniards run livestock within three leagues of the pueblos; he told the missionaries to stop cutting the Indians' hair as punishment; and he tried, from fifteen hundred miles away, to decree an end to illegal use of

Taos pueblo, north house block. John K. Hillers, 1880.   Museum of New Mexico

Indian labor by colonist and missionary alike. Even though abuses persisted, the heads of church and state now greeted each other in public, while ex-custos Perea fumed.[30]

 At Pecos, the missionary effort picked up. Just why Custos Chavarría recalled Fray Pedro de Ortega and moved Andrés Juárez over from Santo Domingo is not clear. Certainly Ortega's abortive attempts to discipline the idolater Mosoyo and to build a church had put him in a compromising position. His smashing of Pecos idols had sorely strained his relations with the people. From all indications, Father Juárez—like the renowned sixteenth-century Franciscan Bernardino de Sahagún—was more tolerant, more willing to accept the Pecos as they were, to learn their language and their ways, and to use this acquaintance to guide them toward a Christian salvation. To change their hearts, he relied not on destruction of pagan symbols, but rather on the infinite grace of God, the God of the New Testament.

 As for Fray Pedro de Ortega, he took up a heavier cross. Assigned to the conversion of Taos, he all but won the martyr's crown. In the beginning, "the idolatrous Indians illtreated him

Juárez to Pecos; Ortega to Taos

to prevent him from remaining there and preaching our holy Catholic faith. For food they gave him tortillas of maize made with urine and mice meat, but he used to say that for a good appetite, there is no bad bread, and that the tortillas tasted fine." When they refused him lodging, he laid up a shelter of branches and persevered in the cold.

First he converted "the principal captain." Others followed and helped him build a decent convento. Then one night as he sat by the fire, an Indian, an ally of "the priests of the idols," leveled an arrow at him. Just as the would-be assassin was about to let fly, a Spaniard's dog startled him. He ran. The dog gave chase. Before he could scale the garden wall, the animal was on him tearing his flesh. They found him dying. There was time only for the friar to absolve and baptize him. "When all those who were not yet baptized and converted saw this punishment from God, they conceived a great love and veneration for the blessed father and [they themselves] were converted and baptized." [31]

Church Building Resumed

While Pedro de Ortega was reportedly winning over the disinclined Taos, Fray Andrés Juárez resumed construction at Pecos. How much he could utilize of what Ortega had done before the stoppage in 1621, Juárez did not say. But by the time Custos Chavarría visited the pueblo, presumably in mid-1622, the structure was taking shape. Fray Andrés, writing to the viceroy on October 2, explained

that a temple is being built in this pueblo de los Pecos de Nuestra Señora de los Ángeles because it has no place to say Mass except for a jacal in which not half the people will fit,[32] there being two thousand souls or a few less. And thus, God willing, it will be finished with His help next year. Therefore I beg Your Excellency, for the love of Our Lord, please order that an altar piece featuring the Blessed Virgin of the Angels, advocate of this pueblo, be given, as well as a Child Jesus to place above the chapel which was built for that purpose. Of all this our Father Custos, fray Miguel de Chavarría, as an eyewitness, will give a fuller account.

Juárez was an accomplished beggar. He also wanted some new priestly vestments because the old ones were "already all torn to pieces." Either he was bidding for an *ayuda de costa* from the royal treasury, the traditional one-thousand-peso initial grant to new churches for bells, altar furnishings, vestments, etc.—which may already have been spent on Pecos —or for a special pious donation. Whatever the case, the astute Franciscan vowed that the altar piece would be installed at Pecos in the viceroy's name so that "the Blessed Virgin might reward the concern of Your Excellency and so that these poor recent converts might be brought to a knowledge of the greatest truth in Our Holy Catholic Faith."

He kept pressing. Pecos was not just any pueblo, "as Your Excellency can verify." To Pecos every year came numerous "heathens, called the Apache nation," people from the plains.

They come to this pueblo to trade, and the items they bring are very important both to the natives and to the Spaniards. Many times when they come they will enter the church and when they see there the retablo and the rest there is, the Lord will enlighten them so that they want to be baptized and converted to Our Holy Catholic Faith. And in all the good that results from the altar piece Your Excellency will share.[33]

That year, 1622, building preoccupied Andrés Juárez. The supply wagons were finally about to return to Mexico City after many months' delay. Like some of his fellow missionaries, Fray Andrés took this opportunity to write the highest-ranking official in New Spain. Of nine letters sent, only his was nonpartisan. He alone confined himself to the immediate needs of his mission, while the others took sides, most of them, like Zambrano Ortiz, vehemently denouncing Governor Eulate and, by implication, their superior who had tried to appease him.

Custos Chavarría was also leaving. After only a year in the missions, he felt compelled to return to Mexico City to defend himself against the barbs of his fellow Franciscans. In letters to the viceroy, the Convento Grande, and the Inquisition, Perea and his party had flayed Governor Eulate, citing again and again his obscene disregard for the viceroy's instructions. At the same time, they had portrayed Custos Chavarría as the governor's toady.

Few friars dared stand by Chavarría. One who did was old Alonso Peinado. He praised the custos' efforts to calm the troubled waters and to propagate the faith, especially among the Pecos, Jémez, Taos, and Southern Tiwas. With another six friars he would have reduced the Piros and Tompiros, "who are on the verge." He had encouraged church construction. At Santa Fe, the foundations had been laid for a convento and a church that Father Peinado believed "will be the best in this land." Evidently he had not seen Pecos.[34]

A Church to Match
the Pueblo

The Pecos project was monumental. The pueblo's size, consequence, and self-respect dictated that its church be the best in the land. Plans called for a nave as wide inside as the largest available pine beams would span, forty-one feet at the entrance, tapering to thirty-seven and a half feet at the sanctuary. Height of ceiling would approximate width. The number of Pecos Indians, that is the size of the potential congregation, determined length—a remarkable one hundred and forty-five feet from entrance to the farthest recess of the apse. Wall thickness varied from eight to ten feet down the sides between buttresses, to twenty-two feet at the back corners where two of the planned towers would rise.[35] Outside, the massive structure, with its rows of rectangular ground-to-roof buttresses up the lateral walls, its six towers, and its crenelated parapet would look as much like a fortress as a church—a reflection not of Father Juárez' fear of attack, but rather of his European heritage.

300,000 Adobes

Such an undertaking laid a heavy burden on the Pecos. Each sun-dried mud block, about 9½ by 18 by 3 inches, weighed forty pounds or so. Gray to black in color and containing bits of bone, charcoal, and pottery, the earth must have been dug from the trash mounds that had accumulated along the edges of the mesilla. The job would require 300,000 adobes. While the men hauled earth and water and the great quantity of wood needed for scaffolding, the actual laying up of walls in Pueblo society was women's work. "If we force some man to build a wall," wrote Fray Alonso de Benavides, "he runs away from it, and the women laugh." [36]

The friars were always quick to condemn Juan de Eulate as an "enemy of churches" when he opposed their construction. Yet his complaints to the viceroy that the missionaries demanded endless free labor from the Indians to build and maintain excessively grandiose structures, that such work kept the natives from cultivating their fields, and that it monopolized the oxen and skills of neighboring colonists, may have been founded as much on fact as on his own greed and irreverence.[37]

The Pecos, no mean builders themselves, had never raised up anything like this before. The whole concept of enclosing within walls forty feet high so immense a volume of unutilized space to the glory of God was foreign to their thinking. Such walls, as well as the buttresses and towers, all of which emphasized the vertical, went against their tradition of building in horizontal layers. Despite the limits imposed on Fray Andrés by the environment—by a friable, impermanent building material of low plastic potential and, to a lesser degree, by

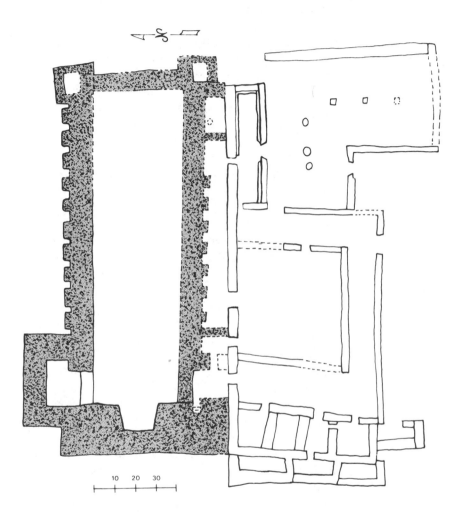

Floor plan of the monumental Pecos church of Fray Andrés Juárez.

a work force untrained in European techniques—he still managed to open the Pecos' eyes with other architectural innovations: winding stairs up the inside of a tower, swinging doors, corbels and crenelations, and many more.

The work took longer than he had reckoned. Seasonal demands on the Pecos, agriculture, hunting, and trading, the inevitable shortages of craftsmen, oxen, or materials, and once again the formidable opposition of Governor Eulate combined to wreck his schedule. In his letter of October 1622 to the viceroy, Fray Andrés had expressed the hope that the church would be finished the following year. It was not. On one of his trips to Santa Fe to say Mass, the Pecos friar and the royal governor had exchanged words over the obeisance a priest should render a governor in church. This led to allegations that don Juan had denied that one should adore the cross. Later the missionary complained that only after three years, more or less, had Eulate granted him "the aid of oxen he had requested from the citizens for construction of the Pecos church." [38] Depending on the date of his initial request, the end of three years would have fallen sometime late in 1624 or in 1625.

In January 1626, New Mexico's seventeenth-century promoter par excellence, Fray Alonso de Benavides, Franciscan custos and agent of the Inquisition, entered Santa Fe with due pomp and ceremony. He stayed more than three years, stimulating vitally the missionary effort. He set out new missions, dedicated churches, and even labored in the vineyard himself among Piros, Jémez, and Gila Apaches. Later, during his vain bid for a bishop's miter, the resourceful Benavides claimed full credit for everything of note that had occurred in New Mexico during his administration. But he did not claim the Pecos project. Fray Andrés Juárez had finished before his arrival.

The Impression of Fray Alonso de Benavides

Still, Father Benavides recognized Juárez' achievement as "a convento and most splendid temple of singular construction and excellence on which a friar expended very great labor and diligence." [39] Adjoining the south wall of the church, the convento, with its rooms and covered walkway secluding the usual interior patio, must have gone up right after the church. On the west side it was two stories. Here Fray Andrés had his quarters, and on the second floor off his cell, a mirador, or enclosed balcony, "which looks out toward the villa [Santa Fe]." [40] Although it is tempting to conjure up a festive dedication on August 2, 1625, the building dates for the monumental Pecos mission, encompassing whatever start

An artist's restoration of the Pecos church by Jerry L. Livingston.
After a painting by Friar Hans Lentz in Hayes, *Four Churches*

Father Ortega may have made, can be drawn no tighter than
1621 and 1625.

Few of Fray Andrés Juárez' contemporaries left descriptions. Yet they must have been impressed. To mounted Spaniards dropping down through piñon and juniper out of the
mountains to the west, come to collect tribute or to trade for
hides and slaves, or to a party of Plains Apaches approaching
from the east, their loaded dog travois inscribing a hundred
parallel lines in the loose dirt, the Pecos church with the sun
on its white plastered walls must have seemed at most a wonder, at least an unmistakable landmark.

Architecturally it was unique, a sixteenth-century Mexican
fortress-church in the medieval tradition, rendered in adobe in
the baroque age at the ends of the earth. No other pueblo
church, with the possible exception of San Gregorio de

Architectural
Marvel

The Mexican fortress-church of Acolman just north of Mexico City.   Gibson, *Aztecs*

Abó, built a decade later and of stone, so completely belied its heritage. Pecos was pure transitional, from transplanted European fortress-church, built of masonry, permanent and dynamic, to New Mexico mission, of earth, field stone, and wood, impermanent and static.

By massing adobe, the friar-architects of New Mexico achieved the height they wanted and, at the same time, gave to their churches distinctive unbroken expanses of exterior wall and a pylon-like silhouette. At Pecos, Juárez conceded to the massive walls. Half a century and half a continent away, Franciscan chronicler Agustín de Vetancurt, wrote of the "magnificent temple" at Pecos "adorned with six towers, three on each side" and with walls "so thick that services were held in their recesses." [41] Yet with his buttresses, Juárez clung to the traditional, as if he wished to create the illusion of masonry. At Pecos, the walls rose almost straight, and the buttresses broke up the smooth exterior texture. Instead of countering the thrust of rib vaulting, as they would have in a Mexican fortress-church, here they bore only the dead weight of a flat roof. Horizontal beam and lintel replaced vault and arch in New Mexico. In other ways too, with windows for example, Fray Andrés may have sought to work the materials at hand into something a European could recognize as a church.

George Kubler, distinguished author of *The Religious Architecture of New Mexico,* would have delighted in analyzing, disassembling, and reassembling Juárez' noble monument. But he and everyone else were wholly fooled by the smaller, cruder eighteenth-century church built right on top of its crumbled ruins. Not until 1967, during excavation and stabilization of the more recent church by the National Park Service, did archaeologist Jean M. Pinkley hit upon the imposing foundations of the parent structure. Her find vindicated both Benavides and Vetancurt. Concluding the preface to a fourth edition of his classic, Kubler paid tribute to Fray Andrés Juárez. Architecturally his church "now emerges as the 'prime object' in seventeenth-century New Mexico." [42]

Missionary's Routine

The great church became at once a revelation and a focus. No Pecos who worked on the structure, no Apache who saw it for the first time, could help but be impressed by this temple to the invaders' God, plainly a virile God who had shown His followers many advanced ways. Neither could an Indian who expressed interest or awe escape hearing more about the love of this God for mankind and His offer of salvation through baptism. This towering new church epitomized the strong ministry of Andrés Juárez.

Custos Benavides, ever prone to pious exaggeration, claimed that Pecos had "more than two thousand Indians, well built houses three and four stories high and some even more. They are all baptized and well instructed under the good administration of Father fray Andrés Juárez, a great minister and linguist." [43] Command of the Pecos language, to whatever degree, must have enhanced Juárez' effectiveness as evangelist, teacher, and administrator, freeing him from utter dependence on the generally ill-trained interpreters. Although Fray Andrés left no description of his regime at Pecos, we can get an idea of what it entailed from Benavides' idealized composite view.

Most of the conventos have only one religious each, and he ministers to four, six, or more neighboring pueblos [not the case at Pecos], in the midst of which he stands as a lighted torch to guide them in spiritual as well as temporal affairs. More than twenty Indians, devoted to the service of the church, live with him in the convento. They take turns relieving one another as porters, sacristans, cooks, bell-ringers, gardeners, waiters, and at other tasks. They perform their duties with as much attention and care as if they were friars. In the evening they say their prayers together, with much devotion, before some santo.

In every pueblo where a friar resides, he has schools for the teaching of prayer, choir, playing musical instruments, and other

A long-waisted
Spanish bell like
those sent to New
Mexico in the 17th
century.
After Boyd,
Popular Arts

useful things. Promptly at dawn, one of the Indian singers, whose
turn it is that week, goes to ring the bell for Prime, at the sound
of which those who go to school assemble and sweep the rooms
thoroughly. The singers chant Prime in choir. The friar must be
present at all of this. He takes note of those who have failed to
perform this duty in order to reprimand them later. When everything is neat and clean, they again ring the bell and each one goes
to learn his particular specialty. The friar oversees everything in
order that these students pay attention to what they are doing. At
this time those who plan to get married come and notify him so
that he may prepare and instruct them according to Our Holy
Council [of Trent]. If there are any persons, either sick or healthy,
who wish to confess in order to receive Communion at Mass, or
who wish anything else, they come to tell him. After they have
been occupied in this manner for an hour and a half, the bell is
rung for Mass.

All go into the church, and the friar says Mass and administers
the sacraments. Mass over, they gather in their different groups.
The lists are examined and note taken of those who are absent in
order that they may be reprimanded later. After roll is taken, all
kneel down by the church door and sing the *Salve* in their own
tongue. This concluded, the friar says: "Praised be the most holy
Sacrament," and dismisses them, warning them first of the care
with which they should go about their daily business.

At mealtime, the poor people in the pueblo who are not ill
come to the porter's lodge, where the cooks of the convento have
ready sufficient food, which is served to them by the friar. Food
for the sick is sent to their houses. After mealtime, it always

happens that the friar has to go to some neighboring pueblo to hear a confession or to see if they are careless in the boys' school where they learn to pray and assist at Mass, for this is the responsibility of the sacristans and it is their duty always to have a dozen boys for the service of the sacristy and to teach them how to help at Mass and how to pray.

In the evening they toll the bell for vespers, which are chanted by the singers who are on duty for the week, and, according to the importance of the feast, they celebrate it with polyphonic chant, as they do for Mass. Again the friar supervises and looks after everything, the same as in the morning.

On feast days, he says Mass in the pueblo very early, and administers the sacraments, and preaches. Then he goes to say a second Mass in another pueblo, whose turn it is, where he observes the same procedure, and then returns to his convento. These two Masses arc attended by the people of the tribe, according to their proximity to the pueblo where they are celebrated.

One of the week days which is not so busy is devoted to baptism, and all those who are to be baptized come to the church on that day, unless some urgent matter intervenes. In that case it is performed any time. With great care the names of those baptized are inscribed in a book; in another those who are married; and in another the dead.

One of the greatest tasks of the friars is to settle disputes of the Indians among themselves, for, since they look upon him as a father, they come to him with all their troubles, and he has to take pains to harmonize them. If it is a question of land and property, he must go with them and mark their boundaries, and thus pacify them.

For the support of all the poor of the pueblo, the friar makes them sow some grain and raise some cattle, because if he left it up to them, they would not do anything. Therefore the friar requires them to do so and trains them so well that with the meat he feeds all the poor and pays the various workmen who come to build the churches. With the wool he clothes all the poor, and the friar himself also gets his clothing and food from this source. All the wheels of this clock must be kept in good order by the friar, without neglecting any detail, otherwise all would be totally lost.[44]

For a dozen and one years, Andrés Juárez kept the Pecos clock running. At times, as he looked out from the steps of his church over the faces of the Pecos gathered, men on one side, women on the other, in the *atrio,* or courtyard that doubled as cemetery, to hear him discourse on the immortality of the soul, he must have felt the despair expressed so often by his fellow missionaries. Would he ever penetrate their hearts? Prodded by native catechists called *fiscales,* they could say by rote the Creed or the Pater Noster, but what did these words mean to them? They plainly enjoyed the rich ceremonialism of the Mass, the singing, and the feast-day processions, but what did they know of the sacrifice of Jesus Christ?

Effects of Juárez' Ministry

Juárez knew that the gobernador they elected annually in compliance with the viceroy's instructions was only a figurehead put forward to deal with the Spaniards. Their traditional headman, whom the Spaniards labeled the cacique, and "the priests of the idols," as Benavides called them, continued to propitiate Corn Mother and all the other intimate forces that ordered the Pueblo world. They simply went underground whenever the missionary put the pressure on. He could punish idolaters at the mission whipping post, along with chronic truants, but that only made them resentful and more secretive. Once he had instructed the Pecos and baptized them, once he had placed the visible church at their disposal, all he could do was keep them going through the motions. For anything more profound, anything resembling genuine "conversion," Fray Andrés waited on the Holy Spirit.

Some of the Pecos, for reasons of their own, may have responded to Juárez' forceful Christian ministry more positively than others. By the end of the century, a vicious intramural rift between progressive and conservative factions would tear the great pueblo apart. If the roots of this rift reached back before the Spaniards' coming—perhaps to a fundamental division between an individualistic, liberal faction of traders influenced by contacts with other peoples and a more traditional, agrarian, community-oriented Pueblo faction—surely the "Christianization" of Pecos by Andrés Juárez increased the tension. It is possible that a group of Pecos, previously joined together in one moiety, or as a clan, a kiva group, or society, decided at this time to align themselves more visibly with the invaders by renovating the "South Pueblo," almost within the shadow of Juárez' church.[45]

The Pecos Become Carpenters

One thing Fray Andrés did in the realm of things material affected Pecos for the rest of its life. It may also have hastened the pueblo's demise. The Franciscan introduced a craft that became a specialty with the Pecos. It afforded them a skill much in demand throughout New Mexico. It brought them some revenue and some esteem. It also gave them a certain freedom of movement, as they went about from mission to settlement plying their skill. Broadening to the individual, this mobility loosened the hold of the community and made it easier for a Pecos and his family to relocate as the pueblo broke up in the eighteenth century. This craft was carpentry.[46]

"It is a mountainous country," Benavides wrote of the Pecos area, "containing fine timber for construction, hence these Indians apply themselves to the trade of carpentry."

During construction of his church, Father Juárez had brought in Spanish craftsmen, probably ship carpenters recruited in Spain in 1604 by Oñate's brother, to train the Pecos men.[47] Carpentry tools were among the standard items freighted north in the mission supply wagons: axes, adzes, small hand saws and long two-man saws, chisels, augers, and planes, as well as spikes, nails, and tacks.[48]

So dedicated to carpentry did the Pecos become that the great purge of 1680 hardly interrupted their work. As soon as the Spaniards reappeared, the carpenters of Pecos went back to work. Eighteenth-century reports tell repeatedly of lumber prepared by the Pecos and delivered to Santa Fe, of doors and window frames and beds made to order for Spaniards and Indians alike, and of skilled woodworking on New Mexico churches. Sometimes their customers failed to pay. In 1733, four Pecos carpenters filed a belated claim against the missionary at Taos for a job they had done on his church "more than ten years before." [49]

Native carpenters. After Códice Florentino, central Mexico, 16th century

Corbel and beam from the 18th-century Pecos church, "collected" in 1869.   Museum of New Mexico

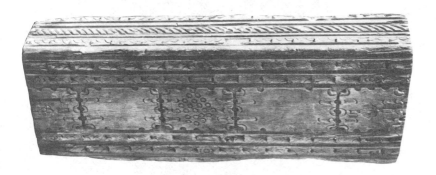

Plains Apaches
and Pecos

Even while he oversaw the myriad details of his ministry to the Pecos—slaughtering a sheep, singing the *Salve Regina,* hoisting a roof beam—Fray Andrés Juárez did not forget the nomads. He had meant what he said in his letter to the viceroy. His mission would become a light unto the Apache nation "so that they want to be baptized and converted to Our Holy Catholic Faith."

He could not have forgotten them if he wanted. Every year about harvest time, from late August to October, they showed up to trade, hundreds of them. Some of them wintered nearby, as Pedro de Castañeda phrased it, "under the eaves" of the pueblo. The arrival of these *vaqueros*—so-called because they followed the vacas de Cíbola, the Cíbola cattle or buffalo— was always an occasion. "I cannot refrain from relating a somewhat incredible though ridiculous thing," recalled Father Benavides as if he had seen it himself,

and it is this. When these Indians go to trade and traffic the whole ranchería goes, including their women and children. They live in tents made of these buffalo skins, very thin and well tanned. They carry the tents loaded on pack trains of dogs harnessed up with their light pack saddles [travois]. The dogs are of medium size. They are accustomed to take five hundred dogs in one pack train, one in front of the other. . . .[50]

Overnight, the open grassy valley that spread out to the east and southeast of the church door was transformed into an Apache rendezvous with clusters of conical skin tipis, run-

A Jicarilla Apache camp. William Henry Jackson, 1884.   Southwest Museum, Los Angeles

ning children, yapping dogs, and the smoke of a hundred fires. One of Oñate's men who had explored east from Pecos in 1598 left a graphic portrayal of these dog-nomads and their tipis as he saw them on the plains, where he

came upon a ranchería of fifty tents made of tanned skins which were very bright red and white in color. They were round like pavilions, with flaps and openings, and made as neatly as those from Italy. They are so large that in the most common ones there is ample room for four individual mattresses and beds. The tanning is so good that even the heaviest rain will not go through the skin, nor does it become hard. On the contrary, when it dries it becomes as soft and pliable as before. As this was so amazing, he made the experiment himself; so, cutting off a piece of leather from a tent, he let it soak, then dried it in the sun, and it remained as pliable as if it had not been wet. The sargento mayor bartered for a tent and brought it to camp. And even though it was so large, as has been stated, it did not weigh more than fifty pounds.

To carry these tents, the poles with which they set them up, and a bag of meat and their pinole, or maize, the Indians use medium-sized, shaggy dogs, which they harness like mules. They have large droves of them, each girt around the breast and haunches, carrying a load of at least one hundred pounds [probably more like fifty to seventy-five pounds]. They travel at the same pace as their masters. It is both interesting and amusing to see them traveling along, one after the other, dragging the ends of their poles, almost all of them with sores under the harness. When the Indian women load these dogs they hold their heads between their legs, and in this manner they load them or straighten their loads. The latter is seldom necessary, for they travel at a pace as if they had been trained with fetters. [51]

Dog travois in use by Comanches and a riotous dog fight, painted by George Catlin, 1834. Catlin, *North American Indians,* II

St. Francis
painted on hide.
Museum of New Mexico

Items of Trade   Trade between Apaches and Pecos had developed in the
sixteenth century soon after the nomads adapted themselves
to the buffalo plains. From mid-century on, volume picked up,
as evidenced by the increasing number of plains artifacts—
Alibates flint knives, flint and bone scrapers, and bone hide-
painting tools—found at datable levels by archaeologists at
Pecos. Because of the near absence of such items in the Tano
pueblos to the west, A. V. Kidder concluded that the Pecos
"may have been more or less monopolistic middlemen for the
westward diffusion" of plains goods.[52]

The nomads brought mainly products of the buffalo—
hides and leather goods, jerked or powdered meat, and tallow.
They also brought tanned skins of other animals, antelope, deer,
and elk; flint and bone tools; salt; and on occasion captives of
the "Quivira nation," their Caddoan-speaking neighbors to

the east. In return, the Pecos gave them maize and other agricultural produce, as well as incidental goods available in the pueblos—painted cotton blankets, pottery, and local turquoise. When harvests were bad and the Pueblos had no surplus to trade, the hungry nomads sometimes fell back on raiding.

In a land as poor as New Mexico, it is no wonder that the invaders sought to profit from the established Pecos-Apache trade. By 1622, Fray Andrés Juárez recognized that the items packed in by the dog-nomads were "very important both to the natives and to the Spaniards." [53] Both relied on the skins for clothing. In addition, said Benavides, the colonists acquired them "for use as sacks, tents, cuirasses, footwear, and everything else imaginable." To dress a skin, the Plains women scraped the rawhide, rubbed in an oily mixture of fat and brains, dried it, then worked it to make it pliable. Smoking rendered it moisture resistant. On some of the buffalo hides meant for use as winter robes, they left the hair; others they scraped thin and tanned until soft as velvet. Such hides and skins became regular items of tribute exacted from the Pecos by their encomendero.[54]

The demands of the Spaniards and the articles they offered for barter—most notably the ubiquitous iron trade knife and later the horse—won a large share of the trade away from the Pecos. Although Coronado found Plains Indian captives living at Pecos as "slaves," the slave trade did not quicken until the Spaniards came to stay. After that, the demand grew so insatiable that Spanish slaving raids directed at the Apaches themselves periodically threatened to wreck the peaceful trade fairs at Pecos and other frontier pueblos. Still, most years they came.

When they did, "the friars always talked to them of God." On one occasion, to hear Father Benavides tell it, certain captains of the Vaquero Apaches entered Santa Fe to see for themselves the famous image of the Assumption of Our Lady which the custos had brought to New Mexico. "The first time they saw it was at night, surrounded by many lighted candles, and there was music. It would be a long matter to relate all my conversations with these captains about their learning how to become Christians." The blandishments worked. The Vaqueros agreed to "a large settlement on a site chosen by them." Just then the devil interfered.[55]

Eager to profit in the slave trade, a successor of the infamous Juan de Eulate, almost certainly don Felipe de Sotelo Osorio, sent out a strong party of Indians to collect as many captives as they could. On the plains, they came upon the

Spaniards Intrude

Vaqueros who had just vowed before the image of Our Lady to become Christians. The eager slavers attacked, killed the chief, and returned with some of the others. Stung by the friars' outcry, the governor reneged and condemned the deed as foul. But the damage had been done.[56]

Father Juárez also worked on the Vaqueros. Not content to sit back and wait for their annual visit to Pecos, he ventured out onto the plains himself, apparently in the company of Spanish traders. He was probably with Capt. Alonso Baca in 1634. Baca and party pressed due east "almost three hundred leagues" to the Arkansas River. There "the friendly Indians who accompanied him," Apaches no doubt, refused to let the Spaniards cross over into Caddoan Quivira.[57]

A generation later, evidently referring to this 1634 expedition, a defendant before the Inquisition admitted that he had gone out on the plains because he wanted the Apaches to make him a captain "as they had done with Capt. Antonio [Alonso] Baca, Francisco Luján, and Gaspar Pérez, father of the one who confesses, and with a friar of the Order of St. Francis named Fray Andrés Juárez." Pérez, an armorer from Brussels who could make trade knives, reportedly "left a son" among the nomads. As part of the elaborate native ceremonial, the Spaniards were supposed to sleep with Apache maidens.[58] Father Juárez, never at a loss for words, this time may have resorted to sign language in defense of his chastity.

Missionary Expansion of Benavides

During the triennium of Alonso de Benavides, 1626-1629, the Franciscans had things pretty much their own way. Their old nemesis Juan de Eulate, relieved in December 1625 by Admiral Felipe de Sotelo Osorio, departed the colony the following autumn with the returning supply caravan. He had not changed. Soon after he reached Mexico City, he was arrested by civil authorities on charges that he had transported Indian slaves to New Spain for sale and that he had sequestered several of the wagons to haul merchandise duty free. Fined and made to pay the cost of shipping the slaves back to New Mexico, don Juan went free. In fact, he turned up later as governor of Margarita, an island off the Spanish Main.

The enduring Fray Esteban de Perea, given leave at last to report in person to his superiors in Mexico City, rode the same caravan as Eulate, his arch adversary. He clutched a packet of documents, the sworn testimony of more than thirty persons heard by Father Benavides sitting as agent of the Inquisition. Still, he would not have the pleasure of seeing the ex-governor do public penance. Even though the Franciscans and the inquisitors accepted his damning reports with thanks, for some reason the Holy Office chose not to prosecute. For his pains, Fray Esteban was reelected custos of New Mexico.[59]

While Perea immersed himself in the business of recruiting thirty more missionaries, the largest contingent ever, and in preparations for the next supply train north, Benavides threw himself into expansion with a vengeance. He had brought a dozen friars himself. He could have used four times as many. Operating in all directions from his residence at Santo Domingo, the hardy prelate carried the gospel himself to the Piros in the Socorro area and to the Tompiros east of there. He utilized well what men he had, both veterans and beginners, thrusting new missions into three Tano and Southern Tiwa pueblos and renewing work at Taos, Picurís, and among the Jémez. He tried also, by pursuing their leaders, to convert the nomads who surrounded the colony "on all sides." Miracles or no miracles, with them he failed.[60]

One of the men Custos Benavides relied on for missionary outreach to the nomads was Pedro de Ortega, formerly of Galisteo, Pecos, and Taos. In 1625, after three trying years with the Taos, Fray Pedro had accepted reassignment to Santa Fe as guardian of the convento and teacher of the boys in the capital, both Spanish and Indian. When Benavides arrived, he appointed Ortega notary of the Inquisition, to serve "with all fidelity, legality, and secrecy." At the stately service of welcome and institution of the new prelate, it was Ortega who rose after the gospel and, flanked by Sargento mayor Francisco Gómez holding the standard of the Holy Office and by the chief constable, read "in loud and intelligible voice" the first formal edict of the faith. It was the feast of Saint Paul's Conversion, January 25, 1625. The Inquisition had come to New Mexico.[61]

Fray Pedro de Ortega among the Nomads

While still at Taos, Father Ortega had heard of an Apache called Quinía "very famous in that country, very belligerent and valiant in war." His people, possibly an ancestral band of the Jicarillas, or perhaps Navajos, ranged the mountains north of Taos both east and west of the Rio Grande. Ortega had tried to convert Captain Quinía. Because the chief was so inclined, claims Benavides, a rival shot him in the chest with an arrow. Ortega and Brother Jerónimo de Pedraza, "a fine surgeon," hastened to Quinía's side and cured him, not with a scalpel but with a religious medal.

For what it was worth in gifts and attentions, Quinía had kept in touch with the friars. He had begged Father Benavides for baptism. "To console him," wrote the custos, "I went to his rancherías . . . and planted there the first crosses. In the year 1628, Father fray Pedro de Ortega baptized him and another famous captain called Manases, who lived near his ranchería. At the time of their baptism, remarkable incidents occurred." [62] But Benavides, who had stirred up more demand for missionaries than he could supply, had no one to assign. The following spring, like manna, reinforcements appeared.

The Return of Perea

Esteban de Perea, custos elect since September 1627, had returned to New Mexico with a flock of twenty-nine friars. One had died en route. At chapter meeting, held on or about Pentecost 1629, he established priorities and made assignments. Most of the Piros and Tompiros, for lack of ministers, still had not been baptized. Perea now allotted six priests and two lay brothers to the task. Two more priests he appointed to the Apaches of Quinía and Manases.

"And since it was the first *entrada* to that bellicose nation of warriors," the new governor don Francisco Manuel de Silva Nieto and a body of armed citizens went along.[63] At one of the Apaches' rancherías, they laid up in a single day "a church of logs, which they hewed; and they plastered these walls on the outside." Franciscans and royal governor, in an exemplary show of cooperation, both dirtied their hands in the work. But no sooner had Silva and the soldiers left than "the devil perverted Captain Quinía." The Indian disavowed his baptism and tried to kill one of the missionaries. Then he and his people moved on. Left alone in the woods, the friars had no choice but to abandon the place.[64]

María de Ágreda and the End of Ortega

A hundred leagues east of Santa Fe and more, beyond the Vaquero Apaches, lived another plains people called the Jumanos, a people who tattooed or painted their faces. The "miraculous conversion" of these "striped" Indians produced superb grist for Benavides' propaganda mill. One way or another, it killed Fray Pedro de Ortega.

Some of the Jumanos on trading visits to the pueblos had developed a special relationship with Fray Juan de Salas of Isleta. Repeatedly they had begged him to return with them and baptize their people. Repeatedly he put them off. Then suddenly, with the arrival of the 1629 caravan, there was an abundance of missionaries, as well as a compelling reason to convert the Jumanos.

At chapter, Custos Perea had read a letter from the archbishop of Mexico concerning the remarkable case of a Spanish Conceptionist Franciscan nun called María de Jesús of Ágreda. Beginning in about 1620, God had miraculously transported her to New Mexico time and again to preach His word to the neglected heathens. The archbishop wanted the friars of New Mexico to investigate the claims "so that they may be verified in legal form." Was it not extraordinary, asked Benavides, that the Jumanos came so regularly every summer begging for baptism? It was as if some person had instilled in them this craving.

When questioned that summer, the Jumanos pointed to a portrait of a nun.

"A woman in similar garb wanders among us over there, always preaching, but her face is not old like this, but young." Asked why they had not told us before, they answered, "Because you did not ask us, and we thought she was around here, too." These Indians repeated this same story in different localities without variation or difference in their accounts.

Venerable Mother María de Jesús de Ágreda preaching to the "Chichimecos" of New Mexico, by Antonio de Castro, printed in Benavides' *Tanto que se sacó,* México, 1730.
Wagner, *Spanish Southwest,* **II**

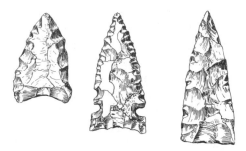

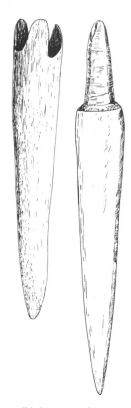

Plains Apache stone
and bone points.
After James H.
Gunnerson,
"An Introduction to
Plains Apache
Archeology—The Dismal
River Aspect,"
Bureau of American
Ethnology, *Bulletin*
173 (Washington, D.C.,
1960)

What more could an apostle ask? Fray Juan de Salas and a companion joined the Jumanos on their return to the plains. After they had traveled more than a hundred leagues, exulted Benavides, a multitude "came out to receive them in procession, carrying a large cross and garlands of flowers." The nun, they said, had shown them how to process and had helped them decorate the cross. So many clamored for baptism that the two friars decided to go back and enlist help. As they prepared to take their leave they blessed the sick, more than two hundred, who "immediately arose, well and healed." [65]

At the same time, it would seem, another apostolic pair and their native interpreters were following a more northerly path that brought them "within view of the kingdom of Quivira." Despite "great dangers and sufferings," they preached and planted crosses at every turn. Then they too headed back to report all they had seen. This party was led by Pecos veteran Fray Pedro de Ortega, who by now had begun to see himself as an apostle of the plains.[66]

Ortega begged to go again. Probably in 1632, probably with Fray Juan de Salas—the accounts vary—Ortega went out to the Jumano settlements, probably on the Río Colorado of present Texas. Although his companion soon returned to the Rio Grande, Fray Pedro stuck it out for six months. He worked hard preaching and catechizing, and he suffered much. According to Benavides' 1634 Memorial, Ortega worked himself to death among heathens and therefore deserved the title of martyr. Writing elsewhere, the same author made the missionary's death among the Jumanos a more conventional martyrdom: "on account of the great zeal of this conversion and because of the suspicion of those idolatrous Indians, they poisoned him with the most cruel poison." [67]

Whether of fatigue or poison, Fray Pedro de Ortega, who had broken up idols at Pecos and had courted Quinía's Apaches, was dead. Except for the exaggerated propaganda of Benavides, so too were missions for the nomads, at least for the time being.

VERDADERA
RELACION, DE LA GRAN'
DIOSA CONVERSION QVE HA AVIDO EN EL
Nuevo Mexico. Embiada por el Padre Fray Eſtevan de Perea, Cuſtodio
de las Provincias del Nuevo Mexico, al muy Reverendo P.Fr.Franciſco
de Apodaca, Comiſſario General de toda la Nueva Eſpaña, de la
Orden de S. Franciſco, dandole cuonta del eſtado de aquellas
còverſiones,y en particular de lo ſucedido en el deſpacho
que ſe hizo para aquellas partes.

¶ *Con licencia del Señor Proviſor, y del ſeñor Alcalde Don Alonſo de Bolaños*
Impreſſo en Sevilla, por Luys Eſtupiñan, en la Calle delas Palmas.Año de 1632.

Alieron deſta Ciudad de Mexico, a quatro de
Setiembre de 1628.años,doze ſoldados,diez y
nueve Sacerdotes,y dos Legos,Religioſos de
S.Franciſco,en compañia del P.Fr. Eſtevan de
Perea Cuſtodio, embiados de la Religioſiſsi-
ma Provincia del Santo Evangelio,con la li-
moſna,y expenſa de ſu Mageſtad, que còCa-
tholico pecho,ſiêdo ſu Ceptro como el Cadu-
ceo de Mercurio;vara vigilante tachonada de
ojos, para la conſervacion deſtas converſiones, en cuya defenſa gaſta la
mayor parte de ſus Reales haberes:vara al fin de la paz,y juſticia,
Con los ya referidos Religioſos fuerõ otros nueve a coſta de la dicha
Provincia,todos con gallardo aliento, y eſpiritu diſpueſto a todo trance
de trabajos,y peligros,oprobrios,y afrètas,por dar a conocer predicãdo
el nombre de Ieſu Chriſto.Con toda alegria,y conformidad, caminarò
haſta el Valle de S.Bartholome,ſin ofrecerſe coſa particular. Aqui ſe re-
freſco la gente cõ algunos alivios para el deſavio con ŷ llegaron:y no lo
fue pequeño en eſta ocaſiò,huyrſe de la manada treinta mulas à las ye-
guas cimarronas,ŷ con muchas diligencias ŷ ſe hizierõn,no parecieron
las quinze. Aqui por ſer la vltima poblaciò, y neceſsitar de baſtimentos
para 150 leguas de deſpoblado,ŷ reſtà haſta el primer pueblo del nuevo
Mexico,

An account of the
western conversions
by Fray Esteban de
Perea, printed in
Sevilla, 1632.
Wagner, *Spanish
Southwest*, I

Missionaries to Ácoma,
Zuñi, and Hopi

In the summer of 1629, Custos Esteban de Perea led a missionary assault on the western pueblos. With Governor Silva, soldiers, ten wagons, and a large remuda, the prelate and eight or ten religious set out for Ácoma on the eve of St. John's Day. One dauntless missionary stayed atop the rock. At Hawikuh, three more chose to abide with the Zuñis. After the first Mass, the ritual act of possession in the name of pope and king, the salvo of arquebuses, the tilting, and the caracoling, governor and custos headed back to Santa Fe while another three friars, with an escort of a dozen soldiers, girded up their loins and pressed on to the Hopis.

Meanwhile, Fray Alonso de Benavides, who remained in New Mexico awaiting the southbound caravan, kept himself busy founding a mission at Santa Clara, his tenth by his own count. Because Custos Perea's commission as agent of the Holy Office had not yet arrived, Benavides continued in that capacity. The Tewas of Santa Clara obliged him by painting the Inquisition's coat of arms in the new church, because "they did not wish any other church to have it." [68]

Benavides
as Lobbyist

When finally he did take his leave in the fall of 1629, Benavides vowed he would return. He never did. Ironically, his influence on the missions of New Mexico increased after his departure. He became a lobbyist. Dispatched by his superiors to the court of Philip IV, the amiable and aspiring religious took to the assignment with gusto. Amid the perfume and lace, the lavish display and the notables of the realm, certain of whom had already sat for the gifted young court painter Diego Rodríguez de Silva y Velázquez, Fray Alonso inhaled the greatness of Spain. Surely His Most Catholic Majesty, once he was informed of New Mexico's "treasures" and of the "many marvels and miracles" that had illuminated the Franciscans' apostolate in that distant land, surely he would want to increase his support. Why should New Mexico not be created a diocese of the church? And why should he, Alonso de Benavides, not be consecrated its first bishop?

His Memorial of 1630, printed at Madrid by royal authority, took the court by storm. The king read it. The council read it. "They liked it so well," wrote Benavides to the friars in New Mexico, "that not only did they read it many times and learn it by heart, but they have repeatedly asked me for other copies."

Benavides Meets
María de Ágreda

In the spring of 1631, Fray Alonso traveled north from the Spanish court for an interview with the Reverend Mother María de Jesús, abbess of the convento of La Purísima Concepción in Ágreda. He carried an order from the Franciscan Father General constraining the nun to tell him everything she knew about New Mexico. Prodded by her confessor and the Father Provincial, she did. In answer to Benavides' leading questions, she gave detailed descriptions of some of the New Mexico friars she had seen on her "flights," including Father Ortega. So many features of the countryside did she recall, even some Benavides had forgotten, that, in his words, "she brought them back to my mind." In his mind, the enraptured friar embellished everything the young abbess said. He begged her to write a letter in her own hand proclaiming God's special concern for the Franciscan missionaries of New Mexico. It made grand publicity.[69]

The Mission Supply
Contract of 1631

While Benavides advertised the missions of New Mexico in Europe at the expense of a sensitive and confused nun, the superiors of his province negotiated a financial agreement with royal officials. This contract, signed in Mexico City on April 30, 1631—the day before Fray Alonso reached Ágreda—

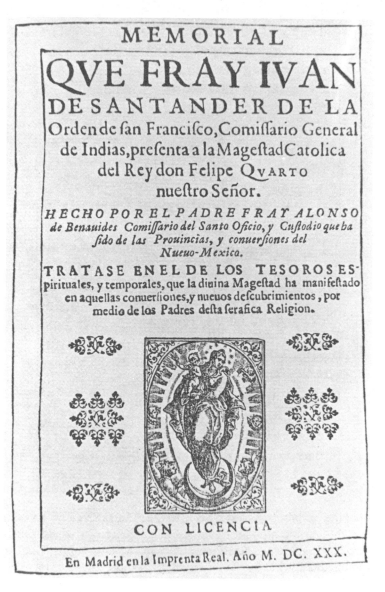

MEMORIAL

QVE FRAY IVAN

DE SANTANDER DE LA
Orden de fan Francifco, Comiffario General
de Indias, prefenta a la MageftadCatolica
del Rey don Felipe QVARTO
nueftro Señor.

HECHO POR EL PADRE FRAY ALONSO
de Benauides Comiffario del Santo Oficio, y Cuftodio que ba
fido de las Prouincias, y conuerfiones del
Nueuo-Mexico.

TRATASE EN EL DE LOS TESOROS ES-
pirituales, y temporales, que la diuina Mageftad ha manifeftado
en aquellas conuerfiones, y nueuos defcubrimientos, por
medio de los Padres defta ferafica Religion.

CON LICENCIA

En Madrid en la Imprenta Real. Año M. DC. XXX.

Title page of Fray Alonso de Benavides' *Memorial,* Madrid, 1630.

spelled out to the last fraction of a peso the amount the crown was willing to spend on these missions. For each item, the negotiators had arrived at a set figure: maintenance of a missionary in the field for the three years between supply caravans (450 pesos for a priest, 300 for a lay brother), outfitting a new missionary (875 pesos), travel expenses for each friar (325), cost of each wagon and its sixteen mules (374 pesos, 4 tomines). The Franciscans assumed the upkeep of the wagons and replacement of spent mules; the crown provided the military escort. By adding the twenty friars being sent out in 1631 to

pal pueblo de la nacion Tanos, que fe dilata por diez leguas en cinco pueblos, adōde aura quatro mil almas bautizadas, con vn Conuento y Iglefia muy buena, y los pueblos las tienen tambien, en que fe les va a dezir Mif-fa defde el Conuento: ay aqui efcuelas de todas Artes, como en los demas.

Nacion Peccos.

AL mifmo Norte otras quatro leguas, fe topa con el pueblo de los Peccos, q̃ tiene mas de dos mil almas, adōde ay vn Conuẽ to y Templo muy luzido, de particular hechura y curiofidad, en que vn Religiofo pufo muy grande trabajo y cuidado; y aunque eftos Indios fon de la nacion Hemes, por eftar aqui folos, y defviados de fu territorio, fe tiene por nacion aparte, aunque es vna mifma lengua: es tierra frigidifsima y poco fertil, aunque da el maiz neceffario para fus habitadores, por-que fiembran mucho Eftan eftos Indios muy biē induftriados de todas Artes, y fus efcuelas de leer, y efcriuir, cantar, y tañer, como los demas.

Description of Pecos
from Benavides'
Memorial of 1630.

the forty-six already in the field, treasury officials came up with a ceiling on the number of missionaries the crown would subsidize in New Mexico, sixty-six. Only in the late 1650s was the ceiling lifted with the addition of four more for the El Paso district.

For thirty-three years the contract stood. It converted mission supply into a business-like and efficient operation. Instead of providing the friars with supplies in kind as before, the treasury now turned over to the procurator-general of the custody a lump sum for the sixty-six missionaries. Everything else was up to the Franciscans. Thanks largely to one remarkable man, Procurator-general fray Tomás Manso, later bishop of Nicaragua, the system ran smoothly and on schedule. Making the arduous round trip with the wagons probably nine times, Manso kept his finger on every detail.

The 1631 contract called for thirty-two wagons, one for every two New Mexico missionaries, excepting the procurator-general and his assistant. These were not the quaint two-wheeled ox carts of the Castaño de Sosa entrada. They were heavy, four-wheeled freight wagons with iron tires, drawn by a team of eight mules, and capable of hauling two tons. On the road, the long train was divided into two squadrons of sixteen wagons, each squadron under the whip of a wagon master. To set them apart, the two lead wagons, like flagships, flew banners displaying the royal coat of arms and their teams were

Fray Tomás Manso

specially caparisoned and wore bells. The squadrons were further broken down into eight-wagon divisions whose lead wagons also flew the royal banner.

The round trip took a year and a half more or less, six months out, six months in New Mexico, and six months back. That left the procurator-general eighteen months to organize and outfit the next northbound train. As long as Father Manso ran the supply service, neither treasury officials nor missionaries could find much to complain about.

Inscription of the Spanish party that stopped at El Morro on March 23, 1632, bound "to avenge the death of Father Letrado." Frederick Webb Hodge, *History of Hawikuh* (Los Angeles, 1937)

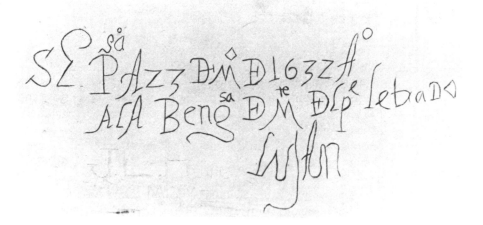

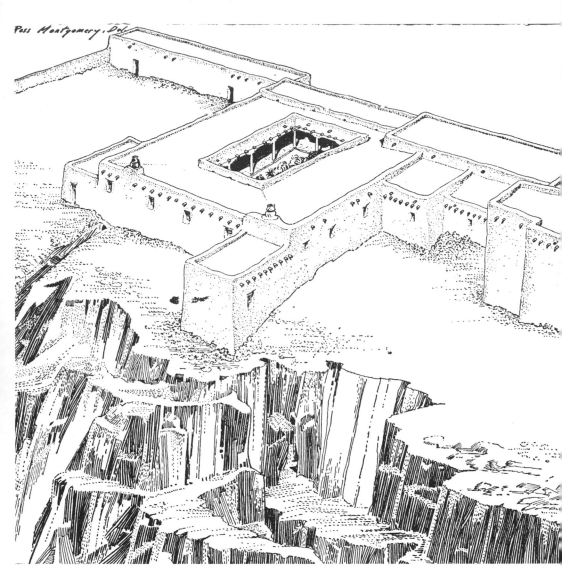

Poss Montgomery, Del.

In practice, the triennial caravan was more than a mission supply service. It was New Mexico's lifeline, the only regularly scheduled freight, mail, and passenger service between the colony and points south. Outbound, royal wagons and Franciscans on muleback, attended by military escort, hundreds of spare mules, and meat on the hoof, were joined by everyone else going to New Mexico, from royal governor to merchants to penniless hangers-on. It was a motley, boisterous train.

On the way back, a similar conglomeration formed around the king's wagons. Governors and ex-governors, claiming the

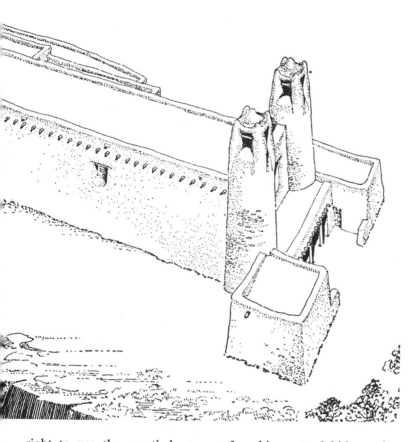

The church built at
Awátovi in the 1630s.
Conjectural restoration
by Ross G. Montgomery.
Montgomery, *Franciscan
Awatovi*

right to use the emptied wagons for shipment of hides, salt,
piñon nuts, and other produce of the province, wrangled with
the friars who saw these exports as fruits of the unlawful exploitation of Indians. Missionary control of the wagons added
yet another dimension to conflict between church and state.[70]

By the early 1630s, the Franciscans had all but covered **Missionary Reverses**
the Pueblo world. From Pecos to Oraibi, from Senecú to Taos,
resident missionaries sought to impose the Christian regime
described by Fray Alonso de Benavides. Opposition by traditional Pueblo leaders, veiled in most of the communities,

erupted violently in the western pueblos, those farthest from the seat of Spanish authority. At Hawikuh on February 22, 1632, the Zuñis put Fray Francisco de Letrado to death and danced with his scalp on a pole. Five days later they caught up with Fray Martín de Arvide, who had set out in search of the Ópata and Pima Indians of Sonora, and killed him too. At the Hopi pueblo of Awátovi, the following year, alleged miracle worker Fray Francisco de Porras died a painful martyr's death when he ate food poisoned by "the priests of the idols." About the same time, the friars pulled back from the Tompiros of Las Humanas and the Jémez of Giusewa, presumably out of fear and frustration.

Disappearance of Alonso de Benavides

The news from New Mexico reached Father Benavides at Rome in time for him to include accounts of these "glorious deaths" in the revised memorial he was preparing for Pope Urban VIII. In every way he knew how, the resourceful Fray Alonso continued to promote the New Mexico missions. His fond hope of becoming the first bishop of Santa Fe seemed at

Fray Alonso de Benavides

times within his grasp. In 1635, back at the Spanish court, he arranged for return passage to the Indies. Then, when the proposal to make New Mexico a bishopric ran into bureaucratic snags, Benavides, the colony's premier propagandist of the seventeenth century, accepted appointment as auxiliary bishop of Goa in Portuguese India. He left for Lisbon at once. Since his name does not appear on any of the standard lists of bishops, it is possible that he died on the outward voyage. It was as if he had sailed off the end of the earth.[71]

Blue Habits for the Friars

The publicity campaign of Alonso de Benavides had put New Mexico on the map. It may also have resulted in a change of color for his brothers' habits. Spanish Franciscans had long pressed the Roman Church to define and endorse the doctrine of the Virgin Mary's Immaculate Conception. Conceptionist Franciscan nuns like María de Jesús of Ágreda, wore the coarse, deep-blue sackcloth cloak symbolic of the

María de Jesús de Ágreda.
Benavides, *Revised
Memorial*

Immaculate Conception. According to Benavides, María de
Ágreda on her miraculous visits to New Mexico most often
dressed in the gray habit of Saint Francis. On other occasions
she appeared in the blue of *La Concepción.* In grateful response
to María's favors through the advocacy of the Immaculate Conception, and as a demonstration in support of the doctrine,
it would appear that the friars of the Holy Gospel province,
mother province of the Order in Mexico, dyed their gray
habits blue, about the color of "the denim used for western
'Levi's.' " [72]

There is no doubt that before the end of the century, and
from then on, the missionary at Pecos wore blue. Just when
the change was ordered is not certain. In Spain, the gifted
María de Ágreda wrote a famous and controversial defense of
the Immaculate Conception, the *Mística Ciudad de Dios,* being
the personal reminiscences of the Virgin as dictated by the

Queen of Heaven herself. After Philip IV visited her at
Ágreda in 1643, María became a confidant of the king. She
asked and received his support of the Immaculate Conception.
Both king and nun died in 1665. In 1670, a Franciscan editor
brought out the *Mística Ciudad*. Two years later, at the request
of the Spanish court, María's cause was introduced at Rome.
Perhaps one of these events, if not an earlier one, had oc-
casioned the change to blue. [73]

**Father Juárez
Leaves Pecos**

The Pecos made no news during the 1630s. They neither
martyred a missionary nor fled their homes. Like most of the
Pueblos, they endured the Spaniards' presence, paid their tribute, and went through the motions of the Roman Catholicism
imposed upon them. Fray Andrés Juárez, the missionary they
had grown accustomed to, pursued his ministry through 1634.
Then, quite suddenly, he was gone. Whether he asked to be
transferred, possibly because of some trouble with the Pecos,
or whether the Father Custos simply decided Fray Andrés had
been there long enough, by early 1635 he had been replaced.

Because most mission records of the period burned during
the purge of 1680—reports of the custodial chapter, correspondence, mission books of baptisms, marriages, and burials—
often the only hope of learning a missionary's whereabouts is

Fray Esteban de Perea, comisario

the Inquisition. Local proceedings of the Holy Office, remitted
periodically to the Tribunal in Mexico City, still survive in
the Archivo General de la Nación. Not only did missionaries
preside over those proceedings, and serve as notaries and as
ratifying witnesses, but they also testified in Inquisition cases.
And more often than not, the notary recorded what missions
they were from.

**Perea as Agent
of Inquisition**

By the time his belated commission as agent of the Holy
Office arrived in 1631, Fray Esteban de Perea had already
turned over to Fray Juan de Salas the burdens of Father
Custos. That freed the crusty Perea to attend to Inquisition
business, which he did until 1638 or 1639, when death finally
caught up with him. The formal reading of an edict of the
faith at Santa Fe in March 1631, combined with Perea's stern

countenance, jolted the populace. "I have noticed," Perea reported to Mexico City, "that before the anathema was read to this simple folk they did not have the fear concerning the [superstitious] use of these powders and herbs which they now so truly show. Their hearts are agitated, and they are afraid." [74]

Perea's investigations opened up a can of night crawlers, the sordid side of frontier life—the love potions concocted with urine or mashed worms as antidote for marital infidelity, the fatal curse of witches who could travel magically in an egg, the diabolical visions. Although Perea dutifully called witness after witness, their testimony did not set him off the way Eulate's offenses against church authority had. Instead it made him sick.

Much of it he laid to racial mixture. There were in New Mexico "so many mestizos, mulattos, and zambaigos, and others [who are] worse, and [also] foreigners; so dangerous and of [such] little moral strength that I am sometimes embarrassed [in making these investigations]." Moreover, Perea thought that the Indians—who as neophytes were exempt from prosecution by the Inquisition—exercised a degrading influence on the Hispanic community in their midst. Frustrated Christian wives testified that Indian servants were the source of powders and potions designed to bring back straying husbands. It was extremely difficult, noted Perea, for persons raised among Indians, even for those who emerged as captains and royal officials, to tell truth from falsehood. [75]

At ten o'clock Thursday morning, May 26, 1633, forty-six-year-old Capt. Tomé Domínguez complied with a summons to appear at the mission of Quarai before Father Perea in the matter of mulatto Juan Antón, alleged bigamist. The captain, a resident of Mexico City, testified that he had been traveling between New Mexico and the viceregal capital the previous summer when at Cuencamé he learned by chance that Juan Antón had a wife there, a black woman who worked at the inn where Domínguez stopped. Antón also had an Indian wife in New Mexico.

To render such testimony as legal evidence in the eyes of the Inquisition, the testifier had to ratify it, either as it stood or with whatever changes he wished to make. This ratification, sometimes executed the same day as the testimony and sometimes years later, required the presence of additional witnesses, *"honestas y religiosas personas,"* at least one, usually two, and in New Mexico, usually Franciscans. Next day, May 27, when Captain Domínguez ratified his testimony without change, Perea relied on only one witness, Fray Andrés Juárez, "because it was impossible to get another." Identified as "preacher and guardian of the Convento de los Ángeles de los Pecos," Juárez cosigned the document with Father Perea, Domínguez, and the friar notary.[76]

This is the last definite reference to Andrés Juárez at Pecos. The following year, 1634, on April 11, he again acted as ratifying witness at Quarai, in another bigamy case. But this time, the notary failed to identify Juárez' mission.[77] Probably he was still at Pecos. It seems likely that his 1634 excursion with Capt. Alonso Baca and company out onto the plains took place while he still served at the gateway. Late in the year the supply wagons arrived. With them came a new governor, friar replacements, and word of the election of Fray Cristóbal de Quirós, twenty-five-year New Mexico veteran, as Father Custos. Soon after, the Franciscans of the custody held their chapter. That body must have confirmed a change of assignment for Fray Andrés Juárez.

He was not leaving New Mexico. Fifty-three years old, he had persevered as a missionary in the colony for twenty-two years, the last thirteen at the populous pueblo of Pecos. Still he refused to retire. In Santa Fe on February 19, 1635, Juárez and another friar witnessed a ratification for Father Perea. Doña Yumar Pérez de Bustillo had testified earlier in the day that the mulatto Juan Antón did indeed marry a Mexican Indian named Ana María at the pueblo of San Felipe. On this occasion, the notary gave the missions of both witnesses. Fray Andrés Juárez, former apostle to the Pecos, was now guardian at the Tewa pueblo of Nambé, a post he would occupy for the next twelve years or more. Fray Domingo del Espíritu Santo, a relative newcomer, had taken over at Pecos. He would not last a year.[78]

If Domingo del Espíritu Santo was the same person as Martín del Espíritu Santo, which is not very likely, he may have come to New Mexico in the Benavides dozen of 1625. Benavides did mention a friar of that name who worked among the Gila Apaches "with great courage during the year 1628." [79] If not, he probably arrived with the caravan of 1634. The earliest extant reference to him in New Mexico, the only reference to him as guardian of Pecos, is the ratification dated February 19, 1635. By mid-1636, he was serving as secretary to Custos Quirós and as guardian of the convento in Santa Fe, where he became involved in the politics of the capital. He died before the supply caravan of 1658-1659 reached New Mexico.[80]

The Basque Ibargaray at Pecos

Another missionary of stronger stuff, a Basque in his late twenties, came out from Santa Fe to live at Pecos. He was

Antonio de Ibargaray. A native of the bustling north-coast villa of Bilbao, Ibargaray, at age twenty-two, had taken the Franciscan habit at the Convento Grande in Mexico City on the feast of San Antonio Abad, January 17, 1629. For his novitiate, the superiors sent him to the province's Convento de San Francisco in Puebla. There he professed on January 20, 1630. He cannot have set out for the missions of New Mexico before the supply caravan of 1634. In February 1635, when Father Perea asked him to act as a ratifying witness, Ibargaray was living at the Santa Fe convento. Transferred to Pecos as guardian before November 1636, the young friar learned rapidly. That month, flaying the royal governor in a letter to the viceroy, Fray Antonio sounded like a veteran.[81]

The issues had not changed. What the governor considered use of the colony's human resources, the friars considered abuse, and vice versa. What the friars demanded in the name of respect for the church, the governor viewed as disrespect for the state, and vice versa. Without local checks or balances on either side, contention was assured. After Silva Nieto, who supported Perea's missionary expansion between 1629 and 1632, royal governors and friars were increasingly at cross purposes. By the end of the thirties, their disagreement had degenerated into a violent, bare-knuckle affair verging on civil war.

Church-State Struggle Renewed

Greedy Francisco de la Mora Ceballos, 1632-1634, cared only about turning a profit, to hear the Franciscans tell it. Delivering quantities of trade knives to certain missions—surely Pecos among them—don Francisco sought to turn conventos into trading posts and missionaries into hawkers. He revived the vale, that little slip of paper entitling the holder to abduct Indian children "as if they were calves and colts." So thoroughly did Mora fleece New Mexico that "the whole land protests." [82]

Francisco Martínez de Baeza, 1635-1637, was no better. After two years of misrule by him, Custos Quirós in desperation sent a special messenger with letters of protest to the Viceroy Marqués de Cadereyta. From Pecos, young Antonio de Ibargaray had opened with a proper courtier's bow: "Once again Your Excellency's great devotion to our holy Order has reached these remote provinces of New Mexico and as a result Your Excellency's chaplains consider ourselves fortunate to have at the present time such a prince governing this New World." He then laid bare for his prince the bad government of Martínez de Baeza.

Ibargaray
Roasts a
Governor

From the moment he became governor he has attended only to his own profit, causing grave damage to all these recently converted souls. He has commanded them to weave and paint great quantities of mantas and hangings. Likewise he has made them seek out and barter for many tanned skins and haul quantities of piñon nuts. As a result he has now loaded eight carretas with what he has amassed and is taking them and as many men from here to drive them to New Spain, thwarting everything His Majesty has ordered in his royal ordinance.

Thus, not since this governor took office, has a single pueblo been baptized. He has refused to lend support to the Faith. Instead he has sought in every way to insult with the ugliest words every minister His Majesty employs here in his royal service converting the natives. Likewise he has sought by force and violence to use the citizens of the villa of Santa Fe and its cabildo [municipal council], because they are poor people, to make utterly untrue reports against the religious of these provinces solely to discredit us with Your Excellency.

The missionary at Pecos understood that Martínez de Baeza had a grudge against him. He hastened to explain. On Sunday he had gone to a preaching station to say Mass. Late the night before, the governor and some soldiers had arrived unexpectedly and unannounced. When the friar went ahead with

Pecos, November 20, 1636,
Your Excellency's chaplain,
Fray Antonio de Ybargaray

the service, not waiting for the guests he did not know he had, Martínez flew into a rage. "I advise Your Excellency of the truth of the matter confident that Your Excellency will sustain us in all as such a fond patron of our holy Order." [83]

The Rowdy
Luis de Rosas

Five months later, in April 1637, the friars rejoiced. A new governor had been installed in Santa Fe. Charged with carrying out his predecessor's *residencia,* the standard judicial review of an official's administration, don Luis de Rosas could have dealt a blow to avarice and exploitation. Instead, he embraced them. Allegedly bribed by Martínez de Baeza, don Luis let the former governor off mildly, then took over his business interests with ravenous intent. He would make this drab colony pay even better, by God. A tough, two-fisted, damn-the-hindmost officer, Luis de Rosas would knock down the man, colonist or missionary, who got in his way.

Pecos interested Rosas from the start. As the main gateway for trade with the Plains Apaches, the eastern pueblo could supply in quantity hides and skins to fill his warehouse and keep native leather workers occupied in the Santa Fe sweatshop he operated. He offered the Pecos incentives. According to witnesses who testified before the failing Esteban de Perea and Custos Juan de Salas in 1638, Rosas would have gladly bartered the Indians' souls for "mantas, hides, and tanned skins."

Ensign Nicolás Enríquez, no friend of Rosas, had heard that the Pecos captains were complaining. The governor had ordered them to collect mantas, hides, and skins and to deliver them at night through a window. In return he would allow the pueblo to name idolatrous leaders, *capitanes de la idolatría,* just as they used to do. The proposal was made, said Enríquez, in the governor's own quarters in front of the Pecos interpreter called Puxavi and Capt. Matías Romero, brother-in-law of armorer Gaspar Pérez. Romero was later accused of illicit trading with the Plains Indians and of taking captives for Rosas to sell. Another witness had it that the governor offered the Pecos leave "to practice idolatry and freedom in their sect or religion," if they would pay their tribute a second time.[84]

Whatever the details, such diabolical meddling in the spiritual lives of his charges must have infuriated Fray Antonio de Ibargaray or his successor at Pecos. Evidently in the fall of 1638, missionary and governor met face to face. "Pretending that he was on the king's business," Rosas and a squad of armed men reined up at Pecos "loaded down with knives to barter with a number of Apache Indians, friends of the baptized natives." From the testimony of Francisco de Salazar, bitter enemy of Rosas and later beheaded as a traitor along with Nicolás Enríquez and six others, the scene unfolded something like this.

To his chagrin, Rosas discovered that the Apaches had nothing left to trade. He blamed the Father Guardian of Pecos. How dare the missionary allow the nomads to trade off all their hides and skins before he arrived? The ranting governor "became so enraged and rash with the minister that he was going to take him to the villa as a prisoner." He ordered him to consume the Blessed Sacrament at once. The friar protested.

Rosas in Fracas at Pecos

He had just eaten and thereby broken the required fast. He would not consume the Sacrament, nor would he leave it.

Just then, "at the ugly words" of the governor, Fray Antonio Jiménez, a seventy-year-old lay brother, came to the guardian's aid. Viciously, Rosas turned on the old man. He ordered him seized and confined to the convento, "to the profound scandal of the natives." He then posted four soldiers armed with arquebuses "in the porter's lodge to guard him. Had the religious not feigned illness he would have taken him publicly as a prisoner to the villa." As a parting threat Rosas sent word to the Father Guardian while he was preaching that the king would "throw out" the Apaches who were there.[85]

The affair was not over. Back in Santa Fe ex-Pecos missionary Domingo del Espíritu Santo confronted the four men who had kept guard over the venerable Brother Antonio. He declared them excommunicate. Rosas was rabid. He detested that friar and "began to persecute him." At the Franciscans' custodial chapter that year, Father Custos Juan de Salas named Fray Domingo guardian of the Santa Fe convento. At the same time, he reassigned from Santa Fe to Picurís the controversial Fray Juan de Vidania, a transfer from the Franciscan province of Michoacán who had earlier been expelled from the Society of Jesus. Vidania, a most passionate and unorthodox religious, was the one friar Rosas esteemed, his "intimate friend."

Taking the reassignment as a personal affront, which it probably was meant to be, the governor sent a squad of soldiers after Vidania and had him returned to the convento in Santa Fe. He then challenged Custos Salas with the fait accompli. Salas backed down. "To keep the peace" he sent Vidania a patent as guardian of Santa Fe. He withdrew Domingo del Espíritu Santo.[86]

Everywhere the Franciscans turned, or so it seemed to them in 1638, there was Rosas, violent, irreverent, and insatiably greedy. Earlier that year, he and a large armed escort had joined five friars on a missionary expedition to the Ópata Indians of northern Sonora. In his eagerness to extract from these natives everything they had to trade, the governor alienated them and ruined the missionaries' debut. His indiscriminate slaving among the nomads, particularly the Apaches, caused the friars further grief. It also hurt the Pecos.

Rosas' Slavers on the Plains

Sometime before October 1638, Rosas sponsored a trading and slaving venture far out onto the plains. The members of this party killed, according to Francisco de Salazar, "a large number of these friendly Apache Indians," the ones who came in seasonally to trade and live in the shadows of Pecos pueblo. The Spaniards had used "many heathen enemies of said Apaches" in the attack, "a practice prohibited by cédula of His Majesty in which he commands that they be left to themselves in their wars." That did not matter to Rosas. What did matter were the captives they brought back. Some of them he set to work in his private labor force. Others he sent for sale to Nueva Vizcaya.

If we can believe Salazar, "the native Christian Indians of Pecos" were horrified. An attack upon these Vaquero Apaches was an attack upon them. The Pecos depended on the goods the Vaqueros brought to the pueblo every fall, not only the dried meat, but also the hides and skins "with which they clothed themselves and paid their tribute." More than that, such slaving raids invited retaliation, an eye for an eye.[87]

One prominent New Mexican, a man who probably had more than a passing interest in the Pecos tribute, stuck by Governor Rosas, just as he had stuck by the Oñates. Addressing the viceroy in the name of the soldiers of New Mexico, Sargento mayor Francisco Gómez praised the governor as a military leader and explorer. He urged the viceroy to continue Rosas in office. The Apaches were no more troublesome now than usual, "but well punished." In fact, said Gómez, they appeared intimidated. If the Franciscans claimed otherwise in their litigations, it should come as no surprise. They had complained about every governor. With them it was force of habit.

In Defense of Governor Rosas

As a result they have this land so afflicted and exhausted that the soldiers despair. This state of affairs is easily understood, since the religious are the masters of the resources of the land and they proceed without a civil judge. The ecclesiastical one they do have here is for throwing the cloak over their faults. The faults they possess in this kingdom are not heard beyond this land, and they are not punished with more than a reprimand, if by chance one is handed down, and that does not hurt them in the slightest. In this way they are masters of the land and of its assets.[88]

Francisco Gómez was not alone in his attack on the heavy-handed Franciscan regime. The Santa Fe municipal council, packed by Rosas, sent to the viceroy a long list of grievances. For the repair of their souls, the several hundred poor and struggling colonists of New Mexico were utterly dependent upon the friars. At the slightest provocation, it was alleged, a citizen could find himself barred from the sacraments, excommunicate, or the object of an investigation by the Holy Office. The influence of not one but three ecclesiastical authorities, all Franciscans in New Mexico, hung like a pall over the lives of

Franciscans' Monopoly

The Franciscan
insignia: the arm
of Christ and the
arm of St. Francis.

the colonists—the local prelate who exercised quasi-episcopal powers and served as ecclesiastical judge ordinary, the agent of the Inquisition, and the subdelegate of the Santa Cruzada who exacted the price of special papal indulgences sold to provide funds for wars against the infidel, in effect a church tax. Each had his staff of notaries and assistants who enjoyed immunity from civil prosecution. So powerful had the Franciscans' monopoly grown, wrote the cabildo, "that, while enjoying the quiet and ease of their cells and doctrinas, they are able to disturb and afflict the land and keep it in [a state of] continuous martyrdom."

The Franciscan bloc also ruled the economy. None of the colonists, according to the cabildo, had herds to match those of the missions. Instead of complaining about the animals of others trespassing on Indian lands, the government-subsidized missionaries should get out of the livestock business. They should distribute their thousands of head of sheep as alms, succoring the impoverished soldier-colonists and at the same time decreasing the burden of labor on the Indians. Every mission kept dozens of Indians at work as cooks, wood carriers, maize grinders, herders, and the like. How could the ordinary citizen hope to survive in a land where many soldiers were too poor to buy horses and arms and where every friar had twenty, thirty, or even forty horses, and arms as well?

The stormy Rosas had an answer—fight. With his own selfish interest always before him, the governor marched into battle on two fronts, political and economic, and in the process rent the colony right down the middle. On the one side stood the embattled Franciscans, joined by a growing assortment of soldier-colonists whom Rosas had stripped of their commissions and encomiendas or had otherwise wronged. With the governor stood the colonists he favored, as well as those, like Francisco Gómez, who gave their first allegiance to the king's man regardless of who he was.

Rosas versus the Friars

Relying on the counsel of Father Vidania, who went over to the governor's side without a backward glance, Rosas assailed the Franciscan power structure in every way he could. He charged Fray Juan de Góngora, subdelegate of the Santa Cruzada, with misconduct and finally drove him from the province. With relish, he forwarded to the Holy Office in Mexico City charges of gross immorality against the missionary of Taos. Death removed testy old Esteban de Perea, and for more than two years there was no local agent of the Inquisition. Emboldened, Rosas and his cabildo challenged the authority of Custos Juan de Salas, and thus his pronouncements and censures, saying that the prelate had never legally presented his credentials to the civil authorities. Salas fought back.

By early 1640, when a Rosas man, excommunicated for slandering the Franciscans, turned up murdered, the hatred spilled over. Father Vidania allowed the excommunicate to be buried in the Santa Fe church. In the fracus that followed, the governor rescued Vidania from his fellow friars, installed him at his side as royal chaplain, banished the others from the villa on pain of death, and closed the convento. Shocked, Custos Salas summoned the missionaries from their posts to an urgent meeting at Santo Domingo. On March 16, they issued a manifesto, signed by Salas and nineteen others, including Father Antonio de Ibargaray and Brother Antonio Jiménez, who together may still have been serving Pecos, as well as ex-Pecos guardians Andrés Juárez and Domingo del Espíritu Santo.

Rosas had boasted that he would seize the Father Custos and expel him from the colony. The other friars vowed to go with him. They blamed the unregenerate governor for what had happened the year before at Taos. They said that he had ordered the Indians not to obey their missionary. As a result, the Taos had rebelled, sacked their church, and put to death Fray Pedro de Miranda, who had replaced the missionary charged with immoral conduct. To consider these grave matters, the friars had come together at Santo Domingo. A number of soldier-colonists joined them.[89]

In April, after voting to return to their missions, the friars chose two of their number to reason with Rosas. The governor personally bloodied their heads with a stick, locked them up for the day, and subjected them to all manner of harassment before he banished them from the villa that evening. The schism was complete.

The Colony Divided

For a year, while the two hostile factions stood off and denounced each other in reports to Mexico City, a number of sorry incidents occurred. Where the blame lay depended upon whose report you read. One of the episodes involved the aging veteran Fray Andrés Juárez. He and a number of other friars, it seemed, had returned to their missions. Juárez was reported at San Ildefonso. According to testimony by anti-Rosas witnesses, the governor dispatched a squadron of soldiers under Capt. Alonso Martín Barba

with the express order that they throw him out of that convento, which they did by force. Said Father fray Andrés Juárez, being as he is a sick man, elderly, and almost a cripple, begged them for the love of God to let him sleep that night in the convento. They did not allow it, and the Father had to leave with the utmost difficulty.

After robbing the convento and driving off the mission livestock, Martín Barba's raiders did the same at Santa Clara and at Nambé. Then Rosas stationed a detachment at San Ildefonso, turning convento into garrison. Father Vidania, whose defense of his patron became more and more frenzied, told a different story. The friars, according to him, had already abandoned the three pueblos before the soldiers rounded up the straying stock. The troops at San Ildefonso were there not on a

Taos pueblo.
Horatio O. Ladd
The Story of New Mexico
(Boston, 1891)

whim of the governor but because the pueblo had been fortified in defiance of civil authority. So it went, and the Pueblo
Indians looked on.[90]

The precise chronology of events from mid-1639 to mid-1641
is impossible to establish from the conflicting testimony. There is
no doubt, however, that most of the Pueblos were involved in one
way or another. At Santo Domingo, they threw up fortifications
against the governor. When Rosas finally mounted a punitive
expedition to Taos, many of the natives migrated out onto the
plains and settled among the Apaches. Other Pueblos fled their
homes in fear and disgust. A missionary to the Jémez died
violently, either at their hands or those of Navajos or Apaches. The
nomads availed themselves of the confusion and raided at will.
The governor's men robbed Sandía and Quarai. At Socorro one of
his irreverent captains reportedly put on a Franciscan habit and
ordered the Indians to kiss his hand.

Sometime around 1640, a lethal epidemic visited New
Mexico. Rough estimates put the death toll among the Pueblos
as high as three thousand, more than ten percent of the population.[91] It was as if their own supernaturals were scourging
them. And Mary of the Angels at Pecos just let them die.

Another governor, Juan Flores de Sierra y Valdez, not a
well man, relieved Luis de Rosas in the spring of 1641. Fray

Hernando Covarrubias, sent out from the Convento Grande, took over as custos and Fray Juan de Salas became agent of the Inquisition. They soon had the apostate Father Vidania behind bars. In Santa Fe, the anti-Rosas faction won control of the cabildo. When the new governor died after only a few months in office, they arrested the former governor, their archenemy, on grounds that he might slip away before his residencia was completed.

**Rosas Defends
Himself**

From "this prison" at Santa Fe, the fearful but still-determined Rosas composed a defense of his administration for don Juan de Palafox y Mendoza, specially appointed royal trouble-shooter to New Spain. He probably entrusted the document, dated September 29, 1641, to the deceased governor's son, who also carried with him the last will and testament of Luis de Rosas.

He had never wanted to be governor of New Mexico, Rosas told Palafox. After fifteen years of loyal military service in Flanders, during which he had risen through the ranks, he had come to New Spain with Viceroy the Marqués de Cadereyta. When the viceroy had assigned him the New Mexico post in 1636, he had protested because of "the bad reputation it has always had for mutiny and seizure of governors." But to no avail. Upon his arrival, alleged Rosas, he had run head-on into the entrenched Franciscans.

"Every convento is a livestock operation and general store owned by the friars," he charged. "During the time I have been in these provinces they have extracted seventy-five two-and-a-half-ton wagons of goods, which from a land so poor amounts to more than extracting millions from Potosí." At one mission, claimed Rosas, he had shut down a sweatshop employing Indian children. That did it. From then on, the friars incited the colony against him.

When he had arrested a criminal, two Franciscans led a mob to the governor's palace and forced the man's release. They made a mockery of royal justice and spat on the authority of the governor. Rosas had sent in his resignation, but the viceroy refused to accept it. Regularly the friars withheld the sacraments from him and from any colonist who would not defame him. They called him foul names and threatened his life. By the time their faction fortified Santo Domingo in defiance of Santa Fe, seventy-three of the colony's 120 soldiers had joined the insurrection. In their effort to depose Rosas, the friars circulated a letter urging the people of New Mexico not to obey him, saying, in Rosas' words, "that I followed the law of Luther and Calvin, that I was practicing an abominable idolatry with a goat, and that I and the citizens of this villa [Santa Fe] were whipping an image of Christ."

The imprisoned ex-governor knew that his allegations about Franciscans fathering bastard children in New Mexico and cheating the royal treasury by accepting subsidies for twelve to fifteen vacant missions would not greatly scandalize Juan de Palafox. What would shock him, Rosas calculated, was the picture of friars fomenting open rebellion against legitimate royal authority, scheming to oust, even to murder, royal officials, and holding a royal governor prisoner while they ruled the colony. This picture Rosas painted in vivid colors.[92]

Once the supply caravan had departed for New Spain that fall carrying his letter, Rosas held his breath. He feared that his enemies might try to murder him before help could arrive. And he was right. They did.

In January of 1642, under cover of a cloak-and-dagger plot complete with unfaithful wife, apparently planted in Rosas' room, enraged husband, and masked avengers, the opposition finally rid the world of the rowdy Luis de Rosas. One wonders if old Fray Andrés Juárez of Fuenteovejuna, the town that had taken justice into its own hands, recalled the precedent. Governor Rosas and Comendador Fernán Gómez, like most tyrants, had a lot in common.

If Juárez or anyone else counted on pardon for the murderers of the king's representative in New Mexico, their hopes faded in the summer of 1642 when the implacable visitor general Juan de Palafox, assumed the viceregency. Palafox stood for royal authority and against the special privileges of the religious orders. He viewed the New Mexico affair as a patent case of "revolt and sedition," crediting the reports of men like Sargento mayor Francisco Gómez and branding the Franciscans the villains in the tragedy. He instructed his governor accordingly.[93]

Under cover of general amnesty granted by Palafox, Gov. Alonso Pacheco y Heredia quietly identified the leaders of the pro-Franciscan, anti-Rosas faction. Then on July 21, he had Antonio Baca and seven other soldier-colonists beheaded in summary fashion. The same day, town crier Jusepe announced the executions to a stunned populace. The governor reiterated the general pardon and ordered every citizen of the colony to rally to the royal standard within two weeks or suffer the death penalty. They knew he meant it. At the end of the decree, he added: "And likewise under said penalty all the Indians captains of the pueblos are to come." [94]

Summary
Executions

Bishop Juan de Palafox,
viceroy in 1642.
Francisco Sánchez-
Castañer, *Don Juan
de Palafox*
(Zaragoza, 1964)

Evidently a delegation from Pecos was there in the crowd on the feast of St. Ann, July 26. Before the governor and the royal standard, there appeared, in the words of the official account,

all the vassals, citizens, and residents of these provinces, likewise the prelate, his definitorium, and the rest of the guardians, and all the principal caciques of the settlements, as proof of loyalty and of the true obedience owed the Royal Majesty. In compliance with the general pardon published by the crier all those who were accomplices of the executed leaders asked for acquittal and immunity, by virtue of which said lord governor ordered issued for their favor and pardon certificates in due form. He also ordered continuation of payment to the thirty soldiers who have enlisted to maintain obedience and the public peace of these provinces.[95]

Still, the sheep refused to lie down with the lion. Inside a month, Governor Pacheco had threatened Custos Covarrubias with banishment or worse if he did not consent to the reburial of a body in the Santa Fe church, the same excommunicate body, since removed, that Father Vidania had let in three and a half years before. The aggrieved relatives of the eight executed men filed criminal charges against Pacheco. Ordered to investigate the conduct of the clergy in New Mexico, the well-respected procurator-general Fray Tomás Manso chose witnesses who whitewashed the friars and damned the memory of Rosas and Vidania. There had been no rebellion, vowed Manso. There had been open rebellion, countered Pacheco.[96]

Nothing had changed. The small ruling minority in New Mexico, far from the seat of authority, remained polarized by self-interest and fear around the office of the governor or the Franciscan-dominated church. At issue, as always, was social and economic control of the Pueblo Indians. Both factions within the Hispanic community recognized the growing danger of Pueblo revolt. The Zuñis, the Jémez, and the Taos had made certain of that. What blinded governors and friars alike was the inability of either faction, in the context of their struggle, to admit any share of the blame.

The Specter of Pueblo Revolt

When the friars of the custody convened at Santo Domingo in 1644, their major concern was defense against the calumny that had made them traitors in the eyes of king and council. They underscored the adverse effect of the Rosas tyranny on the Pueblo Indians, "who are for certain the best Indians in the world." Considering the grinding oppression and indignity these poor natives had suffered at the hands of governors and encomenderos, "even to taking away their children and selling them," it was truly, the friars contended, "a miracle that they have not killed us all."[97]

It was a miracle, to be sure. But in the stifling paternalism of their missions, the friars also wrought oppression and indignity.

When Fray Andrés Juárez, dean of New Mexico missionaries in 1647, addressed the king, he laid the blame as usual to self-serving governors. "May I be cursed of God if they have kept a single command of Your Majesty." They were the scourge of the land, despoiling Indians and colonists, provoking the Apaches, and interfering in the missions. The past governor, don Fernando de Argüello, for selfish reasons of his own, had rebuked a friar for having an Indian whipped. If the missionary tried it again, said the governor, the Indians

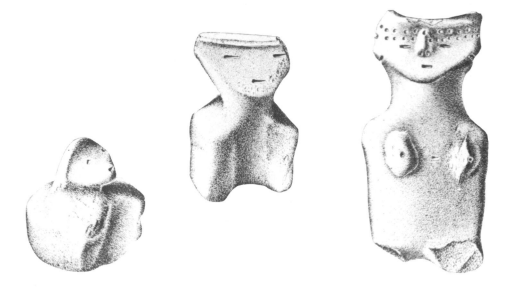

Pecos human effigies, tallest 3″. Kidder, *Artifacts*

should shoot him with arrows. As a result of such blatant discord between secular and religious authority, and the continual exploitation, the Pueblos, alleged Juárez, were no longer obeying their friars and were returning to idolatry.[98]

If the Pueblos were stirring under the whip of mission discipline, it was not alone because the governors interfered, but also because the whip stung.

They had already begun plotting. Governor Argüello, 1644 to 1647, "had twenty-nine Indians hanged in the pueblo of the Jémez as traitors and confederates of the Apaches." In 1650, a revolt, reportedly involving Jémez, Keres, Southern Tiwas, and Apaches, aborted. The Pueblos had arranged to hand over to the Apaches the Spaniards' horse herds, thereby immobilizing their oppressors for the kill. The plan was "to attack in all districts on the night of Holy Thursday, because the Spaniards would then be assembled." But word leaked out. "Many Indians were arrested from most of the pueblos of this kingdom. As a result nine leaders were hanged and many others were sold as slaves for ten years." [99]

Despite the setback of the Rosas years and the ominous stirring of the Pueblos, the friars rallied during the 1650s. Their Sonora adventure, begun in 1645 when five friars went among the northern Ópatas, ended in 1651 or 1652 after Franciscans and alarmed Jesuits worked out a compromise withdrawal, but only after the friars had harvested a considerable crop of souls. During the fifties, the custody finally acted to found missions for the Manso and Suma Indians at El Paso and to the southwest. They stayed well on their side of the line agreed upon with the Jesuits. In 1657, the viceroy approved the Franciscans' bid for twenty missionaries to bring the New Mexico custody up to full quota, plus four extras to minister to Mansos and Sumas.

They would need all the strength they could muster. Another governor, the devious don Bernardo López de Mendizábal, rode north in the same caravan, "another Rosas." [100]

For twenty years no one mentioned Pecos, or so it appears from the documents that survive. From the time of Rosas, who interested himself unduly in the pueblo's trade, to that of López de Mendizábal, who took office in 1659, it was as if Pecos had ceased to exist. This long silence reveals, if nothing else, a certain unobtrusiveness on the part of the people. If some of them abandoned the pueblo or took part in the conspiracy of 1650, the Pecos, unlike the Taos or Jémez, did so unnoticed.

The Pecos Bide Time

Even the names of their missionaries have vanished. From Antonio de Ibargaray, who sat down at Pecos and wrote the viceroy in 1636, and Brother Antonio Jiménez, confined there briefly by Rosas in 1638, to ex-custos Juan González, serving the mission in 1660, the rolls are blank.[101] Afraid for his life in 1640, the Pecos missionary probably moved in with the others at Santo Domingo. Although Pecos may have been relegated for a time to a preaching station of Santa Fe or Galisteo, it is not likely that the friars left such a prominent pueblo or such a fine church and convento unattended for long.

A listing and census of the missions, evidently compiled in 1641, contains the following entry for the Pueblo de los Pecos.

It has a very good church, provision for public worship, *órgano*, and choir. There are 1,189 souls under its administration.[102]

Pecos was listed eighth. The compiler, who had described five of the previous churches as "very good," and the others as not so good, began to color his descriptions on down the line. The churches at Chililí and Isleta were "very fine (*excelentísima*)," the one at Jémez "splendid (*grandiosa*)," at Sandía "excellent (*excelente*)," at Ácoma "exceedingly handsome (*hermosísima*)," and the one the Indians had wrecked at Taos "a handsome temple (*un hermoso templo*)." The slight to Fray Andrés Juárez' magnificent monument at Pecos was the result not of the compiler's careful appraisal of architecture, but rather of his elegant variation of adjectives. He also forgot to mention the convento.

The órgano, shown at Pecos and at sixteen other missions, was probably a small cabinet organ. Extant mission supply lists show shawms, bassoons, and trumpets, but no organs. Such organs could have been made in New Mexico, and destroyed in the revolt of 1680. On the other hand, the same word can also mean *canto de órgano*, or polyphonic music. It could be that all these missions, like some of them during the time of Benavides, had Indians choirs trained in polyphony.[103]

Population Decline   But the poignant thing about this brief entry is the population. Most of the entries are expressed in round numbers, some of them obvious estimates. The figure for Pecos seems to be the result of an actual count, or of a devious friar. If we set aside the pious chroniclers like Benavides and Vetancurt, who kept the number of Pecos steady at "more than two thousand" through most of the century, the decline is appalling.

Father Juárez, who should have known, put the population of Pecos at "two thousand souls or a few less" in 1622. If the 1641 figure is accurate at 1,189—and if both include children—the loss is about forty percent in twenty years. Late in 1694, the count, which definitely included children, was down to 736. In human terms, where three Pecos had lived in 1622, only two lived in 1641, and only one in 1694.[104]

The ministry of Fray Andrés Juárez, 1622 to 1635, was formative in the "Christianization" of Pecos. Digging in the ruins three hundred years later, the astute A. V. Kidder recognized this fact without even knowing the friar's name.

It was probably 1620 or 1630 before domestic animals, china dishes and metal implements became common enough to find their way into the refuse in quantity and so to mark, for the excavator, the beginning of European influence.[105]

That influence, the Pecos now knew, meant more than sheep and flowered plates and trade knives. Much more.

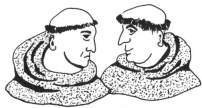

After Códice Azcatitlan,
central Mexico,
16th century

the shadow of the inquisition
1659-1680

Well, Father, if there is no mercy or law of God, put as
many fetters on me as you like; put six pairs on my feet and fifty
on my neck. I swear by Christ—Look here, Father, hang me or
shoot me and with that we shall have done. . . . See, my sons,
how much the Fathers can do, for they hold me a prisoner. . . .
Look, gentlemen, there is no longer God or king, since such a
thing could happen to a man like me. No! No! There is no longer
God or king!

> Gov. Bernardo López de Mendizábal, en route
> to the prison of the Inquisition in Mexico City,
> Santo Domingo, October 6, 1662

"If the custos excommunicated me, I would hang him or
garrote him immediately, and if the Pontiff came here and wanted
to excommunicate me or actually did so, I would hang the Pontiff,
for in this kingdom I am the prince and supreme magistrate. . . ."
Raising with his right hand the cape and cloak he was wearing in
order to show me the pistols he had in his belt, "Now then, we will
consider this affair and Your Reverence and all the other Fathers
Custos of New Mexico will learn what a governor can do."

> Gov. Diego de Peñalosa on the arrest of Fray
> Alonso de Posada at Pecos, September 30, 1663

Seal of the Mexican Inquisition.

Back in the early 1620s, the unshrinking Fray Esteban de Perea, locked in close combat with Gov. Juan de Eulate, had appealed for help to the tribunal of the Inquisition in Mexico City. The Holy Office had responded positively, appointing outbound Custos Alonso de Benavides as its first *comisario,* or agent, for New Mexico.

The Inquisition as a Weapon of the Friars

The Inquisition's presence, comforting to the devout and dreadful to the accused, was broadcast, and reaffirmed periodically, by the formal reading of an Edict of the Faith. For the unburdening of their consciences, anyone with information regarding thought, word, or deed against the Holy Mother Church must come forward and confess it. The local agent had authority to investigate alleged threats to the purity of the Faith by members of the Hispanic community, to summon witnesses and record their testimony, and to recommend and, upon receipt of approval, to execute the arrest and deportation of the accused to Mexico City for trial before the tribunal. Whether the Inquisition's presence in this rude, superstitious, ingrown frontier society made New Mexico a better place to live or not, it did put a formidable weapon in the hands of the friars.

Eulate had left the colony just in time. The governors who succeeded him had cooperated with the friars more or less. Agent Benavides devoted most of his considerable energy to expanding the mission field. Then, during the thirties when church-state relations had deteriorated once again, when the friars really needed the muscle of the Inquisition, local agent Perea grew old and died. The rough and merciless Governor Rosas had taken every advantage. In the sixties, it would be different. Another governor who shared Rosas' greedy expectations and his disdain for the missionaries would find himself shackled in a wagon bound for the prison of the Inquisition in Mexico City.

Because they were considered perpetual minors in the Faith, Indians who retained their Indian identity were exempt from prosecution by the Inquisition, which was not necessarily a blessing. Mission discipline, depending on the friar in charge, could be much more arbitrary and even sadistic. Serious cases involving Indians—apostasy, heresy, and the like—went not to the Holy Office, but to the bishop, or in New Mexico, to the Franciscan prelate. In a society that considered the church an arm of the state and vice versa, crimes against the Faith and treason commingled. In cases of alleged Pueblo sedition, it was the royal governor, generally with consent of the friars, who sentenced them to the gibbet or slave block.

The Pecos may not have understood the workings of the Inquisition, but it touched their lives. Several times during the 1660s, the agent resided at Pecos. Witnesses came and went. Two important Spaniards whom they knew all too well, their encomendero and a plains trader, were arrested and carted away. Then one night, the royal governor rode out to Pecos, entered the convento with armed men, and removed the agent to Santa Fe. Such acts cannot have enhanced the Pueblos' respect for their contentious, overbearing masters. The meticulous, sometimes shocking, and often wearisome records of the Inquisition provide a keyhole view of society in seventeenth-century New Mexico. Seen from there, 1680 comes as no surprise.

Governor López versus Ramírez

Don Bernardo López de Mendizábal, governor of New Mexico from 1659 to 1661, was a petulant, strutting, ungracious criollo with a sharp tongue and enough education to make himself dangerous. Even before the caravan left Mexico City, don Bernardo and Fray Juan Ramírez, another contentious

Don Bernardo López de Mendizábal

criollo, had quarreled over their respective jurisdictions. Ramírez, appointed procurator-general of the New Mexico custody to succeed the illustrious Fray Tomás Manso, had also been elected custos. As the wagons rumbled north, Franciscan prelate and royal governor carried on their own petty war. Ten of the twenty-four friars bound for the missions deserted in protest. López blamed Ramírez and Ramírez blamed López. Both would have their day in court. Both, within three years, would stand accused before the Inquisition.[1]

Arriving in mid-summer 1659, Governor López de Mendizábal took over from Juan Manso while Custos Ramírez relieved Fray Juan González. Ex-governor Manso, younger brother of Fray Tomás, had got on tolerably well with the Franciscans and had aided them in their efforts to found missions in the El Paso area. As was customary, he remained in the colony for López to conduct his *residencia*. Ex-custos Juan González, who had been in New Mexico since at least 1644, stayed on as a *definitor* of the custody and as guardian at Pecos.

Coincidentally, Father González and the Manso clan— Fray Tomás, veteran head of the mission supply service, provincial, and bishop of Nicaragua; his brother Juan, governor from 1656 to 1659; and their nephew Pedro Manso de Valdés, later lieutenant governor—all were born in the tiny, picturesque Asturian seaport of Luarca on Spain's windblown north coast. In America, nineteen-year-old Juan González had pronounced his religious vows on the feast of St. John Chrysostom, January 27, 1624, at the *convento* in Puebla. With studies and ordination behind him, he must have ridden north with his *paisano* Tomás Manso in one of the caravans of the 1630s. He was at Santo Domingo in September 1644 to sign the missionaries' fervent defense of their conduct. Although he may have served during the 1640s or 1650s at Pecos before his term as custos, González did nothing indiscreet or outstanding enough to inscribe himself in the scant records that survive.[2]

The friars' alleged snubs of López de Mendizábal and the governor's refusal to receive Custos Ramírez in Santa Fe as ecclesiastical judge ordinary set the tone of church-state relations for the next two years. What the governor did in the name of Indian reform, and in his own economic best interest, the Franciscans saw as open interference in mission affairs. On his visitation of the colony, which by law every governor was supposed to make, López sought to win over the Indians at the missionaries' expense.

The governor inspected Pecos, probably during the "trade fair" in 1659, but details are lacking. At nearby Galisteo in the presence of ten Spaniards, among them Pecos encomendero Francisco Gómez Robledo, don Bernardo grilled the Indians, men and women, one by one, under pain of death, about the personal life and habits of the missionary. "I am certain," protested Fray Nicolás del Villar, "that no prelate of mine would have made such a rigorous examination of any religious, and with so many and such exquisite questions, as His Lordship made of each of the natives."[3]

López Opposes
Unpaid Labor

More serious than his effort to defame the friars themselves was López' attack on their use of free Indian labor.
Early in his administration, the governor by decree raised the
standard Indian wage from half a real per day to one real plus
food. He then tried to impose it on the missionaries, who had
long enjoyed the services of mission Indians without paying
wages as such. In their defense, the Franciscans cited a 1648
decree by Gov. Luis de Guzmán y Figueroa, based on a royal
cédula, exempting from payment of tribute the pueblo governor
as well as natives employed "in service to the churches and
divine worship," namely "an interpreter, a sacristan, a first
cantor, a bellringer, an organist where there was an organ, a
shepherd, a cook, a porter, a groom." The reference to organ-
ists seems to confirm that the órganos reported earlier in the
1640s at Pecos and other missions were indeed instruments
and not merely choirs skilled in polyphonic chant. Up to the
time of López, the friars had claimed these ten exemptions for
mission staff.[4]

According to much-abused Father Villar at Galisteo, the
cavalier López relieved the women who baked the friar's bread
and told them never to bake for him again. The royal governor
then ordered the other servants of the convento to pay tribute
—tanned skins and mantas—"for no other reason than having
served." When López found out that Villar, who had been at
Galisteo only a year struggling with the Tano language, still
relied on an interpreter "he sent the latter off to a ranch to
break young bulls." Next López had forbidden any Indian to
carry a message for the friar and had removed the native fiscales
of the pueblo, ostensibly because only the king—not the missionaries—could name them. As a result, the friar's hands were
tied, he had no one to bake his bread, no way to preach to the
Indians or impose discipline. In short, his ministry was doomed.[5]

To counter the charges he knew the Franciscans were
lodging with the viceroy, Governor López de Mendizábal set
down charges of his own against them. They ran the usual
gamut, from oppression of mission Indians and wanton misuse
of their quasi-episcopal powers to blatant clerical immorality.
When Franciscan Vice-custos García de San Francisco excommunicated Nicolás de Aguilar, López' heavy-handed agent in
the Salinas district, the governor challenged his authority to act
as anything but a parish priest to the laity. At López' bidding,
witnesses gathered round. Concerning the arbitrary and con-
temptuous use of excommunication and absolution, Juan González Lobón, whom the friars considered a buffoon, testified that
Fray Juan González of Pecos had absolved him "with some

quince bars." The witness claimed that he was not informed why he had been excommunicated. Nevertheless, the friar fined him thirty cotton mantas for which González Lobón gave a draft on his encomienda receipts "to rid himself of his vexation." [6]

To squeeze the colony for every manta and every last fanega of piñon nuts he could, López de Mendizábal relied on his appointed district officers. In New Mexico, the *alcalde mayor,* sometimes called a *justicia mayor,* who presided over local affairs in one of the colony's six or eight districts, or *jurisdicciones,* served unsalaried and at the governor's pleasure. He administered petty justice, settled minor disputes over land and water, supervised the use of Indian labor, rallied the local militia, and helped the friars maintain discipline in the missions—any or all of which could be turned to his own profit and that of the governor. An alcalde mayor could be the missionary's best friend or his worst enemy. In the Salinas missions, the friars branded Nicolás de Aguilar the Attila of New Mexico. [7]

The Alcaldes Mayores

López de Mendizábal's man in the Galisteo (Tanos) district, which also included Pecos, was Diego González Bernal. He, like Aguilar, carried out his governor's orders with gusto, as in the case of alleged fornication against the old friar at Tajique. It is not known how early an alcalde mayor was appointed for the Galisteo-Pecos jurisdiction. Back in the mid-1640s, the friars had accused Governor Pacheco of appointing such officials in most of the mission areas where only Indians lived, "a thing never done before." Although González Bernal surely had predecessors as "alcalde mayor and military chief of Galisteo and its district," their names are lost.

In the documentation for López de Mendizábal's residencia, there is a packet of two dozen letters from him to González Bernal. The governor wrote of his stormy relations with the friars, of competition with them for Pueblo Indian labor, but mainly of day-to-day business affairs. Multiplying this correspondence by the number of the governor's other agents and appointees gives a fair idea of his economic vise grip on New Mexico. [8]

Capt. Diego González:
Tuesday morning or tomorrow night see that three carpenters from that district are here, among them Miguel, to finish seating these doors and windows. Likewise that there are thirty Indians, ten from Galisteo, ten from San Cristóbal, and ten from San Lázaro for [work on] these casas reales; that they bring with them all the gypsum that is ground for whitewashing them; and that the Indian women come to do the whitewashing. See that they bring the boards

I ordered made and ready at Pecos this week, even if it is on horseback, and that they come cautiously and safe from the Apaches I reckon are in the sierra.

Send me a statement regarding the wool and how much is allotted. Urge them to work fast so that all the stockings possible may go in this shipment. I have faith in your attention [to this matter.] God keep you.

Villa [of Santa Fe], September 5, 1660.
Don Bernardo

Capt. Diego González:

From Pecos they have brought only twenty-three fanegas of piñon nuts, in view of which fifteen, according to what you told me, remain to be brought. One need not take notice of Indians turning their backs even though they have been paid, as they have. They brought the two fanegas from there. Let's bring the rest of the shortage. God keep you.

Villa, Feast of the Conception of Our Lady [December 8], 1660. Yours,
Don Bernardo

Señor Diego González:

I appreciate your concern. My foot is better, thank God. I hope He grants you health. These boys brought six short fanegas of piñon nuts in seven packsacks with no more explanation than Javier measured it. If this is the one from [Francisco de ?] Madrid, have them settle up. After all, these are tributes and it [the piñon crop] is in the hills. As for the packsacks, don't write me anything. They must be mine, of those I ordered bartered for at Pecos. I am waiting for them and the piñon nuts that have not come. Nothing else to tell you. God keep you many years.

Villa, December 9, 1660. As always,
Don Bernardo

The Governor and Kachina Dances

Another of the duties of an alcalde mayor was to announce in all the settlements and pueblos of his district, through an interpreter where necessary, the decrees of the governor in Santa Fe. When, to the horror of the friars, López de Mendizábal decreed that the Indians should resume their ceremonial dances, González Bernal did his duty. According to the missionary at Galisteo, the Tanos of that pueblo, San Cristóbal, San Lázaro, and La Ciénaga were only too happy to oblige with "some evil and idolatrous dances called kachinas, from which idolatry followed in these pueblos." Even worse, a rowdy group of Spaniards "had got themselves up in the manner of the Indian kachinas and had danced the dance of that name at the pueblo of San Lázaro and afterwards did the same at their house next to Galisteo." One of them danced in a shocking state of undress. At Pecos, Fray Juan González reported no such brutish goings on.[9]

A ceremonial dance at Zuñi pueblo. *Century* (Dec. 1882)

Jémez kachina masks.   Parsons, *Jemez*

López under Fire   For Bernardo López de Mendizábal, 1660 was the year his fortunes turned. While he and his men kept on extorting a goodly profit in New Mexico, the charges against them were piling up in Mexico City. The first reports critical of the López administration reached the viceroy early that year. He sent copies over to the Holy Office. In the spring, the friars' special messenger and Custos Ramírez, whose supervision of the supply service required him to return to the viceregal capital with the wagons, both testified before the inquisitors against López' regime. Other messengers arrived with atrocity stories: missionaries dishonored and persecuted; Indians, undisciplined, reveling in the old pagan rites "with costumes, masks, and the most infernal chants," goaded by Spanish Christians. If relief did not come soon, one friar told the Holy Office in September 1660, the Franciscans would withdraw from New Mexico.

And it was not only the Franciscans. In an effort to make capital out of former governor Juan Manso's residencia, López de Mendizábal had stalled and then locked up his predecessor.

But Manso, with the aid of disenchanted New Mexicans, had escaped. Within four months, he stood before the tribunal of the Inquisition. López, meanwhile, sent Sargento mayor Francisco Gómez Robledo off to Mexico City with a defense of his actions and a packet of countercharges against the dictatorial, scandal-ridden Franciscans. Unfortunately for don Bernardo, messenger Gómez never made it.

By the end of 1660, the Franciscan superiors had chosen as custos of New Mexico a tough young veteran who had served there during the mid-fifties but who had left before López and his gang took over. He was Alonso de Llanos y Posada González, who signed himself Fray Alonso de Posada.

Fray Alonso de Posada

Don Diego de Peñalosa Briceño

The Holy Office made him its comisario and charged him to carry out the most thorough investigation. The viceroy, who normally would not have appointed another governor for a year, yielded to the outcry from New Mexico and did so in 1660. He chose don Diego Dionisio de Peñalosa Briceño y Verdugo, an accomplished rogue. Together, Posada and Peñalosa would make don Bernardo pay more dearly than he could ever have imagined.[10]

Enter Posada
and Peñalosa

Custos Posada reached the colony first. On May 9, 1661, as agent of the Inquisition, he began hearing formal testimony that quickly opened his eyes. On May 22, he forbade kachina dances and ordered the missionaries to seize every mask, prayer stick, and effigy they could lay hands on and burn them. This they did, to sixteen hundred such objects by their own count. Still, Custos Posada managed to stay out of López' reach until Governor Peñalosa arrived three months later. Almost immediately Peñalosa announced López' residencia. Posada published an Edict of the Faith. The ex-governor stayed away. He said he was ill.[11]

While still in office, López had sacked Alcalde mayor Diego González Bernal. Something had happened between them. Earlier, González had been a loyal servant, dutifully accusing the friars in the Tano missions of driving Indians out of church and refusing the sacraments to Spaniards. Yet during his residencia, the ex-governor would call González "a man with no sense of responsibility, a mestizo by birth." López had even thrown González Bernal in the public jail once "because he exceeded a commission I gave him to put Jerónimo de Carvajal in possession of certain lands." So upset did the prisoner become that he pretended to have lost his mind, whereupon López had ordered him placed in the stocks "to restrain him." Furthermore, López had banished from the capital Diego's kinswoman Catalina Bernal "for being a scandalous person and the bawd for her daughters."

Don Bernardo had experienced no better luck with his next appointee, Antonio de Salas, whom he removed almost immediately "because of the uproars he caused there and for being a comrade of the friars." Salas, also encomendero of Pojoaque, had fallen out with López when the governor made him raze the house he maintained inside that pueblo.[12]

The third alcalde mayor of Galisteo and its district in less than a year was Jerónimo de Carvajal, thirty years old, born in the Sandía district, and owner of the estancia, or ranch, of Nuestra Señora de los Remedios de los Cerrillos, not far from the present-day town of Cerrillos. It was common knowledge that Carvajal's comely young wife Margarita Márquez had been the mistress of Gov. Juan Manso.[13]

López' Residencia
Proclaimed

On Friday afternoon, September 30, 1661, at the bidding of Alcalde mayor Carvajal "all the captains and the people" of Pecos assembled in the pueblo's plaza mayor to hear another proclamation. Carvajal and some other Spaniards had ridden over from Galisteo. Francisco Jutu, a Pecos "conversant in the

Spanish language," stood before the crowd as crier and interpreter. Through him they learned that for a period of thirty
days any person with complaints or claims, civil or criminal,
against former governor López de Mendizábal or his subordinates should appear before the new governor in Santa Fe. Their
grievances would be noted, justice would be done, and damages
would be compensated. All this the Pecos had heard before.[14]

One of the two witnesses who attested the proclamation at
Pecos that afternoon was Diego's younger brother, Antonio
González Bernal. He had been named by Governor Peñalosa to
act as *protector de indios* during the López residencia. His job
was to compile and present all the Indians' claims against the
ex-governor. The Pecos submitted theirs. López still owed them
one hundred pesos for "one hundred parchments and fine
tanned skins" at a peso each. He also owed them for seven
tents of fine tanned skin, worth eight pesos each, or fifty-six
pesos. Nor had he paid them for "a great quantity of piñon
nuts." They could not remember exactly how many fanegas.
They asked that Sargento mayor Diego Romero, who had
taken delivery of the nuts on López' account, state the quantity.[15]

In all, Governor Peñalosa received more than seventy
formal petitions of complaint against his predecessor. Fray
García de San Francisco presented the friars' claims, without
ever mentioning Pecos. Diego González Bernal as attorney
general denounced his former patron on behalf of the Hispanic
community, and Antonio González Bernal spoke for the Indians.
A parade of individuals added claims of their own. Out of all
this, Peñalosa drew up a thirty-three-count indictment against
the ex-governor. López answered, as was customary, count by
count, denying most of the allegations, identifying his enemies,
and explaining the motives for their perjury. Both Father San
Francisco and Diego González Bernal recommended to Governor Peñalosa that he confine López. He did.[16]

In his arrogance, don Bernardo had alienated virtually
everyone except Fray Juan González of Pecos. In the hundreds
of pages of impassioned testimony, there is hardly a mention of
ex-custos González or his mission. When summoned to testify
before Father Posada, the even-tempered Fray Juan made it
very clear that everything he reported against López and his
men was hearsay. It was González whom the imprisoned former
governor asked to hear his confession and administer communion.

López had sent one of his four guards to Custos Posada
during Lent in 1662 requesting the services of a priest. Fray

Nicolás del Villar had balked. The confined former governor did not want Fray Nicolás de Freitas, guardian at Santa Fe and fast friend of Governor Peñalosa, for "plenty of reasons." After those two, Father González was closest. Besides, Posada had delegated him to preach the Santa Cruzada and he would be in Santa Fe anyway. López knew that Fray Juan would not re-

Fray Juan González

fuse him even though it might strain his charity. The guardian of Pecos, unlike the other friars, had not embroiled himself in the affairs of the López administration. For that reason, said don Bernardo, "he always was and is my choice." [17]

Inquisition Closes In on López

While López de Mendizábal languished in confinement, his accusers drew the noose tighter and tighter around his neck. The resourceful Governor Peñalosa wanted to ruin his predecessor without assistance. But it was Father Alonso de Posada, brandishing the terrible authority of the Inquisition, who really brought low the unrepentant don Bernardo.

The Holy Office in Mexico City had already ordered the arrest of three prominent members of the López camp—the notorious Nicolás de Aguilar, alcalde mayor of the Salinas district; Sargento mayor Diego Romero, former *alcalde ordinario,* or municipal magistrate, of Santa Fe; and Sargento mayor Francisco Gómez Robledo, holder of the Pecos encomienda and several others. The arrest of a fourth New Mexican, Cristóbal de Anaya Almazán, was left up to the discretion of Agent Posada. By the spring of 1662, Posada had these orders in hand. Their bearer was none other than ex-governor Juan Manso, spoiling for the chance to square accounts with López de Mendizábal. Another action by the Holy Office made Manso *alguacil mayor,* chief constable, of the Inquisition in New Mexico and charged him with carrying out the arrests. Thus while a similar fate for López was being sealed in Mexico City, the doughty local agent and his constable moved against the four marked New Mexicans. [18]

Arrest and Ordeal of Gómez Robledo

It was still dark. The first thin light of dawn barely shown behind the mountains to the east. Francisco Gómez Robledo, like nearly everyone else this early Thursday morning, lay in bed asleep. Then something intruded, a heavy banging. It could not have been later than five. He stumbled to the door. "Open," came the command, "open in the name of the Holy Office!" He did. Outside in the chill air stood Alguacil mayor Juan Manso, his nephew Maese de campo Pedro Manso de Valdés, and Father Posada's zealous notary Fray Salvador de la Guerra. Oh, God.

They presented the order for his arrest and entered. After he had put on his clothes, "and with hat and cloak," they led him out of his house "which faces on the corner of the royal plaza of this villa" and across to a cell in the Franciscan convento. Guards were posted at door and window. Alguacil Manso ordered Gómez' possessions attached, including his Santa Fe house, his estancia of San Nicolás de las Barrancas downriver in the vicinity of today's Belen, and his encomiendas. He ordered leg irons and chains placed on the prisoner. He told him to designate a person of his choice to assist in the attachment of his property. Gómez named his brother-in-law and compadre Maese de campo Pedro Lucero de Godoy. Outside, it was getting light this May 4, 1662.[19]

A bachelor in his early thirties and the father of two natural children five and six years old, Gómez Robledo would not learn the charges against him for more than year. Yet he must have known that someone had whispered the ugly lie that

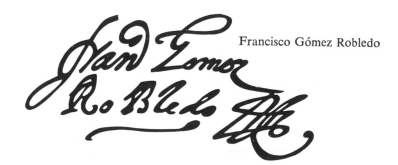

Francisco Gómez Robledo

he was a Jew, just as they had about his father. Born in Santa Fe about 1629, the first son of Francisco Gómez and Ana Robledo, he had been baptized by Fray Pedro de Ortega and confirmed by Fray Alonso de Benavides. On both occasions Gov. Felipe Sotelo Osorio stood as godfather. The elder Francisco, a Portuguese in the service of the Oñates, had held subsequently every office of importance New Mexico had to offer, even that of alguacil mayor of the Inquisition. Until his death at age eighty in 1656 or 1657, Francisco Gómez had been the colony's strongest defender of royal authority as vested in the governor.

Cast in the same mold, Francisco the younger, a heavy-set individual with straight dark chestnut hair, had begun soldiering at age thirteen and had served as councilman and municipal magistrate of Santa Fe. He had carried out numerous commissions for the governors, and like his father had more than once stepped on the friars' toes. His knowledge of the Indian languages served him well. During López de Mendizábal's visitation, Gómez Robledo had stood close at hand. According to some, it was he who counseled the governor that kachina dances were simply not as diabolical as the missionaries avowed. When everyone else backed away from the assignment, it was Gómez Robledo who had ridden for Mexico City with López' defense of himself. That he had been forced at Zacatecas to surrender the dispatch to the northbound Peñalosa was not, he maintained, his fault. In 1662, don Francisco, paterfamilias of the large Gómez clan and pillar of the Hispanic community, held the rank of sargento mayor and served as mayordomo of the religious confraternity of Nuestra Señora del Rosario.[20]

That same Thursday, in the presence of Pedro Lucero de Godoy, Alguacil Manso and the others inventoried Gómez Robledo's house on the plaza. It had "a sala, three rooms, and a patio, with its kitchen garden at the rear." Beginning with "an arquebus, a sword hilt, and a dagger," item by item they proceeded to list all of don Francisco's personal effects—his weapons, horse gear, his complete set of tools for making gun stocks, his household furnishings, clothing, and papers. Among the latter were titles to the Gómez encomiendas:

All of the pueblo of Pecos, except for twenty-four houses held by
    Pedro Lucero de Godoy
Two and a half parts of the pueblo of Taos
Half the Hopi pueblo of Shongopovi
Half the pueblo of Ácoma, except for twenty houses
Half the pueblo of Abó, which Gómez Robledo had received in
    exchange for half of Sandía
All the pueblo of Tesuque, which for more than forty years neither
    Gómez Robledo nor his father had collected because of service
    rendered on contract in lieu of tribute.

There were in addition estancia grants, not only for San Nicolás de las Barrancas but also for a piece of land one league above San Juan pueblo and another on the Arroyo de Tesuque.[21]

After three days, they transferred Gómez to a cell at Santo Domingo next to those occupied by the other prisoners of the Holy Office. There they stagnated and sweat for five months, through the entire summer, seeing "neither sun nor moon." Meanwhile, Father Posada and Alguacil Manso embargoed their properties and sold off enough of their goods to cover the expenses of their imprisonment, their impending journey to Mexico City, and their trials.

At a public auction cried June 30, July 1, and July 2 in the Santa Fe plaza, a variety of Francisco Gómez Robledo's possessions brought 325 pesos. He later charged that Governor Peñalosa rigged the bidding and through his agents knocked down whatever he wanted at a fraction of its value. When Manso had trouble rounding up and separating out don Francisco's stock on the estancia of Las Barrancas, he attached it all with a warning to the other Gómez brothers that they not remove a single head on pain of excommunication and a five-hundred-peso fine. The same penalty applied to unauthorized persons collecting the revenue from the prisoners' encomiendas.[22]

Up to the time the Holy Office made its sudden arrests, New Mexico had seemed big enough for both Custos Posada and Governor Peñalosa. They had even cooperated. In November 1661, for instance, Peñalosa had reaffirmed the exemption from tribute of ten Indians per mission to assist the friars. But when the prelate, officiating as agent of the Inquisition, began ordering alcaldes mayores to impound encomienda revenues, the governor got his back up. Without mincing words, he challenged the Franciscan's jurisdiction over encomiendas, which were royal grants, and admonished him for giving orders to alcaldes. Posada responded that his instructions from the Holy Office were to embargo all property belonging to the prisoners, and encomienda tribute was plainly property. From the summer of 1662 until their showdown at Pecos fourteen months later, relations between governor and prelate degenerated notably.

Posada and Peñalosa Quarrel

Francisco Gómez Robledo and Diego Romero were encomenderos. Cristóbal de Anaya Almazán, as the eldest son in his family, became one soon after his arrest when his father died. By viceregal decree, the number of encomenderos in New Mexico had been limited to thirty-five. These men were the backbone of the colony's defense. In turn for the privilege of collecting the tribute from specified pueblos—customarily twice a year in May and October—they maintained horses and weapons and responded to the governor's call to arms. When a woman or a minor inherited encomiendas, an *escudero,* literally a shield bearer or squire, was appointed as a substitute to render the military service for a share of the tribute. Governor Peñalosa was quite right in insisting on escuderos to serve in lieu of the arrested encomenderos. But the way he handled the matter left little doubt that personal advantage, not defense, was uppermost in his mind.[23]

When they met on the street leading to the governor's palace, Father Posada asked Peñalosa just what he intended to do. Don Diego replied that since Posada had collected the tributes in full for May 1662, without waiting for him to name escuderos, the governor should collect and hold in trust for the escuderos the full proceeds in October. After that, from May 1663 until Mexico City resolved the issue, the revenues should be divided evenly, half for the Holy Office and half to pay the escuderos. When the friar pointed out that he had ordered the May 1662 tribute collected in full because the prisoners had already earned it, Peñalosa turned a deaf ear. Worse, he set up two of his retainers as dummy escuderos so that he could pocket their share of the tribute. In the case of Francisco Gómez Robledo, he passed over four able-bodied brothers to pick Martín Carranza, described by Gómez as "a boy about twelve or fourteen years old whom he [Peñalosa] brought with him, a criollo from Pátzcuaro." [24]

The Pecos Encomienda

Pecos was the richest encomienda in New Mexico, even after a couple of generations of marked population decline. Gómez Robledo reckoned the revenue at 170 units per collection, or 340 per year, "in buckskins, mantas, buffalo hides, and light and heavy buffalo or elkskins." The number of units, or *piezas,* was equivalent to the number of *indios tributarios,* that is, heads of household, a figure the encomendero was doubtless slow to adjust in relation to population decrease. If the twenty-four households of Pedro Lucero de Godoy and the ten households of mission helpers exempt from tribute were added, the total for the pueblo came to 374. Using an average of three persons per household on the low side and four on the high side, a rough estimate of Pecos' population in 1662 fell between 1,122 and 1,496. Compared to his 340 units from Pecos annually, Gómez received 110 from his share of Taos, 80 from half of Shongopovi, 50 from half of Ácoma, and 30 from half of Abó.[25]

Despite the imprisonment of their encomendero and the legal tangle that ensued, someone always came round to collect from the Pecos. For May 1662, Father Posada acknowledged receipt of: "one hundred sixty-eight units in poor buffalo hides, light buffalo or elkskins good only for sacks, heavy buffalo or elkskins, seventy-two buckskins large and small, and some cotton and wool mantas, all of which was valued at one hundred and fifty pesos."[26]

St. Joseph,
painted on hide.
Fred Harvey Collection,
Museum of New Mexico.

In October 1662, by Governor Peñalosa's order, Alcalde mayor Jerónimo de Carvajal, evidently accompanied by Lt. Gov. Pedro Manso de Valdés and Antonio González Bernal, directed the Pecos "captains" to gather in the entire fall tribute and lay it before him. Carvajal then delivered the bundles in person to the governor in Santa Fe, testifying later that Peñalosa kept everything for himself. This collection amounted to: "nineteen cotton mantas, forty-four assorted pieces [of skins], sixty-six buckskins, twenty-one white buffalo or elk-skins, eighteen buffalo hides, sixteen heavy buffalo or elkskins." The Pecos captains also collected what was due from the twenty-four households of Pedro Lucero de Godoy and took it to him at his home.

Again in April 1663, Carvajal returned to Pecos at Peñalosa's bidding, this time to take up half the May tribute: "twenty-nine large buckskins, forty-two assorted pieces of buck-skins, twelve buffalo hides, twelve white buffalo or elkskins, seven heavy buffalo or elkskins." When he turned it over in Santa Fe, the governor forced him, said Carvajal, to alter his statement to read twenty-nine heavy buffalo or elkskins instead of large buckskins. Peñalosa then kept the buckskins, the statement, and all the rest of the delivery. The other half of the May 1633 tribute Pedro Lucero de Godoy, as receiver of his brother-in-law's income, collected on instructions from Father Posada: "thirteen buffalo hides, twenty-two light white buffalo or elkskins, eighteen heavy buffalo or elkskins, thirty buckskins good and bad but most of them good, which in all makes eighty-three units."[27]

It did not seem to worry Diego de Peñalosa that he was twisting the tail of the Inquisition every time his men brought in another load of goods from an embargoed encomienda. The fact was he rather enjoyed it. "And the comisario of this Holy Office," declared a concerned Francisco Gómez Robledo, "seems not to have prevented it, for in such remote places [as New Mexico] there is no justice other than the will of the governor."[28]

López Found Guilty

In the case of ex-governor López de Mendizábal, still under guard in August 1662, nothing could have been further from the truth. In rapid succession, the long arms of the audiencia and the Holy Office reached out to chastise him. Found guilty by the audiencia, or high court of Mexico, on sixteen of the thirty-three charges brought against him during his residencia, López was ordered to pay 3,500 pesos in fines, plus costs, and to settle his debts with friars, colonists, and Indians. Governor Peñalosa stood to profit handsomely. However, at ten o'clock on the night of August 26, Father Posada and Alguacil Manso arrested López. Two hours later, they took into custody his literate, Italian-born, Spanish-Irish wife. All their possessions were attached. Again the Holy Office had foiled the wily Peñalosa.

When it formed up in early October that year, the southbound supply train carried six unwilling passengers. Like his erstwhile aides, the distraught ex-governor López rode fettered in a wagon, doña Teresa, his wife, in a carriage behind. Careful provisions had been made for the security and safe delivery of each prisoner. At Santo Domingo on October 5, for example, Father Posada had turned over Francisco Gómez Robledo to Ensign Pedro de Arteaga who, for one hundred and fifty pesos, guaranteed to see the prisoner behind bars in Mexico City. Arteaga swore to conduct Gómez in shackles "not allowing him the least communication, or that he be given letter, ink, or paper, or that said prisoner be permitted to leave his wagon." Should he fail to carry out his commission, Ensign Arteaga obligated himself to pay back double his salary and suffer whatever other penalities the inquisition might impose.

A hearing before the Inquisition, by Mexican artist Constantino Escalante.
D. Guillén de Lampart, *La Inquisición y la independencia en el siglo XVII*
(México, 1908)

The costs for guard, shackles, food, and incidentals, were
born by the prisoner and paid for out of the sale of his possessions. In addition, the Holy Office required three hundred
pesos in security to cover prison expenses in Mexico City. In
the wagon with Gómez rode two bales wrapped in buffalo or
elkskins, worth two pesos each, containing three hundred
buckskins valued at one peso apiece, along with a single
trunk of his clothing. The dismal journey lasted from fall
through winter to spring. Finally, in April 1663, the head jailer
at the secret prison of the Holy Office checked in one Francisco
Gómez Robledo of New Mexico. Ensign Arteaga had earned
his pay.[29]

Gómez Robledo fared better before the inquisitors than
any of the others. Even though the case against him included
the ominous accusation of Judaism, it proved to be based
mainly on hearsay. Bodily examination by physicians showed
that don Francisco had no "little tail," as one of his brothers
was alleged to have, nor could the scars on his penis be positively identified as an attempt at circumcision. In audience
after audience, answering forcefully and directly, and utilizing

Gómez Robledo
Tried and Acquitted

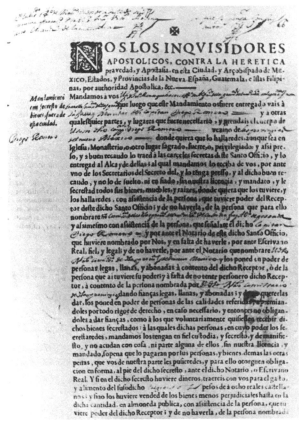

The Inquisition's order for the arrest of Capt. Diego Romero, dated in Mexico City, August 29, 1661 (AGN, Inq., 586)

to the best advantage the long and loyal Christian service of his father, Gómez Robledo earned himself a verdict of unqualified acquittal.[30]

From the pounding on his door that early morning of May 4, 1662, until September 17, 1665, when again in Santa Fe he signed a release of all claims against Father Posada and Pedro Lucero de Godoy, "content and satisfied entirely and fully," the ordeal had cost Francisco Gómez Robledo three years, four months, and fourteen days of his life. In assets, it had cost him several thousand pesos. He got back his personal belongings that had not been sold, his house on the plaza, his titles to lands and encomiendas, as well as an accumulated 875 units of tribute. As for the value of tribute usurped by Governor Peñalosa, 831 pesos, Gómez judiciously requested that the sum be collected by the Holy Office and applied to its chapel in Mexico City. Not that it mattered to them, but in the fall of 1665, the Pecos Indians once again paid their tribute to don Francisco.[31]

por ⟨...⟩ y afsimefmo con afsiftencia de la
perfona que vbiere feñalado el dicho ⟨...⟩
y por ante el dicho Notario, o Efcrivanô Real, los quáles ⟨...⟩
pcios los entregad ante el Notario de los fecreitos defte Santo Officio, y en
nueftra prefencia al dicho Receptor, para que el defpenfero, y proveedor
de los preffos defte Santo Officio, de alli lo alimente. Y afsimefmo traereis
del dicho fecreito vna cama de ropa, en que el fufodicho ⟨...⟩
⟨...⟩ duerma, y los veftidos, y ropa blanca, que vbiere menefter para fu perfona: lo cual entregareis al dicho Alcayde, por ante el dicho
Notario de fecreitos. Y fi para cumplir, y executar lo contenido en efte nueftro Mandamiento, tuvieredes necefsidad de favor, y ayuda, exortamos, y
requerimos, y fi es necefsario en virtud de fanta obediencia, y fopena de ex-
comunion mayor *latæ fententiæ trina canonica monitione præmiffa*, y de ⟨...⟩
⟨...⟩ ducados de caftilla, para los gaftos extraordinarios del dicho
Santo Officio: mandamos à todos, y qualefquier juezes, y jufticias afsi Ec-
clefiafticos, como Seculares de los Reynos, y Señorios de fu Mageftad, que
fiendo por vos requeridos, os den, y hagan dar todo el favor, y ayuda, que
les pidieredes, y vbieredes menefter, y los hombres de guarda, y beftias, que
para traer el fufodicho, y fu cama, y ropa, y prifiones, que mantenimien-
tos de que tuvieredes necefsidad, à los precios, que entre ellos valiere, fin
los mas encarecer. Fecho en Mexico, en la Sala de nueftra Audiencia, firma-
do de nueftros nombres, fellado con el fello menor del Officio, y refrenda-
do de vno de los Secretarios del Secreto del ⟨...⟩

The long-suffering Bernardo López de Mendizábal died in the Inquisition jail before a verdict was reached. The case against doña Teresa was dropped. Ex-alcalde mayor Nicolás de Aguilar, found guilty, had to appear in an *auto de fe,* the public procession of Inquisition prisoners in penitential garb, and to abjure his errors before the tribunal. He was forbidden for life to hold public office and banished from New Mexico for ten years. Cristóbal de Anaya Almazán abjured his errors before the inquisitors and was released. As a condition of his sentence, they ordered don Cristóbal, once he returned to New Mexico, to stand up during Mass on a feast day and publicly recant his false doctrine.[32]

Diego Romero, who appeared as a condemned apostate and heretic in the same auto de fe with Aguilar, made a pathetic showing during his trial. At first he had tried to bluff. Gradually he broke down, implicating his fellow prisoners and admitting what a crude, ignorant, low-life person he was. Accused of incest with **Juana Romero,** allegedly his cousin and the mother of his son, Romero swore that she was no relative at all, but rather "a native of Pecos, of whose issue he does not know, and that his mother raised her from infancy as a mestiza." Later, **Juana** had fallen in with accused madam Catalina Bernal and, according to Romero, had slept with the Father Guardian of the Santa Fe convento. The blond son born to Juana was not Romero's but the friar's, as the resemblance of father and son would prove.[33]

Diego Romero Feted by the Plains Apaches

Certain of the other charges against Diego Romero stemmed from a trading excursion he had led to the plains at the behest of Governor López de Mendizábal. One of Romero's motives, which he admitted during his trial, was to have the Apaches install him "as their captain, as they had done with Capt. Antonio [Alonso] Baca, Francisco Luján, and Gaspar Pérez, father of the one who confesses, and with a religious of

Diego Romero

the Order of St. Francis named Fray Andrés Juárez." [34] Some Pecos Indians joined Romero. Their leader, called El Carpintero, but obviously a trader and diplomat as well, seems to have been a sort of seventeenth-century Bigotes.

Back in the summer of 1660, at the head of a half-dozen Hispanos, their servants, the Pecos contingent, and a pack string of supplies and trade knives, Diego Romero rode tall in the saddle. A large, heavy-set man with curly black hair, he looked forward to cementing trade relations with the Plains Apaches. He would earn the gratitude of Governor López, have some fun, and turn a profit to boot. "Some two hundred leagues" east of the custody of New Mexico, on the "Río Colorado," the traders made camp near the Apache "ranchería or pueblo of don Pedro." Here the heathens feted Romero and El Carpintero with such gusto that the Inquisition knew about it almost before they reached home.

One afternoon a group of about thirty Apaches appeared at the Spaniards' camp and formed a circle around Romero.

They wanted to make him their *"capitán grande de toda la nación apache,"* their chief captain of the entire Apache nation. Four of the heathens left the circle, picked up Romero, and laid him face down on a new buffalo hide spread on the ground. They did the same to El Carpintero. Then they hoisted them shoulder high and began carrying them on the hides in procession "with singing and the sound of reed whistles and flutes, performing their rites."

Arriving at their ranchería, the Apache bearers sat the honored guests on piles of skins in the midst of a circle of two or three hundred Indians. There followed more singing and dancing, during which natives stood on either side of the two men "shaking them." The celebration went on all through the night. There were orations, a mock battle, the smoking of a peace pipe, and, according to Romero's accusers, a heathen marriage rite.

Plains Apaches. After an 18th-century painting on hide (Segesser I) in Gottfried Hotz, *Indian Skin Paintings from the American Southwest* (Norman, 1970)

The Spaniard had reminded his hosts that his father Gaspar Pérez—whose surname, he later told the inquisitors, he had not taken because of don Gaspar's unchristian behavior —had "left a son" among them. He too should have the honor. Accordingly, a new tipi was set up and a maiden brought. Inside on a bed of skins Romero deflowered her. Afterwards the heathens daubed his chest—some said his face and beard— with the girl's blood. They presented him with the tipi and the skins as gifts. They tied a white feather on his head. From then on, said an eyewitness, "he always wore that feather stuck in his hatband." And he swaggered.

Had he not swaggered so much and had the zealous Fray Alonso de Posada not been building his case against the López regime, Romero's feat on the plains might have been told and retold only around campfires. But because it reached the halls of the Holy Office, it was set down and preserved. Here, thanks to that tribunal, is documentary evidence that by 1660 the Spaniards of New Mexico had been using "the French system" for a couple of generations to bind trade connections with Plains Indians. The participation of El Carpintero confirms the continuing role of the Pecos in this trade. Romero, denying that he ever was "married" on the plains, did admit trading a knife for sex on two occasions at another ranchería where the party stayed nine days. He called this place "la ranchería de la Porciúncula," an intriguing link to Pecos, and perhaps to the seminal ministry of Fray Andrés Juárez. [35]

Romero, by throwing his miserable self on the mercy of the inquisitors, had his harsh sentence of service in the Philippine galleys commuted to banishment from New Mexico. But he had not learned his lesson.

Several years later in Guanajuato, under the name Diego Pérez de Salazar, he married a mestiza. The trouble was, he already had a legal wife residing in New Mexico. Before he knew it, he was back in Mexico City, back in the stinking *cárceles secretas*, accused of polygamy. This time, the inquisitors were harsh with Romero. In addition to his appearance in a public auto de fe, "with insignia of a man twice married, conical hat on his head, rope around his neck, and wax candle in his hands," they sentenced him to two hundred lashes, administered as he was paraded through the streets with a crier, and to six years' labor as a galley slave. On October 23, 1678, poor Diego Romero died of "natural causes" in the public jail at Veracruz still waiting for his first galley. [36]

El Carpintero, the "Christian" Pecos Indian, was of course exempt from prosecution by the Inquisition. If, as Franciscan prelate, Father Posada moved to discipline him for his part in the plains episode, the record has not come to light.

The aggressive Alonso de Posada was still in his mid-thirties. Born to Licenciado Alonso de Llanos y Posada and María González in 1626, he hailed from western León, from the villa of Congosto, which translates "narrow pass, or canyon." Not a particularly important place, the cluster of mostly two-storied stone houses roofed with slate or tile occupied an elevated plain high above the Río Sil. "The land is of good quality," according to a nineteenth-century description, "in the main unirrigated for the Sil waters almost none of it because of the depth of the riverbed." As well as wheat, rye, various fruits, and vegetables, the people grew potatoes in abundance. There were trout and fresh-water eels in the river, which has since been dammed in the vicinity of Congosto. From there it flows south and westward toward the sea, commingling with the Río Miño to form a piece of Portugal's northern border.

Custos Posada
Moves to Pecos

The general auto de fe of 1649 in Mexico City.
Alfonso Toro, *La familia Carvajal*, vol. 1 (México, 1944)

On the American side of the Atlantic, the twenty-year-old Alonso had taken the habit of the Franciscans at the Convento Grande, on Saturday, October 20, 1646, at the traditional hour of compline with the entire community present. As a young missionary in New Mexico, he had seen duty at two hardship posts, at the Hopi pueblo of Awátovi between 1653 and 1655, and at Jémez in 1656. Then Fray Alonso returned to Mexico City, where his superiors soon named him custos of New Mexico and sent him back to do battle with Bernardo López de Mendizábal. That he had done with dispatch.[37]

Sometime early in 1663, Father Posada moved out to Pecos, evidently to avoid bumping into Governor Peñalosa. The two men were no longer speaking. Since Christmas Day 1662, when Peñalosa had learned that his hurried shipment of goods purloined from the estate of ex-governor López had been impounded at Parral on orders from Posada, his fury had badly affected his judgment. He derided the Holy Office and composed rude doggerel about inquisitors. On one occasion he was heard to say in a rage that "if the Inquisitors opposed him the way Posada opposed him, he would scour all their assholes." He had made vile threats against Father Posada. And he never missed an opportunity to proclaim his authority as royal governor over any creature in a Franciscan habit.

The showdown began in August 1663. During a dispute over livestock, Peñalosa ordered the arrest of Pedro Durán y Chávez. At Santo Domingo, the prisoner escaped to the church where he invoked the right of asylum. That did not stop Peñalosa. He had Durán y Chávez dragged from the church and jailed in the governor's palace. It was an act Father Posada could not ignore. When a polite letter requesting Durán's return met with a firm refusal, the prelate rode over to Santo Domingo.

To a second request, Peñalosa made no reply at all. With that, the Franciscan started legal proceedings. On September 27, he issued a formal ecclesiastical monition directing the governor to give up the prisoner within twenty-four hours or suffer excommunication. He dispatched a friar to Santa Fe with instructions to make two personal appeals, and, if they did not move Peñalosa, to serve the notice. Fray Alonso then went back to Pecos.

Peñalosa Decides on Arrest   The governor did not bend. Instead, he resolved to make good an earlier threat. He would arrest and deport the arrogant Franciscan. Securing the assent of Lt. Gov. Pedro Manso de Valdés and Fray Nicolás de Freitas, Peñalosa hastily set a dangerous course. It was Sunday, September 30, 1663. A moment of high drama in the long struggle of church and state in New Mexico was about to take place in the convento at Pecos between two strong, unflinching individuals.[38]

Without fanfare, the governor issued a call to arms to a select group of encomenderos. According to a statement by five of them who later sought absolution from Father Posada, "All of us were utterly unprepared, not at all willing, some reaping our wheat, others winnowing theirs, when Gen. Diego de Peñalosa summoned us one at a time without any of us knowing of the others." Each was to mount up, bring his arquebus, and await the governor at a place a quarter-league out of Santa Fe. There they came together. About three in the afternoon Peñalosa rode up. He asked them, "Which way to Pecos?" Told that the road lay before him, he spurred his horse and ordered them to follow.

Before long, don Diego called to Capt. Diego Lucero de Godoy, who rode a fine horse, to go on ahead and ask the native governor "in all secrecy how many friars there are at the pueblo of Pecos and if the Father Custos is there. If by chance you run into him on the road shout to him that something just occurred to you and return in all haste to report to me." Lucero did as ordered. The Pecos governor told him that only Father Posada and Father Juan de la Chica were there. Riding back at a gallop, Lucero missed the main party, which "had taken another trail to the pueblo," but he doubled back to join them as they dismounted under some cottonwoods within sight of the convento.

There were ten or twelve of them. "All proceeded on foot," said the five in their statement,

from behind the kitchen garden toward the convento. The Father Custos, taking a walk or praying, was on a mirador that looks out toward the villa [Santa Fe]. Hearing the rustling, the Father Custos said in a loud voice, "Who goes there?" Gen. Diego de Peñalosa answered, "Friends. Open the door for us, Your Reverence, and give us chocolate." At once the Father Custos ordered the door of the convento opened.[39]

It was sometime between nine and ten at night. Peñalosa posted a guard outside the main door with orders to kill anyone who tried to come out. Some witnesses remembered him saying, "Should St. Francis come out, kill him!" Then the governor and his armed men went inside.

Father Posada recalled their unexpected arrival in these words:

> I was in our cell and the convento was in silence with the doors locked. At the ruckus of some dogs I went out on a balcony or window which forms a part of the cell and I saw some six or seven men with arquebuses in their hands. Some were approaching the convento cautiously.
>
> To find out who they were I said from the window or balcony, "*Deo gratias,* who goes there?" To which Gen. Diego de Peñalosa replied, "It is I."
>
> And I asked him, "Who are you?" He said he was don Diego. I greeted him from above and he said to me, "Open the door, Your Reverence, and let's drink a bit of chocolate." I then ordered the door opened and left our cell to receive the general at the stairway that leads to the patio. I greeted him a second time with all politeness and courtesy and took him straight to our guest cell. [40]

The Franciscan noted that Peñalosa had a pair of horse pistols in his belt. Lieutenant Governor Manso de Valdés entered with arquebus in hand, "apparently with hammer cocked." Obeying an impulse, Francisco de Madrid set his weapon aside. Lucero de Godoy released his hammer. Diego González Lobón came in holding a pistol. Later, before the Inquisition, don Diego de Peñalosa denied that he and his men were any more heavily armed than usual.

Confrontation of Governor and Custos

The most complete account of what happened next is from the pen of Father Posada. Although Peñalosa disputed certain of the details, he did admit before the tribunal of the Holy Office that "he was so impassioned and so blind that without considering more than the harm done to him he resolved to exile said Father Custos from the provinces of New Mexico." [41]

The friar asked the governor what he was doing in the vicinity of Pecos at that hour. "We have come for a refugee," Peñalosa retorted with calculated irony, "and therefore, Your Reverence, you must throw open the doors for us in the name of the king." The Franciscan did.

> "Most willingly," I replied, "but I do not know of any refugee in this convento. If per chance it is I Your Lordship seeks, here I am. There is no need to search for me."
>
> I begged him and his companions to sit down and drink some chocolate. He did so and said to me, "Very well then, Your Reverence, I shall come to the point with you." And while the chocolate was being prepared he began to say certain things with great self-esteem and loftiness regarding my infamy, saying that I was a villain, that there were many such in Asturias, and that if I did not know how to obey the king that he would teach me.

To which I replied, "Sir, I and the Asturians are very much vassals of the king my lord, because we inherit it from our fathers." Don Diego then said that I had no right nor could I say the king *my* lord, but only the king *our* lord, since only he, who was the prince, was entitled to say the king my lord.

Among other things, he insinuated, searching for a way to upset me and make me lose my temper, that he was going to garrote me, that he always carried silk cords to garrote people, that he never did it with one torsion stick but with two because death came quicker. Seeing that he had not made me lose my temper or upset me in this way and that I was responding and speaking to him with great composure and restraint, he tried to catch me in words with theological traps, words used only among theologians.

When I had given him and all his companions chocolate with all graciousness, don Diego de Peñalosa said that it was expedient to the service of God and king that the cell in which I was living be thoroughly searched, to which I responded, "Most willingly."

Taking with him Pedro Manso de Valdés and Diego Lucero de Godoy, with arquebuses in hand, he searched all, even to rummaging through the rubbish. Afterward he said that he also had to search another cell in which I used to live. Without any objection or hesitation I took him to it in person and opened it. He entered with the two arquebusiers and searched it in the same way as the first.

Afterward he went down to the cloister. I told him to search the church and the rest of the cells and workrooms of the convento, to which he replied that he did not wish to go to the church and that it was not necessary to search the rest of the convento.

Back in the guest cell, Peñalosa pressed Posada. He must go to Santa Fe at once, that very night. When the friar explained that it was not his custom to go out at night, and offered instead to give his guests supper and a place to sleep, the governor invited the prelate to step out into the cloister.

When we had gone out, he said to me angrily, "Father, can the custos excommunicate the governor and captain general of this kingdom?"

To which I replied, "Sir, that depends on the case, for if it is one of those contained in canon law, yes, he can, because then the ecclesiastical judge does no more than use and exercise through his office what is ordained in canon law and what the Supreme Head of the Church commands."

To this Gen. don Diego de Peñalosa replied, "if the custos excommunicated me, I would hang him or garrote him immediately, and if the Pontiff came here and wanted to excommunicate me or actually did so, I would hang the Pontiff, because in this kingdom I am the prince and the supreme magistrate, and there is no one who may excommunicate the prince and supreme magistrate."

I replied, "Sir, it is not necessary to bring the person and holiness of the Pontiff into such matters, for it is better to leave His Holiness on the supreme throne he occupies, with the due authority and the respect which all faithful Christians must render to him and with which they regard his person. As for hanging him, he is absent. I am here for Your Lordship to hang, and I shall not be the first religious or priest to die in defense of Our Holy Mother the Roman Catholic Church."

I was worried that someone might have heard us. I made out although at some distance Comisario de la caballería Francisco de Madrid and Capt. Juan Griego who were next to the door of my cell and Capt. Diego Lucero de Godoy who was in a passageway which leads to the patio from outside adjacent to the same cell. It could have been that other persons he brought with him, besides those mentioned, might have heard him because it was night and without light and I could not make them out. While they might not have heard everything clearly, they would have heard some things.

General don Diego, continuing with his replies and propositions, said to me, "Why is Your Reverence seeking to excommunicate me for having ordered don Pedro de Chávez taken from the church of Santo Domingo and held prisoner?"

I replied, "Sir, as an ecclesiastical judge I am obliged to defend the immunity of the Church, and because terms had not been reached for proceeding in the matter judicially, I wrote two letters of supplication to Your Lordship, who, up to now, is not excommunicated or declared such. And with regard to the case concerning immunity, you may state through your attorney, proceeding in legal form, the reasons you had for removing him. And if the reasons of Your Lordship were sufficient basis for doing so, there is no controversy, because the case is one of those contained in the law, as will be seen in the second part of the Decretals, in *Quest.* 4, *Cap.* 8, 9, and 10. And if the case is carried to the use of force it is not necessary to hang the Pontiff of the Roman Catholic Church, for by hanging me the affair may be concluded."

And I replied in this way because he had stated to me for the second time the preceding proposition that he would hang the Pontiff. To this Gen. don Diego de Peñalosa replied, raising with his right hand the cape and cloak he was wearing in order to show me the pistols he had in his belt, "Now then, we will consider this affair and Your Reverence and all the other Fathers Custos of New Mexico will learn what a governor can do. I therefore order Your Reverence in the name of the king to go with me at once to the villa where Your Reverence will see the difficulties cleared up."

I replied, "Sir, these matters need little action, if they are considered with prudence and judgment. There are many authors who clarify the manner in which ecclesiastical and secular judges must deal with them, and therefore neither contention nor anger is necessary."

When the shouting ceased, according to the guards, who had indeed heard the governor saying "many vituperative things," the two men went back inside. Father Posada began taking out books to inform Peñalosa of the immunities a clergy-man enjoyed as Franciscan prelate, ecclesiastical judge ordinary, and agent of the Holy Office. The governor was not impressed. He told the friar to save his breath. Anyone could see that the priest "was the student of a book and that he himself was a clod." Still, said Peñalosa, he knew more than Posada.

A third time the governor told the prelate that he was required in Santa Fe at once. Still protesting the hour, Posada ordered an animal saddled. He wanted to know if he was being taken as a prisoner. Peñalosa said no, he was merely going to honor the governor's palace with his presence. "I shall do so to comply with your command," vowed the grim-faced Franciscan, "but I give notice that I am not going freely." He would force the governor's hand.

Posada Taken
from Pecos

I was outside in the patio about to mount up when it occurred to me to return to the cell. In a loud voice the general commanded Comisario Francisco de Madrid, who was already mounted, to go with me on pretext of my needing something. I realized from his footsteps that the general was following me, and he again entered the cell. At that juncture I knew for certain that they were taking me as a prisoner. In my own cell they placed guards on me, the governor himself serving as one of them.

At that hour, which must have been about eleven at night of said last day of September of last year, 1663, Gen. Diego de Peñalosa, with the accompaniment and escort of all the above-mentioned soldiers, in order to conduct me to the villa of Santa Fe eight leagues from the pueblo of Pecos, disposed that some of the soldiers should go ahead and others behind so that they had me in the middle with His Lordship close to me, conducting me carefully in front of him.

No sooner had they begun the long night's ride when Peñalosa leaned over and said something about the embargo Posada had placed on the goods in Parral. From the tone of the conversation the prelate thought he could feel the governor's mortal hatred. A little less than a league down the trail, "before leaving the milpas of the pueblo of Pecos," he asked again if he was Peñalosa's prisoner. The governor lied. He told the Franciscan that once they reached Santa Fe, he would leave him at the convento. The rest of the way in, recalled the soldiers, "they came chatting on the trail most sociably."

In Santa Fe, the sarcastic Peñalosa insisted that Posada join him at the governor's palace for chocolate. As they came opposite the gallows that had been erected in the center of the plaza "to hang an Indian" said Peñalosa, certain threatening remarks were made. The prelate then disappeared into the casas reales. [42]

The Custos
a Prisoner

About 6:00 a.m. Monday morning, October 1, the Franciscans at the convento in Santa Fe learned what had happened. They were stunned. They had grown used to don Diego's blasphemous threats, but now he had actually done it—locked up the Father Custos. Fray Nicolás de Enríquez, guardian of the convento, reacted swiftly, closing the Santa Fe church and ordering the host consumed. He considered placing all the churches of New Mexico under interdict. "With the utmost anxiety" he penned a hasty note to Fray Antonio de Ibargaray at Galisteo, "definitor and senior Father of this custody," telling him of the prelate's arrest and warning him to be on his guard. "The situation is grave," he concluded, "and to my knowledge without precedent." [43]

Ibargaray had the note by three that afternoon. It only confirmed what he had learned by twenty-nine years' experience in New Mexico—that the governors proceeded, in his words, "as absolute lords, that there is no law other than what they desire, and that not even the immunity of churches is sacred." He knew how to handle the likes of Diego de Peñalosa.

Fray Nicolás de Enríquez'
anxious note to Ibargaray,
October 1, 1663
(AGN, Inq., 507).

Ex-governor López de Mendizábal had characterized Father Ibargaray as "very headstrong and uncontrolled. When Gen. don Juan de Samaniego was governor [1653-1656, while Ibaragaray was custos], this friar seized him and threatened him, telling him that he had trampled the church under foot when he punished the heathen enemy without consulting the religious." But Ibargaray was not as young now, nor was he the prelate. This time he sat down and wrote the Inquisition, urging the tribunal to act "with the utmost dispatch to defend your minister and agent." [44]

For nine days the colony held its breath. The two light field pieces which the governor ordered positioned to prevent the prelate's escape testified to the gravity of the situation. At many of the missions, the friars followed Father Enríquez' lead, locking the churches. They even refrained from celebrating Mass on the feast day of St. Francis, October 4. How Fray Juan de la Chica, who evidently remained at Pecos, answered the questions of the Indians, we can only guess. Surely he made Governor Peñalosa out another Attila.[45]

Meanwhile, inside the governor's palace, Peñalosa and Posada kept up a running argument over their respective authority. Mediators came and went. The governor wanted to expel the prelate for overstepping his ecclesiastical jurisdiction and for sedition. When it became clear to him that he could not build up a strong enough case, he looked for a way out. Father Posada, "in order to avoid greater evils," directed the friars to reopen the Santa Fe church and admit Peñalosa to the sacraments. Although it went against his grain, the dauntless Franciscan finally agreed to drop the whole matter, "insofar as possible," in exchange for an end to the impasse. The governor released him the same day. The ordeal was over.

Father Ibargaray's appeal for help did not reach the Holy Office until early February 1664. In early March, don Diego de Peñalosa made his exit. He knew the inquisitor's file on him was growing, and he had no intention of allowing Father Posada the satisfaction of arresting him as he had arrested his predecessor. Once the governor was gone, Posada set aside the agreement he had accepted under duress and prosecuted the case with vigor. He had no trouble finding witnesses.[46]

Posada Builds His Case

Most of the testimony related in one way or another to Governor Peñalosa's obstruction of Holy Office business and his utter disrespect for the tribunal's authority. He had ignored Inquisition embargoes, appropriating the goods of former governor López and collecting the ecomienda revenues of the arrested New Mexicans. He had seized, opened, and read Inquisition mail. He had terrorized Agent Posada in an effort to force him to release the goods impounded in Parral, even to bodily removing him from Pecos and imprisoning him in Santa Fe. He had made a mockery of ecclesiastical immunity and the right of asylum. Less weighty in the eyes of the inquisitors, but indicative nonetheless, were the accounts of Peñalosa's devil-may-care lack of moral propriety.

He had delighted in flaunting the young mistress he picked up en route to New Mexico. He had sported also with local females. His language was the filthiest, his jokes the most obscene. With undisguised glee, he often made the friars the butt of his crude humor. Testifying before Father Posada at the estancia of Nuestra Señora de los Remedios de los Cerrillos, the alluring doña Margarita Márquez, wife of Alcalde mayor Jerónimo de Carvajal and former mistress of Governor Manso, now in her mid-twenties, offered some examples.

Asked if she had ever heard anyone say that the woman who got pregnant by a governor had her womb consecrated, doña Margarita responded with a variation on the same theme. Don Diego de Peñalosa on his way to New Spain had stopped over to say good-by at the Cerrillos estancia. He had summoned her to his room. Knowing of don Diego's appetites, she had asked her mother to go with her. There, before Margarita, her mother, and another woman, the governor spoke in this low vein, if we can believe the testimony.

He said that the woman who was sleeping with a friar consecrated him. Her husband became the friar's eunuch and would say that he was helpless against the fates. And while the friar was with his wife, the husband would guard the door. If someone appeared the husband would tell him softly, "Do not disturb the Father inside, for he is tending to his compadre's business."

He added that a friar whose balls ached would tell his compadre to play with them. The compadre would say that it would be better if his comadre played with them. Then the husband would call his wife and tell her, "Come here and play with your compadre's balls." [47]

The virile Franciscan may have blushed. Although his varied duties as agent of the Inquisition, even to seeking out such testimony as doña Margarita's, as ecclesiastical judge, and as prelate kept him moving about, Father Posada evidently continued to serve as guardian at Pecos.

It was to the Pecos convento that the released but unrepentant Cristóbal de Anaya Almazán reported in June 1665.

He thrust at the friar an order from the Holy Office releasing his property. He did not present notice of the Inquisition's sentence, as he had been instructed to do, but rather went around boasting that his good name had been wholly restored and that the persons who had testified against him were soon to be arrested. A month later, Posada called his bluff. Not really contrite, Anaya stood at the main altar in the Sandía church during the offertory. It was Sunday morning. He was about to confess before Father Posada and the entire congregation the error of his false doctrine. He had been wrong, he told them, to deny the spiritual relationship of baptizer, baptized, parents, and godparents. Outside afterwards he was as cocky as ever.[48]

In Mexico City meantime, the Inquisition had arrested don Diego de Peñalosa. Formal accusation of the reckless ex-governor ran to 237 articles and took two days to read. When the final sentence was handed down twenty months later, it was harsh—appearance in a public auto de fe, a fine, lifelong exclusion from civil or military office, and perpetual banishment from New Spain and the West Indies. That would have broken most men. Not don Diego.

As the self-proclaimed Count of Santa Fe, the cavalier Peñalosa would reappear first in Restoration England and then at the teeming court of Louis XIV. He offered blueprints for an invasion of mineral-rich Spanish America. His intrigues in fact helped launch the famed Sieur de la Salle for the last time. In 1687, the year La Salle perished violently at the hands of his own men in the wilds of Texas, don Diego died in France. His zestful career, from Peru to Pecos to Paris, had finally closed.[49]

Fray Alonso de Posada, the Franciscan champion who had brought low two of New Mexico's high-and-mighty roguish governors, left the colony with the returning supply wagons in the fall of 1665. Years later he was called upon by the viceroy to report on the lands and peoples east from New Mexico. The Spaniards had heard of Peñalosa's intrigues at the French court. Reliable sources indicated that "the count" had presented to King Louis a plan to capture the provinces of Quivira and Teguayo "assuring him that they are very rich in silver and gold." News that La Salle had sailed added urgency to such reports. Responding in 1686, Father Posada drew in part on his experience at Pecos. Speaking of the Plains Apaches, he wrote:

> While your informant was minister at the pueblo of the Pecos, on a certain occasion a number of rancherías of this Apache nation used to come in to the pueblo to sell hides and

Peñalosa Tried by the Inquisition

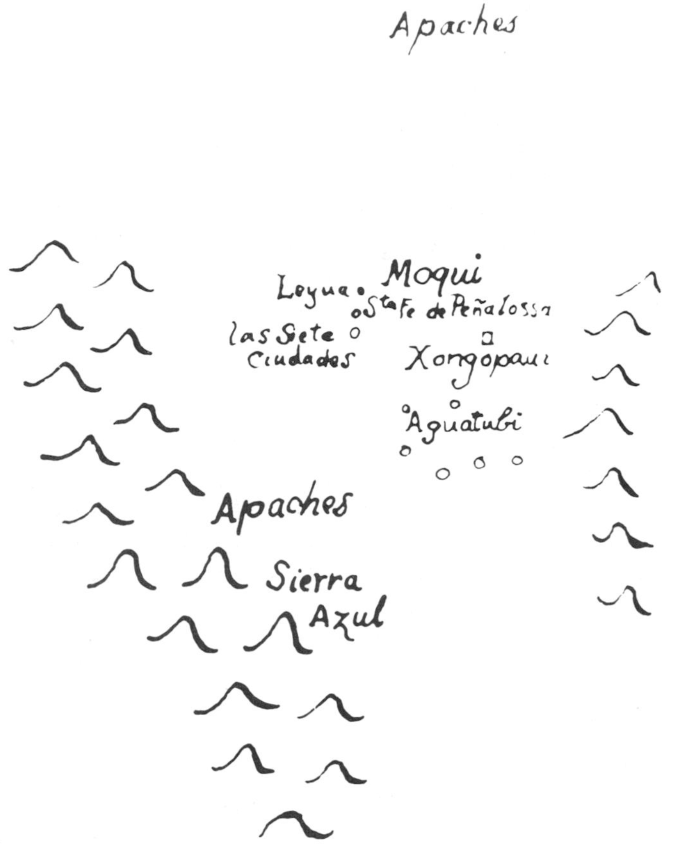

Detail of a French map
of New Mexico, drawn
c. 1675 in conjunction
with Diego de Peñalosa's
invasion plot, showing
the Moqui, or Hopi,
pueblos and a ficticious
place called Santa Fe de
Peñalosa.
From a tracing in the
Library of Congress
(WL 225)

tanned skins. They would bring some Indian males and females, girls and boys, to sell for horses. These were from the Quivira nation, captured in the assaults the Apaches had made in their lands.

Asked many times if they had captured in the Quivira nation or that of the Tejas any earrings or armbands (worn as adornment mostly on the left arm), at the same time being shown objects of gold and silver, they always responded to a man that they had on various occasions killed some famous captains of those nations as well as many other common Indians, but on none of them had they found such things. What they had found were many buffalo hides, deer and antelope skins, maize, and fruits. They said that all the inhabitants of those lands, men as well as women, dressed in tanned skins. From this it may be inferred that there is neither so much gold as is imagined nor so much silver as is said. [50]

The Friars
Reprimanded by
Holy Office

After Posada, no friar ever wielded the authority of the Inquisition in New Mexico the way he had. Fray **Juan de Paz,** his successor in 1665 as both agent and custos, evidently wanted to. Instead, he stirred up such a storm of local resentment that the Holy Office was obliged to reevaluate its role in the colony. Father Paz, it appeared, wanted "to make every affair and case an Inquisition matter," not merely to insure the purity of the Faith but also to intimidate opponents of the friars' regime. If the Franciscans were using the authority of the Holy Office to maintain their privileged ecclesiastical monopoly in New Mexico, that was patently wrong. Having admonished Paz to keep peace with the civil authorities, the inquisitors listened with concern to the complaints that reached them late in 1667.[51]

"We beg you," wrote the Santa Fe cabildo, "to free us of such duress, so many troubles and miseries as we poor soldiers suffer at the hands of these religious." Ever since its founding seventy years before, vast and remote New Mexico had groaned, the municipal council said, under the oppression of litigious Franciscans. The friars were the only ecclesiastical law. They were the judges. They heard and recorded all testimony. Because there were no lawyers in the colony to offer counsel, the citizen stood defenseless and fearful before the arbitrary justice of the Franciscans. For no greater offense than hiring an Indian laborer against the will of a friar, New Mexicans were threatened with prosecution by the Inquisition. Such intimidation was commonplace. What moved the cabildo to appeal at this juncture was not so common.

Fray Nicolás de Enríquez, appointed notary of the Inquisition by Father Paz, had written a scurrilous satire "against this entire kingdom, stripping everyone in it of his dignity, from the governor to this cabildo." The populace clamored for the cabildo to do something. Cristóbal de Chávez went after Fray Nicolás with his dagger, and the friar had to run for his life. To prevent another such scene, the cabildo had petitioned Custos Paz to punish Enríquez and send him back to Mexico City. Instead the prelate embraced this friar and appeared with him in the streets. Worse, under pain of ecclesiastical censure, Paz tried to suppress the case by seizing the pertinent papers, including the cabildo's file copy of the satire, a bootless move since many persons already knew the words by heart. To avoid more litigation with the custos, the cabildo laid the matter before the Holy Office, enclosing a copy of the repugnant satire.

A Satire of New Mexico

The cabildo also made a significant recommendation—that the Holy Office appoint as its local agent a secular clergyman, not a friar. The tithe and the revenue from the confraternity of Nuestra Señora de los Remedios were sufficient to support him. They had already petitioned the bishop of Durango to appoint a secular vicar as ecclesiastical judge ordinary. Although the Franciscan commissary general successfully quashed these attempts to break the Order's monopoly of ecclesiastical justice in New Mexico, they did serve as a warning to overzealous friars.[52]

In the matter of the satire, the attorney of the Holy Office sustained the cabildo. He advised that the inquisitors instruct Agent Paz not to employ Fray Nicolás de Enríquez in any Inquisition business whatever. In addition, a secret investigation should be made to determine if he really was the author, and the cabildo should be assured that any official of the Inquisition guilty of wrongdoing would be punished.[53]

If he was the author, as everyone in New Mexico seemed to think, Enríquez may have penned his controversial satire at Pecos. A native of Zacatecas in his mid-forties, he had probably arrived in New Mexico with Father Posada in 1661. He had been guardian of the Santa Fe convento during the worst of the Peñalosa-Posada feud. After Posada left the colony in 1665, one Fray Nicolás de Echevarría, from the mining town of Sierra de Pinos southeast of Zacatecas, took over as guardian at Pecos. He did not last.[54] By late 1666, when called by Agent Paz to testify against Cristóbal de Anaya Almazán, Fray Nicolás de Enríquez had moved in at Pecos. He did not last either.

By July 1667, three months before the cabildo sent a copy of the satire to the Holy Office, Nicolás de Enríquez testified as guardian of Zia. Just to confuse the succession, it would seem, another Enríquez, aged Fray Diego, a Spaniard who had affiliated himself with the Mexican province in 1626 and evidently no relative, took his place at Pecos. About the same time Fray Juan de Talabán succeeded Father Paz as custos. The latter continued for another year as agent of the Holy Office. The death of Fray Nicolás de Enríquez, probably in 1668, cheated the cabildo of seeing the friar who had allegedly ridiculed an entire colony receive his just deserts.[55]

The colonists rejoiced at the fall of Fray Juan de Paz. Last of the Franciscans in New Mexico to serve simultaneously as custos and as agent of the Holy Office, he had failed to grasp the inquisitors' growing desire to disassociate the authority of the Inquisition and local politics. When they reviewed his proceedings in Mexico City, they decided that impropriety, gross ignorance, and inattention to the obligations of the office had characterized his tenure. They threw out the cases he submitted.

Commenting on his evidence against Juan Domínguez de Mendoza, the inquisitors noted, "All the witnesses who testify against him are friars and it appears that they are inspired by malice." [56]

Just arrived from Mexico City, the cautious new agent, Fray Juan Bernal, probably on the advice of Alonso de Posada, chose as his headquarters the prudently out-of-the-way convento of Pecos. There on January 19, 1669, he swore in as notary Fray Francisco Gómez de la Cadena. The previous notary, appointed by Father Paz in the wake of the Enríquez scandal, was impeded by illness, said Bernal, "and many leagues from this convento of Pecos." Two days later ex-agent Paz signed a hastily compiled inventory of Inquisition papers, formally surrendering them to his successor. They included correspondence, edicts of the Faith, instructions from the inquisitors, and a whole array of confidential cases that Bernal would soon discover were in a horrible mess. [57]

Agent Bernal at Pecos

The son of Bartolomé Bernal, native of San Lúcar de Barrameda on the Andalusian coast, and Beatriz de la Barrera of Sevilla, Juan had been born a criollo in the City of Mexico. On February 12, 1648, at the Convento Grande, he put on the robe of St. Francis. He was only fifteen years and four months old. Twenty years a friar, Bernal was still in his mid-thirties in 1669. As he and his notary worked to bring order out of the jumble left by Paz, which entailed among other things chasing down witnesses who after two and three years still had not ratified their declarations, Bernal would need all the stamina he could muster. [58]

By spring, the new agent had pulled together enough of the loose ends of one case to submit the proceedings to Mexico City. It concerned Bernardo Gruber, a Sonora-based German peddler accused of distributing along with his wares certain mysterious little slips of paper and claiming that "whoever would chew one of these papers would make himself invulnerable for twenty-four hours."

Strange Case of Bernardo Gruber

Father Paz had arrested Gruber straight-away. Since April of 1668, the poor wretch had been locked up in "one of the safest rooms" of Capt. Francisco de Ortega's hacienda in the Sandía district. For the benefit of the inquisitors, Father Bernal characterized as best he could the various witnesses in the case, one "a mulatto, but a truthful man and a good Christian," another "a mestizo and a quiet boy of good reputation and fairly reliable." He explained why it had not been possible to ship Gruber to Mexico City. In so doing, he painted a graphic picture of conditions in New Mexico, dismal at best, even when allowance is made for exaggeration.

New Mexico's
Dire State
in 1669

Sending him at present is all but impossible, Most Illustrious Sir, because this kingdom is seriously afflicted, suffering from two calamities, cause enough to finish it off, as is happening in fact with the greatest speed.

The first of these calamities is that the whole land is at war with the very numerous nation of the heathen Apache Indians, who kill all the Christian Indians they encounter. No road is safe. One travels them all at risk of life for the heathens are everywhere. They are a brave and bold people. They hurl themselves at danger like people who know not God, nor that there is a hell.

The second calamity is that for three years no crop has been harvested. Last year, 1668, a great many Indians perished of hunger, lying dead along the roads, in the ravines, and in their hovels. There were pueblos, like Las Humanas, where more than four hundred and fifty died of hunger. The same calamity still prevails, for, because there is no money, there is not a fanega of maize or wheat in all the kingdom. As a result the Spaniards, men as well as women, have sustained themselves for two years on the cowhides they have in their houses to sit on. They roast them and eat them. And the greatest woe of all is that they can no longer find a bit of leather to eat, for their livestock is dying off.

If God sent rain Bernal would send Gruber. The southbound supply wagons would be leaving in November. Before then, however, he hoped to have instructions from the Holy Office. When nothing arrived until much later, Gruber stayed locked up.[59]

Agent Bernal had his problems. He soon discovered how much work it was to carry on judicial proceedings in a colony so vast and so perilous. "I can neither summon anyone nor go myself to where it can be done, for everyone is afoot, with-

Rain cloud decorations incised on Pecos clay pipes.
Kidder, *Artifacts*

out animals, because the heathen enemy have stolen them."
Father Gómez de la Cadena, his notary, fell ill. On February
4, 1670, in the guardian's cell at Pecos, he swore in another
one, Father Pedro de Ávila y Ayala, who was already living at
the mission. Fray Pedro, a hardy, zealous sort, had traveled in
1668 from the province of Yucatán to Mexico City begging
alms for the sacred places in the Holy Land. When he saw the
supply train forming up for New Mexico, he was overcome,
said the pious chronicler Vetancurt, by a desire to save souls.
He had volunteered and ridden north with Bernal.

On the last day of February, trail-weary Brother Blas de
Herrera, whom Bernal had sent to Mexico City with the
Gruber case eleven months before, reappeared at Pecos with a
packet of documents in response. The inquisitors expressed
their disgust at the way Father Paz had proceeded against the
German. They warned Bernal that local agents did not have
the authority to arrest the accused in such a case without express orders from the Holy Office. In another letter, they reiterated that disrespect for the Franciscans was not an Inquisition matter. An agent must not meddle in affairs that lay beyond the jurisdiction of his office "thus giving rise to much
prejudice and hatred against this Tribunal." The admonition
was for Bernal's own good, "so that with due care he may avoid
what his predecessor has brought about by his ignorance."
Still, no one released poor Gruber.[60]

The only case of record initiated by Agent Bernal was
against an illiterate soldier named Francisco Tremiño, "a man
who swears all day long, and is a desperate character." Several
witnesses who appeared at Pecos that spring of 1670 to denounce Tremiño alleged that he was in league with the devil.

Fray Juan Bernal, agent
of the Holy Office

Fray Pedro de Ávila y Ayala

One of them, Antonio de Ávalos, later described as "a native of New Mexico, of good stature, tall and slender, dark with an aquiline face and crooked nose, and coarse hair," Bernal characterized as "one of the lowliest men in these provinces." As for Tremiño, he lit out for Sonora and was apparently never brought to trial. During Lent some Apaches made off with Bernal's riding animals leaving the agent of the Holy Office "practically afoot." [61]

Gruber Escapes   After twenty-seven months of confinement, Bernardo Gruber escaped. Breaking a window and pushing out one of the heavy wooden bars, he had made his getaway with the help of the Apache servant who was guarding him. Together they had fled south in the night with five horses and an arquebus. On Saturday, June 28, 1670, a distressed and out-of-breath Capt. Francisco de Ortega, who had borrowed a horse to get to Pecos, detailed the entire episode for Father Bernal. Within two days the Franciscan had notified Gov. Juan de Medrano y Mesía of the escape and of the dereliction of the local officials who refused to aid Ortega in pursuit. The governor dispatched Cristóbal de Anaya Almazán with a squad of soldiers and forty Indians. Bernal had Fray Pedro de Avila y Ayala draw up bulletins alerting the agents of the Inquisition in Parral and Sonora. He then sent his notary to inspect the scene and verify Ortega's story. It checked out. The bar had been removed. Gruber was gone. [62]

The following week, when Father Bernal wrote the Holy Office from Sandía, he was feeling very much like Job. Apaches and famine still stalked the land. He still had not straightened out and completed the farrago of Inquisition records, but with God's help he would. The trouble was, he admitted, "they are so mixed up and confused that I do not understand them." Lord knew, he was trying.

> Even though sick with sunburn and other afflictions of this country which I have suffered during certain proceedings in the line of duty, with one arm crippled for several days from running sores, I carry on glady, ever confident that Your Illustrious Lordship will protect me and take me from this country. For even though I have striven to live with the utmost care, and always in seclusion, fraternizing with no one since they attempt to stain my reputation, [it has happened,] as will be seen from a declaration made by Domingo López which I remit to Your Illustrious Lordship with this letter. [63]

Later that summer, there was news of the fugitive Bernardo Gruber. A party of travelers making their way through the forlorn and shimmering desert stretch south of Socorro in mid-

Detail of Bernardo de Miera y Pacheco's 1758 map showing the Jornada del Muerto and a place called Alemán, or the German, in memory of Bernardo Gruber.

July came upon a dead horse tethered to a lonely tree. Nearby they found articles of clothing, apparently Gruber's. A further search turned up his hair, more bits of clothing, and "in very widely separated places the skull, three ribs, two long bones, and two other little bones which had been gnawed by animals."

It appeared that Gruber's Apache companion had killed him for the other horses and the arquebus. If to cover his tracks the wily Gruber had murdered the Apache, tethered the horse, and planted the clothing, no one ever suspected it. In Mexico City, the inquisitors resolved that the dead peddler's wares be sold at auction, that Mass be said for the repose of his soul, and that his bones be given a church burial. Although the life of this luckless German wanderer has long been forgotten, his death gave name to, or at least reinforced the name of the Jornada del Muerto, the Dead Man's Route.[64]

Back in his cell at Pecos, the conscientious Bernal pored over document after document in an effort to conclude every bit of Inquisition business left undone by his predecessor. There was, for example, the matter of four dozen confiscated packs of playing cards that Father Paz had turned over to Maese de campo Pedro Lucero de Godoy, local depositary of the royal treasury. He was to sell the packs at two pesos each in New Mexico commodities. During a period of two years and eight months, Lucero had sold only one pack. Not only were the cards damaged and worm-eaten from five years' storage, but the stamp on them did not correspond. Besides, anyone who wanted playing cards bought them at the store of Governor Medrano, the one store in the colony.

The only way to move the cards, Bernal reckoned, was to sell them to the governor at half price "in the most respected commodity of this country, that it, in standard tanned skins, being the commodity most readily sold in New Spain." The governor consented. At Pecos on November 22, 1670, his agent gave a promissory note for the forty-seven skins. Seven months later in Santa Fe, notary Ávila y Ayala certified receipt of the skins, the same day entrusting them to Lucero de Godoy who added two more for the single pack he had sold at the original price. Finally, on September 4, 1672, Father Bernal ordered Lucero to deliver the skins to Franciscan procurator Fray Felipe Montes who was about to depart with the returning supply wagons. That, to Bernal's relief, was an end to that.[65]

Fray Juan Bernal, sober and unobtrusive, persevered as the Inquisition's agent in New Mexico, seemingly as late as 1679, the year his superiors in Mexico City named him custos. On the roster compiled by the New Mexico chapter in August 1672, Bernal was listed as a definitor of the custody and as guardian not at Pecos but at Galisteo, where eight years later he would suffer a violent death.[66]

His former notary, the ardent Fray Pedro de Ávila y Ayala, accepted the heavier cross of Hawikuh among the Zuñis. Within months he was dead. Western Apaches, emboldened by drought and famine, swept into the pueblo in 1673 killing, burning, and looting. Father Ávila y Ayala died, according to Vetancurt, as a proper martyr should. He fled into the church and embraced a cross and an image of Our Lady. They dragged him out and stripped off his habit. At the foot of a large cross in the patio they stoned him, shot arrows at the writhing nude figure, and finally smashed his head with a heavy bell.[67]

Pecos Glaze V pottery.
Kidder, *Pottery*, II

The new man at Pecos, shown on the August 1672 roster, was Fray Luis de Morales, born at Baeza in the southern Spanish province of Jaén, professed August 26, 1660, at Puebla, and tried as a missioner in New Mexico since 1665. He did not stay at Pecos many years, for in August of 1680 when the Pueblos erupted, Fray Luis died a martyr at his post in San Ildefonso.[68]

As for the Inquisition in New Mexico—personified so boldly in the early 1660s by Fray Alonso de Posada—it hardly functioned during the seventies. The pursuit of Bernardo Gruber seems to have been the last excitement. Agent Bernal's preoccupation with playing cards was indicative.

The tribunal in Mexico City had finally awakened to the fact that its Franciscan agents in New Mexico were reshaping the special province of the Inquisition to fit their local ecclesiastical monopoly and using it as a club in church-state brawls. As a result, the inquisitors had admonished Agents Paz and Bernal to cooperate with the civil authorities. Recognizing the obvious conflict of interest, they no longer appointed the Franciscan custos as comisario of the Holy Office.

Agent Bernal got the message. While insisting on the respect due his office, neither he nor the energetic friar who succeeded him in 1679 went out looking for blasphemers. Like everyone else in New Mexico, they prayed for survival, and hardly heard the expletives.[69]

Famine and invasion—the two calamities lamented by Father Bernal in 1669—cast ever lengthening shadows across the land during the decade of the seventies. Questions of royal or ecclesiastical privilege paled before doomsday predictions. What did it matter that a Franciscan sat as ecclesiastical judge

A Decade of Distress

instead of a secular priest if in truth the barbarians were at the gates? In crisis, the factions of church and state, so long estranged in New Mexico, groped toward mutual aid. At first they fell short.

An Apache Campaign Aborts

Back in February 1668, Gov. Fernando de Villanueva, beset by news of lethal Apache raids on Spanish homes in the Salinas and Piro regions, had appealed to Father Custos Juan de Talabán. A council of war in Santa Fe called for retaliation in force, fifty to sixty soldiers plus Pueblo auxiliaries, for a two-month campaign. The governor begged the custos to throw open mission larders to provision such an expedition and to loan as many horses and mules as needed.

Not so fast, replied the Franciscan. For His own good reasons God had visited upon the whole land "both the plague of locusts that laid waste the fields and also the scourge of crop failure." The custos had been forced to succor some conventos with seed from others to keep missionaries in the field. When Santa Fe was starving, Santo Domingo had sent maize, as had Fray Diego Enríquez of Pecos. Now, starving Santo Domingos were out scavenging for food. Others lined up at the sound of the bell for a dole of maize. Still, despite all this, said Talabán, he would try to scrape together provisions for the campaign. As for the horses, so essential to their scattered ministry, he would have to consult some of the other missionaries. After all, they had acquired these animals through their own diligence and with their alms.

Head of a Pecos horse effigy. Kidder, *Artifacts*

The half dozen Franciscans who gathered at Santo Domingo were unanimous. The custos should solicit from the conventos whatever provisions they could spare—a total of possibly fifty fanegas—as well as a loan of horses and mules. It was not the intention of the friars that blood flow and death follow from this campaign, only that greater misfortune be averted. Their unusual "charitable aid" was being extended in this crisis for defense of Christianity and the churches. Under no circumstances should it be taken as a precedent. Had not the king granted encomiendas to armed men who pledged in return to defend this land at their own expense? As for the animals, the friars demanded a legal guarantee that horses and mules lost or killed during the campaign would be replaced. Without them, how could they get round to administer the sacraments?

Politely, Governor Villanueva thanked Custos Talabán in the king's name for the offer of provisions, but he balked at the guarantee. That hardly seemed appropriate. This was not an adventure or an aggressive war, rather it was a general defense of the realm, of conventos and of friars as well as of everyone else, Christians all. Reconvening his council, the governor presented the friars' offer. No one thought fifty fanegas were enough. Guarantee the horses? Who did the Franciscans think they were? With that, the retaliatory campaign was scrapped.[70]

Don Juan de Medrano y Mesía had assumed the unhappy governorship in November 1668. During the first seven months of his term, Apaches killed, by his tally, six Spanish soldiers and three hundred and seventy-three Christian Indians, stealing more than two thousand horses and mules and as many sheep. In one assault on Ácoma in June 1669, they abducted two Ácomas alive, murdered twelve, and ran off eight hundred sheep, sixty cattle, and all the horses. A small party under Capt. Francisco Javier gave chase, caught the enemy, and were nearly overwhelmed. Cristóbal de Chávez, the dagger-wielding Spaniard who had put the fear of the devil into Father Nicolás de Enríquez, died in the fray. Governor Medrano vowed to launch from Jémez a force of fifty soldiers and six hundred Christian Indians. But he would need the friars' help.

The Apaches Unchecked

"If these voracious enemies are not punished and their milpas not laid waste," wrote the governor, "they will surely devastate this kingdom. That is what those Apaches shout for all to hear and in Spanish! Those of the Gila, the Salineros, and those of La Casa Fuerte have come together"—Apachean groups west of the Rio Grande, including Navajos, ranging from the headwaters of the Gila north to the San Juan. The governor implored Father Talabán to forward to Jémez whatever supplies the conventos could contribute.

Again the Franciscan answered with a tale of woes. Driven by their hunger, even the mission Indians had taken to robbing the conventos. He had been obliged to succor Senecú and Socorro, and now Ácoma. If he had not sent aid to the Tewa conventos of Nambé, San Ildefonso, and San Juan, their ministers would have had to leave. Without the mission dole of seed to the Indians, claimed the superior, "there would not now be an Indian alive." Several of the conventos had already contributed wheat and maize to the governor. From Jémez, aid had gone as well to Galisteo, Sandía, and Zía. Now only Pecos had anything to spare, twenty fanegas of wheat, "and this is taking it from the pueblo's very sustenance."

In addition to the wheat from Pecos, Talabán volunteered two hundred sheep and two dozen cattle, as well as a Franciscan to serve as chaplain. Again, this aid must not be considered a precedent. It was being freely given for defense, to destroy the enemy's crops, not his person. Exactly, replied the

Jémez prayer stick for the dead (15¾″), prayer feather for the dead, and spruce twig prayer stick.
Parsons, *Jemez*

governor who exulted over the friar's response. "I shall remain so grateful for such an act that I shall place it as a blazon on the doors of my house, not forgetting the succor of provisions this holy custody has given me in such need." [71]

The immediate results of the campaign are not known. If the Spaniards and their Pueblo allies did destroy Apache and Navajo crops, they only succeeded in aggravating the western front. The raids did not cease. When the hungry enemies fell on Hawikuh four years later, they utterly consumed it. But at least by then, friars and governors had recognized that only in mutual aid was there any hope of survival.

A Plains Apache
warrior by
Lt. J. W. Abert,
1845.
Abert, *Through the
Country of the
Comanche Indians*
(San Francisco, 1970)

Another theater of Apache warfare stretched across southern New Mexico imperiling the Piro pueblos as well as a long unguarded section of the camino real. East of the Manzano Mountains, the Apaches of Los Siete Ríos had begun pummeling the Salinas pueblos. In one all-out assault, a strategy that became more and more characteristic of the 1670s, Apaches overran the pueblo of Las Humanas at harvest time in 1670, sacked the church, slew eleven residents, and carried off thirty-one captives. In the years to come, no fewer than six Piro and Salinas pueblos perished in drought, famine, disease, and Apache onslaught.[72]

Southern Front
under Assault

Even as Apache war quickened to the south and west, Pecos remained becalmed. As far back as the 1640s and 1650s, there had been mention of random raiding in the area by Apaches from the mountains of northeastern New Mexico, evidently ancestors of the Jicarillas. From time to time, an unwary Pueblo died at their hands almost within the shadow of Pecos. Governor López de Mendizábal had cautioned the Pecos transporting boards to the casas reales in Santa Fe to keep an eye out for lurking Apaches as they came through the sierra. Still, nowhere in the documents chronicling the critical state of affairs in New Mexico does one find reference to the plunder of Pecos.[73]

Trade Fairs at Pecos

The Plains Apaches seemed to have kept coming in annually to Pecos laden with hides and meat and Quivira captives. They preferred to be the middle men in the slave traffic rather than the object of it. Evidently the lure of trade and the diplomacy of Pecos traders like El Carpintero offset the effect of heavy-handed Spaniards operating on the plains. Even though Governor López had sent out in September 1659 "an army of eight hundred Christian Indians and forty Spaniards," even though Governor Peñalosa's man Juan de Archuleta retrieved from the plains about 1662 some of the Taos renegades who had fled their pueblo twenty-two years before—still, Father Posada, at Pecos between 1662 and 1665, observed the annual trade fair. That it continued, despite the calamities that threatened to destroy the colony, explains at least in part why Pecos had provisions to spare. [74]

Father Ayeta
as Deliverer

The man everyone looked to for salvation was thirty-four-year-old Fray Francisco de Ayeta, a tireless Spaniard from Pamplona who took over mission supply in 1674. A decade earlier, at the insistence of the Franciscans themselves, the wagons had been surrendered to a lay contractor, ex-governor Juan Manso. Since then, the missionaries had done nothing but complain. Manso had provided one wagon for every three friars, instead of one for every two as before, and he had overloaded them with commercial cargo. He had delayed delivery, and when the caravans did finally reach New Mexico, he ordered everything dumped at San Felipe, obliging the friars to haul their own supplies from there. After considerable discussion, the crown terminated the old royal contract in favor of a lump-sum annual payment, 330 pesos for each priest and 230 for every lay brother. With the money, Procurator-general Ayeta bought wagons, mules, and the usual supplies and set out for the colony.[75]

The new governor, don Juan Francisco Treviño, the cabildo of Santa Fe, and Father Ayeta, of necessity, all joined hands. New Mexico needed help, help that neither she nor her downtrodden populace could provide. Ayeta agreed to carry a petition to the viceroy. Appearing at court late in the summer of 1676, the Franciscan was convincing. Meantime the provincial chapter elected him custos.

On February 27, 1677, Father Ayeta left again for the north with a caravan conveying not only the regular triennial mission supplies, but also another governor, don Antonio de Otermín; fifty convict soldiers, their commander, and their sergeant as reinforcements for New Mexico's frontiers; one hundred arquebuses; one hundred hilts for swords and daggers; fifty saddles with bridles and spurs; and one thousand horses. One epileptic convict ran away at Parral and six more at El Paso while the caravan waited for the waters to fall. The rest passed muster in the cold at Santa Fe in December 1677.

Fray Francisco de Ayeta

Ayeta now threw himself into the business of defense. The friars must make every sacrifice. There was no talk of precedents. In the hope of making a stand, the custos, "taking the food from the mouths of my religious," ordered more than four hundred fanegas of provisions, two hundred goats, and forty head of cattle placed at the mission of Galisteo to support ten of the soldiers and all the refugees from the deserted Salinas pueblos. He arranged for another similar cache at Senecú, reestabished through "the vigilance, promptness, Christian application, and pious zeal" of Governor Otermín. And in Santa Fe, he had other mission provisions delivered for the remaining soldiers' mess, along with twenty protective leather doublets, without which "they could not go out on campaign, except in great danger."

By September of 1678, the indefatigable Ayeta was back in Mexico City urging another fifty men armed and outfitted as the previous ones but "omitting the thousand horses that went then and applying the three thousand pesos of their value to the

Emergency Defense Measures

maintenance of the men." Moreover, a fifty-man presidio, like the one in Sinaloa, should be established in Santa Fe at royal expense, at least for a decade. When the viceregal government forwarded Ayeta's new proposals to Spain, he loaded up the next shipment of mission supplies and headed north for a third time.

Reining up at El Paso in the heat of mid-summer 1680, he found the great silty-brown river in flood. It was here on August 25 that the strong-willed friar received news from New Mexico that would have caused an Old Testament prophet to cry out in anguish and rend his garments. It had finally happened, "the disaster that has threatened so many times." Father Ayeta fell on his knees in prayer.[76]

Friars and Soldiers Cooperate

The calamities of the 1670s had forced the unruly Hispanic community to pull together. According to Father Ayeta, colonists and missionaries joined in grateful thanksgiving for "such a good governor" as Antonio de Otermín. The Pueblo Indians too had begun to pull together, to a degree the Spaniards would not recognize—until it was too late.

Taking a page from the legendary Cortés, don Juan de Oñate had made a point of his deference to the first humble Franciscans, the servants of the Spaniards' all-powerful triune God. He had entrusted the conversion of the Pueblo Indians to them "for all time." Later governors, like Eulate, Rosas, and Peñalosa, had damned the missionaries, even bloodied their heads. Certain friars, invoking the authority of the Inquisition —Ordóñez, Perea, and Posada—had brought governors to their knees. The unedifying spectacle of jealous, eye-gouging Spaniards at one another's throats cannot have engendered respect among the long-suffering Pueblos.

If the Spaniards, friars and colonists alike, were consistent in anything, it was that the mission Indians should work, produce foodstuffs, and pay tribute. But even in this, they differed as to approach. Fray Pedro de Ortega smashed the objects of the Pecos' worship. Benavides ordered piles of kachina masks and prayer sticks put to the torch. Fray Andrés Juárez seemed to look the other way, so long as the children combed their hair and came to catechism. Governor López de Mendizábal commanded the natives to revive their kachina dances. Encomendero Francisco Gómez Robledo said he saw no harm in the dances. Spaniards at Galisteo undressed and joined in. Then came Fray Alonso de Posada and more bonfires.

Jémez kachina masks. Parsons, *Jemez*

Precursors of Pueblo Revolt

Father Talabán had lamented in 1669 that starving Christian Indians had turned on the friars and robbed and destroyed mission conventos. Particularly among the Piro and

Salinas pueblos—where famine, disease, and Apache aggression had taken a ghastly toll—were the Pueblos showing their defiance of a regime that had brought them nothing but misery. During the administration of Fernando de Villanueva, 1665-1668, certain of the Piros rebelled,

when six Indians were hanged and others were sold and imprisoned. In addition to their crimes and conspiracies they were found in an ambush with the enemy Apaches in the Sierra de la Magdalena, where they killed five Spaniards, among them the alcalde mayor. The latter was killed by one of the six Christian Indians hanged, called in his language El Tanbulita. Despite all these punishments, another Indian governor of all the pueblos of Las Salinas, named don Esteban Clemente, whom the whole kingdom secretly obeyed, formed another conspiracy which was general throughout the kingdom, giving orders to the Christian Indians that all the horse herds of all the districts should be driven to the sierras, in order to leave the Spaniards afoot; and that on the night of Holy Thursday, just as they had plotted during the administration of General [Hernando de Ugarte y la] Concha [1649-1653], they must destroy the whole body of Christians, not leaving a single religious or Spaniard.

But Clemente too was found out and hanged. When they searched his quarters, they found "a large number of idols and entire cooking pots full of idolatrous powdered herbs, feathers, and other trifles." [77]

Pecos clay pipes.
Kidder, *Artifacts*

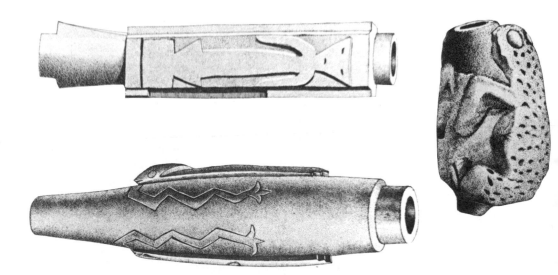

Jémez kiva murals, sketched by R. H. Kern, 1849. Simpson, *Journal*

With the harmony of their life so obviously convulsed, it was little wonder the Pueblos sought to placate the forces that had governed their existence before the Spaniards' coming. Not that they had ever given up the old ways, but they had compromised. They had built Christian churches in their pueblos and let their babies be baptized. They had carried Christian saints in procession. Now the locusts, the disease, and the starving had been visited upon them as unmistakable signs condemning their compromise. And neither the Spaniards nor their saints seemed able to cope.

Witchcraft Trials of 1675

No one had to tell the Spaniards that Pueblo kivas were "places of idolatry where the said apostates offered to the devil the grain and other things they possess." Worse, Pueblo sorcerers killed by witchcraft. In fact, in 1675, Governor Treviño, acting on reports of witchcraft among the Tewa pueblos—the very pueblos Father Talabán had succored six years earlier—had forty-seven alleged sorcerers rounded up and brought to Santa Fe for trial. Accused of bewitching the ailing Fray Andrés Durán, guardian of San Ildefonso, and three other persons, and of having killed seven friars and three Spaniards, the men were found guilty, three were hanged— one each as an example in Nambé, San Felipe, and Jémez— one hanged himself, and the others were sentenced to lashing, prison, or servitude. Meanwhile Capt. Francisco Javier, Treviño's secretary, "gathered up many idols, powders, and other things which he took from the houses of the sorcerers and from the countryside."

But this time the Pueblos called the governor's bluff. Leaving reinforcements in the hills, an armed troop of more than seventy descended on the casas reales to negotiate the release of the prisoners, or, that failing, to kill the governor. Sensing the mood of these uninvited guests, Treviño accepted their eggs and other offerings, gave them some woolen blankets, and reportedly said about the prisoners, lamely, "Wait a while, children; I will give them to you and pardon them on condition that you forsake idolatry and iniquity." [78]

Fray Fernando de Velasco, guardian of the convento at Pecos in August 1680, was an old hand. Born in the ancient port city of Cádiz about 1620—the year Fray Pedro de Ortega broke up the idols at Pecos—he had taken the Franciscan habit thirty years later on August 14, 1650, at Mexico's Convento Grande. Now he was about to celebrate his thirtieth year as a friar. A missionary in New Mexico since the mid-1650s, he had seen service at all the difficult places—at Tajique and Chililí between 1659 and 1661 during the time of Nicolás de Aguilar, the Attila of New Mexico; at Ácoma in 1667; and at the Piro pueblo of Socorro during the early 1670s. By comparison, Pecos was a picnic.[79]

Velasco had a young companion at Pecos, an unaffected twenty-six-year-old lay brother named Juan de la Pedrosa. Invested at the Convento Grande on May 31, 1672, Fray Juan was a native of Mexico City. He had come north with Father Ayeta in the winter of 1674-1675.[80]

By Thursday, August 8, Father Velasco at Pecos knew that something was afoot. His Indians had told him that two Tewas from Tesuque had come round to announce a general uprising of all the Pueblos in league with Apaches, now set for

Fray Fernando de Velasco

the night of August 13. Velasco wrote immediately to Governor Otermín in Santa Fe, and the governor of the Pecos served as runner.

On Friday the ninth, Otermín had the warning from Velasco, another from Father Custos Juan Bernal at Galisteo, and a third from the alcalde mayor of Taos. All agreed. Straight-away the royal governor dispatched Francisco Gómez Robledo to pick up the two messengers from Tesuque. He alerted the other alcaldes mayores. The two Tesuques confirmed their role. They claimed that a tall black man with large yellow eyes, a representative of the Pueblo diety Pohé-yemo, had commanded all the Pueblos to rebel. The devil, said Otermín.

At seven o'clock next morning, August 10, the feast of San Lorenzo, the governor recognized his error. This, not the thirteenth, was the day of reckoning.

A friar who had left Santa Fe at dawn to say Mass in Tesuque had already been murdered. Father Velasco had set out from Pecos for Galisteo. The rebels fell on him in a field within sight of his destination, where the naked bodies of Father Custos Bernal, two other friars, and a number of Spanish men, women, and children stared grotesquely without seeing. Back at Pecos, young Fray Juan de la Pedrosa, two Spanish women, and three children lay dead.[81]

After eighty years of submissive resentment, the Pueblos had finally gone for the jugular.

Design in a Glaze IV Pecos bowl.
After Kidder, *Pottery,* II

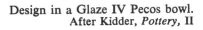

cheir own worst enemies
1680-1704

With regard to the pueblo of Pecos, it has been my experience that these Indians are very loyal. After all, it is of record and well known to this entire kingdom that they dutifully gave warnings of the uprisings of these natives. Aside from not having soldiers to spare, I consider the guard of six men requested by the Rev. Father definitor fray Juan de Alpuente inadvisable. Sending this guard would be to tell these Indians that I doubted their proven loyalty. I am convinced, therefore, that having no guard—even if this Reverend Father refuses to minister to them—is preferable to the unfortunate consequences of their suspecting that they do not have this confidence.

Don Diego de Vargas, Santa Fe, March 14, 1696

Indeed one may allege that these Pecos Indians are loyal because of their outward and public demonstrations, also that in 1680 during the general revolt they gave warning of it to some Spaniards and to the then governor. Yet if one asks about their role in that uprising, they assert as a hard fact that they did not kill Father fray Fernando de Velasco, their minister, and this they allege as a meritorious act. But ask them about Father fray Juan de la Pedrosa, lay religious who was with their Father minister, and likewise about a Spaniard who was at their pueblo of Pecos at the time with his wife and children, and they remain silent.

Fray Francisco de Vargas, Santa Fe, July 6, 1696

Because of the punishment don Felipe, Indian governor of the Pecos, had dealt the five rebellious Indians in 1696, the relatives of the latter toward the end of the year 1700 began to show their resentment and their desire for revenge. They tried at first

to incite the whole pueblo to kill Felipe, but in this they were unsuccessful. After they had committed grave acts of disrespect in
the presence of the Father minister and the alcalde mayor, the
latter informed [Gov. Pedro Rodríguez] Cubero who put the
leaders of this faction in the Santa Fe jail. Breaking their chains,
these Indians fled to the Jicarilla Apaches.

As a result of this, the pueblo of Pecos split into two
antagonistic factions. That of don Felipe prevailed, after one
had attempted to take up arms against the other on five occasions.
The leaders of the other faction, fearing that they would be
destroyed if the rupture came, presented themselves before Cubero
requesting that they be permitted to move to the pueblo of
Pojoaque. Whether they did so is not of record.

Fray Silvestre Vélez de Escalante,
Extracto de Noticias, 1778

Pecos modern painted ware.   Kidder, *Pottery,* I

During the last quarter of the enlightened eighteenth century, when the Spanish crown's pragmatic interest in history and geography pervaded every corner of her vast and vulnerable empire, an intense young Franciscan received permission from the governor in Santa Fe to examine the provincial archives. This was a collection which, in the governor's estimation, "contained nothing but old fragments." Undaunted, Fray Silvestre Vélez de Escalante, not yet thirty but already in failing health, spent hours poring over, copying, and abstracting what documents he could. Among those from the period of the great revolt, he came across a formal complaint by the Santa Fe municipal council against Gov. Antonio de Otermín. Not only did this document present a different version of the outbreak, notably at variance with Otermín's own account, but it also suggested that the Indians of Pecos were their own worst enemies.[1]

Escalante as Historical Researcher

The cabildo put the blame for the revolt of 1680 squarely on Governor Otermín. Because he was either unable or unwilling to govern, or both, Otermín relegated all authority to his secretary of government and war, Maese de campo Francisco Javier, "a man of bad faith, avaricious and sly." Well built, with very gray hair and the scar of an old wound across the left side of his forehead, the cruel Javier had driven the Indians of New Mexico, in the words of the cabildo, "to the ultimate exasperation."

Revolt Laid to Governor Otermín

A short while before the general uprising, Javier had seized at the pueblo of Pecos a camp of Apaches to whom he had given assurance of safe-conduct. Coolly, he distributed some of these captives to his friends and shipped the rest off to Parral for sale. To the Pecos, who gained much of their livelihood from trade with Apaches, the treacherous act of Francisco Javier was grounds for rebellion, or so Fray Silvestre implies. Yet, in the very next sentence, without the least explanation, he tells how the Pecos—or the pro-Spanish faction at Pecos—warned Maese de campo Francisco Gómez Robledo of the impending rebellion well in advance, twenty days, by one account.

Francisco Javier

Gómez Robledo of course told Otermín. Later he appeared before the governor with the native messengers from Tesuque. "My lord," he explained, "here are the two Indians, who freely confess that the uprising is certain." To which Otermín is alleged to have replied, "Have them put in prison until Maese de campo Francisco Javier arrives." A fine way to react in a crisis.

To this excessive confidence [in the unscrupulous Javier] and in-action on the part of Otermín the members of the cabildo attributed the execution of the uprising. This was verified by the rebels in the plaza of Santa Fe, who said, "Give us Francisco Javier, who is the reason we have risen, and we will remain in peace as before." [2]

Double Role of the Pecos   Even after the outbreak, the Pecos played a double role, or rather, they acted in the interest of at least two factions, one of which chanted, "Death to the Spaniards!" and another which evidently did not. The Pecos did not kill their minister, old Fray Fernando de Velasco. Instead, they disclosed to him the plot and saw him off to Galisteo, where the Tanos promptly dispatched him. By most accounts, the Pecos did kill Fray Juan de la Pedrosa and at least one Spanish family. And they did join Tanos and Keres before Santa Fe on August 13 "armed and giving war whoops."

The Siege of Santa Fe   As news of widespread death and devastation in the outlying districts accumulated in Santa Fe, Otermín ordered the residents of the villa to come together and fortify the casas reales, that is, his thick-walled "palace" and the other government buildings on the north side of the plaza. Fray Francisco Gómez de la Cadena, guardian of the Santa Fe convento, and his assistant, Fray Francisco Farfán, consumed the Blessed

Sacrament, packed up the objects of divine worship, and joined the others. When two Indians sent to scout the Galisteo Basin reappeared out of breath with word that "all the Indians of the pueblos of the Pecos, San Cristóbal, San Lázaro, San Marcos, Galisteo, and La Ciénaga, who numbered more than five hundred, were one league from this villa on the way to attack it and destroy the governor and all the Spaniards," the defenders dug in for a siege.

These rebels were saying that now God and Holy Mary, whom the Spaniards worshipped, had died, but the god they obeyed had never died, and therefore they would take possession of the kingdom, having done with all the Spaniards.[3]

Pecos Glaze III
bowl design.
After Kidder,
Pottery, II

   Leading this first wave of rebellious Pueblos was a Spanish-speaking Tano named Juan, whom Governor Otermín had sent out three days before with a letter for Alcalde mayor José Nieto at Galisteo. He rode a horse and sported a priest's sash of red taffeta. Armed like a Spaniard with arquebus, sword, dagger, and leather jacket, Juan agreed to parley

Nuestra Señora de
Guadalupe painted
on hide.
Museum of New Mexico

with Governor Otermín in the plaza. He was not intimidated. He presented the governor with an ultimatum. Many more Indians were on their way to attack Santa Fe. They were bringing two crosses, one white and the other red. If the Spaniards chose the white cross, they would be spared to leave New Mexico. If they chose the red cross and war, they would surely die.

Otermín countered with an offer of pardon. Juan laughed and spurred his horse back across the Río de Santa Fe to the Analco district where the rebels greeted him "with bugle, with solemn pealing of the bells of the San Miguel chapel, and with

Antonio de Otermín

hurrahs, mocking the Spaniards." When the natives began pillaging the abandoned houses of the Mexican Indians who lived in the barrio of Analco and then set fire to the chapel of San Miguel, Otermín dispatched a troop of soldiers to disperse them. But the rebels, taking cover in the gutted houses, put up such a fight that the governor was obliged to join the action himself.

The battle lasted most of the day. Just as the Spaniards put the Pecos and Tanos to rout, hundreds of newly arrived Tewas, Taos, and Picurís, threw themselves at the villa from the other side, drawing the defenders back to the casas reales. When the sun set, the Pecos and Tanos, having suffered heavy casualties, withdrew, leaving the siege of Santa Fe to the Indians of the north. After all, the revolt was their idea.

The siege lasted a week. The Pueblos cut the water supply to the casas reales. They had already begun their victory celebration when a do-or-die force of mounted Spaniards suddenly broke out, caught the besiegers off guard, and trampled some of them under the hoofs of their horses. They claimed to have killed more than three hundred in all. They captured forty-seven. The rest were soon in flight.

Next day, August 21, after he had interrogated and executed the prisoners and provisioned everyone for the road from his own stores, Governor Otermín led the orderly exodus of a thousand refugees out of the villa that had served as seat and symbol of Spanish authority for seventy years. By the Blessed Mother of God, he would be back.[4]

Filing past Santo Domingo, they looked in vain for signs of life. There was evidence of a struggle in the convento. The bodies of three friars, among them ex-custos Fray Juan de Talabán, had been dragged into the church and buried in a common grave. Five more bodies lay outside.

Spaniards Retreat down the Rio Grande

All along the valley, similar scenes of carnage greeted the forlorn column. They halted at the narrows south of San Felipe, not far from the home of swaggering Cristóbal de Anaya Almazán, who had risen to the rank of sargento mayor despite his trial by the Inquisition. His naked body and those of his wife, six children, and several other persons were heaped up at the front door. The revolt had wiped out the entire Anaya clan, save one. Sickened by the sight, Francisco de Anaya, a brother of Cristóbal wounded in the fighting at Santa Fe, thought of his own family, all of them dead. Unlike many of the refugees, don Francisco and a third wife would later return to New Mexico in the train of Diego de Vargas. In 1694, the reconqueror would name him alcalde mayor of the Pecos.[5]

Near the estancia that had been Cristóbal de Anaya's, Otermín summoned a Tano Indian known as Pedro García to appear before him. It was August 25. The day before, while a pack of rebels harried the rear of the retreating cavalcade, this Tano, "who did not want to be a rebellious traitor," tried with his wife and another woman to catch up. The rebels grabbed the two women, but he eluded them and, covered by Spaniards, reached safety. Born, reared, and employed in the household of Alcalde mayor José Nieto, whose estancia lay only a league or so from Galisteo, Pedro now related to Otermín what he had seen and heard during the first days of the revolt.

A Tano Relives the Outbreak

Like a brush fire in the wind, word of the planned uprising had spread from San Cristóbal to all the Tano pueblos, and to Father Custos Juan Bernal. Bernal had alerted Alcalde mayor Nieto and the other Spaniards, who gathered up their families and made for Galisteo. The next day, while Pedro was chopping weeds in a plot of maize on the Nieto estancia, he looked up to see Bartolomé, cantor mayor of the pueblo of Galisteo, coming toward him, his eyes filled with tears.

"What are you doing here?" asked Pedro. The hysterical reply, if Pedro's memory served him, went something like this:

The Indians want to kill the custos and the other Fathers and Spaniards! They say that the Indian who kills a Spaniard will get an Indian woman, whichever one he wants, as his wife. He who kills four Spaniards will take four, and he who kills ten or more will have that many women for wives. They say they have to kill all the servants of the Spaniards and those who speak Spanish.

And they have also ordered that everyone take off their rosaries and burn them. Hurry, get going with your wife and the little orphan girl you have, and perhaps you will be fortunate enough to make it to where the Spaniards are gathered and escape.

Governor Otermín asked Pedro if he knew why the Indians had rebelled. Pedro recalled what Bartolomé had said. The Pueblos were tired of all the work they had to do for the Spaniards and the missionaries. It rankled them that they did not have time to plant for themselves or to do the other things they needed to do. Fed up, they had rebelled.

Later Pedro had learned that the rebels had put to death Custos Bernal and Fray Domingo de Vera at the pueblo of Galisteo. They had martyred Fray Manuel Tinoco of San Marcos and Fray Fernando de Velasco of Pecos within sight of the pueblo as the two missionaries hurried to join Bernal. The roll of Spaniards killed that day included Alcalde mayor Nieto, Juan de Leyva, Nicolás de Leyva, their wives, and their children. Several of the women they kept alive. They ransacked the Spaniards' homes. Meanwhile, the Pecos arrived.

Joining forces, Tanos, Keres of San Marcos, and Pecos had marched off to assault the villa of Santa Fe. Defeated there, they had come back in foul humor. Because six Tanos of Galisteo had been killed and many others badly wounded, the Indians of that pueblo vented their rage on the women captives they held. Three of them, Lucía, María, and Juana, had belonged to Pedro, or so he said. Another named Dorotea was the daughter of Maese de campo Pedro de Leyva. All died.

Concluding his testimony, Pedro explained why he had fled to overtake the retreating Spaniards. Word had come from the Tewas, and from Taos, Picurís, and Utes, that they would annihilate any Indian, or pueblo, who refused to participate in the revolt. For that reason, and because he was a Christian, Pedro had resolved to throw his lot with the Spaniards.[6]

Evacuation of
Río Abajo

As Otermín listened to Pedro's story near the pillaged Anaya house, two hundred and eighty miles downriver Father Francisco de Ayeta received at El Paso the first jumbled reports of the disaster. They came from the Río Abajo. Ever since about 1660, the kingdom of New Mexico had been divided for purposes of administration and defense into two major districts known as the Río Arriba and the Río Abajo, literally the upriver and the downriver sectors of the Rio Grande Valley. The governor commanded upriver, and the lieutenant governor downriver. At La Bajada, where the road from Santa Fe wound down the black basalt descent to the valley just above

Santo Domingo, the traveler passed from Río Arriba to Río Abajo. The uprising of 1680 had cut all Spanish communications between the two regions.

In the Río Abajo, the scared survivors, fifteen hundred of them, had flocked together at Isleta. Assuming that Otermín and everyone else upriver were dead, Lt. Gov. Alonso García and the whole crowd had started south on foot to save themselves. They had with them "a multitude of small children." At El Paso, meantime, Father Ayeta, reacting with his usual vigor, unloaded some of his supply wagons and outfitted a rescue expedition of armed men, friars, and provisions.

When Governor Otermín learned that the Río Abajo people were already retreating downriver, he sent riders ahead with orders for them to stop and wait for him. At Alamillo, north of Socorro, the governor interrogated another Indian, an aged Southern Tiwa man of Alameda captured on the road. What had possessed the Pueblos to forsake their obedience to God and king, Otermín demanded through an interpreter. The old man's reply was direct. "For a long time," he said,

A Tiwa Explains the Revolt

because the Spaniards punished sorcerers and idolaters, the nations of the Tewas, Taos, Picurís, Pecos, and Jémez had been plotting to rebel and kill the Spaniards and the religious, and that they had been planning constantly to carry it out, down to the present occasion. . . . He declared that the resentment which all the Indians have in their hearts has been so strong, from the time this kingdom was discovered, because the religious and the Spaniards took away their idols and forbade their sorceries and idolatries; that they have inherited successively from their old men the things pertaining to their ancient customs; and that he has heard this resentment spoken of since he was of an age to understand.

Painted ceremonial sandstone slab from Pecos.
Kidder, *Artifacts*

United at Fray Cristóbal, the entire Hispanic community of New Mexico—less some 380 colonists and twenty-one Franciscans dead—resumed their inglorious trek southward through the dry Jornada del Muerto.[7]

Upriver, the rebels were celebrating.

Just what the Pecos were doing is difficult to determine. If, as Fray Angelico Chavez suggests, a strapping mulatto named Naranjo, with big yellow eyes and a burning hatred of Spanish injustice, did assume the clever guise of the Pueblo "ancient one" Pohé-yemo and engineer the revolt from a kiva at Taos, he kept to the shadows. The conspicuous leader was El Popé, an ambitious, embittered San Juan medicine man

Pretentions of El Popé

flogged in 1675 at Governor Treviño's orders and harried from his pueblo by Francisco Javier. Once the Spaniards had gone, he took all the credit himself.[8]

El Popé was a paradox. He lashed out against everything Spanish, and he did it as only a Spaniard would. The Pueblos, driven to exasperation by demands for tribute and work and by the persecution of their native religion, had joined together to cast off their oppressors. For a few days or weeks, they had coordinated their efforts. But beyond that, they had no tradition of united political action. It was the Spaniards who had imposed a common sovereignty. Thus El Popé, in his effort to hold together what had been wrought against the Spaniards, ruled in the manner of a Spaniard. He even swaggered like one.

Pecos Glaze I bowl.
After Kidder, *Pottery,* II

Testifying late in 1681, during Governor Otermín's bootless attempt at reconquest, several Pueblo captives described the administration of his would-be native successor.

Popé came down in person, and with him El Saca and El Chato from the pueblo of Los Taos, and other captains and leaders and many people who were in his train, and he ordered in all the pueblos through which he passed that they instantly break up and burn the images of the holy Christ, the Virgin Mary and the other saints, the crosses, and everything pertaining to Christianity, and that they burn the temples, break up the bells, and separate from the wives whom God had given them in marriage and take those whom they desired.

They hacked santos, tore up vestments, and fouled chalices with human excrement. To erase their Christian names and cleanse themselves of the water and holy oils of baptism, El Popé commanded that they wash in the rivers with yucca-root soap. Anyone who harbored in his heart a sympathy for priests or Spaniards would be known by his unclean face and clothes, and he would be punished accordingly. They must not even speak the name of Jesus or Mary or the saints, under pain of whipping or death.

They were ordered likewise not to teach the Castilian language in any pueblo and to burn the seeds which the Spaniards sowed and to plant only maize and beans, which were the crops of their ancestors . . . . all the nations obeyed in everything except in the command concerning Spanish seeds . . . .
[Certain natives] moved by the zeal of Christians . . . Popé caused to be killed immediately. He saw to it that they [the Pueblos] at once erected and rebuilt their houses of idolatry called estufas, and made very ugly masks in imitation of the devil in order to dance the dance of the kachina; and he said likewise that the devil

had given them to understand that living thus, in accordance with the law of their ancestors, they would harvest a great deal of maize, many beans, a great abundance of cotton, squash, and very large watermelons and cantaloupes; and that they could erect their houses and enjoy abundant health and leisure.[9]

In their campaign to eradicate *lo español,* someone demolished the massive Pecos church. The Pecos later claimed that they did not, that the Tewas had done it. And perhaps they had, during El Popé's triumphal tour. Pecos or Tewas, or both, it was no mean feat. The Spaniards said that the rebels "burned" the great monument. The roof and the heavy vigas, the choir loft, and other wooden features would have burned, but not the towering buttressed adobe walls.[10]

Demise of a
Monumental Church

Firing the roof must have been spectacular. The rebels probably heaped piñon and juniper branches and dry brush inside the cavernous structure. When the roof caught and began burning furiously "a strong draft was created through the tunnel of the nave from the clearstory window over the chancel thereby blowing ashes out the door." It was like a giant furnace. When the fire died down, the blackened walls of the gutted monster still stood. To bring it low, Indians bent on demolition clambered all over it, like the Lilliputians over Gulliver, laboriously but jubilantly throwing down adobes, tens of thousands of them. Unsupported by the side walls, the front wall toppled forward facade down, covering the layer of ashes blown out the door. With an explosive vengeance, the Pueblos had reduced the grandest church in New Mexico to an imposing mound of earthen rubble.

They did not raze the entire convento. The two-story west side suffered most. Here the Father Guardian had had his second-floor cell with its mirador looking out in the direction of Santa Fe. The Pecos may have lived in some of the rooms. A circular kiva twenty feet across was dug in the corral just south of the convento and faced with adobes from the fallen church. Bedrock lying close beneath the convento must have thwarted the defiant intrusion of this "house of idolatry" right into the friars' cloistered patio. But the symbolism was clear. The ancient ones had overcome. The saints, mere pieces of rotted wood, were dead.[11]

During the following year, if the Spanish accounts are accurate, the rebel faction at Pecos twice confirmed that they would defy a return of the Spaniards. Their earlier defeat at Santa Fe had not destroyed their rebellious spirit. When a couple of Indian servants who had retreated to El Paso with their Spanish masters ran away and appeared again among the

Pueblos, some of the Pecos who had fought at Santa Fe recognized one of them as an ally of the Spaniards. The traitor paid with his life.[12]

Otermín's Abortive Reconquest

Governor Otermín did attempt a reconquest in the winter of 1681, but it aborted. He and Father Ayeta badly misjudged the temper of the rebels. Moving upriver with their none-too-spirited three hundred soldiers, servants, and Indians, the Spaniards half expected to be greeted as liberators by throngs of repentant Pueblos. The Piro communities lay utterly deserted, so they set fire to them. They captured Isleta by surprise. The friars absolved the people, baptized their infants, and burned the objects of their idolatry. From here, Otermín sent the veteran Juan Domínguez de Mendoza with sixty picked horsemen and some Indians on foot to scout conditions upriver.

As far as Cochití, the wary Domínguez de Mendoza found that the Pueblos, defying driving snow and cold, had taken to the hills. Making his camp in the protected plaza of Cochití, the Spaniard encountered nearby hundreds of rebels gathered on a fortified mesa. Domínguez and his men claimed to recognize among them Taos, Picurís, Tewas, Tanos, Pecos, Keres, Jémez, Ácomas, and Southern Tiwas. In a series of parleys, replete, in the Spaniards' report, with pious rhetoric, embraces, and copious tears of contrition and absolution, the rebels very nearly caught Domínguez in a trap.

The mestizo Alonso Catiti, leader of the concourse, begged for peace and for time to send messengers to all the people so that they would come down to their pueblos and receive the Spaniards. Actually he was buying time to rally his forces. Indian informers told Domínguez that Catiti planned to send into the Spaniards' camp the most comely Pueblo girls and to spring his trap while the enemy enjoyed the carnal pleasures of the bait. Recognizing their peril, the Spaniards beat an orderly retreat to the camp of Governor Otermín.

Just before the entire expedition turned back for El Paso, Father Ayeta expressed his disillusionment. He had expected Pueblos by the hundreds, sorely abused by Apaches and despotic rebel leaders, to fall on their knees and beg for absolution. Instead he had found them "exceedingly well satisfied to give themselves over to blind idolatry, worshipping the devil and living according to and in the same manner as when they were heathen." It was a shock to the evangelist.

This entrada has dispelled the misapprehension under which we have been laboring, namely, that only the leaders would be to blame for the atrocities committed, and that all the rest of the

Jémez kachina masks.
Parsons, *Jemez*

Indians would be found tired of their cruel and tyrannical government, which it was thought was imposed by force. But they have been found to be so pleased with liberty of conscience and so attached to the belief in the worship of Satan that up to the present not a sign has been visible of their ever having been Christians.[13]

If in fact some Pecos were party to Alonso Catiti's "perfidy," it is not likely that the entire pueblo cooperated to repulse the Spaniards. Traditionally aloof and internally divided, the Pecos seem to have maintained their trade and friendly relations with certain of the Plains Apaches, especially those the Spaniards called Faraones, and, whenever it suited them, to have entered into the loose and shifting Pueblo alliances. They had no use for the Tewas, an enmity noted by Spaniards for a century, ever since Castaño de Sosa. By 1689, the Pecos were reported allied with the Keres, Jémez, and Taos "in unceasing war" against Tewas, Picurís, and probably Tanos, their former allies in the attack on Santa Fe. Three years later, the Tanos and Tewas, who had moved in and remodeled the casas reales in Santa Fe, swore that the Pecos and Apaches were their mortal enemies.[14]

What deference, if any, the Pecos practiced toward the various rebel leaders is not apparent. Some Pecos obviously responded to the calls of El Popé and Catiti. But after the initial fall of Popé, which had already occurred by the time Otermín reappeared in 1681, they do not seem to have acknowledged his successor, Luis Tupatú of Picurís. Curiously

Pecos Foreign Policy

El Señor D.n Diego de
Bargas Zapata Lujan, Pon
ze de Leon, Marques de la Na
ba de Barcinas, del Orden de
S.n Tiago, Governador Conqui
tador, Pacificador, y Capitan
General d'el Nuebo Mejico,
perdio la Vida en Canpaña
Rasa por libertar los Va
sos Sacuados en el Sitio
de Bernalillo año
de MDCCIV

Diego de Vargas
(copy of a Spanish
portrait).
Museum of New Mexico

Diego de Vargas' coat of arms.
Espinosa, *Crusaders*

enough, not one of the many Pueblo rebels mentioned by name in the Spanish records of the 1680s was identified as a Pecos.

In sharp contrast, the Spaniards would record by name and deed in the next decade a dozen prominent Pecos. Some would give aid and comfort to the reconquerors. Others, as the fatal rift widened, would press for another revolt.

Had they met, don Diego José de Vargas Zapata y Luján Ponce de León y Contreras, last legitimate male descendant in the noble Vargas line of Madrid, might have looked down his aquiline nose at the criollo **Juan de Oñate.** A strutting aristocrat hungry to perform glorious deeds in an inglorious age, Gov. Diego de Vargas, capable, cocksure, and visibly daring, on February 22, 1691, assumed command of the dispirited New Mexico colony in exile. He found El Paso a hole.

Diego de Vargas Takes Over

The poverty, the misery, and the constant dread of Indian attack had driven many New Mexico refugee families to desert the El Paso settlements. A muster of men capable of bearing arms, counting not only the poorly equipped presidial garrison organized in 1683 but Indian allies as well, turned out scarcely three hundred in all. There were few horses and mules, an acute shortage of grain, and almost no livestock. Sumas, Mansos, and Gila Apaches daily threatened life and property. As he labored to overcome these obstacles, the new governor found himself drawn into Indian wars on the Sonora frontier to the west. Finally, in August 1692—while witches were being hanged in the Massachusetts Bay Colony—don Diego de Vargas embarked on the venture that would make him a national hero.[15]

When the Pecos first heard he was coming, they evacuated their pueblo. At Santa Fe, the Spanish governor had symbolically repossessed the villa, barely averting a battle by his sheer boldness and his confident preparations for a siege. Luis Picurís, formerly called Tupatú, leader of the Tewa-Tano-Picurís alliance, had come down from the north and to all appearances had made his peace with the invaders. Among the enemies of his people, Luis had identified "the nation of the Pecos, which is very numerous, and which maintains friendly relations with the Apaches they call Faraones." Now the Spaniards, accompanied by Luis and many warriors, were marching on Pecos.

Vargas Marches on Pecos

Having camped out of view of the pueblo, Vargas and his soldiers received absolution from Fray Miguel Muñiz de Luna early Tuesday morning, September 23, and advanced. As usual, the governor had instructed the men to cry out five times on their arrival at the pueblo the hymn *"Alabado sea el Santísimo Sacramento,"* Praise be to the Blessed Sacrament. Not until they saw him unsheath his sword were they to shout the *"Santiago!"* and charge.

As the mounted column moved forward through piñon and juniper, scouts picked up the fresh tracks of two Indians on horseback leading in the direction of the pueblo, as if they had alerted the Pecos. Descending a hill and a steep arroyo, they at last came in sight of the imposing earth-colored fortress. Two columns of smoke curled upward, seemingly from the pueblo. Vargas divided his horsemen. They would attack on three sides. Just then, the Indian auxiliaries passed back the word that the rebel Pecos were coming out on horseback. Vargas encouraged his men. If these Indians wanted battle, the Christians "should trample them under foot, capture them, and kill them." But be warned: they could have Apaches with them. Now the Spaniards closed at full gallop.

Pecos was deserted. Believing that the two Indian riders had given the warning only a short while before, Vargas ordered his men to follow what tracks they could. Soon the Spaniards were scattered all over "the mountainous ridge that borders on the maize fields on the other bank of the river from this pueblo, the ravines, ascents, and barrancas." With his guard, the governor rode down into a deep arroyo where one of his servants discovered children's footprints. A shot rang out, echoing through the mountains in the still air. Vargas spurred his horse to where a soldier was descending with an aged Indian woman as his prisoner.

The governor summoned "general interpreter" Pedro Hidalgo, a swarthy, well-built man, thick of beard, with short

A painting on hide of Santiago by Molleno.
Joslyn Museum, Omaha, Nebraska

curly hair and the scar of a burn on his neck. Born and reared in New Mexico and now in his mid-forties, Hidalgo had witnessed the death of one of the missionaries in 1680 and lived to tell about it. Whether or not he understood much of the Towa language of Pecos, as well as Tano, Tewa, and Tiwa, the willing Hidalgo interrogated the old woman for Vargas. Where had the Pecos gone, when, and for what reason, the governor wanted to know. If Hidalgo understood her correctly, her answer revealed that the Pecos were torn.

Vargas Interrogates Pecos Prisoners

The young people had cleared out six days before, as soon as they heard that Vargas was at Santa Fe. The old men of the pueblo wanted to go meet the Spanish governor and sue for peace. The young men had said no and had prevented their elders from going. The few Pecos who stayed behind, while working that morning in their maize fields, had been warned by the two Indian riders.

Another prisoner was brought to Vargas, this one a man who appeared to be about sixty, stark naked. Ordering the woman to give her compatriot one of the skins she wore to cover him up, the Spanish governor had Hidalgo ask him the same questions. He gave the same answers. Vargas decided to make him an emissary. Explaining to the old Indian through Hidalgo that he had come to pardon the Pecos in the name of the king, the Spaniard urged that he go to his people and convince them to return peacefully. No harm would come to them or their property. As a sign of peace, the governor hung a rosary around the Indian's neck. He had him make a little cross just over a quarter-vara long and attached to it a letter as a safe-conduct so that the soldiers would not kill him. Then he embraced the old man and sent him on his way, "repeating to him that he should believe me, and that I would wait at the pueblo for him and his people or for whatever answer they entrusted to him."

Vargas waited four days. He and his soldiers helped themselves to lodging in the pueblo itself, which the governor found to be "very large, and its houses three stories tall, and entirely open." The place was well supplied with maize and all kinds of vegetables. Combing the rocky hills and arroyos that first day, the soldiers rounded up a total of twenty-seven prisoners. They also discovered among the trees caches of animal skins left by the fleeing Pecos, indicative perhaps that the Spaniards had just missed a party of Plains Apache traders. Between two and three that afternoon, another venerable Pecos showed up bearing the cross that had been sent earlier in the day with the first emissary.

The Pecos Divided Again

This second old man told Vargas the same story, that the old people and the women had not wanted to abandon their pueblo, but the young braves, *"los mocetones* who defend them from the enemies who do them harm and engage in war," had compelled them. He also informed the Spaniards that the earlier emissary was in fact the Pecos governor, who now was trying to round up his dispersed people. As an incentive, Vargas vowed that he and his men were ready to move out the moment the Pecos returned to their homes. He reiterated his desire that

Rosary beads and
corroded cross recovered
in excavations at Pecos.
National Park Service
photo by Fred E. Mang, Jr.

the fugitives return to the fold as vassals of the Catholic king
and as good Christians, and that they reconcile their differences
with the Tanos and Tewas, some of whom he had brought with
him, "so that they would be like brothers and do no harm to
one another."

All day Wednesday, Thursday, and Friday the calculating
Vargas attempted to negotiate a return of the Pecos. Three
women, brought in by the Indian allies, greeted the Spanish
governor with the "Praise be to the Blessed Sacrament."
Another old messenger arrived with news that the pueblo's
governor had already gathered some of the people and was
awaiting others. In response, Vargas sent a physically fit younger woman who told him that she was the daughter of a former
Pecos governor. Twice she tried to find her people, the second

time with a soldier escort part of the way, but she failed, or so she said. Summoning a lithe young Pecos male, Vargas hung a rosary around his neck and sent him.

Three more Indian women, two of whom he thought must have been over a hundred years old, were hauled before Governor Vargas, along with a youth who claimed that he had been held captive since 1680. The lad said he was a son of the murdered Cristóbal de Anaya Almazán. Reuniting him with an uncle, Capt. of artillery Francisco Lucero de Godoy, Vargas charged Lucero to teach the boy the armorer's trade. Interrupting his negotiations with the Pecos, the Spanish governor sent an emissary with the standard rosary, cross, and letter to tell the Keres of Santa Ana and Zía that he would soon be coming on a mission of peace. He was losing patience with the Pecos.

On Friday, September 26, about four in the afternoon, the young Pecos runner reappeared with another youth, the only person he had found. The Pecos people had dispersed: the young rebels had threatened to kill the old men who were opting for peace. Disgusted, Vargas had these two, who gave their names as Agustín Sebastián and Juan Pedro, placed with the rest of the prisoners, while he decided what to do next. A report from Domingo of Tesuque, a leader of his Tewa allies, helped him make up his mind.

Scouting in the mountains earlier that day, Domingo and his men had spied three Pecos on a ridge above them. Domingo called to them to come down, that it was safe. The Pecos were wary.

They told him that now they did not want to return to their pueblo. They [the Tewas] were dirty dogs for having made friends and keeping company with the Spaniards, who were liars. They did not want their offers of peace or their friendship. Some of them would go with the Taos and others with the Apaches. Although he said more to them, they paid him no heed and took off whooping through the mountains.

Vargas Withdraws in Peace

To Vargas the message was clear. He was wasting his time.

At this point, don Diego reached one of the most farsighted decisions of his career, or, as he put it a few days later, "I acted with such judicious and prudent resolution." By their refusal to accept his offer of pardon, the Pecos had shown themselves to be, in his words, "rebellious and confirmed in their apostasy." He could punish them, burning their pueblo and their maize in the tradition of his predecessors, or he could release the twenty-eight Pecos he held, leave everything including kivas, "many of which were found in this pueblo," stores, and fields unharmed, and withdraw. He chose the latter course.

Early Saturday morning, he freed the Pecos prisoners with an admonition to tell the others of their good treatment. As a symbol of peace he ordered a large cross set up in the pueblo and others painted on the walls. He left a cross half a vara long and a piece of paper marked with a cross as signs of safe-conduct for the Pecos peace delegation he hoped would come looking for him. Then, taking only the Anaya boy, three Tiwa women with their three infants, and a Spanish-speaking Jumano woman, all previous captives of the Pecos, don Diego de Vargas led his soldiers and allies out of the pueblo past the great mound that had been the church. By three that afternoon, after a strenuous twenty-mile march by "the bad road through the sierra," really only a horse trail, he was back in camp before Santa Fe.[16]

By his restraint at Pecos—something the Pueblos did not expect of Spaniards—Diego de Vargas had cut the ground out from under the young hawks. The soldiers had not even ravaged their kivas. Vargas was gambling. By this act of good faith, he hoped to win an ally.

Three weeks after he had spared Pecos, don Diego returned to collect his due. In the interim, he had triumphantly toured the Tewa pueblos, the relocated Tano pueblos of San Cristóbal and San Lázaro, and Taos, everywhere receiving the formal submission of the natives. He had been obliged to talk the Taos, erstwhile allies of the Pecos, down out of the mountains. After the usual ceremonies and the baptism of ninety-six Indians, two Taos leaders asked to see Vargas in his tent. Speaking through interpreter Hidalgo, the two explained that since they were now all brothers, the Spanish governor should know about a plot against him.

The Peaceful "Reconquest" Rolls On

Two young Taos on their way home from the Zuñi pueblos had come upon a great council allegedly attended by "all the captains of the Zuñi nation as well as the Hopi, Jémez, Keres, Pecos, Faraón Apaches, Coninas of the Cerro Colorado, and many others from other parts." Held near Ácoma, it had lasted three days and three nights. The plan was simple: join forces, ambush and annihilate the Spaniards. Thanking the informants, Vargas called in his Tewa and Tano captains and told them to have their best men at Santa Fe by October 16. He would march first to Pecos, then to the Keres and Jémez pueblos, receiving the homage of each. If they refused, he and his allies would destroy them without quarter. Aware of the friendship between Taos and Pecos, he asked for two swift Taos youths to carry word to the Pecos. He was on his way to make peace. This time he expected their compliance.

From Santa Fe, a buoyant Vargas wrote to Viceroy the Conde de Galve. Counting the villa, he had now "reconquered" thirteen towns for God and king. As for himself, it was payment enough knowing "that no one has been bold enough to undertake what I, by divine grace, have achieved to date." The dispatch, incredibly enough, reached the viceroy in thirty-six days, setting off in the capital a grand celebration, pealing bells, and the festive illumination of the cathedral. Already don Diego was the toast of New Spain.[17]

Reconqueror Welcomed at Pecos

This time the Pecos were waiting for him. They crowded around the entrance to the pueblo, some of them holding aloft arches of evergreen branches. They had set up a cross, "large and very well made." At about two in the afternoon of October 17, 1692, a Friday, as Diego de Vargas and his party of mounted Spaniards approached, they stepped back opening a path. Those who remembered chanted the *Alabado sea.* The Spaniards responded gratefully.

Riding straight into the pueblo with his ensign, who held high the royal standard, the erect, supremely confident Vargas dismounted in the plaza of the house block where he had stayed on his first visit. His officers, his secretary, the interpreter Pedro Hidalgo, and two Franciscan chaplains in their familiar blue habits attended the governor. Some of the several dozen soldiers may have sat their horses to control the crowd in case of trouble. This time Vargas had with him no Indian auxiliaries. Those from El Paso he had sent with the baggage train and spare horses to await him at Santo Domingo. And he had excused the Tewas and Tanos, who had not yet harvested their crops "because of the foul weather they have had."

On that gray fall afternoon, the delicious smell of piñon and juniper fires hung over the teeming plaza while hundreds of Pecos, bundled against the chill in their buffalo robes and blankets, looked on from the rooftops. Vargas through interpreter Hidalgo, delivered a speech, as he had done in all the pueblos. As governor and captain general of the kingdom and provinces of New Mexico and castellan of its armed forces and garrisons by order of His Majesty, he, Diego de Vargas, had come a great distance to restore what belonged to the king, not only this land but also the people, "for he was their lord, their rightful king, and there was no other." They should consider themselves blessed to be vassals of such a king.

The Spanish governor called to the ensign to hoist the

Viceroy the Conde de Galve,
1688-1696.
Rivera Cambas, *Los gobernantes*, I

Charles II, "the Bewitched,"
king of Spain, 1665-1700,
"a cripple in mind and body."
Rivera Cambas, *Los gobernantes*, I

royal banner three times. Hung on a processional staff, it bore also the image of Nuestra Señora de los Remedios, don Diego's special patroness. A squad of soldiers stood at attention with swords unsheathed. Each time the banner went up, Vargas led the crowd in the cry, "Long live the king, our lord! God save him! Charles the Second! King of the Spains, of all this new world, and of the kingdom and provinces of New Mexico, and of these subjects newly won and conquered!" Each time, the soldiers responded, "Long live the king! May he reign in happiness!" Jubilantly, amid cheering, the soldiers threw their hats into the air. Pecos, its lands, and its people had been reconquered. Falling on their knees, the friars intoned the *Te Deum Laudamus*.

Having rendered unto Caesar, Vargas now told the Pecos that the reverend missionary Fathers would absolve them of their grievous apostasy, and of all the other sins they had committed in the course of their revolt, and that aferward they would baptize their children born since 1680. As Christians, he admonished, they must select godparents and bring forward

The Pecos Absolved

their unbaptized. If any of them wished, he himself, the governor and captain general, or one of his men, would serve as godfather.

Fray Francisco Corvera, a native of Manila, headed Vargas' three-man chaplain corps. Fray Cristóbal Alonso Barroso assisted at Pecos, while the third friar, Miguel Muñiz de Luna, ministered to the other detachment at Santo Domingo. Father Corvera delivered a homily. Pedro Hidalgo translated as best he could. The Pecos were instructed to kneel on both knees and to fold their hands. After the friar had intoned the general absolution, he and Father Barroso administered simple baptism to two hundred and forty-eight persons, mostly children, from nursing babies to twelve-year-olds, as parents and godparents filed by. Don Diego stood as godfather to a son of "the captain they obey," and to many others, as did his soldiers. Compadres now, Spaniards and Pecos embraced.

Two years later, the missionary assigned to Pecos would supply the ceremonies to all these simple baptisms in a temporary but proper church, anointing each individual with blessed chrism. Ironically, some of the Pecos men, whose children he baptized in 1692, would bury Father Corvera at San Ildefonso in 1696, a victim of the Tewas' second revolt.

Saturday dawned cold and overcast. It began to snow. As a matter of policy, Vargas had camp pitched outside the pueblo so as not to displace or molest any of the inhabitants. According to the governor's journal, on this inclement morning, interpreter Hidalgo came to his tent with a request from "the old and eminent natives of this pueblo of the Pecos, in a body." They wanted him to appoint pueblo officials, the way the Spaniards did before 1680. By securing his sanction of their leadership, the elders meant to strengthen their hand over the resistance faction. Don Diego consented.

Vargas Installs
Pecos Officials

Speaking again through his interpreter, Vargas told the assembled Pecos that they must elect of their own free will Indians to serve as their pueblo governor, lieutenant governor, alcalde, and alguacil, as well as two fiscales and two war captains. When they had done this, he administered the oath, exhorting them "in the utmost detail through said interpreter to respect and fulfill the duties of their offices to the greater service of Both Majesties." Father Corvera then gave the oath to the two fiscales, whose duties as assistants to the missionaries did not at this time amount to much in the absence of resident priest and church.

When the snow and rain stopped, about two in the afternoon, Vargas gave the order to decamp "despite the bad

Gen. don Diego de Vargas
was here, he who conquered
all New Mexico for our
Holy Faith and the
Royal Crown at his own
expense, in the year
1692. The inscription
on El Morro as drawn
by R. H. Kern, 1849.
Simpson, *Journal*

weather." By three the column had formed up. "Having taken
my leave of these natives," his journal reads, "and having reiterated to them that they should pray and live as Christians,
which they promised me they would do, I set out." Curiously,
don Diego failed to record in his journal, now or on his earlier
visit, the state of the Pecos church. A great heap of melted
adobe, beyond repair, it was evidently not worth the mention.
No matter. Vargas was satisfied. Pecos, whose population he
estimated "from its house blocks and plazas" at about fifteen
hundred, was his, number fourteen on his tally of reconquest.[18]

Taking "the wagon road," they camped that night at abandoned Galisteo and next day passed through San Marcos,
where Vargas noted that "some of the rooms and walls of its
house blocks and dwellings survive, and likewise the walls and
nave of the church as well as those of the convento are in good
condition." Reunited with the rest of his force at Santo Domingo, the tireless reconqueror mapped his route through the
Keres and Jémez pueblos, then westward to Ácoma, Zuñi, and
as far as Awátovi, Walpi, Mishongnovi, and Shongopovi among
the defiant Hopi. Everywhere, demonstrating an almost suicidal
boldness, don Diego de Vargas won the day.

The "Bloodless"
Reconquest Complete

Before Christmas, they were back in El Paso. The final tally, as reported by Vargas to the viceroy, stood at twenty-three pueblos rewon, seventy-four Indian and Spanish captives rescued, and 2,214 Indians baptized. Or, in the words of a news bulletin describing the heroic feat, "An entire realm was restored to the Majesty of our lord and king, Charles II, without wasting a single ounce of powder, unsheathing a sword, or (what is most worthy of emphasis and appreciation) without costing the Royal Treasury a single maravedí."

To make good on this "bloodless reconquest," Vargas had yet to recolonize New Mexico. In the months ahead, he devoted himself zealously to recruiting, fund raising, supply, and to seeking preferment worthy of his deeds. In a long letter to the king, written from Zacatecas in May 1693, don Diego beseeched his sovereign to grant him the title of Marqués de los Caramancheles—two estates near Madrid—"with lordship over them." To continue in the royal service, he also bid for the governorship of Guatemala, or if that be taken, the governorship of the Philippines, or if that be taken, the governorship of Chile, or if that be taken the governorship of Buenos Aires and the Río de la Plata.[19]

"*El hombre propone*," says the Spanish maxim, "*y Dios dispone.*" Man proposes and God disposes. It was the Other Majesty's will that Diego de Vargas die in New Mexico.

Vargas Plans
Recolonization

The second phase of don Diego's task entailed more work and less glory, and it was by no means bloodless. He welcomed the viceroy's praise and his approval of a government-subsidized, one-hundred-man presidial garrison for Santa Fe. Besides those already in the El Paso area, he reckoned he needed as many as forty more priests, plus Custos Salvador de San Antonio, a New Mexico veteran. The twelve thousand pesos offered initially by the viceroy, Vargas considered insufficient to outfit, transport, and maintain for six months the five hundred families of colonists he intended to take. He had decided already where they should settle: 150 families at Santa Fe; 100 in the vicinity of Taos; 50 near Santa Ana; 100 at Jémez; 100 along the Rio Grande from Angostura, south of San Felipe, to Sandía; and 50 at Pecos, bringing the total, incidentally, to 550.

Diego de Vargas' reason for projecting a civil settlement in the vicinity of Pecos—a proposal not realized in fact for another hundred years—was defense.

At the pueblo of the Pecos, a distance of eight leagues from Santa Fe, fifty families could be settled, because it too [like Taos]

MERCURIO
VOLANTE
CON LA NOTICIA

de la recuperacion de las
PROVINCIAS DEL NVEVO MEXICO
CONSEGVIDA
Por D. DIEGO DE VARGAS, ZAPATA, Y LUXAN
PONZE DE LEON,

Governador y Capitan General de aquel Reyno.

ESCRIVIOLA -

Por especial orden de el Excelentissimo Señor CONDE DE
GALVE VIRREY, GOVERNADOR, Y CAPITAN
GENERAL DE LA NUEVA-ESPAñA, &c.

DON *CARLOS DE SIGVENZA, Y*
GONGORA, Cosmographo mayor de su Ma-
gestad en estos Reynos, y Cathedratico Iubilado de Mathe-
maticas en la Academia Mexicana.

Con licencia en Mexico:
EN LA IMPRENTA DE ANTUERPIA
de los Herederos de la Viuda de Bernardo Calderon, año de 1693.

Title page of the
Mercurio Volante,
a tribute to Diego
de Vargas on the
occasion of his "reconquest"
of New Mexico in 1692,
by don Carlos de Sigüenza
y Góngora, New Spain's
most learned professor.
Wagner, *Spanish Southwest,* II

is an Apache frontier and, being so surrounded by very mountainous country, suffers unavoidable ambushes. Settled in this manner, and backed by the military at the villa, it will prevent the robberies and murders that follow from assured entry. It is very fertile land which responds with great abundance to all kinds of crops planted.[20]

They came together at unprosperous El Paso, where for a couple of weeks mission and presidio were inundated by a swarming camp that tripled the population—a hundred soldiers for Santa Fe, some with families, seventy assorted families of colonists, widows and singles and servants, eighteen Franciscans, and an unlisted number of Indian allies, probably twelve hundred persons in all, plus wagons and gear and a thousand mules, two thousand horses, and nine hundred milling head of cattle, sheep, and other sundry stock. More or less formed up, the straggling, motley train began to move out slowly on the feast of St. Francis of Assisi, October 4, 1693, amid great festivity and cursing.

The journey north was a nightmare. The wind blew bitter cold, food ran low, wagon wheels came off, and nearly everyone was sick. Worse, as Vargas and his vanguard of fifty men scouted ahead through the first abandoned pueblos, they began hearing rumors that most of the Indians, fortified on mesa tops, intended to resist. Only the Keres of San Felipe, Santa Ana, and possibly Zía favored the Spaniards' return.[21]

Juan de Ye
Offers Services

At San Felipe, unexpectedly, a Pecos hailed don Diego. Juan de Ye, whom Vargas always addressed as don Juan, had arrived to pay his respects. This was "the captain they obey" whom Vargas had inaugurated as pueblo governor at Pecos the year before, and whose son, like those of so many other native leaders, was his godchild. Apparently, Juan had brought with him his lieutenant governor, alcalde, alguacil, and war captains. Learning of the Spaniards' presence from a Pecos lad who was in Santa Fe when Vargas' two Tano emissaries appeared, Juan had hastened to San Felipe to assure the Spanish governor that the Pecos welcomed his return. He had made that clear to the Tewas and Tanos, and he had come in person to tell don Diego. Whether Vargas sensed it at this stage or not, Juan de Ye, until his probable death on a mission for the Spaniards a year later, was to prove almost indispensable. The reconqueror's refusal to destroy Pecos in 1692 had paid off.

Juan de Ye now briefed the Spanish governor on the fight that lay ahead. As far back as the summer, the rebels who occupied Santa Fe had told Juan to have the Pecos "make many arrows so that all of them together" could attack the Spaniards when they came. A council had been held in the Tewa pueblo of San Juan, at which, according to the Pecos governor, the half-breed Pedro de Tapia had planted a cancerous seed of discontent. An interpreter with the Spanish expedition of 1692 who had since died, Tapia told the Pueblos that Diego de Vargas was a monster. Even though he pardoned them in 1692, his ultimate goal was to slaughter them all, sparing only the children born since 1680. This seed, nurtured in the fertile soil of their guilt, had grown into an effort to unite all the Pueblos against the Spaniards. "If it is true," wrote Vargas about Tapia, "may God forgive him!"[22]

A few days later, cold and complaining, the colonists, along with soldiers, friars, baggage, and animals, caught up. The entire expedition camped on the site of Cristóbal de Anaya's ruined estancia. While Vargas parleyed with a variety of Pueblo delegations and sent out supply details in all directions to trade meat for maize, camp was moved nearer and nearer to Santa Fe. The weather turned colder still, and some of the colonists whispered of deserting.

Juan de Ye stayed with the Spaniards. In fact, four Pecos, mounted and armed, Felipe, Juan, Pedro, and Diego, curious to know what was keeping their governor, showed up in camp one day. Vargas welcomed them and told interpreter Juan Ruiz de Cáceres to make them understand "that I loved them all very much, that they were my children, and that their governor and my compadre, don Juan, knew this well. When they recognized this they were satisfied."

Late the night of November 25, two of Vargas' captains woke him to report that don Juan and the four recently arrived Pecos had urgent news. Shown into the Spanish governor's tent and seated on the ground near his bed, the natives told of a plot to annihilate the entire expedition. This time Francisco Lucero de Godoy interpreted.

A Plot to Annihilate the Spaniards

As usual, Juan put the blame on Tewas and Tanos, along with Picurís and Taos. He identified their leaders, some of whom were feigning friendship. The rebels had called an all-Pueblo junta at La Cienaguilla, seven leagues from Santa Fe. Dividing their forces, they meant to attack the Spanish train simultaneously from front and rear, drive off the animals, and massacre everyone. Should the Spaniards reach Santa Fe, where the native occupants had dug a well inside and laid up provisions to withstand a siege, the plan was to stampede the invaders' horses at night, then fall on the camp. A Spaniard afoot, they were convinced, was no match. But for the refusal of the Pecos and the Jémez to join them, the rebels might already have sprung their trap.

As a Christian, Vargas replied, he would proceed as if he knew nothing of the plot. He intended to give everyone an opportunity to submit peacefully. If the Tanos and Tewas chose war, he would rely, as before, on Nuestra Señora de los Remedios and her Son. He had come not to do harm, but rather to encourage all the Pueblos to live in peace as Christians. He thanked the Pecos for their offer to fight at his side and to steal the rebels' riding horses and mules from the canyon where they had left them, but he prayed it would not come to that. Before dismissing them, Vargas reiterated the affection and esteem he felt for the Pecos, "because they were loyal to the king our lord, Christians, and friends of the Spaniards."

A few days later don Juan was back. He and another Pecos named Juan "of his closest following" said they wanted to see the Spanish governor. Admitted to Vargas' tent about eight in the evening with interpreter Ruiz de Cáceres, they described again the threat posed by the rebel alliance, repeating their offer to capture the enemy's horses. The Pueblo occupants were preparing to defend Santa Fe, where growing numbers of rebels were gathering, and the weather was getting worse. Why, then, the Pecos wanted to know, did the Spaniards not attack? Again Vargas put them off.[23]

Misery in the
Spanish Camp

While he played the diplomatic game, a war of nerves, the Spanish camp was starving. The scant provisions acquired in trade with the Pueblos were not enough. Dissuaded by his officers from going to Pecos in person, the Spanish governor now called in don Juan de Ye. If the Pecos really wanted to aid the Spaniards, they would bring food. "I told him," said Vargas, "that he would demonstrate the strength of the goodwill he felt toward me as a compadre and my relative" if he went to his pueblo and traded for all the flour, maize, pinole, and beans he could get. Don Diego was thinking in terms of seventy or eighty *cargas,* or mule packs, of two fanegas each. Sgt. Juan Ruiz de Cáceres would accompany the Pecos, taking six slaughtered beeves and other trade goods, mules and muleteers, and an escort of twelve soldiers under Capt. Juan Holguín.

The side expedition to Pecos set out about ten in the morning on December 5. It was back by December 9. The haul: an unfulfilling eight fanegas of maize, more or less, and two of maize flour. The Pecos, reported Juan de Ye, were glad to know that the Spanish governor had returned. Don Diego was welcome at their pueblo, where they would load up his mules with provisions, doubtless for an appropriate consideration in trade goods. Don Diego had to explain to the Indian that the Spaniards and their wagons were not proceeding first to Pecos but to Santa Fe instead. Once they had secured the villa, he would go down to Pecos himself to install a missionary. As a sop he presented don Juan with a horse. The Pecos, plainly, were not going hungry that Spaniards might eat.[24]

Vargas and Colonists
in the Snow

When finally they stood in the snow before Santa Fe, the shivering, half-starved colonists were denied shelter within. The Tanos and Tewas made no move to vacate. On December 16, they received Governor Vargas, a procession of soldiers and Franciscans, a cross, and the *Te Deum* inside the walls, but

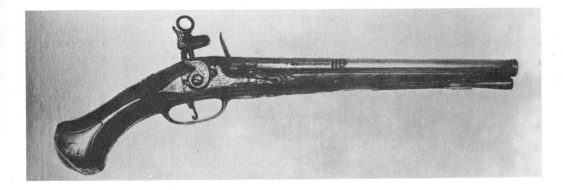

they did so with a foreboding reserve. Still, with his tent set up outside in the cold "a mortar shot from the plaza," Vargas decided to distribute the missionaries.

Officer's pistol made in Madrid, 1703. Brinckerhoff and Faulk, *Lancers*

If the reconqueror appeared calm in the face of the dangers and discomforts of the moment, the friars were perturbed. Everyone in camp knew of "the evil design and perfidy" of the Tanos and Tewas. Again don Juan de Ye came to Vargas' tent. This time he had definite information, relayed from a Zuñi to a Cochití to him. Tewas, Tanos, and Picurís had congregated on the mesa of San Juan with a horde of Apaches. Dressed and armed like Spanish frontier cavalry, with leather doublets, lances, and shields, they would strike Governor Vargas when he least expected it. Meanwhile, they had arranged to steal the Spaniards' horses a few at a time. Don Juan offered to call his Pecos warriors. And again he volunteered to steal the rebels' horses.

Not on their lives were the missionaries going out into the pueblos. Martyrdom was a blessing; suicide was not. In addition to Santa Fe, Vargas wished to thrust ministers into Tesuque, Nambé, San Ildefonso, San Juan, San Lázaro, Picurís, Taos, Jémez, Zía, Cochití, and Pecos. What was he thinking? Had he forgotten his promise to protect the ministers of the gospel as well as the other innocent vassals of the king "who had come with such willingness to settle this land?" How could he ignore the repeated warnings of don Juan de Ye, an Indian who had proven himself "always faithful and honest in all his actions and conduct and who has not left our company in more than a month."

Missionaries Balk and Sign Petition

All eighteen friars signed the petition. That same day, December 18, Fray Diego de Zeinos, secretary of the custody, delivered it to the governor's tent. Whether or not they had their facts straight, they meant to impress upon Vargas the loyalty and the credibility of Juan de Ye.

After all, it was he who at the time of the last uprising in 1680 warned Sargento mayor Francisco Gómez [Robledo], now deceased, twenty days before. And as the time drew closer he repeated the warning eight days before. Seeing that they did not believe him, he told his minister, Fray Fernando de Velasco, "Father, the people are rising to kill all the Spaniards and religious. Therefore, decide where you want to go and I will give you warriors to escape," as in fact he did.

Even had he wished to overrule the friars' protest, Vargas reconsidered. This was no time to send out the missionaries.[25]

The impasse continued. Tension built. An icy wind swirled the snow into drifts. Secure in their walled fortress-pueblo, the native occupants of Santa Fe mocked the Spaniards outside. Vargas doggedly kept up negotiations, all the while struggling to bring in enough food to feed his wretched colony, a few fanegas from this pueblo, five from that. From Pecos, where Sergeant Ruiz de Cáceres and his detachment received another warm welcome, came ten cargas, or twenty fanegas, of flour and ears of maize, as well as regards to don Diego. The long-exiled municipal council of Santa Fe was demanding that Vargas put them in possession of the casas reales. Children were sick and dying. At an open meeting, the leaders of the colony voiced their unanimous resolve: the rebels must go. Inside the walls, meanwhile, the natives worked themselves up for a fight.

The Bloody Battle for Santa Fe

In the brittle pre-dawn cold of December 28, the dark figure of a messenger flitted through camp and disappeared into Vargas' tent. The rebels were about to attack. Ordering trumpet and war drum sounded, the Spanish governor called for don Juan de Ye. Now was the time for the Pecos to prove themselves. "I ordered him to send at once to his pueblo on two swift horses I gave him and alert the young warriors to come well prepared and armed." That day both sides girded for battle. Vargas appealed to the rebels to evacuate the villa peacefully. He might as well have asked each of them for his left foot.

Four Pecos appeared next morning. They reported to Juan de Ye something about their people gathering firewood for the night and staying in the foothills until a Spaniard came for them. Vargas told Francisco Lucero de Godoy to get them. In no time he was back with one hundred and forty Pecos *indios de guerra,* give or take a few. "I received and welcomed them all" said Vargas.

The winter solstice ceremonial, or Shalako, at Zuñi. *Century* (Feb. 1883)

and I embraced their governor don Juan many times and gave him my hand, telling him that he was loyal to His Majesty and a good Christian and that whatever he or any of the people of his pueblo wished they would have a friend in me.

Addressing his entire "army," as men and horses stood there benumbed, their breath escaping in white puffs, don Diego de Vargas reassured them that God and the Blessed Virgin were with them, a fact Fray Diego de Zeinos confirmed. Then all knelt in the snow, recited the general confession, and were absolved by the friar. Mounted up, they moved forward and, met by a hail of shouting, arrows, and rocks, they yelled the Santiago and charged.

This time the Pecos had chosen the winning side. Thirteen years before, they and their Tano allies had fought the beleaguered Spaniards of Santa Fe and lost. Now on the same ground Spaniards and Pecos retook the villa from the Tanos in a hard-fought, two-day battle. Eighty-one rebels died: nine in battle, two by their own hand, and seventy executed. The four hundred who surrendered were allotted among the Spaniards for ten years' servitude. Finally the reconquerors had more than the ritual submission of the Pueblos and the boasts of Diego de Vargas. They had their capital.[26]

Vargas Confirms
His Alliance
with the Pecos

If anything, the Spanish victory at Santa Fe strengthened the alliance between Vargas and don Juan de Ye. Five days later, on January 4, 1694, when the Indian reported a threat to his pueblo, the Spanish governor responded in good faith. Ye, escorted by interpreter Francisco Lucero de Godoy, had come to Vargas' quarters at seven in the morning. An Apache sent by Ye to Pecos had returned in the night with a warning that he had spotted a large force of rebel Tewas, Tanos, Picurís, and Apaches in the mountains behind Santa Fe. They could have been moving on Pecos to avenge their loss of the villa. Vargas expressed his concern. But he was reluctant to leave Santa Fe just yet. He would dispatch don Roque de Madrid, his second-in-command. If, upon investigation, the situation required his presence, don Diego would gladly march to the defense of Pecos.

Madrid took thirty men, saying that he would call for more if needed. Vargas had provided, as usual, that any horses and cueras, the valuable protective leather coats, captured from the enemy be distributed among the members of the expedition. Fray Juan de Alpuente, who rode along as chaplain, would get his first look at Pecos, where two years later he would serve reluctantly as missionary. By four in the afternoon the next day, the column was back. There had been no sign of the rebels. The Pecos to a man, Madrid reported, "were grateful for the sending of these soldiers to protect them. They welcomed them warmly, and, having the Spaniards so firmly on their side, they feel secure." [27]

When Vargas marched out of Santa Fe in February to do battle with the Pueblo rebels dug in on Black Mesa, an "army" of Pecos marched with him. What don Juan de Ye and his following hoped to gain by this close association with the reconquerors, besides the protection of Spanish arms and vengeance on Tewas and Tanos, became increasingly evident that spring. They hoped to restore the traditional role of their pueblo as gateway between the Rio Grande Valley and the plains. The Spaniards had horses and goods, and once they put down rebel resistance, they would impose peace. All this was good for trade.

At least twice, once in March and again in May, don Juan de Ye showed up at the governor's palace with Plains Apaches in tow. The first time there were three of them. They explained to Vargas through an interpreter that they had arrived at Pecos with three tipis of their people. There they had learned of the Spaniards' return. Willingly they had come to render homage to the Spanish governor, to make his acquaintance, and to ask his permission to bring the rest of their ranchería to Pecos to trade "about the end of the rains, which is around October." They told Vargas how they used to come and go trading in peace before the Spaniards had vanished in 1680. This trade had proven beneficial to all concerned. Just so the people they had left at Pecos would know for sure that the Spaniards were back, the three Apaches requested that half a dozen of the reconquerors accompany them that far.

Vargas was delighted. He feted the three and assured them that they and their people would be welcome any time. On his orders, Maese de campo Lorenzo de Madrid, Aide-de-camp Antonio Valverde, an interpreter, and a party of soldiers and settlers rode with them over the mountain. The Pecos staged the kind of festive reception the Spaniards were coming to expect from them. The visiting Apaches

were most pleased at their sight. They presented them liberally with the buffalo meat and tanned skins they had brought, saying that they were going now and that in October, the stated time, the rest of their ranchería would be at this pueblo of the Pecos, to which they [the Spaniards] could come down for the trade fairs as they used to do in the time of those who had left.[28]

But they did not wait until October. On May 2, Juan de Ye presented himself at the casas reales in Santa Fe with a captain of the Apache rancherías of the plains and eight other Indians. Domingo de Herrera interpreted. This Apache had come in response to Vargas' previous invitation. He wanted to confirm the desire of his people to resume trade with the Spaniards when the ears were on the maize, just as in the old days. As tokens of their good faith, he laid before the Spanish governor three buffalo robes and "a campaign tent of light buffalo or elk skins." Vargas asked how far it was to their rancherías. Fourteen days, answered the Apache, and ten to where the buffalo bulls and cows roamed. There was much water, he added.

Juan de Ye and Plains Apaches

Next Vargas asked "the captain of the Apaches Fara-ones" why he was not a Christian. Using his hands, the Indian made signs that they should pour water on his head right then. If the Spaniards would just finish off the rebels, his Apaches would come live in their pueblos and become Christians. That, Vargas allowed, was an excellent thought provided the rebels did not reoccupy them. He explained to the Indian that as an adult he would have to be instructed before baptism. He must learn the prayers which Christians said on their knees. "He trusted me and the Spaniards implicitly," Vargas wrote, "showing by the outward joy of his countenance that he was already a Christian like us." [29]

Two days later at a formal audience, Ye and the first Plains Apache captain, who must have been serving with the Pecos auxiliaries, told Governor Vargas and his staff that the time had come for them and their horses to rest. It was the time for planting milpas, the time for each of them to return to his land. Before they departed, Vargas had some questions for the Apache. While the answers he gave do not rank him with the Turk, the glib plainsman did tell the Spaniards what they wanted to hear.

A Plains Apache Briefs Vargas

As they were having their chocolate, Vargas pointed to a silver dish and asked the Apache if they had anything like that in his land. The native said yes. Within a day's travel, there was a little range of mountains and at its base were some rocks of the same material just over half a vara tall. They called them *hierro blanco,* white iron. So heavy and hard were they that he had no way of breaking off a piece to bring to don Diego. After more questions, the Spanish governor told the Apache that he would pay him anything he wanted for a piece of the rock, "because it is a remedy for eye and heart disease." The Indian asked for an iron ax to break off a piece. "At once," wrote Vargas, "I ordered that it be brought as well as many goods with which I regaled him and likewise a horse he had asked me for, all of which was most pleasing to him."

The governor had also inquired about Texas and Quivira. The kingdom of the Tejas, according to the obliging Apache,

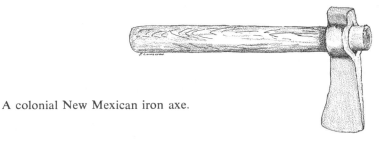

A colonial New Mexican iron axe.

Peso or Pacer, a Plains Apache chief.
National Anthropological Archives, Smithsonian Institution

lay seven days from his ranchería. Asked if there were watering places, he replied that there were rivers in abundance, many buffalo, and much fruit in the summer. Were there Spaniards? In years past there had been, but he did not know if they were still there. This answer satisfied Vargas that the Apache captain was telling the truth, for there had indeed been Spaniards in Texas recently searching for LaSalle. How far was Quivira? Using his fingers, the Indian calculated that the first settlement was some twenty-five to thirty days from his ranchería. His people knew this well because they went to Quivira to make war and capture children to trade for horses.

Vargas reminded the Apache not to forget the white iron. He should bring it when the ears were on the maize, to the pueblo of the Pecos where he and his people were welcome to come and trade with the Spaniards. Vargas would give the citizens of Santa Fe permission to go down to Pecos. He would aid the Apaches in every way, and he would pay well for the hierro blanco.[30]

Spaniards Join Again in Pecos Trade Fair

Evidently the white iron did not pan out. When a Plains Apache captain known to the Spaniards, possibly the same one, sent word through the Pecos late in August that eleven tipis were coming to trade, Vargas made no mention of the metal. Still, he cooperated in every way. At the request of the Pecos war captains, who did not wish to offend the Apaches or miss out themselves, he postponed his campaign against the northern Pueblo rebels and decreed a trading holiday.

Vargas' proclamation of the trading at Pecos was promulgated before large crowds in both of Santa Fe's plazas "to the sound of drum and bugle and in the voice of Sebastián Rodríguez, black drummer." The governor, anxious that his relatively small military force not be weakened further, imposed one restriction. Anyone who wanted to do so could go down to Pecos and enter freely in the trade, except using horses that bore his brand or were otherwise specified "on my account" as needed for war, regardless of who had them now. He who traded such a horse would lose not only the price but the animal as well.

The governor had reason to be pleased. The Pecos fair was visible proof that the kingdom could live in peace, as it had before 1680.[31]

Juan de Ye's Ultimate Sacrifice

During the first six months of his rigorous campaign to restore effective Spanish sovereignty over New Mexico, no Indian, with the possible exception of Bartolomé de Ojeda of Zía, served Diego de Vargas as devotedly or as productively as don Juan de Ye. Whatever his motives, he was always in Santa Fe, or in the field with his Pecos auxiliaries. He entered into Vargas' negotiation to win over the rebels, on several occasions interceding to save the life of an Indian who might favorably influence his fellows.

Once, don Juan came in to ask the Spanish governor's forgiveness for allowing a venerable former governor of the Jémez to live at Pecos. The old man, who still enjoyed considerable respect among his people, according to Ye, could be used to counter the propaganda of the rebellious Tewas and bring the Jémez back down from the mesas. Vargas was willing. But it would take more than diplomacy. When next the Spaniards tried force, don Juan was there with his Pecos. This time it would cost him his life.[32]

On San Juan's Day eve, June 23, 1694, a disgruntled train of colonists entered the gates of Santa Fe to the sparse cheering of the citizenry. This second wave, recruited in Mexico City and shepherded all the way by Franciscan procurador fray Francisco Farfán, increased the population by over two hundred, including three French survivors of the massacred LaSalle colony. No one felt more the need for numbers than Vargas did, but at the same time, with the maize supply so desperately low, he now had to provide for just that many more bellies.

His first priority was to deal swiftly with the rebel Santo Domingos and Jémez, whose harrying raids on the loyal Keres of San Felipe, Santa Ana, and Zía had caused these Indians to doubt the Spaniards' guarantee of protection. As Vargas plotted his move, don Juan de Ye rode in to say that the Rio Grande was up. Even with rafts, the crossing would be risky. Forced to shift priorities, Vargas now rerouted the expedition northward. From the stores of the abandoned rebel pueblos, by purchase, or by force, he would lay in enough maize to see his hungry colony through to harvest time.

His journal entry for July 3 told of a noble but foolhardy act on the part of don Juan de Ye. They had found Taos deserted. Fresh tracks led to the peoples' accustomed refuge, a deep and rugged mountain canyon whose entrance gaped open half a league from the pueblo. A ranchería of Plains Apaches who had come to Taos to trade greeted the Spaniards with handshakes and abrazos. These were mild compared to the demonstrative welcome they gave Juan de Ye, "their friend and acquaintance."

The Apaches arranged a meeting at the mouth of the canyon between Vargas and Francisco Pacheco, governor of the Taos, who suddenly appeared with a menacing number

Parleying with Defiant Taos

Taos pueblo.
E. P. Tenney,
*Colorado: and Homes
in the New West*
(Boston, 1880)

of his men. Ye considered Pacheco an old friend. He interpreted, evidently from Tiwa to Towa, with Sgt. Juan Ruiz de Cáceres or another Towa-Spanish speaker taking it from there. "With great force of words" Ye tried to persuade Pacheco and his people to come down to the pueblo and accept pardon from Governor Vargas. They had done so without harm in October of 1692—why not now? But it was no use.

"Moved by impulse and by fervent Catholic zeal," Diego de Vargas now risked his life, which he recorded in his journal, advancing to where Pacheco stood. The sun had set. Recognizing that he could accomplish little before nightfall, he bid the Taos governor an affectionate good-bye and told him that he would be waiting for him the next day at the pueblo. He had ordered camp made far enough away so that the Spaniards' horses and mules would not damage the Taos' crops. Juan de Ye repeated what Vargas had said. The wily Pacheco, feigning affection and professing the friendship of Taos and Pecos, invited don Juan to stay the night with him so they could discuss at leisure the Spaniards' proposal. Ye accepted.

Immediately Gov. don Juan de Ye, with more joy than if he had been entering his own house, consented most genuinely to stay. Although Sgt. Juan Ruiz de Cáceres and Sargento mayor Francisco de Anaya Almazán told him to consider well what he was doing and not to expose himself because some misfortune might befall him, he replied that he was safe and that he had confidence in Governor Pacheco, his friend.

Sergeant Ruiz suggested to Vargas that he order Ye to return the arquebus he was carrying, which belonged to the gov-

Three Taos leaders, 1870s: Antonio José Atencio, Juan Jesús León, and
Antonio Archuleta.
National Anthropological Archives, Smithsonian Institution

ernor, and his mule as well. Rather than betray a lack of confidence, Vargas rode over to don Juan, who was already dismounted. He repeated the warning of Ruiz and Anaya. The Indian's reply was the same.

He removed his spurs and the powder pouches from his belt, handing them over with the mule and his cloak to the sergeant along with the arquebus and his shield, telling him to look after them for him. He said good-bye to me, giving me an embrace and his hand. He did the same to the others. The Taos looked on attentively with their Governor Pacheco, to whom I repeated "God be with you," and that I would be waiting for him, and for don Juan de Ye, early at my tent to serve him chocolate.

When neither Pacheco nor Ye showed next morning, Vargas rode to the mouth of the canyon. He told his interpreter to shout up to the Taos sentinels that if their governor and don Juan did not appear by one o'clock, the Spaniards would sack the pueblo. No one appeared and Vargas gave the order. Once broken into, the pueblo yielded a wealth of maize. For more than two days they husked and loaded the edible booty, then under cover of darkness headed north into present-day Colorado to double back by the more protected westerly trail of the Ute traders.

A Pecos Glaze V pot. Kidder, *Pottery,* II

As for Juan de Ye, don Diego never saw him again. From two Taos Indians captured July 7 he learned that don Juan was still alive but tied up. Ten days later, safely back in Santa Fe with the maize, Vargas heard that Ye was still missing. Several Pecos Indians "loaded with glazed earthenware to sell" had come to town. A little while later don Lorenzo de Ye, son of don Juan, arrived. His father had not returned to the pueblo. When he had listened to the Spaniard's explanation of how don Juan had gone alone and of his own free will to parley with the Taos, when he had been given his father's weapons and cloak, don Lorenzo was, in Vargas' words, "satisfied but sad about the end that had befallen his father."

Through an interpreter, Diego de Vargas tried "with efficacious words" to express his sympathy. No Spaniard deserved the title reconqueror more than don Juan de Ye, governor of the Pecos. Vargas would never forget him.[33]

Refounding the Missions   For the friars, the reconquest so far had been frustrating. Eager to restore their missions but unwilling to risk their lives foolishly, they had been confined to Santa Fe where they had ministered to the complaining colonists and got in one another's way. Some had served with Vargas on campaign, absolving the men before battle and the prisoners before they were shot. Originally there had been eighteen. On Palm Sunday, April 4, Custos Salvador de San Antonio, who had been openly critical of the governor, and three of the others had departed for El Paso with the wagons and mules sent to the aid of Farfán's colonists. Fray Juan Muñoz de Castro was left in charge at Santa Fe as vice-custos. Late the same month, Vargas began to talk again of refounding missions.

Fresh from a victory of sorts over the rebels on the mesa of Cochití, the reconqueror sent a delegation to the quarters of Vice-custos Muñoz. He would donate to the reestablishment of missions two hundred head of the sheep he had captured. It seemed to him only right, "because of the friendship and the good relations we have with their natives," that the first be founded for the Pecos and the second for the Keres of San Felipe, Santa Ana, and Zía. Until that time he would put the flock in the care of a trustworthy Keres. Another hundred sheep he gave to Muñoz and the thirteen religious in Santa Fe "so that they are assured of meat to eat for a few weeks." He also deferred to the friars first choice of the boys among the Cochití prisoners. For all this Father Muñoz expressed to don Diego the friars' gratitude.[34]

Still, for five long months no mission was refounded. Not until September when Vargas, aided by Pecos, Keres, and Jémez auxiliaries, finally humbled the rebels on Black Mesa

San Ildefonso pueblo, 1880. Museum of New Mexico

and received the allegiance of the Tewa and Tano pueblos, did the time seem right. Then, with "not only moral but physical" assurance of the rebels' genuine submission, the eight missionaries remaining in Santa Fe petitioned Vice-custos Muñoz to send them into the field. It was no coincidence that the first mission they revived was Pecos, pueblo of the deceased don Juan de Ye.[35]

Father Zeinos Installed at Pecos

An earnest priest if ever there was, Fray Diego de Zeinos had served as secretary and notary of the friars since their departure from El Paso. He also bore the title *lector,* which meant that he had been a lecturer in a seminary or university. Whatever his other credentials, Fray Diego was assigned to Pecos.[36]

Governor Vargas set out for Pecos with his usual pomp on Friday morning, September 24, 1694. His purpose was twofold: to carry out the visitation required by his office and to install Father Zeinos. With him went the royal standard, his staff, the presidial garrison, Vice-custos Muñoz, Zeinos, and the three other friars assigned to San Felipe, Santa Ana, and Jémez. Making good time over the mountain, they entered the pueblo of the Pecos early the same afternoon in time for the customary formalities.

The assembled natives had heard it all before. They had anticipated this day. "They promised," according to Vargas' journal,

that they would build their church in order that divine worship might be celebrated in greater decency than at present. They have provided for the construction of a chapel which they proved by showing me the beams to roof it.

I, said governor and captain general, instructed them at length, speaking and conferring with the cacique and governor whom they have had and likewise with the captains and the old Indian leaders and warriors through interpreters Capt. Francisco Lucero de Godoy and Sgt. Juan Ruiz de Cáceres. They responded unanimously, saying that they were most pleased that I had come to conduct the visitation and brought them the above-mentioned Reverend Father Lector for their minister. They had rebuilt for him its very ample and decent convento and residence.

Vargas thanked the old Pecos governor and his natives for "their superior effort." He told them that "in order to live civilly" they must elect and present to him their pueblo officials. He made no secret of his support for the incumbent governor. "Indeed, when they understood my will, they asked me that it be thus, saying that it was their will." At two in the afternoon, the Pecos put forward their slate, returning to the Spanish governor the symbolic staffs of office so that he might present them anew and administer "in His Majesty's name the oath they must swear in legal form by God Our Lord and the sign of the Holy Cross." Sworn in were:

Diego Marcos, governor
Agustín [Sebastián], lieutenant governor
Pedro Pupo and Salvador Tunoque, alcaldes
[Diego] Unfeto, jailer
Pedro Cristóbal Tundia, constable
Antonio Quoac, Pedro Cochze, Diego Ystico, and Agustín
    Guocho, fiscales
Juan Chiuta, head war captain
Pedro Lucero Tuque, Miguel Echo, Juan Omvire, Miguel Himuiro,
    Juan Diego, Diego Stayo, don Lorenzo de Ye, and Agustín
    Tafuno, war captains.

Francisco de Anaya Almazán

According to Vargas, the Pecos then asked him to appoint Sargento mayor Francisco de Anaya Almazán, "a most worthy person," as alcalde mayor and military chief of their pueblo. Before the revolt of 1680, the alcalde mayor of the Tanos had administered Pecos as well. Anaya, in fact, had held the office for a time in the mid-1660s. Now, with the Tanos dispersed and the Galisteo Basin deserted, the governor named an alcalde mayor for Pecos alone, giving him the oath, the writ of title, and the staff of office.

Anaya Named Alcalde Mayor

Described in 1681 as a man of "medium build, protruding eyes, a thick and partly gray beard, and wavy chestnut hair," the veteran don Francisco de Anaya must have been in 1694 at least sixty-one. He had outlived two wives and was wed to a third, Felipa Cedillo Rico de Rojas. With María de Madrid, who must have been a relative if not his fourth wife, he alternated as godparent for dozens of Pecos children in the next nineteen months. Vargas called him "a linguist and old soldier." By all accounts, don Francisco, unlike his pre-revolt predecessors, cooperated with the missionary in every way.

Before Governor Vargas led his retinue back to the Rio Grande to perform similar rites at San Felipe, he "asked them the name of the patron saint of this chapel which is to be transferred to the church they will rebuild and erect anew in the coming year." They told him that they wished to retain the patroness who had been theirs before the deluge of 1680, Nuestra Señora de los Ángeles de la Porciúncula. With that, Vargas concluded the visitation. The mission at Pecos, after a lapse of fourteen years, was reborn.[37]

Zeinos as Pastor and Advocate of the Pecos

The ministry of Fray Diego de Zeinos was a success while it lasted, about one year. In less than three weeks, he could boast a temporary church. Constructed by the Pecos, presumably under the supervision of the friar and Alcalde mayor Anaya, it utilized the massive, still-standing north wall of the convento. It lay atop the leveled mound covering the south wall of the pre-1680 church and measured inside roughly twenty by sixty or seventy feet. The nave paralleled that of its monumental predecessor but the orientation was reversed: the altar was at the east end, the entrance at the west.[38]

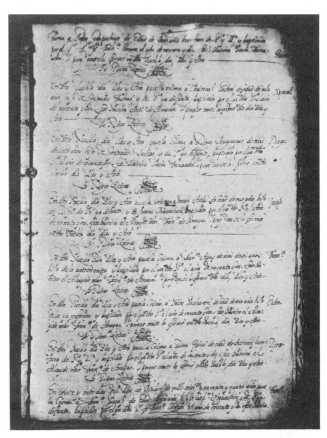

A page from the Pecos book of baptisms, October 26-27, 1694. Among the children baptized simply in 1692, who later received full ceremonies, was eleven-year-old José Astipi, son of the deceased don Juan de Ye (fourth entry from top). Alcalde mayor Anaya stood as godfather.

Between October 11, 1694, and September 7, 1695, Father Zeinos baptized 103 Indians, mostly infants and children. Francisco de Anaya stood as godparent for seventeen of them, María de Madrid for twelve. The new resident missionary also celebrated full solemn baptism with all the prayers and ceremonies for 240 of the 248 persons baptized in the simple form by Father Corvera in 1692, running through as many as twenty-two in one day. So that a complete record might be kept in the Pecos book of baptisms, Zeinos had each of these 240 appear with a godparent, not necessarily the same one as in 1692. Anaya thus became godfather to three children of the deceased don Juan de Ye, and to twenty-three others, while María de Madrid collected forty-three more godchildren.[39]

To ingratiate himself with his new charges, Father Zeinos appeared in Santa Fe with a petition. Because the Pecos had demonstrated their loyalty by warning the Spaniards in 1680 and again during the reconquest, he thought they deserved a reward, "some exemption or privilege." He requested Vargas to confirm the Pecos' loyalty and forward the petition to the viceroy. The governor did so the same day. In Mexico City the viceroy's attorney pointed out that the Pueblos of New Mexico were already exempt from tribute and labor, the usual reward in such cases. That left Governor Vargas free to express to the Pecos his profound thanks in the name of the king, no more no less.[40]

On the first day of November 1694, a new custos arrived in Santa Fe. He was Fray Francisco de Vargas, a Spaniard himself but unrelated and unattracted to the lofty don Diego de Vargas. The two had already clashed, when Fray Francisco

Custos Vargas Asks Questions

Fray Francisco de Vargas, Custodio

had been custos before, over mission property in the El Paso district. Now the friar had something else on his mind.

Someone, perhaps ex-custos San Antonio, had complained to the superiors that Vice-custos Muñoz de Castro had used duress to install Father Zeinos and the other friars in missions where there were no soldiers for their protection. The superiors wanted a full report on the state of these missions. The ever-efficient custos drew up a ten-point questionnaire that went straight to the mark. "First Your Reverence will declare what motivated you to go to the mission and whether you were forced to do so by any prelate."

Fray Diego de Zeinos of Pecos was still secretary of the custody. In mid-December, he reported to Santa Fe to assist the custos with the questionnaire. In his legible, studied hand, Fray Diego penned the original which would be submitted to Mexico City with the replies of the individual missionaries. Then he went back to Pecos to answer the questions himself. The first one posed no problem for him.

To the first point I say that the motivating and even ultimate reason for my having come to this pueblo of Pecos was the one that brought me to this holy and venerable custody, namely, the object of converting souls redeemed with the precious blood of Our Redeemer. No force on the part of any prelate preceded my coming to this pueblo. Rather, with the minds of the missionaries favorably disposed to the least suggestion, they all went gladly to their assignments.

The rest of his answers showed the capable Father Zeinos to have been neither a sorry pessimist nor a visionary romantic, but rather a realist with faith. The Pecos, adults as well as children, were attending catechism, he said, "whenever they are able." With respect to prayer, "I found them so far removed that most did not know how to cross themselves." Very gradual instruction seemed to him the best remedy.

How many of the persons they had baptized had since died? The custos wanted to know. This figure, if any, indicated the success of their ministry, particularly in the case of innocent children. Of all the individuals Zeinos had baptized or annointed with holy oils, nine children and three adults had died, a dozen souls who otherwise would not have known God's grace. He averred that in all but one case, he had been advised immediately when someone was in danger from sickness, a claim few of his successors would make. None of the Pecos had applied to him for marriage, yet on his own initiative he had already united eleven couples who had been living together illicitly.

The Population of Pecos in 1694   There were, according to his records, 736 native residents of Pecos: 186 men, 230 women, and 320 children under the age of twelve or thirteen. Two years earlier, Diego de Vargas had estimated the pueblo's population, based on the number and size of its house blocks, at more than twice that many, or about 1,500. Either Vargas' guess was badly off, or a good many members of the resistance faction had lived up to their threat and not returned. Even if some had stayed away, there were others still living at Pecos who spoke against reconciliation with Spaniards. Before long they and their "pro-Spanish" brothers would be at each other's throats.

The temporary church was described by Zeinos as "a chapel, not large but decent and fitting for celebrating the Holy Sacrifice of the Mass." Asked whether the Pecos provided him with food, he replied that they "do for me what they can to help succor me and supply my needs." He admitted that New Mexico's winters were severe and the country poor. "It is without resource for humans until we get a new shipment." Still, the friars did not accuse the Pueblos of stinginess. Former vice-custos Muñoz, responding to a personal grilling by Custos Vargas, said that even in the Jémez, Tewa, and Tano pueblos, where the natives were experiencing scarcities, they provided their friars with some tortillas at least. "The better supplied pueblos, e.g., Pecos and the Keres pueblos, provided more, but only maize and tortillas."

In the matter of idolatry, Fray Diego had not actually caught the Pecos at it, but he had reason to believe they did engage in it. "I beg the Father of the Heavens to grant me the enlightenment to recognize and remedy it," he prayed. At San Juan, where the natives had been observed using rocks as altars for offerings of "meal, feathers, and other things," their friar had "corrected them."

Trusting not in himself but in the Almighty, the earnest Zeinos expressed hope for the future. The harvest of souls

Jémez altars and altar paintings. Parsons, *Jemez*

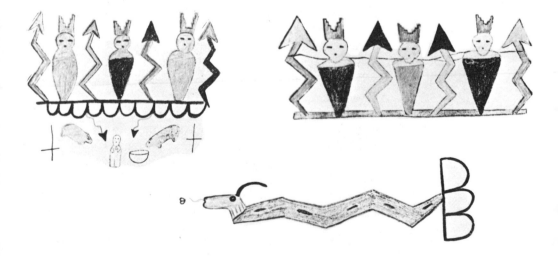

was potentially great, and the Pecos, in his words, "do not present poor prospects." Still, no one said it was going to be easy.

We must always fear future setbacks because of the utter fickleness and inconstancy we have experienced in the Indians. Still, this fear has not been enough (thank God) to turn us away from our first purpose. Indeed we stand ready to die if necessary for that Lord who, blameless, gave his life for ours.[41]

The Unfortunate Accident of Fray Diego de Zeinos

Almost everyone agreed. Fray Diego de Zeinos was an ideal missionary. He gave patient instruction and fervent sermons. He had begun learning the Pecos language. In recognition of his ability, Custos Vargas continued him in office as secretary and notary of the custody. His brothers elected him definitor. The Holy Office of the Inquisition appointed Zeinos its comisario for New Mexico. Then, without warning, his career was ruined.

On September 7, 1695, a Wednesday, a group had gathered around the baptismal font in the temporary Pecos church. Fray Diego was intoning the prayers in Latin and going through the rites of a solemn baptism for a baby girl born to Ana María Pijunguechi and Pedro Juan Ucaevo. He named her in Christ Angelina Rosa. Through his interpreter, probably Felipe, he explained to the godmother, María Somocee, the spiritual relationship and obligations she had just assumed. It was Zeinos' last Pecos baptism.

Next day in one of the rooms of the refurbished convento, Fray Diego picked up an arquebus. Certain that the weapon was unloaded, he ran his hand over it to examine the lock. It fired. A Pecos Indian fell dead, evidently one of the man servants or boys who had access to the convento. The friar was horror-struck.

Whether or not the incident happened just that way, which is what the documents say, it ended Zeinos' ministry to the Pecos. Further testimony disclosed that Alcalde mayor Anaya, who came and went as a familiar member of the convento household, had loaded the arquebus without telling Fray Diego. Why the religious was handling the weapon in the first place no one said. Perhaps with that in mind, Custos Vargas later recalled Zeinos and suspended his authority to say Mass.

The Pecos took the accident in their stride. They neither rose against the friar nor sought revenge. They recognized that it was not his fault. They could see how it grieved him. A group of them set out at once for Santa Fe to inform Governor Vargas what had happened. They also appeared before Vice-custos Juan Daza at Santo Domingo to plead in the friar's behalf. Later, when they learned that Custos Vargas had returned from El Paso, a second delegation made up of Lt. Gov. Agustín Sebastián, Cacique Damián, the alcaldes, and the war captains went up to the villa. Through Alcalde mayor Anaya and interpreter Felipe they appealed to Governor Vargas to intercede with the custos. They begged in the name of Diego Marcos, their governor, who was ill, and all the people of the pueblo that Father Zeinos be allowed to remain at Pecos.

Favorably impressed, Diego de Vargas sent them over to the prelate's quarters so that the Franciscan could see how devoted they were to Father Zeinos. Even though the royal ensign Antonio de Valverde accompanied them with a request from Governor Vargas, Custos Vargas did not give them the assurance they sought. When the royal governor rode out to Pecos on a visitation October 21, the whole pueblo met him with the same plea. "I was," admitted Diego de Vargas, "perplexed." Only the custos could assign a missionary. But just to demonstrate his friendship for them, he agreed to go with them in person to see the prelate.

Diego de Vargas Defends Zeinos

October 27 was the day. Between ten and eleven in the morning they processed across the open plaza to the Franciscans' makeshift "convento"—royal governor, Lt. Gov. Luis Granillo, Secretary of government and war Domingo de la Barreda, Alcalde mayor Anaya, and the Pecos. Custos Vargas saw them coming and met them at the door of his cell. The governor greeted the prelate, told him that the Indians were from Pecos, and requested leave to enter and kiss his hand. The Franciscan consented.

This time when Governor Vargas reiterated the Pecos' petition, Custos Vargas had an answer. Father Zeinos, he explained, had requested permission to travel to Mexico City on Inquisition business, a request the prelate could not deny. In that case, countered Diego de Vargas, it would be well if the Franciscan superior assured the Pecos that Zeinos, on his return, would be reassigned to their pueblo. Governor Vargas then turned to the Pecos and explained that their minister was going to see the Padre Grande to get a license to say Mass again.

To that they responded that one of them would go to Mexico City to bring him back so that he would not stay there. I told them that I would give them a license for not one alone but for two, three, or four to go so that they would see as far as I was concerned that they had achieved all they had asked of me. With that we took our leave of the Very Reverend Father Custos together. For my part I much regretted not being able to console these Indians, for they told me that the women and children were crying to come see me and the Very Reverend Father Custos and the minister and comisario Fray Diego de la Casa Zeinos.

Earlier the same day Governor Vargas had admitted a petition by Father Zeinos in his own behalf. After reviewing the shooting incident, the friar had pointed to the Pecos' remarkable efforts to retain him as their minister, which served, in his opinion, "as an endorsement of my person and proof of my innocence." But he wanted something in writing.

Therefore, looking as I must to the honor of my sacred Order and also to my personal reputation, I petition Your Lordship please to order that I be given a certified affidavit, signed by Your Lordship and countersigned by your secretary of government and war, of all the efforts of these Indians, my parishioners, before Your Lordship. . . . God Our Lord as my witness, I have not intervened or had the slightest part in these vigorous efforts and opportune petitions. Rather these Indians on their own, because they liked me, of their own free will made these most urgent efforts [in my behalf].

The governor was happy to oblige, almost too happy. He lauded Zeinos' ministry at Pecos and stressed the importance of the pueblo, "among the largest with an apparent population of more than eight hundred persons of all ages." He urged that the superiors hasten this missionary's return to his post. Because Pecos, like the other recently revived missions, was

Fray Diego de Zeinos

in effect a new mission after fourteen years of apostasy, it seemed unwise to substitute another missionary for one they liked. At Zeinos' request, the Santa Fe cabildo also addressed to the viceroy, his council, and the religious superiors a warm endorsement in the friar's behalf.

One wonders. This near-canonization of Fray Diego by the civil authorities, the fervent desire of the Pecos to retain his services, and the constant presence with them of Alcalde mayor Francisco de Anaya—it all sounds contrived. One wonders if the governor might not have been using the episode to embarrass the prelate. Whatever, Fray Diego de Zeinos left New Mexico, perhaps in the company of some Pecos. Sadly, "the missionary they liked" never returned.[42]

The Pecos did not like the next one, nor did he like them. He never trusted them. Among Diego de Vargas' original eighteen, Fray Juan Alpuente, definitor and former lecturer in philosophy, had served the reconqueror most often as military chaplain. He had volunteered first for Zía, partly because he wanted to administer the saving sacraments to Indians, partly to get out of Santa Fe "because I am by nature violent and I recognize in my conscience that I only live when I live alone." He had seen Pecos first when he accompanied the unneeded relief expedition of Roque de Madrid. He had been with Vargas at Taos when don Juan de Ye failed to return. Now in mid-November, like it or not, Fray Juan found himself Father Guardian at Pecos.[43]

The Reluctant Ministry of Juan Alpuente

Partly to ease the loss of Father Zeinos and partly to provide for Governor Vargas' pet Pecos, Custos Vargas assigned a compañero, or assistant, to Father Alpuente. He was Fray Domingo de Jesús María, one of eight members of the new Franciscan missionary college at Querétaro who had answered the Father Commissary General's call to join in the reconquest. Temporarily under obedience to the custos in New Mexico, these eight were not incorporated in the province of the Holy Gospel but retained their affiliation with the college, which was of no consequence to the Pecos, who did not like Fray Domingo either.[44]

To make matters worse, the winter of 1695-1696 was another starving time in New Mexico. A plague of worms and a drought during the previous growing season had ravaged the harvest, particularly among the struggling colonists. Again the northern Pueblos were restive. The relocated Tanos, uprooted once more when Governor Vargas founded the villa of Santa Cruz de la Cañada, twenty-two miles north of Santa Fe, had taken to the hills. Rumors, threats, and fears of new revolts were common. But because such rumors tarnished his image as reconqueror, Diego de Vargas was inclined to minimize them.

Nevertheless, in December 1695, he got up out of his sickbed and summoned the Pueblo leaders, "his children." He told them that he had had reports of agitators stirring up their people. He reminded them of the war they had just suffered. Surely they preferred the peace of his administration. As usual in don Diego's journal, they went away "pleased."

New Rumors
of Revolt

Not everyone minimized the threat. Lieutenant Governor Granillo thought a note from Father José Díez of Tesuque urgent enough to deliver it to the governor on Sunday, February 26, at midnight. It warned that the Pecos were about to rebel.

Next day, the pueblo governor of Tesuque arrived to verify the report. He had heard it from a Tewa of Nambé who had just come from Pecos. This lone Indian, fearing that the Pecos would kill him if he did not go along with them, agreed that the Tewas would also rise. The leader of the plot was said to be don Lorenzo de Ye, son of ex-governor Juan de Ye. First they would murder Father Alpuente and the Spaniards, then go off to live at "La Piedra Blanca where they have an old pueblo." [45]

Anti-Spanish sentiment at Pecos, given new life by the elimination of don Juan de Ye, by the shooting incident, the removal of Zeinos, or the indiscretion of Alpuente, may have coalesced around don Lorenzo de Ye, whose father had died futilely serving the Spaniards. If the leaders of the resistance faction really were sending out invitations to the Tewas—consistent enemies of the Pecos—to join them in revolt, they must have been desperate.

Friars Ask for Guards

From where the friars knelt, all the signs pointed to a repeat of 1680, a general rising of all the Pueblos. Early in March, a concerned Custos Vargas convened the definitory. They would petition the governor for mission guards. Failing that, each would face a dilemma, whether to remain in the relative safety of the villa or return defenseless to his mission and probable death.

Diego de Vargas admitted their petition, but shifted the burden to them. He would do what he could, given the dearth of his forces, when each missionary specified for him how many men he needed. The custos responded at once. Each minister must state how large a guard he considered adequate, or if he could do without.

Fray Juan Alpuente of Pecos answered first. As a definitor, he was already in Santa Fe, where he had been spending most of his time anyway. He took the rumors of an impending revolt as fact. Accordingly,

I answer and in conscience request six soldiers (to protect the sacred vessels and my person) under the following conditions: First, that they are armed with weapons, powder, and shot. Second, that they are God-fearing so as not to cause unrest and scandal in the pueblo. For if I tell and preach to the Indians to give up their concubines and live as God commands, they might see the soldiers having intercourse with Indian women and say to my face,

Potshuno, a Tewa warrior of Nambé, photographed by John K. Hillers, 1879.
B. M. Thomas Collection, Museum of New Mexico

"Why do you scold us, Father, for the Spaniards do the same?"
And the third is that the maintenance of these soldiers be charged
to their salaries because the convento cannot support them.

Fray Juan Alpuente, Difinidor

Fray José Díez of Tesuque, whose mission lay no more
than three leagues north of Santa Fe, wanted twelve well-
armed soldiers. He had already reported the Pecos plot. A
Tano had told Roque de Madrid that the uprising was set for
the next full moon, only eight days off. Already the Tanos had
hauled provisions up into the mountains and had built horse
traps at the ascents. Painfully aware of the gathering storm,
the friars continued their ministry. "The minister of Pecos
knows that the Indians of his pueblo are carrying their provisions to La Peña Blanca, yet he persists in ministering to
them."

Díez was torn. How could he say Mass in conscience
before apostates who had already consented to the uprising?
He knew they had by what Pecos Alcalde mayor Francisco de
Anaya had said to Governor Vargas in front of four priests.
Now it was Tewas inciting Pecos. Two Indians of Tesuque had
gone to Pecos with an appeal: "Already the time is short.
Only you are not with us. The Spaniards are dropping from
hunger. Only twenty are strong." Seized, these two were
whipped at Anaya's orders. If Díez excommunicated them to
keep them out of church, they would use it as grounds for
rebellion. Yet he could not bear to celebrate the Mass before
them.[46]

When all the alarms were in, the friars had made a point.
But so had Diego de Vargas. Simple arithmetic exposed the
folly of their requests. They had asked for ninety men or more.
The governor had only one hundred. Of those, sixty were
needed for the two detachments that alternated guarding the
horses, ten more guarded the entrance to Santa Fe, and
twenty-six had to escort the pack train of provisions and livestock coming from El Paso. That left four. As a compromise
don Diego agreed to provide at his own expense six temporary
four-man mission guards: at San Juan, Nambé, Picurís, Taos,
and the two Jémez pueblos.

As for Pecos, the six-man detachment requested by Father Alpuente was not only unnecessary, it was an insult. Rather than assign soldiers and cause the Pecos to doubt the royal governor's confidence in them, he frankly preferred that Father Alpuente not return to his mission. What did the Pecos have to do to prove their loyalty? Don Diego suggested that Alpuente consider the kindness these Indians had shown his predecessor. Instead of committing some outrage as a result of the accidental shooting, as one might have expected from "barbarous people," they grieved with the Padre. If Fray Juan Alpuente had any cause for alarm, it could only be the pueblo's frontier location, not the Pecos themselves.[47]

Obviously the governor did not believe them. Custos Vargas told the friars assembled in Santa Fe that he could not force them back to their missions alone, nor could he prevent them from going. After discussing the pros and cons of martyrdom, he asked each missionary for his decision. Armed with these, he replied to the governor's halfway proposal, listing one by one the friars' verdicts.

Alpuente refused to return to Pecos. His assistant, who had remained at the pueblo, told of harassment and a death threat. The Pecos had ridiculed Fray Domingo de Jesús María as he preached with a crucifix in his hands. Frightened, he had carried the sacred vessels to his cell for safe keeping. At midnight on March 21, Indians had entered the cell and taken the vessels, as well as the keys to the entire convento and church. Two Pecos came to him and told him to run, begging him not to expose them. His fear grew when he noticed Faraón Apaches mixing with the Pecos. One ranchería had camped at the pueblo and another at the river. Then "a heathen, crying, told him by signs that they were going to cut off his head." That was too much. "He does not dare administer this pueblo or any other."

The Pecos Abuse Fray Domingo

The custos begged the governor to send soldiers to remove the religious objects and the livestock from the missions. Once again the Pueblos were bent on freedom to practice their idolatry. The upheaval was imminent.[48]

Diego de Vargas gave ground. The presence of Faraón Apaches at Pecos permitted him to accede to Father Alpuente's demand for six soldiers without losing face. After three weeks, he would withdraw four of them leaving two "to guard the friar's person and to accompany him at night whenever he is called to administer the holy sacraments." As for Santa Clara, San Juan, and San Cristóbal, he had no more troops to send. If the missionaries were scared, they would simply have to evacuate.[49]

JUNE 4, 1696

On the day of the second Pueblo revolt, June 4, 1696, Diego de Vargas summons a hundred Pecos warriors to Santa Fe (SANM, II, no. 60a).

A few days later as he forwarded to the viceroy the friars' representations, Diego de Vargas all but called them cowards. Their "fears and timidity" had got a hold on them. "It has been for me, I assure Your Excellency, one continuous bout." Their woes, he added, "were enough to oppress the most care-free spirit." Ten weeks later, five of the cowards were dead.[50]

Fray Domingo de Jesús María got out just in time. He, Fray José Díez, and Fray Jerónimo Prieto were recalled to the Querétaro college, where some of the religious from Mallorca

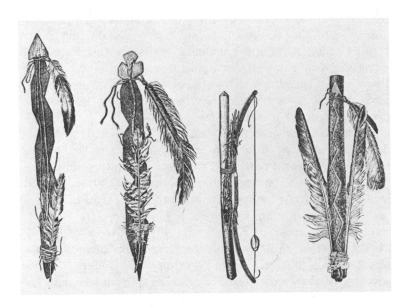

Jémez prayer sticks.
Parsons, *Jemez*

had walked out after a dispute with their brethren from the Spanish mainland. Custos Vargas hated to lose the three, but there was nothing to do but comply with the special order. Fray Domingo departed May 15, the other two May 16.[51]

The blow the "fearful Franciscans" expected, but Diego de Vargas did not, fell Monday, June 4. In the Jémez, Tewa, Tano, and Tiwa pueblos of the north, it was August 10, 1680, all over. The vengeful Pueblos ran amok. Spanish settlers, twenty-one in all, were denuded and put to death and their bodies strewn about. At San Ildefonso, rebels fired the church and convento with Fathers Francisco Corvera and Antonio Moreno inside. Near the convento of twice-relocated San Cristóbal, they tossed the bodies of two more Franciscans, partially stripped, faceup grotesquely, in the form of a cross. A San Diego de los Jémez, the Indians called Father Francisco de Jesús María Casañas to confess a dying woman. It was a ruse. Clubbing him dead, they threw the body at the church door where wild beasts later consumed much of it. Thus Casañas, one of the Queretarans who stayed, gained a place in his Order's martyrology as protomartyr of the Propaganda Fide colleges in North America.[52]

Not so widespread or so costly in terms of body count as 1680, still, this second revolt would take Diego de Vargas six months to suppress, six trying months of skirmishes, of destruction and theft of crops and animals, of executions and offers of pardon, of Pueblos snifting for survival. The Keres of

Revolt of 1696

San Felipe, Santa Ana, and Zía stuck with the Spaniards, as did most of the Tewas of Tesuque. Neither did the Pecos revolt. Again, as in the reconquest, Pecos auxiliaries served alongside the Spaniards on almost every campaign. Yet the Pecos were divided, worse than usual. For the first time, Spaniards recorded the violence of factionalism at Pecos. The pueblo was about to split wide open.

The first excited reports said the Pecos had risen. Confident that they were wrong, Governor Vargas dispatched orders to Alcalde mayor Francisco de Anaya to evacuate the missionaries and come on the double to Santa Fe with one hundred loyal Pecos warriors. Anaya arrived during the night of June 5 with the two remaining Queretarans, Fray José García Marín, who had just replaced Father Alpuente at Pecos, and Fray Miguel de Trizio of San Juan de los Jémez, who, lucky for him, was at Pecos nursing García. Next day, don Felipe Chistoe, governor of the Pecos, appeared with his war captains and the one hundred auxiliaries, some mounted and some afoot. Vargas had been right.[53]

To verify the carnage in the nearest Tewa pueblos, the governor made a quick two-day inspection taking his aides, twenty soldiers and armed civilians, Alcalde mayor Anaya, don Felipe, and the one hundred Pecos. At Nambé the hard-bitten Fray Juan Alpuente, again chaplain, officiated at the burial of victims. To bury the dead friars at San Ildefonso pueblo, Vargas called for the Pecos Indians and the soldiers "to cover them with a wall and adobes the rebels had torn down from the church itself for the reason that they could not be moved because they were whole. The fire had not burned them, but rather the smoke and heat suffocated them because the enemy Indians had cut off the ventilation."[54]

A Terrible Plot at Pecos   Back in Santa Fe, the cooperative Felipe Chistoe of Pecos, who was not among the nineteen pueblo officials installed by Vargas twenty months before, came to don Diego in confidence with a dreadful scheme. He wanted the royal governor's sanction.

The faction at Pecos headed by Diego Umbiro, "old and principal personage of this nation," had been cooperating with the rebels "by treaty and council." Cachina, a war captain with a large following, and two other prominent Pecos were also among the leaders plotting the Spaniards' overthrow. What don Felipe wanted was license to execute them.

He asked if I would issue an order for him to hang them. He feared that they would cause the people of the pueblo to rise and obey them because the majority were of their following and feared them greatly. I answered him, "Yes, if you yourself know that you have trustworthy Indians to execute their hanging, you can call them to your house at night for the purpose of discussing the people of the risen pueblos. In this way you can succeed for sure in taking their lives." This seemed fine to him and he said he would do it.

Two days later, Monday, June 11, the arrival at Pecos of two rebel agitators played into don Felipe's hands. One of them, a Jémez called Luis Cunixu, flaunted "an eight-sided gilded brass reliquary containing various relics, among them a piece of wood of the cross and an ecce homo [literary, 'behold the man,' an image of Christ, scourged, crowned with thorns, wearing a red robe, and holding a reed in His bound hands]." It had belonged to Father Casañas, who was now dead, the Indian bragged. The other rebel, Diego Xenome of Nambé, had allegedly spent the entire winter traveling from pueblo to pueblo, even to Zuñi and Hopi and the Apaches, spreading the gospel of revolt. Don Felipe knew they had come to enlist the Pecos. He pretended to go along with them.

As governor of the pueblo, he bade the rebel emissaries, their principal Pecos sympathizers, and enough trusted members of his own faction to enter a kiva. What he was about to do in the close, semi-darkness of the kiva that day would have repercussions that not even he could anticipate.

He asked the principales of the opposing faction what they thought of the uprising. Diego Umbiro spoke for them. To kill the Spaniards, Umbiro said, was good. Spaniards were, after all, "of different flesh." The people who had revolted were Indians like they, the Pecos. "And the rest of his following, Cachina and the others, answered in like manner."

Then don Felipe made his move. Getting up from where he sat and brandishing his pueblo governor's staff, he announced with gravity, "Here we are the king's men!" With that, his followers seized the five principal men of the opposition. They hanged Diego Umbiro, Cachina, and two others. The fifth, a youth "who was gaining a following" among the Pecos, got away. The deed was done.

Next day don Felipe turned Luis Cunixu and Diego Xenome over to Governor Vargas. They told their stories and were shot.[55]

Despite this terrible show of "loyalty," Father Custos Vargas did not trust the Pecos. What if they had given warnings in 1680 and spared Father Velasco: they would not deny

Executions in a Pecos Kiva

Restored kiva, Pecos National Monument.
National Park Service photo by Fred E. Mang, Jr.

the murders of Fray Juan de la Pedrosa and a Spanish family. They just kept silent.

And if one asks them about the church they had then, the vestments, etc., they give as an excuse that the Tewas burned them. From which it follows logically that they either did take part in that outrage or had not the courage to defend their church and vestments. Therefore if at present they are given a minister and they kill him (the more likely because of their friendship with the Faraón Apaches, with whom they could rise and withdraw to La Piedra Blanca, and because it is notorious that said pueblo is divided into factions from the declarations that the governor of the pueblo has made and his punishment of their leaders), they will give the excuse they gave for the church and vestments.

Why risk it? the prelate asked the governor. This time Diego de Vargas heeded the alarmist friar and provided the guard, mules, and muleteers to remove everything of value from Pecos. He sent Alcalde mayor Anaya to raise eighty Pecos warriors for the next campaign and "to tell these Indians in advance that the provisions and sheep, as well as the religious objects, were being removed only to secure them from attack by rebels or by Apaches allied with the rebels." Father Antonio de Acevedo, guardian of the Santa Fe convento, rode down to Pecos with the pack train on Saturday, July 7, said Mass at the pueblo early next day, and was back in the villa with provisions, sheep, and religious gear about two o'clock Sunday afternoon.[56]

Church Possessions Removed

Ten days later while Anaya was at Pecos preparing the auxiliaries Governor Vargas had requested, a Pecos lad ran up to him saying that a crowd of rebels was in the mountains only two leagues away. They were Taos, Picurís, and Tanos coming to assault Pecos. They were afoot. Anaya wrote Vargas immediately asking for powder and ball. Vargas sent it. He thought the rebels might steal the Pecos horses and ride on Santa Fe. He postponed his campaign. But the threat vanished. The rebels turned back for Taos. Anaya saw their tracks and the signs they had drawn in the dirt on the trail, which his Pecos interpreted for him.

The cross was meant to explain that the ones who had made the tracks were Christians like them, and not Apache Indians who were not Christians, and that whoever followed the Spaniards as Christians they would kill. That is what they say the war club means and the line [across the trail], which the Pecos did not want to cross over.[57]

Whatever his motives—and they may have sprung from a purely Pecos grudge or from personal ambition akin to that of

El Popé—don Felipe Chistoe pursued his purge of the opposition with deadly vengeance. When he learned that Pock Face (*Caripicado*), the youth who escaped the hanging, had ventured back into the pueblo under the cover of night, he loaded his arquebus and went looking for him. When he caught sight of him at a distance he fired. The ball entered the temple. Pock Face fell dead.

To prove that he had killed the rebel, don Felipe took his retinue and went up to Santa Fe with trophies. Governor Vargas entered the Indian's arrival in his journal for August 30, 1696.

So that it might be of record with me, he presented me the head, hand, and foot. All the citizens of the villa saw them, marveling at the loyalty of this Indian. I thanked him and gave him a gift, as well as the others.[58]

Rebuilding   The provisions packed up on muleback from Pecos in July had saved the day for Custos Vargas and the nine refugee friars crowded into the convento at Santa Fe. By August, the prelate had quit griping at Diego de Vargas and gone back to his mission at Santa Ana. The governor, passing through that pueblo on his return from a stand-off before the great rock of Ácoma, noted the progress Father Vargas had made on his building project. He had finished a convento and had amassed the materials, the adobes and timbers, for construction of the church. "He had brought the carpenters of the pueblo of Pecos to hasten working these timbers and likewise the doors, which he specified and the carpenters took the measurement in order to make." Again the carpenters of Pecos were in demand, as they would be throughout the eighteenth century—carpenters and native auxiliaries.

Custos Francisco de Vargas, the friar who had expressed such vehement distrust of the Pecos two months before, in September went to their pueblo himself to supervise a remodeling of the temporary church that Zeinos had built. Diego de Vargas, meanwhile, campaigned against the Taos with his usual contingent of Pecos. Late in October, they chased down some of the Picurís who were fleeing eastward with Apaches across the mountains. Fatigued and half-frozen, the royal governor and his advance party made it back to Pecos on November 7 after eleven days of driving snow and sleet.

The prelate and the governor embraced. There were no harsh words at this meeting. Don Diego was made welcome over chocolate in the convento. The priest explained that he had celebrated the feasts of All Saints and All Souls, November

1 and 2, in the enlarged Pecos church. Governor Vargas of course complimented him on the splendid job he had done.

I noted that by his order and with the plan he gave those Indians and the assistance rendered by their alcalde mayor, he had added to the body of the church, giving it more height for the clerestory. Likewise he had built a sanctuary of two steps for the main altar; he had up the walls for the sacristy; and he had enclosed the patio with a wall with its door for entrance from said convento.[59]

The Pueblo revolt of 1696 had backfired. By forcing a decision in Mexico City, it had strengthened the Spaniards' hand. New Mexico must never be evacuated again, whatever the cost. Another such humiliation of Spanish arms and the whole northern frontier might rise. Therefore, the precarious colony must be reinforced with more settlers, provisions, tools, and livestock. The revolt of 1696 not only assured the presence of many more Spaniards in New Mexico, but also by its failure to attract all the Pueblos, it crushed forever the prospect of another 1680.

Diego de Vargas Replaced

Through crisis after crisis Diego de Vargas had ruled with the iron fist that circumstances seemed to demand. He had effectively muzzled criticism and had broadcast his noble deeds as far as his name would carry them. When the crown failed to reward him with a promotion, he bid for a second five-year term as governor and captain general of New Mexico. But he was too late. His replacement, don Pedro Rodríguez Cubero, arrived on July 2, 1697, thereby unleashing a local struggle for power and preferment that saw the reconqueror crudely vilified and held in Santa Fe for nearly three years.[60]

The Franciscans, meanwhile, played the local factions to whatever advantage they could and gradually restored their missions. Straight-away Rodríguez had a proper convento built for them in Santa Fe. The viceroy approved the request of Custos Vargas raising the number of friars from thirteen priests and one lay brother, the low ebb, to twenty priests and a lay brother. Missions like Pecos that had slipped to the status of visitas were again staffed with resident missionaries. Other friars, fired by the old zeal, braved considerable hostility to entrench themselves again on the rock of Ácoma and at Zuñi. At Laguna, they founded an entirely new mission for a congregation of Pueblo displaced persons. They even ventured as far as the Hopi pueblos, but there they failed. When the people of Awátovi showed themselves ready to receive the Spaniards back, the others, evidently motivated by an old intratribal grudge, annihilated that pueblo.

LA Villa de Santa Feé, Cabeçera de las Provincias de la Nueva Mexico, informa à V. S². en el pleito que figue contra Don DIEGO DE VARGAS, ZAPATA, Y LVJAN, Governador que fue de aquel Reyno, y Provincias, fobre diferentes exceffos que el fufo dicho, fus Miniftros, y Criados executaron en el tiempo de fu govierno, cantidades que percibió para fu manutencion, y no convirtió en el fin â que fe deftinaron, que deve reftituir á fu Mageftad, é interefados, y fobre que no buelva à governar dicho Reyno; proponiendo fu informe en cinco puntos, que fe expreffaràn.

A   Excm

Review of the lawsuit brought by the municipal council of Santa Fe against Diego de Vargas, printed in México, 1703. Wagner, *Spanish Southwest*, II

At Pecos, a parade of at least half a dozen friars administered the mission between 1697 and 1700. From the bunching of their entries in the book of baptisms, it would appear that they spent a goodly portion of their time in the relative security of Santa Fe, venturing out to Pecos only when the occasion or the spirit moved them, a practice observed, for better or for worse, during much of the eighteenth century.

When Fray Juan Álvarez, the new custos, made his visitation of Pecos on November 5, 1697, he found everything in order, almost. He told Fray Alonso Jiménez de Cisneros, who had been in charge since March, to sign the account book in receipt of the mission's movable assets. He reminded the missionary that "with regard to these and all other things the maximum growth of the missions is a religious and Christian obligation, both in the realm of the spiritual and in the other." [61]

Almost independent of the daily round observed in church and convento, a grim struggle gripped the pueblo only a few hundred feet away. The memory of don Felipe Chistoe's executions in the summer of 1696 had set Pecos against Pecos. The families and clans of Diego Umbiro, of Cachina, and of Pock Face did not forget.

The Pecos as Their Own Worst Enemies

Toward the end of the year 1700, the enemies of don Felipe tried to incite the entire pueblo to rise up and kill him. Failing that, they made known their hatred in other ways, openly committing acts of grave disrespect toward him, even in the presence of their missionary and the alcalde mayor. Fearing further violence, the alcalde mayor notified Governor Rodríguez Cubero. The governor had the ringleaders arrested and hauled up to the Santa Fe jail. But they soon broke out and fled to the Jicarilla Apaches. The struggle continued at Pecos.

On at least five different occasions, the two factions stood at the brink of civil war. Each time don Felipe prevailed. Fearing ruin if the final rupture came, the leaders of the opposing faction petitioned Governor Rodríguez Cubero to let them move to the deserted Tewa pueblo of Pojoaque. For some reason, he must have denied their petition, for in 1707 Pojoaque was resettled by "Tewas." Like don Lorenzo de Ye,

Pedro Rodríguez Cubero

the principal opponents of Felipe Chistoe seemed simply to disappear. Some may have taken up with Apaches or gone with their families to live in other pueblos. Still, their removal cannot have healed so deep a rift. [62]

Don Felipe endured. In the early spring of 1702, he headed a Pecos delegation summoned to Santa Fe by Governor Rodríguez Cubero. The Tewas and Taos were reported plotting revolt again in league with Apaches. The Pecos governor, who was described as about forty years old, gave his testimony in Spanish and interpreted for the others but could not sign. He assured the royal governor that the Pecos were quiet and peaceful. No pueblo had invited them to rebel. They had learned from some "Apaches de la Trementina," which means in Spanish the Turpentine Apaches, that the Tewas and Taos wanted Trementinas and Jicarillas to help them kill the Spaniards. The Apaches had refused because the Spaniards were the source of "what they needed, such as horses, knives, hoes, and other goods." [63]

The Death of Diego de Vargas

Felipe Chistoe was there in 1704 when Diego de Vargas died. Vargas, who finally got away from Rodríguez Cubero, had vindicated himself and returned to New Mexico as the Marqués de la Nava de Barcinas for a second term as governor. Still the nobleman on horseback, the sixty-year-old Vargas proclaimed a campaign against the Faraón and Siete Ríos Apaches. Leading his troops through the Río Abajo, the reconqueror fell ill. They carried him back as far as Bernalillo. There on April 8, he died.

Don Felipe, governor of the Pecos, had headed the list of Pueblo auxiliaries on Vargas's last campaign. He had brought Pecos war captains Miguel, Diego, Pedro, and Agustín and forty-two fighting men, many more than had come from any of the other pueblos.. By his actions in the revolt of 1696, Felipe had firmly committed the Pecos to an alliance with the Spaniards. It was an alliance that long outlived him, one that lasted as long as there were Pecos able to fight. [64]

Don Diego de Vargas Zapata Luján Ponce de León

The fatal rift at Pecos, betrayed only vaguely in the years before, broke wide open under the stress of revolt and reconquest. Pecos turned on Pecos. None would forget the executions of 1696. For whatever reasons, some had committed themselves to the Spaniards' presence—at a later date they would have been styled progressives—while others—the conservatives—resisted it just as grimly.

Rent from within, shaken by don Felipe's purge, the fortress at the gateway between pueblos and plains stood less firm before the Comanches and the epidemics to come.

chapter VII

pecos and the friars
1704-1794

Inasmuch as I have had word that at the pueblo of Pecos a partially subterranean room in the form of a kiva or *coi* [a kiva within a house block] has been built apart from the pueblo under the pretext of the women getting together to spin; inasmuch as its door should open on the street, and the king our lord (God save him) has ordered all his ministers to observe with utmost diligence that such rooms are not built in the pueblos because of the great superstitious and idolatrous abuses that are committed, as is of record; and inasmuch as there are in addition to this one others in said pueblo, I order the alcalde mayor of that district to go immediately and ascertain if it is true. If it is, he will make them destroy and demolish it immediately.

> Gov. Juan Ignacio Flores Mogollón, Santa Fe,
> January 20, 1714

They use kivas, of which some pueblos have more, others less. There are sometimes nine in one pueblo, as at Pecos, and one in others, as at Nambé. Some of them are underground, and others are above ground with walls like a little house, and of them all, some are round while others are rectangular. . . . These kivas are the chapter, or council, rooms, and the Indians meet in them, sometimes to discuss matters of their government for the coming year, their planting, arrangements for work to be done, or to elect new community officials, or to rehearse their dances, or sometimes for other things.

> Fray Francisco Atanasio Domínguez, 1777

Viceroy Francisco Fernández
de la Cueva Enríquez, Duque
de Alburquerque, 1702-1711,
and signature.
Rivera Cambas,
Los gobernantes, 1

If Fray Alonso de Posada had been resurrected in eighteenth-century New Mexico, he would hardly have recognized the place. Not that the Jornada del Muerto or the Sierra de Sandía looked any different; not that the mainly agricultural subsistence-level economy had changed, or the pattern of trade and hostilities with surrounding nomads, or the drought, disease, and isolation, but rather, the colony's very reason for being. The Pueblo revolts and the reconquest by Diego de Vargas—set in the larger context of an increasingly secular world—had thrust up a watershed. The blood of the martyrs flowed back to the age of spiritual conquest, the age of Fray Juan de Padilla and Fray Alonso de Benavides, while the tide of the future ran on toward the mundane, toward colonial rivalry, solicitation of sex in the confessional, and even constitutions. Defense had replaced evangelism.

The 18th-Century
Revolution
in New Mexico

Friars no longer dictated the affairs of the colony. The primary concerns of the Spanish Bourbon kings and their colonial bureaucracy were defense and revenue, not missions. Where missionaries held or strengthened imperial frontiers, as they did in New Mexico, they continued to receive compensation from the crown. Still, the mission payroll declined in proportion to that of the military. In 1763, thirty-four Franciscan priests received an annual *sínodo,* or royal allowance, of 330 pesos each, and one lay brother, 230, for a total of 11,450 pesos—as compared to 32,065 pesos for the Santa Fe garrison. The salaried presidial, too often ill-equipped, poorly trained, and abused by his officers, had replaced the soldier-encomendero. In New Mexico, the formal encomienda system did not survive 1680.[1]

No longer did Franciscans control the economic lifeline of the colony. The government-subsidized mission supply service that operated for much of the seventeeth century was not restaged in the eighteenth. Instead, like everyone else, the friars made their own arrangements for freighting. The missions' combined wealth, using the word loosely, fell in proportion to that of the steadily expanding Hispanic community. Few pre-revolt families returned. The settlers who came with Vargas and those who came later wrought, in effect, "a new and distinct colonization." By 1799, a census, including the El Paso district, showed 23,648 of them—and only 10,557 Indians.[2]

Although friars continued as the only priests to the vast majority of New Mexicans, they saw their monopoly of the local church seriously undermined in the eighteenth century. Three bishops of Durango actually appeared in the colony on visitations—Benito Crespo in 1730, Martín de Elizacoechea in 1737, and Pedro Tamarón in 1760. Crespo appointed New Mexico-born don Santiago Roybal, whom he had previously ordained at Durango, as his vicar and ecclesiastical judge in Santa Fe, an opening wedge for the secular clergy.

A Franciscan still served as agent of the Inquisition, but his authority was only a shadow of what it had been. Compromised by the "flexible orthodoxy" of reforming Bourbons, the Holy Office now too often spent its energy hairsplitting or protecting its own privileged status. As guardian of traditional Hispanic values against the blasphemy of the Enlightenment, it had little business on an illiterate frontier. Unless the governor of New Mexico happened to profess French philosophy, Protestantism, or Freemasonry, unless he had two wives or was grossly immoral, he ran little risk of accusation, arrest, or trial by the Inquisition, even when he trod on the friars' toes. At times, in fact, the tables were turned. Denunciation of the missionaries themselves for solicitation or worse became a weapon of the laity.[3]

Most of the bluerobes ministered faithfully to their motley flocks of Indians and Hispanos, even under the most trying conditions. Some were sorely perplexed by the conflict inherent in being both missionary and parish priest, striving to observe with the right hand the Rule of St. Francis, while accepting with the left, fees for services rendered. Some broke under the strain. A few were scoundrels. Overall, it would seem, the quality of the clergy did decline in eighteenth-century New Mexico. Within the Order, missionary momentum shifted from the provinces to the newly formed missionary colleges whose gray-robed friars answered the call to Coahuila-Texas, the Californias, and Sonora-Arizona. Nothing wounded the

Francisco Cuervo y Valdés

dedicated, beleaguered New Mexico missioner more than the gaping disparity between the pious expectations of the seventeenth century and the scabby reality of the eighteenth.

Diego de Vargas, heroic reconqueror and strutting peacock, was dead. The viceroy, then the Duke of Alburquerque, hastily appointed a governor ad interim, one don Francisco Cuervo y Valdés, knight of the Order of Santiago, who entered Santa Fe in March 1705. By the end of that year, Cuervo had recruited enough settlers to found a new villa in the Bosque Grande de doña Luisa, the future Albuquerque. He had arranged for the repeopling of Galisteo with some of the dispersed Tanos. He had waged war on Navajos and Apaches, and he had presented to don Felipe Chistoe of Pecos and to other loyal Pueblo leaders "suits of fine woolen Mexican cloth like that used by the Spaniards" along with "white cloth for shirts, as well as hats, stockings, and shoes." The rest of the time, don Francisco spent trying to convert his interim appointment to a regular one.

The Pueblo Indians considered Cuervo a savior, or so he tried to convince the crown. At a concourse of their leaders who came together in Santa Fe in January 1706, these natives, on their own volition says the document, begged through their protector general, Alfonso Rael de Aguilar, that "don Francisco Cuervo y Valdés be continued and maintained in this administration for such time as is His Majesty's will, so that they might enjoy not only the blessings of peace but might also make progress in those things which they hoped to achieve

The Administration of Cuervo y Valdés

through his Catholic and successful programs, of which they were very certain because of what they had already experienced of his prompt and sure actions." Representing the Pecos, as usual, was the Spanish-speaking don Felipe Chistoe.[4]

Along with the Pueblo leaders' plea that he be retained in office, Cuervo sent to the viceroy a supplication by Custos Juan Álvarez. The missions of New Mexico desperately needed vestments, chalices, and bells. They needed reinforcements, another thirteen friars in addition to the twenty-one already granted. Payment of their travel expenses had fallen three years behind. They lacked even wine and candles for Mass. In some missions, according to the prelate, "the chasuble is of one color, the stole of another, and the maniple of still another; and, they are without bells with which to call the people to catechism." To document his statement Father Álvarez supplied a mission-by-mission account of the custody.

> At the pueblo of the Pecos Indians, ten [others said seven or eight] leagues distant from the villa of Santa Fe, is Father Preacher fray José de Arranegui. The road which is rough and mountainous is closed by snows and continually [endangered] by the enemy Apaches. This mission has no bell. It has a set of the vestments that His Majesty gave in 1698, with a chalice. It has no chrismatories, except some glass vials, one broken. There are in this pueblo about a thousand Christian Indians, children and adults. This mission needs two ministers, both because of the many people and because of the closing of the road and the continual presence of the enemy. They are beginning to build the church. This mission is called Nuestra Señora de Porciúncula de los Pecos.[5]

Fray José de Arranegui

A Basque from the salty coastal villa of Lequeitio, half way between Bilbao and San Sebastián, Fray José de Arranegui had professed at the Mexican Convento Grande on April 20, 1695, and had already begun his ministry in New Mexico by the year 1700. Pecos, where he baptized, married, and buried between August of 1700 and August of 1708, seems to have been his first and perhaps his only missionary assignment. How often he actually resided at the pueblo is hard to tell, but probably not often. For much of the time he served as notary and minister of Santa Fe as well. As secretary, he cosigned Custos Álvarez' glum report of January 1706. [6]

Despite their inclination to look on Pecos as a visita of Santa Fe, the Franciscans did superintend the construction of a proper new church at the waning pueblo. Curiously, less is known about the building of this one than about either Zeinos' temporary reconquest chapel or the great pre-Revolt monument of Andrés Juárez. Custos Álvarez said about Pecos, "They are beginning to build the church." But he said the same thing about fifteen other pueblos, including Ácoma where the massive, seventeenth-century structure had survived 1680 almost intact. Perhaps by sometime in 1705, Arranegui had made a start.

New Church at Pecos

An equally elusive statement, by the hyperobservant Father Visitor fray Francisco Atanasio Domínguez in 1776, suggests 1716-1717 as the completion date. After counting the roof beams, "well wrought and corbeled" by Pecos carpenters, thirty-eight over the nave, twenty over the transept, and ten over the sanctuary, Domínguez noted a brief Latin inscription "on the one facing the nave: *Frater Carolus*. The inference is," he continued, "that a friar of this name was the one who built the church, but it is impossible to identify him since the individual is not identified by his surname." [7]

Fray Carlos José Delgado

The only friar named Carolus, or Carlos, who ministered at Pecos, or for that matter anywhere in the custody up to 1776, was an eighteenth-century Andrés Juárez named Carlos José Delgado. Described later as an "apostolic Spaniard," Delgado had been recruited from the province of Andalucía for the missionary college of Querétaro, had transferred to the province of the Holy Gospel, and in 1710 had arrived in New Mexico where he was to labor for forty years.

The Apostolic
Fray Carlos

By August 4, 1716, Fray Carlos, "ministro presidente" at Pecos, was bent over a desk in the convento decorating the title page of a new book for *patentes,* the official letters of exhortation and instruction from Franciscan superiors, which were regularly copied into such books at all the Order's houses. Although Delgado's baptismal and burial entries, which might have mentioned a "new church," are missing, his marriage entries survive, and they are distinctive. He wrote in

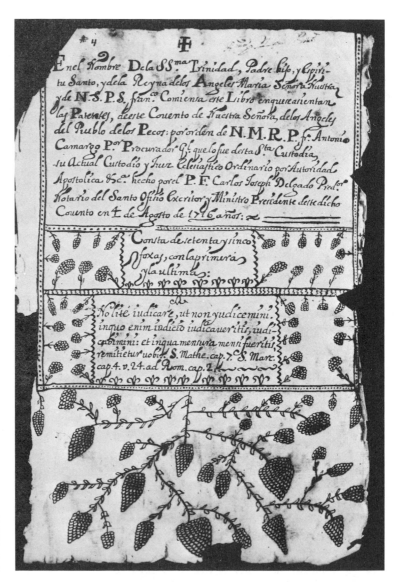

The artistic Father Delgado's title page of the Pecos book of patentes, August 4, 1716 (AASF).

a heavy, legible hand, and he filled the margins with garlands of curious, snowball-like flowers. Chronologically, the entries are bunched, seven in December-January 1716-1717, seventeen in April-May 1717, and three in October 1717, suggesting that he too divided his time between Santa Fe and Pecos.[8]

"The construction was done," wrote Fray Juan Miguel Menchero in 1744, "through the industry and care of the Fathers of the mission without having spent even a half-real of His Majesty's funds." The church, in his estimation, rated the adjectives "beautiful and capacious." Like Zeinos' chapel, it faced west, and it sat entirely on top of the mound covering Andrés Juárez' much larger fallen temple. The new church had barely three thousand square feet of floor space, compared to well over five thousand in the Juárez structure. But now there were fewer Pecos, not half as many.[9]

This was the fourth and final Pecos church. As late as 1846, eight years after the last few Pecos had abandoned the pueblo, artist John Mix Stanley of Lt. W. H. Emory's command sketched the deteriorating structure much as Father Domínguez had described it in 1776. Emory's comment that the details of the church "differ but little from those of the present day" is as true now as then.

Its facade, flanked by twin bell towers rising barely above the flat roof, could hardly have been more typical of New Mexico church architecture. Between the bell towers, which jutted forward several feet forming a shallow narthex, and above the eight-foot-tall, two-leaved door, ran a wooden balcony with balustrade and roof. To get out onto it, said Domínguez, one exited from the choir loft through a window.

Unlike the monumental, seventeenth-century Juárez church, this one had neither buttresses nor crenelations, but it did have a transept. The floor plan was cruciform. In profile, the roof line ran straight back from the bell towers and stepped up at the transept allowing for a wooden-grated "transverse clearstory light." The outside, or north side, of the building presented one great expanse of adobe wall broken only by a single high window at the north end of the transept. On the south side, which looked out over the convento, there were at least three high windows.

To reach the main door in 1776, it was necessary to enter the cemetery through a gate in the high wall directly in front. The porter's lodge and two-story convento were on the right. Once across the cemetery and inside, Father Domínguez found the dim interior of the church "rather pleasant." Above his head as he entered was the choir loft, to his right a door

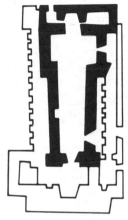

Floor plan of the smaller, 18th-century Pecos church (solid areas) superimposed on that of the 17th-century structure.

Top Nuestra Señora de los Ángeles, a panel in gesso relief, and an angel on a decorative piece from an altar screen, both reportedly from the church at Pecos. Photographed in 1920 in the collection of L. Bradford Prince. Museum of New Mexico

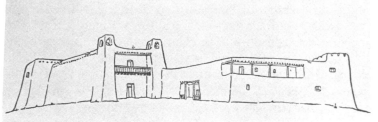

The Pecos church and convento, a drawing by Horace T. Pierce based on Father Domínguez' description in 1776. Adams and Chavez, *Missions*

leading through Zeinos' dilapidated chapel to baptistery, sacristy, and convento beyond. The church floor was packed earth. Under it lay most of the baptized persons who had died over the previous sixty or seventy years.

Five steps led up to the sanctuary. Over the main altar, a movable wooden one, hung an old, framed oil painting of Nuestra Señora de los Ángeles and another, somewhat newer, of Nuestra Señora de la Asunción, as well as eight lesser oils arranged around the other two. In both arms of the transept stood wooden altars surmounted by paintings, some on buffalo hide. Evidently the Pecos church boasted no statuary at all.

Virtually nothing escaped Domínguez' eye. In the nave, there was a well-constructed wooden pulpit in its usual place on the epistle side, and on the gospel side "a pretty wooden confessional on a platform," then a long bench with legs. He described the sacristy and inventoried everything he found, item by item, from chasubles to thurible to missal. Next he toured the convento downstairs and up, identifying cells, store-rooms, and stables. Upstairs, only the rooms on the south side were usable in 1776. The others needed repair. Good miradors looked out to the south and the west, and in the southwest corner stood a fortified tower. "When there are enemies," he noted, "a stone mortar is installed in it." [10]

In all, the physical plant at Pecos was more than adequate. The church, constructed sometime between 1705 and 1717, may even have deserved the adjectives "beautiful and capacious." If the friars' ministry to the Pecos in the eighteenth century proved ineffectual, as some of them admitted it did, the reasons lay beyond a proper church and a place to live. Those they had.

For one thing, their ministry lacked continuity. Few of the friars stayed at Pecos long enough to implement a regimen, to learn the language, or to win the people's confidence. Between 1704 and 1794, the Pecos saw a constant parade of missionaries, at least fifty-eight. In the previous century, the able Andrés Juárez had lived with them for thirteen years, from 1621 to 1634. Now during the same length of time, 1721 to 1734, eleven different missionaries signed the Pecos books. Not that they were intensifying their ministry, much as they might have wished to, quite the contrary.

Hit-or-Miss
Ministry
at Pecos

Mostly they were *ministros interinos,* temporary pastors visiting from Santa Fe to provide a minimum of essential services and the sacraments, for the custody was almost always undermanned. Besides that, the superiors found themselves hard put to keep their missionaries in the field. Time and again they had to reiterate the prohibition against coming to Santa Fe without permission. Relatively speaking, Santa Fe was civilized and secure. Between Apaches and Comanches, the pueblo of Pecos was perilous and isolated. Its people, too, were dying off. The population dropped steadily, from perhaps seven or eight hundred early in the century to a mere ninety-eight adults and forty-four children in 1792.[11]

Despite their beautiful and spacious church, their Christian veneer, and their commitment to military and trade alliances with Spaniards, the Pecos, like most Pueblos, held tenaciously to their traditional society and religion. To them, the friars' neglect was salutary. To them, Father Domínguez' matter-of-fact acceptance of their nine kivas in 1776 was a triumph of sorts. Diego de Vargas had spared the kivas, but a couple of his successors, harking back to the anti-idolatry campaigns of the previous century, had not.

Admiral don José Chacón Medina Salazar y Villaseñor, Marqués de la Peñuela, who bought the governship of New Mexico for five years and succeeded Cuervo in 1707, had declared war on kivas. To him and to Custos Juan de la Peña, they represented all that was secretive and diabolical in Pueblo paganism. Not all the friars agreed. Nevertheless, on orders from Peñuela and accompanied by Peña, Sargento mayor Juan de Ulibarrí toured the pueblos, demolishing kivas and pronouncing against native dances.[12] Later, when his administration was under fire, Peñuela took testimony from the Pueblos themselves to show that they harbored no ill feelings toward him or Ulibarrí. As usual, the Spaniards put words in the Indians' mouths and then transcribed them in proper legal form.

Dutifully, the Pecos delegation reported to the casas reales in Santa Fe: Juan Tindé, governor; Felipe Chistoe, cacique; José Tuta, war captain; Agustín and Santiago, alcaldes; and Pedro Aguate, interpreter. Testifying on July 8, 1711, they affirmed that neither the royal governor nor Ulibarrí had done them any harm. Ulibarrí, who had been alcalde mayor of Pecos and Galisteo, had not come to their pueblo on the visitation ordered by Peñuela. The Pecos may have been speaking in general terms when "they stated that they did not or do not hold against him his having got rid of their kivas and prohibited the dances. They recognize first, as the Christians

Peñuela's War on Pueblo Religion

El Marqués de la Peñuela

they are, that having rid them of said kivas, scalps, and dances was indeed a service." Those, of course, were the Spaniards' words, not the Pecos', as the next royal governor would find out soon enough.[13]

Peñuela, meanwhile, found himself confronted by angry Franciscans. His ally, Custos Juan de la Peña, had died in 1710. The new prelate, Fray Juan de Tagle, a close associate of former governor Cuervo, evidently believed the charges against Peñuela lodged in Mexico City by a couple of disgruntled New Mexicans: that the governor had abused and exploited the Pueblo Indians and had usurped the trade of the province. Peñuela fought back, denouncing Father Tagle to the Franciscan commissary general in the bitterest terms. Not only had the prelate prejudiced the Indians against the governor so thoroughly that they no longer heeded his orders, but he had also encouraged the missionaries to disobey their king. In his scandalous effort to win the Indians' allegiance, Tagle had traveled from pueblo to pueblo inciting them to dance.

Peñuela versus the Friars

Worse, Fray Francisco Brotóns, one of the custos' circle later accused of soliciting sex, had allegedly urged the Taos to construct two underground kivas. These were the places, Peñuela reminded the Father Commissary, where the Pueblos carried on their infernal idolatry, "where they commit sundry offenses against God Our Lord, performing in them superstitious dances most inconsistent with Our Holy Catholic Faith, from which have resulted diverse witchcraft and things most improper." Despite the governor's general demolition of these kivas, with the full cooperation of the deceased custos, Father Tagle now tolerated every abuse. As a result, the Indians were getting out of hand.

In this fight, which divided friars as well as laity, the Pecos sided with Peñuela. According to him, they were bitter because Custos Tagle had removed their minister, the Mexican veteran Fray Diego de Padilla, whom they liked, and had substituted a much younger man, Fray Miguel Francisco Cepeda y Arriola, who badly mistreated them. "Because of this," Peñuela continued,

their governor don Felipe Chistoe felt obliged to flee to this villa, abandoning his privileges, and saying that if they did not remove from his pueblo said Father, successor of Father fray Diego de Padilla, they would have to rise and take off for the sierra. With much cajolery he was compelled to return to his pueblo, but this was not enough to compensate for the removal of Father Padilla and what may result from it. I leave the matter to the superior consideration of Your Reverence.[14]

Attire of dancers in the corn dance at Santo Domingo as drawn by Julian Scott, 1891.
Thomas Donaldson, *Moqui Pueblo Indians of Arizona and Pueblo Indians of New Mexico*
(Washington, D.C., 1893)

Another matter rankled the governor, a shameless viola-
tion of his jurisdiction. The viceroy had forwarded to New
Mexico two titles, one creating don Domingo Romero of Tesuque native governor and captain general of the Tewas, Taos,
Picurís, Keres, Jémez, Ácomas, Zuñis, and all the northern and
western frontiers of the province, and another granting don
Felipe Chistoe of Pecos the same rank over Pecos, Tanos,
Southern Tiwas, and "the frontiers and valleys of the east."
Somehow, alleged Peñuela, the devious Custos Tagle had appropriated the titles, conferring Romero's because he was a
partisan and withholding Chistoe's because he was not. The
prelate then had the audacity to request, through his vice-
custos at Santa Fe, that governor Peñuela make the formal
presentations at a ceremony before the assembled native
leaders.[15]

The entire weighty issue of whether or not to suppress
the Pueblos' ancient customs, their kivas and dances, their way
of painting and adorning themselves, their heathen attire, even
their privilege of carrying Spanish weapons, came to a head
during the administration of Peñuela's successor, Juan Ignacio
Flores Mogollón, native of Sevilla, ex-governor of Nuevo León,
an infirm, aging bachelor.

Hardly had Flores been in office a year when he learned that the Pecos had built a partially subterranean room outside the pueblo "under the pretext of the women getting together to spin." It was a kiva, he knew. And they had others. Emboldened by the precedent of Peñuela, the resolute Flores decided on his own to obliterate this evil once and for all. On January 20, 1714, he decreed the destruction of all kivas and *cois*. The latter were unauthorized rooms having only a roof entrance and hidden in a pueblo house block. The decree said nothing about consultation with the Franciscans. In this case, the state was acting unilaterally.

The Demolition of Pecos Kivas

First, the governor ordered his alcalde mayor of Pecos, Capt. Alfonso Rael de Aguilar, prominent soldier and citizen of New Mexico since the reconquest, to go at once to that pueblo and investigate. If the reports were true, he was to make the Pecos raze the abominable structures,

admonishing said Indians that if they wish to build a room where the women may get together to work it must be inside the pueblo in a public place near the convento or the casas reales [16] with its door onto the street so that those who enter and leave, and what they do inside, may be known.

Don Juan Ignacio Flores Mogollón

Moreover, Rael was to have Pecos Gov. Felipe Chistoe and Lt. Gov. Juan Diego el Guijo appear in Santa Fe before Flores to explain their negligence in this matter. The decree was routed to all the alcaldes mayores

so that each one may publish it in his district and destroy whatever kivas there may be. They are to notify the natives of these pueblos that they are not to rebuild them under pain of a hundred lashes administered without pardon at the post and subjection to four years in a sugar mill or sweatshop.

Alcalde mayor Rael carried out his governor's orders to the letter. His account, of particular interest to archaeologists today, follows in full.

In the pueblo of Nuestra Señora de los Ángeles de los Pecos on January 23, 1714, I, Capt. Alfonso Rael de Aguilar, alcalde mayor and military chief of this pueblo and its district, in execution and due fulfillment of the above order issued by don Juan Ignacio Flores Mogollón, governor and captain general of this kingdom and provinces of New Mexico and castellan of its forts and garrisons for His Majesty, proclaimed and made it known to don Felipe Chistoe, governor of this pueblo, and his lieutenant, Juan Diego Guijo.

Having heard and understood, they said that they would obey and appear before the governor and captain general. Then immediately I went in the company of Capt. Sebastián de Vargas, my lieutenant alcalde mayor, to examine the kivas. I found four in this form: One halfway between the two house blocks, subterranean. I entered it by the ladder placed in the square door of the roof. It had a hearth where they build a fire. On top of this kiva I found a holy cross of wood stained red which apparently they had just put in place a short time before. In the vicinity of the door near the ladder there was about a load of firewood which I ordered removed and the kiva destroyed. It was entirely closed up, unroofed, and filled with rock. There remained not a sign or a trace that there had been on that site and in that place any kiva at all. [17]

The two that were opposite [or in front of] the first house block made with walls, with their doors in the roof, their ladders in place, their hearths where they build fires, were also destroyed and razed to the ground, level with the foundations.

The fourth was in the second house block next to a stable of Governor don Felipe. The walls of this one were not demolished because they are joined to those of the house block. It was unroofed and the vigas that crossed and continued into some rooms of the apartment of some Indians were sawed off. In this kiva I found three cowhides, a small box containing tobacco and three cigarette butts, and a fire that was on the hearth, from which it was known that they had slept in the kiva.

So that it is thus of record I put it in the form of a legal writ which I signed with my lieutenant on said day, month, and year as above.

Alfonso Rael de Aguilar
Sebastián de Vargas [18]

 Sebastián de Vargas

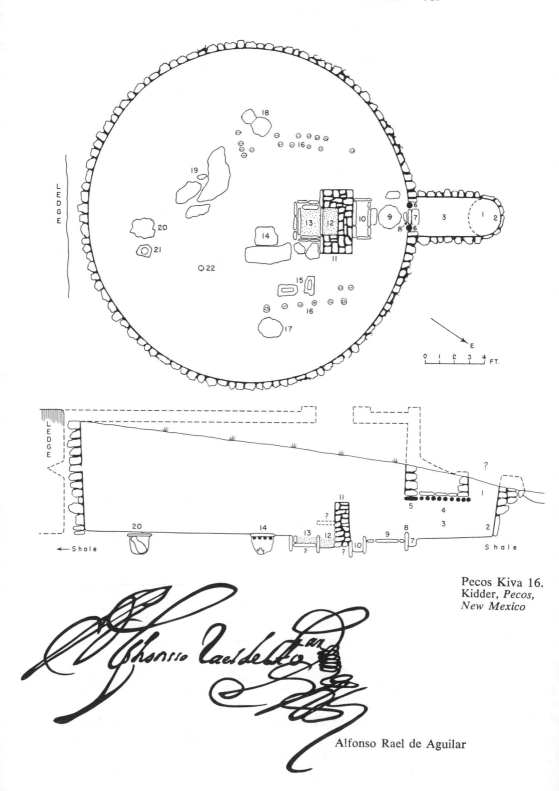

Pecos Kiva 16.
Kidder, *Pecos,*
New Mexico

Alfonso Rael de Aguilar

Felipe Chistoe cannot have watched the rape of his peoples' sacred places without regret. But he said nothing. Life would go on. They would build new kivas. This vicious act by the Spaniards did not justify war or flight. Chistoe and the Pecos had too much to lose. The Spaniards had made him what he was, the most important Pueblo leader on the eastern frontier. They led the campaigns in which he and his auxiliaries profited from booty. And of course they supplied many of the trade goods that lured the plains peoples to Pecos every year. Life would go on.

Some of the missionaries may not have been so sure of that as Chistoe. Time had not yet erased the memory of 1680 and 1696. Surely God in his wisdom and grace was enlightening the Pueblos. There were signs. Why provoke them with direct attacks on their customs, so long as these did not obstruct the preaching of the gospel? Of course not all the missionaries could agree on what constituted an affront to God and what did not.

Other Christian Reforms

Governor Flores was not through yet. The Pueblos had permitted the destruction of their kivas. Why not proceed with other Christian reforms? Why not disarm them of all but their native weapons; why not curtail their intercourse with known hostiles; why not forbid them to paint themselves and dress like heathens? They should instead be made to dress like Christians so everyone could distinguish them from the enemy. This time, Flores would ask for opinions not only from soldiers but also from friars. After all, he did not have to heed them.

Regarding the weapons, it had come to his attention that the Pueblos "possessed many firearms, swords, and cutlasses." Not only did these pose a threat in case of rebellion, but too often they found their way into the hands of heathens. The civil and military men were agreed. At a junta held in Santa Fe on July 6, 1714, they urged that the Pueblos be disarmed quickly before they had a chance to hide their weapons. The friars disagreed. While the royal ordinances forbidding Indians the use of Spanish weapons should indeed be enforced in most places, beleaguered New Mexico was different. Here, they argued, where distances were great and Spanish troops few, the Christian Indians needed such weapons to defend themselves. Moreover, if the governor tried to remove them, he might touch off a new Pueblo revolt. Why not let the viceroy decide?

"Believing that there was no cause for such fear," as he put it, Flores forged ahead. The alcalde mayor of each district was told to gather up the weapons without delay, while the dispossessed owners reported to Santa Fe for a compensatory payment. The penalties for failure to comply were stiff: for Spaniards who sold weapons to the Indians, fifty pesos and four years on the Zuñi frontier for the first offense, and for the second, a hundred pesos and ten years at Pensacola; for mulattoes and mestizos two hundred lashes and two years on an ore crusher; and for Indians caught again with Spanish weapons, loss of those weapons without compensation, fifty lashes, and sale to a sweatshop.

Again they began at Pecos, where eight muskets and a carbine were seized. One of them belonged to don Felipe Chistoe, and that was a problem. Not only did this Indian, because of his outstanding record of loyalty, possess a patent from the former viceroy Conde de Galve licensing him to carry such arms, but he also had a letter from the current viceroy conferring on him the perpetual governorship of Pecos and on his right-hand man, Juan Tindé, the perpetual lieutenant governorship. Wisely, Flores made an exception. He paid the other Pecos, but he returned the gun to don Felipe Chistoe.[19]

Disarming the Pueblos

Having voted to disarm the Pueblos, the same junta of July 6 considered the related problem of native dress and adornment. These Indians still painted themselves with "earths of different colors" and wore feathers as well as skin caps, necklaces, and earrings as they had before their conversion. What bothered the governor and the military men was not so much that these practices were offensive to God, but rather that they were being used as a cover for illicit activities on the part of the Pueblos. If Christian natives dressed like heathens, how could anyone tell friends from foes?

Capt. Juan García de la Riva, like most of the others, believed that the Pueblos should not be allowed to go about looking like heathens, but he added that he had heard it said that in the winter they painted their faces with red ochre to protect their eyes from the glare of the snow. Veteran Capt. Tomás López Olguín was against the Pueblos painting themselves or entering church with feathers on their heads or ears. "It is an open abuse, like the kivas were." Moreover, said López Olguín, the Pueblos, in the guise of heathens, were stealing stock. He gave an example. A mule from the rancho of El Torreón had turned up at Pecos with the brand altered, "a thing the Apaches are not accustomed to do." When accused of stealing such animals the Pecos denied it, saying that they bought them from the Plains Apaches. That, López

Zuñi warriors in native attire.
Century (May 1883)

Olguín declared, was a lie. The Apaches came to Pecos to
buy animals not sell them. And lastly, "he had heard it said
that these Pecos have come in the company of Apaches to
kill in the area upriver from this villa."

An Expression
of Tolerance
Because of the gravity of the issue, Custos Tagle requested the opinions of the missionaries in the field. Two of
them agreed with the governor; others maintained that the
Pueblos were being falsely accused. Fray Antonio Aparicio of
Pecos refused to comment, recommending only that such a
serious matter be referred to the viceroy for a decision. Some
expressed their fear of Pueblo unrest if the Spaniards tried
to curtail such ancient and relatively innocuous practices.

After all, wrote Fray Antonio de Miranda from Ácoma, "there are many incongruous customs among us and completely permitted." Spanish women painted their faces and Spanish men wore "ribbons, plumes, and other profane dress." This time Governor Flores listened to the friars. [20]

"I have come to realize," he confessed to the viceroy, "that to make the Indians change their dress would be for them more lamentable than having removed their kivas and weapons." As a result, he decided not to act until he had word from the viceroy. In Mexico City, too, they listened to the friars. A top-level junta recommended that the viceroy order the governor of New Mexico not to make any sudden moves, rather gradually by "good and gentle measures" to wean the Pueblos from their traditional dress and customs "to a civil and Christian life, without using force or violence." [21]

Governors Peñuela and Flores were the last to mount concerted attacks on Pueblo culture. Succeeding governors interested themselves in the natives as an exploitable resource and as allies against the quickening raids of the nomads. Except for an occasional unusually zealous or idealistic friar, the missionaries too adopted a more patient and tolerant attitude. Commenting on these early attempts to crush Pueblo "superstition and idolatry," Fray Silvestre Vélez de Escalante admitted in the late 1770s "that afterward, despite various measures taken at different times by governors and prelates to extinguish these dances and kivas, the same Indians have reestablished them little by little and they maintain them today." [22]

It had come to a calculated, practical coexistence. Responding in 1714, Fray Antonio de Miranda, the veteran missionary at Ácoma, had summed up in these words the prevailing attitude of the eighteenth century.

As Catholics the Indians are obliged to detest all heathen ceremony. However, in such a critical case, one must exercise the prudence of the serpent and the simplicity of the dove, because violence will result in more harm than one bargains for. Christ, our Life, removed the weight of the Law and rendered it easy and light. *Jugum enim meum suave est, et onus meum leve.* [For my yoke is easy, and my burden is light. Mat., 11:30.] With a load so weightless, and of such ease, one must carry the natives (weak sheep) with the patience of the gardener cultivating a recently planted garden. Little by little he removes the weeds, and through patience he comes to see the garden free of darnel. But to will that the new plant bear leaves, flowers, and fruit all at once is to will not to harvest anything. [23]

Small Pecos ceremonial vessels.
Kidder, *Pottery,* II

Governors and Friars
Renew Competition

In the eighteenth century, as in the seventeenth, the Pueblo Indians remained for the royal governor and his alcaldes mayores, and for the friars, New Mexico's most readily exploitable resource. Naturally, a governor who had paid exorbitantly for the office expected an exorbitant return. But with no mines, no cochineal, no customs houses, such a return was by no means assured. By default, therefore, Pueblo Indian weaving, buffalo hides, and the soft tanned animal skin became "the principal object and attraction of the governors. They are," in the words of Fray Andrés Varo, "the rich mines of this kingdom." [24]

To hear the missionaries tell it, the governors were avaricious, cruel, tyrannical brutes utterly devoid of scruples or a sense of duty. Rather than nurture or protect the Pueblos, they exploited them mercilessly, exacting their goods, their labor, even their women, while neglecting both the administration and the defense of this unhappy kingdom. Obviously they hated and maligned the Franciscans who called them down. To hear the governors tell it, the missionaries were the ones who forced the Indians to labor without pay, who appropriated their maize, and who entered into trading ventures while neglecting their spiritual obligations. After more than a century, their critics pointed out, the friars still did not know the Pueblo languages; after more than a century, the Pueblos still had to confess through interpreters.

Regardless of who were the worse oppressors, governors or missionaries, both parties in their ardor seemed to agree that the Pueblos were indeed oppressed. But how badly is difficult to say. Certainly for don Felipe Chistoe and don Juan Tindé, with their titles, their fancy ceremonial Spanish dress, their privileges, and their influence over native auxiliary troops and native trade, both in constant demand by the Spaniards, life was not all that miserable. Nor were the Pueblos slow to take advantage of a fight between Spaniards, to play one set of "protectors" off against the other.

When it suited their purpose, or there was no other way, they asserted whatever a particular governor or custos wanted to hear. No, answered Chistoe and Tindé in 1711, Governor Peñuela had never taken advantage of them. He had never summoned the Pecos all at once to work on the churches, the governor's palace, or the other public buildings in Santa Fe "but rather thirty, twenty-five, twenty, or six have gone." He had always fed them and paid them well in trade knives or awls for their carpentry and other work.[25] Yet, a dozen years later, when local politics dictated, the same two Pecos, Chistoe and Tindé, pressed their claims against a domineering governor.

The residencia, or judicial review of every governor's administration upon leaving office, offered the Pueblos a means of expressing their grievances, that is, when the residencia judge was impartial, unbribed, or an enemy of the departing executive. In the case of the controversial, rags-to-riches opportunist don Félix Martínez, whose residencia was held belatedly in 1723, there were Spaniards, including the aging Pecos alcalde mayor Alfonso Rael de Aguilar, who for one reason or another wanted the Indians to speak up. The Pecos demanded compensation from Martínez for the personal labor that had caused them to lose their crops, payment for two thousand boards he ordered them to cut, dress, and haul to "his palace or houses he built," and two horses, the agreed-upon price, owed to Chistoe for an Indian boy acquired from heathens and sold to Martínez. In this case, the judge ordered Martínez to pay.[26]

Judicial Review as a Check on the Governors

Another opportunity for the Pueblos to be heard was the royal governor's general visitation, provided of course that their grievances were not against him or his partisans. The self-serving Antonio de Valverde y Cosío, who, like his rival Martínez, had risen through the ranks since the reconquest, reined up at Pecos with his retinue in August 1719. Alcalde mayor Rael had announced in July the upcoming visit.

The Pecos Present Claims

All gathered in "the casas reales," or *casa de comunidad*, a building seventy feet or so west of the convento. This structure, like similar ones built and maintained by the Indians in other pueblos, was a visible reminder that the Pecos were vassals of the Spanish king. Here the alcalde mayor or his deputy took lodging and sometimes resided. Here, too, travelers who stopped at the pueblo could expect room, board, and feed for their animals, as did the first bishop to visit Pecos in defiance of the Franciscans. On the doors of the casas reales were posted the decrees of the royal governor, and here, on his visitation, the governor reiterated to the Pecos the desire of their king that they receive the benefit of his justice. If anyone had injured or offended them or owed them a debt, they should step forward and so state.[27]

While the account of Valverde's visitation says only that the Pecos filed "several claims" which the governor ordered "promptly and faithfully settled in full," the records of other visitations are much more explicit. By listening at the door of the casas reales to the claims presented by Pecos carpenters and traders, one glimpses the day-to-day intercourse between these Indians and their neighbors. Before Gov. Gervasio Cruzat y Góngora on July 28, 1733:

Miguel Jaehi, Indian of the pueblo of Nuestra Señora de los Ángeles de los Pecos, asks and claims of Francisco Velázquez, soldier of the royal presidio of the villa of Santa Fe, one door, for which he offered him a horse bit. He had not paid in more than twelve years. [The governor] ordered that it be paid. He was paid with a large Mexican hoe.
Diego Jastimbari, Indian of said pueblo, asks and claims of Diego Gallegos, citizen who lives across from Cochití, one red roan he-mule he took from his nephew. [The governor] ordered that it be paid. He was paid with a musket. Alonso Benti, Juan Diego Guojechinto, Diego Chumba, and Antonio Chunfugua, Indian carpenters of said pueblo, ask and claim of the Rev. Father fray Juan José [Pérez] de Mirabal,[28] minister of the pueblo of Taos, twenty-four trade knives, six apiece, for the work they did on the church dressing timbers, now more than ten years ago. The Reverend Father will be notified.
Lorenzo de Chillu, Indian of said pueblo, asks and claims of Cristóbal, Indian of the pueblo of Nambé, one horse for two mantas, one painted cotton, the other wool, now two years past. [The governor] ordered that it be paid. [29]

Twelve years later in the casas reales, Gov. Joaquín Codallos y Rabal sat in judgment of other small claims, all of which he allowed and ordered paid.

Lorenzo, Indian of said pueblo and war captain, states that Bartolo Olguín, citizen of Ojo Caliente, owes him a horse that he borrowed when don José Moreno [Codallos' alcalde mayor of Pecos and Galisteo, 1744-1748] went on a buffalo hunt by order of Col. don Gervasio Cruzat. . . . Agustín, Indian of said pueblo, claims of a son of Lt. Andrés Montoya also named Andrés a calf

A colonial New Mexico bed.   Museum of New Mexico

for a half-fanega of piñon nuts, two standard buckskins, and one heavy buffalo or elkskin he sold to him. . . . Agustín, Indian of said pueblo claims of the heirs of Diego, Indian and former governor of the Indians of the pueblo of Cochití, four fanegas of wheat for a bed he sold to the said deceased Diego. . . .

In conclusion, Governor Codallos exhorted the Pecos through an interpreter, in the prescribed form, to respect royal justice and decent living, as well as their missionary, and

to take special care, as His Majesty charges, to raise poultry, cattle, and sheep and to cultivate their lands, neither living in idleness nor as vagabonds but working in their own pueblo in their fields; likewise to obey their superiors, governor, and captains in whatever they command conducive to the service of Both Majesties. [30]

The Pecos recognized the irony in these rhetorical preachments. How were they to respect their royal governor and alcalde mayor on the one hand and their minister and the Father Custos on the other, the agents of Both Majesties, when so often they were bitterly at odds? Guided by self-interest and a will to survive, and, one suspects, sometimes intimidated or or simply confused, the mission Indians more often than not took the governor's side, even when their position roundly contradicted their missionary.

The minister at Pecos in 1731 was a fighter. Described by a fellow Franciscan as "an anvil when it comes to work," the

Father Esquer Damns
Governor Bustamante

steadfast, undaunted Fray Pedro Antonio Esquer administered not only his own mission but, whenever needed, the villa of Santa Fe as well. He had first signed the Pecos books on February 24, 1731, when he baptized three infants. Little over three months later, there occurred an event which Father Esquer had been awaiting eagerly: the residencia of the venal, blaspheming, immoral Gov. Juan Domingo de Bustamante. Given the opportunity, the Pecos missionary unburdened his conscience with gusto.

Fray Pedro Antonio Esquer

In a lengthy and impassioned indictment, during the course of which he warned the residencia judge that Bustamante had planted spies in his house, Esquer charged the governor with extorting, tyrannizing, intimidating, and perverting soldiers, citizens, and Indians. He told how Bustamante had been trained in corruption by ex-governor Valverde, his uncle and father-in-law, originally a poor man who had risen to wealth by cheating the soldiers and Indians of El Paso and who, by connivance, had secured the governorship of New Mexico. To cover his muddy tracks, Valverde had bought the governorship for his nephew for twenty thousand pesos. After nine years and two months in office, Bustamante, Esquer alleged, "now has some 200,000 pesos, rather more than less, and is the owner of wrought silver, coach, slaves, fine clothes, household furniture, pack train with not a few draft mules, and not a few horses." In the friar's opinion, Bustamante was an irreverent ogre without a single redeeming grace. "We can indeed say in Catholic truth that we have suffered martyrdom during the time of his administration."

Esquer labeled the governor's subordinates "fruit of the same tree." They corrupted the Indians, teaching them to lie and be deceitful, even to one another. This was dangerous, for even Indians could recognize the many injustices that lay so heavy on the land, and in such recognition grew the seeds of revolt. "As a result," the Pecos friar confessed, "we suffer torment beneath the death-dealing club for the truths inherent in the Holy Gospel, because the Indians live like Moors without a lord, serving only the alcaldes mayores, who deny them a fair wage, restrain them from doing good, and supply them with lies and evil." [31]

Maybe he was right. Maybe the Pecos were cowed. Whatever their reasons, they lauded Governor Bustamante. Testifying at his residencia, Antonio Sidepovi, *indio principal* and governor, pled ignorance of any wrongdoing on Bustamante's part and agreed that the royal governor had acted as a protective father to the people of Pecos. He had bought their maize

Juan Domingo de Bustamante

when no one else would, and he had paid them in "mattocks, axes, plowshares, and other tools." He had helped the pueblo progress, nurtured the Faith, and defended the Pecos from their enemies. In fact, Governor Bustamante, his alcaldes mayores for Pecos and Galisteo, who were Alfonso Rael de Aguilar and Manuel Tenorio de Alba, and all his other officials had "administered justice with complete fairness, without being brought gifts or bribes, and they had treated the people of his pueblo well with complete love and affection." [32]

In taking the governor's side, the Pecos acknowledged who could do them the most good, and the most harm. Their missionaries' influence had begun to wane. In the lives of the Pecos, the alcaldes mayores, minions of the governors, offered more continuity. Some of them served a decade or longer. Most were native-born New Mexicans. They were the ones who regulated trade and sounded the call for native auxiliaries. In the eighteenth century, the casas reales had replaced the convento as the focus of Spanish influence at Pecos.

By 1731, the Franciscans of New Mexico were very much on the defensive. It was difficult enough coexisting with the likes of Juan Domingo de Bustamante, but at least governors came and went. Now a challenge of more lasting consequence faced them. After two centuries of nominal jurisdiction, the bishop of Durango had begun to press with vigor his claim to New Mexico. In 1725, Bishop Benito Crespo had gotten as far north as El Paso on an episcopal visitation. Five years later—

New Mexico Visited by Bishop Crespo

at the invitation of Governor Bustamante—he came again and insisted on proceeding up the Rio Grande, the first bishop ever to do so.

It was a warm day in July 1730. As His Most Illustrious Lordship don Benito, twelfth bishop of Durango, approached the pueblo of Pecos attended by his entourage, Fray Juan George del Pino hid upstairs in the convento. The bishop's secretary rode on in advance. When he noticed the bishop's cook standing outside the convento, he yelled at him to get away from there and go to the casa de comunidad. "Under no circumstances did His Most Illustrious Lordship wish to stop or to dine in the convento." At that, Father Pino leaned out of the mirador and offered the convento, saying that all was ready. He had made no preparations in the casa de comunidad. He would of course comply most willingly with the decision of His Most Illustrious Lordship. Just then, he caught sight of the bishop's party coming up the trail.

Alerting the convento servants as he went, the friar rushed downstairs, through the convento, and into the church to receive the bishop at the church door. Solicitous to show all due respect, but not subordination, Father Pino welcomed the eminent visitor, begging earnestly that he deign to accept the hospitality of the convento where a meal was waiting. The prelate responded graciously but firmly. He would accept the meal, but not in the convento. "With that, he took his leave of the Father, who afterward ordered that the food be transferred to said casa de comunidad." [33]

The nice maneuvering that day at Pecos by bishop and friar was no game. Outspoken Custos Andrés Varo, on orders from his superiors in Mexico City, maintained steadfastly that the custody was not subject to the episcopal authority of the Durango see. Just as steadfastly, Bishop Crespo maintained that it was. The two, who had met at El Paso and traveled upriver together, had negotiated a temporary compromise. The bishop would refrain from making a formal visitation of the churches, baptisteries, mission books, and the like, and he would publish no edicts. But he would be received in the churches by the friars, and he would be allowed to preach and to perform the rite of confirmation. Both men were at pains not to do or to say anything that might prejudice their cases in the future.

Crespo Finds Fault with Franciscans   Although he maintained his episcopal decorum throughout, Benito, bishop of Durango, found much that displeased him in Franciscan New Mexico. Writing to the viceroy from Bernalillo and El Paso, he leveled a number of serious allega-

Benito, Bishop of Durango

tions. The king, who paid forty royal allowances annually in support of these missions, had every right to expect the services of forty missionaries, yet the bishop had found seven lacking, and from what he was told, "they have been lacking for a long time." On the basis of one brief visit, he recommended consolidation, one friar for several pueblos, one for Pecos and Galisteo, one for San Juan, San Ildefonso, and Santa Clara, and so on. He charged that the friars lacked the zeal to convert the peoples who bordered on the pueblos but were content instead simply to trade with them. In the pueblos themselves, he claimed to have seen signs of paganism, idolatry, apostasy, "and the reciprocal lack of love" between missionaries and Indians.

Perhaps the bishop's most serious charge, the one he kept returning to, was that none of the missionaries knew the native languages. Not only did this demonstrate, in his opinion, a woeful lack of dedication "when the languages are not so difficult," but it also meant that the friars were aliens in their own missions. Moreover, the church's precept requiring annual confession and communion went unfulfilled in New Mexico since the Indians refused to confess "except at the point of death because they do not want to confess through an interpreter."

That was not entirely fair, countered Fray Juan Antonio Sánchez. He himself knew Tewa. So did Fray José Irigoyen. Fray Pedro Díaz de Aguilar and Fray Juan José Pérez de Mirabal each knew a Pueblo language, the former Keresan and the latter Tiwa as spoken at Taos. Many others had a start learning several. That, in fact, was the problem, according to Sánchez. Every time a missionary mastered a few words of one language, the superiors transferred him somewhere else. What did they expect?

Before he left the custody, Bishop Crespo appointed Santa Fean don Santiago Roybal, a secular priest he had ordained in Durango for the purpose, as his vicar and ecclesiastical judge, an act of dubious legality. He also posted a schedule of fees for marriages, burials, etc., and took one last

Jesuit Father Ignacio Keller, en route to the Hopi pueblos in
1743, is repulsed by Apaches. Detail after a map, c. 1748,
drawn in conjunction with a visitation by Fray Juan Miguel Menchero.

dig at the Franciscans. The fees they had been charging were,
he said, both arbitrary and exorbitant.[34]

In fairness to the friars, it should be said that the crusading Bishop Crespo was prejudiced. Like his predecessor, Pedro
Tapis, he was strongly pro-Jesuit. Seven years before, he had
had the sacred rites making him bishop performed in Mexico
City at the Jesuit church of La Profesa. He warmly endorsed
a Jesuit takeover of the apostate Hopi pueblos, and he was
always, sometimes openly, sometimes by implication, comparing the Franciscan missions unfavorably with those of the
Jesuits. Besides, there was more than a little truth in the friars'
contention that Crespo had come to New Mexico uninvited by

them, had spoken mainly with their enemies, had ignored their merits and the adverse circumstances of their ministry, and had catalogued only their faults. Still, some of what the bishop had said was true, and the Franciscans of New Mexico knew it.[35]

For the next thirty years, during which the charges and countercharges varied little, the friars strained to defend themselves and the sacredness of their Order from a convenient alliance of bishops and governors and, at the same time, to put their missionary house in order. Considering the odds against them, even their limited success was a credit. They persevered.

Busy, enterprising Fray Juan Miguel Menchero, preacher, censor of the Holy Office, procurator of the custody of the Conversion of St. Paul, and visitor by order of the Franciscan commissary general for New Spain, enjoyed being a superior. Sent out from Mexico in 1731, in the wake of Bishop Crespo's visitation, it was his task to marshal the friars' defense and to correct whatever abuses he found.

Menchero Calls
for Rededication

Arriving jaded and sweaty at El Paso in early July, Fray Juan Miguel issued the usual official letter announcing his visitation. He cited his authority from the Father Commissary General and proclaimed a list of mandates. Every missionary must keep in his mission a book of expenses and income from crops and livestock. There must be no women cooks in the conventos "so as to avoid the scandal that can follow from it." Inspired by the zeal of the "old Fathers," the present friars should dedicate themselves to the upkeep and repair of their churches and conventos, "repairing drains and other things that can cause their destruction." But the crux of the letter had to do with language.

First, Spanish should be taught at every mission, as the king had ordered repeatedly. Primers, catechisms, and readers should be distributed according to the number of catechumens. And second, to prevent the scandal of it being said that the friars administered confession to Indians only through interpreters, to the discredit of their holy habit,

we admonish all Your Reverences to devote special effort to learning the [native] language, each of you at the mission where obedience has placed you, with the assurance that he who complies with this our mandate will be recognized. Likewise for this reason, insofar as our religious life permits, you will not be transferred to another mission, except when the contrary is judged the more proper course. And especially will the effort of those who devote themselves to writing or having a grammar made of said language be recognized. [36]

It was a good try. None of their relatively short-term, part-time missionaries in the eighteenth century seemed to know the Towa language of the Pecos. A few of them, like Francisco de la Concepción González, 1749-1750, and Juan José Toledo, 1750-1753, strained mightily to transliterate the difficult Pecos names, names like Extehahuotziri, Sejunpaguai, Guaguirachuro, Huozohuochiriy, and Timihuotzuguori. But if any of them attempted even a simple word list or vocabuary, it has not come to light.

Before he could get on with his visitation, Father Menchero, as supply man of the custody, had to deliver the goods purchased in Mexico City for the missionaries against their annual royal allowances. Because of Bishop Crespo's allegations, Menchero was especially scrupulous in his accounting.

Mission Supply   The supplies for Pecos, which evidently were supposed to last three years, came to 807 pesos 4 reales, 503 on account and the remainder advanced against the 330-peso allowance for 1731. In August, missionary Pedro Antonio Esquer of Pecos checked the goods against the list in Santa Fe and signed a receipt before witnesses. It was up to him to have the stuff hauled out to Pecos.

By far the most costly items, valued together at more than two hundred pesos, were two cases of fine chocolate. Other boxes, trunks, and odd bundles contained sugar, cinnamon, saffron, and other spices; olive oil, candle wax, and fine-cut tobacco; majolica, china, and pewter dishes; two habits, two cowls, a cloak, and two cords; quantities of cloth of different varieties; a ream of paper, razors, a brass washbasin, comb, mirror, and 500 bars of soap; assorted kitchen utensils, tools, bridles, needles, and pins; a set of vestments of flowered silk and a Nuestra Señora de Guadalupe; and, for the teaching of Spanish, two sets of primers, two dozen catechisms, and two dozen readers; as well as numerous other goods not readily available at the ends of the earth.[37]

To begin his formal visitation, Father Menchero accompanied Esquer down to Pecos, where he found everything in accord with the dictates of the Council of Trent. In the privacy of a cell in the convento, he put to the missionary a series of questions under vow of holy obedience. Had he observed faithfully the Institute, Rule, and Constitutions of the Order? Did he administer the Holy Sacraments to Indians and Spaniards? Had Custos Varo done his duty in everything, including the distribution of the tithes to the poor? To everything Esquer answered yes.[38]

MISSÆ PROPRIÆ
SANCTORUM
TRIUM ORDINUM
FRATRUM MINORUM
S. P. N.
FRANCISCI,

Ad formam Missalis Romani redactæ, & exactius examinatæ conformiter Breviario, à SS. D. N. Innocentio Papa XII. approbatæ, novoque Kalendario, & Rubricis locupletatæ.

ANTVERPIÆ,
EX TYPOGRAPHIA PLANTINIANA
M. D C C X X I V.

A Franciscan missal printed in Antwerp in 1724.
Museum of New Mexico

Back in Santa Fe after visiting several of the missions, Menchero paused to address "certain things worthy of attention." Henceforth, no missionary was to order Indians to work outside the mission "unless payment is made to them in advance." No friar was to charge an Indian any fee whatsoever for administering the sacraments. Considering "the malice and passion that reigns in this kingdom," he must not accept anything, under any circumstances, even if offered freely. For the sake of decency and cleanliness, Menchero appealed to them to get the nests of swallows out of their churches. Any friar

Fray Juan Miguel Menchero, Comisario Visitador

who showed up in Santa Fe without permission of the vice-custos and good reason would be subject to six months at the mission of Zuñi for the first offense, and for subsequent offenses, arrest by "the secular arm" and summons before the custos.

Lastly, he pleaded with the friars to get along with government officials. If an alcalde mayor did something "contrary to the service of God, the welfare of the Indians, and the will of the Catholic Majesty"—like forcing them to herd stock in various places without pay—the missionaries were to try prudent and fraternal persuasion. If that did not work, they should report the offense to the vice-custos, who would take it up with the governor. "From the unity of Your Reverences with the great zeal of His Lordship," quoth Menchero rhetorically, "better service to Both Majesties is bound to result."[39]

He might as well have been beating his head against an adobe wall.

Bishop Elizacoechea at Pecos

As for bishops, another soon came visiting, despite the unsettled question of his legal right to do so. This time, the friars backed down. Crespo's successor, Doctor don Martín de Elizacoechea, "bishop of Durango, the kingdom of Nueva Vizcaya, its confines, and the provinces of New Mexico, Tarahumara, Sonora, Sinaloa, Pimas, and Moqui, of His Majesty's council, etc.," rode up to Pecos with his Basque suite late in August of 1737. He was permitted free access to the church, the mission books, and everything else.

"Having inspected the church of said pueblo," read the note in the Pecos book of baptisms, "its baptismal font, oils and holy chrism, the sacristy, vestments, altar stone and altar, and having said the responsories in the form prescribed by the Roman Ritual, he declared that everything was appropriately decent and according to law." He expressed his thanks to Pecos missionary Fray Diego Arias de Espinosa de los Monteros and encouraged him to continue the good work. He included no

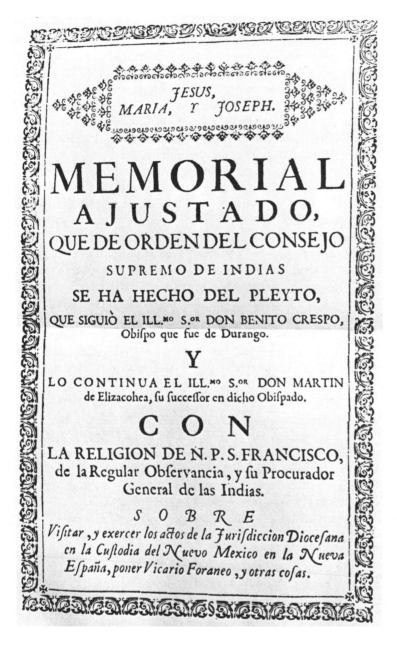

JESUS,
MARIA, Y JOSEPH.

MEMORIAL
AJUSTADO,
QUE DE ORDEN DEL CONSEJO
SUPREMO DE INDIAS
SE HA HECHO DEL PLEYTO,
QUE SIGUIÒ EL ILL.ᴹᴼ S.ᴼᴿ DON BENITO CRESPO,
Obiſpo que fue de Durango.

Y
LO CONTINUA EL ILL.ᴹᴼ S.ᴼᴿ DON MARTIN
de Elizacohea, ſu ſucceſſor en dicho Obiſpado.

CON
LA RELIGION DE N. P. S. FRANCISCO,
de la Regular Obſervancia, y ſu Procurador
General de las Indias.

SOBRE
*Viſitar , y exercer los actos de la Juriſdiccion Dioceſana
en la Cuſtodia del Nuevo Mexico en la Nueva
Eſpaña, poner Vicario Foraneo , y otras coſas.*

Title page of a brief of the lawsuit brought by Bishops Crespo and Elizacoechea against the Franciscans over episcopal jurisdiction in New Mexico. Wagner, *Spanish Southwest,* II

admonition to learn Towa. Whether the bishop spent the night in the convento or in the casas reales, the note did not say.[40]

In the twenty-three years that elapsed between Elizacoechea's visitation and that of a successor, the friars came to see bishops as the lesser of two evils. The governors were their real scourge.

While neglecting Pecos, where the Comanches began to make themselves felt in the late 1730s, the Franciscans directed their apostolic labors to the west. Old Fray Carlos Delgado went out to the apostate Hopi pueblos in 1742 and led back a migration of hundreds of refugees, mostly descendants of the Tiwas who had fled during the 1680s. He also opened up the Navajo field for his brethren, claiming thousands of conversions. Later in the 1740s, the irrepressible Fray Juan Miguel Menchero picked up the initiative.

These new spiritual conquests were the friars' best answer to their critics, a demonstration to the world that the missions of New Mexico were still "living vineyards of the Lord" and their missionaries true heirs of the apostles. Yet the governors opposed them, maliciously, it seemed to them. When reports by the outspoken Fray Andrés Varo reached the viceroy, he decided to send a member of his household, don Juan Antonio de Ornedal y Maza, to New Mexico to get the facts. Instead, Ordenal got together with the hot-headed, youthful Gov. Tomás Vélez Cachupín, another member of the viceroy's "family," and "hell conspired" to roast the missionaries of New Mexico as they had never been roasted before. But they did not wither. Rather they fought hellfire with hellfire.[41]

Despite the crescendo of royal governors and missionaries having at one another, life at Pecos changed little. Every year there were fewer people. A squad of Spanish soldiers moved in west of the convento beyond the casas reales to help defend them against assault by the Comanches. Governor Codallos y Rabal petitioned the Franciscan commissary general in 1744 to remove Fray Juan José Hernández, on-again-off-again minister at Pecos, because, in Codallos' words, "every day I receive pitiful complaints from the Indians because of his bad treatment of them." [42]

Six years and six missionaries later, the Pecos governor and the cacique, responding through an interpreter, answered the vice-custos' questions about Fray Francisco de la Concepción González just the way they were supposed to. He was never absent from the mission. He said Mass on Sundays, he instructed them and their children daily in the catechism, and he spoke to them in Spanish "so that they might learn the language." He charged no fee for baptisms, marriages, or burials, or for celebrating the patron saint's feast, August 2. He succored the pueblo when in need. Never had he taken anything from their homes or corrals. Never had they woven mantas for him. Willingly they planted four fanegas of wheat and half a fanega of maize for his sustenance and that of four boys, a bell-ringer, a porter, a cook, and three grinding women. They also provided firewood for the convento.[43]

Father González, their missionary for part of 1749 and 1750, had scars to show, figuratively speaking, from his battles with royal governors. Gaspar Domingo de Mendoza, 1739 to 1743, had accused him of complicity in the alleged native uprising plotted by one Moreau, a French immigrant later sentenced to die. As a result, the friar's superiors had recalled him to Mexico City and had subjected him to judicial inquiry. A fellow missionary, testifying in González' behalf, swore that his conduct had been exemplary, that he had always tried to keep the peace by preaching the gospel. Moreover, he had repaired the churches and conventos of Santa Fe and Nambé and had rebuilt the Tesuque church from the foundations up, begging the means from among the citizenry and donating a large part of his own royal allowance.

Acquitted and back in New Mexico, the undaunted Father González had run afoul of Governor Codallos. When the friar objected to the governor's use of some Tesuque laborers, whom Codallos allegedly had taken away from catechism and church construction and then had failed to pay, and when the missionary refused to perjure himself in Codallos' behalf, the governor's friendship turned to mortal hatred. He vowed to break the insubordinate friar. And in that spirit he revived the old charges.[44] But Gonzáles outlasted Codallos and moved out to Pecos late in the summer of 1749. While there, he compiled the most accurate census of the pueblo to date, correcting in the process the wild guess of Custos Varo.

Contrary to what Varo said, there were not as many Pecos at mid-century as there had been fifty years before, not nearly as many. Disease, emigration, and attacks by hostile Plains Indians had cut their number in half. Finding no census in the provincial archive in 1749, Varo had estimated the pueblo's population at more than a thousand. Father González counted each and every one, but he did not bother to add them up. Someone else, taking issue with Varo, noted on González' census "there are probably 300 persons here." Actually there were 449: 255 adults and 194 children.

Except for Agustín, who headed the list as cacique, and Francisco Aguilar, evidently an Indian or a thoroughly accepted mixed-blood, González valiantly rendered the native surnames of every adult male and nearly every woman along with his or her Christian given name. He grouped them according to where they lived, but in such a way as to drive an archaeolo-

The Pecos Census of 1750

gist up the wall. He began, it would seem, with the South
Pueblo and then moved north.

> East side of the community house block (*cuartel de la comunidad*)
>   36 adults, 40 children
> west side of said house block
>   50 adults, 35 children
> small plaza (*placita*)
>   29 adults, 15 children
> plaza
>   88 adults, 70 children
> east side of plaza house block
>   52 adults, 34 children.[45]

**Bishop Tamarón
Made Welcome**

During the 1750s, while the population of Pecos fell from
499 to 344, the governors kept the Franciscans pretty well
muzzled. When, in 1759, a third bishop of Durango announced
his intention to visit New Mexico, the friars were almost eager.
They wanted to talk. This bishop, the untiring, practical, wide-
eyed Dr. Pedro Tamarón y Romeral, the bluerobes made welcome, in his words, "as if they were secular priests."[46]

The bishop and his suite, which included a corpulent
black valet who "must have excited the Indians' imagination,"
rode in the company of Custos Jacobo de Castro and an armed
escort over the mountain from Santa Fe to Pecos on Thursday,
May 26, 1760. Despite the weight of his responsibilities, His
Most Illustrious Lordship was enjoying himself. "He was one
of those inveterate tourists who delight in new scenes and little-
frequented places and have a flair for collecting odd bits of
interesting information." [47]

The Pecos came out on horseback to meet him, performing "many tilts to show how skillful and practiced they are in
riding." Fray Francisco Javier Dávila Saavedra, a native of
Florida now in his mid-forties, awaited him at the church door.
Inside, Bishop Tamarón administered the sacrament of confirmation to 192 Pecos, although, as he later admitted, it
caused him considerable mental anguish. The adults simply
were not properly instructed. During the ceremonies, one of
the principal men, Agustín Guichí, a Pecos carpenter, seemed
to be studying the bishop's every move.

In the course of his inspection, Tamarón charged Father
Dávila to prepare a book of confirmations so that these and
subsequent ones might be legally recorded. He asked why
there had been no marriage entries in more than a year. No
marriages had been performed, Dávila replied.

Left First page of the 1750 Pecos census, in the hand of Fray Francisco de la Concepción González (BNM, leg. 8, no. 81).

Below Bishop Pedro Tamarón y Romeral, a sketch from his portrait at the cathedral in Durango.

With the Pecos books before him, the bishop began to lecture the friar. One thing more than any other "saddened and upset" him. It was the same thing that had dismayed Bishop Crespo thirty years before. In all these years, the friars had failed to learn the native languages or to teach the Pueblos intelligible Spanish.

The Language Problem

His Most Illustrious Lordship charged him exceedingly to try his utmost to dispose the Indians, his parishioners, to confess annually, for it has been said that they do not do so, but rather leave it only for the point of death, the reason being that said Father missionary does not understand them. He has two alternatives, either have them learn the Spanish language or work up an interrogatory for confessions in their language.

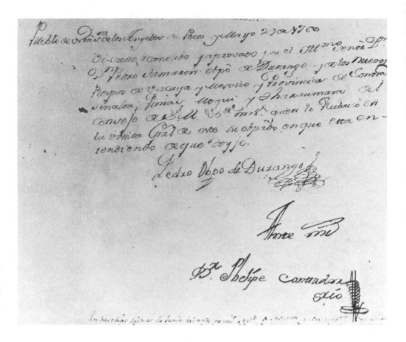

Notice of Bishop
Tamarón's visitation,
May 29, 1760, in the
Pecos book of burials
(AASF).

It was not only confession. The Pueblos, in the opinion of Bishop Tamarón, were woefully ignorant of the chief truths and duties of the Christian faith. They could recite in unison some of the catechism, but since they did not understand Spanish, they had no idea what they were saying. For one thing, he ordered Father Dávila to give up the current practice of having the native fiscales, or catechists, lead the Pecos in group recitations. Rather, each individual should be examined separately.

Again language was the key. Interpreters, who only added to the confusion, were not the answer. The friars simply had to come to grips with the Pueblo languages. He commanded them to. He begged them to. He offered to pay the printing costs of native-language catechisms and guides to confession. Still, after repeated and vehement admonitions, the custos and missionaries "tried to excuse themselves by claiming that they could not learn those languages."

It was, to be sure, the friars' most glaring failure in New Mexico, and some of them admitted it. But it was not all their fault. The Pueblos had learned by the eighteenth century that the surest defense of their traditional culture was to guard their languages. By refusing to surrender this key to their closed Pueblo world, they not only blocked Christian invasion, but they insured as well its quiet permanence.

Those few friars who did learn a Pueblo language in the eighteenth century did so most often at Zuñi or one of the other western pueblos where the people were not so much under the eye of the Spaniards and not so secretive. In utter frustration, Castro related to Bishop Tamarón how his friars were thwarted by Pueblo interpreters who seemed to be deliberately confusing them or by "the rebelliousness of the people." The bishop himself had admitted that in matters of trade and profit "the Indians and Spaniards of New Mexico understand one another completely." Yet when it came to the catechism, the Pueblos were ignorant.[48]

That was no accident. The Spaniards' Christian zeal, diluted in eighteenth-century New Mexico, was no longer a match for the reinforced tenacity of the Pueblos.

Three months after Bishop Tamarón's visitation, there occurred at Pecos one of the most delightful events in the annals of New Mexico's past, at least when viewed from the twentieth century. The bishop had an account of it published to illustrate the marvelous workings of Christian divine retribution. It also said something about the Pecos after a century and a half of domination by Both Majesties, after assaults by smallpox and Comanches, after the violence of their own discord, and after the reduction of their people by eight of every ten. Their spirit had not broken.

A Memorable Burlesque at Pecos

It was mid-September, about harvest time. They must have been feeling glad. There were a few soldiers on escort duty at the mission, but the missionary was probably off in Santa Fe. The Pueblos had long featured "sacred clowns" in their ceremonials, clowns who, unlike the rest of the people, could ridicule even the supernaturals. Why not ridicule a bishop?

The originator of this performance was one of the Indian principal men of that pueblo, called Agustín Guichí, a carpenter by trade. He made himself bishop, and, in order to present himself to his people as such, he designed and cut pontifical vestments. Making the mitre of parchment, he stained it with white earth. Out of a cloak (*tilma*), he made a cape like the cope used at confirmations, and he fashioned the rochet out of another cloak. He made a sort of pastoral crosier from a reed.

The aforesaid Agustín donned all this, mounted an ass, and two other Indians dressed themselves up to accompany him in the capacity of assistants. One took the part of the Father Custos. They put a garment like the Franciscan habit on him, and they painted the other black to represent my man. These two also rode on similar mounts, and, after all the Indian population had assembled along with others who were not Indians, to the accompaniment of a muffled drum and loud huzzas, the whole crew, followed by the three mounted men with Agustín, the make-believe bishop garbed as such in his fashion, in the middle, departed for the pueblo. They entered it at one o'clock on the fourteenth day of September 1760. They went straight to the plaza, where the Indian women were kneeling in two rows. And Agustín, the make-believe bishop, went between them distributing blessings. In this manner they proceeded to the place where they had prepared a great arbor with two seats in it. Agustín, who was playing the part of the bishop, occupied the chief one, and Mateo Cru, who was acting the Custos, the other.

And the latter immediately rose and informed the crowd in a loud voice that the bishop ordered them to approach to be confirmed. They promptly obeyed, and Agustín, garbed as a bishop, used the following method of confirming each one who came to him: He made a cross on his forehead with water, and when he gave him a slap, that one left and the next one came forward. In this occupation he spent all the time necessary to take care of his people, and after the confirmations were over, the meal which had been prepared for the occasion was served. Then followed the dance with which they completed the afternoon. On the next day the diversion and festivities continued, beginning with a Mass which Bishop Agustín pretended to say in the same arbor. During it he distributed pieces of tortillas made of wheat flour in imitation of communion. And the rest of the day the amusement was dancing, and the same continued on the third day which brought those disorders and entertainments to an end.

On the fourth day, when the memorable Agustín no longer found occupation in the mockery of his burlesque pastimes as bishop, he went about the business of looking after his property. He went to visit his milpa, or maize field, which was half a league away near the river. Then he sat down at the foot of a juniper tree opposite the maize. He was still there very late in the afternoon as night was drawing in, when a bear attacked him from behind, so fiercely that, clawing his head, it tore the skin from the place over which the mitre must have rested. It proceeded to the right hand and tore it to pieces, gave him other bites on the breast, and went away to the sierra.

According to the investigation of this singular event conducted by don Santiago Roybal, vicar of Santa Fe, the mortally wounded Agustín repented. He acknowledged to his brother that "God has already punished me." As he lay in his house dying, he called for his son and told him "to shut the door." Then in confidence he admonished him, "Son, I have committed a great sin, and God is punishing me for it. And so I order that you and your brothers are not to do likewise. Counsel them every day and every hour."

Agustín confessed his terrible sin, through interpreter Lorenzo, to Fray Joaquín Rodríguez de Jerez, who afterward administered extreme unction. Then he died. The friar interred his mutilated body on September 21 in the Pecos church.[49]

Fiscal Juan Domingo Tarizari testified that he had examined the bear's tracks. It had come straight down out of the sierra, had mauled Agustín, and had gone back without even entering the milpas to eat maize. This was strange behavior for a bear. A bear simply did not attack a man unless the man was chasing the bear. To Bishop Tamarón, the message was clear.

The Most High Lord of Heaven and Earth willed this very exemplary happening so that it should serve as a warning to those remote tribes and so that they might show due respect for the functions of His Holy Church and her ministers, and so that we might all be more careful to venerate holy and sacred things; for the punishment that befell [Agustín Guichí] does not permit us to attribute its noteworthy circumstances to mere worldly coincidence.[50]

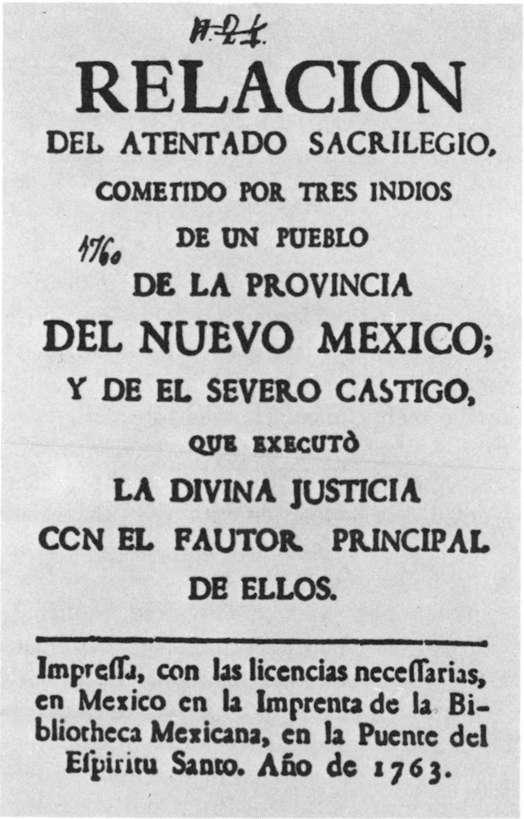

RELACION

DEL ATENTADO SACRILEGIO,

COMETIDO POR TRES INDIOS

DE UN PUEBLO

DE LA PROVINCIA

DEL NUEVO MEXICO;

Y DE EL SEVERO CASTIGO,

QUE EXECUTÒ

LA DIVINA JUSTICIA

CCN EL FAUTOR PRINCIPAL

DE ELLOS.

Impreſſa, con las licencias neceſſarias, en Mexico en la Imprenta de la Bibliotheca Mexicana, en la Puente del Eſpiritu Santo. Año de 1763.

Title page of Tamarón's six-page *Narrative of the Attempted Sacrilege Commited by Three Indians of a Pueblo of the Province of New Mexico and the Severe Punishment Divine Retribution Inflicted upon the Main Perpetrator among Them,* México, 1763.
Wagner, *Spanish Southwest,* II

In the generation after Agustín's memorable burlesque, the gods, both Christian and Pueblo, frowned on Pecos. Not that it was all smallpox, Comanches, famine, and death, but the Four Horsemen did gallop through these years with devastating clatter. Immersed in their own problems, not the least of which was manpower, the Franciscans neglected Pecos more and more, to the point in the 1770s and 1780s that they expected the people to come up to Santa Fe for baptism and marriage. The statistics, devoid though they are of human pathos, of the whimper of a dying child, chart the pueblo's unrelenting downward course.

Population			Baptisms	Marriages	Burials
1706	c.1000	1700-1709		124	
		1710-1719		94	
		1720-1729		65	
1730	544	1730-1739	230	56	138
		1740-1749	202	76	134
1750	449	1750-1759	186	50	98
1760	344	1760-1769	123	17	50
1776	269	1770-1779	30		
1789	138	1780-1789	40	33**	51**
1799	159*	1790-1799x	57	18	51

  * includes some refugee Tanos
 ** no entries for 1780-1781, time of great smallpox epidemic
  x first Spaniards and genízaros at San Miguel del Vado, 1798-1799
    (150 by 1799)

Before he was through with his thankless assignment, Fray Francisco Atanasio Domínguez, chosen comisario visitador in 1775 because of his capacity for incisive observation, his meticulousness, and his candid integrity, would cause his superiors to rue their choice. He was too incisive, too meticulous, too candid. Worse, he was a perfectionist, although not without a redeeming wit and sense of the ridiculous. The superiors wanted a report on conditions in the custody, which they knew were bad, but evidently they had not expected to be told, in such painful detail, just how bad.

The conscientious, Mexico City-bred Father Domínguez hit it off with Col. don Pedro Fermín de Mendinueta, a native of Navarra thirty-five years in the royal service. Mendinueta, who reflected the heightened attention to duty of Charles III's bureaucracy, had governed New Mexico for nearly a decade. In the spring of 1776, while Domínguez and his two companions shared Mendinueta's table, visitor and governor talked.

The Santa Fe church and convento. Horace T. Pierce's
drawing based on the 1776 description by Father Domínguez.
Adams and Chavez, *Missions*

"In the private conversations we two had during those
days," Domínguez reported to his provincial, "he asked me for
a friar for the Pecos mission, giving me good reasons, among
them the long time those souls have gone without spiritual
nourishment." The visitor agreed and at once assigned one of
his companions, the youthful Fray José Mariano Rosete y
Peralta. But just as Rosete was leaving, a letter arrived from
Fray Silvestre Vélez de Escalante of Zuñi. Vélez, who would
join Domínguez that summer in an attempt to reach Alta California by striking northwestward from Santa Fe, asked that
Rosete be named assistant at Zuñi. The visitor consented, and
"the mission of Pecos remained as before."

It was as if the friars of Santa Fe, who were supposed to
be looking after Pecos, along with Galisteo and Tesuque, had
forgotten the mission existed. During 1767 and 1768, Mendinueta's first two years in New Mexico, they had celebrated
twenty-one baptisms for the Pecos, but since then only fifteen
in seven years. During his entire tenure to date, nine years,
they had entered in the Pecos books only two marriages and
seven burials. "The lord governor deplores this," Domínguez
continued, "but he is satisfied with the reasons I have given
him to persuade him that not everything can be as we should
like."

Mendinueta was satisfied but not satisfied. When the
Father Visitor began to speak and gesture earnestly of explorations north and west from New Mexico, and of all the
heathen peoples crying out for baptism, the governor stopped
him cold with a question. "If there are not enough fathers for
those already conquered, how can there be any for those that
may be newly conquered?" It was a good question, one calculated, in Domínguez' words, to "chill a spirit ardently burning
to win souls." [51]

In late May or early June 1776—as sweat ran down the
necks of delegates to the Second Continental Congress in

Franciscan Neglect
of Pecos

The Meticulous
Visitation of Domínguez

Philadelphia, two thousand miles away—Fray Francisco Atanasio Domínguez conducted his visitation at Pecos, the most thorough ever. He began with a brief description of the physical setting.

The pueblo and mission of Nuestra Señora de los Ángeles de Pecos is 7 leagues southeast of Santa Fe at the foot and lower slope of the Sierra Madre [later, the Sangre de Cristo] mentioned at the said villa. It is located and established on a good piece of level ground offered by a low rock, which is easy to climb. This rock is more or less boxed in between a sierra and a mesa. The sierra [the Tecolote Range] lies to the east, about 3 or 4 leagues from the pueblo, and the mesa to the west, about a quarter of a league from it. The buildings are on the said rock, surrounded by a fence, or wall, of adobe [stone].

He moved on next to the meticulous portrayal, paraphrased earlier in this chapter, of church and convento. He did not bother with the casas reales, saying only that a former alcalde mayor, Vicente Armijo, had taken the balusters from the western mirador of the convento and put them in the casas reales.[52] To feed the missionary, when they had one, and his convento staff, the Pecos tended five pieces of ground: a "beautiful" walled vegetable garden abutting the cemetery on the west and four large milpas north, west, and south of the kitchen garden not more than a quarter-league away. They would not tell him what the yield was. Instead, "they do say uproariously that wheat, maize, etc., are sown, except for chile, and that a sufficient amount is harvested." Since there was no missionary, they had planted these field for themselves.

The Pueblo in 1776

As for the pueblo itself, the only entrance through the long low peripheral wall from the outside, said Domínguez, was a gate facing north.

A short distance from the entrance are some house blocks, or tenements all joined at the corners (*cuarteles o lienzos todos unidos por las esquinas*),[53] which form a little plaza within. One enters through a gate in the middle of the tenement facing east. Of these four tenements the two that face east and west are very wide. On top in the center they have dwellings that overlook both the little plaza inside which they enclose and the outside and are like the top section of a long and narrow tomb.

Beyond this little plaza to the south is another tenement, or house block, like the two described. The only difference is that it stands alone and is very long, extending from north to south. Farther beyond to the south are the church and convento.[54] Everything appears very large and can only be seen in perspective up from the north and down from the south.

By comparing Domínguez' word picture, as sketchy as it is, with the house blocks Father González listed in his 1750 census, and with the maps of A. V. Kidder's excavations, it is possible to correlate the lot. The two wide "tenements" on the east and the west of Domínguez are the "east side of plaza house block" and "plaza" of González, that is, the east and west sides of Kidder's main Pecos "quadrangle." The entrance midway along the east side, cited by Domínguez, shows clearly on the maps of Kidder. The third of Domínguez' "four tenements," which he did not describe, probably because it was a less impressive extension of the first two, is the "placita" of González and the U-shaped extremity at the south end of Kidder's quadrangle.

Pecos from the north: main pueblo, south pueblo, church and convento. An artist's restoration by S. P. Moorehead. Kidder, *Pecos, New Mexico*

The Domínguez tenement that "stands alone and is very long, extending from north to south" would seem to be the "community house block" of González and the mysterious "south pueblo" of Kidder. From the vantage of a hawk circling high over the elongated mesilla of Pecos in 1776, one would have seen the main pueblo complex at the northern tip, the long, thin south pueblo in the middle, and the mission compound at the southern end. The two pueblos, evidently both occupied when Alfonso Rael de Aguilar destroyed the kiva halfway between them in 1714, had continued to house the Pecos through most of the eighteenth century, even though the people's diminishing numbers would have permitted consolidation in one or the other.[55]

Father Domínguez counted one hundred "families" at Pecos, or 269 persons. Their language, he observed, was one with Jémez. "It is very different from all the other languages of these regions, and its pronunciation is closed, almost through clenched teeth." Rather matter-of-factly, and without commentary, he added that the Pecos spoke Spanish "very badly." Availing themselves of wood from the sierra, most of them were good carpenters.

Fray Francisco Atanasio Domínguez, Minister

The Pecos as Christians

Regarding their observance of the Christian faith, Domínguez, surprisingly enough, deemed the Pecos "devout and well inclined," which hardly squares with what he had to say later about the Pueblos in general. Alcalde mayor José Herrera assured the visitor that even though the Pecos had no missionary, they understood that their children "must go to the church daily to recite the catechism with the fiscal." On Saturday mornings and on feast days, everyone went to say the rosary. For baptisms and marriages, they journeyed up to Santa Fe where the friars would keep the Pecos books until a missionary returned to their pueblo. "With regard to burials," Domínguez noted, "if an Indian dies, the others perform the offices, etc."

Devout or not, the Pecos were in a bad way. Comanche raiding had forced them to give up their irrigated fields northeast of the pueblo along the Pecos River. Out of fear of this enemy, they no longer hauled the good water half a league up from the river, where swam, according to Domínguez, "many delicious trout." They relied instead on "some wells of reasonably good water below the rock." Even arable land dependent on rain, if it lay at a distance from the pueblo, was too dangerous to work.

Therefore, but a very small part remains for them. Since this is dependent on rain, it has been a failure because of the drought of the past years, and so they have nothing left. As a result, what few crops there usually are do not last even to the beginning of a new year from the previous October, and hence these miserable wretches are tossed about like a ball in the hands of fortune.

Governor Mendinueta had given them a dozen cows, which, taken with the eight the Comanches had left them, brought their herd to twenty. Once the Pecos had been rich in horses. Now they had twelve in all, "sorry nags" Domínguez called them. "Today these poor people are *in puribus,* fugitives from their homes, absent from their families, selling those trifles they once bought to make themselves decent, on foot, etc." [56]

Back in Santa Fe, Domínguez filled in briefly as minister of the villa, and thus as missionary of Pecos in absentia. In mid-June, he had a new book of baptisms begun for Pecos and on July 23, six days before he and Father Vélez de Escalante set out on their "splendid wayfaring" into the Great Basin, he made the first entry. Domingo Aguilar, of the prominent Pecos Aguilar clan, and his wife María Rosa had appeared at the church door in Santa Fe carrying a three-month-old son. Why had they delayed so long? the Padre inquired. They had been away from their pueblo, they told him, "looking for something to eat." [57]

The actions of some of his brethren had scandalized Father Domínguez, probably more than they should have. When he listed for his superiors all twenty-nine friars resident in the custody, including himself, he made no comment about thirteen who apparently were doing their job. Eight he classified as old and ill, or just ill, and one as blind. Two were drunks. Another, he alleged, lived openly with a married woman and another was an unruly, brawling trader "at the cost of the Indians' sweat." One each he characterized as

Domínguez Characterizes His Brethren

"ungovernable and living in scandal," "not at all obedient to rule and a trader with heathens," and "not at all obedient to rule and an agitator of Indians." [58]

The timely advent of forty-six friar recruits from Spain aboard the warship *El Rosario* in 1778 enabled the superiors to dispatch seventeen new men to the custody straight-away. Replacing the ailing and the unsuited, they brought the total to thirty-five, "leaving three as extras on hand to fill vacancies as has been customary." A neat listing, drawn up soon after, matching men and missions showed Fray José Manuel Martínez de la Vega at Pecos. If he really served there, it was only on the fly, and he baptized no one. He was soon at Alburquerque. Fray José Palacio, who signed himself "ministro de esta misión de Pecos," celebrated one baptism at the pueblo in 1779 and three in 1780. He may even have been resident for a time. [59] Then, unexpectedly, the smallpox hit, carrying off so many people that the royal governor urged reducing the number of missions.

Smallpox Ravages
the Province

The toll was ghastly. At Santo Domingo in February and the first week of March 1781, at least 230 Indians died. Up and down the river the count at several pueblos exceeded a hundred. The plague spread. Evidently many died at Pecos, but the burial records are lost. [60] Two censuses of the eastern pueblo, one before and one after, tell the tale:

1779   94 men, 94 women, 23 boys, 24 girls, or 235 persons
1789   62 men, 58 women, 6 boys, 12 girls, or 138 persons.

Reporting on May 1, 1781, the governor put the total number of men, women, and children dead in the contagion of 1780–1781, probably the worst ever, at 5,025, a quarter or more of the entire population. Under these circumstances, why, the governor asked, should not some of the desolated missions be joined together and the total number subsidized by the crown reduced proportionately, say to twenty.

Consolidation
of Missions

Ever since the visitation of Bishop Crespo in 1730, consolidation had been a dirty word with the missionares of New Mexico. Now the governor, the highly touted, economy-minded, military hero Juan Bautista de Anza, had them against the wall. His superior, the Caballero de Croix, first commandant general of the Provincias Internas and vice-patron of the church in this recently formed northern jurisdiction, liked the idea. No matter that the friars protested. Croix cut their missions to twenty. [61]

Teodoro de Croix, the
Caballero de Croix.
Thomas, *Teodoro de Croix*

In the case of Pecos, consolidation was merely a clerical
matter. For the previous two decades, while maintaining the
status of a mission and thus its claim to a full-time missionary
supported by royal allowance, Pecos had been treated in effect
as a visita, or preaching station, of Santa Fe. Since the stipend
went to the man and not to the mission, as was confirmed
several times in the 1780s, it was up to the custos to place his
men wherever he thought they would do the most good. By
formally attaching Pecos to Santa Fe as a visita in 1782, consolidation simply acknowledged a fact of long standing. Given
the hard times, Pecos, with its steadily declining native population and no nearby Hispanic communities, no longer warranted
the services of a full-time minister.

It worked as before. To regularize certain human relations in the eyes of the church, Fray Francisco de Hozio, minister at Santa Fe and "pro ministro" of Pecos, ordered chief catechist Lorenzo to bring all the people who needed marrying up to the villa. Ten Pecos couples showed and, on January 4, 1782, in mid-winter, all were duly married. Three weeks later, Custos Juan Bermejo, who also served as chaplain of the Santa Fe presidio, rode over to Pecos with a military escort to baptize two new babies. Soldiers stood as godfathers, and the friar signed as custos and pro ministro of Pecos "for lack of a minister." While he was there, Bermejo married one more couple and, at a nuptial Mass, veiled all ten previously joined in Santa Fe on the fourth. [62]

Pecos Exempted from War Tax   Later in 1782, because of their poverty and their losses to smallpox the year before, the Pecos, along with Zuñis and Hopis, missed their chance to contribute to the war against England and, indirectly, to the independence of the United States. The king had decreed that all free subjects of the colonies donate something to the war chest, each Indian and mixed-blood one peso, and each Spaniard two. But after Governor Anza and Custos Bermejo had visited Pecos in August of 1782, they conceded that the poor people of that pueblo should be exempt. And the commandant general agreed.[63]

A 1784 Spanish real,
the size of a dime,
found at Pecos during
excavations in 1966.
National Park Service
photo by Fred E. Mang, Jr.

Preoccupied as they were with personal Indian diplomacy
and defense, subjects of the next chapter, both Anza and his
successor don Fernando de la Concha still managed to keep
a close eye on mission affairs, much too close to suit the friars.
The governors chided the missionaries about the Indians'
ignorance of Christian doctrine and urged stricter enforcement
of attendance. In turn, Custos José de la Prada, in 1783,
bewailed Anza's interference, especially in placing missionaries.
The following year, a delegation of New Mexico friars turned
up in Arizpe to complain about Anza before Commandant
General Felipe de Neve and to answer charges the governor
had preferred against them. They resented everything from his
consolidation plan and his juggling of mission allowances and
boundaries to his partisan judgments and false accusations.

Interference Charged by Missionaries

Unfortunately, the Franciscans themselves were too badly
divided to do much about the meddling of the governors. This
disharmony ran deeper than the routine lack of fraternal
charity deplored by their superiors from time to time. This was
criollo versus peninsular Spaniard, *americano* versus *gachupín,*
a malady that pervaded all of colonial life, as old as the first
generation born in the Americas, yet now, in the age of revolutions and independence, all the more virulent.

Franciscans Divided

Under Anza, a rare criollo governor, and Custos Bermejo,
a Spaniard who allied himself with Anza, the gachupín friars

Fernando de la Concha

in New Mexico charged blatant discrimination. In 1782, they cited nine specific cases. This tension between American and European friars, a tension that built during the years leading up to independence, explains their preoccupation with an old policy of the province known as the *alternativa*. It provided rotation of office, with superiors chosen alternately from americanos and gachupines, as well as equality of representation on the definitory and even throughout a missionary field like New Mexico. When they should have been pulling together, some of the friars were instead competing, concerned during the 1780s and 1790s with a growing imbalance in favor of the gachupines.[64]

Governor Concha Inspects Pecos

The Pecos had already assembled, as many of them as there were in October 1789. Don Fernando de la Concha, flanked by soldiers and his secretary, listened without understanding as the interpreter intoned in Towa the threefold purpose of his visitation. The royal governor would hear their claims, he would take a census, and he would review their weapons and accoutrements of war. The Pecos alleged no injuries by government officials, either to their lands or to their possessions. They did make certain petty claims which the governor settled forthwith. Of the 138 Pecos enrolled, Concha judged forty men well mounted and armed and fit for military service. Even though they confessed only on their deathbeds and did not understand Spanish, he concluded that the Pecos were "not among the worst instructed in the Christian doctrine." After he had delivered the usual sermon, the Spanish governor departed as quickly as he had come.[65]

The arrival in Santa Fe of Custos Pedro de Laborería and a band of missionaries "to be employed in the missions," late in August 1790, put pressure on Concha to raise the number of missions again. He compromised. In consultation with Laborería, he came up with a plan "altering in a small way the consolidation Col. don Juan Bautista de Anza, my predecessor, effected in 1782." He reelevated Pecos and three other pueblos from visitas to full-fledged missions, and he approved the assignment of missionaries. With some reservations, he recommended two extra missionary allowances. The viceroy, he knew, was for holding the line. After all, Anza's consolidation had been saving the crown 3,695 pesos annually, while, in the viceroy's words, "all the goals of service to God and king continue to be achieved." [66]

That same year, 1790, while federal marshals counted people in the new United States of America to determine representation and taxation, the Viceroy Conde de Revillagigedo also called for population counts from every corner of New Spain. They were to show name, ethnic group, age, family status, and occupation of adults, as well as the number and ages of all dependent children. That fall, Father Severo Patero and Alcalde mayor Antonio José Ortiz, both of Santa Fe, compiled the rolls for their district which also embraced the missions of Pecos and Tesuque.

The Census of 1790

The Pecos census of 1790 differed from the one of 1750 in several ways, other than the very obvious two-thirds drop in total population, from 449 to 154. For one thing, Father Patero made no effort at all to list native names. He put down only the Spanish given name, supplying in six cases a Spanish surname: José Miguel de la Peña, Tomás de Sena, Domingo Aguilar, Lorenzo Sena, Antonio Baca, and Matías Aguilar. He gave their ages, most of them doubtless guesses, but he provided no hint where anyone lived in the pueblo. Considering all Pueblos farmers, he did not bother with occupation. Although he titled the roll "Census of the Indians of Pecos," he listed first "don José Mares, Spaniard, age 77, widower, one son, 13." Evidently Mares, a retired soldier and plains explorer, was living at Pecos in 1790 as an Indian agent or local administrator of the Comanche peace signed four year earlier.[67]

Four years later, in 1794, there were 180 Indians at Pecos, including some Tano families, a rare increase of nearly twenty percent, but no Spaniards were listed.[68]

When Viceroy Revillagigedo sent off to Spain late in 1793 his 430-paragraph report on the missions of New Spain, including the 1790 census figures from New Mexico, he lamented the spiritual backwardness of the Pueblo Indians. "The saddest thing," he wrote,

Religious Coexistence in New Mexico

is that after the more than 200 years the Indians of New Mexico have been reduced they are as ignorant of the Faith and religion as if they were just starting catechism, giving evidence of this regrettable truth in many notorious cases and in fact.

Viceroy the Conde de Revillagigedo II, 1789-1794.
Rivera Cambas, *Los gobernantes,* I

It is true that they baptize the recently born Indian, but it is also true that they never use any other name than the one his parents gave him from the first thing they saw after the infant's birth, for example Mouse, Dog, Wolf, Owl, Cottonwood, etc. And thus everyone calls him in their language, and he forgets entirely the saint's name given him at baptism.

When the Indian reaches the age of six or seven he must attend instruction morning and afternoon. But this is achieved only with difficulty, and as a result, since the beginnings of their

Christian education are so feeble and cease the day of their marriage or in the first years of their youth, they forget very rapidly the little they learned, abandoning themselves to their evil inclinations and customs and dying not much different than heathens.

They are heathens underneath and very given to the vain respect and superstitions of their elders. They have a natural antipathy for everything to do with our sacred religion. Few confess until the moment of death, and then the majority by means of an interpreter, and in order to get it over they do no characteristic Christian works nor do they contribute a thing in gratitude to God and king. [69]

At least the viceroy had no favorites. The customs of the Spaniards and mixed-bloods of New Mexico, he allowed, were not much better. Father Domínguez would have said amen to that.

Whatever the reasons, the friars had failed to impose upon the Pueblos more than a patchy veneer of Christianity. For all their zeal, they had not stamped out kivas or kachinas, either by violent suppression or by gentle persuasion. They had not broken the Pueblos' pagan spirit. They had not learned their languages. In fact, during the eighteenth century, they had come grudgingly to accept coexistence. They kept on baptizing and marrying, but by now they recognized that spiritual conquest had eluded them, that the ultimate salvation of the Pueblo Indians lay beyond their means. "May God Our Lord destroy these pretexts so completely," Father Domínguez prayed, "that these wretches may become old Christians and the greatest saints of His Church." [70]

El Vado Grant

Late in 1794, as the Spanish-born minister of Santa Fe, Tesuque, and Pecos advocated the use of "more rigor than gentleness" to enforce Indian attendance at Mass and catechism, one Lorenzo Márquez, citizen of Santa Fe, stood before Lt. Col. Fernando Chacón, the new governor of New Mexico. Márquez and fifty-one other men, finding their present lands and waters insufficient for the support of their growing families, formally petitioned for a grant of vacant land on the Pecos River at a place "commonly called El Vado." [71]

For the pueblo de los Pecos the settlement of that grant was the beginning of the end.

pecos, the plains, and the provincias internas
1704-1794

The trade that the French are developing with the Comanches by means of the Jumanos will in time result in grave injury to this province. Although the Comanche nation carries on a like trade with us, coming to the pueblo of Taos, where they hold their fairs and trade in skins and Indians of various nations, whom they enslave in their wars, for horses, mares, mules, hunting knives, and other trifles, always, whenever the occasion offers for stealing horses or attacking the pueblos of Pecos and Galisteo, they do not pass it up. Indeed, during the five-year term of don Joaquín Codallos, my predecessor, the number of Pecos who perished at their hands reached one hundred and fifty.

They have such a grudge against these two pueblos that I find it necessary to garrison them with thirty presidial soldiers and to keep scouts out, so that by detecting them in time they can warn me and I can sally to meet them. . . . I have fortified these two pueblos of Pecos and Galisteo with earthworks and towers at the gates capable of defending them against these enemies, since the presidio cannot always keep the garrison there because it has many places to cover.

> Gov. Tomás Vélez Cachupín to the viceroy, Santa Fe, March 8, 1750

Top Details from Bernardo de Miera y Pacheco's 1758 map.

Above Comanche feats of horsemanship, a painting by George
Catlin, 1834.
Catlin, *North American Indians*, II

The plains had always been a paradox. At once a source
of riches, of hides and meat and ideas, and of death, of thieves
and raiders, the benefits to the Pecos had long outweighed the
detriments. Sad for them, as for the Saline pueblos before
them, the scales reversed in the eighteenth century.

By 1750, their vital locale at the gateway between pueblos
and plains had become a curse instead of a blessing. Sorely
weakened by internal dissension and emigration, by pestilence,
warfare, and interruption of trade, the "citadel" that once
fielded five hundred warriors and struck fear into neighboring
peoples now depended for defense on Spanish military aid and
diplomacy. Not that the Pecos fighters had gone soft. They
were just too few.

As late as the 1690s, it can be argued that the Pecos held
the balance of power, that without their aid, Diego de Vargas
might well have lost New Mexico. Vargas said almost as
much himself, and he rewarded the Pecos accordingly. Yet
with the death of the two enduring Pecos dons, Felipe Chistoe
in the mid-1720s and Juan Tindé in 1730, that era passed. A
half-century later when Juan Bautista de Anza rode down to
Pecos to negotiate a peace and save New Mexico from the
ravages of invasion, it was not a Pecos he embraced, but a
Comanche.

By dint of its location, the pueblo of the Pecos maintained
a strategic importance despite its declining population. The
Spaniards could not afford to lose it. Otherwise, Santa Fe lay
open from the southern plains. The place, then, became more
important than the people, a shift reflected even in the Spaniards' name for the pueblo. At the beginning of the century
they invariably called it *el pueblo de los Pecos,* the pueblo of
the Pecos people. Later it became simply *el pueblo de Pecos,*
Pecos pueblo, the place.

More and more the significance of Pecos was seen in its relationship to Hispanic Santa Fe. Daring Frenchmen who blazed "the Santa Fe Trail" in the 1730s and 1740s thanked God to reach Pecos, but they did not stop there. Those imperial strategists in Mexico City and Madrid who conceived defense plans embracing the entire northern "provincias internas," from the Mississippi Valley to the Californias, could see that a road from San Antonio or from St. Louis struck the province of New Mexico at Pecos. It was a port of entry. Then, in the very last years of the century, with the settlement of San Miguel del Vado at the river crossing ten leagues east, even that distinction was lost.

The Pecos as
Auxiliaries

The Pecos did not fade overnight. The Spaniards continued to think of them very much as people, albeit exploitable second-class people, well into the eighteenth century, as long as their pueblo remained a major center of trade with the Plains Indians, as long as Pecos auxiliaries fought at their side.

Until the 1730s, the Pecos on any given campaign were likely to outnumber the fighting men from any other pueblo. Routinely, Fray José de Arranegui noted on July 1, 1702, the death of Francisco Fuu, husband of María Tugoguchuru, killed by the Jumanos "when Gov. Pedro Rodríguez Cubero sent out 56 Indians from this pueblo." Early in the spring of 1704, don Felipe Chistoe and forty-six Pecos answered the call for what proved to be Diego de Vargas' last campaign, three times as many men as from any other pueblo. A decade later, Governor Flores Mogollón dispatched a much larger force into the same area against the same foe, into the Sierra de Sandía against Faraón Apaches. This time, of the 321 auxiliaries summoned from fifteen pueblos to the rendezvous at Santo Domingo, one hundred were Pecos. Zía with thirty-six was second.[1]

They must have gone out on dozens of such campaigns. There were almost certainly Pecos with Sargento mayor Juan de Ulibarrí in 1706 on his touted trip to El Cuartelejo, more than a hundred leagues northeast of Santa Fe. Again that year, word had reached the villa from the Picurís remnant who had fled from Vargas back in 1696 and since then had been living among the "Cuartelejo Apaches." They wanted to come home. In response, Governor Cuervo y Valdés charged Ulibarrí to ransom them and escort them back.

Ulibarrí, Cuervo's alcalde mayor of Pecos and newly refounded Galisteo, named Capt. José Trujillo substitute alcalde for the duration, bolstered his forty Hispanos with a hundred

Indian auxiliaries "from the pueblos and missions of this kingdom," and set out north from Santa Fe in mid-July. In seven weeks he was back. Not only had he seen El Cuartelejo and entered into friendly relations with the local Apaches, but he had also learned of Frenchmen among their enemies the Pawnees and had taken possession of this delightful region for Spain. Moreover, he had "liberated" the famous leaders don Lorenzo and don Juan Tupatú and some sixty Picurís, a few of whom settled at Pecos. [2]

Whoever the Pharaoh, or Faraón, Apaches were to the Spaniards, they cannot have been so confused in the minds of the Pecos. Perhaps at times, the same Apache band did alternately raid and trade at Pecos. More likely, it was the Spaniards' loose classification, their admission that "they all look alike," that made the Faraones the special friends of the Pecos one minute and the foes of Pecos auxiliaries the next.

Faraón Apaches as Friends and Foes

There is no doubt from the Vargas journals that certain Plains Apaches, sometimes labeled Faraones, reestablished trade at Pecos during the 1690s, a trade they maintained into the 1730s, at least until the Comanches convulsed the southern plains. It is also clear from burial entries at Pecos and from other sources that other Apaches, also termed Faraones, preyed on the Pecos during this same period.

They struck any time of year without warning. Diego Suuchan, a married man, died in July 1697 a quarter-league from the pueblo when "the Apaches slit his throat" or decapitated him. On March 6, 1701, Father Arranegui buried Pedro Pui, about twenty-four, an orphan, "killed by the Apaches at the river." He buried four more victims, one a woman, in the spring of 1703. In August 1704, Apaches killed Francisco Antonio "and brought in his body." The body of Francisco Guatori, unmarried, the fourth death attributed to Apaches in 1705, "did not turn up, only his bones." Because of a lost book, the burial record at Pecos breaks off abruptly early in 1706 not to resume until mid-1727. Meantime, in 1711, the Marqués de la Peñuela asked the Pecos to confirm that he had responded with soldiers "when their enemies the Apaches have done them harm, as he did when they killed don Pedro, native governor of the pueblo, and Lt. Col. Juan Páez Hurtado went in pursuit." [3]

If the Spaniards were confused, the Pecos themselves made a clear distinction between the Faraones of the plains and the Faraones who regularly took refuge in the Sierra de Sandía. The latter they branded "thieving Indian pirates" and murderers. In August of 1714, while many of the Pecos men

Mounted Pueblo (?) Indian auxiliaries versus unidentified Apaches.
After an 18th-century painting on hide (Segesser I) in Gottfried Hotz,
Indian Skin Paintings from the American Southwest (Norman, 1970).

were on campaign in the Sandías, seven Apaches, identified by
the Pecos themselves as members of the Sandía band, showed
up at the pueblo. A couple of older men and five women and
children, this was no war party. No matter, the Pecos were for
killing them on the spot. José de Apodaca, agent of Alcalde
mayor and master blacksmith Sebastián de Vargas, said no.
He notified Vargas, who came down from Santa Fe and took
this motley bunch back with him to appear before Governor
Flores.

Agustín, a Pecos who knew both the Apaches' language
and Spanish, interpreted, hardly an impartial officer of the court.
Through him, all the Apaches told different stories. Their
captain had sent them to see if the Pecos were alert because
others were coming to steal. They had come peacefully seeking food. They wanted to trade. They had come from the
Cerro de las Gallinas beyond the Sandías. They had come from
the Cerro de las Cebollas. There were twenty tents with their
captain. There were two women with their captain. With that,
interpreter Agustín "stated that he had told the truth and just
what the Apaches had said, neither adding nor omitting a
thing."

A couple of days later don Juan Tindé and several of his people stood before the governor to explain why they had wanted to kill these Apaches. Felipe Chistoe interpreted for those who did not speak Spanish. All agreed. These Faraones had killed a Pecos during the time of Governor Cuervo y Valdés (1705–1707). Besides, "they are thieving Indian pirates who make their base in the Sierra de Sandía from which they sally forth to rob horses and cattle from the pueblo of Galisteo, said pueblo of Pecos, Santo Domingo, Bernalillo, and other ranchos." Even the Apaches who came in peace to trade at Pecos knew the Faraones of the Sandías to be bad, horse-stealing Indians.

Governor Flores did not vacillate. He sentenced the two adult males to work on an ore crusher where they were to be kept shackled to prevent their return to thievery. He gave an old woman to a citizen of Santa Cruz de la Cañada. The remaining two women and two boys were to be sold in Sonora or elsewhere to persons who would try to make Christians of them. The governor accepted Alfonso Rael de Aguilar's offer to buy them and transport them out of New Mexico for two hundred pesos, a sum he promptly distributed as follows: fifty pesos to the Third Order of St. Francis, fifty to Alcalde mayor Vargas for bringing in the Apaches, twenty-five to the governor's secretary for his services, and the remainder to the honest poor.[4]

A year later when the governor held councils of war to consider a punitive expedition against raiding Plains Apaches, called variously Chipaynes (sometimes Chilpaines or Chipaindes), Limitas, Trementinas, or Faraones, the native governor of Taos pointed out a conflict of interest. The Pecos, he said, should not be allowed to go. They and these Faraones were virtually one people. Back when the Pecos were reduced, this Taos averred, the Faraones had left them and fled out onto the plains. Since then, these fugitives had been wont to mingle during the trading at Pecos and then, on leaving, to steal from the district of Santa Cruz de la Cañada, from Picurís and Taos, and from the friendly Jicarilla Apaches who came to trade at Taos. Naturally the Pecos would warn their old partners. Capt. Félix Martínez also objected to the Pecos going, but for a different reason. With the presidio undermanned and the Pecos auxiliaries out on campaign, he thought the Faraones might circle round and attack the weakened pueblo.

But the Pecos did go, thirty of them under Chistoe and Tindé "with muskets." And they took the blame. The whole force—37 soldiers, 18 settlers, and 146 Pueblo auxiliaries—commanded by Juan Páez Hurtado, left from Picurís on August 30, 1715, picked up Jicarilla allies en route, and ended up on the Río Colorado, the Canadian of today, only to discover that the Apaches they were after had decamped. With supplies running low they turned back. "I presume," wrote the disappointed Páez about his vanished enemy, "that from the trading conducted at Pecos they got word that the Spaniards were coming after them."

Not only did the Páez fiasco reveal the heated rivalry between Taos and its regular Apache trading partners on the one hand and Pecos and its Plains "Faraón" partners on the other, but it also said something about the Pecos. Plainly they knew one Faraón from another.[5]

Trade Fairs at Pecos   The annual fall trade gatherings at Pecos, sometimes called *rescates* and sometimes *ferias,* held up as long as the Plains Apaches did. Governor Peñuela, accused of usurping "the trade that comes to the pueblos and frontiers of Taos, San Juan, and Pecos," answered his critics in 1711. The Pecos, at Peñuela's bidding, testified

that they are and have always been involved in trade, and that they enjoy very great advantage from the Apache Indians, Faraones, Chipaynes, and Jacindes, who are accustomed to come to their pueblo most years. The Pecos buy from them buffalo meat, lard, grease, buckskins, buffalo hides, buffalo or elkskins, and some Apache children slaves [and other Plains Indian captives] whom they capture from the enemies with whom they wage war. These the Pecos buy from said Apaches for a horse or two at most and sell them to the Spaniards for four or five horses, from which they realize very great profits. [6]

Peñuela, at pains to show how his employment of Pecos Indians on church construction in Santa Fe benefited them in their trading, explained why he had paid each worker two awls instead of the usual trade knife. Earlier in the year, he had sent to Parral for thirty dozen "Madrid knives." These, along with many other goods on the governor's account, had been lost en route in an attack by hostile Suma Indians. Unable to acquire any iron elsewhere, Peñuela ordered some iron bars intended for use in the mines broken up as well as plowshares for the presidio's fields. From this, master blacksmith Sebastián de Vargas made a great quantity of awls, two of which the governor gave to each Indian.

Vargas, in 1711 lieutenant alcalde mayor of Pecos and Galisteo, swore that he had seen the Pecos trading the awls to good advantage with heathen Apaches for buffalo or elk-skins and meat. "He also saw how some of said Pecos Indians were taking to the Apaches a bowl-shaped basket of tobacco and with it an awl for which they got a skin." [7]

Pecos Alcalde mayor Sebastián de Vargas acknowledges receipt of fifty pesos, his share from the sale of some Faraón Apaches, September 9, 1714 (SANM, II, no. 210).

When the Chipayne Apaches showed up at Pecos in August 1711 with their skins and captives to trade "as they customarily do some years," they sold out quickly and left. Later Capt. Juan García de la Riva discovered that he had bought not a heathen Plains Indian youngster but a Spanish-speaking Christian lad abducted from the Rio Grande missions of Coahuila. Ordering everyone else who had acquired a captive from the Chipaynes to bring him or her in for examination, Peñuela identified three more Christians. He warned their new owners to treat them as such, then wrote to the governor of Coahuila via the governor of Nueva Vizcaya and the corregidor of Zacatecas asking what he should do. The response, if any, has not come to light. [8]

It was customary in New Mexico for the alcalde mayor of the district to open and preside over the trading. As unobtrusively as possible, he was to set fair prices and to maintain order. All parties presumably benefited from such supervision, and the heathens were spared "the excesses and injuries that arise from the insatiable greed of the citizens of this kingdom." Often Indians who had come in peace to trade had been provoked to anger by the Hispanos' misdeeds. The trouble was that hardly anyone could agree on the line between beneficial regulation of trade and monopolistic exploitation by the governor and his alcaldes mayores.

The citizens were always complaining of interference by the alcaldes. In 1725, Gov. Juan Domingo de Bustamante, later accused by the friars of lining his pockets in every conceivable way, decreed for the record that no alcalde obstruct or alter the customary free trade in captives brought by the heathens to the Taos Valley, San Juan, and Pecos. He dispatched the original to each of the three alcaldes in turn for his acknowledgement and signature. As was standard, each official made a copy and posted it on the door of the local casas reales. Alcalde mayor Manuel Tenorio de Alba tacked up the decree at Pecos on October 1.⁹

Trade in Captive Indians

Although in volume and worth the trade in buffalo hides and fine tanned skins far exceeded the "ransom" of non-Christian captives, no item was more important to the local Hispanos or more avidly sought after than these human *piezas.* Mostly they were children or young women, for their men died fighting, were put to death, or were too tough to "domesticate." No Hispano of New Mexico, however lowly his station, felt that he had made good until he had one or more of these children to train as servants in his home and to give his name. Men wanted to present them to their brides as wedding gifts. They were as sure a symbol of status as a fine horse.

Baptized and raised in Hispano homes, these captive Apache, Navajo, Ute, Comanche, Wichita, or Pawnee children assumed the culture of their new surroundings and lost their tribal identity, or, as the anthropologists say, they were acculturated and detribalized. When they came of age, they generally married others of their kind or, in some cases, a Hispano or a Pueblo Indian, further blurring their heritage. As a class in New Mexico they were called *genízaros.*

When captive children were acquired by the Pueblo Indians, they were of course baptized and given a Christian name to satisfy the friars, but they remained Indians so long as they kept to an Indian environment. Nor did they seem to lose their old identity so fast, at least not for a generation or so. It was the same with foreign Pueblos, who turned up in the Pecos books as Miguel Zía, Lorenzo Picurí, Antonio el Queres, or Antonio Tano; hence, Catalina la Yuta, Juan Antonio Jicarilla, and Juana Manuela Jumana. Although the exclusiveness of Pueblo society naturally limited the practice of keeping captives among them, some Pueblos did. On December 28, 1743, for example, after Fray Agustín Antonio de Iniesta had baptized two Apache girls at Pecos, he noted that "both of them belong to Antonio, the governor of this pueblo, who stood as godfather."

Coronado had found slaves from the plains living at Pecos. Along with trade contacts, "under the eaves" of their pueblo and out on the plains, the presence of these foreigners among them may have "contaminated" the typical Pueblo community with Plains individualism and self-assertiveness, at least among members of the more susceptible trading faction. Whatever the effect, it must have continued throughout the eighteenth century, for the missionaries assigned to Pecos kept baptizing, marrying, and burying a potpourri of Utes, Pawnees, Wichitas, unspecified Apaches, Jicarilla Apaches, Carlana Apaches, and a good many others identified simply as the children of "heathen parents." [10]

For the Franciscans of New Mexico, the traffic in heathen children presented both an opportunity and a dilemma. The superiors vacillated. In 1700, the custos forbade the friars to acquire the ransomed offspring of Apaches or other heathens, even for the sake of making Christians of them or training them to serve in the convento. It laid the missionaries open to charges of acquisitiveness, trading, and keeping human chattel. The prohibition was reiterated often enough to indicate that the practice continued. In 1738, Custos Juan García did so once more: "Again we direct that the religious abstain from attending the trading, much less from acquiring *piezas* to sell and going armed for this purpose." [11] Yet, in 1749, Custos Andrés Varo conceded that they still did so.

> The heathen Indians [who commit hostilities] come back to the pueblos in peace bringing buffalo hides and deerskins and some Indian children they have captured in the wars they wage among themselves. The citizens and *gente de razón*, Spaniards, and Pueblo Indians trade for them with horses, mules, knives, awls, clothing, beads, and other things. Once in a while the religious of the mission to which they come trades for some skins, and if he manages to ransom some Indian it is to add him to the pueblo. [12]

A ruckus at the Pecos "fair" early in August, 1726, illustrates how fights could break out between an officious alcalde mayor and greedy traders. To hear Alcalde mayor Manuel Tenorio tell it, he was simply doing his duty, opening trade between the heathens and the many Hispanos who had collected

Rowdy Traders
at Pecos, 1726

that day and setting prices "favorable to the citizenry as is customary." But this time, a rowdy bunch of traders led by twenty-three-year-old Diego Manuel Baca of Santa Fe cut him short. Scandalously ignoring Tenorio and the office he held, they set up shop on their own and "in their ambitious greed" commenced trading straight-away. Seeing their hostile mood and how many of them there were, the alcalde judiciously withdrew and looked for witnesses who would testify to this outrage.

Coincidentally, don Pedro de Rivera, appointed by the viceroy to conduct an exhaustive inspection of northern frontier defenses, was still in Santa Fe. A Spanish-born member of his party had commissioned Alcalde mayor Tenorio to get him a good heathen child during the trading at Pecos. The Pecos missionary, Fray Antonio Gabaldón, also wanted a *pieza pequeña*. When the heathens arrived laden with buffalo meat to trade to the Pecos but with only a few captives, Tenorio's attempt to select the best two for his customers before opening the trading to anyone else evidently set off the row.

Baca incited the others, yelling that the trading was for the people not for government officials. Pushing and shoving, they bid the four or five captives up to three and four horses each, plus bridles, "getting the worse of the bargain." It served them right, said Tenorio, who recorded the testimonies of four witnesses in his faltering hand and sent them off to Governor Bustamante.[13]

Meantime, the aggrieved citizenry had prevailed upon certain of the friars to lay bare before Inspector Rivera the avaricious, stifling, illegal trade practices employed by Bustamante and his alcaldes to squeeze the New Mexico turnip dry. When the governor found out, according to one friar, his pleasant toleration of the Franciscans turned to mortal hatred.[14]

Among the humble exports packed south by New Mexico's "merchants," buffalo hides and bales of tanned skins acquired in trade at Pecos and elsewhere ranked high. Up through the 1730s and 1740s, the era of Procurador general fray Juan Miguel Menchero, the Franciscans still freighted mission supplies north in wagons leased from private contractors, and merchants, both importers and exporters, still shipped their goods by agreement with the friars. Some New Mexicans made annual trips to the government-run stores in Chihuahua. Apparently certain of the friars were tempted too. In a report to Menchero, one conscientious missionary suggested that "the religious not be permitted to leave New Mexico for the villa of Chihuahua with the citizenry or for any other reason

because this is usually [an excuse] to trade in tanned skins, buffalo hides, and other goods, all of which is foreign to the religious state." [15]

Later in the century, the great annual exodus of Chihuahua, the *cordón* or *conducta*, as it was called, a raucous party of four or five hundred New Mexico traders and stockgrowers, with mule trains, soldier escort, and countless sheep, still carried the hides and skins from the plains. By then, however, Taos had far outstripped Pecos in volume.

The reasons were several, the same ones that account for the pueblo's steadily declining population. Certainly the most dramatic was the appearance of a hard-riding, hard-fighting Plains people who began to war with the Pecos in the 1730s and who favored Taos for trade. Not that this people killed so

Opposite A trade knife or *belduque,* descended from the all-purpose European peasant knife. After Sidney B. Brinckerhoff and Pierce A. Chamberlain, *Spanish Military Weapons in Colonial America,* 1700-1821 (Harrisburg, Pa., 1972)
Above Pack train at Taos pueblo, by Henry R. Poore. Elbridge S. Brooks, *The Story of the American Indian* (Boston, 1887)

many Pecos—a misconception set in motion by Governor Vélez Cachupín in 1750—but that they so turned the southern plains world upside-down that the Apache trading partners of the Pecos, their suppliers, were scattered about like chaff in the wind.

This people was the Comanche.

The Rise of the Comanche Nation

The Comanche did not spring at full gallop from the head of a mythological buffalo. Their advent was almost meek. Drawn out of the basin and range country west of the Rockies by trade, horses, and the plains, they arrived in New Mexico about the turn of the eighteenth century in the tow of the Utes, fellow Shoshonean speakers. Almost immediately, allied bands of Utes and Comanches began contending with the semi-sedentary Jicarillas for hunting and trading grounds. By the second decade of the century, they had these Apaches begging the Spaniards for baptism. Their horse stealing under guise of peace, their murderous raids on the northern settlements, and their interruption of Apache trade had the Spaniards cursing their "barbarity." In 1719, Governor Valverde resolved to teach them a lesson.

Mustered at Taos in September, this was no token force —sixty presidials, forty-five settlers, and 465 Pueblos, later

Comanche women and children by George Catlin, 1834.
Catlin, *North American Indians,* II

joined by nearly two hundred Apaches. This was war. Fray
Juan George del Pino of Pecos rode as chaplain. Strung out,
Spaniards in front, pack animals in the middle, and native
auxiliaries at the rear, with scouts ranging the flanks, they advanced northeastward through the pleasant valleys of Jicarilla
and Carlana Apaches who pointed to the ravages committed by
the enemy. Near the Arkansas River, they came on several
deserted Comanche camps marked by cold fires and the tracks
of travois poles leading away. The Cuartelejo Apaches clamored
for Spanish aid, against Utes and Comanches, against Pawnees
and Jumanos, against westward-moving Frenchmen who gave
firearms to their enemies. But winter was coming. Valverde
could not go on. He had not even seen a Comanche.[16]

By the time of Brigadier Pedro de Rivera's visit in 1726,
the Comanches, "a nation as barbarous as it is warlike," had
earned a notoriety of their own.

Their origin is unknown, because they are always on the move and
in battle array, for they war with all tribes. They halt at any
camp site and set up their campaign tents, which are made of
buffalo hide and transported by large dogs which they raise for this
purpose. The men's clothing covers no more than the loins, the women's
falls below the knee. As soon as they conclude the trade that brings them
there, which is confined to tanned skins, buffalo hides, and the Indian
children they capture (because they kill the adults), they withdraw,
continuing their wandering until another time.[17]

Small cross found
east of the Pecos
church where Apaches
camped.
Gunnerson and Gunnerson,
"Evidence"

Displaced Apaches

If the Pecos felt any pressure from the Comanches during
the 1720s, the Spaniards did not record it. There is not even a
reference to Comanches trading at Pecos. By the mid-1730s,
however, the disruption these new plainsmen were causing had
begun to strain the symbiotic trade relationships the Pecos had
long enjoyed with certain Apache bands. Over the years to
come, the quiet dissolution of this trade probably figured more
heavily in the decline of Pecos than all the notorious Comanche
assaults put together.[18]

For the first time, displaced Jicarillas, formerly the special
allies of rival Taos, began to appear in the Pecos books. Something was certainly going on during January 1734 when Fray
Antonio Gabaldón catechized, baptized, and buried in the
Pecos cemetery five Apaches. One he said was "a captain of
the Apaches." Three were Jicarillas: a woman about ninety
who had suffered an arrow wound in the heart, a boy, and a
little girl. The following month he baptized another Jicarilla
child "of heathen parents." These refugees, running from Co-

manches or other Apaches, had sought shelter at Pecos. In 1738, Fray Juan George del Pino, assured by the interpreter and the Pecos catechists of a Jicarilla woman's constancy and "moved by charity and the fear of her ill health, administered to her the water of baptism in the manner and form prescribed by the manual for adults." She had been living at Pecos for three years.[19]

Comanche Assaults But it was the assaults that made news. Even though the first two Pecos deaths attributed to Comanches occurred in 1739, the really newsworthy attacks began in the 1740s during the governorship of Joaquín Codallos y Rabal. Why the Comanches, or one division of them, wanted to destroy Pecos and Galisteo is not clear. Certainly the Pecos had long been associated in trade with Apaches, and now they harbored Jicarillas. Whatever the reasons for the Comanches' grudge, they came not merely to steal horses but to vanquish as well.

Joaquín Codallos y Rabal

Few details of the first blow survive. It fell on San Juan's Day eve, June 23, 1746. The Comanches fought as if possessed. With a burning log, they tried to fire church and convento. The Pecos beat them back putting up so stiff a defense that the attackers finally withdrew after killing a dozen inhabitants, including two women, three children, and three Jicarilla Apaches. They abducted a Pecos boy seven years old, and they took off with the pueblo's horses.

Reacting with unusual speed Lt. Gov. Manuel Sáenz de Garvisu, with fifty presidial soldiers, some civilians, and Indians from Pecos and Galisteo, gave chase. They found the boy dead on the trail "from arrows and hatchet blows." As they began to close, the Comanches, slowed by the stolen horses, wheeled around "in a great multitude" to do pitched battle.

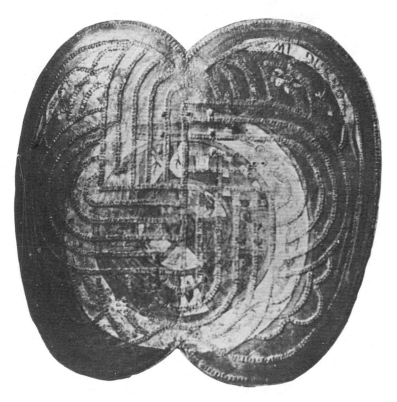

Spanish officer's shield,
or *adarga,* of three-ply
bull hide.
Brinckerhoff and Faulk,
Lancers

More than sixty of the enemy died according to Spanish count. But of far greater concern to the governor, nine soldiers and one civilian were killed. In brash defiance, Comanches hit Galisteo two weeks later, killing an old man who was herding some cows.

Reporting to the viceroy, Governor Codallos told how the Comanches were guided by apostates from New Mexico who knew the waterholes, ranches, and settlements. Besides that, they were a numerous nation and so well disciplined in warfare that they had defeated other Plains tribes and taken their lands. Codallos wanted greater authority so that he could carry "open and formal war" to the Comanches' own country. Following normal procedure, the viceroy requested an opinion of the Marqués de Altamira, his chief military advisor.

What riled Altamira was the loss of ten Spaniards without "more punishment to the enemy than killing about sixty of them." As a result, the Comanches were "elated, vainglorious, and proud," as their subsequent attack on Galisteo demonstrated. Emboldened by a succession of victories over other

Indians, and now by this affront to Spanish arms, these Comanches were obviously taking the offensive. They were jubilant over killing one Spanish soldier, Altamira opined, even at the loss of a hundred of their own, "which because of their barbarousness and their numbers is of small consequence to them." In sum, the governor, utilizing Comanche prisoners and the good offices of the missionaries, should offer the barbarians peace. If they refused, he should "banish them from that entire area." [20]

A Battle at Pecos,
1748

Although he won a satisfying victory in 1747, the overall effectiveness of Governor Codallos' Comanche policy can be judged by what took place at Pecos on Sunday, January 21, 1748. The afternoon before, near sundown, a messenger, whose face betrayed anxiety, delivered a note at the governor's palace. Snow lay on the ground. The air was brittle cold. Codallos read the note. It was from Fray José Urquijo of Pecos. A large force of Comanches had massed at the Paraje del Palo Flechado, only two and a half leagues from the pueblo. Urquijo feared an attack. Codallos showed the note to Fray Juan Miguel Menchero, outspoken special agent of the Franciscan commissary general. Menchero had recently coordinated a large-scale Gila Apache campaign—a role unbecoming a friar, some of his brethren said. Menchero cursed the luck. He was ill. He would have to send his secretary Fray Lorenzo Antonio Estremera.

Codallos ordered the drum beaten. It was getting dark. Most everyone was inside by a fire. "In a villa, the capital of a kingdom, where there are more than 950 Spaniards and mixed-bloods and more than 550 Indians," according to one report, "only 25 persons, counting citizens and soldiers, assembled." Ten of them he dispatched for horses seven leagues away. With the other fifteen and Father Estremera, he mounted up and headed for Pecos. It was hard going, Estremera recalled, "the night black, the road bad, and the snow deep." But they made it, about two in the morning.

Heroics of
Governor Codallos

No one was asleep. The Pecos and their missionary were distraught, say the reports, all of which made Governor Codallos the man of the hour. Ascertaining first the direction from which the enemy was coming and roughly how many there were, more than 130, all mounted, he began giving orders. The Pecos assured him that Comanches did not attack at night. They had until daybreak.

He told the pueblo officials to get the women, children, and old men up on the roof tops and bar all doors. A dozen of the old men waited in the convento to protect the mis-

A Comanche warrior, after a George Catlin painting.
Samuel G. Goodrich, *The Manners, Customs and Antiquities of the Indians of North and South America* (Boston, 1849)

sionary. The young men, the *mocetones,* armed with bow and arrows, shield, lance, and war club, rallied around him. There were about seventy, among them some heathen Jicarillas "of those who live in peace in the shelter of this pueblo." Through an interpreter, the governor explained his plan. Since all the pueblo's horses were out to winter pasture and those of the governor's men spent, they would have to go out against the Comanches on foot. It was absolutely necessary, he told them, that everyone stay together. They must not scatter. The rest of the night, while scouts kept watch around the pueblo, they remained under arms.

About eight o'clock, the Spanish-speaking Pecos stationed in one of the church towers shouted that the Comanches were coming up on the convento side, many more than a hundred, all on good horses. It was time. Swiftly they followed the governor through the gateway, soldiers, civilians, Indians, and Father Estremera, who had seen to their Christian preparation "with acts of contrition and general absolution for all exigencies." Taking up a position a short distance beyond the convento, everyone well together, they obeyed Codallos' order not to fire until the enemy committed himself, and then only on command.

The Comanches advanced "with such an outcry and screaming to strike fear that only the presence of mind and energy of Gov. Joaquín Codallos, aided by God, could have overcome such boldness." When they were no more than a pistol shot away, the governor moved his men forward in order and the battle was joined.

The Spanish "square" held. Firing several volleys point-blank, using their lances and bowmen to good advantage, the governor's force repelled the cavalry assault, inflicting a goodly number of casualties. Startled, the Comanches withdrew a short distance "skirmishing with great agility." Most of them wore *cueras,* the protective leather coats, and carried a large shield, lance, bow and arrows, and some a sword or war club. During the lull, they picked up their dead and wounded, placing them across their horses.

Meanwhile, eager to see what was going on, the old men Codallos had left in the convento told Father Urquijo that they would be right back. Slipping out and heading for a good vantage, they were spotted by one of two additional Comanche parties coming up to join the others. It was no contest. The Comanches ran them down. Eleven died. In addition, said Father Estremera, a Jicarilla had been killed in the battle, one civilian wounded, and a soldier's horse slain.

The other two columns of Comanches rode in defiance by the governor a musket shot away and took their places with the rest. Now there were three hundred more or less. Promptly Codallos ordered his force to fall back on the convento little by little, the Indians first. The enemy watched. Just then on the road from Santa Fe, they saw the troops and extra horses coming to reinforce the governor. From a distance, the column seemed larger than it was. The Comanches withdrew to a hill a quarter-league from the pueblo. The men and horses from Santa Fe joined the others in convento and pueblo. A short while later, the enemy departed the same way they had come. "Thus it was assured," Father Estremera exulted,

in God and by God (based on what I had seen myself) that the generalship, courage, and discipline of the lord governor were the reasons the enemy barbarians did not finish off the entire pueblo by killing and capturing its natives, for this was their avowed intention. All the Indians thanked the governor a thousand times and embraced him for having delivered them. The Reverend Father minister did the same with great feeling and offered to commend him to God as long as he lived.

Opposite A page from the Pecos burial book December 14, 1728-January 1, 1729, recording the deaths of eleven persons during the measles epidemic (AASF).

Catharina
Agustin   En catorce de Di[cie]e del año de mil setecientos, y veinte, y ocho
Maria   altaron los Fiscales murio en una cassa de Catharina Pin-
             guechi viuda de edad de sesenta a poco mas, o menos a
             Agustin Quinpelloqui de edad de veinte, y ocho a, poco mas, o
             menos, casado con Maria Dutu, y a Maria Sonle, de e-
             dad de treinta a poco mas o menos casada con sus

Maria Perez = y en año dia, mes, y año murieron Maria Citela
             cru de edad de quarenta a poco mas, o menos casadas con Agus-
Christoualtin cru = y Christobal Suonisi casado con Catharina Sirisi
             de edad de sesenta a poco mas o menos estan enterrado
             en esta Yglesia, y[o] q[ue] conste lofirme
                                          Anto[nio] Sabaleta

Maria   En veinte, y dos de Di[cie]e del año de mil setecientos, y veinte, y
Catharina   ocho murieron Maria Jutu de edad de sien a poco mas
Barba   o menos resciuio el S[antisi]mo S[acramen]to de la Penitencia Viuda = Cathari-
Agustin   na Sarbula = y Agustin Sarbulo esta enterrado en esta
Barb.   Yglesia y[o] q[ue] conste lofirme
                                          Anto[nio] Sabaleta

Juana   En treinta, y uno de Di[cie]e de mil setecientos y veinte y ocho
             a murio resciuio el S[antisi]mo S[acramen]to de la Peni[tenci]a Juana Soms-
m[igue]l   ouchi Viuda de edad de ochenta a poco mas o menos.
Miguel   a Miguel fuecoro de edad de quarenta, y cinco a poco mas o
             menos casado con Catharina Diteguo esta enterrado en esta
             Yglesia, y[o] q[ue] conste lofirme —
                                          Anto[nio] Sabaleta

Año DE 1529 =

Juana Sarbula En primero de Ene[r]o del año de mil setecientos, y veinte, y nueve
Agustin   murio Maria Sarbula = y Agustin Ja[?] Viudo de edad de
               setenta a poco mas, o menos resciuio los S[antisi]mos Sacram[en]tos es-
               tan enterrado en esta Yglesia, y caza q[ue] conste es mi[?]
                                          Anto[nio] Sabaleta

That same afternoon Father Urquijo buried in the church the bodies of thirteen men who had died in the battle. The funeral rite was held next day. For the consolation of the Pecos, Codallos left a squad of soldiers. Six weeks later, when he wrote to the viceroy, he enclosed Father Estremera's sworn account of the battle at Pecos, so that his most excellent lordship, if he deemed it meet and proper, might commend the governor of New Mexico to the king.[21]

The Scourge of Epidemic Disease

Less newsworthy than the Comanche assault of 1748, but more lethal, was an unnamed epidemic that swept New Mexico late that summer. Sixty-eight persons died at Santa Fe between July and September. Father Urquijo was ordered to the villa to help. During his absence, at least fifteen Pecos children expired as well as three single men "without receiving the sacraments because," in the words of Fray Andrés García, "it is the custom of these mission Indians to notify the Father when there is no chance." The bunching of deaths in the Pecos burial books, more or less complete for the years 1695–1706 and 1727–1828, reveals major epidemics almost every decade:

1696 (fever)	1748
1704	1759
1728–1729 (measles)	1780–1781 (smallpox)
1738 (smallpox, in 18 weeks 26 young children died)	1800 (smallpox)
	1816 (smallpox)
	1826.

And there were others. Over the years, epidemic disease claimed many more lives at Pecos than did the violent assaults of Plains raiders.[22]

Against the Comanches, hero Codallos had won some and he had lost some. At a junta convened in 1748, the consensus was that this now formidable Plains people, despite their barbarous perfidy, should be permitted to trade at Taos. New Mexicans were not prepared to do without the skins, meat, horses, and captives only the barbarians could supply. Besides, it brought them within the sphere of Christian influence and saved their captives from probable death.[23]

Vélez Cachupín Takes Over

In the spring of 1749, Governor Codallos, praised by Fathers Estremera, Menchero, and Varo for his defense of Pecos, yielded to his successor. Young, full of ambition, and not a little impetuous, don Tomás Vélez Cachupín was already in the habit of exaggerating his own merits and the faults of others. Writing to the viceroy after a year in office, Vélez

Tomás Vélez Cachupín

Cachupín claimed that Comanches had killed one hundred and fifty Pecos Indians during the administration of his predecessor, between 1743 and 1749.[24] Picked up by two fervent Franciscans, equally prone to exaggeration and eager to embarrass the governors any way they could, suddenly the Pecos dead exceeded one hundred and fifty, and now at one blow!

According to Fathers Juan Sanz de Lezaun and Manuel Bermejo, whose avowed purpose was to defend the persecuted and calumnated church and lay bare the incompetence and malice of New Mexico's governors,

A Massacre that Never Happened

soon after the arrival of Codallos as governor, the Pecos came to ask him for permission to go to the country of the Comanches to prepare buffalo meat. Aware of the great danger and warned by experienced persons, nevertheless, guided by his own self-interest, he granted them the permission. It is assumed that beforehand they did various carpentry jobs for him at his house.

Permission granted, with the proviso that they bring him [buffalo] tongues, almost the entire pueblo of Pecos set out. At a short distance an ambush of Comanches fell on these Pecos. The dead exceeded 150. Few escaped, the reason this pueblo is destitute of people.

Immediately don Manuel Sáenz, lieutenant of the presidio, set out with fifty men, citizens and soldiers. An ambush of these Comanches set out after them and killed ten Spaniards. The rest, some afoot and others on horseback, fled for the pueblo of Pecos. As a result, this fierce enemy has the Spanish troops in such a state that merely on hearing their name all tremble. And for all this, who is to blame but the governors? Not only do they favor the enemy, but when it is time to muster the troops to punish them, they have them diverted to other things in their personal service. They do not punish them because of the interest they have in their trading activities.[25]

There are, no doubt, elements of truth in this tale. The buffalo hunt and the carpentry have a valid ring. The account of Lieutenant Sáenz de Garvisu's chase squares precisely with the pursuit of June 1746. Some of the other stories the two friars told can be verified elsewhere. The Comanches, they said, had sent word early in 1750 that they were coming to Taos to trade. Warned that he should protect Galisteo and Pecos, the impulsive Governor Vélez Cachupín, "carried away by his caprice and greed," headed straight for Taos with all his soldiers. "In an instant the enemy struck Galisteo killing nine or ten Indians." In the Galisteo burial book, there is an entry of December 12, 1749, for eight men killed by Comanches attacking the pueblo. But nowhere is there corroborating evidence that more than a hundred and fifty Pecos died in "a cleverly laid Comanche ambush." [26]

In fact, there is evidence to the contrary. Father Menchero had estimated the population of Pecos at 125 families in 1744. Father Francisco de la Concepción González counted everyone in 1750, a total of 449 persons. The discrepancy is not great enough, nor does the 1750 census show an abundance of widows. If indeed "almost the entire pueblo of Pecos" had walked into a Comanche ambush in the 1740s, Father Manuel de San Juan Nepomuceno Trigo, who visited the pueblo as vice-custos in 1750, should have known about it. If he did, his statement in 1754 was a distortion. "The mission is invaded daily by the barbarians," wrote Trigo, "but the Pecos are such valiant warriors that the enemy is always defeated." [27]

Still, the extravagantly heightened story that more than a hundred and fifty Pecos perished at one Comanche blow has persisted. It is the easiest way to explain the demise of the once populous pueblo—easy but erroneous. An example of the mid-century polemics of friars and governors, this exaggeration, suggested by Governor Vélez Cachupín and avidly embellished by the two Franciscans, should be taken for what it was—a blatant piece of propaganda.[28]

The Defense of Pecos and Galisteo

After the assault on Galisteo in December 1749, Governor Vélez Cachupín took the Comanche grudge against Pecos and Galisteo seriously. Like his predecessor, he provided, on paper at least, detachments of fifteen soldiers at each pueblo. The large compound west of the Pecos convento, the so-called "presidio," probably dates from the 1740s and 1750s. Alcalde Mayor José Moreno and a squad of soldiers had stood as marriage witnesses at Pecos as early as February 1747, although they may simply have been passing through on patrol. The friars confirmed that Governor Codallos had left troops to guard the pueblo after his heroics there in January 1748. That April, the military-minded Father Menchero wrote of fifteen-man detachments at both Pecos and Galisteo. Like others posted on outlying New Mexico frontiers, these detachments rotated and, like the parent presidio in Santa Fe, rarely if ever mustered at full strength.

Vélez Cachupín, in his letter of March 1750, to the viceroy was the first to mention that he had fortified Pecos and Galisteo "with earthworks (*trincheras*) and towers (*torreones*) at the gates." Just what form the earthworks took is difficult to say, but the towers at the gates have been well substantiated at Pecos by archaeologist A. V. Kidder. In the north or main pueblo, he excavated four of them and identified a likely fifth, all "strategically placed" to command the four entrances. He termed them "guardhouse kivas," and he recognized that they were of late construction. But because he surmised that they were entered by a hatchway in the roof, because they were fitted out like kivas, and because they seemed not "to have been mentioned in the early Spanish accounts," Kidder refused to assign them a primarily defensive role. Probably he was right about their ritual significance, albeit secondary. The kiva-like

The kivas of Pecos (not all in use concurrently). Four "guard-house kivas" marked H, I, J, K.
Kidder, *Pecos, New Mexico*

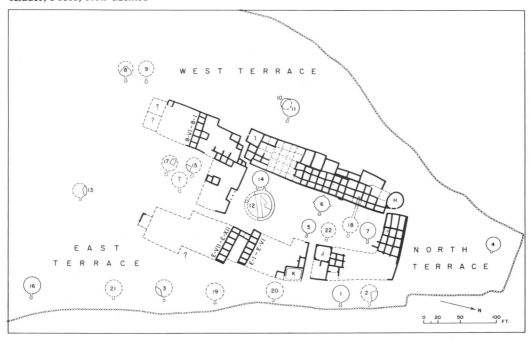

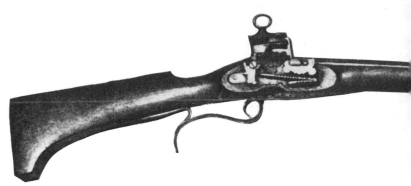

An 18th-century Spanish escopeta, a light musket widely used on the

fire pit, deflector, and ventilator simply provided the best heating system for these chambers. These, it would seem, were Vélez Cachupín's defensive torreones.[29]

For the next half-century, until the Spanish settlements took hold at the river ford beyond, the governors guarded the Pecos gateway as best they could. To back up the arms of the Pecos Indians, which in 1752 consisted of 107 fighting men with 3,313 arrows, seventeen lances, four swords, and no cueras, they garrisoned the place sporadically and provided a small arsenal. In 1762, Alcalde mayor Cayetano Tenorio was responsible at Pecos for "1 small campaign cannon, 3 pounds of powder, and 250 musket balls." Somewhat expanded, the Pecos arsenal in 1778 included "18 muskets, 9 pounds of powder, 300 balls, 1 bronze cannon of two-pounder caliber with its carriage and other accessories, 4 balls of grape shot, ramrod, and wormer." [30]

Comanches Hurl Themselves at Galisteo

After treating and trading with Comanches at Taos in July 1751 and cautiously accepting their promises of peace, Governor Vélez Cachupín four months later saw his defenses tested by Comanches. The Indian scouts he employed to watch the approaches to Pecos and Galisteo had grown lazy. At dawn on November 3, 1751, without warning, a hell-bent army of three hundred Comanches or more "hurled themselves at the pueblo of Galisteo in an attempt to enter and sack it. The squad of ten soldiers which I had as a precaution there," Vélez reported,

together with the Indians, positioned themselves behind an earthwork and fired upon the enemy. They repulsed the assault, killing six and wounding others badly. The enemy made a second attempt, but likewise were repelled. Chastised, they did not renew the

northern frontier.   Brinckerhoff and Faulk, *Lancers*

attack, but remained an hour in the neighborhood of the pueblo, a musket shot away, firing the sixteen muskets they had and shooting their arrows at the entrance to the earthwork where the squad was. The latter answered their fire. Having achieved nothing except the killing of twelve cows that happened to be outside the pueblo, the enemy withdrew suddenly, as is their custom in such cases.

Vélez Cachupín was furious. "My heart leaped," as he put it, "with an ardent desire to give them a taste of our arms and show them something else than the kindness with which I had treated them and dealt with them at Taos." Taking personal command of the punitive force, the brash young governor caught up with the Comanches on the sixth day, and, by his own account, handed them such a drubbing, killing a hundred or so and releasing the others after firm but kind words, that they contented themselves with peaceful trade for the remainder of his term. At this time, too, he learned that not all Comanches shared the grudge against Pecos and Galisteo, only certain leaders.[31]

Despite the nasty things the friar partisans of ex-governor Codallos said about Vélez Cachupín, he, like Vargas before him and Anza after him, seemed to grasp intuitively the key to peace with the raiders: an active personal diplomacy backed by proven prowess in battle and a supply of gifts or trading opportunities. In his instructions to his successor, Vélez cautioned that the heathens would test him to see what manner of man he was. He must go to the fairs at Taos, conveying both confidence and friendship, and he must see to the Comanches' protection from the other tribes while trading, particularly from the Utes who had broken with them late in the 1740s. He must sit down and smoke with them, even "permit their

Diplomacy of Vélez Cachupín

The Virgin of the
Immaculate Conception
by Bernardo de Miera
y Pacheco, a panel
from the altar screen
of the former 18th-
century church at
Nambé pueblo.
Museum of New Mexico

familiarities and take part in their fun at suitable times."

As for the displaced Plains Apaches, the Carlanas, Palomas, Cuartelejos, and Chipaynes, they should also be wooed. During the winter of 1751–1752, three hundred men of these tribes had taken refuge near Pecos. Although the friars baptized and buried some of their young and their infirm, these Apaches camped outside the pueblo and were never counted on Pecos censuses. Viewing them as a ready reserve in the event of Comanche hostility, Governor Vélez Cachupín had succeeded in keeping them there. He had sought to prevent a close alliance between them and the horse-thieving Faraones and Natagés, or Mescaleros. When the men ventured out onto the plains to hunt or rendezvous with relatives, they left their women and children in the safety of Pecos. These Apaches, he noted, made much better plains scouts than the Pueblos.

The natives of Pecos and Galisteo who ably guarded the approaches to their pueblos should be kept alert. To insure the continuation of his successful policies at the eastern gateway, Vélez Cachupín recommended to the next governor that he retain Alcalde mayor Tomás de Sena, "who, because of his kindness, is greatly loved by the Indians. If he should be separated from them," Vélez counseled, "you could not find anyone who would wish to serve in that office." [32]

But his successor did. Eager to put his own stamp on New Mexico affairs, Francisco Antono Marín del Valle, a vain, less bold individual who governed from 1754 to 1760, soon broke Vélez Cachupín's delicate web of alliances. The Apaches left the vicinity of Pecos. The Comanches took to raiding again. And the new alcalde mayor of Pecos and Galisteo went out on campaign.

Marín del Valle Wrecks the Comanche Peace

Don Bernardo de Miera y Pacheco, lured north from El Paso by the offer of an alcaldía mayor, was an "engineer," soldier, merchant, painter, and, most important to Governor Marín, an accomplished map maker. After he had accompanied the governor on his visitation, Miera drew in 1758 an elaborate, illuminated map of the entire kingdom of New Mexico, one of a number he would compile and draw over the next quarter-century. On it, northeast of Pecos and north of the Río Colorado (the Canadian), he sketched a village of tipis. Below it, he wrote the words "tierra de Cumanches," and above it, drew a delightful leaping buffalo. Well to the south, on the west side of the Río Pecos not far from modern Fort Sumner, he labeled another cluster of tipis "Apaches Carlanes." [33]

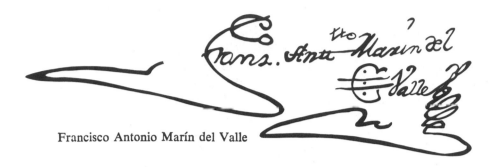

Francisco Antonio Marín del Valle

While he held the office of alcalde mayor of Pecos and
Galisteo between 1756 and 1760, don Bernardo claimed to
have gone out on three campaigns against the Comanches. He
also tried unsuccessfully to refound old cannon. He stood
several times as godfather to Plains and Pecos Indians, as did
his wife and his son, don Manuel. Before Governor Marín,
his patron, stepped down, Miera painted for him a very special
map in color showing New Mexico and "the provinces, enemy
and friendly, that surround it." Replaced as alcalde mayor by
Marín's successor in 1760, don Bernardo Miera remained in
New Mexico for the rest of his life pursuing his varied interests, a prominent citizen who was never quite as prominent
as he wished.[34]

**French Threat
to New Mexico**

No problem exercised the governors of New Mexico more
during the eighteenth century than defense against the heathen
peoples on its borders, unless perhaps it was convincing the
bureaucrats in Mexico City and Spain, who did not know a
Comanche from a Pecos, how serious it was. It galled them
that mere rumors of a few exotic Frenchmen somewhere out
on the plains brought a more excited response than ten Apache
raids. Diego de Vargas had used vague reports of a French
threat in 1695 to win additional military aid for the colony.
Other governors too were quick to relay every shadow of a
Frenchman, real or imagined.

They were out there, to be sure, trading guns and liquor
and working their Indian diplomacy westward from the Illinois country and from the lower Mississippi Valley as well. A
real scare came in 1719 when the European War of the Quad-
ruple Alliance and the Valverde expedition to the Arkansas
coincided. Although he never saw a Frenchman, the cautious
Valverde reported what the friendly Apaches told him about
French forts, guns, and military advisers among their Pawnee

Bernardo de Miera y Pacheco

enemies. The next year, when Pawnees annihilated the follow-up expedition of Lt. Gov. Pedro de Villasur, some of the survivors swore that there had been Frenchmen among their assailants.[35]

The Mallet Brothers

Thanks to the diplomacy of Étienne Véniard de Bourgmont among the Plains Apaches in 1724, the door to New Mexico lay open. But Bourgmont's return to France, Comanche-Apache warfare, and lingering resentment over the Villasur massacre intervened. Some illicit trade may have got through. For sure, in 1739, when Pierre and Paul Mallet and six or seven companions from the Illinois country dropped down via Taos to Santa Fe, they and their French contraband were cordially welcomed. Two of them, "Petit Jean" and Moreau, decided to stay, becoming Juan Bautista Alarí and Luis María Mora, the first a good citizen and the second an alleged rabble-rouser and sorcerer sentenced to die in the plaza of Santa Fe.

The others, after months of riotous hospitality, returned —several back to Illinois and several down the Canadian, the Arkansas, and the Mississippi to New Orleans. The latter, departing through Pecos late in the spring of 1740, carried a letter from a friend in Santa Fe, don Santiago Roybal, the vicar, to his counterpart in Louisiana. Roybal wanted French goods badly, and he enclosed a list. He thought a lucrative trade could be got up between the two provinces across the plains "because we are not farther away than 200 leagues from a very rich mine, abounding in silver, called Chihuahua, where the inhabitants of this country often go to trade." That kind of talk excited the Sieur de Bienville, governor of French Louisiana.[36]

The party Bienville sent to Santa Fe with a letter to the governor aborted, but a lone Frenchman, evidently a deserter from Illinois, dragged into Pecos early in June 1744. Governor Codallos told Sgt. Juan Felipe de Rivera to take a couple of

A knot of presidial
soldiers besieged,
perhaps members of
Pedro de Villasur's
ill-starred expedition
to the plains in 1720.

After an 18th-century
painting on hide
(Segesser II) in
Gottfried Hotz,
*Indian Skin Paintings
from the American
Southwest* (Norman,
1970)

soldiers to the pueblo of "Nuestra Señora de la Defensa de
Pecos," enlist four Pecos Indians, and bring this unidentified
intruder in "well secured." Interrogated in Santa Fe, he gave
his name as Santiago Velo (Jacques Belleau, Bellot, or Valle?)
and confessed that he was a native of Tours who had served as
a soldier in Illinois. Codallos had no use for him. Dispatching
the Frenchman's statement directly to the viceroy and Velo
himself to the governor of Nueva Vizcaya, he washed his
hands of the matter.[37]

Meanwhile, out on the plains other Frenchmen were working for peace between the Wichitas, their allies, and the Comanches. With that accomplished in 1746 or 1747, the way

A friar in trouble
perhaps Fray Juan
Mingues, the chaplain
killed in the massacre
of Villasur's command
in 1720.

After an 18th-century
painting on hide.
(Segesser II) in
Gottfried Hotz.
*Indian Skin Paintings
from the American
Southwest* (Norman,
1970)

again lay open to Santa Fe. By early 1748, Codallos had word that thirty-three Frenchmen had come to the Río de Jicarilla and traded quantities of muskets to the Comanches for mules. The next three Frenchmen, deserters from the Arkansas post who turned up at a Taos fair in the spring of 1749, were Governor Vélez Cachupín's problem. Two were carpenters by trade, the other a tailor, barber, and bloodletter. Vélez put them to work in the governor's palace and requested of the viceroy that they be allowed to stay.

Another pair arrived with an errant refugee Spaniard. Vélez cursed Gov. Gaspar Domíngo de Mendoza for entertaining the Mallet party, "the first who entered," and permitting them to return to French territory with favorable reports of New Mexico.[38] In November 1750, that mistake came home to roost. Four Frenchmen appeared at Pecos. One was no stranger. It was Pierre Mallet.

He had set out from New Orleans with trade goods and letters from the governor and merchants of Louisiana. Only six days short of Pecos, the party had run into some Comanches who were spying on Pecos hunters. These jovial theives pro-

Bachiller Santiago Roybal

ceeded to despoil Mallet and his companions of most of their goods. With a dozen spent horses, they had made Pecos, where Lt. Gov. Bernardo de Bustamente y Tagle met them.

Taken into custody, they were escorted to Santa Fe and then on down to El Paso where Governor Vélez was waiting. He declared them illegal aliens and confiscated what goods they had left. These were evaluated and cried three times at public auction. Since no one bid on them, the El Paso merchant who had appraised them bought them himself for 420 pesos, six reales. The buyer was also a soldier, a painter, and a map maker, don Bernardo de Miera y Pacheco, later alcalde mayor of Pecos and Galisteo. Vélez Cachupín used the money to send the prisoners to Mexico City, and that was that.[39]

Just at noon on August 6, 1752, four days after the Pecos patronal feast, Fray Juan José Toledo was roused from his cell by a commotion. One of the servants motioned for him to come quickly. Outside the cemetery wall stood a couple of

Poor Chapuis and Feuilli

Charles III, king of Spain, 1759-1788.   Brinckerhoff and Faulk, *Lancers*

bedraggled-looking Europeans, one of them holding a French flag on a stick, or as Toledo described it, a piece of white linen with a cross on it. They and their guide Manuela, a runaway Aa Indian servant of Esteban Baca, had been brought in from the Río de las Gallinas by Jicarilla and Carlana Apaches.[40] They had with them a string of nine horses carrying packs of sealed trade goods. Fray Juan, a thirty-six-year-old native of Mexico City knew no French. Jean Chapuis sounded to him like Xanxapy, very close if one sounds the Mexican x's, and Louis Feuilli, like Luis Fuixy. Ordering the goods unloaded and placed in the convento, Toledo saw to his guests, and then wrote a hasty note to Governor Vélez Cachupín, who had it the same evening.

Next day, Alcalde major Tomás de Sena reined up outside the convento. With sign language, he communicated as best he could that the Frenchmen had been summoned to appear before the lord governor in Santa Fe. Sequestering goods and horses, he packed the lot to the villa. The French tailor, who after three years in Santa Fe had picked up some Spanish, interpreted.

The story the two told of sanction by French officials, their grand plans for opening trade, and the invoices of their merchandise, convinced Governor Vélez Cachupín that this was a matter for the viceroy. Their wares, all manner of dry goods, hardware, and fancy items, from silk garters and lace, hawk bells and mirrors, to embroidered beaverskin shoes and ivory combs, the governor sold at auction. When the viceroy decided that this was a matter for the king, hapless Chapuis and Feuilli, professing all the while their ignorance that such trade was illegal, were shipped off to Spain. Their attempt to open the Santa Fe Trail had been precisely seventy years too soon.[41]

If other Frenchmen tried the Pecos gateway, their fates are not recorded. A decade later, as the Seven Years War wound down, France transferred Louisiana to Spain. Not only did the Spaniards inherit the elaborate French system of Indian diplomacy and subsidies, which would influence their own less liberal Indian policy, but also a vast and vulnerable new frontier. The contest for North America had come down to Spaniards and Englishmen.

In New Mexico, meantime, it all hung on war and peace with "the barbarous Indians."

Between 1760, the year an anonymous imperial strategist recommended the creation of a separate northern viceroyalty in New Mexico, and 1776, the year the crown set in operation the

The Rising
Comanche Tide

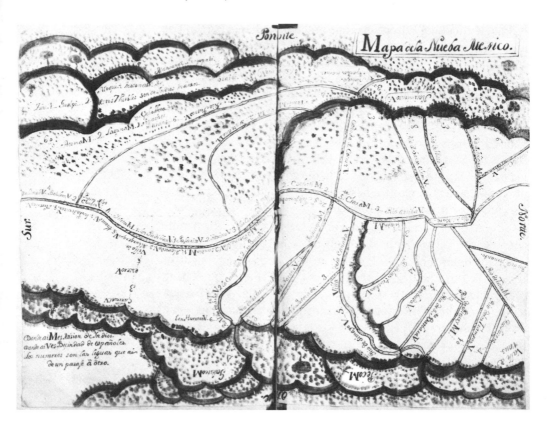

An anonymous sketch map of places and distances in New Mexico in the 1760s. M stands for missions, V for Spanish settlements. The numbers are distances in leagues (AGN, Tierras: Civil, 426). Courtesy of the Archivo General de la Nación, Mexico

unified General Command of the Provincias Internas, almost a viceroyalty, the *indios bárbaros* ran wild.

At Pecos, trade with Apaches declined as Comanche hostility heightened. Although Jicarillas and their allies continued to live in and around the mountains north and east from Santa Fe and Pecos, no one mentioned Pecos "fairs." The pueblo's population fell from 344 to 269. The Franciscans neglected it. No longer did the friars bother to enter in the book of burials the Pecos dead. From time to time, however, they showed up in the governor's routine body counts. On January 13, 1772, for example, "9 Comanches killed two Indians of the Pueblo of Pecos who went out to look for their oxen." That was not the whole story, but it was a telling part of it.[42]

Gov. Francisco Marín del Valle was an adherent of the eye-for-an-eye school, or better, many heathen eyes for one Spanish eye. During his administration and those of his two short-term successors, violence begot violence. To avenge the spectacle of Taos dancing with two dozen Comanche scalps before their very eyes, the Comanches rallied a huge war party and descended on the Taos Valley in August 1760. Their seige and plunder of the Villalpando house, where dozens of Spanish men, women, and children perished or were carried off alive, so impressed Bernardo de Miera y Pacheco that he related it in the legend of one of his maps nineteen years later.

Although Marín's retaliation failed, Gov. Manuel Portillo Urrisola enticed the Comanches to Taos late in 1761 and succeeded in killing "more than four hundred." By "this glorious victory," he had hoped to inspire such dread in all heathens that New Mexico would be left in peace. But he was worried. His successor had arrived. This official spoke of summoning the Comanches to talk. Tomás Vélez Cachupín was back.[43]

Again Vélez embraced Comanches, sat and smoked with them, and negotiated an exchange of prisoners. He condemned the arrogant Portillo, "who never wished to hear them speak directly to him." But even though don Tomás demonstrated again during his second term, 1762-1767, how Spaniards could reason with Comanches, the man who followed him, for one reason or another, was not up to it. Don Pedro Fermín de Mendinueta, whose eleven-year administration was the longest in New Mexico's history, and probably the bloodiest, never commanded the Comanches' respect the way Vélez Cachupín had. He was always on the defensive.[44]

Not that Mendinueta wanted all-out war. He recognized that New Mexico was too weak, almost prostrate. Still, his superiors cried for blood, for the vindication of Spanish arms. Much of the time he spent trying to get the scattered Hispanos to come together in compact defensible communities, or *placitas*. Never able to win a great enough victory to dictate lasting peace, the governor vacillated as a matter of policy. Writing of the Comanches in 1771, he admitted as much.

Mendinueta Vacillates

The alternate actions of this nation at the same time, now peace, now war, demonstrate their accustomed faithlessness, either because of a premeditated principle of the entire nation or because their captains do not enjoy the superiority necessary to impose obedience and each individual does what he pleases, accommodating himself to enter in peace whenever he deems it advantageous and making war whenever his barbarous nature dictates.

Since it is impossible to reduce them to obedience to one or more captains or to limit their freedom so that they do not do as they fancy, I have adopted the policy of admitting them to peace whenever they ask for it and come with their trade goods and of waging war whenever they assault our frontiers and commit plunder. From war alone, all that results is loss of life and property, but from the alternate this poor citizenry gains some good, as occurred at the last two fairs, or *rescates,* of which I have spoken.

His-oo-san-chees,
The Little Spaniard,
famed Comanche
warrior, after a
painting by George
Catlin, 1834.
Catlin, *North
American Indians*, II

Pedro Fermín de Mendinueta

Indeed at little cost they bought nearly 200 horses and mules, 12 muskets with ammunition, and a considerable number of buffalo hides, essential in this kingdom and profitable to trade in Nueva Vizcaya, as well as some Indian captives who are added to the body of Our Holy Faith.

If the viceroy had any better policy to suggest, Governor Mendinueta was ready to listen.[45]

For Pecos, traditional target of the Comanches, the now-peace-now-war regime of Fermín de Mendinueta meant mostly war. This was not war in the conventional sense, nor was there any reliable pattern to it. One time the attackers came in the dead of winter, hundreds strong, hurling themselves at the pueblo, and the next in spring or summer when only a dozen or so lay in ambush for workers in the fields, wood cutters, or hunters. The irregularity of this war, the not knowing, must have taken as great a psychological toll as physical.

Like the serial stories filed by a war correspondent, Mendinueta's letters to the viceroy make up a chronicle. March 10, 1769: a Pecos reports fresh Comanche tracks some leagues from the pueblo. They lead in the opposite direction. Nevertheless, Alcalde mayor Tomás de Sena sends scouts and waits up at Pecos all night. When the sun rises next morning, the scouts still have not returned. Believing that the Comanches must have been after Apaches, the people let out their livestock without telling Sena.

Hardly had they done so when they were assaulted on all sides by more than 200 Comanches who made every effort to enter the pueblo. They did not succeed because of the vigorous defense put up by the Indians with their alcalde mayor. They did run off 42 horses and kill part of the cattle, while the cattle still in the corrals were unharmed. Three Pecos Indians were wounded by gunshots, and as the enemy withdrew they killed another who, because he was old, had not been able to keep up with the scouts and was returning to his pueblo. Eight of the enemy died. Many were wounded, which was evident from the many bloody arrows found after the battle. When they withdrew they burned the tents [of the dead] and their bows and cueras, of which many fragments were found, and they killed part of the horses and mares.

The Pecos blamed this attack on their war captain, who had given the wrong location of the tracks. Mendinueta complained that he often received misinformation. No one saw the enemy, but everyone reported false alarms.[46]

Early on a winter morning in December 1770, two Pecos venture out of their pueblo. A short distance down the trail some thirty Comanches jump them. It is over in an instant.

The raiders also recapture sixteen horses stolen from them by Apaches who had come in close to Pecos.

On April 5, 1771, forty Comanches assail the pueblo but are beaten off. The following month the alcalde mayor, probably Vicente Armijo, catches up with five Comanches rustling horses and kills all five with no casualty among the Indians who accompanied him. Again Comanches attack Pecos on September 5. Again they are repulsed. Later in the month, the governor sends the lieutenant of the Santa Fe presidio and two squads of soldiers. One squad escorts the Pecos to their fields to harvest and bring in their wheat. Despite the Comanches, who show themselves and shoot a few arrows from a distance, the soldiers, the Pecos, and their alcalde mayor fall back in good order with wheat and livestock. This time, the Comanches ride off.

A month later they are back, an estimated five hundred strong. A smoke signal sent up by scouts alerts the Pecos and the squad of soldiers. The enemy, dismounted, tries to force one of the gates. They fail, losing five men killed and many wounded. Not always are the Pecos scouts so effective. Late that same fall, on November 25, five of them sally out of the pueblo at dawn right into an ambush. All die, along with an oxherd.[47]

Eye for an Eye   The worst war losses suffered by the Pecos during these years occurred in 1774. That spring, forty of them had left their pueblo to join a body of civilians and a soldier escort, bound perhaps on their annual trip to the salines. Because of the Pecos' "extreme want," Governor Mendinueta had granted them permission to hunt buffalo before joining up. But the Comanches took them off guard. Eleven were killed, one captured, and the rest fled, "losing their meager baggage." At three p.m. on August 15, the Pecos out working their milpas looked up to see a hundred Comanches bearing down on them. They scattered, but not in time. Seven men and two women died. Seven others were carried off.[48]

This time the punitive expedition came through. The Comanches, reunited, were celebrating. "So many were the tents that they could not make out where they ended." Charging right into them, the Spaniards cut a bloody swath, then formed a square and held off the enemy all day before retiring in order that evening. An even greater victory followed a month later. Mendinueta, availing himself of the New Mexicans' momentary high spirits, marshaled a force of six hundred soldiers, militiamen, and Indians and sent them out under don Carlos Fernández, an aging but thoroughly proven campaigner. Taking another encampment by surprise, the Spanish force killed or captured "more than four hundred individuals," recovered a thousand horses and mules, and eagerly divided among them the tipis and other spoils of the Comanches.[49]

Still, these triumphs did not end the war. In the months ahead, Comanches killed two Pecos cutting firewood, three sowing their fields, and one in a skirmish. In all, if the gov-

Carlos Fernández

ernor's figures are anywhere near accurate, between 1769 and 1775, some fifty Pecos must have died *"a manos de los Comanches."* No wonder Father Domínguez found them in 1776 cultivating only the fields within shouting distance of the pueblo. No wonder they had only a dozen sorry nags. No wonder they did not go to the river for a swim.[50]

Already a hero, forty-two-year-old Lt. Col. Juan Bautista de Anza rode into Santa Fe late in 1778 with a confidence that bordered on cockiness. Unlike most of his predecessors, he already knew an Apache from a Pueblo. He was a frontiersman, born and reared in the presidios of Sonora. As swaggering as his position demanded, yet brave enough to close in hand-to-hand combat, Anza was a natural leader of fighting men. He had recently sat for a portrait in Mexico City. Feted at the viceroy's palace for opening the overland road from Sonora to Alta California, don Juan was still not too proud to embrace a Navajo or smoke with a Comanche. In that regard, he was every bit the equal of Vargas or Vélez Cachupín.

And the time was right. He had just come from a series of meetings in Chihuahua with don Teodoro de Croix, first commandant general of the Provincias Internas. For more than a decade, reform-minded Spanish bureaucrats had been looking at the defense of the northern frontier as a whole. The Marqués de Rubí's inspection of 1766-1768, the resultant *Regla-*

Anza Takes On the Comanches

José de Gálvez.
José Antonio Calderón
Quijano ed., *Los
virreyes de Nueva
España en el reinado
de Carlos III*, vol. I
(Sevilla, 1967)

mento of 1772 delineating the presidial cordon from the Gulf
of Mexico to the Gulf of California, and the unified general
campaigns of the redheaded Irish wild goose, Commandant
Inspector Hugo O'Conor, had all followed in rapid succession.

Then, in 1776, don José de Gálvez, formerly the king's
archreformer in New Spain, had become minister of the
Indies. Within months, his vision of a northern jurisdiction
independent of the viceroy and devoted to pacifying, developing, and defending New Spain's most exposed frontier was a
reality. The six northern governors, from Texas to California,
henceforth would answer to the commandant general. He
would communicate directly with the king through Gálvez.
Although the main object of the General Command was defense, the royal instructions as usual suggested a more noble

Juan Bautista de Anza,
evidently painted in
Mexico City, 1776-1777.
Museum of New Mexico

purpose: "the conversion of the numerous heathen Indian tribes of northern North America." [51]

One of the decisions confirmed at the Chihuahua meetings would have a direct if belated effect on the Pecos. The Spaniards had resolved to seek peace and alliance with the Comanches against warring Apaches. There were precedents, particularly on the Texas frontier. Anza gave the project highest priority, setting aside temporarily the opening of a road to Sonora, the disrupting of the Gila Apache-Navajo alliance, and other pressing matters. Plainly, the Comanches, epitomized now by a fierce and implacable war leader named Cuerno Verde (Green Horn), were the kingdom's cruelest scourge. Before he parleyed, the new governor had first to show them who he was. That he did in 1779.

A Comanche village by George Catlin, 1834.   Catlin, *North American Indians,* II

A Signal Victory
over Comanches

The muster at San Juan was set for mid-August, a time the Comanches might have expected to find them in their fields instead. In all, nearly six hundred men took part, none evidently from the overexposed pueblo of Pecos. Outfitting the dirt-poor militiamen and shaking the column down, Anza led them not by the traditional route east from Taos but north into Colorado and then east. Joined by two hundred Comanche-hating Utes and Apaches, to whom the governor explained his spoils policy of equal shares, the expedition pushed on to and across the Arkansas River. Somewhere north of present-day Pueblo they came upon a large body of Comanches setting up the pole frames of their tipis along Fountain Creek. The scene resembled a Catlin painting. The mountains towered to the west.

Anxiously observing the Spaniards "drawn up in a form they had never before seen," the Comanches dropped everything, jumped on their horses and took off. After six or eight miles of pursuit across the grassy plain, the Spaniards and their Indian allies began to catch up. The Comanches wheeled around. Eighteen of the bravest died in the scattered melee. The women and children who ran to their fallen men were captured as were more than five hundred horses. Back at the half-made camp, the spoils were so plentiful that a hundred horses could not carry them all.

Learning that this camp was to have been the rendezvous and site of a victory celebration upon the return from New

Mexico of Cuerno Verde himself, Anza doubled back, in his words, "to see if fortune would grant me an encounter with him." It did.

Somewhere in view of 12,334-foot Greenhorn Mountain, the bold Cuerno Verde, who knew of his people's recent defeat, had the temerity to attack six hundred men with only fifty. Judging from his own diary and the outcome, Anza's tactics were brilliant. Cutting Cuerno Verde and his staff off in an arroyo, he moved in for the kill. "There without other recourse they sprang to the ground and, entrenched behind their horses, made in this manner a defense as brave as it was glorious. . . . Cuerno Verde perished, with his first-born son, the heir to his command, four of his most famous captains, a medicine man who preached that he was immortal, and ten more." [52]

The distinctive headdress of Cuerno Verde with its prominent green horn, and that of his second-in-command Jumping Eagle, were sent by a jubilant Anza to Commandant General Croix as trophies with a pledge to work for even "greater things now and in the future." Although his greatest achievement, the Comanche peace, would take another six years to consummate, this victory over Cuerno Verde had broadcast Anza's fame to every member of the Comanche nation. There would be no shame in coming to terms with this man. At Pecos, meanwhile, other died at their hands. [53]

For reasons best known to themselves, the Comanches in 1785 began treating seriously of peace. Beyond the elimination of Cuerno Verde, reasons advanced by others include heavy losses in the smallpox epidemic of 1780-1781, military pressure by other tribes armed by the Spaniards on the east Texas frontier, a slow drift southward with corresponding diversion of raiding sphere from oft-plundered New Mexico to richer regions, Anza's refusal to admit their trade so long as they remained hostile, and the appeal of the titles and gifts and supplies offered by alliance. Perhaps the choice of Pecos as an access to Santa Fe and as the new focus of their trading would be no shame in coming to terms with this man. At Pecos, meanwhile, others died at their hands. [53]

The Comanche Peace

Anza made one thing clear. It was all or nothing. Each of the three major branches of the Comanche nation, the Jupe or Yupe (the people of the timber), the Yamparika (the root eaters), and the Cuchanec or Cuchantica (the buffalo eaters), had to concur. At a council on the Arkansas in November, attended by representatives of all but the snowbound northern Jupes and the easternmost Cuchanecs, they all did. It was resolved that Ecueracapa, leading chief of the Cuchanecs, speak

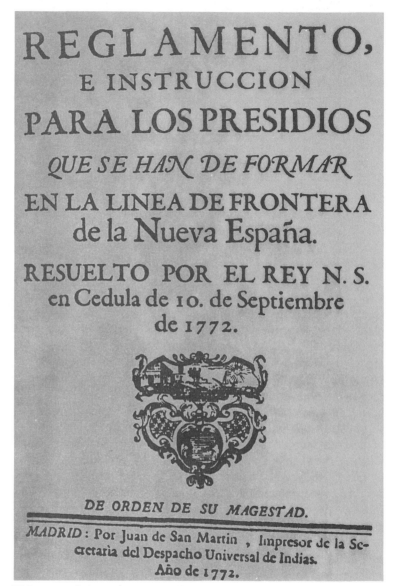

REGLAMENTO,
E INSTRUCCION
PARA LOS PRESIDIOS
QUE SE HAN DE FORMAR
EN LA LINEA DE FRONTERA
de la Nueva España.

RESUELTO POR EL REY N. S.
en Cedula de 10. de Septiembre
de 1772.

DE ORDEN DE SU MAGESTAD.

MADRID: Por Juan de San Martin , Impresor de la Se-
cretaria del Despacho Universal de Indias.
Año de 1772.

Title page of the *Reglamento* of 1772 governing the frontier
military, Madrid, 1772.
Wagner, *Spanish Southwest,* II

for the others at Santa Fe. When José Chiquito, likely a *genízaro,* strayed from a party of Spanish buffalo hunters into Comanche hands, Ecueracapa made him and two Comanches his emissaries to the Spanish governor. He begged entrance though Pecos. Anza should warn the Jicarilla Apaches to let him pass.

Feted in Santa Fe for four days, given horses and gifts for themselves and a horse and cap of fine scarlet for Ecueracapa, the emissaries could hardly wait to report back to their chief. Anza ordered them to take with them thirteen Pecos Indians and a Spaniard, evidently José Manuel Rojo. They departed Santa Fe on January 3, 1786. Meanwhile, a renegade bunch of Comanches tried to subvert the peace, killing Juan Sandoval, a Pecos, outside the pueblo. But diplomacy overcame. Ecueracapa so outdid himself to entertain the returning emissaries and their guests that they "never tired of elaborating on it when they got back to the province."

On a cold day in February, the Pecos looked out on a rare sight, Comanches setting up their tipis in peace. A resplendent Ecueracapa rode on up to Santa Fe where Juan Bautista de Anza was waiting to receive him with honors due a visiting chief of state, with military escort, the municipal council turned out, pomp and an applauding crowd.

Ecueracapa loved it. "His harangue of salutation and embrace of the governor on dismounting at the door of his residence exceeded ten minutes." Inside they talked of terms. A tense moment followed when Anza presented the Comanche chief and his staff to a Ute delegation, mortal enemies since mid-century. The very name "Comanche," applied to the plains nation by the Spaniards, derived from a Ute word for enemy, or "anyone who wants to fight me all the time." It had taken the governor hours of parleys to bring the Utes to the brink of reconciliation. "After several accusations and apologies by both parties this was achieved and formalized in their manner, chiefs and attendants exchanging their garments with their counterparts."

After three days of conferences and festivities in Santa Fe, after Ecueracapa and the Ute chief had been regaled equally "to avoid jealousy which might prejudice their recent friendship," Anza led them and a colorful, polyglot concourse over the mountain to Pecos. There they would draw up the preliminary articles of peace.

The Comanches who had camped before Pecos came out to meet the governor, "manifesting their great joy and delight." When he dismounted "at his own quarters," they crowded around him, some two hundred of them. "All, one by one, came up to embrace him with such excessive expressions of affection and respect that they were by no means appropriate to his rank and station." One of the governor's emissaries on the plains described how Comanches embraced him and rubbed their faces against his. Here Anza was at his best.[55]

Conference at Pecos

Comanche war leaders by George Catlin, 1834.

Retiring to the lodging prepared for him, the governor took his midday meal in the company of the Comanche captains, some of whom wore such earthy names as Rotten Shoe, He Plays Dirty, and The Vermin. Anza's superior, Commandant General Jacobo Ugarte y Loyola, an old campaigner himself, painted a portrait in words of these Comanches after a delegation of them visited him in Chihuahua late the same year:

All of these Indians are robust, good looking, and extremely happy. Their faces show forth the martial, frank, and generous character that distinguishes this nation from the others of this frontier. Their dress is decent, fashioned from buffalo skins they provide themselves. They paint their faces with red ochre and other earths, highlighting their eyelids with vermillion. They love adornments and sport them especially in their hair which they wear braided and intertwined with imitation gold buttons, colored glass beads, ribbons, and whatever other thing that glitters. Yet in odd contrast, the women are slovenly. Their hair is cut, which among them is a sign of slavery and abjection. They enjoy no more respect than what their owners bestow in proportion to how they serve them. [56]

That afternoon, the business of making peace continued. Bare from the waist up, Tosapoy, who occupied third place in the Cuchanec order, delivered a moving harangue. As a token

Catlin, *North American Indians,* II

of good faith, on his knees he presented to Anza a Spaniard from Santa Fe, young Alejandro Martín, who had been a captive among them for eleven years. The governor now affirmed tentatively, pending the commandant general's approval, the five points presented in Santa Fe by Ecueracapa: 1) a new and lasting peace; 2) permission for the Comanches to move closer to New Mexico; 3) access to Santa Fe through Pecos and free trade at the latter place; 4) an alliance and redoubled war against the Apaches; and 5) acknowledgment before other Comanche leaders, since only Cuchanecs were then in attendance at Pecos.

In compliance with the last point, the Spanish governor gave to Ecueracapa his own sword and banner and arranged that his staff of office be displayed to members of the tribe who were not present. The Comanches, in response, dug a hole in the dirt and refilled it, "performing various ceremonies suggesting that in so doing (as they said and as is customary among them) they were for their part also burying war." After many other Comanches had acknowledged the peace, either in Santa Fe or on the plains, Anza submitted the articles to Ugarte. The commandant general added some commentary and clarification but he approved the pact essentially as it was drafted at Pecos on February 28, 1786.[57]

Next day in the new atmosphere of good feeling, Anza presided over a trade fair at Pecos. It was Ash Wednesday. Voluntarily "all the Comanche and Ute captains with the rest of the individuals of both nations present" accompanied the governor to receive the ashes at service. Afterwards, he published a decree designed to restrain the Hispanos' usual outrages during the trading and to set the rules. The old 1754 price list would govern, with two exceptions: trade knives and horses. Two knives would bring only one buffalo hide, and thirteen of the same, a single average horse. A decade earlier, describing what went on at Taos, Father Domínguez had written:

> The Comanches usually sell to our people at this rate: a buffalo hide for a *belduque,* or broad knife made entirely of iron which they call a trading knife here; "white elkskin" (it is the same [buffalo] hide, but softened like deerskin), the same; for a very poor bridle, two buffalo skins or a vessel like those mentioned; the meat for maize or corn flour; an Indian slave, according to the individual, because if it is an Indian girl from twelve to twenty years old, two good horses and some trifles in addition, such as a short cloak, a horse cloth, a red lapel are given; or a she-mule and a scarlet cover, or other things are given for her. . . .
>
> They are great traders, for as soon as they buy anything, they usually sell exactly what they bought; and usually they keep losing, the occasion when they gain being very rare, because our people ordinarily play infamous tricks on them. In short, the trading day resembles a second-hand market in Mexico, the way people mill about.[58]

The infamous tricks were precisely what Anza wanted to avoid.

> Then on the ground designated for the fair he marked out two lines so that the contracting parties, each positioned on the outside of one, could exhibit and hand over to each other in the space between whatever goods they had to exchange. With this arrangement, the presence of that chief [Governor Anza], the opportune positioning of troops, official overseers, and the abolition of the abusive contributions that the latter used to charge the heathens as a fee for permission to trade, this fair took place in ideal calm and good order.
>
> The Comanches exchanged at it more than 600 skins, many loads of meat and tallow, 15 horses, and 3 muskets to their entire satisfaction, without experiencing the slightest affront. As a result, grateful and pleased with this new method, they proclaimed publicly that they know now more than ever the truth of our peace, and by virtue of the justice and consideration shown them were bound to be faithful always, and that the advantages they had gained would prompt them to repeat such trading with even greater determination transferring the larger part, if not all, of their fairs to the pueblo of Pecos.[59]

During the following months, Anza worked to secure Ecueracapa's preeminent position as captain general of the entire Comanche nation. And he succeeded. By April 1787, he had in hand a final treaty with all three branches. Ecueracapa had gone after Apaches and sent in tally sheets of his kills. His people had come again to trade at Pecos. Despite the replacement of Anza in 1787 and the death of Ecueracapa in 1793, despite the utter failure of the Jupes to settle down in the pueblo they asked the Spaniards to build for them on the Arkansas, despite troublesome hostilities of Utes, Navajos, and Jicarillas with Comanches, the alliance of Comanches and Spaniards embarked upon at Pecos in 1786 stood unbroken for a generation.[60]

In the fading light of afternoon, the Pecos made out riders approaching. As they drew closer, they could see that they were Comanches escorting a couple of Spaniards "with flag unfurled." Actually one was a Frenchman called Pedro Vial, a gunsmith and Indian trader now in the service of Spain. It was May 25, 1787. At the bidding of the governor of Texas, the explorer Vial had just made his way cross-country clear from San Antonio.

Plains Exploration

A couple of months later, old José Mares, long-time Spanish soldier at Santa Fe and scout, stopped over at Pecos. He was going to try it in reverse, from New Mexico to San Antono, taking with him Cristóbal de los Santos, who had been with Vial, and interpreter Alejandro Martín, the young man presented to Anza at the Pecos peace conference the year before. They also made it, by a shorter route, and returned. Vial followed in 1788-1789 with a trek from Santa Fe to Natchitoches to San Antonio and back, and in 1792-1793 to St. Louis round trip. Always they came and went through Pecos, New Mexico's eastern port of entry.

As individual feats of exploration, these lonely voyages across the plains were prodigious. As moves on the international chessboard of North America, they were singularly puny. Spanish imperialists wanted to bind the Provincias Internas and Spanish Louisiana, to secure the middle of the continent from Englishmen out of Canada, Anglo-Americans shoving west, and conniving Frenchmen who wanted their American empire back. The explorations of Vial and "interpreter" Mares, in the words of Viceroy Revillagigedo, "have been and can be very important and conducive to counteract the dangerous designs of foreign powers." In the long run, they proved not very conducive at all.[61]

Comanche tally of casualties and spoils in battle with Apaches, 1786 (AGI, Guad., 287).   Thomas, *Forgotten Frontiers*

For a few short years, it looked as though Pecos might recover. The murderous assaults had ceased. The eastern gateway lay open. Trade picked up. "In the short time since my arrival," exulted Gov. Fernando de la Concha in 1787 three months after taking office, "seven fairs have been held at the pueblo of Taos, a very considerable one at that of Pecos, and another at Picurís, the most noteworthy since up to now none has taken place at this pueblo." [62]

Concha was as careful of the Comanche peace as Anza had been. He treated with their delegations, provided maize as relief when drought temporarily drove the buffalo herds from their ranges, and regularly distributed gifts to them and the other allied tribes. Each spring when the caravan from Chihuahua pulled into Santa Fe, these heathen allies lined up for the dole. Bolts of bright cloth and quantities of hats, shoes, knives, mirrors, rope, strings of beads, coral, vermillion, indigo, bars of soap, cigarettes, and *piloncillos,* those hard-as-rock little cones of raw sugar, were a small enough price to pay. When treasury officials held up the four thousand pesos in 1790 for "extraordinary expenses of peace and war," Concha appropriated the funds allotted for the missionaries' allowances, assuring the commandant general in 1791 that the Franciscans had "gladly agreed to wait until this year." A bald, forced loan, it clearly showed the governor's priorities. [63]

Nurturing Comanche Peace

A Lipan Apache warrior, after a painting by Arthur Schott. W. H. Emory, *Report on the United States and Mexican Boundary Survey,* vol. 1 (Washington, D.C., 1857)

As the regular port of entry and trade for the Comanches after 1786, Pecos became almost an agency town. To make the peace work, Anza and Concha relied on "interpreters," Spaniards or mixed-bloods who knew the natives' language and customs, who knew where they could be found when the governor wanted them, who handled the delicate business of grievances and infractions, in effect, Indian agents. José Mares, the elderly plains explorer who headed the Pecos census of 1790 and who lived at the pueblo with his thirteen-year-old son, was evidently one of these.

Juan Bautista de Anza

On occasion, Indian diplomacy demanded tact of the highest order. Not long after the Comanche peace had been signed at Pecos, a group of "Lipan Apaches" showed up to test it or at least to share in the benefits. They asked "that they be permitted to re-establish the commerce which 35 or 40 years ago they carried on at the Pueblo of Pecos," before they had gone south for fear of the Comanches. The traders of New Mexico were glad to see them back and urged the governor to admit their petition. The Comanches were appalled. If the Spaniards made peace with these Apaches, who would the Comanches have left to fight? They would become mere women!

Recognizing the conflict, the commandant general instructed Governor Concha to keep the peace only with Comanches, Utes, Navajos, and Jicarillas, the so-called "four allied tribes," and to make war on Apaches by any other name. By 1790, scattered deaths attributed to Apaches began appearing in the Pecos book of burials. Yet, on occasion, the lure of profit and the ransom of captives prevailed. In 1791, "a party of Llanero and Mescalero Apaches" came to Pecos to get what they could for ten captives "and to barter various goods and buffalo hides." [64]

The Gateway Displaced

By the end of the century, Spanish settlement at the river ford had superseded Pecos pueblo as port of entry and agency town. "Interpreters" to the Comanche nation moved down to San Miguel del Vado. Hispano *comancheros* and *ciboleros,* a breed of plains traders and hunters in the tradition of Diego Romero, made their bases there. Instead of waiting for the Comanches to come to them, they took themselves to the Comanches. Even though the occasional color and hubbub of trade fairs broke the routine at Pecos well into the nineteenth century, the recovery set in motion by the Comanche peace had passed.

Still, for another forty years, Pecos refused to die.

Spanish soldier's
pistol, c. 1780.
Brinckerhoff and Faulk,
Lancers

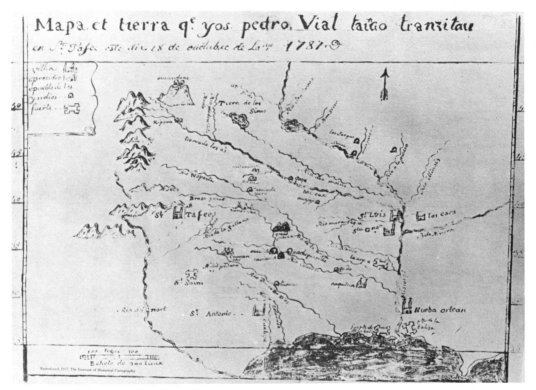

Pedro Vial's arena, 1787:
Santa Fe center left, St.
Louis center right, New
Orleans lower right.
Carl I. Wheat, *Mapping
the Transmississippi
West, 1540-1861*, vol. 1
(San Francisco, 1957)

chapteR IX

towaRò extinction
1794-1840

There is a pueblo called Pecos, which must have been one of the largest in former times. Those people worked hard. But today there cannot be forty Indians of both sexes. It is a shame. It could be resettled with other people.

Custos Isidoro Barcenilla, 1815

Never, Most Excellent Sir, will we look with indifference on an action which has caused us almost total ruin. Our loss could hardly be greater. We see ourselves despoiled of the land on which we, from our eldest to the youngest of our people, have spilled the sweat of our brows, working it in such a way that it might furnish us our subsistence. Will it be reasonable or just that others profit from our labor, without any remuneration? It hardly seems possible. That decision bears not the least semblance of equity. We commit to the wisdom of Your Excellency all the injuries that must be our lot as a consequence of such violent despoilment.

Petition of the Pecos Indians, March 9, 1829

This village, anciently so renowned, lies twenty-five miles eastward of Santa Fé, and near the *Rio Pecos,* to which it gave name. Even so late as ten years ago, when it contained a population of fifty to a hundred souls, the traveller would oftentimes perceive but a solitary Indian, a woman, or a child, standing here and there like so many statues upon the roofs of their houses, with their eyes fixed on the eastern horizon, or leaning against a wall or a fence, listlessly gazing at the passing stranger; while at other times not a soul was to be seen in any direction, and the sepulchral silence of the place was only disturbed by the occasional barking of a dog, or the cackling of hens.

Josiah Gregg, *Commerce of the Prairies,* 1844

Josiah Gregg.
Gregg, *Commerce*

If, as Josiah Gregg claimed, the last of the Pecos could be
seen in the 1830s gazing off to the east, their thoughts were
probably less bound up with the return of "Montezuma" than
with the plains themselves, source of the wealth and the danger
that once had made their pueblo the strongest of them all.
Now as calicoes, hairpins, and hardware, the richest trade in
the history of the plains, jolted by in the beds of Pittsburgh
wagons, the Pecos had no part in it. They were too few now
to be of any use—as converts to Christianity, as vassals or
allies, as traders or carpenters. The priest came only when he
had to, or not at all. The settlers in the valley encroached on
the land of their fathers. Pecos was dying.

Dwindling
Remnant

For the venerable pueblo at the eastern gateway, the turn
of the century was a watershed. The New Mexico census of
1799 was the last to show Pecos with more Indians than non-
Indians, 159 to 150. Five years before, in 1794, there had been
no "*españoles y castas*" at all, no plaza or settlement of Hispanos dependent on the interim missionary of Pecos. With the
petition of Lorenzo Márquez and his fifty-one land-poor *com-
pañeros,* admitted by Gov. Fernando Chacón on November 25,
1794, the eastern pueblo's traditional isolation began to break
down.

Settling
San Miguel del Vado

[Fernando de] Chacón

The caravan in sight of Santa Fe.   Gregg, *Commerce*

Their reasons for requesting a large settlement grant were the usual ones. "Although we all have some pieces of land in this villa [Santa Fe], they are not sufficient for our support, both because they are small and because of the great shortage of water and the crowd of people who make it impossible for all of us to enjoy its use." Since the Comanches by the mid-nineties appeared firmly committed to peace, New Mexicans could now contemplate the grass and good bottoms in the valley of the Río Pecos with an eye to possession. Márquez and company had already staked out a fine uninhabited site.

Twenty-odd miles downriver southeast of Pecos pueblo, it lay at the place where the trail to the plains crossed the river, "where," according to the petition, "there is space enough not only for the fifty-one of us [fifty-two counting Márquez] who ask but also for as many in the province who are destitute." They described the boundaries of this new Eden simply: "in the north the Río de la Vaca [Cow Creek] from the place called La Ranchería to El Agua Caliente; in the south El Cañón Blanco; in the east La Cuesta and Los Cerritos de Bernal; and in the west the place commonly called El Gusano [South San Isidro]."

Thirteen of the fifty-two men who applied were *genízaros,* those ransomed Indians and their descendants who lived as Hispanos, exactly twenty-five percent. Although more genízaros would move to the area later, the settlers themselves fostered the quarter-truth that his was "a genízaro settlement" in order to win concessions from church and state. Twenty-five of the fifty-two had firearms. All of them pledged as one "to enclose ourselves in a plaza well fortified with bulwarks and towers and to make every effort to lay in all the firearms and munitions we possibly can."

That sounded good to Governor Chacón. At his orders, don Antonio José Ortiz, alcalde mayor of Santa Fe, rode out next day to put the El Vado grantees in possession. First he read to them the conditions of the grant: 1) it was to be common, not for them alone but for future settlers as well; 2) they must be armed with firearms or bows and arrows, muster periodically, and all have converted to firearms at the end of two years—those who had not would be expelled; 3) they must build the plaza within the stipulated boundaries of the grant—"During the interim they should locate at the pueblo of Pecos, where there is sufficient lodging for the said fifty-two families;" 4) the alcalde of Pecos was "to set aside a small portion of these lands [presumably those of the pueblo] so that said families may plant them for themselves at their pleasure, but without their children, heirs, or a substitute being able to inherit them;" 5) everyone must share in work on the plaza, irrigation ditches, and other projects in the common good. They agreed.

Conditions of the Grant

"Therefore," wrote Alcalde Ortiz in the standard language of land grants,

I took them by the hand and stated in loud and intelligible voice that in the name of His Majesty (God save him), without prejudice to his Royal Estate or that of a third party, I had conducted them over these lands. They pulled up grass, threw rocks, and shouted "Long live the king," taking possession of said lands quietly and peacefully without the least opposition.[1]

Antonio José Ortiz

Evidently it took them some time to get themselves together. Although Lorenzo Márquez and Domingo Padilla, two of the El Vado grantees, or their Indian namesakes, showed up as early as the 1780s in the Pecos books as godfathers and marriage witnesses, no one identified as a settler of El Vado appeared until late 1798. Until they had homes up and fields planted, most of them preferred to leave their families in Santa Fe. Interestingly enough, the first entry for an El Vado resident, dated November 28, 1798, records the marriage of Juan de Dios Fernández, "citizen (*vecino*) of El Vado and formerly an Indian of Pecos," to María, daughter of grantee Juan Armijo, "performed with the consent of their parents." A few Pecos, it would seem, did join the El Vado settlements, but very few.[2]

Allotting
Farm Lands By early 1803, the plaza, puesto, or población of San Miguel del Vado boasted fifty-eight heads of family. Having persevered the required five years, they had earned their legal stake in the community. In recognition, Governor Chacón "by verbal order" dispatched don Pedro Bautista Pino, who later gained a wider fame as New Mexico's delegate to the Spanish Cortes of 1810-1813. It was March, just before planting time.

Pedro Bautista Pino

Don Pedro's job was to allot the available farm lands among all the families. "Because of the many bends of the river," measuring the total was a pain.

He began at the north. With the help of the interested parties he marked off the requisite number of parcels, trying as best he could to make them all equally desirable. Most were 50 or 65 varas wide, measured along the irrigation ditch, a few were 100 or 130 varas, and the largest 230. To match family and parcel, Pino had them draw lots. Then on a list next to the name of each, he entered the number of varas. One piece was reserved for the magistrate of the community, and a smaller surplus parcel to support three Masses annually for the souls in Purgatory. After the drawing, he marked the northern boundary at "a hill on the bank of the river above the mouth of the acequia that contains these lands," and in the south "the promontory of the hill of the pueblo and cañada they call Los Temporales." That left room for expansion southward.

Finally, don Pedro called them all together and admonished them to put up promptly, solid landmarks of rock. That would prevent disputes. None of them, he concluded, was free to sell or otherwise alienate his land for a period of ten years, beginning that day, March 12, 1803. After he had gone through the same routine two days later at the settlement of San José del Vado, three miles upstream from San Miguel, distributing farm land to forty-five men and two women, Pedro Bautista Pino made ready to ride back to Santa Fe. The settlers crowded around him. Nine years later he recalled the scene in his book.

During the administration of Señor Chacón, I was commissioned to found at El Vado de[l Río] Pecos two settlements, and to distribute lands to more than 200 families. After I concluded this operation, and upon taking leave of them (having refused the fee they were going to give me for my labor), my heart, at that moment as never before, was overcome with joy. Parents and little children surrounded me, all of them expressing, even to the point of tears, their gratitude to me for having given them lands for their subsistence.[3]

The presence of so many Spaniards and mixed-bloods making love, giving birth, and dying on the Río Pecos, at first far away downriver, but still within the jurisdiction of the mission, should have meant closer attention to Pecos by the Franciscans. And it did for a time. Then, as the disparity widened, as the El Vado settlements propagated and Pecos shrunk further and further, the priest moved out to El Vado and visited the Pecos less often than when he had resided in Santa Fe.

Spiritual Neglect of Pecos

For the missionaries of New Mexico—whose priest-to-parishioner ratio had been thrown all out of proportion by the Hispano population spiral—overworked, undersupported, and often demoralized, it became a question of numbers. In 1794, there were 165 Pecos Indians and no settlers at El Vado; in 1820 only 58 Pecos, but by then 735 settlers. The friars responded accordingly.

Baptisms, marriages, and burials of Pecos Indians and settlers of the El Vado district:

	Baptisms		Marriages		Burials	
	Pecos	El Vado	Pecos	El Vado	Pecos	El Vado
1795	5	0	2	0	9	0
1800	2	8	1	4	18	2
1805	0	14	1	12	2	11
1810	1	30	1	11	5	14
1815	0	24	0	5	3	12
1820	1	35	0	8	not available	
1825	1	176	1	40	1	97[4]

Whether justified by numbers or not, Christian nurture of Mission Nuestra Señora de los Ángeles at Pecos during this period can be summarized in one word—neglect. The same thing can of course be said of the colony as a whole. At the very end of 1799, when the authorities were again considering the creation of a diocese of New Mexico, as they did every so often, the province, including El Paso, was composed of nine districts with 23,648 Spaniards and mixed-bloods and 10,557 Indians, or a total population of 34,205.

The villa of Santa Fe, with its 120-man presidial garrison and its population of 3,450 Spaniards, was the seat of a district that also included the missions of Tesuque and Pecos. In all, the province had twenty-six Indian missions. For the support of a missionary at each, the king provided the annual 330-peso allowance, except at Zuñi where 900 pesos were allotted for two. The few secular priests dispatched from Durango to serve the four villas did not often stay long in poor New Mexico. Seculars ministered at Santa Fe and El Paso, but the Franciscans were left to care for both Alburquerque and Santa Cruz de la Cañada. The missions were nine friars short. Pecos as usual was vacant.

Whoever filled the vacancy at Pecos, at least on paper, should reside in the mission and gather to him the new establishment or settlement of Spaniards and mixed-bloods on the Río Pecos. Although it is rather distant, for now there is no other means of administering this settlement since it is not yet duly established. But in time it will inevitably need a minister.[5]

Interim Ministers from Santa Fe

During the 1790s, the assistant pastor at Santa Fe, a Castilian Spaniard named Buenaventura Merino, had been assigned to look after the Pecos. He came round every few months. He also saw to the Tewa pueblo of Tesuque, just north of Santa Fe. Born on February 24, 1745, at Villavicencio de los Caballeros in the diocese of León, the forty-year-old Merino had landed in America in 1785 with a group of recruits for the missionary college of San Fernando de México, supplier of Franciscans to Alta California. He had hated the rigorous routine at the college. After four and a half years of it, he threw in with the disillusioned Fray Severo Patero, just back from Spain's aborted Nootka Sound colony. Together they petitioned the viceroy for permission to serve in New Mexico. The college's superior, who pointed to the crying need for missionaries in California, chose to release them, and the two had shown up in Santa Fe in September of 1790.

Reporting on his ministry in 1801, Father Merino put the total population of Pecos pueblo at 59 males and 64 females. There were 182 settlers downriver at San Miguel del Vado, 85 of them men and boys and 97 women and girls. Characterized by the friar as "very poor," both Hispanos and

Fray Buenaventura Merino

Indians grew maize, wheat, and a few vegetables in fields irrigated by the Río Pecos, but only enough to subsist. They ran only a few head of cattle and no sheep or goats "because the enemies do not let them increase." Filling out the rest of the questionnaire, Merino declared that in his district there were no industries or commerce worth mentioning, no bridges over the river, and no good timber for the royal navy.[6]

Merino's successor, Fray Diego Martínez Arellano, a discouraged Mexican veteran who began ministering at Pecos and El Vado in the spring of 1802, greeted his reassignment after two years as a blessing. Writing his last entry in the book of baptisms, he let his feelings show. He could not find the parents of the Pecos baby girl he had just baptized. The reason was plain. "All the Indians," noted Martínez, "live publicly in concubinage because the officials, both Spaniards and Indians, tolerate it. And the minister can do nothing to remedy it because they tell him he is being indiscreet."[7]

Their next minister, one of the newly arrived peninsular Spaniards, stayed around longer, but devoted almost all his time to El Vado. Thirty-five-year-old Fray Francisco Bragado y Rico, from the neighborhood of tiny Villalonso and Benafarces in the diocese of Zamora, Castilla la Vieja, had "no degrees other than being a Christian, priest, and friar of Our Father St. Francis." [8] He appeared at Pecos in June 1804 and very soon took up the cause of the settlers.

It was not right that "the genízaros" of the new settlement had been denied Mass and the word of God simply because they lived so far from Pecos over "a bad and very perilous road." They deserved a chapel of their own, where they could be baptized, married, and buried without an all-day journey. They had in fact already begun one by December of 1804 when Bragado petitioned the bishop of Durango for permission. "This settlement," he wrote, "is composed of one hundred and twenty families, all poor and unfortunate people with no greater resource for their subsistence than their own labor and no greater possessions than the little land with which Our Sovereign (God save him) has succored them." It worked. By the following spring, they had the permission. [9]

Governor Chacón
Damns the Friars

On the last day of 1804, Governor Chacón filed a state-of-the-missions report. It stung worse than the knotted cords of the *disciplina,* the scourge. According to him, the missionaries were gouging the poor citizenry who depended on them alone for the sacraments. They charged exorbitant fees, disregarding the schedules set by the distant bishops of Durango. If someone could not pay a baptismal or marriage fee, the friars set them to work. It was common on the death of a poor colonist, said Chacón, that the friar suddenly became the deceased's sole heir, while the legitimate heirs found themselves reduced to utter penury.

If anyone thought the Franciscans confined their venal practices to Hispanos, the stiff-necked Chacón meant to set him straight. The Indians had to pay to celebrate their mission's patronal feast, or else it was cancelled. It was customary, too, every All Souls Day, November 2, after the harvests were in, for the Indians of all the pueblos to enter the churches laden with offerings of produce of every kind. These went to the friars. When an Indian died, his family paid the missionary for the funeral Mass in livestock if possible, or, despite the natives' legal exemption, in personal service, "especially the friar who treated them well." For years, Chacón alleged, some ministers had let the Indians sell off portions of the four leagues of land each pueblo enjoyed under the law, thus contributing further to their charges' privation.

Provincia del Nuevo Mexico — Misiones y Curatos de la misma.

Noticia de las Misiones y curatos, actualmente existentes en la citada Provincia, con expresion de sus Ministro, Sinod. y n.º Almas.

Misiones	Ministros	Años de ser.	Sinodos Sinodal	de l. Paz	Indios Varones	Mugeres	Total	Esp. y cast. Hombres	Mugeres	Total	Total de Almas
San Geronimo de Taos	1	1	330	idem	228	276	558	435	392	827	1385
San Lorenzo de Pecuries	1	1	330	idem	133	131	264	284	290	574	838
San Juan de los Cavalleros	1	1	330	idem	104	125	229	1053	1020	2088	2317
Santo Tomas de Abiquiu	1	1	330	idem	86	85	171	667	711	1378	1549
Santa Clara	1	1	330	idem	110	090	200	563	504	1067	1267
San Ildefonso	1	1	330	idem	133	122	255	125	121	246	501
San Francisco de Nambe	1		330	idem	091	072	163	016	017	33	196
N. S. de Guadalupe x Pojuaque					043	044	87	105	106	211	298
San Diego de Tesuque	1	1	330	idem	073	076	149	114	113	227	376
N. S. d. los Angeles x Pecos	1	1	330	idem	052	073	125	220	217	437	562
San Buenaventura x Cochiti	1	1	330	idem	319	346	665	279	314	593	1258
Santo Domingo					191	165	356	67	82	149	505
San Felipe	1	1	330	idem	168	116	284	256	215	471	755
N. S. de los Dolores x Sandia	1	1	330	idem	164	160	324	207	183	390	714
San Diego x Xemes	1	1	330	idem	159	159	318	213	219	432	750
Nuestra S. de la Asumpcion x Sia	1	1	330	idem	134	144	278				278
Santa Ana					240	263	503	34	22	56	559
San Agustin de la Ysleta	1	1	330	idem	234	238	472	217	212	429	901
N. S. de Belem	1	1	330	idem	049	59	108	990	893	1883	1991
Villa Capital x Santa Fe	1							1374	1513	2887	2887
Villa de Sta. Cruz de la Cañada	1							1140	1062	2202	2202
Villa de Alburquerque	1							1918	1955	3873	3873
San Esteban x Acoma	1	1	330	idem	369	363	732				732
San José de la Laguna					473	435	908	053	054	107	1015
N. S. de Guadalupe x Zuñi	1	1	450	idem	707	752	1459	003	002	005	1464
Compañia Presidial	1	1	480	idem				349	387	736	736
Totales en 1804	22	19	6540	120 a Mar	4314	4294	8668	10637	10614	21304	29909
Existian en 1802	24	21	7200	idem	4328	4191	8509	10319	1025	21222	29713
Notas Diferencias	2	2	660		14	113	99	263	289	79	178

1804 census of the missions and parishes of New Mexico (AGI, Mex., 2737).

Addressing himself to the Franciscans' spiritual care of the Pueblos, the governor dragged out all the old allegations. Few of the Indians confessed annually, waiting instead until moribund, when they did so only through an interpreter. None of the missionaries in 1804 had a knowledge of the native languages, "nor," claimed the governor, "do they exert the least effort or application to acquire it." For the most part, the Pueblos understood Spanish but preferred not to use it, especially the women. The friars left religious instruction to other Indians, the fiscales—a scandal in Chacón's book.

No religious attends this essential activity. Since they were prohibited the punishment of the Indians at their discretion and the custom of employing them to serve, they abandon them under the pretext of not being able to control them, protesting that they neither pay attention nor obey them. Generally they treat the Indians badly, abusing them in word and deed whenever they have the opportunity. As a result, the Indians look upon them with spite and as their worst oppressors.[10]

A Church for
El Vado

Father Bragado endured at Pecos almost six years. He saw the rowdy mixed-breed communities of San Miguel and San José del Vado almost double in size. Evidently work was progressing on the San Miguel church, but not without incident. Once in the summer of 1805 when Manuel Baca, interim deputy justice of the district, ordered Ignacio Durán, in charge at San José, to beat the drum for the people to come work on

Manuel Baca, Teniente

the church, not everyone assembled. Reyes Vigil and his sons refused. When Durán ordered them, Vigil told him that he could "eat shit, eat a bucket of shit!" Afterwards, at Vigil's corral, the two got into a name-calling, rock-throwing, hair-pulling brawl. Because only a part of the record survives, the outcome of the ensuing legal action is not known.[11]

As their priest, Bragado found himself very much involved in the lives of the El Vado settlers. Early in 1809, he and Teniente de justicia Manuel Baca appeared together before

Custos José Benito Pereyro to forgive each other and to drop the proceedings they had entered into. They vowed not to re-kindle this or past differences. When the custos informed Gov. José Manrique of the reconciliation, the governor warned that it was not genuine. All Baca wanted was to bring to his side the woman who had been the cause of the trouble. Father Bragado had better watch his step.[12]

Whether or not the Baca affair hastened his departure, Bragado cleared out early in 1810, the moment a replacement was available. The custos transferred him to San Ildefonso and assigned in his place Fray Juan Bruno González, an untried Spaniard who had arrived in Santa Fe on February 26 and who found himself minister of Pecos and El Vado on March 12. Like his predecessors, he soon learned that the settlers were as unreliable as the Pecos when it came to notifying the Father that someone was dying. He stayed not quite one year.[13]

The San Miguel del Vado church as sketched by Lt. J. W. Abert in 1846.
Abert, *Western America in 1846-1847* (San Francisco, 1966)

Rebellion in New Spain

As Fray Juan Bruno ministered on the Río Pecos, he heard the ghastly news of 1810. Unless inured by the incredible plague of events that had rendered his homeland a satellite of the monster Napoleon, the Spanish Franciscan must have blanched. A mad diocesan priest drunk with the heady spirits of the French Revolution, one Miguel Hidalgo, had raised the cry of independence and liberty at a little town northwest of Mexico City. The rabble had risen. They killed and burned and looted in an orgiastic caste war that threatened briefly to envelope the entire heartland of New Spain. But because the rebels were ill organized and unsustained, royal forces had taken the offensive. Before Father González left Pecos, they had captured Hidalgo. He was to be shot.

The Priest Moves to El Vado

Twenty-seven-year-old Fray Manuel Antonio García del Valle, a native of Mexico City, did not stand on tradition. Granted, he had been appointed minister of the mission of Pecos, and it was still the cabecera, or seat of the "parish," but he saw no earthly reason for him to reside in a dying Indian pueblo when the large majority of his parishioners lived ten leagues or so downriver. After relieving González in March 1811, he baptized thirty-two infants for the settlers of El Vado before a Pecos Indian couple finally had a baby. That year the settlers at last finished the chapel of San Miguel del Vado.[14] Why should he not reside there?

To make his change of residence legitimate, Father García del Valle needed the approval of the see of Durango. The people of El Vado must send a petition. It was first-rate, a real propaganda piece. They chose José Cristóbal Guerrero, a genízaro of Comanche origin, to represent San Miguel and San José, two hundred and thirty heads of family "well instructed in the obligations of Christians." They made the most of the fact that Comanches, not really that many according to the books, were joining their communities and taking instruction

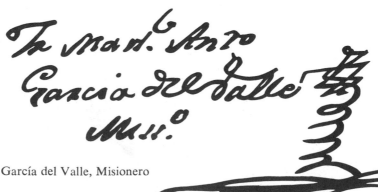

Fray Manuel Antonio García del Valle, Misionero

San Miguel del Vado, 1846.   Abert, *Report*

for baptism. Not only did this swell their numbers, but it also cemented the peace between Comanches and Spaniards. "As a result," they predicted with chamber-of-commerce élan, "it is to be expected that within a few years these will be the most populous settlements in the province of New Mexico."

In sharp contrast stood the dying mission of Pecos. Only thirty families of Indians lived there "and of so little capacity that they received only the sacraments of baptism and matrimony." Fray Manuel, missionary at Pecos, had indicated to the settlers his willingness to move to El Vado. They requested therefore that he be allowed to do so, with the obligation of visiting Pecos with an escort once a month. Early in 1812, the diocese approved. For better or for worse, the Pecos had lost their resident minister for good.[15]

That same year in far-off Cádiz, capital of the resistance in French-occupied Spain, don Pedro Bautista Pino published for the benefit of his fellow delegates to the Cortes and the world at large an *Exposición sucinta y sencilla de la provincia del Nuevo México.* His goal was reform. Hoping to win for New Mexico the often-proposed diocese, he proclaimed the sorry state of the church in his province. All of New Mexico, with twenty-six Indian pueblos and one hundred and two Spanish communities, had only two secular priests and twenty-two Franciscans. Distances were great. As a consequence, many New Mexicans did without spiritual care. The absence of a bishop, moreover, had caused them, in Pino's words, to suffer "infinite harm."

Pino and the Spanish Constitution

Not since 1760 had their *primado pastor* visited New Mexico. For half a century no one had been confirmed. They had forgotten that there was a bishop. Ecclesiastical discipline foundered. Many who needed a dispensation to marry, but who were too poor to travel to Durango to obtain one, lived and raised families in sin. It was a crime that a province producing nine to ten thousand pesos annually in tithes had not seen the face of its bishop in more than fifty years. "I, who am older," Pino confessed, "never knew how bishops dressed until I came to Cádiz."[16]

He was convincing. The Cortes voted in favor of a diocese and a seminary college for New Mexico. On the Río Pecos a skeptical Father García del Valle took part in the excitement as the El Vado settlers elected their "parochial elector" under the liberal Spanish Constitution of 1812, a thoroughly new experience.[17]

But none of it came to anything. Napoleon let Ferdinand VII go. Once home on the Spanish throne, the king abolished the constitution, dissolved the Cortes, and nullified all its legislation. And that was that. As the people said, *"Don Pedro Pino fue, don Pedro Pino vino."*

Enduring
Comanche Peace

For the most part the Comanches kept the peace. By the 1790s, it was habit. Even though the pueblo of Pecos declined visibly, even though more and more "comancheros" were taking the commerce of New Mexico out onto the plains, still the Comanches honored the tradition begun at the peace conference of 1786. They came to Pecos to trade, and they came to parley.

When Tampisimanpe, the Eastern Comanche captain, reined up at Pecos in July 1797, he wanted to trade and parley. He wanted to see Governor Chacón confirm a "general" of the Comanche nation. It had been prearranged. The other Comanche captains had gathered. Next day at a solemn junta presided over by the Spanish governor, Canaguaip of the Cuchanticas received "a plurality of votes," whereupon Chacón recognized him in the king's name.

I presented to him in proof thereof a baston with head of silver and a medal of the same. To distinguish him further I gave him, among other articles, a long dress coat of trimmed scarlet cloth, bestowing on him in addition two fanegas of maize, one arroba of *punche* [local tobacco], and a tercio of piloncillo [raw sugar candy] for him to regale his household.

Before they departed, the Comanches presented to the governor two Spaniards, servants of a French trader abducted on the plains by unfriendly heathens. The governor sent them off to Chihuahua to see the commandant general.[18]

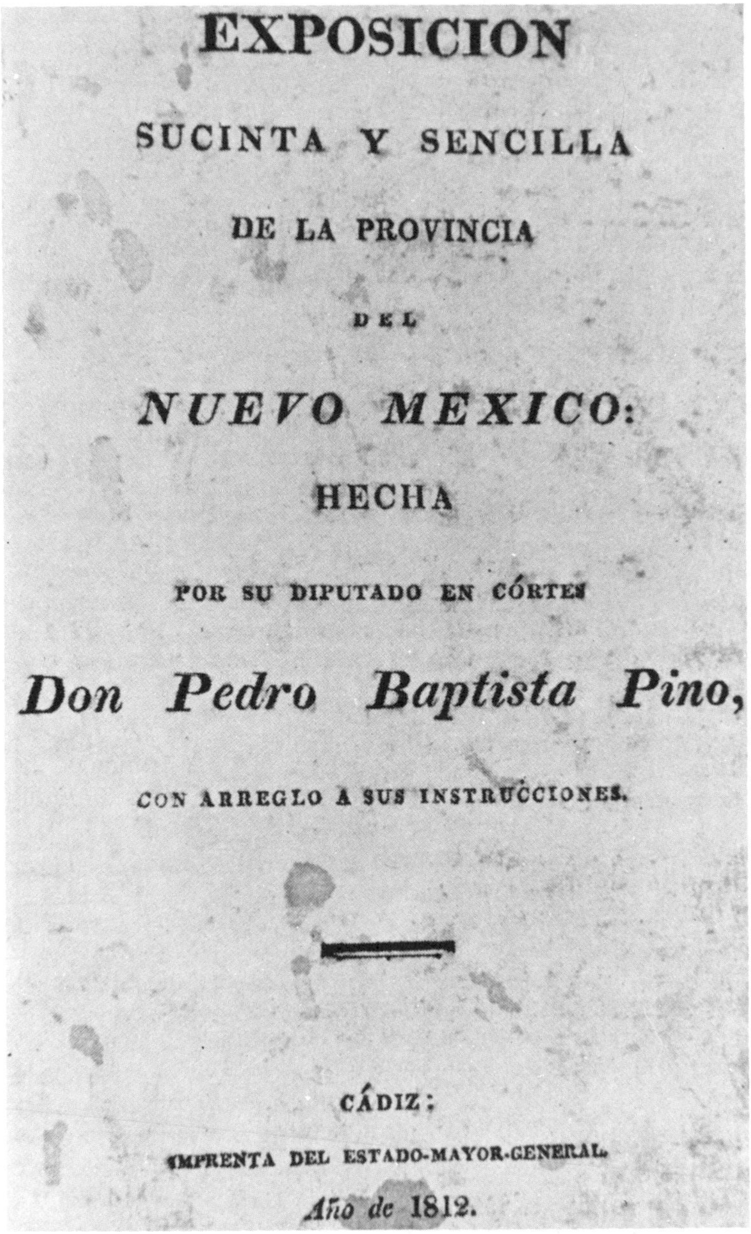

EXPOSICION

SUCINTA Y SENCILLA

DE LA PROVINCIA

DEL

NUEVO MEXICO:

HECHA

POR SU DIPUTADO EN CÓRTES

Don Pedro Baptista Pino,

CON ARREGLO Á SUS INSTRUCCIONES.

CÁDIZ:

IMPRENTA DEL ESTADO-MAYOR-GENERAL.

Año de 1812.

Title page of Pedro Bautista Pino's brief description of New Mexico, Cádiz, 1812. Carroll and Haggard, *Three New Mexico Chronicles*

On occasion, Comanche leaders tried to put one over on the Spaniards. Chacón caught the Yamparika captain Guani-coruco at it in 1804. This Indian had traveled to Chihuahua, probably in the annual trade caravan, for an interview with Commandant General Nemesio Salcedo. He had several things on his mind.

First, he was unhappy with interpreter Juan Cristóbal who neglected to carry the reports of the Comanches to Governor Chacón. He asked permission for a son of his, one José María who had received baptism at Chihuahua in 1803, to live at San Miguel del Vado and serve as interpreter there and at Pecos during the trading. He also requested license to hold the trade fairs at Pecos because, on route through the mountains from that pueblo to Santa Fe, their animals suffered and Apaches killed their women and children who followed along behind. Guarnicoruco had another son whom he believed should be named captain of the Yamparikas. Lastly, he volunteered to guide Spaniards to the Cerro Amarillo, fifteen days east of Pecos and El Vado, so that they could determine whether it was gold or some other metal. Salcedo, requesting that the governor keep him informed, passed these maters on for Chacón's attention.[19]

The New Mexico governor was frank. Guanicoruco was a liar. Interpreter Juan Cristóbal had not been assigned to the Yamparikas since Chacón took office. José María Gurulé was not a son of Guarnicoruco, rather a Skidi Pawnee genízaro who had once been a captive of the Comanches. Chacón had sent him to El Vado as Comanche interpreter with the first settlers. But because of Gurulé's unruly conduct, cheating, and horse thieving, the governor had removed him "at the petition of the entire nation" and put paid interpreter Alejandro Martín in his place. As for Guarnicoruco's request to trade at Pecos, that was absurd. "I have not heard," wrote Governor Chacón,

that in the twenty years the Comanche nation has been at peace with this province they have carried on their trading at any other place than the pueblo of Pecos, eight leagues from this capital, the very place Guarnicoruco refers to. I or one of my subordinates attend the trading with an appropriate escort to maintain good order between Spaniards and heathens.

If Chacón tried to elevate Guarnicoruco's son, who was only fourteen or fifteen years old, he would lose the confidence of the rest of the nation. If this Indian knew where to find the Cerro Amarillo, let him bring in some samples. When Guarnicoruco showed up in Santa Fe, the Spanish governor reproached him for misleading the commandant general. Perhaps, the Indian replied, the interpreter had misunderstood what he was trying to say.[20]

Ferdinand VII, king of Spain, 1814-1833.   Rivera Cambas, *Los gobernantes,* I

Zebulon Montgomery Pike by Charles Willson Peale.   Independence National Historical Park

The Spanish quest for a Cerro Amarillo or Cerro de Oro in Comanche territory, the enduring enmity of certain Apache bands, and a heightened United States threat across the plains all coincided early in 1804. A far-ranging prospector and buffalo hunter named Bernardo Castro had just ridden into Santa Fe from his second bootless excursion in search of the magic mountain. He claimed to have seen it once before, but only fleetingly by night. Frustrated by deep snows in his attempt to pack a couple of loads of meat up to the villa, Castro decided to go back to El Vado to get them. At the same time, he meant to check out a "very rich vein of silver" two or three leagues from there. Chacón had advised him to wait until it warmed up, but Castro replied that he did not know how to stand idle.

Early in March, the teniente de justicia of Pecos and El Vado notified the governor of Castro's fate. A scouting party of twenty men under Diego Baca had picked up fresh tracks they reckoned were Apache, of seven afoot and two on horseback. They feared the horses might be Castro's. They were. That same day, Baca found the frozen bodies, Castro and José Antonio Rivera. He had them packed up to the mission of Pecos where Fray Diego Martíncz Arellano gave them Christian burial, noting for the record that they had been "killed by Apaches while searching for the mine of the Río de Tecolote."

The same day that Fray Diego put Castro's body in the ground, Diego Villalpando, whom Castro had left among the Comanches Orientales, appeared in Santa Fe. He had been beyond Natchitoches with a dozen Spaniards out of San Antonio. A few days after parting with these men, Villalpando had noted among the Comanches an abundance of loot. He surmised that the heathens had killed these Texans for their large herd of horses and mules. When the Comanches heard that the Spanish troops had ridden out of San Antonio to repel "some Englishmen or Americans," they headed for that villa. One Comanche who did not go for lack of a horse made known his desire to kill Villalpando. It was then that the New Mexican had made his escape.[21]

The mention of Americans might well have caused Chacón to curse. The year was 1804. Thomas Jefferson had just stretched the United States constitution around sprawling, ill-defined Louisiana. Lewis and Clark were outfitting in St. Louis. From then on, right down to 1821, Spanish officials from San Antonio to Santa Fe would damn the Anglos, real or imagined, the likes of Zebulon Montgomery Pike, who came seducing the Plains Indians, filibustering, or just looking for commerce—honest or otherwise.

While Comanches came and went, and once in a while an American or two, the real everyday enemy on the Río Pecos remained the Apache. In the mission book of burials, it was as if a line had been drawn at 1786. Before that, for a half-century, all deaths resulting from hostilities were attributed to Comanches, after that only to Apaches. The friars did not identify them as Jicarillas, Mescaleros, or others. But between 1790 and 1803, the entries for at least five Pecos Indians included the terse explanation "killed by Apaches." In 1804, it was Bernardo Castro and his companion, while six months later, four more El Vado settlers. Time and again settlers and Indians went after them, mustering sometimes at the pueblo and sometimes downriver at El Vado. For the most part, it was like chasing the wind. One seemingly typical militia force set out from San Miguel del Vado in mid-December 1808. They came from all over and included ten genízaros from Santa Fe and ten from San Miguel. For a total of 148 men there were 47 firearms and 263 rounds of ammunition. The rest carried only bow and arrows.[22]

Lure of Trade on the Plains

For the average mixed-blood or genízaro who drew a plot of ground at El Vado in 1803, it was not the prospect of a good year for maize or beans that excited him most, but rather the vision of hunting or trading on the plains. There could be profit in that. The case of Juan Luján, "Indian settler" who owned a 65-vara parcel, was probably not unique. He had walked to the Río Tesuque to see if he could talk Bartolo Benavides, a retired soldier, into going halves with him on an animal to use for buffalo hunting. He failed. On the way home, as chance would have it, he came upon a horse strolling unattended along the road toward Tesuque, or so he later claimed. Since a dog had just bitten him and walking was painful, Luján caught the horse and rode back to El Vado. The Tesuques came looking and charged him with theft. He said he was going to return the animal. For his error Juan Luján spent a month at labor on public works.[23]

Near Rebellion in New Mexico

Lt. Col. Joaquín del Real Alencaster, governor from 1805 to 1808, very nearly lost New Mexico, not to Apaches or Anglos, but to the people themselves. Times were hectic, to be sure. Competition for the loyalty of the Plains tribes quickened. Unwelcome American traders and explorers kept showing up in Santa Fe. Whether he was following orders or not, Real Alencaster's rude attempt to curtail the irregular plains traffic out of the province almost caused a rebellion.

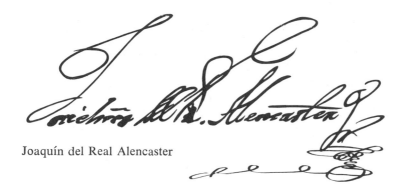

Joaquín del Real Alencaster

Spanish lance blade. Brinckerhoff and Faulk, *Lancers*

At San Miguel on the Río Pecos, don Felipe Sandoval called a meeting, ostensibly to raise funds for the feast of the Virgin of Guadalupe. Juan Antonio Alarí, teniente de justicia of the Pecos-El Vado subdistrict, accused by the people of being a tyrannical bully for the governor, spied on the meeting. He was right. The Virgin was only a cover.

Sandoval was urging the people of San Miguel and San José to ignore the repressive measures of the governor and his henchmen. They should go to the Comanches and trade as usual. Just let the bastards try and stop them. The people of La Cañada and the Río Arriba were with them. At that, "with a garrote and clubs," Alarí broke up the meeting, and arrested Sandoval.

When it was learned that Sandoval and José García de la Mora, "defender" of the people of the Río Arriba, had been hauled before the governor, a mob from the north started for the capital. Only when they had been given assurance that neither Sandoval nor García was in jail did they turn back. From testimony taken in Santa Fe, a number of additional grievances emerged: the limit on what New Mexicans could take in the annual caravan to Chihuahua, the prohibition against selling sheep to the Navajos, the collection of grain from the poor citizens of the Río Arriba to feed the Santa Fe garrison. When Real Alencaster sent the proceedings off to the commandant general, he included charges of sedition against Felipe Sandoval. This time nothing had come of it. In 1837, the mob would behead an unpopular New Mexico governor.[24]

Don Alberto Maynez, who took over from Real Alencaster in 1808, was at pains to let the people of New Mexico know that they were at liberty to trade with the heathen nations and also with Nueva Vizcaya. All they needed was government

approval and passports, these only to make certain the number
of armed men per trading party was sufficient. Felipe Sandoval
was vindicated. By 1814, he served as municipal councilman
in Santa Fe and as protector of New Mexico's Indians. The settlers on the Río Pecos, with or without government sanction,
kept on hunting and trading among the Comanches, enjoying
"the best relations with that heathen nation . . . calm and at
peace as always." [25]

Maintaining the
Comanche Dole

Still, the New Mexicans were no fools. They knew that the
only things that kept the Comanche "barbarians" at peace were
trade and gifts. They knew that while they bartered cloth,
hunting knives, and beads for horses and mules with one band,
other Comanches were stealing more in Texas, Coahuila, or
Nueva Vizcaya. When the Comanche general Soguara arrived
in the fall of 1818 with "more than a thousand" of his people
to trade, don Facundo Melgares, New Mexico's fat but singularly astute and energetic governor, gave out gifts until his
warehouse was almost bare. He begged the commandant general to send more, posthaste. [26]

Exactly a year later, Manuel Antonio Rivera, a plains
guide from San Miguel del Vado who had spent the summer of
1819 among the Comanches, testified in Santa Fe that General
Vicente was en route to see Melgares with news that "many
Anglo-Americans were coming to attack this province." Vicente
wanted to assure the Spanish governor "that the Comanches
and he were prepared to fight the Americans because they advance taking Comanche horse herds and captives and because
the Spaniards of New Mexico are their friends and the lord
governor their *tata* [dad]." [27]

Just how deep the Comanches' friendship ran was evident
in August 1821 when Tata Melgares' gifts played out. Much
of the viceroyalty had already pronounced for Agustín de
Iturbide and independence. There was fighting elsewhere. Commandant General Alejo García Conde, who embraced independence that very month, could spare nothing for gratification of
allied tribes. As the disgruntled Comanches rode back from
Sante Fe through the El Vado district, they took out their
frustrations en route, killing livestock, sacking several houses,
stealing, and raping two women. "So as not to upset the
peace" the settlers did not stand up to them. But they were
furious.

These outrages, protested Manuel Durán of El Vado, were
the result of having cut off the customary Comanche dole. Did
the governor recognize the implications? "This could be the
cause of our losing their fidelity to the alliance we have with

St. Anthony of Padua, a retablo by the anonymous New Mexico santero "A. J.," 1882. Museum of New Mexico

them." He begged Melgares to solicit contributions for an emergency fund. The governor agreed. He knew full well that all the province's heathen allies might rebel if not supplied the usual gifts. Circulating the El Vado plea, he urged the other districts to forward whatever they could to gratify the barbarians "and escape desolation and death." [28]

There were tense moments, to be sure, but the Comanches never did go on the offensive against New Mexico the way they had before 1786. The tradition of trade and forbearing intercourse prevailed. Never was the 1812 prediction of El Vado

Recounting Comanche depredations, Manuel Durán of El Vado warns Governor Melgares that cutting off the dole may wreck the New Mexico-Comanche alliance, August 21, 1821 (SANM, II, no. 3008).

promoters realized, never did great numbers of Comanches come to live as Christians on the Río Pecos. But some did, and their names are scattered through the parish records.

That Indians of Pecos pueblo and Comanches continued to come in frequent contact, during "fairs" and on the plains, is beyond question, and perhaps, as one early anthropologist said, many Pecos "spoke Comanche as well as their own tongue." It seems doubtful, however, based on the same church records, that "there was much Comanche blood in the tribe." [29] As far as Pecos and Comanches were concerned, the hachet buried in 1786 stayed buried. But that did not always mean, literally, that they lay down together.

As they passed back and forth on the dirt track from Santa Fe to El Vado, breaking their journey at Pecos, more than a few Hispanos noted good land along the river, land that the Indians of the dying pueblo were not cultivating, vacant land ripe for the taking.

The Pecos Pueblo League

In 1813, the year after Father García del Valle had moved down to San Miguel, an enterprising trio of "Spaniards and citizens of Santa Fe," by name Francisco Trujillo, Bartolomé Márquez, and Diego Padilla, requested "several pieces of land, unappropriated, untilled, and unimproved at the place called Las Ruedas, located in the environs of the pueblo of Pecos." Once the site of a prehistoric Pecos satellite community, Las Ruedas lay about four miles downriver from the pueblo, near present-day Rowe. Their ownership of such lands, the promoters averred, would in no way prejudice the settlers at San Miguel. Neither would it encroach in the direction of Pecos on "the boundaries of the league (which is ordered set aside for every Indian pueblo), not by far." [30]

The famous "pueblo league" was a legal fiction. Before the eighteenth century, the Pueblo Indians seem to have been entitled under Spanish law to whatever lands they habitually occupied or used. Sometime after 1700, however, there evolved the doctrine of a given league, a sort of recognized minimum right of the Pueblos. In the case of Pecos, it was a minimum indeed, one eventually imposed by the growing Hispano presence and the pueblo's decline. In Spanish law, current use was the key. No matter that the Pecos had farmed or otherwise used more land historically, they were no longer using it in the nineteenth century. Measured one league, or 5,000 varas, in each of the cardinal directions from the cross in the mission cemetery, the standard "pueblo grant" thus contained four square leagues, roughly twenty-seven square miles, or more than 17,350 acres.

The
Upper Pecos Valley

The only extant Spanish land title to Pecos pueblo is a clumsy forgery. One of the so-called Cruzate grants, allegedly made to eleven different pueblos in 1689, it was apparently part of a large-scale nineteenth-century scheme. Nevertheless, the description of the Pecos "grant" was accurate: "to the north one league, and to the east one league, and to the west one league, and to the south one league, and these four lines measured from the four corners of the pueblo leaving aside the church which is to the south of the pueblo." [31]

So long as the Pecos had no neighbors, there was no reason for them to go out and measure their grant on the ground. After the Trujillo-Márquez-Padilla petition of 1813, there was every reason. But since that petition, forwarded by Gov. José Manrique to the commandant general, got lost in the bureaucracy, the earliest recorded measurement of the Pecos league took place in August of 1814.

Juan de Dios Peña, retired ensign of the Santa Fe garrison, and two companions were bidding for a grant just north of Pecos on both banks of the river. A settlement there, the would-be grantees declared, "will serve as a defensive outpost against the enemy Apaches and other barbarians." By order of Governor Manrique and commission of Santa Fe's constitutional alcaldes, Protector de indios Felipe Sandoval went to Pecos and in the company of Peña and local Alcalde Juan Antonio Anaya "we proceeded to measure to the satisfaction of the native principal men of the pueblo the league which from time immemorial His Majesty (God save him) has granted them to the four points of the hemisphere." On this occasion they did not say where they began the measurement.[32]

A Land Grant to the North

For some reason—probably related to the restoration of Ferdinand VII and the reversal of reforms by the Cortes—Peña's 1814 petition was not acted upon. The following year, after there had been a change of governors, he tried again and was successful. Sometimes called the Cañón de Pecos, or the Cañón de San Antonio del Río Pecos, this, or a part of it, eventually became the Alexander Valle grant. Assured by Felipe Sandoval that "said site is independent of the league and farm land of the natives of that pueblo, at a normal distance, and very much separated from the property of said pueblo," Gov. Alberto Maynez sent Santa Fe Alcalde mayor Matías Ortiz out to put Peña in possession. "Beginning at the cross in the cemetery," said Ortiz, "I measured the league upriver and, having completed in full the Indians' league, in the surplus I took don Juan de Dios by the hand" and went through the usual routine. By starting at the cemetery cross, well south of the pueblo itself, Ortiz had lopped off just that much good irrigable land to the north.[33]

The legal battle began in 1818. Juan de Aguilar of Santa Fe, one of Peña's two companions, believed that he had been defrauded. Three years before, he claimed, he had duly acquired a piece of land "in the place known as the surplus of Pecos." Later, the Pecos Indians had protested and called for a new measurement. The alcalde of El Vado, don Vicente Villanueva, complied. In so doing, Aguilar contended, he had deviated from

Vicente Villanueva

established practice in two regards. First, he had begun from "the edge of the pueblo" instead of the cemetery cross, and second he had used a one hundred-vara measuring cord instead of the standard fifty-vara cord. "As a result several properties have been prejudiced." Aguilar begged Gov. Facundo Melgares to address himself to these two points.

Responding the same day to an order from the governor, Alcalde Villanueva defended his measurement. He had indeed used a one hundred-vara cord. To have used a shorter one, he alleged, would have been prejudicial to the Indians because of the irregular, broken terrain. He had wet the cord and stretched it to get the kinks out and then staked it taut. Aguilar and his sons had stretched it again until it broke. With them and "the other settlers of the rancho" looking on, Villanueva had measured one hundred varas on the repaired cord "to everyone's satisfaction," shouting out the count as he went.

That "several properties" had been prejudiced was a lie, said Villanueva, only Aguilar's. Actually one other property lay even farther inside the northern boundary of the Pecos league, but the owner, who did not want it, had died and his heirs wanted it even less. Villanueva had made a couple of other measurements for the settlers with the cooperation of the Pecos. As for his point of origin, the alcalde explained it in these words.

It is true that it has been customary (and I have done so myself) to begin at the cemetery cross. This has been done not because of a set rule; rather because all the pueblos (except this one) have the church more or less in the center. This pueblo, to the contrary, as a consequence of its long site has the church more than a hundred varas away from one end of the pueblo in the opposite direction from the part the natives are defending. Therefore I deemed it just that it be begun, in all directions, from the pueblo as center.

If the governor took any action, the record of it has long been separated from Aguilar's challenge and Villanueva's response. The precedent, however, was set.[34]

Meantime, Trujillo, Padilla, and Márquez had persisted. Submitting a new petition dated May 26, 1814, they asked this time for

A Land Grant
to the South

an unimproved site, located at the place called Los Trigos as far as El Gusano, independent of the league of the Indians of the pueblo of Pecos, in order that we may, without injury to the latter or to any third party, establish our small stock ranches to pasture animals toward some betterment of our standard of living, to clear and plow a few pieces of land for planting, whether it be wheat or maize, knowing full well that we will not prejudice those adjoining us in any way.

The area known as Los Trigos, which gave name to the grant, pressed even closer to Pecos than Las Ruedas, extending from the latter to the present headquarters of the Forked Lightning Ranch. Eight or ten miles downriver, El Gusano, today's South San Isidro, was the western boundary call of the San Miguel del Vado grant and later the focus of a bitter boundary dispute.

Governor Manrique, observing the letter of prevailing reform legislation, had passed the petition on to the Santa Fe municipal council for its approval. Convinced that the grant would not encroach on the prior rights of Pecos Indians or El Vado settlers, the council at its meeting of July 30, 1814, recommended that Trujillo and companions be put in possession "whenever it is convenient." But then word of the king's restoration reached Santa Fe. Trujillo and company waited another year.

On June 22, 1815, Governor Maynez had set them straight. They could pasture their stock on the vacant lands that lay between Pecos and El Vado, but, if there were space enough, so could any other citizen. Only such lands as they might cultivate and fence, as well as the lots for their houses and corrals, would be covered by royal grant. That, years later, set the lawyers dancing an intricate step. Moreover, to make certain the Pecos league was being observed in full, the governor sent Matías Ortiz and the petitioners to Pecos. There on October 20, 1815, said Ortiz, "I measured a fifty-vara cord and handed it over to the Pecos Indians so that they might measure it to their satisfaction. Then, having measured [on the ground] a hundred cord lengths to their entire satisfaction, I set their boundary."[35]

Now, both downriver and up, the land was taken. Although there was a lag between the issuance of these grants and their actual settlement, the Pecos soon had next door neighbors.

"Mexican woodman."
John T. Hughes,
Doniphan's Expedition
(Cincinnati, 1847)

The Onslaught of Settlers

Evidently Santa Fe promoter Esteban Baca, who rounded up sixteen willing derelicts in 1821, would have moved right into the pueblo. In his application for a settlement grant, which seems to have been lost in the independence shuffle, don Esteban did not mince words. He understood that there were now only eight or ten Pecos Indian families left, and all that land going to waste. Their church was falling down. Their minister had abandoned them. Because they were so few, "and having no title," the Pecos were plainly in peril. Besides, the king wanted vacant lands peopled and planted. Therefore, reasoned Baca, his people, "leaving to the Indians whatever land they can cultivate," would move in, reverse the downward population trend, rebuild the church, and bring in a minister. It was, if nothing else, a very good try.[36]

The real onslaught began in 1825. That year Gov. Bartolomé Baca and the Diputación Provincial, New Mexico's token legislature under the Mexican constitution of 1824, in effect threw open the Pecos league. A typical grant of lands allegedly uncultivated by the Pecos for many years went to the illiterate Rafael Benavides and several companions. Its boundaries were "to the east the little springs that are on this side of the Río de la Vaca [Cow Creek], to the west the river, to the north the trail that comes down from Tecolote, and to the

Bartolomé Baca

south the boundary of Diego Padilla [one of the Los Trigos grantees]." The word spread. One Luis Benavides pleaded in March 1825, the same month he retired from military service, for a "small property in the surplus land of the natives of Pecos to sow a few maize plants and some wheat" for his large family and "relief from so many miseries." [37]

With or without grants, they came. Almost overnight dozens of families settled "the Cañón de Pecos." Beginning with the baptisms of two male Roybal infants in the mission church, April 16, 1825, mention of Hispanos from the Cañón de Pecos became more and more frequent. This in fact was the beginning of the present-day village of Pecos. By the early 1830s, the priest at San Miguel del Vado was listing settlers merely "from Pecos," and in May of 1834 he buried a boy "in the chapel of Pecos." Plainly they were there to stay.[38]

The few remaining Indians of the pueblo did not surrender to encroachment without a fight. When proceedings in their favor, supposedly sent by the governor in 1825 to the Mexican congress, "went astray," they tried again the following

The Pecos
Fight Back

year. Alcalde Rafael Aguilar, his lieutenant Juan Domingo Vigil, and "General" José Manuel Armenta, all Pecos Indians, appealed to the Diputación to halt the unlawful alienation of their lands. Some recipients of these grants were speculating. Without having acquired any legal rights to the land or having occupied it the required five years, they had begun selling it off. Others had already planted at the insistence of don Juan Vigil, one of the grantees with Rafael Benavides. "It is not nor has it been our desire," the Pecos insisted, "that they give them our lands." What the Indians had not planted, they used as pasture for their livestock.

Had they no rights as citizens under God and the nation? "Well we know that since the conquest we have earned more merits than all the pueblos of this province." If grants were to be made, they should be of land truly vacant, "as it is at Lo de Mora, at Las Calandrias, at El Coyote, at El Sapelló, on the plains of the lower Río Pecos, as it is on the lower Río Salado and the Río Colorado [the Canadian]." Those were truly lands without owners—a fact certain Apaches and Comanches would surely have challenged.[39]

At least they had bought time. None of the settlers, came the word from Santa Fe, could sell or otherwise alienate Pecos lands until the government resolved the matter. When Gov. Antonio Narbona finally had in hand the information he had requested from the constitutional alcalde of El Vado, he reported to the Mexican minister of domestic and foreign affairs. Narbona was bluntly on the side of the settlers.

[Antonio] Narbona

The lands in question at Pecos amounted to "8,459 varas" on both sides of the river, "abandoned," in the governor's words, "many years back." The forty-one settlers involved had had to clear what they had been given. These lands, according to the governor, lay farther than half a league from the pueblo. The Indians, no more than nine families, not even forty persons, still possessed a full league in the other directions, largely unattended and unworked. No wonder these Indians were the poorest people in New Mexico. They had always refused to mingle with the Hispanos, hence "their barbarous state." Narbona had little sympathy for them.

His suggestion was to break up the Pueblo communes, to give each Indian individual property rights. That way the Indians themselves would progress toward civilization, and lands that lay barren would be brought under cultivation. Otherwise, the Pueblos would remain "mere slaves to their ancient customs," as Narbona put it.

None of them has any authority to transfer property, not even to succor himself. At the same time, that which their pueblo cedes to them, imperfectly and with many limitations, is only enough to make them miserable and keep them in the decadence that even they themselves recognize.[40]

Narbona's rhetoric solved nothing. His ebullient successor, Manuel Armijo, inherited the problem. The settlers divided into factions. In March 1829, thirty-one individuals, who were "settled in the Cañón de Pecos," signed or put their x's on a document at the "Ciénaga de Pecos" reiterating their opposition to others who had been granted land in that area. There simply was not enough to go around.

That same month, the Pecos protested again. Rafael Aguilar and José Cota, representing the pueblo, beseeched the Mexican governor to hear them. It had now been five years since their lands had been invaded by settlers. Apparently the governor had ordered that these intruders be given final title. Still, the Pecos begged him to consider

how great must be the pain in our hearts on seeing ourselves violently despoiled of our rightful ownership, all the more when this violent despoilment was executed while they threatened us with the illegal pretext of removing us from our pueblo and distributing us among the others of the Territory. Please, Your Excellency, see if by chance the natives of our pueblo for whom we speak are denied property and the shelter of the laws of our liberal system. Indeed, Sir, has the right of ownership and security that every citizen enjoys in his possessions been abolished?[41]

It was a good question, good enough that a commission was named to consider it. Carefully weighing the petition of the Pecos along with other documents bearing on the case, the commission came up with a surprisingly unequivocal two-point answer, which the Diputación enacted.

1) That all the lands of which they have been despoiled be returned to the natives of the pueblo of Pecos
2) That the settlers who have possession of them be advised by the alcalde of that district that they have acquired no right of possession because said grant was given to lands that have owners.[42]

Now it was the effected settlers' turn to cry violent despoilment. The case went to court.[43] Whatever the details, the decision did not adversely effect the lineal descent of the full Pecos league in the courts. Whether the settlers actually got off the pueblo's land is another question. From the El Vado church records and the subsequent settlement pattern, it is plain that they did not.

When the pitiful remnant of Cicuye, the eastern fortress-pueblo, finally resolved to abandon the place, the persistent invasion of their lands beginning in 1825 must surely have been a factor.[44]

Santa Fe
Trade

Late in 1818, after an absence of more than eight years, the aging fifty-year-old Fray Francisco Bragado returned to the Pecos Valley. He settled in at San Miguel del Vado. When the spirit moved him, which was not very often if the church records are any indication, he climbed on a mule or horse and rode with an escort to the mission of Pecos. More often than not, the Pecos who cared came to him.

While he sat by a fire or in the shade of a portal at San Miguel, Father Bragado rarely lacked topics to chew over with his cronies. Times were changing at a dizzy pace. He could talk elections. Under the reimposed Spanish constitution, which seemed a cruel mockery to traditional monarchists, even the few Indians at Pecos elected a municipal government in January 1821, Quanima as alcalde and Rafael as the one councilman.[45] Then there was all the talk of Mexican independence. As a peninsular Spaniard, but a rather down-to-earth sort, the Franciscan must have had mixed feelings about that.

From his vantage at El Vado, he witnessed the opening of the Santa Fe trade, a business that would reorient New Mexico's economy and pave the trail for the United States Army a quarter-century later. Enterprising, semi-literate "Captain" William Becknell was the first. Gambling on a cordial reception

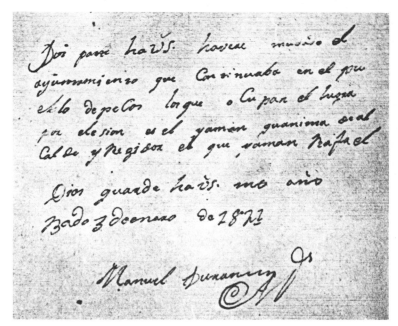

The Pecos remnant elects a municipal government under the Spanish Constitution of 1820 (SANM, II, no. 2954).

by Governor Melgares, he and a company of twenty to thirty men had set out from Missouri with their merchandise lashed aboard pack animals. In mid-November of 1821, they pulled into San Miguel. Up in Santa Fe they made a killing, commercially speaking. The next year they were back with wagons. In 1825, the year Father Bragado died, goods estimated at $65,000 passed over the Río Pecos ford. San Miguel was the port of entry, the ancient pueblo of the Pecos no more than a curious relic up the trail a ways.[46]

The hapless Thomas James and party, forced by Comanches on the plains to hand over much of their merchandise as a guarantee of safe passage, had crossed the ford at San Miguel only two weeks after Becknell. James was the earliest Anglo-American visitor to describe in detail the pueblo of Pecos, or the Fort as he called it. Despite the quarter-century that elapsed between his overnight stay on November 30-December 1, 1821, and the publication of his *Three Years among the Indians and Mexicans* in 1846, the word picture he painted was essentially accurate. He mentioned nothing of Montezuma, a perpetual fire, or a huge voracious snake.

Leaving San Miguel, which James described as "an old Spanish town of about a hundred houses, a large church, and two miserably constructed flour mills," the Missourians fell in with a company of New Mexicans.

Mexican muleteers and pack train.   Gregg, *Commerce*

We stopped at night [November 30, 1821] at the ancient Indian
village of Peccas about fifteen miles from San Miguel. I slept
in the Fort, which encloses two or three acres in an oblong, the
sides of which are bounded by brick [stone] houses three stories
high, and without any entrances in front. The window frames
were five feet long and three-fourths of a foot in width, being
made thus narrow to prevent all ingress through them. The lights
were made of izing-glass [selenite] and each story was supplied
with similar windows. A balcony surmounted the first and second
stories and moveable ladders were used in ascending to them on
the front. We entered the Fort by a gate which led into a large
square. On the roofs, which like those of all the houses in Mexico
are flat, were large heaps of stones for annoying an enemy. I
noticed that the timbers which extended out from the walls about
six feet and supported the balconies, were all hewn with stone
hatchets. The floors were of brick, laid on poles, bark and mortar.
The brick was burned in the sun and made much larger than
ours, being about two feet by one. The walls were covered with
plaster made of lime and izing-glass. I was informed by the
Spaniards and Indians that this town and Fort are of unknown
antiquity, and stood there in considerable splendor in the time
of the Conquerors. The climate being dry and equable and the
wood in the buildings the best of pine and cedar, the towns here

March of the Santa Fe caravan.   Gregg, *Commerce*

suffer but little by natural decay. The Indians have lost all tradition of the settlement of the town of Peccas. It stood a remarkable proof of the advance made by them in the arts of civilization before the Spaniards came among them. All the houses are well built and showed marks of comfort and refinement. The inhabitants, who were all Indians, treated us with great kindness and hospitality. In the evening I employed an Indian to take my horses to pasture, and in the morning when he brought them up I asked him what I should pay him. He asked for powder and I was about to give him some, when the Spanish officer forbade me, saying it was against the law to supply the Indians with amunition. Arms are kept out of their hands by their masters who prohibit all trade in those articles with any of the tribes around them. On the next day in the evening we came in sight of Santa Fe.

On Epiphany, Sunday, January 6, 1822, in Santa Fe the wide-eyed, waspish Thomas James witnessed New Mexico's celebration of Mexican independence. To hear him tell it, he was indispensable, erecting the seventy-foot liberty pole and running up the first flag. But his heart was not in it. The revelry scandalized him, or so he said. "No Italian carnival," he reckoned, "ever exceeded this celebration in thoughtlessness, vice and licentiousness of every description."

Mexican
Independence

Religious medal
struck in the
United States for
the Mexican market.
Gregg, *Commerce*

An unforgettable day, Gov. Facundo Melgares called it in
his official report. Surely some orator likened the coming of the
Three Kings to the coming of the Three Guarantees—Independence, Religion, and Union. There were salvos, processions
and pageants, and, as on most public occasions, Indian dances
in the plaza. James, who wrote in retrospect during a time of
intense anti-Mexican feeling, never tired of comparing the low-
life Hispanos of New Mexico to the sober and industrious
Pueblo Indians. He admired the people of San Felipe who
"danced very gracefully upon the public square to the sound
of a drum and the singing of the older members of their
band" during the second day's festivities. "About the same
time," he remembered,

the Peccas Indians came into the city, dressed in skins of bulls and
bears. At a distance their disguise was quite successful and they
looked like the animals which they counterfeited so well that the
people fled frightened at their appearance, in great confusion from
the square.[47]

**The Last
Franciscans**

Francisco Bragado y Rico, who in 1805 had secured
license from the bishop for a chapel at San Miguel del Vado,
twenty years later was laid to rest in that chapel in a box
on the gospel side of the sanctuary. He died on January 4,
1825, "fully conscious and well disposed," consoled by Fray
Teodoro de Alcina de la Boada of Nambé. His passing was
attended by a sign, which Father Alcina dutifully recorded.

Father Alcina records the remarkable death of Fray Francisco
Bragado, January 4, 1825 (AASF).

Twenty-six hours after the Reverend Father's death as Juan José
Salazar was washing his face with vinegar, he noticed that blood
came from a cut, which they had given him when they shaved him,
as fresh as if he were alive, and ran to the tip of his chin. Miguel
Lucero observed the same thing, as did several others who were
present. As a record and perpetual memorial I enter it in this very
book with the alcalde of the district who was present when the two
above-mentioned persons related the occurrence.[48]

Bragado's successor, Fray Juan Caballero Toril, another fifty-year-old native of Spain, made every effort to minister to the Indians who still inhabited the crumbling pueblo of Pecos. Although he no longer identified the chapel at San Miguel as "belonging to the mission of Nuestra Señora de los Ángeles de Pecos" after December 1825, Caballero took seriously his obligation to say Mass at Pecos at least once a month.

It was not easy. The friar and Alcalde Gregorio Vigil nearly came to blows over the escort required for a safe trip to the mission. When Caballero complained to Governor Narbona during Holy Week in 1827, the governor addressed a stern warning to the alcalde. If Vigil did not see to an escort for the minister so that he could carry the sacraments to the natives of Pecos, perhaps the priest would abandon San Miguel and move back up to the mission. Father Caballero had his escort that same day.[49]

Late in 1827, amid rumors of Spanish plans to invade and reconquer Mexico, the Mexican national congress decreed the expulsion of peninsular Spaniards from the republic. Several Spanish Franciscans left New Mexico as a result, among them Father Caballero. On the last day of February 1828, he signed a detailed inventory of everything he had found in the San Miguel chapel and sacristy, all that had been added during his ministry, as well as items borrowed from the mission of Pecos. Among the latter were a broken metal cross, a little box with lock and key containing the silver cruets of holy oils and chrism, and some molds for making altar breads. The following month, Governor Armijo wrote to an unnamed priest, probably Father Alcina, telling him to take over at San Miguel whether Caballero, who said he was ill, left or not. He left.[50]

Fr. Teodoro Alcina

During the remainder of 1828, Fray Teodoro Alcina alternated at San Miguel with Fray José de Castro. They were both European Spaniards, but too old and too much needed in priest-poor New Mexico for expulsion. Alcina, from Palafox in Gerona, had spent thirty-five of his sixty-two years in New Mexico. Castro would bury him at Santa Cruz de la Cañada in

1834. Only a year younger, Castro himself, a native of San Salvador del Cristinado in Galicia, was dead by late 1840.[51]

The books of baptisms, marriages, and burials assigned to Mission Nuestra Señora de los Ángeles de Pecos, which, like its missionaries themselves, had spent most of the previous century at Santa Fe or El Vado, ended in 1829. On June 2, 1828, Father Castro had performed the last recorded baptism of an Indian by a Franciscan at Pecos, for eight-day-old José Manuel, son of Rafael and Paula Aguilar. The following November, the dutiful Father Alcina visited the mission and baptized the infant son of settlers from the Cañón de Pecos. His burial entry at San Miguel on December 3 was the last by a friar. On January 1, 1829, don Juan Felipe Ortiz, diocesan priest from Santa Fe, took over. After better than two centuries the Franciscan ministry on the Río Pecos had come to a close.[52]

In 1833, when the first bishop, the stern and tireless José Antonio Laureano de Zubiría y Escalante, actually came to San Miguel del Vado on a visitation, he was appalled. Because of an acute shortage of ministers, the secular priest of Santa Fe was riding out on circuit. The fabric was a mess, the accounts hopeless, and the church "utterly deprived." Lord have mercy. "With much grief and sorrow," the bishop's secretary noted in the book of baptisms, "he has observed that this parish church lacks even the most essential things for the celebration of the divine mysteries."

He did not even mention the mission of Pecos.[53]

Hanging On

They were still there, thirty or forty of them, like the ghostly survivors of a science fiction tragedy, haunting the ruins that once had housed their civilization. Digging there in the twentieth century, archaeologists could tell how it had gone, "the bunching up or huddling . . . the long, slow decay eating its way northward in both the South Pueblo and the Quadrangle." [54]

They could not survive much longer. Just as well. The Hispanos wanted their lands so much that they had threatened in the previous decade to remove them bodily and scatter them among the other pueblos. Now they were too few to cope. Still the old woes persisted—plains raiders, emigration, even, if the fantastic story spun for a late nineteenth-century romantic has any basis in fact, internal dissension,[55] and of course disease.

Despite the introduction of vaccination against smallpox in New Mexico as early as 1805, when inoculated children

Bishop José Antonio Laureano de Zubiría of Durango.   Museum of New Mexico

were used as living vials to transport the vaccine, the dread disease, sometimes in league with other killers, still took its toll. By 1810, if not before, the children at Pecos had been vaccinated. In the summer of 1815, with the disease "already around," Governor Maynez had ordered the deputy justice at El Vado to send someone up to Santa Fe to be trained in how to give vaccinations, and also a child to carry the vaccine fresh. The following year, in December alone, at least eighteen Pecos died, of what Father García del Valle did not say, but all eighteen were adults.

Perhaps vaccination was allowed to lapse. On a visit to Pecos in March 1826, Father Caballero had buried seven in two days, all of them children. To a community of only forty persons, that was a terrible loss. Again in the winter of 1831-1832 smallpox stalked the El Vado settlements, and probably Pecos, the usual rest stop on the trail up to Santa Fe. Tradition has it that "mountain fever" or a "great sickness" finally led to abandonment, but that still has not been diagnosed.[56]

Over the years, a succession of Plains Indian raiders had tested their valor against the fortress-pueblo of Pecos: Apaches, Comanches, and Apaches again. In the 1820s, when it was hardly more than a ruin, others tried their hand. These so-called "barbarians of the north" were likely Cheyennes and Arapahos. On the night of June 16, 1828, they steathily surrounded Pecos "closing even to the houses." Detecting them just in time, the Pecos "repelled them, firing on them." Next morning, according to a report by Juan Esteban Pino from the Cañón de Pecos, "they [the Pecos?]" followed the heathens' tracks "up onto the mesa by El Picacho toward the Rincón de las Escobas." From the tracks, they estimated that there were a considerable number headed as if for Galisteo.

While the memory of this sort of thing probably figured in their decision to abandon the pueblo a decade later, it is too much to credit the new raiders with "bringing to a dismal end the history of the proudest pueblo in all New Mexico." [57] The valley's proliferating Hispanos, even while encroaching on mission lands with their crops and livestock, did offer more inviting spoils and some safety in numbers.

Individual Pecos Indians who moved away from the pueblo during these final years are difficult to follow. Some certainly did. José Chama, for example, "native of Pecos" who married Juana Arias at San Miguel in 1817, a dozen years later showed up as a resident of Antón Chico. A witness to the Chama-Arias union, Miguel Brito, who was described in 1820 in the baptismal book as an "indio y vecino de Pecos," in 1821

was counted an infantry member of the El Vado militia, along with Chama. More than a decade after the final exodus, Lt. James H. Simpson of the United States Army was told at Jémez that there were only eighteen Pecos left in 1849. Fifteen lived at Jémez, one at Santo Domingo, one at Cañón de Pecos, and one at Cuesta in the El Vado district. Even today there are people in the village of Pecos who claim that great great grandmother was a Pecos Indian. And maybe she was.[58]

The Abandonment of Pecos Pueblo

For years the faithful remnant of the Pecos nation had suffered reason enough to abandon their ancestral pueblo. What finally compelled them to do it is not known, although some wondrous myths have been invented to account for it. The year, tradition has it, was 1838, one year after a rabid New Mexico mob beheaded Gov. Albino Pérez.

The move was calculated. They packed up their ceremonial gear, and, again according to tradition, arranged with the local Hispanos to take care of the church and celebrate the feast of Nuestra Señora de los Ángeles, la Porciúncula, every August 2, which they do to this day. The refugees may have broken their trip at Sandía. Their final destination, eighty miles west of Pecos by trail, was Jémez, the only other pueblo that spoke the Towa language. Some of them may have had second thoughts and gone back. But they did not stay.[59]

A New Mexican ranch.
Horatio O. Ladd,
The Story of New Mexico
(Boston, 1891)

Commenting on the Pecos migration eleven years after it happened, a talkative Jémez told Lieutenant Simpson that

> during one of the revolutions of the country, when he was quite a youth, this tribe, being very much harassed by the Spaniards, (Mexicans,) asked permission of the people of Jémez to come and live among them. They not only granted them permission to do this, but sent out persons to help them get in their crops, and bring them and their property to their new abode. When they arrived, they gave them houses and fields.[60]

There were seventeen or twenty of them, led by Juan Antonio Toya. Father Caballero had recorded Toya's name and that of his wife María de los Ángeles at Pecos in 1826 when he baptized their seven-day-old son José Francisco. José Cota, or Kota, another of the emigrants, had joined with Rafael Aguilar in the fight to save the Pecos lands in 1829. By 1838, they and the others had reached their decision. They would go, at least for a while.[61]

Tourists and Tall Tales

One year later, in September of 1839—a year that saw a quarter of a million dollars in goods rumble past on the Santa Fe Trail—the irrepressible Matthew C. Field, actor, journalist, and rover, spent the night with Dr. David Waldo in the Pecos church. His article about the "dilapidated town called *Pécus*," which he guessed rightly "in its flourishing days must have been inhabited by not less than two thousand souls," soon appeared in the New Orleans *Picayune*. "The houses now are all un-roofed," he wrote,

and the walls crumbling. The church alone yet stands nearly entire, and in it now resides a man bent nearly double with age, and his long silken hair, white with the snow of ninety winters, renders him an object of deep interest to the contemplative traveller. The writer with a single American companion once passed a night in this old church, entertained by the old man with a supper of hot porridge made of pounded corn and goat's milk, which we drank with a shell spoon from a bowl of wood, sitting upon the ground at the foot of the ruined altar by the light of a few dimly burning sticks of pine. In this situation we learned from the old man the following imperfect story, which is all the history that is now known of the city of the Sacred Fire.

Whereupon, in purple prose, Field launched into the tale of how Montezuma had chosen the Pecos as his people and

Our Lady of the Angels in place over the altar in the Pecos village church of San Antonio, 1880. Photo by Ben Wittick. El Paso Centennial Museum

had commanded them to keep a sacred fire burning in a cave until his coming again. Josiah Gregg claimed to have seen it smouldering in a kiva. For centuries the Pecos remained faithful to the trust. "Man, woman, and child shared the honor of watching the holy fire, and the side of the mountain grew bare as year after year the trees were torn away to feed the consuming torch of Montezuma." Then "a pestilential disorder came in the summer time and swept away the people." Only three were left: a venerable chief, his daughter, and her betrothed. The old man expired. The lovers grew weak. Just before death overcame them, the young man had an idea.

Taking a brand from the fire, he grasped his beloved by the hand and led her out of the cave. "A light then rose in the sky which was not the light of morning, but the heavens were red with the flames that roared and crackled up the mountain side. And the lovers lay in each other's arms, kissing death from each other's lips, and smiling to see the fire of Montezuma mounting up to heaven."

Wash-u-hos-te,
a Pecos man at Jémez,
probably by R. H. Kern,
1849.
Simpson, *Journal*

Still, Matt Field did not reckon he had done justice to
the old man's story.

He told it in glowing words and with a rapt intensity which the
writer has endeavored to imitate, but he feels that the attempt is a
failure. The scene itself—the ruined church—the feeble old man
bending over the ashes, and the strange tones of his thin voice
in the dreary midnight—all are necessary to awaken such interest
as was felt by the listeners. Such is the story, however, and there
is no doubt but that the legend has a strong foundation, in truth;
for there stands the ruined town, well known to the Santa Fé
traders, and there lives the old man, tending his goats on the hill
side during the day, and driving them into the church at night.
. . . It was imperative upon us to leave the place before day light
that we might reach our destination (San Miguel) early the next
morning, so that we could not gratify our curiosity by descending the cavern ourselves, but we gave the old man a few bits of
silver, and telling him that the story with which he had entertained us should be told again in the great United States, we
each pocketed a cinder of the sacred fire and departed.[62]

Pecos, stylized and
deserted, 1846.
Abert, *Report*

Montezuma, the perpetual fire, and a great serpent god
"so huge that he left a track like a small arroyo" were off
and running.[63]

The era of Pecos as monument had begun. The living
pueblo was dead.

The pueblo of Jémez by R. H. Kern.   Simpson, *Journal*

epilogue

Actually, neither people nor place really died. They simply parted company.

At Jémez pueblo, the Pecos refugees settled into homes and planted fields provided by their hosts, but they did not forget who they were. They spoke the same language, noted Lt. James H. Simpson in 1849, but they "differ somewhat in their religious customs." They did not forget even as one generation followed upon the next. Studying Jémez in the early 1920s, anthropologist Elsie Clews Parsons came away with the impression

that in the ceremonial organization there exists something of a cleavage between the "Pecos race" and the old-timers of Jemez. In particular I recall the scorn expressed by a Pecos descendant in opining that "these Jemez people don't know anything," and in describing a meeting of the Old Men where it was plain that the only ones who knew anything were the chiefs of the Pecos societies, including the chief of the *tab ö´ sh* who had married into Pecos lineage.

The Jémez people had welcomed the remnant of powerful Pecos. These immigrants, headed by Juan Antonio Toya, brought with them religious objects and practices to add to those of Jémez. They brought with them the Pecos bull, and fetiches, and the Pecos Eagle Catchers' society. And they brought an image of Nuestra Señora de los Ángeles, La Porciúncula, whose feast, August 2, the pueblo of Jémez began to celebrate along with that of its own patron San Diego. Not everything they carried from Pecos stayed at Jémez however. In 1882, for example, Judge L. Bradford Prince "obtained" from Pecos immigrant Agustín Cota a wooden plaque of Our Lady of

the Angels from the mission church at Pecos, or so Cota led Prince to believe.

They did not forget. From time to time they made pilgrimages back to their ancestral home, where they continued to maintain shrines. Another link, forged mainly of paper by agencies of the United States government, bound the displaced Pecos and the memory of the land they had once occupied. For more than a century, from 1855, when a claim to the Pecos league was filed in behalf of "the inhabitants of Pecos Pueblo," until 1959, when the Indian Claims Commission dismissed the last Pecos bid for additional compensation, the existence of a recognizable community of Pecos Indians at Jémez vaguely disquieted those who took up the land in their absence.

Not that the Pecos ever seriously thought of reoccupying their league. They were too few. Besides, Hispanos had long been farming the good land along the river. What they wanted, they explained to Superintendent of Indian Affairs Michael Steck in 1864, was permission to sell the 18,763.33 acres confirmed to them by Congress. Steck promised to ask the commissioner in Washington. The claimants, all residents of Jémez, now numbered seven men and twenty-five women and children. Because the Pecos Pueblo grant included several hundred acres of fine farm land "and one of the best water powers in the Territory," its sale, Steck thought, could bring $10,000 or more. Later in 1864, the government issued a patent. Juan Antonio Toya now had a paper.

Four years hence, Toya and ten others, four of them women, put their x's on paper and their grant in the hands of indispensable, resilient, sometimes drunken John N. Ward, special agent to the Pueblos, their friend. For $10.00 they sold to Ward the northern quarter outright, that portion already encroached upon by Hispano residents of Pecos village. At the same time, they gave him power of attorney to sell the rest in their behalf. Ward cast about for a buyer. The U.S. Supreme Court, meantime, lent its support, deciding in *United States v. Joseph* (1876) that the Pueblo Indians were not wards of the government and therefore, like other citizens, could dispose of their property as they saw fit.

By 1872, Ward had found his buyer, the debonair Las Vegas merchant and speculator Frank Chapman. The price to the Pecos for their three-quarters was $4,000, the price to Ward for his quarter, $1,300. That should have been that, as far as the Pecos were concerned, but it was not. Forty years down the road—after title to the grant had changed

Opposite
"The watch for Montezuma" by Paul Frenzeny and Jules Tavernier. *Harper's Weekly* (May 22, 1875)

Agustín (Cota) Pecos, last of his pueblo, died 1919. Photographd by Kenneth M. Chapman, 1902. Museum of New Mexico

hands several times, at least once over a meal in a New York restaurant, after "a large hotel scheme for the ruins of Pecos" was scrapped and a fortune made cutting railroad ties, after purchase by the mercantile firm of Gross, Kelly and Company —the Supreme Court reversed itself. It found in *United States v. Sandoval* (1913), marvelous to relate, that the Pueblo Indians had been wards of the government after all. Therefore they could not have alienated their lands. Therefore Gross, Kelly and Company's paper title was invalid, or was it? Therefore the Hispanos of Pecos village were illegal squatters, or were they?

The outcry was resounding. Dozens of lawyers hurried into the fray, along with champions of Indian rights like John Collier and Stella Atwood. One estimate put the number of non-Indian, property-holding trespassers on Pueblo grants at three thousand. Were they all to be ejected and the lands restored to the Indians? Were they to be compensated? Or were they to stay put and let the government compensate the Indians? And what about a long-abandoned pueblo like Pecos? On the advice of white friends, Pablo Toya, son of Juan Antonio, requested in 1921 a certified copy of the patent to the Pecos Pueblo grant. The paper issued to his father had been lost.

The three-man Pueblo Lands Board, created by Congress in 1924 to identify all valid non-Indian holdings within the external boundaries of recognized Pueblo Indian grants or purchases and to assess the Pueblo's losses, did not get around to Pecos until 1929. Even though the pueblo had been abandoned under the previous sovereignty of Mexico, the Board reasoned that the United States government, by confirming the

grant to the Pecos remnant at Jémez, had obligated itself to protect the Indians' interest, which it had failed to do. As a result, the Indians claiming Pecos ancestry—whose numbers based on church records were now estimated as high as 250—deserved an award.

A somewhat exaggerated 19th-century sketch of Pecos.
William M. Thayer, *Marvels of the New West* (Norwich, 1888)

In the meantime, Gross, Kelly and Company had filed suit to quiet title on the whole grant. Rather than do battle in the courts with the exising village of Pecos, the company gave up its claim to the northern half in return for a quitclaim to the southern 9,831 acres. That settled that. The Pueblo Lands Board found in 1930 that the 339 adverse claims to Pecos lands had legally and utterly extinguished all Indian title to the entire 18,763.33-acre grant. None of the land was recoverable. As compensation, the Board recommended $1.50 per

Abandoned "Catholic Church" and convento, Pecos, 1846, by John Mix Stanley. Emory, *Notes*

acre, based upon "approximate average value from the occupancy of this territory in 1846 to the present time," which amounted to an award of $28,145.00. In 1931, Congress appropriated that sum to the Bureau of Indian Affairs for the Pecos remnant at Jémez. Again that should have been that.

But in 1946 the Indian Claims Commission Act, intended to settle once and for all Indian claims against the United States for loss of aboriginal lands, opened the door again. Instead of seeking to establish the Pecos Indians' shadowy claim to aboriginal territory, which, in the hands of competent expert witnesses might have been made to encompass all the drainage of the Pecos River for at least sixty miles from Terrero to Antón Chico, attorneys for the "Pueblo de Pecos" attacked only the amount of the previous award. It was, they alleged in a petition filed July 30, 1951, both "inadequate and insufficient." In response, the government alleged that the Pueblo de Pecos was not now a proper party to bring suit. The Pecos remnant and the Jémez, it seemed, had been merged in 1936 into the consolidated Pueblo de Jémez. Only it could bring suit.

Undaunted, the lawyers for the Pecos in 1955 bid to amend their original petition by making the claimant all-inclusive: the "Pueblo de Pecos, Pueblo de Jémez, and Pueblo de Jémez acting for and on behalf of Pueblo de Pecos." They further moved to include "a plea of lack of fair and honorable dealings" on the part of the Pueblo Lands Board. It worked.

Over government objections, the Commission allowed the a-
mended petition.

Finally heard on its merits in 1959, the Pecos plea fell
short. The Commission, after reviewing the dealings of the
Pueblo Lands Board, could find no evidence of negligence or
unfairness. Since neither the Pecos nor the United States had
appealed the decision at the time, the initial award stood as
"a final judgment fixing the value of the lands and water rights
lost by the Pecos Pueblo." Such a judgment was not subject to
review or revision by the Indian Claims Commission. Case
dismissed.

Still, they have not forgotten. Emboldened by the precedent of the Taos Blue Lake decision in 1971, which returned to
the ownership of Taos pueblo an object of religious veneration,
the Pecos have asked the New Mexico Department of Fish and
Game to return to them the cave at Terrero, sixteen miles up
the Pecos River from their former pueblo. It is sacred ground,
they say.

While the last of the Pecos "kept the faith" at Jémez, a
motley procession of traders, soldiers, and tourists was track-
ing through the ruins of their former homes, scratching graffiti,
pocketing souvenirs, and recounting the fantastic tales of "a
lost civilization."

If Thomas James heard the tales in 1821, he did not
repeat them. Ten years later, Albert Pike heard them all

"Astek Church,"
actually the main
pueblo ruin, Pecos,
1846, by
John Mix Stanley.
Emory, *Notes*

right—Montezuma, the eternal fire in a cave, and worship of a giant snake—but he did not fix them precisely on Pecos. That came soon enough. An article by "El Doctor Masure" in the *Santa Fe Republican* of September 24, 1847, told of a visit in 1835 to the "furnace of Montezuma" at Pecos. Josiah Gregg, too, said that he had descended into a Pecos kiva and "beheld this consecrated fire, silently smouldering under a covering of ashes, in the basin of a small altar."

Ever since the sixteenth century, Spanish chroniclers had associated ruins north of Mexico with the origin of the Aztecs and with Montezuma. The legendary pre-conquest feathered serpent had slithered northward even earlier. When, in the romantic atmosphere of the nineteenth century, Pecos became a bona fide and easily accessible ruin, it is no wonder that such specters took up residence here. "Ere the May-flower drifted to Plymouth's snowy rock, this vestal flame was burning. . . . and yet till Montezuma shall return—so ran the charge—that fire must burn."

Artist John Mix Stanley, with the invading Army of the West in 1846, sketched both mission church and pueblo ruins, and in House Executive Document No. 41 of the Thirtieth Congress, First Session, the former was labeled "Catholic Church" and the latter "Astek Church." Army engineers W. H. Emory and J. W. Abert related the Montezuma legend at Pecos, where "the fires from the *'estuffa'* burned and sent their incense through the same altars from which was preached the doctrine of Christ" and where "they were said to keep an immense serpent, to which they sacrificed human victims."

Yet no one topped young Pvt. Josiah M. Rice, who passed by in 1851 with Col. Edwin V. Sumner's command. "There are," claimed Rice, "many traditions connected with this old church, one of which is that it was built by a race of giants, fifty feet in height. But these, dying off, they were succeeded by dwarfs, with red heads who, being in their turn exterminated, were followed by the Aztecs."

Pondering Montezuma's alleged birth at Pecos and his vow to return, the astute Adolph F. Bandelier in 1880 ascribed the tale to "an evident mixture of a name with the Christian faith in a personal redeemer, and dim recollections of Coronado's presence and promise to return." Of course it may also have become a convenient ruse employed by the Pueblos to mislead inquisitive whites. Lt. John G. Bourke, contemporary of Bandelier and ethnologist in his own right, found the Montezuma story "among the Pueblos who have had most to do with Americans and Mexicans and among no others." No matter,

thought historian Ralph Emerson Twitchell in 1910. "This
story is the veriest rot."

The big snake, in whose veracity Bandelier refused to
believe "until I am compelled," persisted nonetheless. In 1924,
a grandson of Mariano Ruiz, chief informant of Bandelier, recited what he had heard his grandfather tell about the Pecos
snake. This account appeared in Edward S. Curtis' *The North
American Indians,* volume 17.

The snake, he said, was kept in an underground room in the
village, and at stated intervals a newborn infant was fed to it.
The elder Ruiz was asked to assume the duty of custodian of the
sacred fire, an annual office, which he declined because he had
observed that the fire-keeper always died soon after being released from confinement in the subterranean chamber where the
fire burned. (Whether the fire and the serpent were housed in the
same cell the grandson did not know, but possibly such was the
case and the refusal of Ruiz to accept the proffered position was
really due to his horror at the idea of spending a year in proximity
to the reptile. But there appears to be no good reason why he
should not have imparted this information to Bandelier, if such
was the case.) Strolling about the environs of the village, Ruiz
one day came upon his most intimate friend bowed in grief. To
the Mexican's inquiry the Indian responded that his newborn
child had been condemned to be fed to the snake, that already
he had been forced to yield several children to the sacrifice, and
had vainly hoped that this one would be spared. This was the
first time Ruiz had heard that children were fed to the snake.
He proposed that they hoodwink the priests, and acting on his
advice the Indian poisoned a newborn kid with certain herbs,
wrapped it up as if it were a baby, and threw it to the reptile.
That night terrifying sounds issued from the den as the great
snake writhed in its death agony, and in the morning it lay with the
white of its belly exposed. The populace was utterly downcast, for
this presaged the extinction of the tribe.

Some observers recorded more mundane theories of why
the Pecos had departed. Certainly disease and warfare had
figured prominently in the pueblo's decline. Santa Fe trader
James Josiah Webb, passing through in 1844, surmised that
the inhabitants "had become so reduced in numbers that they
were unable to keep their irrigating ditches in repair, and
other necessary community labor, to support themselves in
comfort." Looking at it from a different angle, Indian Agent
John Greiner asserted in 1852 that the Pecos had been
"annoyed beyond endurance by the Mexicans living in their
houses and seizing their property by piecemeal." Finally they
had given up. "The pueblo of Pecos is now a mass of ruins,"
reported John Ward in 1867.

The few original inhabitants were compelled to abandon the village about eight years previous to our government's taking possession of the country in 1846. They left in consequence of their reduced circumstances and numbers and the encroachments of Mexican citizens in general.

After the Pecos had gone, the pot hunter, the scavenger, and the transient pretty much wrecked the place. A few sorry souls haunted habitable corners of the ruins for a decade or so—Matt Field's wizened goatherd, fugitive Juan Cristóbal Armijo wanted for murdering a Mormon peddler, the old woman and her comely daughter of "dark and meaning eye" who so titillated Richard L. Wilson as he gathered his *Short Ravelings from a Long Yarn, or Camp March Sketches of the Santa Fe Trail.* One unfortunate of the 1841 Texan-Santa Fe expedition, Thomas Falconer, remembered being herded with his fellow captives into the ruins of Pecos pueblo. "It is a walled enclosure, in which a few persons lived; but," he added, "the houses within were made more ruinous than on our arrival, by the Mexican soldiers, who made fires of the materials."

Mexican landowners.
John T. Hughes,
Doniphan's Expedition
(Cincinnati, 1847)

The north end of the main quadrangle stood longest. "The dwellings," James Madison Cutts said in his journal entry of August 17, 1846, "were built of small stones and mud; some of the buildings are still so far perfect as to show three full stories." A comparison of Stanley's sketch with the rendering by German artist Heinrich Balduin Möllhausen twelve years later illustrates the rapid moldering of the pueblo proper. Already by 1858, great mounds buttressed and filled the walls of the lower stories, mounds that would continue to grow and thereby entomb for the archaeologist what lay beneath.

The same dozen years also brought the hulking church to the brink. Möllhausen, like almost every writer before him, commented on the woodwork in the building, carved and painted, especially the hefty beams and corbels. Above them, the roof had begun rotting away, and, in places, the sunlight shown through. The German's painting of the Pecos church in 1858 is the last to show the structure essentially intact. Shortly thereafter a Polish squatter named Andrew Kozlowski tore into it. His widow told Bandelier that when they had arrived in 1858 the beams were still in place. Kozlowski pulled many of them down to build houses, stables, and corrals. He also, she said, tried to dig out "the corner-stone," but in that he failed.

In 1866, when landscape painter Worthington Whittredge portrayed the building's southern profile, nave roof and towers were absent.

By Bandelier's day, the church had definitely gone to ruin. "In general," he wrote in 1880,

the vandalism committed in this venerable relic of antiquity defies all description. It is only equalled by the foolishness of such as, having no other means to secure immortality, have cut out the ornaments from the sculptured beams in order to obtain a surface suitable to carve their euphonious names. All the beams of the old structure are quaintly, but still not tastelessly, carved; there was . . . much scroll-work terminating them. Most of this was taken away, chipped into uncouth boxes, and sold, to be scattered everywhere. Not content with this, treasure-hunters, inconsiderate amateurs, have recklessly and ruthlessly disturbed the abodes of the dead. "After becoming Christians," said to me Sr. Mariano Ruiz, the only remaining 'son of the tribe' of Pecos, still settled near to its site, "they buried their dead within the church." These dead have been dug out regardless of their position relative to the walls of the building, and their remains have been scattered over the surface, to become the prey of relic-hunters. The Roman Catholic Archbishop of New Mexico [Jean Baptiste Lamy] has finally stopped such abuses by asserting his title of ownership; but it was far too late. It cannot be denied, besides, that his concession to Kozlowski to use some of the timber for his own purposes was subsequently interpreted by others in a manner highly prejudicial to the preservation of the structure.

The Pecos church, 1858, by Heinrich Balduin Möllhausen. The artist visited Pecos on June 15, 1858, but probably did not paint this romantic watercolor until after his return to Berlin in the autumn of that year. Housed in the Museen Preussischer Kulturbesitz, Museum für Völkerkunde, Berlin, the painting was destroyed in the bombing of the city during World War II. The print, from a pre-War negative, was provided by the Museum through the courtesy of David H. Miller, Cameron University

Even in ruin it was impressive.

"I am dirty, ragged & sunburnt," Bandelier exulted from Pecos on September 5, 1880, "but of best cheer. My life's work has at last begun."

The great Swiss-American pioneer ethnologist had only just arrived in the Southwest a few days before. From the train, he had caught his first glimpse of Pecos. Its setting was all colors,

to the left, the towering Mesa de Pecos, dark pines clambering up its steep sides; to the right, the broad valley, scooped out, so to say, between the *mesa* and the Tecolote ridge. It is dotted with green patches and black clusters of cedar and pine shooting out of the red and rocky soil. Scarcely a house is visible, for the *casitas* of adobe and wood nestle mostly in sheltered nooks. Beyond Baughl's [siding], the ruins first strike his [the tourist's] view; the red walls of the church stand boldly out on the barren *mesilla;* and to the north of it there are two low brown ridges, the remnants of the Indian houses.

To alert the less observant tourist, the Santa Fe Railway Company later erected on the north side of the tracks opposite the ruins an immense signboard proclaiming Pecos a wonder of the Southwest. In a sense, Bandelier did the same thing. His notably meticulous report—even to mention of the broken Anheuser-Busch beer bottles—based on ten exhilarating days of

"Pecos Church,
New Mexico,"
by Worthington
Whittredge, 1866,
oil on cardboard,
9⅜ x 22⅛ inches.
Courtesy M. Knoedler
and Co., New York

field investigation, alertcd the archaelogist to the potentials of the Southwest.

Curiously, Bandelier never followed up his initial study at Pecos. Eight years later, in 1888, he did meet at Jémez a trio of the Pecos remnant: José Miguel Vigil, Agustín Cota, who was at the time governor of Jémez, and José Romero. Aside from the Spanish names of six other Pecos Indians "still alive," and the native names for Pecos pueblo and four nearby ruins, he got very little out of them. Ethnohistorian Frederick Webb Hodge and archaeologist Edgar L. Hewett, who interviewed Vigil and Cota on several occasions between 1895 and 1902, did better. Hewett's 1904 article "Studies on the Extinct Pueblo of Pecos" listed twenty-two Pecos clans, discussed the archaeology of the upper Pecos Valley and the aboriginal range of the Pecos people, fixed the year of the abandonment at 1838, and recorded the native names of the seventeen refugees. Relying mainly on Pablo Toya, son of the deceased Juan Antonio, the persistent Mrs. Parsons added three more refugees and figured out genealogies.

Meantime, Pecos had been on display in California. A sixteen-foot-long model of the mesa top showing reconstructed church, South Pueblo, and main Quadrangle was a prominent attraction in the New Mexico building at the 1915 San Diego Panama-California Exposition. That same year, the trustees of

Adolph F. Bandelier

Above
Adolph F. Bandelier
in 1882. Photographed
by W. Henry Brown.
B. M. Thomas Collection,
Museum of New Mexico

The hulking church
ruin with Glorieta
Mesa as backdrop
Photographed by
H. T. Hiester,
early 1870s.
Museum of New Mexico

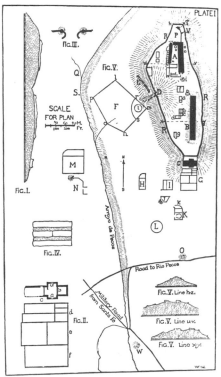

Top
Adolph F. Bandelier at Pecos, 1880.
Photographed by George C. Bennett.
Museum of New Mexico

Above
Nave, transept, and sanctuary, early 1870s.
H. T. Hiester.
Museum of New Mexico

Bandelier's general plan of the Pecos ruins,
1880. Bandelier, "Visit"

Phillips Academy, Andover, Massachusetts, resolved to exca-
vate a site in the Pueblo area "large enough, and of sufficient
scientific importance, to justify work upon it for a number of
years."

No one at the time quite guessed what the excavation of
Pecos would yield. The thirty-year-old Harvard man appointed
to direct it, only the sixth archaeologist to earn a Ph.D. in the
United States, already had wide experience in the Southwest.
He had suggested Pecos. Genial, modest, penetrating, and full
of ideas, Alfred Vincent Kidder knew what he was after.
Solidly trained in field method by a prominent Egyptologist, he
was spoiling to raise New World archaeology above the old
antiquarianism that concentrated on the collecting of showy
specimens for museums and to move it in the direction "of
systematic, planned research and of detailed analysis of data
followed by synthesis."

Previous excavations in the Southwest had resulted in an
array of loose pages. At Pecos, which proved vastly richer
and more complex than he had imagined, Kidder found the
index. Digging in the dark, loamy soil that had built up and
eventually buried the cliff on the east side of the pueblo, in what
Kidder called "the greatest rubbish heap and cemetery that had
ever been found in the Pueblo region," he uncovered neatly
statified deposits containing quantities of broken pottery, pottery that could be classified,

an orderly superposition of all these types, the oldest naturally
lying at the bottom, later ones above, and the latest at the top.
With the sequence of the pottery types thus established, it becomes
a perfectly simple matter to arrange all sites containing one or
more of them in their true chronological order. The same principle
is also used in the local work at Pecos: graves, for example, with
offerings of Type 3 pottery must be older than graves containing
Type 4; rooms filled with Type 6 rubbish must have been
abandoned after rooms filled with refuse of Type 5, etc.

When he got past the middens to the pueblo ruins themselves, Kidder discovered not the large single structure he had
anticipated, but another sequence. The historic town of "wret-
chedly bad masonry" had been laid out on top of the tumbled walls
of previous buildings, and the latter over at least two earlier layers
of dwellings. This situation thrust him into a study of the "mecha-
nics of pueblo-growth."

In the course of ten summers at Pecos between 1915 and
1929, two events broadcast the coming of age of American
archaeology. The first was the publication in 1924 of Kidder's
An Introduction to the Study of Southwestern Archaeology,

with a Preliminary Account of the Excavations at Pecos, which has been called "the first detailed synthesis of the archaeology of any part of the New World." The second, in August 1927, was an informal, precedent-setting reunion of Southwestern field researchers at what became known as the "Pecos Conference." Here, at Kidder's invitation, he and his colleagues reached fundamental agreement on cultural sequence in the prehistoric Southwest, definitions of stages in that sequence, and standardization in naming pottery types. When the fiftieth anniversary Pecos Conference convened in 1977, there was high praise for Alfred Vincent Kidder, who in pursuit of his vision made Pecos the most studied and reported upon archaeological site in the United States.

Preservation also came. Simultaneous with Kidder's opening field session in 1915, Jesse L. Nusbaum of the Museum of New Mexico had directed the removal of tons of debris from the old church, which, roofless and cruelly weathered, still stood nearly its full height at the transept. His crews then stabilized undercut walls with massive cement footings. In 1920, before Gross, Kelly and Company sold its share of the Pecos Pueblo grant, Harry W. Kelly and Ellis T. Kelly, his wife, along with the company deeded an eighty-acre tract, including mission church and pueblo ruins, to Roman Catholic Archbishop Albert T. Daeger. As agreed, Daeger in turn deeded the historic parcel to the Board of Regents of the Museum of New Mexico and the Board of Managers of the School of American Research in Santa Fe. Created a New Mexico State Monument in 1935 and a National Monument in 1965, enlarged several times over by a donation of land from Mr. and Mrs. E. E. Fogelson, owners of the Forked Lightning Ranch, Pecos in 1976 is well on the way to becoming what Kidder envisioned in 1916—"an educational monument not to be rivalled in any other part of the Southwest."

This is the day of "environmental statements" and "interpretive concepts" and "master plans," of "resource management" and "visitor use." Under the superintendence of the National Park Service, excavation, research, and stabilization continue. In 1967, when archaeologist Jean M. Pinkley, trenching to find a wall of the eighteenth-century porter's lodge as described by Father Domínguez, hit instead the buried rock foundations of Fray Andrés Juárez' mammoth church, she laid bare a truth that had eluded Bandelier, Hewett, and Kidder. At the same time, she made seventeenth-century pious chronicler Alonso de Benavides, who had portrayed the Pecos church in superlatives, less the liar.

Alfred V. Kidder

Top
Looking not unlike Butch Cassidy and the Sundance Kid,
a relaxed Alfred Vincent Kidder (second from left) and
Carl E. Guthe, his assistant (far left), pose before the
field shack at Pecos with some of the gang, 1916.
Museum of New Mexico

Above
The great Pecos trash heap. Kidder's crew deepens the cut to
nineteen feet, first season, 1915.
Kidder, *Southwestern Archaeology*

Top
Trenching into the main Pecos ruin, 1920.
"Here we found a most complex state of affairs;
a jumble of early walls, some fallen, others
partly incorporated into the bases of later
structures." Kidder, *Southwestern Archaeology*

Above
Skeletons in the deep Pecos rubbish.
Kidder, *Southwestern Archaeology*

Working Cut 3, Test X, in the eastern Pecos
midden, 1915. Kidder, *Southwestern Archaeology*

Jesse L. Nusbaum's crew digging out the 18th-century Pecos church ruin, 1915. Museum of New Mexico

The Pecos maze: excavation of the main pueblo. Heavy lines are part of late quadrangle, irregular light lines trenches, and dots burials. Kidder, *Pecos, New Mexico*

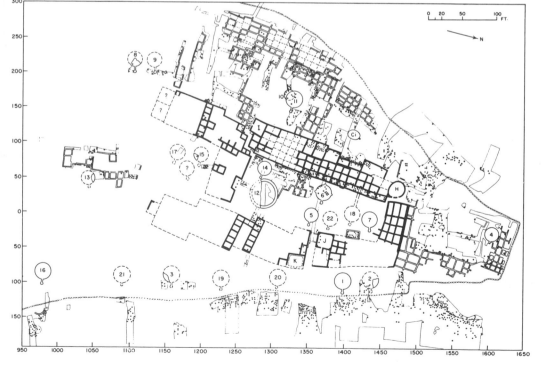

The north terrace, oldest portion of
the main Pecos ruin, looking up
the Pecos Valley.
Kidder, *Southwestern Archaeology*

Deterioration of Pecos main quadrangle,
looking north. Upper photograph by
George C. Bennett, 1880. Lower
photograph, 1915.
Museum of New Mexico

A. V. Kidder contemplates burials in
the Pecos church, 1915.
Museum of New Mexico

"The view of Pecos, as it now lies, without the least addition," wrote Lt. J. W. Abert in his journal entry for September 26, 1846,

would form a beautiful picture, and more than a picture, for every cloud, every degree that the sun moves, gives such varied effects to the landscape, that one has a thousand pictures; but their effects are so fleeting, that although they last long enough to delight the spectator, it would yet perplex the artist to catch these changes. For my part, I tried, and tried in vain, until at last some large night herons came sweeping over my head, and warned me that the shades of evening were drawing on, when I returned to camp.

National Park Service excavations of Pecos church and convento, 1967. National Park Service photo by Fred E. Mang, Jr.

On a similar day, August 3, 1975, closest Sunday to the feast of Our Lady of the Angels, a procession strung out along the path west of the convento ruins on the way to celebrate Mass in the roofless church. The clouds and their effect were just as Abert had described them, the shades of color and light just as fleeting. The tenth archbishop of Santa Fe, smiling, walked in front. Behind him, the men of Pecos village carried the restored painting of Nuestra Señora de los Ángeles as a banner. From Jémez, a delegation of the Pecos remnant had come to take part, and from Washington, D.C., New Mexico's two United States senators.

In one sense, the scene was complete in itself—the pageantry of the moment, the tolerant presence of three cultures, the glory of the natural surroundings—enough to delight anyone. Yet for the spectator who knew something of the history of the living Pueblo de los Pecos, another dimension lay behind the scene, a dimension that stretched far back beyond the time when the people and the place had parted company.

Pecos on the eve of excavation, 1915. Museum of New Mexico

appendix I

the population of pecos

Italicized entries in the population column are most likely firsthand information; asterisks denote San Miguel del Vado and environs.

YEAR(S)	POPULATION	SOURCE
1500-1600	"little less than 2,000"	Kidder, *Pecos, New Mexico*
1540-42	*"as many as 500 warriors"*	Castañeda, I:12, Hammond and Rey, *Narratives*
1581	500 houses (Nueva Tlaxcala: Pecos?)	Gallegos of Rodríguez-Sánchez Chamuscado expedition, Hammond and Rey, *Rediscovery*
1583	"about 2,000 men armed with bows and arrows"	Pérez de Luján of Espejo expedition, Hammond and Rey, *Rediscovery*
1622	*"2,000 souls, a few less"*	Fr. Andrés Juárez to the viceroy, Oct. 2, AGN, Civil, 77
1620s	"more than 2,000 souls"	Fr. Alonso de Benavides, *Memorial*, 1630, and *Revised Memorial*, 1634
c. 1641	*1,189*	Report on the missions, anon. and undated, NMHR, vol. 4 (1929), pp. 47-48
1662	c. 1,100 to 1,500	Rough estimate based on encomienda tribute, AGN, Tierras, 3268
1680	"more than 2,000 Christians"	Vetancurt, *Teatro Mexicano*, 1698
1692	about 1,500	Diego de Vargas, Oct. 17, J. M. Espinosa, *First Expedition*
1694	*736 (186 men, 230 women, 320 children)*	Fr. Diego de Zeinos, Dec. 28, BNM, leg. 3, no. 6

YEAR(S)	POPULATION	SOURCE
1695	"more than eight hundred persons of all ages"	Diego de Vargas, Oct. 27, SANM, II, no. 58
	eight hundred persons	Santa Fe Cabildo, Nov. 8, BNM, leg. 4, no. 11
1706	"about a thousand Christian Indians, children and adults"	Fr. Juan Álvarez, Jan. 12, Hackett, *Documents,* III
1714	100 Pecos auxiliaries summoned for an Apache campaign, three times the number from any other pueblo	Gov. Juan Ignacio Flores Mogollón, Aug., SANM, II, no. 209
1730	*521 (98 [198?] families)*	Bishop Benito Crespo., Sept. 8, Adams, *Tamarón's Visitation*
1744	125 families	Fr. Juan Miguel Menchero, Hackett, *Documents,* III
1749	"estimate . . . more than 1000, counting children and adults"	Fr. Andrés Varo, BNM, leg. 8, no. 57
1750	*449 (255 adults, 194 children)*	Fr. Francisco de la Concepción González, BNM, leg. 8, no. 81
1752	*318 (127 heads of family, 111 children) (107 fighting men)*	Gov. Tomás Vélez Cachupín, AGN, PI, 102
1760	*344 (158 families)*	Bishop Pedro Tamarón, Adams, *Tamarón's Visitation* (Fr. Juan Agustín de Morfi, 1782, quotes Tamarón's 1760 figures for 1765, Thomas, *Forgotten Frontiers*)
1765	*532 [332?] (138 families)*	Nicolás de LaFora? NMHR, vol. 50 (1975), p. 350
1776	*269 (100 families)*	Fr. Francisco Atanasio Domínguez, Adams and Chavez, *Missions* (Antonio Bonilla, 1776, AGN, Historia, 25, uses Varo's 1749 estimate)
1779	*235 (94 men, 94 women, 23 boys, 24 girls)*	Gov. Juan Bautista de Anza, Nov. 1, BNM, leg. 10, no. 59
c. 1779	84 families	Fr. Juan Agustín de Morfi, 1782, Thomas, *Forgotten Frontiers*

YEAR(S)	POPULATION	SOURCE
1789	*138 (62 men, 6 boys, 58 women, 12 girls)*	Gov. Fernando de la Concha, Oct. 28, HL, Ritch
1790	*152*	Concha, Nov. 1, AGN, PI, 161 (picked up by Revillagigedo, 1793)
	154 (56 families)	Antonio José Ortiz and Fr. Severo Patero, Nov. 9, SANM, II, no. 1096a
1792	*142 (61 families, with 44 children)*	Estado de las misiones, July 16, BNM, Leg. 10, no. 83
1794	*180 (50 families, with 43 children)* including some Tano families	Estado actual, BNM, leg. 10, nos. 70 and 82
	165 (79 male, 86 female)	Misiones de la custodia . . . 1793-1794, Nov. 3, 1795, AASF, 1795, no. 13
1799	*159 Indians* *150 Hispanos**	Estado que muestra las jurisdicciones, BNM, leg. 10, no. 74
1799	*118 Indians (56 male, 62 female)* *178 Hispanos (83 male, 95 female)**	Fr. Buenaventura Merino, June 10, 1801, Cathedral Archive, Durango.
1800	*123 Indians (59 male, 64 female)* *182 Hispanos (85 male, 97 female)**	Same as above
1804	*125 Indians (52 male, 73 female)* *437 Hispanos (220 male, 217 female)**	Noticia de las misiones, Dec. 31, AGI, Mex., 2737
1808	*132 Indians (59 male, 73 female)* *646 Hispanos (326 male, 320 female)**	Noticia de las misiones, Dec. 30, SANM, I, no. 1191
1810	*135 Indians (59 male, 76 female)* *662 Hispanos (321 male, 341 female)**	Noticia de las misiones, Dec. 31, HL, Ritch
c. 1811	"30 fighting men"	Pedro Bautista Pino, *Exposición*, 1812
1811-12	30 Indian families 230 heads of Hispano families*	José Cristóbal Guerrero of El Vado petitions for a resident priest, AASF, 1812, no. 14

YEAR(S)	POPULATION	SOURCE
1815	no more than 40 persons of both sexes	Anonymous complaint, AASF 1815, no. 7
1820	*58 Indians (28 male, 30 female)* *735 Hispanos (356 male, 379 female)**	Noticia de las misiones, [Dec. 31,] SANM, II, no. 2950
1821	8 or 10 families	Esteban Baca petitions for lands at Pecos, Feb. 10, SANM, I, no. 130
	54 Indians (26 male, 28 female) *738 Hispanos (366 male, 372 female)**	Noticia de las misiones, Dec. 31, SANM, II, no. 3094
1823	*90 persons*	Padrón general, MANM
1826	not even 40 persons (no more than 40 families)	Gov. Antonio Narbona, Oct. 14, SANM, I, no. 1371
1831-32	"not more than fifteen or twenty men"	Albert Pike, *Prose Sketches and Poems,* 1834
1830s	"about a dozen, comprizing all ages and sexes"	Josiah Gregg, *Commerce of the Prairies,* 1844
1838	17 persons (7 men, 7 women, 3 children) abandon Pecos pueblo for Jémez	Edgar L. Hewett, "Studies," 1904
	20 persons (12 male, 8 female)	Elsie Clews Parsons, *Jemez,* 1925
1849	18 persons (15 at Jémez, 1 each at Cañón de Pecos, Cuesta, and Santo Domingo)	James H. Simpson, *Journal,* 1852

appendix ii

notable natives of pecos

YEAR(S)	NATIVES	REMARKS
1540-1542	"Cacique" and "Bigotes"	Pecos leaders in dealings with the Coronado expedition
1583-1590s	"Pedro Oroz"	Abducted by Espejo; taught Mexican donados Pecos language
early 1620s	Francisco Mosoyo	"Great idolater" encouraged by Gov. Eulate
late 1630s	Puxavi	A Pecos interpreter at time of Gov. Rosas
1660	El Carpintero	Feted with Diego Romero in Plains Apache ceremonial
1661	Francisco Jutu	Pecos crier and interpreter
1680, 1692-94	Juan de Ye	Pecos gov.; said to have warned Spaniards in 1680; Vargas' most trusted Pueblo ally; failed to return from peace mission to the Taos resisters' camp
1694	Diego Marcos	Gov. installed by Vargas, Sept. 24
1695	Damián	Cacique at Pecos
1696	Lorenzo de Ye	Son of Juan; rumored plotting revolt
1696-1720s	Felipe Antonio Chistoe	"Pro-Spanish" Pecos leader; Vargas' ally in 1696; chief of auxiliaries; perpetual governor; bilingual

YEAR(S)	NATIVES	REMARKS
1696	Diego Umbiro, "Cachina," and two not named	Leaders of "anti-Spanish" faction; hanged by Chistoe
1696	Pock Face (Caripicado)	Young anti-Spanish leader shot by Chistoe; head, foot, and hand presented to Vargas
1690s-1728	Pedro de la Cruz	Long-time Pecos leader
c. 1700-30	Juan Diego Tindé	Chistoe's right-hand man; leader; bilingual; d. Feb. 15, age 60
c. 1711	Pedro	Pecos governor killed by Apaches
1712-40s	Juan Diego de Yescas, alias el Guijo	Interpreter, principal man
1712-	Antonio de Aguate	Interpreter
1714	Agustín	Interpreter who knew both Apache language and Spanish
1729	Agustín Cache	Cacique, "about ninety," died Jan. 11
1731	Antonio Sidepovi	Governor who testified at Bustamante residencia
1730-50s	Francisco Aguilar	First (?) of the prominent Pecos Aguilar family
1740s	Antonio de los Ángeles	Pecos governor who owned several Apaches; "a Tano"?
1743	Miguel	Cacique
1750	Agustín and Antonio Pousoi	Cacique and governor, head 1750 census
1760	Agustín Guichí	Carpenter and principal man; impersonator of Bishop Tamarón; mauled by bear; buried Sept. 21
	Mateo Cru	Played the Father Custos in Guichí's burlesque
1750s-60s	Lorenzo	Long-time interpreter
1780s and 90s	Lorenzo Tilli, Domingo Aguilar, and Lorenzo Sena	Fiscales mayores in charge when no missionary at Pecos
1786	Juan Sandoval	Last known Pecos killed by Comanches
1798	Juan de Dios Fernández	"Citizen of El Vado and formerly an Indian of Pecos" marries María Armijo, Nov. 28
1802	José	Sacristán mayor, d. July 1

YEAR(S)	NATIVES	REMARKS
1802	Santiago Calabacitas	D. Apr. 18, 1825, without the sacraments "because of the laziness of the Indians"
1810	Juan Trébol	Fiscal
1812	Bartolo Vigil	First (?) of Vigil family at Pecos pueblo
1817	José Chama	Married Juana Arias of Santa Fe; residents of Antón Chico, 1829
	Miguel Brito and Francisco Moya	"Indios y vecinos de Pecos"; Brito a member of El Vado militia, 1821
1821	Quanima	Elected alcalde of Pecos pueblo "ayuntamiento" under Spanish constitution
1820s	José Cota	With Rafael Aguilar petitions for return of Pecos lands, 1829; a José Kota among last Pecos emigrants, 1838
1820s	Rafael Aguilar	Regidor, 1821, and several times alcalde of Pecos; leads fight to save Pecos lands
1825	Agustín Cota	
1825	Juan Antonio Armenta	Marries widow María de los Ángeles
1826	Juan Antonio Toya	Likely the Antonio Toya, "governor," who led the emigration to Jémez in 1838; "full-blooded Comanche" (Bandelier) or captive of Comanches (Parsons)
	Juan Domingo Vigil and Juan Manuel Armenta	With Aguilar appeal to Diputación Provincial to halt giveaway of Pecos lands; Armenta "70" in 1825
1828	José Manuel Calabazas	Godfather to José Manuel, son of Rafael Aguilar, b. June 2
1834	María Petra	Last (?) Pecos mentioned in El Vado books; parents "unknown"
1902	José Miguel (Vigil) Pecos (Zu-wa-ng)	One of emigrants of 1838 dies at Jémez, uncle of Agustín (Cota) Pecos
1919	Agustín (Cota) Pecos (Se-sa-fwe-yah)	Last survivor of 1838 Pecos emigration dies at Jémez

appendix III

the franciscans of pecos

Abbreviations: G, identified as guardian of convento at Pecos; M, Mexico City; NM, New Mexico; P, Puebla; SC, San Cosme; Sp, Spain; V, died violently.

FRIAR	BORN	PROFESSED	TO NEW MEXICO	AT PECOS	DIED	REMARKS
Juan de Padilla	Andalucía, Sp (to New Sp 1529)		1540	1540, 1541, 1542	1542, Quivira, V	Co-discoverer of Pecos with Hernando de Alvarado
Luis de Úbeda	Sp (to New Sp 1534)		1540	1541, 1542-?	?, NM	Left at Pecos by Coronado
Francisco de San Miguel	c. 1530	Apr. 18, 1571, P	1598	Sept.-Dec. 1598	after 1602	Built first church at Pecos?
Pedro Zambrano Ortiz, G	c. 1586, Canary Is.	Oct. 27, 1610, M	1616	c. 1617-c. 1620	after 1636	Built first Pecos convento
Pedro de Ortega, G	Mar. 1593, M	May 8, 1612, M	1618	c. 1620-late 1621	c. 1632, NM, V?	Broke up Pecos "idols;" began massive second church
Andrés Juárez, G	c. 1582, Fuente-ovejuna, Córdoba, Sp	Dec. 5, 1609, M	1612	late 1621-34	after 1647, NM?	Built greater part of, and completed, second church and convento; introduced carpentry; linguist; longest term missionary at Pecos
Domingo del Espíritu Santo, G				1635	before 1659, NM	
Antonio de Ibargaray, G	c. 1602, Bilbao, Vizcaya, Sp	Jan. 20, 1630, P	1634	1636-?	Still alive in Feb. 1668, NM?	Later custos and oldest friar in the custody

Name	Birthplace	Profession	Arrival	Service	Death	Notes
Antonio Jiménez, lay bro.				1638		"Arrested" by Gov. Rosas
Juan González, G	c. 1604, Luarca, Asturias, Sp	Jan. 27, 1624, P	by 1644	?-1662	after 1686, M?	Ex-custos
Alonso de Posada, G	c. 1626, Congosto, León, Sp	c. Oct. 20, 1647, M	by 1653	1662-65		Custos and agent of the Inquisition; arrested at Pecos by Gov. Peñalosa
Juan de la Chica			before 1659	1663	after 1668, NM?	Present at Posada's arrest
Nicolás de Echevarría, G	c. 1616, Sierra de Pinos, Zacatecas	May 26, 1638, M	by 1644	1665-66		
Nicolás de Enríquez, G	c. 1623, Zacatecas		prob. 1661	1666-67	early 1669, NM	Alleged author of satire
Diego de Enríquez, G	Sp	incorp. 1626	after 1659, by 1665	1667-68		
Juan Bernal, G	Nov. 1632, M	Feb. 13, 1649, M	1668-69	1669-71	1680, Galisteo, V	Agent of the Inquisition; custos in 1680
Francisco Gómez de la Cadena			after 1659, by 1665	1669		Inquisition notary
Pedro de Ávila y Ayala		incorp. 1668	1668-69	1670-71	1673, Hawikuh, V	Inquisition notary; killed by Apaches
Luis de Morales, G	Baeza, Jaén, Sp	Aug. 26, 1660, P	1665	1672-?	1680, S. Ildefonso, V	
Fernando de Velasco, G	c. 1619, Cádiz, Sp	Aug. 15, 1651, M	before 1659	?-1680	1680, within sight of Galisteo, V	
Juan de la Pedrosa, lay bro.	Apr. 1654, M	May 31, 1673, M	1675	1680	1680, Pecos, V	
Francisco Corvera	Manila	Feb. 6, 1684, M	El Paso 1691	1692	1696, S. Ildefonso, V	With Vargas 1692
Cristóbal Alonso Barroso	Lisbon	Mar. 5, 1685, M	El Paso 1691	1692, 1700	after 1703	With Vargas 1692

FRIAR	BORN	PROFESSED	TO NEW MEXICO	AT PECOS	DIED	REMARKS
Diego de (la Casa) Zeinos, G			El Paso by 1692	1694-95		Built temporary church; withdrawn from Pecos after shooting incident
Juan Alpuente, G			1693	1695-96		Left Pecos for fear of revolt
Domingo de Jesús María	Sp (to New Sp 1692)		1693	1696		Member of College of Querétaro; recalled before revolt of 1696
José García Marín, G	Sp (to New Sp 1692)		1693	1696		Member of College of Querétaro; evacuated to Santa Fe during revolt of 1696
Francisco de Vargas	Sp (to New Sp 1664)		El Paso 1691	1696		Custos; remodeled Zeinos' temporary church
Alonso Jiménez de Cisneros, G			Cochití by 1696	1697-98		
Miguel de Trizio, G	Sp (to New Sp 1692)		1693	1698		Member of College of Querétaro
Francisco Farfán	c. 1643, Cádiz, Sp	July 2, 1662, M	before 1680	1698-99		
Diego de Chavarría	c. 1661, Tacuba, M	Mar. 6, 1679, M	El Paso by 1689	1699		Vice-custos 1698
Miguel Muñiz de Luna	Puebla	Feb. 13, 1684, P	El Paso 1691	1699-1700	after 1729	With Vargas 1692
José de Arranegui	Villa de Lequeitio, Vizcaya, Sp	Apr. 20, 1695, M	by 1700	1700-08		May have begun fourth Pecos church; divided time between Pecos and Santa Fe
Juan de Tagle		Apr. 20, 1695, M	El Paso by 1699	1708	after 1720	
Diego de Padilla	M	Oct. 5, 1680, M	El Paso by 1693	1709-11	after 1712	"Ministro presidente del pueblo, y visita de Galisteo;" liked by the Pecos

Name	Origin	Profession/Ordination	First assignment	At Pecos	After	Notes
Miguel Francisco Cepeda y Arriola	Puebla	May 5, 1704, P	Bernalillo by 1709	1712		Mistreated the Pecos, according to Gov. Peñuela
Lucas de Arévalo	Sp (to New Sp 1706?)		by 1709	1712-14		Pecos missionary when Rael de Aguilar demolished kivas; chaplain with Páez Hurtado on plains, 1715
Antonio Aparicio	Sp (to New Sp 1706?)		El Paso by 1708	1714-15		
Jerónimo de Liñán		Dec. 17, 1706, M	Alburquerque by 1711	1716-18		Accused by Pino and Irazábal of soliciting sex in the confessional, 1718
Carlos José Delgado	c. 1677, Sp (to Querétaro col. 1708)	Fran. prov. of Andalucía	1710	1716-17	after 1752	Evidently finished fourth Pecos church; missionary in NM forty years; "apostolic Spaniard"
Juan George del Pino	c. 1688, M	Dec. 17, 1706, M	S. Ildefonso by 1717	1718-21, 1729-31, 1737-38	after 1753	Chaplain on 1719 Valverde expedition to the plains
Francisco Irazábal			Zuñi by 1707	1722	after 1729	Knew Zuñi language
Diego Arias de Espinosa de los Monteros	Pto. de Santa María, Sp	June 10, 1714, P	Galisteo by 1723	1723, 1736-37	c. 1748	
Antonio Gabaldón	c. 1700, Puebla	Oct. 1, 1717, P	Galisteo by 1723	1724-29, 1730, 1733-34	after 1760	Only 24 years old in 1724
José de Irigoyen	c. 1698, Puebla	Mar. 19, 1716, P	Galisteo by 1725	1726	after 1760	
José Antonio Guerrero	M	Jan. 1, 1706, P	Tesuque by 1714	1727	after 1742	
Juan Sánchez de la Cruz	Sp (to New Sp 1717)		Taos by 1719	1728	after 1746	
Manuel Zambrano	M	Oct. 20, 1711, P	San Felipe by 1727	1730	after 1763	

FRIAR	BORN	PROFESSED	TO NEW MEXICO	AT PECOS	DIED	REMARKS
Pedro Antonio Esquer	Sevilla, Sp	July 7, 1711, M	Galisteo by 1724	1731-32, 1734, 1735, 1739, 1741, 1745	after 1749	Damned Gov. Bustamante
Cayetano de Otero	c. 1701, Galicia, Sp	Jan. 29, 1725, P	Zuñi by 1731	1732-33	after 1768	
Francisco Manuel Bravo Lerchundi	Puebla	Dec. 30, 1700, P	Ácoma by 1730	1733, 1734-35		
Juan José de Oronzoro	Puebla	July 10, 1717, P	S. Clara by 1733	1736	after 1763	
Juan José Pérez de Mirabal	Málaga, Sp	May 19, 1720, M	Taos by 1722?	1738-39	after 1763	
José de Eguía y Lumbre			Santa Cruz by 1732	1739-40		
Jacinto González	Cádiz, Sp	Sept. 24, 1730, P	Zuñi by 1733	1740, 1743	by 1769	Interim minister for Hernández
Antonio Zamora	M	Oct. 9, 1714, M	by 1740	1741-42	after 1764	
Juan José Hernández	Tlaxcala	Apr. 27, 1730, SC	Ácoma by 1741	1742-47, 1757-58	after 1769	Charged by Gov. Codallos with abusing the Indians
Juan Antonio Sánchez	Puebla	Feb. 9, 1713, P	c. 1718	1743		
Agustín Antonio de Iniesta Márquez	c. 1709, Toluca	May 2, 1735, P		1743-44	by 1774	
José Urquijo	M	June 14, 1732, M		1747-48, 1754-55	by 1769	At Pecos during Comanche attack Jan. 21, 1748; attended both Pecos and Galisteo
Andrés José García de la Concepción	c. 1720, Puebla	May 29, 1736, P	c. 1746	1748-49, 1763	after 1779, M	At Pecos "one year" (Domínguez, 1776); "old and ill," 1777
Pedro Ignacio Pino	M	Apr. 27, 1730, M	Zia by 1741	1749?	Dec. 9, 1767, Ácoma	Named to Pecos, May 1, 1749, but may never have got there

						Author of 1750 Pecos census
Francisco de la Concepción González	Santander, Sp	Jan. 28, 1727, M	by 1740	1749-50		
Juan José Toledo	c. 1716, M	July 14, 1732, M	Ácoma by 1743	1750-53	by 1774	Received French traders at Pecos, 1752; denounced to Inquisition in 1771 for saying fornication no sin
Manuel José Rojo	c. 1718, M	Feb. 5, 1736, SC	c. 1750	1751-52	Apr. 17, 1789, Santa Fe	"Four months" at Pecos (Domínguez, 1776); "old and ill," 1777; blind from c. 1785
Miguel Gómez Cayuela	c. 1699, Andalucía, Sp (to New Sp 1743)	c. 1726, Sp	by 1745	1753-54, 1755-56	by 1774	Petitioned to leave NM from Pecos, 1754, after his ten years
Miguel Campos				1755		There during visitation of Custos Jacobo de Castro
Joaquín Mariano Rodríguez de Jerez	c. 1714	c. 1731		1755, 1756-57, 1760-61	after 1772	Confessed and buried Agustín Guichí who impersonated Bishop Tamarón
José García de Noriega	c. 1730, M	Jan. 1, 1747, M	Zuñi by 1758	1758-59	after 1775	At Pecos "one year" (Domínguez, 1776); blind in 1777
Francisco Javier Dávila Saavedra	c. 1715, Florida	June 30, 1739, Veracruz	El Paso by 1750	1759-60, 1761	after 1782	At Pecos during Tamarón visitation; "sicker than all the others," 1777
Estanislao Mariano de Marulanda	c. 1734, Ozumba	July 12, 1750, M	Zuñi by 1759	1761-62, 1776	after 1779	"Three years at Pecos" (Domínguez, 1776)
Antonio Brizuela	c. 1729, M	June 6, 1749, M	Galisteo by 1761	1762		
José Manuel Martínez de la Vega	c. 1734, M	Jan. 14, 1753, M	c. 1766	1764-67	Apr. 10, 1789, Anamiquipa	
Manuel Antonio de Santa Cruz y Burgoa	c. 1729, Vizcaya, Sp	c. 1751, M		1767-1768		
José de Burgos	c. 1732, Veracruz	Feb. 22, 1749, P	Santa Fe by 1760	1771, 1784-86, 1787-88	Sept. 13, 1788, Santa Fe	"Preceptor de gramática;" "a notorious drunkard," 1777
Joaquín Ildefonso Rodríguez	c. 1714	c. 1730	Santa Fe by 1763	1772-73	by 1774	Sorely "persecuted" by civilians; demented?

FRIAR	BORN	PROFESSED	TO NEW MEXICO	AT PECOS	DIED	REMARKS
Patricio de Jesús Cuellar	c. 1733, Tulantzingo	Nov. 17, 1749, P	Santa Fe by 1766	1774	c. 1779	Also pronounced "a notorious drunkard" in 1777
Francisco Atanasio Domínguez	c. 1740, M	c. 1757, M	El Paso, 1775	1776	by 1805	Briefly served Pecos at Santa Fe "for lack of a minister"
José Medrano	c. 1738	c. 1758	Sandía by 1772	1776-77	after 1785	At Santa Fe; Pecos "for lack of a minister"
Juan José Llanos	c. 1736, Toluca	Oct. 20, 1754, M	Nambé by 1771	1777-78	after 1787	
Andrés de Claramonte	c. 1737, M	Dec. 21, 1758, M	Picurís by 1764	1777	1800	
José Palacio		Nov. 18, 1745, M	1776	1778, 1779-80	Apr. 23, 1785, Bernalillo	"Ministro de esta misión de Pecos"
Tomás Salvador Fernández	Veracruz	Nov. 16, 1768, M	Laguna by 1777	1781	after 1787	"Ministro de esta misión de Pecos"
Francisco de Hozio	Jan. 8, 1752, Miranda de Ebro, Castilla, Sp (to New Sp 1777)	c. Oct. 1722, Bilbao	S. Ildefonso by 1780	1782, 1786-87, 1788-89, 1790	Sept. 24, 1823, Santa Fe	Long-time presidial chaplain at Santa Fe
Juan Bermejo	c. 1733, Sp (to New Sp 1777)	c. 1761	Santa Fe by 1779	1782		"Custodio y pro-ministro . . . por falta de ministro"
José Carral	Sp (to New Sp 1777)		Isleta by 1779	1782-84		"Pro-ministro" of Pecos and minister of Santa Fe
Francisco Martín Bueno	Sp (to New Sp 1777)		Jémez by 1779	1789-90	Apr. 21, 1790, Santa Fe	Minister of Santa Fe and Pecos
Severo Patero			1790	1790-91		Incorp. from Col. de San Fernando; left NM 1793
Buenaventura Merino	Feb. 24, 1745, Villavicencio de los Caballeros, León, Sp	Oct. 19, 1760, Medina de Río Seco (to New Sp 1785)	1790	1792-93, 1794-1800	Mar. 17, 1806, Santa Fe	Incorp. from Col. de San Fernando
Juan Fernández de la Sierra	Sp (to New Sp 1777)		San Juan by 1779	1793-94		Accused of soliciting sex

						Ministro interino
Diego Muñoz Jurado	c. 1749, Santa Eufemia, Córdoba, Sp (1777)	c. 1766	Taos by 1779	1794		
José Pedro Rubín de Celís	c. 1765, Puebla	c. 1782	c. 1793	1794	after 1821	"Ministro encargado del Pueblo de Pecos"
Diego Martínez Arellano	Nov. 11, 1752, Ameca Ameca, Chalco	Apr. 24, 1776, M	1790	1802-04	after 1827	
Francisco Bragado y Rico	c. 1769, Villalonso, Zamora, Sp	c. 1788, Villalón, Galicia	1802	1804-10, 1818-25	Jan. 4, 1825, San Miguel del Vado	Obtained license for San Miguel del Vado chapel, 1805; buried in it by Father Alcina
Juan Bruno González	c. 1777, Los Hoyos, Soria, Sp		1810	1810-11	after 1826	
Manuel Antonio García del Valle	c. 1784, M		1810	1811-18	June 1834, Sandía	Obtained bishop's license to reside at El Vado and visit Pecos "at least once a month," 1812
Juan Caballero Toril	c. 1775, Pedroche, Córdoba, Sp	c. 1793, Prov. Sta. Ma. de los Ángeles	1810	1825-28		Argued with alcalde of El Vado over escort to visit Pecos; evidently expelled with Spaniards, 1828
Teodoro Alcina de la Boada	Mar. 1, 1766, Palafox, Gerona, Sp	c. 1783, Gerona	1793	1825, 1828	May 29, 1834, Santa Cruz de la Cañada	He and Castro last Franciscans to serve Pecos; Alcina's final entry Dec. 3, 1828
José de Castro	c. 1767, San Salvador del Cristinado, Galicia, Sp (1795)	c. Aug. 1788	1802	1828	by late 1840	
DIOCESAN PRIESTS:						
Juan Felipe Ortiz			Santa Fe by 1825	1829, 1832-33	after 1853	
José Francisco Leyva y Rosas			Alburquerque by 1817	1829-32	after 1850	
José Vicente Chávez			Belén by 1826	1833-34	after 1850	
Rafael Ortiz			by 1824	1834-35	after 1851	

appendix iv

encomenderos and alcaldes mayores

YEAR(S)	ENCOMENDEROS	REMARKS
before 1620- c. 1656	Francisco Gómez?	A Portuguese; to N.M. c. 1605; leading citizen; sargento mayor, etc. Suc. by his son
c. 1656-80	Francisco Gómez Robledo	Born Santa Fe c. 1628; tried by Inquisition 1660s and acquitted; maese de campo

Alcaldes Mayores of Galisteo (Tanos)
and District Including Pecos

c. 1659-61	Diego González Bernal	Agent of Gov. López; removed by him
1661	Antonio de Salas	Appointed and removed by Gov. López
1661-65	Jerónimo de Carvajal	Born in Sandía dist. c. 1630; owner of Cerrillos. estancia
1664	Francisco de Anaya Almazán	Born N.M. c. 1633; family perished in revolt of 1680; he returned with Vargas
?-1680	José Nieto	He and family killed by Tanos, Aug. 10, 1680

Alcalde Mayor of Pecos
(Galisteo abandoned)

1694-96-?	Francisco de Anaya Almazán	Helped build temporary third Pecos church

YEAR(S)	ALCALDES	REMARKS
	Alcaldes Mayores of Pecos and Galisteo (Refounded, 1706)	
c. 1705-c. 1710	Juan de Ulibarrí	B. San Luis Potosí; to N.M. 1694; sargento mayor and procurador; led exped. to plains to liberate Picurís, 1706
1706	José Trujillo	Alcalde mayor of Santa Cruz; app. by Ulibarrí as lt. alcalde of Pecos to serve in his absence
1711-14	Sebastián de Vargas	Master blacksmith; lt. alcalde mayor
1714-20s	Alfonso Rael de Aguilar	Sargento mayor; destroyed Pecos kivas, 1714
1725-c. 1738	Manuel Tenorio de Alba	Capt. in 1732; frequent godfather at Pecos
c. 1739-43	Manuel Sáenz de Garvizu	Native of Spain; Codallos' lt. gov.; lost 10 men pursuing Comanches e. from Pecos, 1746
1744-48	Juan José Moreno	Native of Spain; 42 in 1745
1746	Miguel de Alire	Interim alcalde in Moreno's absence
c. 1749-56	Tomás Antonio de Sena	Blacksmith and armorer
1755	Francisco Aguilar	Lt. alcalde mayor
1756-c. 1760	Bernardo de Miera y Pacheco	Cartographer and jack-of-all-trades lured to N.M. by Gov. Marín del Valle
c. 1760-62	Cayetano Tenorio	Son of Manuel?
1762-69	Tomás Antonio de Sena	Reappt. by Gov. Vélez; reg. mine of N.S. de los Dolores
early 1770s	Vicente Armijo	Took balusters from convento mirador and put them in the casas reales
	Jerónimo Leyva	Armijo's lt.
1776-	José Herrera	Alcalde mayor at time of Domínguez visitation
1782-90s	Antonio José Ortiz	Alcalde mayor of Santa Fe district, which now incl. Pecos; put El Vado grantees in possession, 1794

YEAR(S)	ALCALDES	REMARKS
	Tenientes de Justicia of Pecos and El Vado (Under District of Santa Fe)	
1790s-1800	Domingo Anselmo Santiesteban	Vecino of Sta. Fe living at Pecos; d. Pecos, Sept. 12, 1800
1802-03	Antonio Vigil	
1804	Lorenzo Antonio Marín	
1805	Juan Antonio Alarí	Quashed alleged sedition in El Vado settlements
1807	Tapia	
1809, 1813-14, 1820	Manuel Baca	He and Fr. Francisco Bragado dispute and reconcile, 1809
1815	Juan Antonio Anaya	Assisted at measurement of Peña grant, 1814
1818	Vicente Villanueva	Measured Pecos "league"; killed by Apaches near Las Ruedas, c. 1822
	Alcaldes Constitucionales of El Vado	
1821	Manuel Durán	Sent results of Pecos pueblo "ayuntamiento" election to Gov. Melgares
1825	Diego Padilla	Long-time resident of El Vado area; grantee
1826	José Ramón Alarid	Reported to Gov. Narbona about Pecos lands
1827	Gregorio Vigil	He and Father Caballero disagreed over escort to visit Pecos
1828	José Miguel Sánchez	Cosigned inventory of San Miguel del Vado chapel with Caballero
1829	Santiago Ulibarrí	

appendix v

miera's 1758 map of new mexico

Late in the fall of 1756, while a combined force of more than three hundred presidial soldiers and Indian auxiliaries tracked Apaches on the upper Gila River and cursed the broken terrain, the Viceroy Marqués de las Amarillas fumed. How was he to know where anything was on the northern frontier? What he needed was maps, reliable maps, "showing in detail the rivers, mountains, mining towns or mines discovered, presidios and missions," and more. On December 19, 1756, the viceroy dispatched to each of his six northern governors an order for a map. Because he considered the making of such maps a matter of good administrative practice on their parts, he stipulated that the governors themselves, not the royal treasury, pay costs. Furthermore, the finished products, accompanied by statements of conditions in the respective provinces, were to be in his hands promptly.

Gov. Francisco Antonio Marín del Valle of New Mexico (1754-1760) smiled as he read the order. He had stolen a march on the viceroy. Already he had searched the archives in vain for a map of New Mexico. Then he had searched New Mexico in vain for an individual who could make him one. Strained relations between Marín and the Franciscans all but ruled out a friar as cartographer. Not until early 1756, when don Bernardo de Miera y Pacheco moved to Santa Fe, "of his own free will"—evidently enticed by the offer of a political appointment as alcalde mayor—did the governor have his man.

Miera, a versatile Spaniard who had settled in the El Paso district in 1743, had served as engineer and map maker in the general offensive of 1747, "Father Menchero's campaign," and had thereby gained firsthand knowledge of much of western New Mexico. Two years later, he had plotted the Río del

Norte from El Paso downriver to La Junta. Once in New
Mexico, as alcalde mayor of Pecos and Galisteo, he rapidly
familarized himself with eastern New Mexico on three campaigns against the Comanches.

Don Bernardo would accompany Marín on his official
tour of inspection and, at the governor's expense, he would map
the entire province. From late June until December 1, 1757,
they were in the field. By the end of April 1758, Miera's elaborate map was ready. The governor enclosed, as a letter of trans-
mittal, his own commentary on military and Indian affairs and
sent the packet south.

The viceroy was pleased. He complimented Governor
Marín for getting the job done despite the lack of previous
maps. In addition, he ordered Marín to leave for his successor
a map and report similar to those submitted, as well as a
detailed diary of campaigns, so that the new governor might
orient himself quickly, before self-seeking locals led him astray.

The 1758 Miera map of New Mexico reproduced here is
only one—probably the most complete—of several maps
drawn by don Bernardo for Marín del Valle. The governor
himself mentioned that he had sent the viceroy an earlier one,
presumably by Miera since there were no other cartographers
about. Later, on a mission to the Hopi pueblos, Miera mapped
for Marín the provinces of Hopi and Navajo. And, if the
governor obeyed orders, he further commissioned don Bern-
ard to draw for the next executive a chart of all New Mexico
similar to the one of 1758. Perhaps as a token of his appreciation for his patron, the artistic Miera created in addition a very
special map (reproduced above following page 166). Using as
his canvas a thirty-by-forty-inch piece of local cotton cloth
treated with size, he painted in color the kingdom of New Mexico and all the surrounding provinces. He dedicated it to Marín.

Well into the twentieth century, the original of Miera's
1758 map and Governor Marín's accompanying report reposed
in volume 39 of the Californias section, Archivo General de la
Nación, Mexico City. There Herbert E. Bolton catalogued
them in 1913. In 1925, don Rafael López, director of the
archive, approved a skillful tracing of the map. Only the
smallest details and a few words (e.g., ojo for ojos, Comanches
for Cumanches, Picurí for Picurís) gave it away. Lansing B.
Bloom found map and report still in their assigned place in
1930 when he photographed them and thousands of other
documents for the University of New Mexico. But in 1951,
when the archive microfilmed Californias 39 for The Bancroft
Library, University of California, only a poor photocopy of

the tracing remained. Original map and report had vanished.

The following reproduction of Miera's 1758 map is, strictly speaking, a 1977 tracing, slightly restored, based on inferior prints from Bloom's film of the missing original. Because of the map's size, about 26 X 32 inches, Bloom had shot it in eight sections. Unfortunately he did not keep the camera at the same distance from the object or even level. The several sections, as a result, were somewhat distorted and did not match up. The negatives had been destroyed. By rephotographing the old prints and using an enlarger to bring all sections to the same scale, and by tilting the easel to minimize the distortion, National Park Service photographer Gary G. Lister pieced the whole thing together again.

Time and wear had partially effaced a few words on the original. By comparing various prints of the 1758 map, the 1925 tracing, and other Miera maps, each such word was recovered. A complete transcription was compiled. Thus armed, Jerry L. Livingston, a talented Park Service illustrator, began the painstaking business of tracing and redrawing Miera's New Mexico.

So little graphic material has survived from eighteenth-century New Mexico that the 1758 Miera map is important in itself. It is of even more interest when compared with known examples of don Bernardo's later cartography. The statistical data found in the map's margins were compiled during Governor Marín's inspection tour of 1757. Full title, legend, and text follow in translation.

MAP which don Francisco Antonio Marín del Valle, Governor and Captain General of this kingdom of New Mexico, ordered drawn in conjunction with the tour of inspection he made of his jurisdiction, to which is added part of [Nueva] Vizcaya and Sonora and the provinces of Navajo, Hopi, and Gila, and in the margins of which are set forth the people who compose this jurisdiction, Indians as well as Spaniards, non-Indians, and soldiers, all vassals of His Majesty.

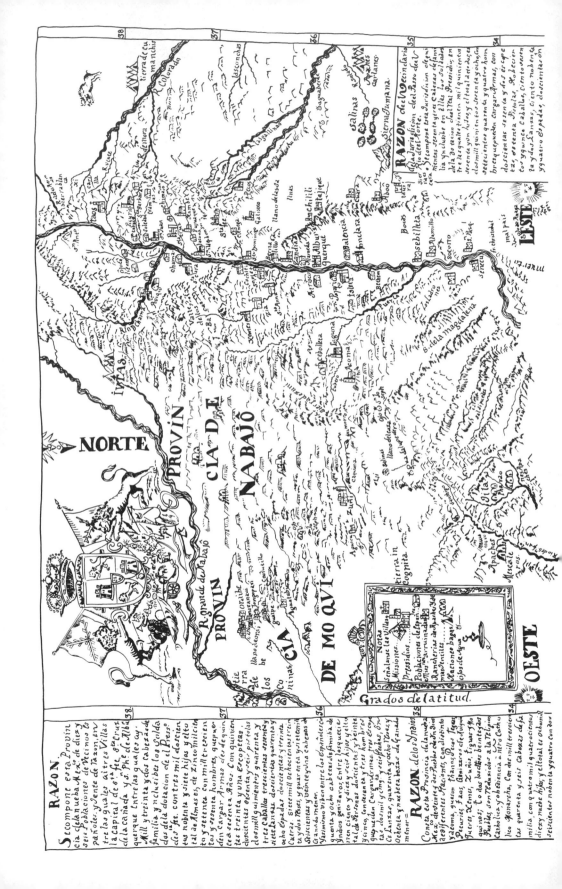

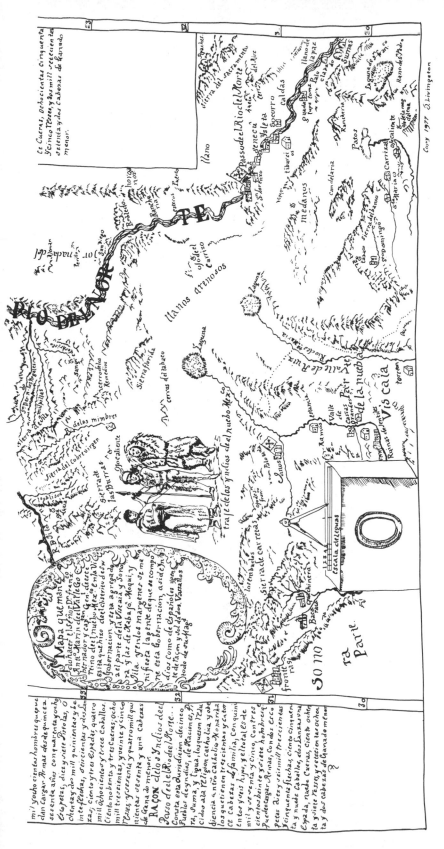

Symbols

The villas are marked	+
Missions	🏛 ... Ruined missions
Presidios	👥 ... Rancherías of Apaches and other heathens
Settlements of Spaniards	🏚 ... Roving tribes
	◡ ... Springs

Cory 1977 S. Livingston

DESCRIPTION This province of New Mexico is composed of sixteen settlements of Spanish and non-Indian citizens; three are villas: the capital of Santa Fe, Santa Cruz de la Cañada, and San Felipe de Alburquerque. In these settlements there are 1,032 heads of family, including the soldiers of the garrison of the Santa Fe presidio, with 3,297 children. Their total population is 5,170, with 1,360 men between the ages of fifteen and sixty capable of bearing arms. They have 531 muskets, 266 pistols, 2,543 horses, 367 lances, 248 swords, 230 buffcoats, 7,832 head of cattle, and 47,621 head of sheep.

Likewise there live among the Spaniards 58 heads of family of genízaro Indians, who have 116 children, and a total of 225 persons, with 63 men capable of bearing arms. They have 3 muskets, 2,056 arrows, 11 lances, 48 head of cattle, and 89 head of sheep.

DESCRIPTION of Indians. This province of New Mexico is made up of twenty-two pueblos of Indians of different tribes with distinct languages. They are Tanos, Pecos, Tewas, Picurís, Taos, genízaros of Abiquiú, Queres,, Jémez, Zuñis, Tiwas, and Hopis. All of the said twenty-two pueblos are converted to the Catholic religion and obedience to our Catholic Monarch. There are 2,346 heads of family, with 4,419 children, and the total is 8,694, with 2,800 men between fifteen and sixty capable of bearing arms. They have 48 muskets, 17 pistols, 82,520 arrows, 602 lances, 103 swords, 4,813 horses, 193 buffcoats, 8,325 head of cattle, and 64,561 head of sheep.

DESCRIPTION of the Indians of El Paso del Río del Norte. This district is made up of five pueblos of Indians of the Piro, Suma, and Tiwa tribes converted to the Catholic religion and obedience to our Catholic Monarch. There are 314 heads of family, with 506 children, and the total is 1,065, with 327 men capable of bearing arms. They have 2 muskets, 16,350 arrows, 159 horses, 2 lances, 1 sword, 9 buffcoats, 187 head of cattle, and 783 head of sheep.

DESCRIPTION of the citizenry of the district of El Paso del Río del Norte. This district is composed of 563 heads of family, including the soldiers of the garrison of the royal presidio, who among them have 1,561 children. The total of all is 2,568, with 744 men capable of bearing arms. They have 262 muskets, 70 pistols, 915 horses, 162 lances, 194 swords, 211 buffcoats, 855 head of cattle, and 2,772 head of sheep.

aBBReviations

AASF   Archives of the Archdiocese of Santa Fe, Albuquerque: B, baptismal books; M, marriage books; Burial books

AGI   Archivo General de Indias, Sevilla, Spain: Guad., Audiencia de Guadalajara; Mex., Audiencia de México

AGN   Archivo General de la Nación, México: Inq., Inquisición; PI, Provincias Internas

AW   *Arizona and the West*

BL   The Bancroft Library, University of California, Berkeley: BRP, Bolton Research Papers; M-M, Mexican Manuscripts; NMO, New Mexico Originals

BNM   Biblioteca Nacional, México, Archivo Franciscano, New Mexico Documents

DII   *Colección de documentos inéditos relativos al descubrimiento, conquista y organización de las antiguas posesiones españolas de América y Oceanía*, 42 vols. (Madrid, 1864-1884)

EP   *El Palacio*

HL   Huntington Library, San Marino, California: Ritch, Ritch Collection

LEP   Libro de entradas y profesiones de novicios de este convento del Padre San Francisco de México, 1562-1680, BL, M-M 216-18

MANM   Mexican Archives of New Mexico, State Records Center and Archives, Santa Fe

NMHR   *New Mexico Historical Review*

SANM   Spanish Archives of New Mexico, State Records Center and Archives, Santa Fe

SGNM   Surveyor General of New Mexico, State Records Center and Archives, Santa Fe

notes

Chapter I, pages 3-7

1. Standard works on the Coronado expedition are Herbert E. Bolton, *Coronado, Knight of Pueblos and Plains* (Albuquerque, 1949); George P. Hammond and Agapito Rey, *Narratives of the Coronado Expedition, 1540-1542* (Albuquerque, 1940); and George Parker Winship, "The Coronado Expedition," *Fourteenth Annual Report of the Bureau of Ethnology*, Smithsonian Institution, 1892-1893, Part 1 (Washington, D.C., 1896), pp. 329-613. See also A. Grove Day, *Coronado's Quest* (Berkeley and Los Angeles, 1940).

2. Informes de los conquistadores y pobladores de México y de otras partes de la Nueva España, México, folio 203, Archivo General de Indias, Sevilla, Spain (AGI), Audiencia de México (Mex.), legajo 1064. Francisco A. de Icaza, *Conquistadores y pobladores de Nueva España: diccionario autobiográfico*, 2 vols. (Madrid, 1923), II, p. 289. Hammond and Rey, *Narratives*, p. 88.

3. Informes de los conquistadores, ff. 179, 190; Icaza, *Conquistadores*, II, pp. 222, 254-55. Hammond and Rey, *Narratives*, p. 90. Pascual Madoz, *Diccionario geográfico-estadístico-histórico de España y sus posesiones de ultramar*, 16 vols. (Madrid, 1845-1850), VIII, pp. 34-35.

4. Juan Troyano to the king, México, Dec. 20, 1568, AGI, Mex., 168. Francisco del Paso y Troncoso, *Epistolario de Nueva España, 1505-1818*, 16 vols. (México, 1939-1942), X, pp. 262-77.

5. For the earlier career of Padilla in New Spain and a lively characterization, see Fray Angelico Chavez, *Coronado's Friars* (Washington, D.C., 1968), pp. 14-27, 46-47. This study cuts through "the pious imaginings" of the later chroniclers to get at what can be known of the sixteenth-century Franciscans brought together by the Coronado expedition. See also Chavez, ed., *The Oroz Codex* (Washington, D.C., 1972), p. 94n.

6. The earliest use of the name Pecos by Spaniards occurs in the testimony of Castaño de Sosa's soldiers in 1591. See below, p. 48.

7. An enlightening discussion of how news traveled during this period is Carroll L. Riley, "Early Spanish-Indian Communication in the Greater Southwest," *New Mexico Historical Review* (NMHR), vol. 46 (1971), pp. 285-314.

8. Coronado's testimony, Sept. 3, 1544, Hammond and Rey, *Narratives*, pp. 324-25. Pedro de Castañeda, Relación de la jornada de Cíbola, I:12. The entire Relación was transcribed and translated in Winship, "Coronado Expedition." A more recent English rendering is

in Hammond and Rey, *Narratives*, pp. 191-283. Riley, "Communication," pp. 303-04.

9. Father Padilla's brief but graphic account of the trip as far as the Rio Grande pueblos is translated in Hammond and Rey, *Narratives*, pp. 182-84. Chavez, *Coronado's Friars*, pp. 49-53, offers a somewhat revised translation.

10. Castañeda, II:5.

11. Between 1915 and 1929 archaeologist Alfred Vincent Kidder supervised extensive excavations at Cicuye-Pecos and its environs. The publications that resulted, a number of which appear in the Bibliography, were many, and included *An Introduction to the Study of Southwestern Archaeology with a Preliminary Account of Excavations at Pecos*, rev. ed. (New Haven, 1962), first published in 1924. After nearly twenty-five years away from the Southwest in the Maya field, Kidder returned to pull together *Pecos, New Mexico: Archaeological Notes* (Andover, 1958). In conclusion (pp. 307-22), he mused about the decline of Pecos and hinted at "some inner defect" which he believed might have been factionalism, a condition endemic in Pueblo society. Kidder also pointed out, as others had, that Pecos and Jémez, despite their common language, were "extraordinarily unlike" (p. 320).

12. Castañeda, I:12. Kidder, *The Artifacts of Pecos* (New Haven, 1932) contains excellent descriptions and photographs of bird-bone flageolets and other musical instruments and of various items of personal adornment.

13. Padilla as quoted in Chavez, *Coronado's Friars*, pp. 51-52.

14. The text of the requerimiento is published in English in Charles Gibson, ed., *The Spanish Tradition in America* (New York, 1968), pp. 58-60. For background, see Lewis Hanke, *The Spanish Struggle for Justice in the Conquest of America* (Philadelphia, 1949), pp. 31-36.

15. The manuscript reads *"ocho patios grandes cada uno con su corredor."* Relación del suceso, AGI, Patronato, 20, and translated in Hammond and Rey, *Narratives*, pp. 284-94. The outstanding discussion of Pecos architecture is Kidder's *Pecos, New Mexico*.

16. Castañeda, II:4-5. The author of the Relación del suceso, who was with Alvarado, if not Alvarado himself, said that the people of Cicuye "neither plant cotton nor have turkeys because it is fifteen leagues east of the river [the Rio Grande] close to the plains where the cattle roam." Another account claimed that the Pecos had "plenty of maize, beans, and frijoles and some turkeys." Relación postrera de Cíbola, Spanish text and translation in Winship, "Coronado Expedition," also translated in Hammond and Rey, *Narratives*, pp. 308-12.

17. Ibid. Relación del suceso. Castañeda, I:12-13, 15. Bolton, *Coronado*, pp. 179-91. Declarations of Juan Troyano, México, June 9, 1544, and Melchor Pérez, Guadalajara, Aug. 12, 1544, AGI, Justicia, 1021, pieza 4, The Bancroft Library, University of California, Berkeley (BL), Bolton Research Papers (BRP), no. 393. Once the Spaniards had learned from the Arawak Indians in the Caribbean the word cacique, meaning chief, they spread it all over the Americas. In New Mexico it is still used by non-Indians to distinguish a pueblo's "chief priest," the final authority in all matters, from its governor, the "front man" who deals with outsiders. It is most unlikely (Bolton, *Coronado*, pp. 179-80) that Cacique, a leader of the conservative agrarian establishment at Cicuye, accompanied Bigotes and the delegation to Hawikuh.

18. Castañeda, I:13. Castañeda alone among the chroniclers says that Coronado at this point ordered Alvarado back to Cicuye to get the gold bracelet or bracelets. When Bigotes and Cacique denied their existence, the captain arrested the two. Coronado's testimony of September 3, 1544, makes it appear that Alvarado was already at Tiguex with the prisoners when the general arrived from Zuñi. Ham-

mond and Rey, *Narratives,* pp. 326-27.

19. Bolton, *Coronado,* pp. 201-30. Chavez, *Coronado's Friars,* pp. 52-54. Riley, "Communication," pp. 303-06.

20. Castañeda, II:5. Coronado's testimony Sept. 3, 1544. Hammond and Rey, *Narratives.* There is still disagreement among anthropologists concerning the identity of the Teyas. The recent interpretation of Dolores A. Gunnerson, *The Jicarilla Apaches: A Study in Survival* (DeKalb, Ill., 1974), pp. 12-74, making them ancestors of the Eastern or Plains Apaches, has been roundly challenged by Morris E. Opler in a review article in *Plains Anthropologist,* vol. 20 (1975), pp. 150-57. It would appear that Baltazar de Obregón, writing in 1584, had got the allusion to the Teya seige of Cicuye mixed up with one of the actions of the Coronado expedition. He had Coronado attacking Cicuye with artillery for eighty days (elsewhere over forty)! Still, the pueblo held out, compelling the Spaniards to leave the land of this "valiant and indomitable people." Historia de los descubrimientos antiguos y modernos de la Nueva España y Nuevo México, 1584, AGI, Patronato, 22, ramo 7, BL, BRP, no. 406, translated by Hammond and Rey as *Obregón's History of 16th Century Explorations in Western America* (Los Angeles, 1928), pp. 18, 335.

21. Coronado's testimony, Sept. 3, 1544, Hammond and Rey, *Narratives,* p. 331.

22. Relación del suceso. Bolton, *Coronado,* pp. 230-35.

23. Castañeda, I:19, 21.

24. This is the interpretation of Albert H. Schroeder, "A Re-analysis of the Routes of Coronado and Oñate into the Plains in 1541 and 1601," *Plains Anthropologist,* vol. 7, no. 15 (Feb. 1962), pp. 2-23. Bolton thought the expedition built its bridge over the Pecos River near Anton Chico.

25. Waldo R. Wedel, *An Introduction to Kansas Archeology,* Bureau of American Ethnology, Bulletin 174 (Washington, D.C., 1959), pp. 60-65.

26. Castañeda, I:21. Bolton, *Coronado,* pp. 238-304.

27. Juan de Contreras quoted by Bolton, *Coronado,* p. 303. Pérez denied that he was present. Pérez, Aug. 12, 1544, AGI, Justicia, 1021.

28. Castañeda, I:22. Bolton, *Coronado,* pp. 305-12. A native of Borobia, east of Soria, Tristán de Luna y Arellano, by his own admission "the friend and associate of viceroys and principal men in New Spain," in 1559 led a large, ill-fated sea expedition to colonize La Florida. See Herbert Ingram Priestly, *Tristán de Luna, Conquistador of the Old South* (Glendale, 1936).

29. Chavez, *Coronado's Friars,* pp. 41-43, 58-62.

30. Jaramillo's narrative, Hammond and Rey, *Narratives,* pp. 295-307. Jaramillo stated further that some Indians from New Spain stayed because Brother Luis did. Two blacks, one named Sebastián who belonged to Jaramillo and the other owned by Melchor Pérez, also remained behind. None of the other chroniclers mentions them. In 1583 Antonio de Espejo met one of the Mexican Indians still living at Cicuye. See below, p. 43.

31. Castañeda, III:4. Chavez, *Coronado's Friars,* pp. 28-29, 55, 62-72. As an explanation of Fray Luis de Úbeda's choice of Cicuye, Chavez suggests that the elderly lay brother might have stayed there previously in 1541 while the army was off exploring.

32. Ibid., pp. 73-74.

Chapter II, page 31

1. Troyano to the king, México, Dec. 20, 1568, AGI, Mex., 168. Paso y Troncoso, *Epistolario,* X, pp. 262-77.

2. For a lucid treatment of the Chichimeca War and what it meant to subsequent Spanish expansion northward, see Philip Wayne Powell, *Soldiers, Indians, and Silver: The Northward Advance of New Spain 1550-1600* (Berkeley and Los Angeles, 1952), and on Zacatecas, Peter John Bakewell, *Silver Mining and Society in Colonial Mexico, Zacatecas, 1546-1700* (Cambridge, 1971).

3. Fray Cintos de San Francisco to Philip II, México, July 20, 1561, Joaquín García Icazbalceta, ed., *Códice franciscano, Nueva colección de documentos para la historia de México*, vol. 2 (México, 1941), pp. 217-28. See the editor's introduction to Alonso de Zorita, *Life and Labor in Ancient Mexico*, ed. Benjamin Keen (New Brunswick, N.J., 1963), pp. 46-50. Chavez, *Oroz Codex*, pp. 273-76. In 1585, the Third Mexican Provincial Council of the Church, which heard a renewed Franciscan plea for peaceful persuasion, roundly condemned war by fire and blood. Stafford Poole, " 'War by Fire and Blood,' The Church and the Chichimecas 1585," *The Americas*, vol. 22 (1965), pp. 115-37.

4. Kieran R. McCarty, "Los franciscanos en la frontera chichimeca," *Historia Mexicana*, vol. 11 (1962), pp. 321-60. Powell, "Franciscans on the Silver Frontier of Old Mexico," *The Americas*, vol. 3 (1947), pp. 295-310. J. Lloyd Mecham, *Francisco de Ibarra and Nueva Vizcaya* (Durham, N.C., 1972). Hammond and Rey, *Obregón's History*. Robert C. West, *The Mining Community in Northern New Spain: The Parral Mining District, Ibero-Americana*, vol. 30 (Berkeley and Los Angeles, 1949).

5. Viceroy Conde de Coruña to the king, México, Nov. 1, 1582, Hammond and Rey, *The Rediscovery of New Mexico, 1580-1594* (Albuquerque, 1966), pp. 123-24. Testimonies of Pedro Bustamante and Hernán Gallegos, México, May 16, 1582, ibid., pp. 127-38.

6. Chavez, *Oroz Codex*, pp. 336-40. Chavez argues that Brother Rodríguez was a dupe of the mercenary soldiers from the beginning. See also his article "The Gallegos Relación Reconsidered," NMHR, vol. 23 (1948), pp. 1-22. Hammond and Rey, *Rediscovery*, p. 8, aver that "these men . . . were moved by a spirit of Christian idealism and sacrifice in bringing the light of civilization to new lands and peoples, a desire to serve both God and king, and the hope of bettering their own fortunes." Baltazar de Obregón said that Rodríguez was from Ayamonte and Santa María from Valencia. Hammond and Rey, *Obregon's History*, pp. 268-69.

7. Hammond and Rey, *Rediscovery*, summarize the expedition of 1581-1582 in their introduction, pp. 6-15, 51-63, and publish the documents in translation, pp. 67-150. Another account is in the same editors' *Obregón's History*, pp. 268-313.

8. The Franciscan chronicler Fray Pedro Oroz credited the three friars with naming New Mexico. Chavez, *Oroz Codex*, pp. 337-38. Cf. Lansing B. Bloom, "Who Discovered New Mexico?," NMHR, vol. 15 (1940), pp. 105-07.

9. For a discussion of the identity of Nueva Tlaxcala, see Hammond and Rey, *Rediscovery*, pp. 59-60. Schroeder does not agree that Gallegos' Nueva Tlaxcala was Cicuye, or Pecos. He opts for the pueblo of Gipuy on Galisteo Creek. Schroeder and Dan S. Matson, eds., *A Colony on the Move: Gaspar Castaño de Sosa's Journal, 1590-1591* (Santa Fe, 1965), p. 158. Even though the rest of the details are inconclusive, the alleged size of the pueblo would seem to favor Pecos. Gallegos claimed that the natives of this pueblo communicated by signs, while Pedro de Bustamante mentioned "an interpreter of these natives." This interpreter may have been the Mexican Indian from Coronado's expedition mentioned at Pecos in connection with the visit of Espejo in 1583.

10. Chavez, *Oroz Codex*, p. 338, and "Gallegos Relación," pp.

9-15, follows Adolph Bandelier in fixing the place of Santa María's death just south of Paa-ko pueblo. Marjorie F. Lambert, *Paa-ko, Archaeological Chronicle of an Indian Village in North Central New Mexico* (Santa Fe, 1954) pp. 5-7, believes that the friar had traveled well south of this Tano pueblo into the territory of the eastern Tiwas or the Tompiros. Hammond and Rey, *Rediscovery,* p. 222.

11. Rodrigo del Río de Losa, before Nov. 1, 1582, quoted in Bloom, "Who Discovered New Mexico," p. 106.

12. For summary and documents of the 1582-1583 expedition, see Hammond and Rey, *Rediscovery,* pp. 15-28, 153-242, and *Obregón's History,* pp. 315-39.

13. Report of Antonio de Espejo, Santa Bárbara, Oct. 1583, Hammond and Rey, *Rediscovery,* pp. 213-31.

14. Pérez de Luján's account, ibid., p. 204. Neither Espejo nor Obregón mentions this event.

15. Obregón, Historia, Hammond and Rey, *Obregón's History,* p. 335.

16. Ibid., pp. 335-36. Pérez de Luján's account.

17. Hammond and Rey, *Rediscovery,* p. 236. See the editor's introduction in Chavez, *Oroz Codex.*

18. Ibid., p. 62.

19. Hanke, *Aristotle and the American Indians* (Bloomington, Ind., 1959), pp. 74-88.

20. Philip II to Viceroy Conde de Coruña, Madrid, Apr. 19, 1583, AGI, Mex., 1064. François Chevalier, *Land and Society in Colonial Mexico: The Great Hacienda,* trans. Alvin Eustis, ed. Lesley Byrd Simpson (Berkeley and Los Angeles, 1966), pp. 46-47, 148-84.

21. Excerpt of Marqués de Villamanrique to Luis de Velasco, Texcoco, Feb. 14, 1590, Hammond and Rey, *Rediscovery,* pp. 296-98. Hammond and Rey (ibid., pp. 28-48), basing their summary on "Castaño's Memoria" and other primary sources (pp. 245-320), present the Castaño entrada in a less favorable light than do Schroeder and Matson in their edition of the Memoria alone. The Memoria was printed twice in *the Colección de documentos inéditos relativos al descubrimiento, conquista y organización de las antiguas posesiones españolas de América y Oceanía* (DII), 42 vols. (Madrid 1864-1884), IV, pp. 283-354, and XV, pp. 191-261.

22. Testimony of Cristóbal Martín, Las Milpas, Aug. 24, 1591, et al., AGI, Mex., 220.

23. Castaño's Memoria. Schroeder and Matson, in *Colony on the Move,* pay particular attention to the expedition's route and provide photographs and excellent maps of the country traversed.

24. The first use of the name Pecos by Europeans is usually attributed to the Oñate expedition of 1598.

25. Castaño's Memoria, DII, XV, pp. 221-22.

26. Martín. Aug. 24, 1591, AGI, Mex., 220. Alonso Jáimez, who commented on the ignominious return of Heredia and company, corroborated Martín's account, adding that the Spaniards had left their gear in certain rooms of the pueblo. Testimony of Jáimez, Siete Mártires, July 10, 1591, ibid.

27. Castaño's Memoria, DII, XV, pp. 223-41. Schroeder and Matson comment (*Colony on the Move,* pp. 81-103) at length on the description of Pecos as it relates to the archaeological work of Kidder and others. The testimonies of Martín and Jáimez, both participants, confirm the Memoria's account of the battle, though they are far less detailed. They mention seeing for certain only one dead Pecos. AGI, Mex., 220.

28. Castaño's Memoria, DII, XV, pp. 252-53.

29. Velasco to Morlete, México, Oct. 1, 1590, Hammond and

Rey, *Reconquest*, pp. 298-301.

30. See Powell, *Soldiers, Indians, and Silver*, pp. 181-223.

31. Velasco to the king, México, Feb. 23, 1591, Hammond and Rey, *Rediscovery*, pp. 301-03.

32. Castaño to Velasco, "the Río del Norte route," July 27, 1591, et al., ibid., pp. 305-20.

33. Velasco to the king, México, Feb. 28, 1592, ibid., pp. 312-14.

Chapter III, pages 68-77

1. Chevalier, *Land and Society*, pp. 148-84. The remarkable 1589 contract between Villamanrique and Lomas is in AGI, Patronato, 22, and printed in DII, XV, pp. 54-80. A historical novel by Philip Wayne (Powell), *Ponzoña en Las Nieves* (Madrid, 1966), captures the bitterness of the Lomas-Urdiñola rivalry.

2. Hammond and Rey have published in translation most of the Oñate documents along with an editorial summary in *Don Juan de Oñate, Colonizer of New Mexico, 1595-1628*, 2 vols. (Albuquerque, 1953). Some of the same documents, and some others, were published earlier in both Spanish and English by Charles Wilson Hackett in *Historical Documents relating to New Mexico, Nueva Vizcaya, and Approaches Thereto, to 1773. Collected by Adolph F. A. Bandelier and Fanny R. Bandelier*, 3 vols. (Washington, D.C., 1923-1937), I, pp. 193-487. For a prose translation of Gaspar Pérez de Villagrá's epic *Historia*, covering events through the battle of Ácoma, see *History of New Mexico by Gaspar Pérez de Villagrá, Alcalá, 1610*, trans. Gilberto Espinosa (Los Angeles, 1933).

3. Appointment of Oñate, Velasco, México, Oct. 21, 1595, Hammond and Rey, *Oñate*, I, pp. 59-64. Hammond and Rey, *Rediscovery*, pp. 48-50, 323-26.

4. Monterrey to the king, México, Feb. 28, 1596, Hammond and Rey, *Oñate*, I, pp. 82-85.

5. Oñate to Monterrey, Río de las Nazas, Sept. 13, 1596, Hackett, *Documents*, I, pp. 352-66. Hammond and Rey, *Oñate*, I, pp. 169-79. The documents concerning the Ulloa inspection are in ibid., pp. 94-168.

6. Monterrey to the king, México, Nov. 15, 1596, and the king to Monterrey, Madrid, Apr. 2, 1597, et al., ibid., pp. 183-96. Hackett, *Documents*, I, pp. 376-95, and for the Ponce de León bid, pp. 280-349.

7. The record of the second inspection is in Hammond and Rey, *Oñate*, I, pp. 199-308.

8. Velasco to the king, México, May 26, 1592, Hammond and Rey, *Rediscovery*, pp. 314-16.

9. See Robert Ricard, *The Spiritual Conquest of Mexico*, trans. Lesley Byrd Simpson (Berkeley and Los Angeles, 1966); Chavez, *Oroz Codex*; McCarty, "Los franciscanos;" and France V. Scholes, "Problems in the Early Ecclesiastical History of New Mexico," NMHR, vol. 7 (1932), pp. 32-74. Volume 3 of Agustín de Vetancurt, *Teatro Mexicano: descripción breve de los sucessos exemplares de la Nueva-España en el nuevo mundo occidental de las Indias*, 4 vols. (Madrid, 1960-1961), is a history and description of the province of the Holy Gospel, first published in 1697, by its official chronicler.

10. Monterrey to the king, México, May 11, 1596, Hammond and Rey, *Oñate*, I, pp. 92-93. Ricard, *Spiritual Conquest*, pp. 239-63.

11. Memorial to the viceroy, n.d., Hammond and Rey, *Oñate*, I, pp. 77-80. Monterrey to the king, México, May 1, 1598, ibid., pp. 386-89.

12. Act of taking possession, Apr. 30, 1598, and Itinerario, 1596-1598, AGI, Patronato, 22, Hammond and Rey, *Oñate*, I, pp. 329-36, 309-28.

13. Relación de la jornada y descubrimiento de las vacas de Cíbola, San Juan Bautista, Feb. 23, 1599, AGI, Patronato, 22, Hammond and Rey, *Oñate*, I, pp. 398-405. Itinerario, 1596-1598.

14. Relación de como los padres de San Francisco se encargan de las provincias del Nuevo México, San Juan Bautista, Sept. 8, 1598, AGI, Patronato, 22. It is strange that Hammond and Rey did not publish this important document.

15. Itinerario, 1596-1598, AGI, Patronato, 22; Villagrá, *History*, pp. 147-54.

16. Obediencia y vasallaje a su magestad, San Juan Bautista, Sept. 9, 1598, AGI, Patronato, 22, Hammond and Rey, *Oñate*, I, pp. 342-47.

17. Relación de la jornada y descubrimiento de las vacas, and Itinerario, 1596-1598, AGI, Patronato, 22.

18. Declaration of San Miguel, San Gabriel, Sept. 7, 1601, AGI, Mex., 26, Hammond and Rey, *Oñate*, II, pp. 673-75.

19. Fray Francisco Antonio de la Rosa Figueroa, Becerro general menológico y cronológico de todos los religiosos que de las tres parcialidades conviene, a saber Padres de España, Hijos de Provincia, y Criollos, ha habido en esta Santa Provincia del Santo Evangelio desde su fundación hasta el presente año de 1764, Newberry Library, Chicago, Ayer Collection. Another less orderly version of essentially the same thing, with some added notes on later friars, is the Prontuario general y específico y colectivo de nomenclaturas de todos los religiosos que han habido en esta Santa Provincia del Santo Evangelio desde su fundación, University of Texas Library, Austin, Latin American Manuscripts. Cited hereafter as Becerro and Prontuario. Declaration of San Miguel, Sept. 7, 1601, AGI, Mex., 26. Vetancurt does not even mention Father San Miguel.

20. See Stanley A. Stubbs, Bruce T. Ellis, and Alfred E. Dittert, Jr., " 'Lost' Pecos Church," *El Palacio* (EP), vol. 64 (1957), pp. 67-92; Kidder, *Pecos, New Mexico*, pp. 329-32; and Alden Hayes, *The Four Churches of Pecos* (Albuquerque, 1974). No certain documentary reference to this "lost" Pecos church has yet turned up. It is most unlikely that Fray Luis de Úbeda, the simple lay brother left at Pecos by Coronado in 1542, built it. None of the subsequent sixteenth-century visitors mentioned a church. The first missionary regularly assigned to the pueblo was San Miguel, who stayed only three months late in 1598. For twenty years after that, Pecos had no resident missionary. The consensus today is that the friars next assigned to the pueblo, between 1617 and 1621, built this first Pecos church. But this theory does not square with a telling statement by Fray Andrés Juárez, builder of the massive "second" Pecos church. Writing in October 1622, Juárez emphasized the pueblo's dire need for the church he was erecting, saying that until it was finished the *only* place he had to say Mass was a *jacal,* or adobe hut, in which not half the people would fit. Juárez to the viceroy, Pecos, Oct. 2, 1622, AGN, Civil, 77. Presumably by then San Miguel's 1598 structure was a ruin, having been stripped of its roof and many of its adobes by the Indians after the friar's hasty departure. Admittedly this too is conjecture.

21. The documents concerning the Ácomas' defiance and their defeat are translated in Hammond and Rey, *Oñate*, I, pp. 425-79. See also Villagrá, *History*, pp. 164-268.

22. Oñate to the viceroy, Mar. 2, 1599, Hammond and Rey, *Oñate*, I, pp. 480-88.

23. Declaration of Jusepe Gutiérrez, San Juan Bautista, Feb. 16, 1599, ibid., pp. 416-19, and *Rediscovery*, pp. 323-26.

24. Scholes and Bloom, "Friar Personnel and Mission Chronology, 1598-1629," NMHR, vol. 19 (1944), pp. 320-30.

25. Declaration of Bartolomé Romero, San Gabriel, Oct. 3, 1601, AGI, Mex., 26, Hammond and Rey, *Oñate*, II, pp. 708-11. Romero

also mentioned a church built at one of the Jémez pueblos under the supervision of Fray Alonso Lugo, originally assigned there in September 1598. These early references to New Mexico churches affirm the possibility that San Miguel did indeed build the first Pecos church.

26. Declaration of Ginés de Herrera Orta, México, July 30, 1601, Hammond and Rey, *Oñate,* II, pp. 643-57.

27. Declaration of San Miguel, San Gabriel, Sept. 7, 1601, et al., ibid., pp. 672-91.

28. Escalona to the viceroy, San Gabriel, Oct. 1, 1601, and to his prelate, same date, ibid., pp. 692-700. Fray Pedro de la Cruz, et al., to the viceroy, Cuernavaca, Nov. 13, 1602, ibid., pp. 980-83.

29. Investigation of conditions in New Mexico, México, July 1601, ibid., pp. 623-69. Report of the colonists who remained in New Mexico, San Gabriel, Oct. 1601, ibid., pp. 701-39. Scholes and Bloom, "Friar Personnel," pp. 323-27.

30. Oñate to the viceroy, San Gabriel, Aug. 24, 1607, Hammond and Rey, *Oñate,* II, pp. 1042-45.

31. Montesclaros to the king, México, Mar. 31, 1605, ibid., pp. 1001-05. The king to Montesclaros, Madrid, June 17, 1606, ibid., pp. 1036-38. Velasco to the king, México, Dec. 17, 1608, et al., ibid., pp. 1067-74.

32. Velasco to the king, México, Feb 13, 1609, et al., ibid., pp. 1075-1105. Scholes, "Royal Treasury Records Relating to the Province of New Mexico, 1596-1683," NMHR, vol. 50 (1975), pp. 10-13.

33. See Scholes' vivid studies "Church and State in New Mexico, 1610-1650," NMHR, vol. 11 (1936), pp. 9-76, 145-78, 283-94, 297-349, vol. 12 (1937), pp. 78-106, and "Troublous Times in New Mexico, 1659-1670," ibid., pp. 134-74, 380-452, vol. 13 (1938), pp. 63-84, vol. 15 (1940), pp. 249-68, 369-417, vol. 16 (1941), pp. 15-40, 184-205, 313-27. Both were published separately by the Historical Society of New Mexico (Albuquerque, 1937, 1942). Because the separates are long out of print and scarce, I will cite the installments in NMHR with volume and page. Another seminal study by Scholes is "Civil Government and Society in New Mexico in the Seventeenth Century," NMHR, vol. 10 (1935), pp. 71-111.

34. Velasco's instructions to Peralta, México, Mar. 30, 1609, Hammond and Rey, *Oñate,* II, pp. 1087-91.

35. Scholes and Bloom, "Friar Personnel," pp. 330-36. Father Peinado entered the Franciscan novitiate at the Convento Grande in Mexico City on June 15, 1574, and professed on June 26, 1575. Libro de entradas y profesiones de novicios de este convento del Padre San Francisco de México, 1562-1680, BL, Mexican Manuscripts (M-M) 216-18. This useful source, cited hereafter as LEP, includes only those friars who entered the Order at the Convento Grande, not those invested in Spain or elsewhere.

36. Scholes, "Church and State," XI, pp. 30-50.

37. Fray Francisco de Velasco to the king, Apr. 9, 1609, Hammond and Rey, *Oñate,* II, pp. 1093-97.

38. Excerpts from pertinent articles of the 1573 ordinances were included in the discussion about modifications of Oñate's contract. Ibid., pp. 585-607, 744-45, 958-66.

39. Scholes, "Civil Government," pp. 78-79, 102.

40. Witnesses in the 1601 Valverde investigation claimed that Oñate had not yet allotted any pueblos in encomienda. Hammond and Rey, *Oñate,* II, pp. 630, 641. Evidently he began doing so not long afterward, although details are scarce. In 1606 Oñate attested that he had previously granted the pueblo of Santiago de Jémez to Juan Martínez de Montoya. Scholes, "Juan Martínez de Montoya, Settler and Conquistador of New Mexico," NMHR, vol. 19 (1944), p. 340.

41. Working backwards hypothetically from the early 1660s when

Francisco Gómez Robledo held the entire pueblo of Pecos in encomienda, we may assume that he inherited it from his father Francisco Gómez, one of New Mexico's most prominent soldier-colonists. The elder Gómez, who had previously served the Oñate family, had come to the colony midway through don Juan's governorship. For a sketch of the Gómez clan, see Chavez, *Origins of New Mexico Families* (Santa Fe, 1954), pp. 35-37. Describing an event that took place about 1621, Capt. Francisco Pérez Granillo alluded to the Pecos encomendero without saying who he was. Declaration of Pérez Granillo, Santa Fe, Jan. 27, 1626, AGN, Inquisición (Inq.) 356, ff. 264v-65.

Chapter IV

1. Scholes and Bloom, "Friar Personnel," pp. 332-36.
2. Scholes, "Early Ecclesiastical History."
3. The saint with the flowing white beard, whose appearance at Ácoma was described by the soldier-poet Pérez de Villagrá, has been identified as either St. Paul or St. James. Villagrá, *History*, pp. 264-65. Alonso de Benavides, *Fray Alonso de Benavides' Revised Memorial of 1634*, eds. Frederick Webb Hodge, George P. Hammond, and Agapito Rey (Albuquerque, 1945), pp. 126-27, 166, 196-97.
4. Pedro Zambrano Ortiz, was the son of Tomé Ubero and Juana García Zambrano, also natives of the Canary Islands. LEP, no. 565. Rosa Figueroa, Becerro. Testifying in 1621 Zambrano stated that "two years before, a little more or less," he had been guardian of the convento at Pecos. Declaration of Zambrano, Sandía, Aug. 18, 1621, AGN, Inq., 356, ff. 282v-83v. Scholes and Bloom, "Friar Personnel," NMHR, vol. 20 (1945), pp. 58, 66.
5. Fr. Andrés Juárez to the viceroy, Pecos, Oct. 2, 1622, AGN, Civil, 77, exp. 14. Francisco J. Santamaría, in his *Diccionario de Mejicanismos* (México, 1959), defines the word *jacal* (from Nahuatl *xacalli*) as "a hut, commonly made of adobe, with a roof of straw or tajamanil [strips of wood]." It is also used in New Mexico for log and adobe construction. For a summary of the South Pueblo puzzle to 1958, see Kidder, *Pecos, New Mexico*, pp. 106-09, 121. He came to believe that neither Coronado's men nor those of Castaño had mentioned this South Pueblo because "low and perhaps discontinuous structures would have failed to impress them." Schroeder and Matson, *Colony on the Move*, p. 93, do not think the South Pueblo was there at all in 1540 or 1590.
6. Scholes, "Church and State," XI, p. 146.
7. Eleanor B. Adams and John E. Longhurst, "New Mexico and the Sack of Rome: One Hundred Years Later," NMHR, vol. 28 (1953), pp. 243-50.
8. Zambrano, Aug. 18, 1621, AGN, Inq., 356, ff. 282v-83v. Scholes catalogues the friars' manifold charges against Eulate in "Church and State," XI, pp. 146-51.
9. Three examples of these vales are in AGN, Inq., 356, ff. 275-76. Fray Pedro de Ortega, Zambrano's successor at Pecos, claimed that three or four such permits were used in the pueblo while he was there. Declaration of Ortega, Sandía, Sept. 2, 1621, ibid., ff.288-89.
10. Zambrano, Aug. 18, 1621, AGN, Inq., 356, ff. 282v-83v. Zambrano to the viceroy, Galisteo, Oct. 7, 1622, AGN, Civil, 77, exp. 14. Declarations of Zambrano, Santo Domingo, Apr. 20, 1626, AGN, Inq., 356, ff. 261-61v, 277-81. Zambrano to the viceroy, Nuevo México, Nov. 6, 1636, AGN, Provincias Internas (PI), 35, exp. 3.
11. Benavides, *Revised Memorial*, p. 97. LEP, no. 605. Rosa Figueroa, Becerro.

12. Declaration of Ortega, Santa Fe, Jan. 27, 1626, AGN, Inq., 356, ff. 265-65v. Ortega, Sept. 2, 1621, ibid., ff. 288-89.

13. "In view of the extreme rarity of stone 'idols' in the Southwest, it is remarkable that no less than four should have been found in the comparatively small amount of digging done at Pecos." Kidder, *Artifacts of Pecos*, p. 86. This work by Kidder contains excellent illustrations and descriptions of a variety of Pecos ceremonial objects. See also Lambert, "A Rare Stone Humpbacked Figurine from Pecos, New Mexico," EP, vol. 64 (1957), pp. 93-108, and Kidder, *Pecos, New Mexico*, pp. 233-35. On the basis of his excavations of Pecos kivas —meticulously detailed in the latter volume—Kidder believed that the missionaries "in the early 1600's" may have ordered one prominent kiva burned and at least five others filled with refuse. Ibid., pp. 236-40. This, too, may have been part of Father Ortega's campaign.

14. Gómez, a leader of the New Mexico encomendero class, and an encomendero himself, almost certainly bequeathed his encomiendas to his son, Francisco Gómez Robeldo, later the Pecos encomendero of record. That the elder Gómez who became, in the words of Chavez, "the most outstanding military official in New Mexico during his lifetime" should have held the Pecos encomienda, considered the richest in the province, stands to reason. Chavez, *Families*, pp. 35-36.

15. Declaration of Pérez Granillo as recorded and affirmed by Ortega, Santa Fe, Jan. 27, 1626, AGN, Inq., 356, ff. 264v-65. Ortega, Sept. 2, 1621, ibid., ff. 288-89. Zambrano, Aug. 18, 1621, ibid., ff. 282v-83. Scholes, "Church and State," XI, p. 169. Since Pérez Granillo, testifying in January 1626, stated that the incident had taken place about five years before, and since the customary time for collecting tribute was either May or October, the date was probably October of 1620 or the following May.

16. Mrs. Edward E. Ayer translated Benavides' words in *The Memorial of Fray Alonso de Benavides, 1630* (Chicago, 1916), p. 22, as follows: "a monastery and a very splendid [*luzido*] temple, of distinguished workmanship and beauty." The Spanish (p. 103) reads *"un Convento y Templo muy luzido, de particular hechura y curiosidad."* Peter P. Forestal, *Benavides' Memorial of 1630* (Washington, D.C., 1954), p. 23, has it "a friary and a very magnificent church of unique architecture and beauty." In his revised manuscript Memorial of 1634, Benavides wrote *"un convento y iglesia de particular hechura y curiosidad muy capaz en que cabe toda la gente del pueblo,"* which Hodge, Hammond, and Rey, *Benavides' Revised Memorial*, p. 67, rendered "a convent and church of peculiar construction and beauty, very spacious, with room for all the people of the pueblo."

17. See the discussion of church placement with regard to native resistance, mutual distrust, room for development, and other factors in George Kubler, *The Religious Architecture of New Mexico*, 4th ed. (Albuquerque, 1972), pp. 15-23.

18. Chavez, "The Carpenter Pueblo," *New Mexico Magazine*, vol. 49, nos. 9-10 (1971), pp. 27-28.

19. Hayes, *Four Churches*, p. 20.

20. Declarations of Fr. Pedro Haro de la Cueva, Fr. Andrés Juárez, and Fr. Andrés Bautista, Sandía, Aug. 22, 1621, and Sept. 2, 1621, AGN, Inq., 356, ff. 286-88, 289v-90. Ortega, Sept. 2, 1621, ibid., ff. 288-89. Chavez, *Families*, pp. 63, 95, 105.

21. Zambrano, Aug. 18, 1621, AGN, Inq., 356, ff. 282v-83.

22. Scholes, "Church and State," XI, pp. 150-56.

23. LEP, no. 554. Madoz, *Diccionario*, VIII, pp. 230-33.

24. The play, probably written several years before, first appeared in print in volume twelve of the author's works published in Madrid in 1619.

25. Scholes and Bloom, "Friar Personnel," XIX, pp. 330-31.

The friar signed his name in only one way. It looks like Juárez but could as easily be Suárez. The mark that appears above the signature could be a dot of the J or an accent on the a. Contemporaries also wrote his name Xuárez or Zuárez. All are variant spellings of a surname derived from the word *suero* (serum) extended to mean blood, family, or race. Benavides, in his 1634 Memorial, used the Portuguese spelling, Soares.

26. For a glimpse of Archbishop-Viceroy García Guerra and the world he lived in, see Irving A. Leonard, *Baroque Times in Old Mexico: Seventeenth-Century Persons, Places, and Practices* (Ann Arbor, 1966), pp. 1-20.

27. A listing of the supplies procured by Ordóñez, with prices and names of merchants and craftsmen from whom he bought them, is in AGI, Contaduría, 714-15. A reimbursement voucher in Romero's favor is in ibid., 850.

28. Pérez Huerta, Relación verdadera, AGN, Inq., 316. Scholes, "Church and State," XI, pp. 30, 58-59, which includes a transcription of the pertinent passage.

29. Zambrano, Aug. 18, 1621, AGN, Inq., 356, ff. 282v-83. Pérez Huerta, Relación verdadera, AGN, Inq., 316. Scholes, "Church and State," XI, pp. 44-45.

30. Ibid., pp. 151-60.

31. Benavides, *Revised Memorial*, pp. 97-98.

32. Juárez to the viceroy, Oct. 2, 1622, AGN, Civil, 77, exp. 14. This statement all but rules out the possibility that Juárez' immediate predecessors, Zambrano or Ortega, built the "lost" church northeast of the pueblo. Even though it was small, he would not have described it— had it been standing or in use—as a jacal.

33. Ibid.

34. Peinado to the viceroy, Chililí, Oct. 4, 1622, et al., AGN, Civil, 77, exp. 14.

35. The dimensions are from Hayes, *Four Churches*.

36. Benavides, *Memorial* (Ayer), p. 121.

37. Such complaints were common in sixteenth-century New Spain where the friars were accused of building overly sumptuous and costly structures to the detriment of the Indians. See Ricard, *Spiritual Conquest*, pp. 170-75.

38. Declaration of Juárez, Santo Domingo, June 13, 1626, AGN, Inq., 356, ff. 273v-74. Declaration of Alonso Varela, Santa Fe, May 19, 1626, ibid., ff. 269-69v.

39. Benavides, *Memorial* (Ayer), p. 103.

40. Benavides referred to church and convento as one. There is no reason to believe that Father Juárez after he completed the church waited long to lay up the convento (Hayes, *Four Churches*, pp. 23-28) or that he was not the builder of the two-story west side mentioned in the 1660s. Francisco de Madrid et al., Santa Fe, Apr. 22, 1664, AGN, Inq., 507, ff. 343v-46.

41. Vetancurt, *Teatro Mexicano*, III, p. 277.

42. Kubler, *Religious Architecture*, p. xii. Jean Pinkley, rediscoverer of the Juárez church, died before the project was finished. Roland S. Richert and Alden C. Hayes carried on. Hayes's *Four Churches* is a summary of "the archeology of the historic structures at Pecos."

43. Benavides, *Revised Memorial*, p. 67.

44. Ibid., pp. 100-02. See Ricard's *Spiritual Conquest* for a detailed analysis of the sixteenth-century missionary regime in New Spain, of which the later New Mexican experience was, in most respects, an offshoot.

45. On the basis of fragmentary evidence, archaeologists venture for the South Pueblo "a late occupation with considerable repair and remodeling." Kidder, *Pecos, New Mexico*, p. 108. Considerable adobe

construction, potsherds, and other refuse indicate that it was lived in during the seventeenth century, but precisely when is still in doubt. Benavides wrote of intra-pueblo civil wars between "warriors" and "sorcerers," which Hodge discounted completely as a Mexican characteristic wrongly ascribed to the Pueblos. Benavides, *Revised Memorial,* pp. 42-43, 238.

46. Chavez, "Carpenter Pueblo,", pp. 32-33, ranks the emigration of Pecos carpenters in third place behind Comanche hostility and disease as a probable cause of the pueblo's drastic eighteenth-century decline. He does not mention internal dissension.

47. Benavides, *Revised Memorial,* p. 67. Hammond and Rey, *Oñate,* II, pp. 994-1000. The names of the master carpenters who taught the Pecos are unknown. An entry-by-entry reading of the seventeenth-century section of Chavez' *Families* failed to turn up a single carpenter.

48. See the lists of items shipped with Benavides in 1625. Benavides, *Revised Memorial,* pp. 117-18.

49. Visitation of Gov. Gervasio Cruzat y Góngora, Pecos, July 28, 1733, Spanish Archives of New Mexico, State Records Center and Archives, Santa Fe (SANM), Series II, no. 389. See also nos. 323 and 470.

50. Benavides, *Memorial* (Ayer), pp. 55-56, 80.

51. Hammond and Rey, *Oñate,* I, pp. 400-01. A preliminary report on Apache camp sites near Pecos is James H. and Dolores A. Gunnerson, "Evidence of Apaches at Pecos," EP, vol. 76, no. 3 (1970), pp. 1-6.

52. Kidder, *Pecos, New Mexico,* pp. 313-14, and *Artifacts,* pp. 42-44. Dolores A. Gunnerson, "The Southern Athabascans: Their Arrival in the Southwest," EP, vol. 63 (1956), pp. 346-65. See also Charles L. Kenner, *A History of New Mexican-Plains Indian Relations* (Norman, 1969), pp. 4-12. In the words of Dolores Gunnerson, *Jicarilla Apaches,* p. 18, Pecos "seems to have been the most important center for trade with the Plains Apaches even before Coronado's time."

53. Juárez to the viceroy, Oct. 2, 1622, AGN, Civil, 77, exp. 14.

54. Benavides, *Memorial* (Ayer), pp. 55, 153. Robert H. Lowie, *Indians of the Plains* (Garden City, N.Y., 1963), p. 67. As used in New Mexico, the Spanish terms for hides and skins referred more to the quality of the piece than to the animal from which it came. The word *gamuza* (Spanish for the small goat-like European antelope, or chamois), which I have translated "buckskin," was used for the tanned skin of either antelope or deer. The buckskin became a standard unit of trade, valued at one peso in the seventeenth century, like the Anglo-American "buck" for a dollar. The *cuero de cíbola* was a buffalo rawhide. *Anta* (Spanish for elk, moose, and sometimes buffalo) referred to the tanned skin of a buffalo or elk. For lack of a better phrase, I have translated it "buffalo or elkskin." I have rendered the terms *anta gorda* and *anta delgada,* indicating thickness, "heavy" and "light." *Anta blanca,* which I have left "white buffalo or elkskin," had a particular meaning in New Mexico, according to Fray Francisco Atanasio Domínguez. It meant a large, specially prepared buffalo (or elk?) skin used as a "canvas" for a painting. Adams and Chavez, *The Missions of New Mexico, 1776, A Description by Fray Francisco Atanasio Domínguez, with Other Contemporary Documents* (Albuquerque, 1956), pp. 17, 252. A *tecoa,* which I have made a "fine tanned skin," was of good enough quality for use as tipi material. Testimonio de las demandas, Santa Fe, Oct. 29, 1661, AGN, Tierras, 3286.

55. Benavides, *Revised Memorial,* pp. 91-92.

56. Benavides, *Memorial* (Ayer), pp. 56-57, 155-57.

57. Fr. Alonso de Posada, who resided at Pecos between 1663 and 1665, described briefly the 1634 Alonso Baca expedition in a report he

was asked to prepare during the LaSalle scare. Posada, *Informe*, ca. 1686, AGN, *Historia*, 3. This document, printed in various places, appeared most recently in *Documentos para servir a la historia del Nuevo México* (Madrid, 1962), pp. 460-84. S. Lyman Tyler and H. Darrel Taylor edited and translated it as "The Report of Fray Alonso de Posada in Relation to Quivira and Teguayo," NMHR, vol. 33 (1958), pp. 285-314.

58. Trial of Diego Pérez Romero, 1662-1665, AGN, Inq., 586; summarized by Scholes in "Troublous Times," XV, pp. 392-98. Chavez, *Families* p. 87. For the volatile Gaspar Pérez' own brush with the Inquisition, see Scholes, "First Decade of the Inquisition in New Mexico," NMHR, vol. 10 (1935), pp. 226-28. Cf. below, pp. 194-96.

59. Scholes, "Church and State," XI, pp. 162-64, and "First Decade of the Inquisition," pp. 201-06.

60. Scholes and Bloom, "Friar Personnel," XX, pp. 72-80. Benavides, *Revised Memorial*.

61. Ibid., pp. 97-98. The appointment of Ortega as notary of the Holy Office as well as his account of Benavides' grand entrance into Santa Fe are included as appendices on pp. 125-29.

62. Ibid., pp. 89-90. Gunnerson, *Jicarilla Apaches*, pp. 70-74, 78-79.

63. Bloom, ed., "Fray Estevan de Perea's *Relación*," NMHR, vol. 8 (1933), p. 226.

64. Benavides, *Revised Memorial*, p. 90.

65. Ibid., pp. 92-95. Vetancurt, *Teatro Mexicano*, III, pp. 260-61. For a discussion of the various striped peoples called Jumanos by the Spaniards, see Scholes and H. P. Mera, "Some Aspects of the Jumano Problem," *Contributions to American Anthropology and History*, vol. 4, no. 34 (1940), Carnegie Institution Publications, no. 523, pp. 265-99. The Jumanos of the plains may have been Coronado's Teyas. Schroeder, "Re-Analysis," p. 20.

66. Benavides, *Revised Memorial*, p. 99. Account of the conversion of New Mexico presented to the Sacred Congregation of the Propagation of the Faith, Apr. 2, 1634, ibid., p. 164.

67. Posada, *Informe*, says that Ortega, whose first name he had wrong, stayed six months "and no harm befell him." Although Benavides implies that Fray Pedro met his end on the plains, it is possible that Ortega took over from Fray Francisco de Letrado at the pueblo of Las Humanas and died there in 1632 or soon after. That could account, at least in part, for the long interruption of missionary activity at that pueblo. Benavides, *Revised Memorial*, pp. 71, 96, 99. Account of the conversion, ibid., p. 164.

68. Benavides, *Revised Memorial*, p. 69. Bloom, "Perea's *Relación*," pp. 226-34.

69. Benavides, Tanto que se sacó de una carta, May 15, 1631, *Revised Memorial*, pp. 135-49. For a convincing account of how the enraptured and enthusiastic Benavides used María de Ágreda, unwittingly bringing her to the attention of the Inquisition, see T. D. Kendrick, *Mary of Agreda: The Life and Legend of A Spanish Nun* (London, 1967), pp. 28-45.

70. Again Scholes is the authority. See his "The Supply Service of the New Mexican Missions in the Seventeenth Century," NMHR, vol. 5 (1930), pp. 93-115, 186-210, 386-404, which includes the text of the 1631 contract.

71. Benavides, *Revised Memorial*, pp. 10-17, 76-80.

72. Chavez, "The Unique Tomb of Fathers Zárate and de la Llana in Santa Fe," NMHR, vol. 40, pp. 105, 113-14 n. 6. This is Fray Angelico's interpretation, which he admits is a guess.

73. See Kendrick, *Mary of Agreda*, and Carlos Seco Serrano, ed., *Cartas de Sor María de Jesús de Ágreda y de Felipe IV*, in *Biblioteca de Autores Españoles*, vols. 108-09 (Madrid, 1968).

74. Perea quoted by Scholes, "First Decade of the Inquisition," p. 217.

75. Ibid., pp. 214-26.

76. Declaration and ratification of Tomé Domínguez, Quarai, May 26-27, 1633, AGN, Inq., 380, exp. 2, ff. 250-50v. Scholes, "First Decade of the Inquisition," p. 228.

77. Ratifications of Nicolás Ortiz, Adrián Gutiérrez, and Nicolás de Ávila, Quarai, Apr. 11, 1634, AGN, Inq., 380, exp. 2, ff. 238-39v. Scholes, "First Decade of the Inquisition," p. 229.

78. Declaration and ratification of Yumar Pérez de Bustillo, Santa Fe, Feb. 19, 1635, AGN, Inq., 380, exp. 2, ff. 254v-55.

79. Scholes thinks this one mention of Fray Martín del Espíritu Santo might refer instead to the martyr Martín de Arvide. Benavides, *Revised Memorial*, pp. 83, 251.

80. Scholes, "Church and State," IX, pp. 293 n. 14, 316. Scholes and Bloom, "Friar Personnel," XIX, pp. 332n, XX, 66n. Scholes, "Supply Service," p. 209. Domingo del Espíritu Santo does not appear in the LEP or elsewhere under that name.

81. Antonio was the son of Juan de Ibargaray and Elvira (illegible). LEP, no. 840. Rosa Figueroa, Becerro. Ratifications of Alonso Martín Barba and Inés Montoya, Santa Fe, Feb. 18-19, 1635, AGN, Inq., 380, exp. 2, ff. 243v-44v. Ibargaray to the viceroy, Pecos, Nov. 20, 1636, AGN, PI, 35, exp. 3

82. Perea quoted by Scholes in "Church and State," XI, pp. 284-86.

83. Ibargaray to the viceroy, Nov. 20, 1636, AGN, PI, 35, exp. 3. The letter was published in *Autos sobre quejas de los religiosos franciscanos del Nuevo México, 1636,* ed. Vargas Rea (México, 1947), pp. 25-28. Fernando Ocaranza, *Establecimientos franciscanos en el misterioso reino de Nuevo México* (México, 1934), pp. 57-62, summarized the several friars' letters. Scholes, "Church and State," XI, pp. 286-90.

84. Declaration of Fr. Juan de San José, Quarai, July 28, 1638, AGN, Inq., 385, exp. 15, ff. 5-6. Declaration of Cristóbal Enríquez, Sandía, Sept. 11, 1638, ibid., ff. 16-16v. Scholes, "Church and State," XI, pp. 297-302. Chavez, *Families,* pp. 28, 97.

85. Declaration of Francisco de Salazar, Santa Fe, July 5, 1641, AGI, Patronato, 244, ramo 7. Scholes, "Church and State," XI, p. 327. Jack D. Forbes, *Apache, Navaho, and Spaniard* (Norman, 1960), p. 132, mistakenly had Rosa taking the priest of Pecos as a captive to Santa Fe. The name of Fray Antonio Jiménez was supplied by witnesses testifying before Fray Tomás Manso in August 1644. AGI, Patronato, 244, ramo 7. He may have been one of two unidentified lay brothers in New Mexico at the end of 1629. Scholes and Bloom, "Friar Personnel," XX, p. 72. Nothing else is known about him.

86. Declarations of Pedro Varela, Agustín de Carbajal, and Alonso Baca, Santo Domingo, Aug. 19 and 20, 1644, AGI, Patronato, 244, ramo 7.

87. Salazar, July 5, 1644, ibid.

88. Francisco Gómez to the viceroy, Santa Fe, Oct. 26, 1638, AGN, PI, 34.

89. Scholes, "Church and State," XI, pp. 302-22. Salas et al., Santo Domingo, Mar. 16, 1640, AGI, Patronato, 244, ramo 7. A number of documents, including the cabildo's report to the viceroy, Feb. 21, 1639, have been translated in Hackett, *Documents,* III, pp. 47-74.

90. Declaration of Carbajal and Baca, Aug. 19 and 20, 1644, AGI, Patronato, 244, ramo 7. In September 1638, Juárez was described as "preacher and guardian of the convento of San Francisco de Nambé and definitor of the custody, fifty-nine years old or a little more or less." Declaration of Juárez, Sandía, Sept. 11, 1638, AGN,

Inq., 385, exp. 15, f. 7v. That made him three years older than he would have been had he really been twenty-six at his investiture on December 4, 1608.

91. Scholes, "Church and State," XI, pp. 322-25.

92. Luis de Rosas to Juan de Palafox, Santa Fe, Sept. 29, 1641, BL, M-M 1908.

93. Scholes, "Church and State," XII, pp. 78-87.

94. Gov. Alonso Pacheco y Heredia, Santa Fe, July 21, 1643, AGI, Patronato, 244, ramo 7.

95. Gov. Pacheco, Santa Fe, July 26, 1643, ibid.

96. Scholes, "Church and State," XII, pp. 87-98.

97. Fr. Juan de Salas et al. to Fr. Juan de Prada, Santo Domingo, Sept. 10, 1644, AGI, Patronato, 244, ramo 7. Antonio de Ibargaray and Domingo del Espíritu Santo were among the twenty-one friars who signed. Andrés Juárez, perhaps too ill to travel, did not.

98. This letter, summarized by Scholes in "Church and State," XII, pp. 98-100, is cited as Juárez to the king, Oct. 23, 1647, AGN, Reales Cédulas, 3, no. 103. The noncommittal royal decree in response is there but the letter is not.

99. Declaration of Diego López Sambrano, Hacienda de Luis Carbajal, Dec. 22, 1681, Hackett and Shelby, eds., *Revolt of the Pueblo Indians of New Mexico and Otermín's Attempted Reconquest, 1680-1682*, 2 vols. (Albuquerque, 1942), II, pp. 298-99. Declaration of Juan Domínguez de Mendoza, Río del Norte, Dec. 20, 1681, ibid., p. 266.

100. Scholes, "Supply Service," pp. 192-96. Charles W. Polzer, "The Franciscan Entrada into Sonora, 1645-1652: A Jesuit Chronicle," *Arizona and the West* (AW), vol. 14 (1972), pp. 253-78.

101. Both Ibargaray and González served terms as custos, the first from sometime in 1654 until April 1656, and the second from sometime after that until the summer of 1659. Scholes, "Troublous Times," XII, pp. 141-42. It is not known how long after 1636 Ibargaray remained at Pecos or how long before 1660 González arrived.

102. Certificación de las noticias, Madrid, May 24, 1664, AGI, Mex., 306. For a translation and corrected dating of the document, see Scholes, "Documents for the History of the New Mexican Missions in the Seventeenth Century," NMHR, vol. 4 (1929), pp. 46-51, and "Correction," NMHR, vol. 19 (1944), pp. 243-46. The Spanish reads: *"tiene muy buena iglesia, culto divino, órgano, y cap.a de música."*

103. See Lincoln Bunce Spiess, "Church Music in Seventeenth-Century New Mexico," NMHR, vol. 40 (1965), pp. 5-21. Cf. below, p. 176.

104. Juárez to the viceroy, Oct. 2. 1622, AGN, Civil, 77 exp. 14. Fr. Diego Zeinos to Fr. Francisco de Vargas, Pecos, Dec. 28, 1694, Biblioteca Nacional, México, New Mexico Documents (BNM), leg. 3, no. 6.

105. Kidder, *Artifacts of Pecos*, p. 4.

Chapter V, pages 174-175

1. Scholes describes the tribulations and the trials of both men in "Troublous Times" and "Supply Service."

2. Rosa Figueroa, Becerro. Fr. Juan de Salas et al. to Fr. Juan de Prada, Santo Domingo, Sept. 10, 1644, AGI, Patronato, 244, ramo 7. Father González took office as custos sometime between 1656 and 1659. Scholes, "Troublous Times," XII, p. 141. Inquisition testimony places him at Pecos as early as June 1660 and as late as July 1662. AGN, Inq., 587, exp. 1, ff. 168-69, and 586, exp. 1, ff. 41-42.

AGN, Inq., 587, exp. 1, ff. 168-69, and 586, exp. 1, ff. 41-42.

3. Fr. Nicolás del Villar to Fr. Juan Ramírez, Galisteo, June 14, 1660, ibid., 587, exp. 1, ff. 29-30. Hackett, *Documents*, III, pp. 151-52.

4. Gov. Luis de Guzmán y Figueroa, Santa Fe, June 30, 1648, quoted in a decree of Gov. Diego de Peñalosa, Santa Fe, Nov. 4, 1661. The document is fully transcribed by Scholes in "Troublous Times," XII, pp. 170-74.

5. Villar to Ramírez, June 14, 1660, AGN, Inq., 587, exp. 1, ff. 29-30. Scholes, "Troublous Times," XII, pp. 418-19.

6. Declaration of González Lobón, Santa Fe, June 14, 1660, AGN, Inq., 587, exp. 1, ff. 168-69. Chavez, *Families*, p. 39. Scholes, "Troublous Times," pp. 422-27.

7. Scholes, "Civil Government," pp. 91-93.

8. Letters of López de Mendizábal to González Bernal, Santa Fe, May 1660-July 1661, AGN, Tierras, 3286. Scholes, "Church and State," XII, p. 90. See the testimony of Nicolás de Aguilar before the Inquisition as translated in Hackett, *Documents*, III, pp. 169-71. Chavez, *Families*, p. 40.

9. Declarations of González and Villar, Santa Fe, Sept. 26 and 27, 1661, AGN, Inq., 593, exp. 1, ff. 52-53v, 59v-61. Scholes, "Troublous Times," XII, pp. 407-09.

10. Ibid., pp. 161-64, 434-41.

11. Ibid., pp. 441-47, and XIII, pp 63-66. The complete record of López' residencia, the only one come to light for a pre-1680 New Mexico governor, is the third part of a three-volume López-Peñalosa collection, the Concurso de Peñalosa, in AGN, Tierras, 3268, 3283, and 3286.

12. Descargos de López de Mendizábal, Santa Fe, Oct. 29, 1661, AGN, Tierras, 3286. Hackett, *Documents*, III, p. 194. Chavez, *Families*, p. 100.

13. Declarations of Carvajal, Santa Fe, Sept. 28, 1661, AGN, Inq., 593, exp. 1, f. 62v, and Cerrillos, May 26, 1664, ibid., 507, ff. 286-86v. Scholes, "Troublous Times," XII, pp. 136-38. Chavez, *Families*, p. 15.

14. Carvajal, Pecos, Sept. 30, 1661, AGN, Tierras, 3286.

15. Testimonio de las demandas, Santa Fe, Oct. 29, 1661, ibid. Scholes, "Troublous Times," XII, pp. 394-96.

16. Scholes neatly summarizes charges and countercharges in "Troublous Times," XIII, pp. 66-79. Father San Francisco claimed that López had cost fourteen missions nearly 9,000 head of livestock. Pecos was not one of the fourteen. Diego González Bernal, former alcalde mayor of the Tanos-Pecos jurisdiction, fled New Mexico shortly after presenting the charges against López. Hackett, *Documents*, III, p. 138.

17. López de Mendizábal to Posada, Santa Fe, Apr. 14, 1662, AGN, Inq., 587, exp. 1, ff. 198-99. Declaration of González, Santa Fe, Sept. 26, 1661, ibid., 593, exp. 1, ff. 137v-38v.

18. Scholes, "Troublous Times," XII, pp. 447-50.

19. Juan Manso, Writ of arrest, Santa Fe, May 4, 1662, et al., AGN, Tierras, 3268.

20. Proceso contra Gómez Robledo, AGN, Inq., 583. Scholes, "Troublous Times," XII, pp. 439-41. Gómez the younger was described in 1681 as fifty-three years old, "married, of good stature and features with red hair and mustache, and partly gray." Chavez, *Families*, p. 36.

21. Juan Manso, Inventory, Santa Fe, May 4, 1662, et al., AGN, Tierras, 3268. Declaration of Lucero de Godoy, Pecos, June 29, 1663, ibid.

22. A complete accounting of Gómez' assets and expenses during his bout with the Inquisition, 1662-1665, is ibid.

23. Scholes, "Troublous Times," XV, pp. 249-54. Declaration of Peñalosa, México, June 30, 1665, AGN, Inq., 507, ff. 442v-46. Hackett, *Documents,* III, p. 258.

24. Declaration of Gómez Robledo, México, Apr. 24, 1663, AGN, Tierras, 3268. Testifying in 1661, Carranza said he was a native of Valladolid in Michoacán, about fifteen years old, and an aide and servant of Peñalosa. Declaration of Carranza, Santa Fe, Nov. 1, 1661, AGN, Inq., 593, exp. 1. Indictment of Peñalosa, México, Oct. 7-8, 1665, ibid., 507, ff. 454-56v.

25. Gómez Robledo, Apr. 24, 1663, AGN, Tierras, 3268.

26. Posada, Santo Domingo, July 15, 1662, ibid.

27. Lucero de Godoy, June 29, 1663, ibid. Carvajal, May 26, 1664, AGN, Inq., 507, ff. 286-86v. Articles 150-52 of the indictment of Peñalosa, México, Oct. 7-8, 1665, AGN, Inq., 507, ff. 498-99. Hackett, *Documents,* III, p. 260.

28. Gómez Robledo, Apr. 24, 1663, AGN, Tierras, 3268.

29. AGN, Tierras, 3268. Scholes, "Troublous Times," XV, pp. 254-66.

30. Ibid., pp. 410-14. Proceso contra Gómez, AGN, Inq., 583.

31. AGN, Tierras, 3268

32. Scholes, "Troublous Times," XV, pp. 369-417.

33. Proceso contra Romero, AGN, Inq., 586. Article 17 of charges and Romero's reply, México, Sept. 19, 1663, ibid., ff. 93, 97v-98.

34. Declaration of Romero, México, Aug. 29, 1663, ibid., f. 86v. The document has Antonio Baca, which may be a slip for his brother Alonso. Scholes, "Troublous Times," XV, p. 394, has Alonso.

35. Declarations of Juan de Moraga, Bartolomé de Ledesma, and Felipe de Albizu, who were with Romero, et al., AGN, Inq., 586, Declaration of Romero, México, Oct. 12, 1663, ibid., f. 110.

36. Segunda causa contra Diego Romero, 1676-1678, ibid., 629, exp. 2. Kessell, "Diego Romero, the Plains Apaches, and the Inquisition," *The American West,* vol. 15, no. 3 (May-June 1978), pp. 12-16.

37. LEP, no. 1027. Scholes and Bloom, "Friar Personnel," XX, pp. 77n, 82n. Madoz, *Diccionario,* VI, pp. 563-64.

38. Scholes, "Troublous Times," XV, pp. 260-62, 266-68, and XVI, pp. 15-32. Publication of testimony against Peñalosa, México, Nov. 23, 1666, AGN, Inq., 507, f. 632v. Posada had heard belated testimony against ex-governor López de Mendizábal at Pecos early in August. Declaration of Francisco Ramírez, Pecos, Aug. 3, 1663, ibid., 587, exp. 1, ff. 236-37v.

39. Francisco de Madrid et al. to Gov. Juan de Miranda, Santa Fe, Apr. 22, 1664, ibid., 507, ff. 343v-46.

40. Declaration of Posada, certified copy, Santa Fe, May 24, 1664, ibid., ff. 347-58v.

41. Peñalosa's defense, México, Oct.-Dec. 1665, ibid., ff. 565-65v. Scholes, "Troublous Times," XVI, pp. 196-97

42. Posada, May 24, 1664, AGN, Inq., 507, ff. 347-58v. Madrid et al., Apr. 22, 1664, ibid., ff. 343v-46.

43. Enríquez to Ibargaray, Santa Fe, Oct. 1, 1663, ibid., f. 99.

44. Ibargaray to the Holy Office, Galisteo, Oct. 1, 1663, ibid., ff. 98-99v. López de Mendizábal's defense as extracted in Hackett, *Documents,* III, p. 215. Old Ibargaray was still guardian at Galisteo late in 1667. Ratification of Fr. Fernando de Velasco, Sandía, Nov. 13, 1667, AGN, Inq., 608, exp. 6, f. 388.

45. Declaration of Fr. Nicolás de Echavarría, Santo Domingo, Mar. 1666, ibid., 507, f. 763. Virtually nothing is known about Fray Juan de la Chica, save that he was a priest, that he had arrived in New Mexico before 1659 and was still there in 1665, that he spent some time in Santa Fe, and that he was at Pecos when Governor Peñalosa

arrested Posada. See Scholes, "Supply Service," pp. 209, 403.

46. Scholes, "Troublous Times," XVI, pp. 28-35. Posada to the Holy Office, Santo Domingo, June 8, 1664, AGN, Inq., 507, ff. 105-08.

47. Declaration of Margarita Márquez, Cerrillos, May 26, 1664, ibid., ff. 288v-89v. Scholes, "Troublous Times," XVI, pp. 35-38.

48. Posada to the Holy Office, Santo Domingo, July 14, 1665, AGN, Inq., 666, exp. 10, ff. 536-36v. Scholes, "Troublous Times," XV, pp. 407-10, and XVI, pp. 314-15, 319. There is an April 1664 reference to Posada as "present guardian" at Pecos. Madrid et al., Apr. 22, 1664, AGN, Inq., 507, ff. 343v-46.

49. Scholes, "Troublous Times," XVI, pp. 184-205.

50. Posada, Informe, ca. 1686, AGN, Historia, 3. See also Tyler and Taylor, "Report of Fray Alonso de Posada," and Hackett, ed., *Pichardo's Treatise on the Limits of Louisiana and Texas,* 4 vols. (Austin, 1931-1946), I, pp. 155-59.

51. Scholes, "Troublous Times," XVI, pp. 313-20.

52. The cabildo of Santa Fe to the Holy Office, Santa Fe, Oct. 25, 1667, AGN, Inq., 610, ff. 123-24v.

53. Nicolás de las Infantas y Venegas, México, Apr. 11, 1668, ibid., f. 121.

54. The son of Juan de Echevarría and María Ramírez, Nicolás entered the Franciscan Order with eighteen others on May 25, 1637, at the Convento Grande. He was twenty-one. By 1644, he had made it to New Mexico. His name did not appear on a 1659 roster: he had either left temporarily or been overlooked. In 1663, he served at Picurís; in 1665, he was a definitor of the custody; by March 1666, he had been named guardian at Pecos; and in 1668, he was at Sandía. Declaration of Echevarría, Santo Domingo, Mar. 1666, AGN, Inq., 507, f. 763. LEP, no. 954.

55. Nicolás de Enríquez was a transfer from the Franciscan province of Jalisco. At the foot of the declaration he gave at Santo Domingo, Dec. 13, 1666—when he was described as guardian of Pecos and a little over forty-four—a note was added early in 1669 explaining that he had not ratified his testimony because he had died. AGN, Inq., 666, exp. 10, ff. 556-58. The other Enríquez was a definitor and guardian at Pecos as of Nov. 13, 1667, when he acted as a ratifying witness. Ibid., 608, exp. 6, ff. 388-88v.

56. Quoted by Scholes, "Troublous Times," XVI, pp. 319-20.

57. Appointment of notary, and inventory of Inquisition papers, Pecos, Jan. 19 and 21, 1669, AGN, Inq., 608, exp. 6, ff. 411, 400-03v. Gómez de la Cadena, who was forced because of illness to give up his post as notary in February 1670, had served in Santa Fe between 1665 and 1670. In 1671-1672 he was at Tajique and Chililí, in 1672 at Isleta, and in 1679-1680 back in Santa Fe. He survived the Pueblo revolt of 1680.

58. LEP, no. 1099.

59. Bernal to the Holy Office, Santo Domingo, Apr. 1, 1669, AGN, Inq., 666, exp. 5, ff. 373-74. A translation of the letter, along with excerpts of other documents in the Gruber case, is in Hackett, *Documents,* III, pp. 271-77. Scholes, "Troublous Times." XVI, pp. 320-21.

60. Holy Office to Bernal, México, Oct. 20 and 25, 1669, quoted by Scholes, ibid. Bernal to the Holy Office, Sandía, July 8, 1670, and appointment of notary, Pecos, Feb. 4, 1670, AGN, Inq., 614, ff. 280-80v, 283-83v. Vetancurt, *Teatro Mexicano,* IV, pp. 286-87.

61. The Tremiño case is in AGN, Inq., 616, exp. 1. Hackett, *Documents,* III, pp. 278-79. Chavez, *Families,* p. 8. Bernal to the Holy Office, July 8, 1670, AGN, Inq., 614, ff. 280-80v.

62. Declaration of Ortega, Pecos, June 30, 1670, et al., ibid., 666, exp. 5.

63. Bernal to the Holy Office, July 8, 1670, ibid., 614, ff. 280-80v.

64. Francisco del Castillo Vetancurt to Juan de Ortega, Parral, Sept. 1, 1670, translated in Hackett, *Documents,* III, p. 277. Chavez, "La Jornada del Muerto," *New Mexico Magazine,* vol. 52 (Sept.-Oct. 1974), pp. 34-35.

65. Bernal, Pecos, Nov. 10, 1670, et al., AGN, Tierras, 3286.

66. Although Bernal may have continued as guardian at Pecos as late as the 1672 chapter meeting, the last positive reference to him at that mission concerns the playing cards and is dated November 1670. See Bloom and Lynn B. Mitchell, "The Chapter Elections in 1672," NMHR, vol. 13 (1938), pp. 111, 113.

67. Vetancurt, *Teatro Mexicano,* IV, pp. 286-87. Adams and Chavez, *Missions,* p. 197n. Excavating in 1966 within the old church at neighboring Halona, today's Zuñi, National Park Service archaeologists came upon a headless skeleton presumed to be that of Ávila y Ayala. A badly crushed skull, also thought to be his, had been unearthed in 1917 near the altar steps at Hawikuh. Louis R. Caywood, *The Restored Mission of Nuestra Senora de Guadalupe de Zuni, Zuni, New Mexico* (St. Michaels, Ariz., 1972), pp. 39-40.

68. Rosa Figueroa, Becerro. Scholes, "Mission Supply," p. 404. Bloom and Mitchell, "Chapter Elections in 1672," p. 113.

69. Scholes, "Troublous Times," XVI, pp. 321-27.

70. Gov. Villanueva, Santa Fe, Feb. 18, 1668, et al., BNM, leg. 1, no. 29.

71. Gov. Medrano y Mesía to Custos Talabán, Santa Fe, June 16 and 19, 1669, et al., ibid., no. 32. Frank D. Reeve, *History of New Mexico,* 2 vols (New York, 1961), I, pp. 239-41.

72. See Forbes, *Apache, Navaho, and Spaniard,* pp. 156-76.

73. López claimed that during the month of August 1660 Apaches killed 27 Christian Indians in their fields and carried 2 away alive—17 from the Piro pueblos, 5 from Ácoma, 2 from Santo Domingo, 3 from Jémez, 1 from Taos, "and another from a bit beyond the pueblo of the Pecos." López to the viceroy, Santa Fe, Oct. 24, 1660, AGN, Tierras, 3286.

74. Fr. García de San Francisco et al. to the viceroy, Santo Domingo, Sept. 8, 1659, AGN, Inq., 593, exp. 1, ff. 249-56v. Gunnerson, *Jicarilla Apaches,* pp. 92-95.

75. Scholes, "Mission Supply," pp. 386-403.

76. A file of documents dealing with Ayeta's aid to New Mexico, 1677-1680, is translated in Hackett, *Documents,* III, pp. 285-326. See also Hackett and Shelby, *Revolt,* I, pp. lxxix-lxxxvi.

77. Declaration of Diego López Sambrano, Hacienda of Luis de Carbajal, Dec. 22, 1681, ibid., II, pp. 292-303.

78. Ibid. Declarations of Luis de Quintana and Fr. Francisco de Ayeta, Hacienda of Luis de Carbajal, Dec. 22 and 23, 1681, ibid., II, pp. 285-92, 305-18.

79. Velasco was the son of Fernando de Velasco and Ángela Grozo, both natives of Cádiz. LEP, no. 1154. He had apparently also served at Sandía in 1659. Scholes and Bloom, "Friar Personnel," XIX, pp. 334n, 335n, XX, 81n. For his involvement with the notorious Nicolás de Aguilar, see Hackett, *Documents,* III. Testifying at Santo Domingo on November 7, 1667, he said he was minister at Ácoma and about forty-nine years old. AGN, Inq., 608, exp. 6, ff. 386v-88.

80. A son of Nicolás de la Pedrosa and Antonia Cárdenas, both of Mexico City, Juan was eighteen years and one month old at his investiture. LEP.

81. Otermín, Santa Fe, Aug. 9 and 10, 1680, Hackett and Shelby, *Revolt,* I, pp. 3-7. Otermín to Ayeta, near Socorro, Sept. 8, 1680, ibid., pp. 94-105.

Chapter VI

1. For the career and writings of the remarkable Silvestre Vélez de Escalante, see Adams, "Fray Silvestre and the Obstinate Hopi," *NMHR,* vol. 38 (1963), pp. 97-138, and "Letter to the Missionaries of New Mexico," *NMHR,* vol. 40 (1965), pp. 319-35. The lengthy introduction to Hackett and Shelby, *Revolt,* based on the documents published therein, chronicles events from 1680 to 1682.

2. Vélez de Escalante, Extracto de noticias, BNM, leg. 3, no. 1. After a brief, unfinished survey of the discovery and conquest of New Mexico from secondary sources, Vélez de Escalante covered in considerable detail the period from the administration of Governor Otermín to that of Félix Martínez, from 1678 to 1717, basing his study on the documents he examined in Santa Fe between 1776 and 1779, some of which have since been lost. Unfortunately, his numerous other duties and his worsening health cut short the project. An inaccurate copy of the second half of the study was published initially in 1856 and most recently in *Documentos para servir a la historia del Nuevo México,* pp. 324-459. Eleanor B. Adams has prepared the entire original manuscript for publication.

3. Vélez de Escalante, Extracto. Otermín, Santa Fe, Aug. 9-13, 1680, and Otermín to Ayeta, near Socorro, Sept. 8, 1680, Hackett and Shelby, *Revolt,* I, pp. 3-13, 94-105. A list of the friars killed, compiled in 1680, has Taos as the scene of Fray Juan de la Pedrosa's death, evidently an error. Ibid., p. 110. Vetancurt, *Teatro Mexicano,* III, p. 273, IV, p. 227.

4. Vélez de Escalante, Extracto. Otermín, Santa Fe, Aug. 13-21, and Otermín to Ayeta, Sept. 8, 1680, Hackett and Shelby, *Revolt,* I, pp. 12-19, 94-105. The accounts, which vary in other small details, do not make clear whether the battle with the Pecos and Tanos was fought on the thirteenth or the fifteenth.

5. Otermín, Aug. 24, 1680, Hackett and Shelby, *Revolt,* I, pp. 21-22. Chavez, *Families,* pp. 4-5, 125.

6. Vélez de Escalante, Extracto. Otermín, Aug. 24-26, 1680, and Declaration of Pedro García, Aug. 25, 1680, Hackett and Shelby, *Revolt,* I, pp. 22-26. Confusing the Tano Pedro García with a Tewa captured August 23, Vélez de Escalante calls him Antonio.

7. Hackett and Shelby, *Revolt,* I, Declaration of Pedro Nanboa, Alamillo, Sept. 6, 1680, ibid., pp. 60-62. Scholes, "Civil Government and Society," p. 91. Henry Warner Bowden, "Spanish Missions, Cultural Conflict and the Pueblo Revolt of 1680," *Church History,* vol. 44 (1975), pp. 217-28, agrees with Pedro Nanboa. "The cultural antagonism between Spaniard and Pueblo had fundamentally religious roots, and an adequate understanding of the 1680 hostilities must give them priority" (p. 227).

8. Chavez, "Pohé-yemo's Representative and the Pueblo Revolt of 1680," *NMHR,* vol. 42 (1967), pp. 85-126.

9. Declarations of Juan of Tesuque, Pedro Naranjo, and of Juan Lorenzo and Francisco Lorenzo, Río del Norte, Dec. 18-20, 1681, Hackett and Shelby, *Revolt,* II, pp. 233-38, 245-53. Vélez de Escalante, Extracto.

10. Fr. Francisco de Vargas to Diego de Vargas, Santa Fe, July 1696, SANM, II, no. 60b. Vetancurt, *Teatro Mexicano,* III, p. 278.

11. Hayes, *Four Churches,* pp. 22-23, 32-35.

12. Declaration of Josephe, Río del Norte, Dec. 19, 1681, Hackett and Shelby, *Revolt,* II, pp. 238-42. Evidently paraphrasing, Vélez de Escalante, Extracto, says that the traitor came among the Pecos, was recognized, and was immediately executed by them.

13. Declaration of Ayeta, Hacienda de Luis de Carvajal, Dec. 23, 1681, Hackett and Shelby, *Revolt,* II, pp. 305-18. Alonso Catiti, who lived as an Indian at Santo Domingo, was a natural son of Capt. Diego Márquez of Los Cerrillos, one of the Spaniards beheaded in the wake of Governor Rosas' murder. Chavez, *Families,* p. 69.

14. Vélez de Escalante, Extracto. Diego de Vargas, Sept. 16, 1692, J. Manuel Espinosa, ed., *First Expedition of Vargas into New Mexico, 1692* (Albuquerque, 1940), p. 106.

15. See Espinosa's narrative, patently pro-Vargas *Crusaders of the Río Grande* (Chicago, 1942), pp. 25-59. Another, less satisfactory account, relying on Espinosa's earlier doctoral research, is Jessie Bromilow Bailey, *Diego de Vargas and the Reconquest of New Mexico* (Albuquerque, 1940).

16. Vargas, Sept. 22-27, 1692, AGN, Historia, 37, and as translated by Espinosa, *First Expedition,* pp. 119-35. Chavez, *Families,* pp. 4, 47-48. Vargas later distinguished between "the short road through the mountains" from Santa Fe to Pecos, used by the Indians on foot and by persons on horseback, and "the wagon road" via Galisteo. Vargas to the viceroy, El Paso, Jan. 12, 1693, AGI, Guad., 139, and Espinosa, *First Expedition,* pp. 278-89.

17. Vargas to the viceroy, Santa Fe, Oct. 16, 1692, SANM, II, no. 53. Espinosa, *Crusaders,* pp. 76-83, and *First Expedition,* pp. 158-65.

18. Vargas, Oct. 16-18, 1692, SANM, II, no. 53, and Espinosa, *First Expedition,* pp. 166-70. Vargas described in detail the ceremonies performed at Santa Fe on September 14 and at Tesuque on September 29. Thereafter, as at Pecos, he simply referred to his previous descriptions, saying "in the same manner I reclaimed, revalidated, and proclaimed possession, in behalf of His Majesty, of both this pueblo and its land as well as its natives, his vassals." Father Corvera, who had professed at the Convento Grande on February 8, 1684, was ministering in the El Paso area by 1691. His companion, Father Barroso, a native of Lisbon, professed March 5, 1685, also at the Convento Grande. He too was at El Paso by 1691, and served at Socorro del Sur at least as early as April 1692. Both worked in New Mexico after the recolonization. Rosa Figueroa, Becerro. Chavez, *Archives of the Archdiocese of Santa Fe, 1678-1900* (Washington, D.C., 1957), pp. 9, 10, 16.

19. Espinosa, *Crusaders,* pp. 82-111.

20. Vargas to the viceroy, Jan. 12, 1693, AGI, Guad., 139.

21. Espinosa, *Crusaders,* pp. 112-35.

22. Vargas to Luis Granillo, Nov. 14, 1693, SANM, II, no. 54a. Both the SANM original and the AGI copy read that Vargas intended, according to Tapia's lie, to put everyone to the sword, sparing only those twelve to fourteen *and older.* This must be a slip.

23. Vargas, Nov. 24-25, 30, 1693, SANM, II, no. 54b. Vargas to the viceroy, Santa Fe, Jan. 20, 1694, AGI, Guad., 140. Espinosa, *Crusaders,* pp. 136-42.

24. Vargas, Dec. 5 and 9, 1693, SANM, II, no. 54b. Espinosa, *Crusaders,* p. 147, incorrectly has Roque de Madrid leading the food detail to Pecos.

25. Since none of the documents of 1680 identify the Pecos governor or individual who warned Gómez, there really is no evidence to dispute the friars' claim that it was Juan de Ye. Fr. Salvador de San Antonio et al. to Vargas, Dec. 18, 1693, AGI, Guad., 140. Vélez de Escalante, Extracto, transcribed the complete petition and Vargas' courtly reply. Vargas, Dec. 17-18, 1693, SANM, II, no. 54b. Espinosa, *Crusaders,* pp. 149-52. Espinosa appended Pacheco to Fray Fernando de Velasco's name apparently mistaking P.e (Padre) for P.o (Pacheco).

26. Vargas, Dec. 21, 23, and 29, 1693, and Vargas to the viceroy,

Jan. 20, 1694, AGI, Guad., 140. Espinosa, *Crusaders*, pp. 152-62.

27. Vargas, Jan. 4-5, 1694, AGI, Guad, 140. Vélez de Escalante, Extracto, suggests that the Pecos may have been testing the Spaniards, turning in a false alarm to see if they would come to their aid.

28. Vargas, Mar. 27, 1694, SANM, II, no. 55d.

29. Vargas, May 2, 1694, ibid. Espinosa (*Crusaders*, p. 183) assumes that the Apache capitan of the rancherías of the plains and the captain of the Apaches Faraones were one and the same, and he may be right. It is hard to tell from Vargas' journal.

30. Vargas, May 4, 1694, SANM, II, no. 55d. Surely Vargas would have sent someone or gone himself to investigate this "white iron" if, as Espinosa says, it was a day's journey *from Santa Fe*.

31. Vargas, Aug. 26-28, 1694, SANM, II, no. 55h.

32. Vargas to the viceroy, Santa Fe, June 2, 1694, BL, New Mexico Originals (NMO).

33. Vargas, July 3-7, 17, 1694, SANM, II, no. 55g-55h. Vargas to the viceroy, Santa Fe, Sept. 1, 1694, SANM, II, no. 55j. Espinosa, *Crusaders*, pp. 184-98.

34. Vargas, Apr. 28, 1694, SANM, II, no. 55d. Espinosa, *Crusaders*, pp. 178-82, 213n. Chavez, *Archives*, p. 18.

35. Fr. Antonio Carbonel et al. to Muñoz de Castro, Santa Fe, Sept. 22, 1694, BNM, leg. 4, no. 7.

36. Zeinos sometimes signed Diego de la Casa Zeinos. Rosa Figueroa does not seem to have included him in the provincial Becerro.

37. Vargas, Sept. 24, 1964, Huntington Library, San Marino, Calif., Ritch Collection (HL, Ritch). There had been two reconquerors named Francisco de Anaya Almazán, the old sargento mayor and a young aide-de-camp, presumably uncle and nephew. The latter had drowned in the Rio Grande. Chavez suggests that this unfortunate youth was the son of Cristóbal de Anaya rescued at Pecos in 1692. *Families*, pp. 4, 125.

38. Hayes, *Four Churches*, pp. 23, 35, 50-51.

39. Other godparents with Spanish surnames were Antonio de Almazán, Francisco Madrid, Sebastiana Madrid, Antonio Montaño, and Diego Romero. Although the marriage and burial entries for Zeinos' administration are missing, the record of Pecos baptisms, marriages, and burials is nearly complete from the reconquest to abandonment, from 1694 to 1838, except for a hiatus in burials between 1706 and 1727 and another in baptisms between 1700 and 1725. This record, the richest single documentary source for the period, is preserved in the Archives of the Archdiocese of Santa Fe (AASF), now housed in Albuquerque. All the extant books of baptisms (B), marriages (M), and burials (Bur) have been numbered. Those for Pecos are B-19 (Box 22); B-20 (Box 22); M-10, Galisteo (Box 6a); M-18 (Box 11); M-19 (Box 11); M-20 (Box 11); Bur-9, Galisteo (Box 6a); Bur-18 (Box 9).

40. Zeinos to Gov. Vargas, admitted in Santa Fe, Oct. 14, 1694, et al., and Opinion of the fiscal, México, Nov. 20, 1694, AGI, Guad., 140.

41. Zeinos to Custos Vargas, Pecos, Dec. 28, 1694, and Custos Vargas to the missionaries, Santa Fe, Dec. 20, 1694, BNM, leg. 4, no. 8. Muñoz de Castro to Custos Vargas, Santa Fe, Jan. 4, 1695, BNM, leg. 3, no. 6. Vargas, Noticias ciertas, Dec. 1694, BNM, leg. 4, no. 6. Zeinos confirmed that he had baptized seventy children to date, which accords with the baptismal book and shows that the extant record of his baptisms at Pecos is complete. According to a list compiled by a successor, Zeinos celebrated 36 marriages during his year at Pecos. AASF, M-18, Pecos (Box 11).

42. Zeinos to Gov. Vargas, admitted in Santa Fe, Oct. 27, 1695,

and Gov. Vargas, certification, Santa Fe, Oct. 27, 1695, SANM, II, no. 58. Santa Fe cabildo to the viceroy et al., Santa Fe, Nov. 8, 1695, BNM, leg. 4, no. 11. Espinosa's statement (*Crusaders,* p. 229) that the shooting incident at Pecos "fanned smouldering embers" of insurrection in New Mexico seems unfounded.

43. Between November 18, 1695, and April 29, 1696, Alpuente performed 28 baptisms at Pecos. He married five couples. On December 5, 1695, during a visitation by Custos Vargas, he began a new book of burials. By May 1, 1696, he had recorded ten burials, the last two of which he seemed to enter twice. All were buried in the church. According to Alpuente, one died of a cough, four of a cough with pain in the side, and five of a fever. AASF, M-18, Pecos (Box 11). Alpuente to Custos Vargas, Zía, Dec. 28, 1694, BNM, leg. 3, no. 6.

44. Michael B. McCloskey, *The Formative Years of the Missionary College of Santa Cruz of Querétaro, 1683-1733* (Washington, D.C., 1955), pp. 70-71. See also Isidro Félix de Espinosa, *Crónica de los Colegios de Propaganda Fide de la Nueva España,* ed. Lino Gómez Canedo (Washington, D.C., 1964), pp. 227, 491-95. If Domingo de Jesús María was the José de Jesús María on the list, and apparently he was, he crossed the Atlantic in 1692 in a mission of twenty-eight Spanish friars recruited for the college by Fray Pedro Sitjar. The record is in AGI, Contratación, 5545A. Friars of the Querétaro college wore gray habits, not the blue of the Holy Gospel province.

45. Gov. Vargas, Santa Fe, Mar. 8, 1696, SANM, II, no. 59. Espinosa, *Crusaders,* pp. 228-43. La Piedra Blanca, or sometimes La Peña Blanca, evidently somewhere above the mother pueblo, may be the Arrowhead Ruin (LA:251), a fourteenth-century offshoot of Pecos up Glorieta Canyon some five miles to the northwest. For a description see Jane Holden, "A Preliminary Report on Arrowhead Ruin," EP, vol. 62 (1955), pp. 102-19, and Kidder, *Pecos, New Mexico,* pp. 49-51.

46. Custos Vargas to the missionaries, Santa Fe, Mar. 9, 1696, and replies, BNM, leg. 4, no. 24e.

47. Gov. Vargas, Santa Fe, Mar. 14, 1696, and Custos Vargas to Gov. Vargas, Santa Fe, Mar. 13, 1696, SANM, II, no. 59.

48. Custos Vargas et al. to Gov. Vargas, Santa Fe, Mar. 22, 1696, ibid.

49. Gov. Vargas, Santa Fe, Mar. 22, 1696, ibid.

50. Gov. Vargas to the viceroy, Santa Fe, Mar. 28, 1696, ibid. Vélez de Escalante, in his Extracto, quoted from this letter when condemning the governor for his cavalier attitude.

51. Fr. Pablo Sarmiento, Querétaro, Jan. 17, 1696, and Custos Vargas to the Father Commissary General, Santa Ana, May 17, 1696, and Fr. Diego de Salazar, Querétaro, Aug. 21, 1696, BNM, leg. 4, nos. 19, 23, and 22. McCloskey, *Formative Years,* pp. 73-74. Whether or not the trio traveled together some of the way, Fray Domingo arrived at the college on August 19, the other two on August 21.

52. I. F. de Espinosa, *Crónica,* p. 494. J. M. Espinosa, *Crusaders,* pp. 244-71.

53. Vargas, June 4-7, 1696, SANM, II, no. 60a. Twichell translated the entries about the revolt from Vargas' journal, June 4-17, in "The Pueblo Revolt of 1696," *Old Santa Fe,* vol. 3 (1916), pp. 333-73. A Spaniard, García Marín was recruited from the Franciscan province of Burgos for the Querétaro college. He, like Trizio and Domingo de Jesús María, crossed in the mission of 1692. Espinosa, who must have misread *indiano* for *indigno,* is wrong that García was American-born (*Crusaders,* p. 213n). García to Custos Vargas, Santa Clara, Dec. 31, 1694, BNM, leg. 3, no. 6.

54. Vargas, June 8, 1696, SANM, II, no. 60a.

55. Vargas, June 11-12, 1696, ibid. Testifying in Santa Fe, Diego

Xenome told how the Pecos had tied him up and taken him down into the kiva where Governor Felipe informed him that they "had already killed those who were partisans of the Tewas." Espinosa, *Crusaders,* pp. 250-54.

56. Custos Vargas said that there were at Pecos 66 packsacks of maize, 8 fanegas of wheat, and a number of the 74 head of sheep he had placed there. Custos Vargas to Gov. Vargas, Santa Fe, admitted July 6, 1696, and Gov. Vargas, Santa Fe, July 6-8, 1696, SANM, II, no. 60b. Gov. Vargas, Santa Fe, Nov. 23, 1696, AGI, Guad., 141. Espinosa, *Crusaders,* pp. 260-61. Among the Pecos assets Father Alpuente had turned over to Father García Marín in May were half a dozen pigs (four boars and two sows), plus the increase of another boar and sow and seven ·young. AASF, M-18, Pecos (Box 11).

57. Gov. Vargas, July 19-20, 1696, and Anaya to Vargas, Pecos, July 17 and 19, 1696, SANM, II, no. 60b.

58. Gov. Vargas, Aug. 30, 1696, SANM, II, no. 60c.

59. Gov. Vargas, Santa Fe, Nov. 23, 1696, AGI, Guad., 141. Espinosa, *Crusaders,* pp. 281-88. Vargas' journal for Oct. 22-Nov. 9, 1696, has been translated by Alfred Barnaby Thomas in *After Coronado, Spanish Exploration Northeast of New Mexico, 1696-1727,* 2nd ed. (Norman, 1966), pp. 53-59.

60. For details of the struggle, on both the local and national levels, and the eventual restoration of Diego de Vargas, see Espinosa, *Crusaders,* pp. 307-62.

61. There are four pages from the Pecos account book sewn in at the end of the baptisms, marriages, and burials found in AASF, M-18, Pecos (Box 11). They give the dates, between 1697 and 1699, on which each friar signed in receipt. The six who served the mission between 1697 and 1700 are as follows (the first and last entries by each in the extant, incomplete books of baptisms, marriages, and burials appear in parenthesis):

Fr. Alonso Jiménez de Cisneros took over in March 1697 and surrendered his accountability for the mission on February 6, 1698. (June 14, 1697-Jan. 24, 1698)

Fr. Miguel de Trizio signed in receipt on March 1, 1698. (Mar. 7, 1698-Aug. 29, 1698)

Fr. Francisco Farfán on October 13, 1698, signed for everything in the account book plus 30 fanegas of wheat, some more not yet reaped because it was not ripe, 50 sacks of maize, and some on the ear. On July 4, 1699, he left everything including the keys in the charge of Damián, convento interpreter, evidently for Fray Diego de Chavarría. (Nov. 20, 1698-July 4, 1699)

Fr. Diego de Chavarría never did sign in receipt, though he baptized four persons at Pecos on September 6, 1699.

Fr. Miguel Muñiz de Luna on September 18, 1699, received "this convento and everything attached to it" from Damián and interpreter Rafael. (Nov. 3, 1699-June 27, 1700, including 34 marriages)

Fr. José de Arranegui. (Aug. 12, 1700-Aug. 28, 1708)

For more on these friars see Appendix III.

62. Vélez de Escalante, Extracto. Vélez' brief account of factionalism at Pecos, written over seventy years after the fact on the authority of documents since lost, is translated in full at the beginning of this chapter. Because the population figures for these years are so scattered or unreliable, no exodus from Pecos around the turn of the century is evident. See Appendix I. Pecos families, who according to tradition came directly from Pecos pueblo, did show up in other communities. See, for example, Charles H. Lange, *Cochití, A New Mexico*

Pueblo, Past and Present (Carbondale, 1968), p. 407, and Kidder, *Pecos, New Mexico,* p. 317.

63. Declarations of Felipe Chistoe, et al., Santa Fe, Mar. 3, 1702, BL, NMO.

64. Vargas, Mar. 27-Apr. 2, 1704, SANM, II, no. 99. Espinosa, *Crusaders,* pp. 356-62. See Oakah L. Jones, Jr., *Pueblo Warriors and Spanish Conquest* (Norman, 1966), pp. 65-68. In the document, don Felipe was listed first among the Pueblo auxiliaries and identified as governor of the Pecos. Next came chief of scouts José de Naranjo, who was not, as Jones says, from Pecos.

Chapter VII, pages 301-309

1. Certificación de las mercedes, limosnas, consignaciones de misiones, pensiones, y ayudas de costa, México, Dec. 22, 1763, BL, M-M, 339. For the development of the frontier military in the eighteenth century, see Max L. Moorhead, *The Presidio: Bastion of the Spanish Borderlands* (Norman, 1975).

2. Estado que muestra las jurisdicciones, 1799, BNM, leg. 10, no. 74. Chavez, *Families,* pp. x-xiv.

3. Fr. Carlos José Delgado, Informe, Santa Bárbara, Mar. 27, 1750, Hackett, *Documents,* III, pp. 425-30. Richard E. Greenleaf, "The Mexican Inquisition and the Enlightenment, 1763-1805," NMHR, vol. 41 (1966), pp. 181-96. Adams, *Bishop Tamarón's Visitation of New Mexico, 1760* (Albuquerque, 1954), pp. 1-33, provides a summary of the jurisdictional dispute between the bishops of Durango and the Franciscans of New Mexico.

4. Alfonso Rael de Aguilar et al., Santa Fe, Jan. 10, 1706, AGI, Guad., 116, and Hackett, *Documents,* III, pp. 366-69.

5. Fr. Juan Álvarez to Gov. Cuervo y Valdés, admitted in Santa Fe, Jan. 7, 1706, and Álvarez, Informe, Nambé, Jan. 12, 1706, AGI, Guad., 116, and Hackett, *Documents,* III, pp. 369-78.

6. AASF, M-18, M-19, Pecos (Box 11). Chavez, *Archives.* Rosa Figueroa, *Becerro.*

7. Adams and Chavez, *Missions,* p. 209. The manuscript record of the entire Domínguez visitation is in BNM, leg. 10, no. 43. For an interesting and detailed account of the construction of a contemporary church in Santa Fe, for which Pecos carpenters supplied boards and planks, see Kubler, *The Rebuilding of San Miguel at Santa Fe in 1710* (Colorado Springs, 1939). Perhaps Andrés González, the master builder, a native of Zacatecas who had come to New Mexico in 1693, was also employed on the Pecos project.

8. The next marriage entry after Delgado's last is dated May 6, 1718. AASF, M-19, Pecos (Box 11), and Patentes, Book II (Box 2), Pecos. For a brief sketch of his career see Adams and Chavez, *Missions,* pp. 331-32. Probably the outstanding Franciscan to serve in eighteenth-century New Mexico, the enduring Delgado deserves a biographer.

9. With his estimate of 1,000 Christian Indians at Pecos in 1706, probably on the high side by 200 or 300, Álvarez made it the largest pueblo in New Mexico, except for Halona at Zuñi with 1,500. Álvarez, Informe, Jan. 12, 1706, AGI, Guad., 116. Fr. Juan Miguel Menchero, Informe, Santa Bárbara, May 10, 1744, BNM, leg. 8, no. 17, and Hackett, *Documents,* III, pp. 395-413.

10. Adams and Chavez, *Missions,* pp. 208-14. Kubler, *Religious Architecture,* pp. 85-87. Hayes, *Four Churches.* Both Hayes and Kubler reproduce the 1846 Stanley sketch.

11. Estado de las misiones, Santa Fe, July 16, 1792, BNM, leg.

10, no. 83. My Appendix I shows clearly the relentless decline in the pueblo's population. For a complete listing of Pecos friars see Appendix III. Chavez, *Archives,* cites repeated warnings to the missionaries not to come to Santa Fe without permission. These, of course, did not apply to friars on the staff of the Santa Fe convento who visited Pecos periodically when there was no resident.

12. Custos Peña had reported the destruction of kivas to his superiors on July 31, 1709. Chavez, *Archives,* p. 23. Only the day before, he had inspected the Pecos books, probably in Santa Fe, AASF, M-19, Pecos (Box 11).

13. Declaration of Juan Tindé et al., Santa Fe, July 8, 1711, BNM, leg. 6, no. 4.

14. Gov. Peñuela to Fr. Luis Morete y Teruel, Santa Fe, May 25, 1712, BNM, leg. 6, no. 3. Vélez de Escalante, Extracto, cited a similar scathing letter to the viceroy, date May 30, which was later referred to the Franciscan commissary general for appropriate action. Father Diego de Padilla had begun administering the mission of Pecos and the visita of Galisteo in 1709. Only his marriage entries survive in the Pecos books, the earliest dated June 11, 1709, and the last April 9, 1711. The entries of Father Cepeda, his successor, run only from April 19, 1712, to August 21, 1712. AASF, M-19, Pecos (Box 11).

15. Fr. José de Haro to Gov. Peñuela, n.d. and Mar. 5, 1712, BNM, leg. 6, no. 3.

16. This is the earliest specific reference I have to the *casas reales,* or *casa de comunidad,* at Pecos, not to be confused with the government buildings in Santa Fe. Such community houses, built in many pueblos during the seventeenth century, were New Mexico's inns. Here outsiders could transact business or find lodging without invading the Indians' homes. A 1680 document drawn up in El Paso refers to "the casas reales, which the common people call casas de comunidad." See Hackett and Shelby, *Revolt,* I, pp. 36, 201.

17. From Rael's description, this could be the restored kiva between the south and north pueblos at Pecos National Monument, Kiva 16, which, reckoned Kidder, "had had to be given up, perhaps because of ecclesiastical pressure, either before 1680 or, more probably, soon after the reconquest. Glaze VI and modern sherds testify to the lateness of its abandonment. Whatever the cause, the kiva roof was removed. . . . Those parts of the structure that remained protruding were thoroughly robbed of stone (absence of building stones in the fill)." *Pecos, New Mexico,* p. 202. One discrepancy is that Rael said this kiva was filled with "rock," and the archaeologists found earth.

18. Gov. Flores Mogollón, Santa Fe, Jan. 20, 1714, and Rael de Aguilar, Pecos, Jan. 23, 1714, BL, NMO. The reports of all but one of the other alcaldes are appended. Alfonso Rael de Aguilar, who accompanied Vargas in both 1692 and 1693, had a soldier son of the same name, also active in New Mexico in 1714. From the signature on this document, it is clear that Alfonso the elder was the alcalde mayor. No mention was made of Fray Lucas de Arévalo, the Pecos missionary at this time, or of Custos Tagle.

19. Gov. Flores Mogollón to the viceroy, Santa Fe, Sept. 14, 1714, BNM, leg. 6, no. 16. The viceregal fiscal in his opinion of November 2, 1714, and a junta general on January 22, 1715, upheld Governor Flores' action, further instructing him to inventory the purchased weapons and to hand them out only "for necessary engagements in the royal service." Ibid. Vélez de Escalante, Extracto. Jones' statement that the viceroy supported the view of the friars and reversed Flores' decision (*Pueblo Warriors,* p. 90) would seem to be in error. Certainly, in practice, the prohibition was soon relaxed.

20. Gov. Flores Mogollón, Santa Fe, July 5, 1714, et al., SANM,

II, no. 207. Vélez de Escalante, Extracto.

21. Junta general, Mexico City, Jan. 22, 1715, BNM, leg. 6, no. 16. Flores to the viceroy, Sept. 14, 1714, BNM, leg. 6, no 16.

22. Vélez de Escalante, Extracto.

23. Miranda to Flores, Ácoma, [July 1714], SANM, II, no. 207. Vélez de Escalante copied Father Miranda's entire letter into his Extracto.

24. Fr. Andrés Varo, Informe, El Paso, Jan. 29, 1751, BNM, leg. 9, no. 17. Henry W. Kelly quotes this passage from Varo (NMHR, vol. 16, p. 178) in his "Franciscan Missions of New Mexico, 1740-1760," NMHR, vol. 15 (1940), pp. 345-68, and vol. 16 (1941), pp. 41-69, 148-83 (also Albuquerque, 1941). Kelly pulls together an account of the vehement church-state conflict at mid-century.

25. Declaration of Juan Tindé et al., July 8, 1711, BNM, leg. 6, no. 4.

26. Antonio Becerra Nieto, judgment of Pecos claims, Janos, Aug. 16, 1723, SANM, II, no. 323. For some idea why Martínez had enemies among the Spaniards of New Mexico see Ted J. Warner, "Don Félix Martínez and the Santa Fe Presidio, 1693-1730," NMHR, vol. 45 (1970), pp. 269-310.

27. Valverde visitation, Pecos, Aug. 21, 1719, SANM, II, no. 309. For a brief archaeological description of the Pecos casas reales, which measured 145 feet long by 30 to 40 feet wide, see Hayes, *Four Churches*, pp. 53-58.

28. Pérez de Mirabal, whose earliest entries in the Taos books date from 1722, later served at Pecos during 1738-1739. Adams and Chavez, *Missions*, p. 337.

29. Cruzat y Góngora visitation, Pecos, July 28, 1733, SANM, II, no. 389. Valverde y Cosío visitation, Pecos, Aug. 21, 1719, SANM, II, no. 309.

30. Codallos y Rabal visitation, Pecos, Aug. 27, 1745, SANM, II, no. 470. When Gov. Enrique de Olavide y Michelena visited Pecos on September 5, 1738, none of the Indians presented claims, but they heard the same old exhortation. BL, NMO.

31. Declaration of Fr. Pedro Antonio Esquer, Santa Fe, after June 10, 1731, BNM, leg. no. 38. Fr. Juan Antonio Sánchez to the Father Provincial, México, c. 1731, BNM, leg. 7, no. 25. AASF, B-19, Pecos (Box 22); M-20, Pecos (Box 11); Bur-18, Pecos (Box 9).

32. Declaration of Antonio Sidepovi, Santa Fe, June 26, 1731, BL, NMO. In the residencia of Gaspar Domingo de Mendoza (1739-1743), two Pecos testified, giving brief, uninformative, and always favorable answers: Antonio de los Ángeles, "a Tano" and governor of the pueblo, and Miguel, the cacique. Declarations, Santa Fe, Dec. 29, 1743, BL, NMO. There are several other residencias from the first half of the eighteenth century at which Pecos Indians either did not testify or joined in the whitewash.

33. Fr. Andrés Varo, Carta diaria, July 5-Sept. 27, 1730, BNM, leg. 7, no. 24. For some reason, Father Pino used consistently the English form George instead of the Spanish form Jorge.

34. Bishop Crespo to the Viceroy Marqués de Casafuerte, Bernalillo, Sept. 8, and El Paso, Sept. 25, 1730, translated by Adams, *Tamarón's Visitation*, pp. 95-106. See also pp. 13-16. Fr. Francisco de Lepiane, Informe, México, 1728, BNM, leg. 7, no. 14. Fr. Juan Antonio Sánchez to the Father Provincial, c. 1731, BNM, leg. 7, no. 25.

35. John Augustine Donohue, *After Kino, Jesuit Missions in Northwestern New Spain, 1711-1767* (Rome and St. Louis, 1969), pp. 17-18. A good example of the friars' impassioned defense of the custody is Sánchez to the Father Provincial, c. 1731, BNM, leg. 7, no. 25.

36. Fr. Juan Miguel Menchero, Patente, El Paso, July 3, 1731,

AASF, Patentes, Book II (Box 2), Pecos. Chavez, *Archives*, p. 32. By the later 1740s, when Menchero was again functioning as comisario visitador, the missionaries of New Mexico still had not improved their knowledge of the native languages. It deeply pained their superiors in Spain and Mexico that "in the more than one hundred and fifty years since its conquest there has not been an assiduous friar who was stimulated by zeal and superior conduct to compose a grammar of the many and varied languages of this Holy Custody." Fr. Juan José Pérez de Mirabal, Patente, Santa Fe, Jan. 5, 1748, BNM, leg. 8. no. 36.

37. Fr. Pedro Antonio Esquer, Receipt, Santa Fe, Aug. 21, 1731, BNM, leg. 7, no. 56. Exactly nineteen years later, another Pecos missionary, along with a number of his brethren, accused Menchero of mismanaging the funds, charging for goods not sent, and inflating the statements with items not for their use. Declarations of Fr. Francisco de la Concepción González, Pecos, Aug. 21, 1750, BNM, leg. 8, no. 80.

38. Menchero, Visitation, Pecos, Aug. 24, 1731, BNM, leg. 7, no. 44a. The same day Menchero, with his secretary Fray Antonio Gabaldón, made the usual notation in each of the mission books stating that it conformed to the dictates of the Council of Trent.

39. Menchero, Patente, Santa Fe, Sept. 4, 1731, AASF, Patentes, Book II (Box 2), Pecos.

40. Notice of visitation, Aug. 29, 1737, signed by Elizacoechea and his secretary Pedro de Echenique, AASF, B-19, Pecos (Box 22).

41. See Adams, *Tamarón's Visitation*, pp. 16-19; Kelly, "Franciscan Missions;" and Hackett, *Documents*, III, pp. 388-501.

42. Codallos y Rabal to Father Commissary General, Santa Fe, June 4, 1744, BNM, leg. 8, no. 10.

43. The number of helpers in the convento, ten, had remained the same for over a century, while the population of Pecos had dropped by two-thirds or more. Fr. Manuel de San Juan Nepomuceno y Trigo, Visitation, Pecos, Aug. 21, 1750, BNM, leg. 8, no. 80. Trigo, Informe, Istacalco, July 23, 1754, BNM, leg. 9, no. 30, and Hackett, *Documents*, III, pp. 459-68. When Custos Jacobo de Castro visited Pecos on June 26, 1755, the Pecos told him essentially the same thing about Fray Miguel Campos, who had even exempted them from growing the wheat and maize for his table. BNM, leg. 9, no. 31.

44. Declaration of Fr. José Irigoyen, Tlatelolco, Oct. 24, 1748, BNM, leg. 8, no. 38. On Moreau see Hackett, *Pichardo's Treatise*, III, p. 352, and *Documents*, III, pp. 391, 401, and Chavez, *Families*, p. 239.

45. Padrones de las misiones que tiene la custodia de la Nueva México formados el año 1750, BNM, leg. 8, no. 81. Kelly, "Franciscan Missions," XV, pp. 362-63, reproduces these figures with some apparent typos. The González census of Pecos is undated. His first and last entries in the mission books are dated August 3, 1749, and August 25, 1750. AASF, B-19, Pecos (Box 22), and Bur-18, Pecos (Box 9). Kidder, *Pecos, New Mexico*, p. 327, who appears to arrive at totals of 450 and 448, figures the average number of children per couple at 1.86. For a tentative correlation of González' house blocks and those described by Domínguez in 1776, see below, pp. 345-46.

46. Adams, *Tamarón's Visitation*, pp. 17n, 19-33.

47. Ibid., p. 21.

48. Ibid., pp. 48-50, 78-79. Notice of Tamarón's visitation in Pecos book of baptisms, May 29, 1760, AASF, B-19, Pecos (Box 22). On Dávila see Adams and Chavez, *Missions*, pp. 163-64, 331.

49. The page on which the record of Agustín's burial must have appeared was removed from the Pecos book before the folio numbers were added. AASF, Bur-18, Pecos (Box 9). Perhaps Agustín Guichí, principal man and carpenter, was the cacique Agustín of the González census in 1750.

50. Bishop Tamarón extracted this account from the record of his visitation and had it published as *Relación del atentado sacrilegio, cometido por tres indios de un pueblo de la provincia del Nuevo México; y de el severo castigo, que executó la divina justicia con el fautor principal de ellos* (México, 1763). Adams, *Tamarón's Visitation*, pp. 50-53.

51. Fr. Francisco Atanasio Domínguez to Fr. Isidro Murillo, Santa Fe, June 10, 1776, Adams and Chavez, *Missions*, pp. 277-80. Pecos books, AASF. An introduction to the visitation, the superiors' instructions, and Domínguez' letters are all included in Adams and Chávez, *Missions*.

52. Domínguez did not say that former alcalde Armijo still lived *at Pecos;* rather that "he is still alive, but he is no longer alcalde."

53. The word *lienzo* can mean the face or front of a building, a stretch of wall, or the curtain of a fortification, i.e., the part of the wall between bastions. Domínguez seems to be using it to mean a more-or-less linear section of house block, in the sense of one side of a quadrangular building. Following Adams and Chavez, I have translated it "tenement" for lack of a better word.

54. This short sentence is omitted in Adams and Chavez, *Missions*, p. 213.

55. See particularly figures 21 and 22 (pp. 64, 67) in Kidder, *Pecos, New Mexico,* and his discussion of the South Pueblo, pp. 106-09.

56. Adams and Chavez, *Missions*, pp. 208-14, 181, and BNM, leg. 10, no. 43.

57. AASF, B-20, Pecos (Box 22). In an impassioned plea of 1780 begging Mendinueta to return and save New Mexico from Juan Bautista de Anza, his successor, two disgruntled New Mexicans claimed that the Pecos and Galisteos were crying out for their former benefactor. The people of Galisteo wanted to abandon the pueblo for a place where they could live without suffering such hunger. Vicente de Sena and José Miguel Peña to Mendinueta, Arizpe, June 21, 1780, BNM, leg. 10, no. 60.

58. Domínguez to Murillo, Aug. 16, 1777, Adams and Chavez, *Missions*, pp. 297-300, and BNM, leg. 10, no. 46. The day after Domínguez compiled this list, evidently at El Paso, the earnest young Fray Silvestre Vélez de Escalante, whom he had left upriver as vice-custos, addressed an official letter to the brothers admonishing them to mend their ways. See Adams, "Letter to the Missionaries."

59. Documents relating to the mission of 1777-1778 conducted from Spain to the Holy Gospel province by Fr. Juan Bautista Dosal are in AGI, Contratación, 5546, and AGI, Mex., 2732. At least six friars later assigned to Pecos were among this group: Fathers Hozio, Bermejo, Carral, Martín Bueno, Fernández de la Sierra, and Muñoz Jurado. See Appendix III. Estado en que se hallan las misiones, 1778-1813, BNM, leg. 10, no. 52. Colocación de los religiosos misioneros, c. 1779, BNM, leg. 10, no. 56.

60 Simmons, "New Mexico's Smallpox Epidemic of 1780-1781," NMHR, vol. 41 (1966), pp. 319-26. The Pecos burial book is missing for this period. The following year, 1782, the Galisteo books of burials and marriages were assigned to Pecos. AASF, Bur-9, Galisteo (Box 6a), M-10, Galisteo (Box 6a). Evidently the smallpox epidemic was the final blow to Galisteo, which was not mentioned as a living pueblo after 1782. Although most of the survivors emigrated to Santo Domingo, some Tano families turned up at Pecos in the 1790s. Estado actual de las misiones, Belén, Sept. 1, 1794, BNM, leg. 10, nos. 70 and 82.

61. Anza had first suggested reducing the number of missions as an economy measure in a report of November 1, 1779. Croix to Anza, Chihuahua, Sept. 15, 1781, and Pedro Galindo Navarro, Dictamen,

Arizpe, Aug. 6, 1781, SANM, II, nos. 831 and 832. Conde de Revillagigedo, *Informe sobre las misiones, 1793, e instrucción reservada al Marqués de Branciforte, 1794,* ed. José Bravo Ugarte (México, 1966), pp. 52-53. Resumen de los padrones, Nov. 1, 1779, BNM, leg. 10, no. 59. Fernando de la Concha visitation, Pecos, Oct. 28, 1789, HL, Ritch.

62. AASF, M-10, Galisteo (Box 6a), and B-20, Pecos (Box 22). A table reflecting Anza's consolidation shows Pecos still appended to Santa Fe in 1788 under Father Hozio and its statistics combined with the villa's. Galisteo is no longer listed. Estado actual de las misiones, Mar. 19, 1789, BNM, leg. 10, no. 85.

63. Croix to Anza, Arizpe, Aug. 12, 1781, and Jan. ??, 1783, SANM, II, nos. 827, 828, and 850b. Chavez, *Archives,* p. 41. During his visitation of Pecos on August 22, 1782, Governor Anza served as a witness to a marriage performed by Custos Bermejo. AASF, M-10, Galisteo (Box 6a).

64. See Chavez, *Archives,* pp. 41-45. Estado en que se hallan las misiones, 1778-1813, BNM, leg. 10, no. 52.

65. Concha visitation, Pecos, Oct. 28, 1789, HL, Ritch. Concha cosigned and appended to the record of his visitation church inventories. The rather cursory one for Pecos, dated November 1, 1789, was compiled by Fr. Francisco Martín Bueno, minister of Santa Fe and Pecos.

66. Revillagigedo, *Informe,* p. 53. Concha to Jacobo Ugarte y Loyola, Santa Fe, Nov. 12, 1790, SANM, II, no. 1096. Plan a que me parece indispensable en el día se extiendan las misiones, Concha, Santa Fe, Nov. 1, 1790, AGN, PI, 161. Cf. Estado actual de las misiones, Mar. 19, 1789, BNM, leg. 10, no. 85.

67. Padrón de los indios de Pecos, Patero and Ortiz, Santa Fe, Nov. 9, 1790, SANM, II, no. 1096a. Kidder, *Pecos, New Mexico,* pp. 327-28. José Mares seems to have been the 24-year-old José Julián Mares who enlisted in 1746 as a soldier in Santa Fe and the uncle of the Juan Domingo Mares, who acted as godfather to a child at Pecos on January 6, 1765. Chavez, *Families,* p. 220. AASF, B-19, Pecos (Box 22). In 1787-1788 he had explored a route via Comanche and Taovaya villages to San Antonio in Texas and back. Bolton, *Texas in the Middle Eighteenth Century* (Austin, 1970), pp. 129-30. See below, pp. 407-09. In his 1790 compilation, Concha made the population of Pecos 152 Indians, evidently leaving Mares and his son off. Plan a que me parece indispensable, Nov. 1, 1790, AGN, PI, 161.

68. Estado actual de las misiones, Sept. 1, 1794, BNM, leg. 10, nos. 70 and 82.

69. Revillagigedo, *Informe,* p. 55. Cf. Adams and Chavez, *Missions,* pp. 254-58.

70. Adams and Chavez, *Missions,* p. 258.

71. San Miguel del Vado Grant, Surveyor General of New Mexico, State Records Center and Archives, Santa Fe (SGNM), no. 119. Estado actual de las misiones, Sept. 1, 1794, BNM, leg. 10, nos. 70 and 82.

Chapter VIII, pages 360-361

1. Lista de los naturales, [Santa Fe, Aug. 1714,] SANM, II, no. 209. SANM, II, no. 99. AASF, M-18, Pecos (Box 11). For an interesting, if confused, note on the 1702 expedition see Thomas, *After Coronado,* p. 14.

2. El Cuartelejo, on the basis of archaeological evidence, seems to have been located in Scott County, Kansas. Wedel, *Introduction to Kansas Archeology,* pp. 467-68. Thomas, *After Coronado,* pp. 16-22, interpreted Ulibarrí's route, opting instead for east-central Colorado,

and published the diary, pp. 59-80. See also Kenner, *New Mexican-Plains Indian Relations,* pp. 24-27, Jones, *Pueblo Warriors,* pp. 73-77, and Gunnerson, *Jicarilla Apaches,* pp. 170-79. Ulibarrí, Appointment of José Trujillo, Santa Fe, July 11, 1706, HL, Ritch. Evidently some of the Picurís caught by Vargas in 1696 settled at Pecos. Some of those returned by Ulibarrí may also have done so. Several likely candidates identified in the extant Pecos books were Antonio Tigua (1702), Bernabé Picurí (1702, 1722), Miguel Tupatú (1714), and Lorenzo Picurí (1728). AASF, M-18 and M-19, Pecos (Box 11), and Bur-18, Pecos (Box 9).

3. Declaration of Juan Tindé et al., Santa Fe, July 8, 1711, BNM, leg. 6, no. 4. AASF, M-18, Pecos (Box 11).

4. Autos y diligencias que se han seguido contra unos indios gentiles apaches faraones, Santa Fe, Aug.-Sept. 1714, SANM, II, no. 210.

5. Juan Páez Hurtado, Diario, Aug. 30-Sept. 18, 1715, et al, BL, NMO. Thomas has translated the diary and most of the related documents in *After Coronado,* pp. 80-98. Jones, *Pueblo Warriors,* pp. 90-94, discusses the campaign. The Faraones, later pushed southward, eventually became a component of the Mescaleros. For a full discussion of the process, see Schroeder, *A Study of the Apache Indians,* Part III "The Mescalero Apaches" (New York, 1974).

6. Declaration of Juan Tindé et al., July 8, 1711, BNM, leg. 6, no. 4.

7. Declaration of Sebastián de Vargas, Santa Fe, [Aug. 1711,] et al., BNM, leg. 6, no. 4.

8. Peñuela, Santa Fe, Aug. 5, 1711, BL, NMO. Peñuela to the viceroy, Santa Fe, Oct. 20, 1711, BNM, leg. 6, no. 4.

9. Bustamante, Santa Fe, Sept. 17, 1725, SANM, II, no. 340.

10. AASF, B-19, Pecos (Box 22). Kidder, *Pecos, New Mexico,* p. 314. "The term 'genízaro' has been derived from the Turkish *yeni,* new, and *cheri,* troops; hence the English 'Janizary,' a member of a body of Turkish infantry made up of slaves, conscripts, and subject Christians. In Spanish, the word came to be applied specifically in different periods and situations to various non-typical groups or blood mixtures. In New Mexico, it was used to designate non-Pueblo Indians living in more or less Spanish fashion. Some of them were captives ransomed from the nomadic tribes, and their mixed New Mexico-born descendants inherited the designation." Adams and Chavez, *Missions,* p. 42 n. 72.

11. Custos Juan García, Patente, Isleta, June 27, 1738, AASF, Patentes, Book II (Box 2), Pecos. See Chavez, *Archives,* pp. 21, 27, 157, 161, 164.

12. Custos Andrés Varo, Informe, Santa Bárbara, Jan. 29, 1749, BNM, leg. 8, no. 57.

13. Capt. Manuel Tenorio de Alba, Pecos, Aug. 3, 1726, et al., SANM, II, 340a. The record of the 1724-1728 general military inspection and the *Reglamento* that resulted are in Pedro de Rivera, *Diario y derrotero de lo caminado, visto y observado en la visita que hizo a los presidios de la Nueva España septentrional,* ed. Vito Alessio Robles (México, 1946). See also Moorhead, *The Presidio,* pp. 27-46. A little over a month after Tenorio's troubles with the traders, Fray José Irigoyen baptized at Pecos a little Panana, or Pawnee, girl. AASF, B-19, Pecos (Box 22).

14. Fr. Juan Antonio Sánchez to the Father Provincial, México, c. 1731, BNM, leg. 7, no. 25. Ocaranza, *Establecimientos franciscanos,* pp. 179-91.

15. Fr. Lorenzo de Saavedra, Breve noticia, n.d., BNM, leg. 7, no. 14. Moorhead, *New Mexico's Royal Road: Trade and Travel on the Chihuahua Trail* (Norman, 1958), pp. 41-54.

16. Thomas, *After Coronado,* pp. 26-33, and documents, pp. 99-133. Kenner, *New Mexican-Plains Indian Relations,* pp. 28-30.

17. Rivera, *Diario y Derrotero,* p. 55. On the ways of the Comanches, see Ernest Wallace and E. Adamson Hoebel, *The Comanches, Lords of the South Plains* (Norman, 1952).

18. Two very different explanations of the displacement of Jicarillas, Cuartelejos, Faraones, and others by Comanches are advanced by Schroeder, *Apache Indians,* and Gunnerson, *Jicarilla Apaches.*

19. AASF, B-19, Pecos (Box 22), Bur-18, Pecos (Box 9).

20. Viceroy Juan Francisco de Güemes y Horcasitas to Codallos y Rabal, México, Oct. 26, 1746, BL, NMO. The Pecos burial book shows only six deaths in 1746, none of them attributed to Comanches. A folio could be missing. AASF, Bur-18, Pecos (Box 9). Chavez, *Families,* p. 277.

21. Codallos y Rabal to the viceroy, Santa Fe, Mar. 4, 1748, enclosing the declaration of Father Estremera, Santa Fe, Jan. 28, 1748, SANM, Series I, no. 1328. Charles F. Lummis published both friar's account and governor's letter in Spanish and English as "Some Unpublished History: A New Mexico Episode in 1748," *Land of Sunshine,* vol. 8 (Jan. 1898), pp. 74-78, and (Feb. 1898), pp. 126-30. Inexplicably, Twitchell, *The Spanish Archives of Mexico,* 2 vols. (Cedar Rapids, 1914), I, pp. 148-51, includes Lummis' translation of the letter not under no. 1328 but under no. 499, which has absolutely nothing to do with it. Two other accounts are in Menchero to the viceroy, Santa Fe, Apr. 24, 1748, BNM, leg. 8, no. 47, and Fr. Andrés Varo quoted by Fr. Pedro Serrano, Informe, 1761, BNM, leg. 9, no. 53, Hackett, *Documents,* III, pp. 479-501. AASF, Bur-18, Pecos (Box 9).

22. AASF, Bur-18, Pecos (Box 9), and Bur-9, Galisteo (Box 6a). Chavez, *Archives,* pp. 231-40.

23. Hubert Howe Bancroft, *History of Arizona and New Mexico 1530-1888,* (San Francisco, 1889), pp. 249-50.

24. Vélez Cachupín to the viceroy, Santa Fe, Mar. 8, 1750, AGN, PI, 37, exp. 2, and translated in Hackett, *Pichardo's Treatise,* III, pp. 325-29. There is no mistaking what the governor said: he wrote out the number *ciento y cincuenta,* a hundred and fifty. Perhaps that was the number killed in all New Mexico during Codallos' rule. From 1743 to 1749 inclusive, the Pecos book shows a total of 112 deaths, only 15 of which are blamed on Comanches. No entry for the 12 killed during the June 1746 attack is included. AASF, Bur-18, Pecos (Box 9).

25. Sanz de Lezaun and Bermejo, Informe, Zía and Santa Ana, Oct. 29, 1750, BNM, leg. 8, no. 67. For an idea of the basis of the two friars' bias, see Kelly, "Franciscan Missions," XVI, pp. 61-67.

26. Ibid., pp. 181-82. Chavez, *Archives,* p. 31. There is a passing reference in the record of Codallos' 1745 visitation to a buffalo hunt led by don José Moreno (alcalde mayor of Pecos and Galisteo, 1744-1748) during the administration of Governor Cruzat y Góngora. See above, p. 322.

27. Trigo, Informe, Istacalco, July 23, 1754, BNM, leg 9, no. 30, and Hackett, *Documents,* III, pp. 459-68. If Governor Vélez Cachupín's figures are correct for 1752, a much greater drop in Pecos' population, from 449 in 1750 to 318 in 1752, occurred during his own administration. Estado general y particular, Vélez Cachupín, 1752, AGN, PI, 102.

28. Kelly, "Franciscan Missions," XVI, pp. 181-82, relates the story as the friars told it, "one last and dramatic episode . . . to illustrate the seriousness of the Indian menace and the culpable failure of the governors to protect the Kingdom." Others, e.g. Chavez, "Carpenter Pueblo," p. 32, have retold it as fact. Hayes, *Four Churches,* p. 14, follows Kelly but judiciously substitutes "many" for the "more than 150" Pecos killed. Kidder, *Southwestern Archaeology,* p. 86, basing his account in 1924 on "stories still current among the Mexicans in the valley," called the ambush "the death blow." By 1958, however, in

Pecos, New Mexico, pp. 313, 316-17, he was no longer willing "to assign full responsibility for Pecos' extinction to Comanche hostility." The "legendary ambush," he had concluded, must have been exaggerated in the retelling and probably "dealt with a somewhat lesser disaster which may have overtaken some party of Pecos buffalo hunters who had ventured too far or too incautiously into Comanche country."

29. Vélez Cachupín to the viceroy, Mar. 8, 1750, AGN, PI, 37, exp. 2. See also the documents cited above in note 21. Kidder, *Pecos, New Mexico,* pp. 219-26. Hayes, *Four Churches,* pp. 53-55. Squad leader Bartolomé Maese was present at Pecos, along with Alcalde mayor Tomás de Sena, in December 1750 when a blind and venerable Carlana Apache man begged for baptism. AASF, B-19, Pecos (Box 22).

30. Noticia del armamento, pertrechos, y municiones, Dec. 30, 1778, SANM, II, no. 751. Razón de los pertrechos de guerra, Feb. 4, 1762, AGN, PI, 102. Estado general y particular, Vélez Cachupín, 1752, AGN, PI, 102.

31. Vélez Cachupín to the viceroy, Santa Fe, Nov. 27, 1751, Thomas, *The Plains Indians and New Mexico, 1751-1778* (Albuquerque, 1940), pp. 68-76, who translated this document and others related, mistakenly made Pecos, not Galisteo, the scene of the November 3 assault (p. 68).

32. Vélez Cachupín, Instructions to Francisco Marín del Valle, Aug. 12, 1754, Thomas, *Plains Indians,* pp. 129-43. Vélez Cachupín to the viceroy Santa Fe, Sept. 29, 1752, ibid, pp. 118-25. See also Robert Ryal Miller, ed., "New Mexico in Mid-Eighteenth Century: A Report Based on Governor Vélez Cachupín's Inspection," *Southwestern Historical Quarterly,* vol. 79 (1975-1976), pp. 166-81.

33. Miera y Pacheco, Mapa que mandó hacer el Señor Don Francisco Antonio Marín del Valle, c. 1758, AGN, Californias, 39, and reproduced below, Appendix V, pp. 510-11. Chavez, *Families* pp. 229-30. The death of Juan Diego, a Pecos buried January 1, 1758, was attributed to Comanches. AASF, Bur-18, Pecos (Box 9).

34. Miera y Pacheco, Mapa del reino del Nuevo México, c. 1760, Dirección General de Geografía y Meteorología, Tacubaya, D.F., Colección de Orozco y Berra, no. 1148, and reproduced above following p. 166. Bolton, *Pageant in the Wilderness: The Story of the Escalante Expedition to the Interior Basin, 1776* (Salt Lake City, 1950), pp. 11-13.

35. For background see Thomas, *After Coronado,* and Henry Folmer, *Franco-Spanish Rivalry in North America, 1524-1763* (Glendale, Calif., 1953).

36. Folmer, "Contraband Trade between Louisiana and New Mexico in the Eighteenth Century," NMHR, vol. 16 (1941), pp. 262-63, quotes Roybal's letter. Declaration of Pierre Mallet et al., Hackett, *Pichardo's Treatise,* III, pp. 349-52. Gunnerson, *Jicarilla Apaches,* pp. 222-25, discusses the French diplomacy that opened the way to New Mexico.

37. Diligencias judiciales en orden a la averiguación de la persona de Santiago Belo, 1744, SANM, II, no. 456. Codallos y Rabal to the viceroy, Santa Fe, Mar. 4, 1748, SANM, I, no. 1328. Folmer, "Contraband Trade," pp. 264-65.

38. Bolton, "French Intrusions into New Mexico, 1749-1752," in John Francis Bannon, ed., *Bolton and the Spanish Borderlands* (Norman, 1964), pp. 154-63.

39. The documents concerning the return of Mallet are translated in Hackett, *Pichardo's Treatise,* III, pp. 333-63.

40. At Pecos on May 3, 1757, Fray Juan José Hernández baptized María Andrea, an adult of the so-called A or Aa tribe, with Bernardo de Miera y Pacheco's wife and his son Manuel serving as godparents. Simmons, "The Mysterious A Tribe of the Southern Plains," *The Changing Ways of Southwestern Indians: A Historic Perspective,* ed. Albert

H. Schroeder (Glorieta, N.M., 1973), pp. 73-89, has concluded that the Aa Indians were Skidi Pawnees.

41. Testimonio de los autos . . . sobre haber llegado dos franceses cargados de efectos que conducían de la Nueva Orleans, AGN, PI, 34, exp. 3. Both Hackett, *Pichardo's Treatise,* III, pp. 363-70, and Thomas, *Plains Indians,* pp. 82-110 (including the invoices), have translated documents relating to poor Chapuis and Feuilli.

42. Pedro Fermín de Mendinueta to the viceroy, Santa Fe, Mar. 30, 1772, AGN, PI 103. For the background, enactment, and functioning of the General Command, see Luis Navarro García, *Don José de Gálvez y la Comandancia General de las Provincias Internas del Norte de Nueva España* (Sevilla, 1964).

43. Portillo Urrisola to Bishop Tamarón, Santa Fe, Feb. 24, 1762, Adams, *Tamarón's Visitation,* pp. 58-62. Adams and Chavez, *Missions,* pp. 4, 251-52.

44. Thomas, *Plains Indians,* pp. 33-48, 148-56. Jones, *Pueblo Warriors,* pp. 131-47. Navarro García, *Gálvez,* pp. 244-50.

45. Mendinueta to the viceroy, Santa Fe, May 11, 1771, AGN, PI, 103.

46. Mendinueta to the viceroy, Santa Fe, Apr. 27, 1769, ibid.

47. Mendinueta to the viceroy, Santa Fe, Apr. 27, 1769, Jan. 18, May 11, Aug. 18, 1771, and Jan. 4, 1772, ibid. The governor reported similar raids in his letters to the viceroy of March 30, 1772, May 14, 1773, and October 16, 1773. Ibid.

48. Mendinueta to the viceroy, Santa Fe, June 20, 1774, ibid., and Sept. 30, 1774, AGN, PI, 65, exp. 10. Thomas, *Plains Indians,* pp. 169-73, translated the latter from an AGI copy.

49. Mendinueta to the viceroy, Santa Fe, Oct. 20, 1774, ibid., pp. 173-77. The Fernández victory, basis of the New Mexico folk drama "Los Comanches," has been somewhat confused over the years. See Kenner, *New Mexican-Plains Indian Relations.* p. 29n.

50. Mendinueta to the viceroy, Santa Fe, Mar. 30, May 12, and Aug. 18, 1775, AGN, PI, 65, exp. 10. The last two are in Thomas, *Plains Indians,* pp. 179-84. Adams and Chavez, *Missions,* pp. 213-14. During these years the Franciscans recorded in the Pecos book only four burials. One of them was for José Antonio, September 19, 1772, killed by Comanches. AASF, Bur-18, Pecos (Box 9).

51. Navarro García, *Gálvez,* pp. 275-81. See also Thomas, *Teodoro de Croix and the Northern Frontier of New Spain, 1776-1783* (Norman, 1941) and Moorhead, *The Presidio.*

52. Thomas, *Forgotten Frontiers: A Study of the Spanish Indian Policy of Don Juan Bautista de Anza, Governor of New Mexico, 1777-1787* (Norman, 1932), pp. 64-71, along with a translation of Anza's diary, Aug. 15-Sept. 10, and his covering letter to Croix, Nov. 1, 1779, pp. 121-42.

53. In April, June, October, and November 1783 the minister of Santa Fe noted in the Pecos book the burials of Francisco Pancho Pamie, José Francisco Aguilar, Lucas Ponhana, and Andrés Tonui, all "killed by Comanches." AASF, Bur-9, Galisteo (Box 6a).

54. On the Comanche peace, in addition to Thomas, *Forgotten Frontiers,* pp. 71-83, 292-342, in which the documents are translated, see also Moorhead, *The Apache Frontier: Jacobo Ugarte and Spanish-Indian Relations in Northern New Spain, 1769-1791* (Norman, 1968) pp. 143-69.

55. Relación de los sucesos ocurridos en la Provincia del Nuevo México con motivo de la paz concedida a la Nación Comanche, Nov. 17, 1785-July 15, 1786, AGN, PI, 65, exp. 2, and translated from an AGI copy by Thomas, *Forgotten Frontiers,* pp. 294-324. Francisco Javier Ortiz to Anza, Santa Fe, May 20, 1786, ibid. Wallace and Hoebel,

Comanches, pp. 4-5. AASF, Bur-9, Galisteo (Box 6a).

56. Ugarte y Loyola to the Marqués de Sonora, Chihuahua, Jan. 4, 1787, AGN, PI, 65, exp. 2. Moorhead, *Apache Frontier,* pp. 156-59.

57. Artículos de paz concertados y arreglados en la villa de Santa Fe y pueblo de Pecos, 1786, AGN, PI, 65, exp. 2, and translation by Thomas, *Forgotten Frontiers,* pp. 329-32.

58. Adams and Chavez, *Missions,* p. 252.

59. Relación de los sucesos, AGN, PI, 65, exp. 2. I have seen no specific documentation for an earlier Comanche trade fair at Pecos. Out of force of habit, Moorhead, *Apache Frontier,* p. 147, asserts incorrectly that this one too was held at Taos.

60. Relación de los sucesos, AGN, PI, 65, exp. 2. Moorhead, *Apache Frontier,* pp. 147-69. Ronald J. Benes, "Anza and Concha in New Mexico, 1787-1793: A Study in New Colonial Techniques," *Journal of the West,* vol. 4 (1965), pp. 63-76. Thomas, "San Carlos, A Comanche Pueblo on the Arkansas River, 1787," *The Colorado Magazine,* vol. 6 (1929), pp. 79-91. Simmons, *Border Comanches: Seven Spanish Colonial Documents, 1785-1819* (Santa Fe, 1967), pp. 23-31.

61. Revillagigedo to Pedro de Nava, Apr. 30, 1793, as quoted in Noel M. Loomis and Abraham P. Nasatir, *Pedro Vial and the Roads to Santa Fe* (Norman, 1967), pp. 392-93. Not only does this work set these explorations in context but it also includes translations of the diaries. See also Nasatir's synthesis *Borderland in Retreat: From Spanish Louisiana to the Far Southwest* (Albuquerque, 1976).

62. Concha to Ugarte y Loyola, Santa Fe, Nov. 10, 1787, AGN, PI, 65, exp. 1.

63. Pedro de Nava to Revillagigedo, Chihuahua, June 24, 1791, AGN, PI, 65, exp. 16. Moorhead, *Apache Frontier,* pp. 166-69.

64. Nava to Revillagigedo, June 24, 1791, AGN, PI, 65, exp. 16. Simmons, ed., "Governor Anza, the Lipan Apaches and Pecos Pueblo," EP, vol. 77, no. 1 (1970), pp. 35-40.

Chapter IX, pages 417-419

1. San Miguel del Vado Grant, SGNM, no. 119. See Albert James Díaz, *A Guide to the Microfilm of Papers relating to New Mexico Land Grants* (Albuquerque, 1960). Estado actual . . . 1794, BNM, leg. 10, no. 82. Estado que muestra las jurisdicciones . . . 1799, ibid., no. 74.

2. AASF, B-20, Pecos (Box 22), M-10, Galisteo (Box 6a), Bur-9, Galisteo (Box 6a). There are other scattered references to Pecos Indians living at San Miguel del Vado or at some other of the numerous satellite communities that sprang up in the valley, but they do not add up to a significant exodus. Fray Angelico Chavez' statement that El Vado was settled by Hispanos, genízaros, and "also by Indians of other pueblos, including more progressive Pecos Indians, who entered into a genízaro status and thus contributed to the depopulation of their pueblo" is too strong. Chavez, *Archives,* p. 205.

3. H. Bailey Carroll and J. Villasana Haggard, eds., *Three New Mexico Chronicles* (Albuquerque, 1942), pp. 8n, 215 n. 2. San Miguel del Vado Grant, SGNM, no. 119. SANM, I, no. 887. Although Pino did not mention the five-year residency requirement, it applied to similar community grants made by Governor Chacón, for example the Cebolleta Grant at the foot of Mount Taylor. Reeve, "Navaho Foreign Affairs, 1795-1846," part I, 1795-1815, NMHR, vol. 46 (1971), pp. 108, 121. Juan de Dios Fernández, the former Pecos Indian, was not listed among the recipients of farming lands at either San Miguel or San José. One of the San Miguel genízaros, José María Garduño, who

received 130 varas of land in the distribution, was arrested four years later in Chihuahua as a vagrant. SANM, II, no. 2043.

4. AASF, B-20, Pecos (Box 22), M-10, Galisteo (Box 6a), Bur-9, Galisteo (Box 6a).

5. Estado en que se hallan las misiones . . . 1778-1813, et al., BNM, leg. 10, no. 52. Estado actual . . . 1974, ibid, no. 82

6. Fr. Buenaventura Merino, Santa Fe, June 10, 1801, Cathedral Archive, Durango. Merino, who signed the Pecos books between May of 1792 and February 1802, had entered the Order at the convento in Medina de Río Seco on October 18, 1759, had professed his religious vows there on October 19, 1760, and had studied philosophy for three years, sacred theology for three, and moral theology for a year and a half. Elected preacher in 1768, he served subsequently in the conventos of Almazán and Atienza. Nómina de los religiosos, June 28, 1803, BNM, leg. 10, no. 77. Chavez, *Archives,* p. 166. Merino and Fr. Severo Patero to the viceroy, Colegio de San Fernando de México, Mar. 30, 1790, et al., AGN, PI, 161, part 7.

7. Baptismal entry, Feb. 26, 1804, AASF, B-20, Pecos (Box 22).

8. Nómina de los religiosos, June 28, 1803, and Noticia de los religiosos, 1815, BNM, leg. 10, nos. 77 and 78.

9. Bragado y Rico to the bishop of Durango, Pecos, Dec. 11, 1804, license granted, Durango, Feb. 22, 1805, endorsed by Gov. Joaquín del Real Alencaster, Santa Fe, Apr. 30, 1805, AASF, 1804, no. 14. Bragado also stood by the El Vado settlers in a dispute over the ten pesos for the license which Governor Chacón apparently had misappropriated. Diego Manuel Baca et al. to alcalde de primer voto, Puesto del Vado, May 24, 1805, AASF, 1805, no. 6.

10. Noticia de las misiones, Chacón, Santa Fe, Dec. 31, 1804, AGI, Mex., 2737.

11. Bartolomé Fernández, San Miguel del Vado, July 28, 1805, et al., SANM, II, no. 1867.

12. Pereyro to Manrique, Santa Clara, Mar. 8, 1809, and Manrique to Pereyro, Santa Fe, Mar. 10, 1809, SANM, II, no. 2209.

13. Manrique to Nemesio Salcedo, Santa Fe, Mar. 19, 1810, SANM, II, no. 2302. AASF, B-20, Pecos (Box 22), M-10, Galisteo (Box 6a), Bur-9, Galisteo (Box 6a).

14. Although García del Valle began on March 8, 1811, baptizing babies at the El Vado settlements, he did not mention a church there until late September. Up until then he had been burying El Vado people at Pecos. But on September 28, he buried a girl "in this chapel of San Miguel." On September 30, he baptized a child "in this parish church of San Miguel del Vado belonging to the mission of Nuestra Señora de los Ángeles de Pecos." He celebrated the first wedding "in the church of San Miguel" on October 14, 1811. Ibid.

15. Guerrero to the gobernador de la mitra, c. 1811, and response, M. Cosío, Durango, Feb. 6, 1812, AASF, 1812, no. 14.

16. Carroll and Haggard, *Three New Mexico Chronicles,* pp. 50-53. Pino's entire *Exposición* is reproduced photographically on pp. 211-61.

17. Manuel Baca et al., San Miguel del Vado, Jan. 16, 1814, SANM, II, no. 2527.

18. Chacón to Pedro de Nava, Santa Fe, Nov. 18, 1797, SANM, II, no. 1404. Kenner, *New Mexican-Plains Indian Relations,* pp. 56-57. On August 21-22, 1809, Gov. José Manrique was called down from Santa Fe to parley with Comanches at Pecos pueblo. SANM, II, no. 2237.

19. Salcedo to Chacón, Chihuahua, Jan. 16, 1804, SANM, II, no. 1703.

20. Chacón to Salcedo, Mar. 28, 1804, no. 75, SANM, II, no 1714.

Alejandro Martín turns up again and again in the Pecos-El Vado books. Chacón identified Gurulé as an Indian of the Aa tribe.

21. Chacón to Salcedo, Santa Fe, Mar. 28, 1804, no. 73, SANM, II, no. 1714. AASF, Bur-9, Galisteo (Box 6a).

22. Juan Lucero, San Miguel del Vado, Dec. 16, 1808, SANM, II, no. 2193. See also nos. 2178 and 2194. Gov. Alberto Maynez had ordered a force to assemble at Pecos pueblo in July 1808. Maynez, Santa Fe, June 11, and Dionisio Valle to Maynez, Pecos, July 6, 1808, SANM, II, nos. 2111, 2136. Capt. Francisco Amangual, en route from San Antonio in Texas to Santa Fe, on June 17 reported that Capt. Dionisio Valle and his men were camped at Pecos mission. Next evening Amangual's party camped there too and found nearby a small spring in an arroyo of white sand. Loomis and Nasatir, *Vial,* pp. 507-08. For an informative treatment of comancheros and ciboleros, the plains traders and hunters, see Kenner, *New Mexican-Plains Indian Relations,* pp. 78-114.

23. Declaration of Juan Luján, Santa Fe, Jan. 11, 1806, SANM, II, no. 1948.

24. Sumaria información indigatoria sobre covocatoria, conmoción, y escándalo cometido entre los vecinos de las jurisdicciones Tenencia de Pecos y Alcaldía de la Cañada, 1805, SANM, II, no. 1930. For the United States threat to New Mexico, and plains diplomacy during these years, see Loomis and Nasatir, *Vial,* and Nasatir, *Borderland in Retreat.*

25. Manuel Baca to Gov. José Manrique, San Miguel del Vado, June 1, 1813, SANM, II, no. 2492. Felipe Sandoval, Santa Fe, Aug. 17, 1814, SANM, I, no. 703. Maynez, Santa Fe, June 14, 1808, SANM, II, no. 2114.

26. Melgares to Alejo García Conde, Santa Fe, Oct. 8, 1818, Thomas, ed., "Documents Bearing upon the Northern Frontier of New Mexico, 1818-1819," NMHR, vol. 4 (1929), p. 156. García Conde to Melgares, Durango, Nov. 9, 1818, SANM, II, no. 2771. Kenner, *New Mexican-Plains Indian Relations,* p. 63, says that "Melgares reported the arrival at Pecos of more than a thousand Indians under Chief Soguara, 'to trade in this province, according to custom' " (also p. 56). They probably did arrive at Pecos, although the documents do not specify the place.

27. Declaration of Manuel Antonio Rivera, Santa Fe, Oct. 8, 1819, SANM, II, no. 2850.

28. Manuel Durán to Melgares, El Vado, Aug. 21, 1821, and Melgares to the alcaldes, Santa Fe, Aug. 25, 1821, SANM, II, nos. 3008, 3010.

29. John Peabody Harrington, "The Ethnogeography of the Tewa Indians," *Twenty-Ninth Annual Report of the Bureau of American Ethnology* (Washington, D.C., 1916), p. 478.

30. Trujillo et al., Santa Fe, Aug. 21, 1813, SANM, I, no. 1005.

31. Gov. Domingo Jironza Petrís de Cruzate, El Paso, Sept. 25, 1689 (spurious?), SGNM, no. F. Twitchell, *Spanish Archives,* I, pp. 466-69, includes a transcription of the Spanish with several slips. The Pecos Pueblo grant, he says on page 478, "was surveyed in 1859 for a little over 18,763 acres and was patented in 1864." For the pueblo league see Myra Ellen Jenkins, "Spanish Land Grants in the Tewa Area," NMHR, vol. 47 (1972), pp. 114-16.

32. Felipe Sandoval, Santa Fe, Aug. 17, 1814, et al., SANM, I, no. 703.

33. Matías Ortiz, Santa Fe, June 30, 1815, et al., SANM, I, no. 18. Twitchell, *Spanish Archives,* I, pp. 193-96.

34. Villanueva to Melgares, El Vado, Aug. 19, 1818, and Juan de Aguilar, petition admitted, Santa Fe, Aug. 19, 1818, SANM, I, no. 56. Twitchell, *Spanish Archives,* I, pp. 30-31.

35. Los Trigos Grant, SGNM, no. 8, and Twitchell, *Spanish Archives*, I, pp. 296-97. Reportedly, about 1822 Vicente Villanueva was killed near Las Ruedas and the Los Trigos grant temporarily abandoned.

36. Esteban Baca et al., Santa Fe, Feb. 10, 1821, SANM, I, no. 130. A census dated December 31, 1821, showed Pecos with 26 men and 28 women. SANM, II, no. 3094.

37. Luis Benavides, Santa Fe, Mar. 8, 1825, SANM, I, no. 138. Rafael Benavides et al., Santa Fe, Mar. 1, 1825, SANM, I, no. 135. Also SANM, I, no. 388.

38. San Miguel del Vado, baptisms, 1829-1839, B-1 (box 40), marriages, 1829-1846, M-1, (box 20), and burials, 1829-1847, Bur-1 (box 18), AASF. These take up where the last Pecos mission books leave off. The two Roybal boys were 1) José Polonio, son of José María Roybal and Juana Sena, godparents Tomás Maese and Bárbara Aguilar, and 2) José Casildo, son of Miguel Roybal and Ignacia Herrera, godparents José Luis Armijo and Juana Armijo. From the Pecos and El Vado church records a fairly complete roster of the early families of the Cañón de Pecos area could be compiled.

39. Rafael Aguilar et al., Pecos, Mar. 12, 1826, SANM, I, no. 1370. Twitchell, *Spanish Archives*, I, p. 378.

40. Narbona to ministro de relaciones interiores y exteriores, Santa Fe, Oct. 14, 1826, SANM, I, no. 1371. A translation of this document is appended to Florence Hawley Ellis, *A Reconstruction of the Basic Jemez Pattern of Social Organization, with Comparisons to Other Tanoan Social Structures* (Albuquerque, 1964), pp. 59-61. José Rámon Alarid to Narbona, El Vado, Aug. 21, 1826, SANM, I, no. 62.

41. Aguilar and Cota to the governor, Santa Fe, Mar. 9, 1829, and Pedro González et al. to Santiago Ulibarrí, Ciénaga de Pecos, Mar. 1, 1829, SANM, I, no. 288.

42. Commission report by "Pino, Arce, Baca," n.d., Pecos Pueblo Grant, SGNM, no. F.

43. José María Paredes to Ramón Abreu, México, Feb. 11, 1830, SANM, I, no. 1369. Domingo Fernández et al. to the jefe político, Santa Fe, May 7, 1829, SANM, I, no. 288. All the grantees of the 1825 Rafael Benavides grant joined with Fernández in the protest. See SANM, I, nos. 284-87, for Fernández grants.

44. The preceding paragraphs are a rather cursory treatment of Pecos lands up into the Mexican Period. Attorney Em Hall, a resident of the village of Pecos since 1970, is currently at work on a complete study of the subject.

45. Manuel Durán to Melgares, El Vado, Jan. 3, 1821, SANM, II, no. 2954.

46. Josiah Gregg, *Commerce of the Prairies,* ed. Moorhead (Norman, 1954), pp. 13-16, 331-32n. In a privately printed, seven-page pamphlet Marc Simmons takes issue with Gregg, arguing that Becknell's purpose right from the start was trade with Santa Fe. *Opening the Santa Fe Trail, One Hundred and Fifty Years, 1821-1971* (Cerrillos, N.M., 1971).

47. Thomas James, *Three Years among the Indians and Mexicans* (Philadelphia and New York, 1962), pp. 80-90. As an antidote to the biased James account, take the equally biased account by Governor Melgares in David J. Weber, ed., "An Unforgettable Day: Facundo Melgares on Independence," NMHR, vol. 48 (1973), pp. 27-44.

49. Narbona to Caballero, Santa Fe, Apr. 17, 1827, and Vigil to Caballero, San Miguel del Vado, Apr. 17, 1827, AASF, 1827, nos. 24 and 25, also nos. 11-12, and 22-23.

50. Caballero's last entry in the Pecos-San Miguel books was for a baptism on March 4, 1828. AASF, B-20, Pecos (Box 22). Armijo, Santa Fe, Mar. 3, 1828, AASF, 1828, no. 13. Inventario de los uten-

cilios y alajas, San Miguel del Vado, Feb. 28, 1828, ibid., no. 12. It would seem that Chavez, *Archives*, p. 98, who says that San Miguel was still "a chapel under Pecos mission," misread the document. Certain items borrowed from the mission belonged to Pecos, not the chapel itself.

51. Nómina de los religiosos, June 28, 1803, and Estado general de esta Santa Custodia, 1817, BNM, leg. 10, nos. 77 and 80. Chavez, *Archives*, pp. 196, 237.

52. AASF, B-20, Pecos (Box 22), M-10, Galisteo (Box 6a), Bur-9, Galisteo (Box 6a). A search of the San Miguel books turned up the baptism at San Miguel of a baby girl "from the pueblo of Pecos" as late as March 21, 1835. The priest was Rafael Ortiz, the infant's parents "unknown."

53. Notice of Bishop Zubiría's visitation, San Miguel del Vado, Sept. 29, 1833, AASF, B-1, San Miguel del Vado (Box 40).

54. Kidder, *Pecos, New Mexico*, p. 66. Actually it was Adolph F. Bandelier who first commented on this "path of ruin" during his visit to the site in 1880. "This decay is the same in both houses [i.e., Kidder's South Pueblo and Quadrangle]; the path of ruin from S.S.E. to N.N.W. indicates its progress. It shows clearly that, as section after section had been originally added as the tribe increased in number, so cell after cell (or section after section) was successively vacated and left to ruin as their numbers waned, till at last the northern end of the building alone sheltered the poor survivors." Bandelier, "A Visit to the Aboriginal Ruins in the Valley of the Rio Pecos," *Papers of the Archaeological Institute of America*, American Series, Vol. 1 (Boston, 1881), p. 133.

55. Charles Fletcher Lummis, *The Man Who Married the Moon and Other Pueblo Indian Folk-stories* (New York, 1894), pp. 137-46.

56. See Bloom, *Early Vaccination in New Mexico*, Publications of the Historical Society of New Mexico, no. 27 (Santa Fe, 1924). AASF, Bur-9, Galisteo (Box 6a), and Bur-1, San Miguel del Vado (Box 18). Kidder, *Pecos, New Mexico*, p. 313.

57. Kenner, *New Mexican-Plains Indian Relations*, p. 75. Juan Esteban Pino to Juan José Arocha, Cañón de Pecos, June 17, 1828, Mexican Archives of New Mexico, State Records Center and Archives, Santa Fe (MANM).

58. James H. Simpson, *Journal of a Military Reconnaissance from Santa Fé, New Mexico, to the Navajo Country* (Philadelphia, 1852), p. 21. Revista de armas, Primer Compañía de Milicias, Manuel Baca, El Vado, Sept. 9, 1821, SANM, II, no 3028. AASF, B-20, Pecos (Box 22), and M-10, Galisteo (Box 6a). I have extracted the vital data from every extant baptismal, marriage, and burial entry in the Pecos books down to 1810. By then entries for El Vado residents had inundated the natives'. A careful study of these books to the end, to 1829, and the San Miguel books after that, would probably turn up other Pecos emigrants, as well as basic data on settlement patterns in the valley.

59. Tradition in support of a second evacuation, involving only five persons, is strong. In 1880 Adolph Bandelier heard from E. Vigil that the last fourteen Pecos had appeared before Gov. Manuel Armijo in 1840 and declared that they could no longer maintain themselves at their own pueblo. As a consequence, they wished to accept the invitation of the Jémez, tendered in 1838. Juan Esteban Pino had bought most of their lands. The rest they had given to Mariano Ruiz, who had come from Jémez to Pecos in 1837. Ruiz told Bandelier that the last five Pecos, "Antonio (*gobernador*, and still living at Jemez), Gregorio, Goya, Juan Domingo, and Francisco," were removed to Jémez by Jémez officials in 1840. Bandelier, "Visit to the Aboriginal Ruins," pp. 124-25, and *The Southwestern Journals of Adolph F. Bandelier, 1880-1882*, eds. Lange and Riley (Albuquerque, 1966), pp. 77, 84. Kidder, *Pecos, New*

Mexico, p. 317. Harrington, "Ethnogeography of the Tewa Indians," pp. 477-78. Lummis, *The Man Who Married the Moon,* pp. 143-45. Among surviving documents for 1840 in the MANM there seems to be no record of the Pecos appearing before Armijo.

60. Simpson, *Journal,* pp. 22-23.

61. Edgar L. Hewett, "Studies on the Extinct Pueblo of Pecos," *American Anthropologist,* vol. 6 (1904), pp. 426-39, provided a list of the names in the Pecos dialect of the seven men, seven women, and three children who vacated the pueblo in 1838. Elsie Clews Parsons, *The Pueblo of Jemez* (New Haven, 1925), pp. 130-35, working at Jémez a couple of decades later, brought the list up to twenty and supplied some of the refugees' Spanish names. Unfortunately the Jémez books of baptisms, marriages, and burials for the 1830s and 1840s, which might aid in fixing the date of the Pecos immigration, are missing. A crude draft of some baptismal entries (AASF, 1840, no. 8) reveals two sons born to Juan Antonio Toya and Juana María at Jémez—Juan Pablo, baptized on June 30, 1840, and José San Juan, baptized Christmas Eve 1841. Francisco and Guadalupe were listed as the paternal grandparents, with Mariano San Juan and María the maternal set. María of Jémez served as the godparent of both infants.

62. John E. Sunder, ed., *Matt Field on the Santa Fe Trail* (Norman, 1960), pp. 50-51, 247-51. Gregg, *Commerce,* pp. 188-90. In the Quadrangle, at the southwest corner of the northern house block, Bandelier thought he had found the room where the sacred fire was kept. "Great interest attaches to this apartment, from the fact that, according to Sr. Mariano Ruiz, the sacred embers ("braza") were kept here until 1840, in which year the five last remaining families of Pecos Indians removed to their cognates at Jemez, and the 'sacred fire' disappeared with them. Sr. Ruiz is good authority on that point, since, as a member of the tribe ("hijo del pueblo"), he was asked to perform his duty by attending to the embers one year. He refused, for reasons which I shall hereafter state. The facts—that the fire was kept in a sort of closed oven, and that the front opening existed—made it unnecessary to search for any other conduit for smoke and ventilation. The fire was kept covered, and not permitted to flame." Bandelier, "Visit to the Aboriginal Ruins," p. 82.

63. For a summary of the Montezuma and sacred snake legends of Pecos, see Simmons, *Witchcraft in the Southwest: Spanish and Indian Supernaturalism on the Rio Grande* (Flagstaff, Ariz., 1974), pp. 127-34. Also Bandelier, "Visit to the Aboriginal Ruins," pp. 125-26; Edward S. Curtis, *The North American Indian,* vol. 17 (Norwood, Mass., 1926), pp. 19-21; and Helen H. Roberts, "The Reason for the Departure of the Pecos Indians for Jemez Pueblo," *American Anthropologist,* vol. 34 (1932), pp. 359-60.

BIBLIOGRaphy

Archives and Collections

Archives of the Archdiocese of Santa Fe, Albuquerque (AASF)
Archivo General de Indias, Sevilla, Spain (AGI)
    Audiencia de Guadalajara (Guad.)
    Audiencia de México (Mex.)
    Contaduría
    Contratación
    Justicia
    Patronato
Archivo General de la Nación, México (AGN)
    Californias
    Civil
    Historia
    Inquisición (Inq.)
    Provincias Internas (PI)
    Reales Cédulas
    Tierras
Bancroft Library, University of California, Berkeley (BL)
    Bolton Research Papers (BRP)
    Mexican Manuscripts (M-M)
    New Mexico Originals (NMO)
Biblioteca Nacional, México (BNM)
    Archivo Franciscano, New Mexico Documents
Cathedral Archive, Durango, Mexico
Dirección General de Geografía y Meteorología, Tacubaya, Mex.
    Colección de Orozco y Berra
Huntington Library, San Marino, California (HL)
    Ritch Collection (Ritch)
Newberry Library, Chicago
    Ayer Collection
State Records Center and Archives, Santa Fe
    Mexican Archives of New Mexico (MANM)
    Spanish Archives of New Mexico (SANM)
      Series I
      Series II
    Surveyor General of New Mexico (SGNM)
University of New Mexico, Zimmerman Library
    Special Collections
University of Texas Library, Austin
    Latin American Manuscripts

Books, Articles, and Miscellaneous Works

Abel, Annie Heloise, *The Official Correspondence of James S. Calhoun,* Washington, D.C., Office of Indian Affairs, 1915.

Abert, J. W., *Report of Lieut. J. W. Abert of His Examination of New Mexico, in the Years 1846-1847,* 30th Cong., 1st sess., House Ex. Doc. No. 41, Washington, D.C., Wendell and Van Benthuysen, 1848.

————, *Western America in 1846-1847: The Original Travel Diary of Lieutenant J. W. Abert, who mapped New Mexico for the United States Army,* ed. John Galvin, San Francisco, John Howell Books, 1966.

Adams, Eleanor B., *Bishop Tamarón's Visitation of New Mexico, 1760,* Albuquerque, Historical Society of New Mexico, 1954.

————, "Fray Silvestre and the Obstinate Hopi," *New Mexico Historical Review,* vol. 38 (1963), pp. 97-138.

————, ed., "Letter to the Missionaries of New Mexico," by Fray Silvestre Vélez de Escalante, 1777, *New Mexico Historical Review,* vol. 40 (1965), pp. 319-35.

Adams, Eleanor B., and Fray Angelico Chavez, *The Missions of New Mexico, 1776: A Description by Fray Francisco Atanasio Domínguez with Other Contemporary Documents,* Albuquerque, University of New Mexico Press, 1956, 1976.

Adams, Eleanor B., and John E. Longhurst, "New Mexico and the Sack of Rome: One Hundred Years Later," *New Mexico Historical Review,* vol. 28 (1953), pp. 243-50.

Autos sobre quejas de los religiosos franciscanos del Nuevo México, 1636, ed. Vargas Rea, México, 1947.

Bailey, Jessie Bromilow, *Diego de Vargas and the Reconquest of New Mexico,* Albuquerque, University of New Mexico Press, 1940.

Bakewell, Peter John, *Silver Mining and Society in Colonial Mexico, Zacatecas, 1546-1700,* Cambridge, Cambridge University Press, 1971.

Bancroft, Hubert Howe, *History of Arizona and New Mexico, 1530-1888,* San Francisco, The History Company, 1889, Albuquerque, Horn and Wallace, 1962.

Bandelier, Adolph F., *Final Report of Investigations among the Indians of the Southwestern United States, Carried on Mainly in the Years from 1880 to 1885,* 2 vols., *Papers of the Archaeological Institute of America,* American Series, Vols. 3 and 4, Cambridge, Mass., John Wilson and Son, 1890-1892.

————, "The 'Montezuma' of the Pueblo Indians," *American Anthropologist,* vol. 5 (1892), pp. 319-26.

————, *The Southwestern Journals of Adolph F. Bandelier, 1880-1882,* ed. Charles H. Lange and Carroll L. Riley, Albuquerque, University of New Mexico Press, 1966, *1883-1884,* 1970, *1885-1888,* and Elizabeth M. Lange, 1975.

————, "A Visit to the Aboriginal Ruins in the Valley of the Rio Pecos," *Papers of the Archaeological Institute of America,* American Series, Vol. 1, Boston, A. Williams and Co., 1881, pp. 35-135.

Bannon, John Francis, ed., *Bolton and the Spanish Borderlands,* Norman, University of Oklahoma Press, 1964.

—————, *The Spanish Borderlands Frontier, 1513-1821,* Albuquerque, University of New Mexico Press, 1970.

Barker, S. Omar, "Pecos Ruins: Newest National Monument," *New Mexico Magazine,* vol. 44 (June-July 1966), pp. 30-31, 38.

Benavides, Alonso de, *Benavides' Memorial of 1630,* trans, Peter P. Forrestal, ed. Cyprian J. Lynch, Washington, D.C., Academy of American Franciscan History, 1954.

—————, *Fray Alonso de Benavides' Revised Memorial of 1634,* eds. Frederick Webb Hodge, George P. Hammond, and Agapito Rey, Albuquerque, University of New Mexico Press, 1945.

—————, *The Memorial of Fray Alonso de Benavides, 1630,* trans. Mrs. Edward E. Ayer, Chicago, privately printed, 1916.

Benes, Ronald J., "Anza and Concha in New Mexico, 1787-1793: A Study in New Colonial Techniques," *Journal of the West,* vol. 4 (1965), pp. 63-76.

Bloom, Lansing B., *Early Vaccination in New Mexico,* Publications of the Historical Society of New Mexico, no. 27, Santa Fe, Santa Fe New Mexican Publishing Corp., 1924.

—————, ed., "Fray Estevan de Perea's *Relación,*" *New Mexico Historical Review,* vol. 8 (1933), pp. 211-35.

—————, "Who Discovered New Mexico?," *New Mexico Historical Review,* vol. 15 (1940), pp. 101-32.

Bloom, Lansing B., and Lynn B. Mitchell, "The Chapter Elections in 1672," *New Mexico Historical Review,* vol. 13 (1938), pp. 85-119.

Bolton, Herbert E., *Coronado, Knight of Pueblos and Plains,* Albuquerque, University of New Mexico Press, 1949.

—————, "French Intrusions into New Mexico, 1749-1752," in John Francis Bannon, ed., *Bolton and the Spanish Borderlands,* Norman, University of Oklahoma Press, 1964, pp. 154-63.

—————, *Guide to Materials for the History of the United States in the Principal Archives of Mexico,* Washington, D.C., Carnegie Institution, 1913, New York, Kraus Reprint, 1965.

—————, "The Mission as a Frontier Institution in the Spanish-American Colonies," *American Historical Review,* vol. 23 (1917), pp. 42-61.

—————, *Pageant in the Wilderness: The Story of the Escalante Expedition to the Interior Basin, 1776,* Salt Lake City, Utah State Historical Society, 1950.

—————, *Spanish Exploration in the Southwest, 1542-1706,* New York, Charles Scribner's Sons, 1908, Barnes and Noble, 1967.

—————, *Texas in the Middle Eighteenth Century: Studies in Spanish Colonial History and Administration,* Berkeley, University of California Press, 1915, and reprint, Austin, University of Texas Press, 1970.

Bourke, John G., "Bourke on the Southwest," ed. Lansing B. Bloom, *New Mexico Historical Review,* vols. 8-13 (1933-1938), *passim.*

Bowden, Henry Warner, "Spanish Missions, Cultural Conflict and the Pueblo Revolt of 1680," *Church History,* vol. 44 (1975), pp. 217-28.

Boyd, E., *Popular Arts of Spanish New Mexico,* Santa Fe, Museum of New Mexico, 1974.

Brinckerhoff, Sidney B., and Odie B. Faulk, *Lancers for the King, A Study of the Frontier Military System of Northern New Spain, With a Translation of the Royal Regulations of 1772,* Phoenix, Arizona Historical Foundation, 1965.

Brugge, David M., "Pueblo Factionalism and External Relations," *Ethnohistory,* vol. 16 (1969), pp. 191-200.

—————, "Some Plains Indians in the Church Records of New Mexico," *Plains Anthropologist,* vol. 10 (1965), pp. 181-89.

Carroll, H. Bailey, and J. Villasana Haggard, eds., *Three New Mexico Chronicles,* Albuquerque, The Quivira Society, 1942.

Castañeda, Pedro de. See Winship; also Hammond and Rey, *Narratives.*

Catlin, George, *North American Indians: Being Letters and Notes on Their Manners, Customs, and Conditions, Written during Eight Years' Travel amongst the Wildest Tribes of Indians in North America, 1832-1839,* 2 vols., Edinburgh, John Grant, 1926.

Caywood, Louis R., *The Restored Mission of Nuestra Senora de Guadalupe de Zuni, Zuni, New Mexico,* St. Michaels, Arizona, St. Michael's Press, 1972.

The Century Illustrated Monthly Magazine, vol. 25-26 (Nov. 1882-Oct. 1883).

Chapman, Charles E., *Catalogue of Materials in the Archivo General de Indias for the History of the Pacific Coast and the American Southwest,* Berkeley, University of California Press, 1919.

Chavez, Fray Angelico, *Archives of the Archdiocese of Santa Fe, 1678-1900,* Washington, D.C., Academy of American Franciscan History, 1957.

—————, "The Carpenter Pueblo," *New Mexico Magazine,* vol. 49 (Sept.-Oct. 1971), pp. 26-33.

—————, *Coronado's Friars,* Washington, D.C., Academy of American Franciscan History, 1968.

—————, "The Gallegos Relación Reconsidered," *New Mexico Historical Review,* vol. 23 (1948), pp. 1-21.

—————, "La Jornada del Muerto," *New Mexico Magazine,* vol. 52 (Sept.-Oct. 1974), pp. 34-35.

—————, *Origins of New Mexico Families in the Spanish Colonial Period,* Santa Fe, Historical Society of New Mexico, 1954.

—————, ed., *The Oroz Codex,* Washington, D.C., Academy of American Franciscan History, 1972.

—————, "Pohé-yemo's Representative and the Pueblo Revolt of 1680," *New Mexico Historical Review,* vol. 42 (1967), pp. 85-126.

—————, "Some Original New Mexico Documents in California Libraries," *New Mexico Historical Review,* vol. 25 (1950), pp. 244-53.

—————, "The Unique Tomb of Fathers Zárate and de la Llana in Santa Fe," *New Mexico Historical Review,* vol. 40 (1965), pp. 101-15.

Chevalier, François, *Land and Society in Colonial Mexico: The Great Hacienda*, trans. Alvin Eustis, ed. Lesley Byrd Simpson, Berkeley and Los Angeles, University of California Press, 1966.

Coke, Van Deren, *Taos and Santa Fe: The Artist's Environment, 1882-1942*, Albuquerque, University of New Mexico Press, 1963.

Colección de documentos inéditos relativos al descubrimiento, conquista y organización de las antiguas posesiones españolas de América y Oceanía, 42 vols., Madrid, 1864-84.

Cumberland, Charles C., *Mexico: The Struggle for Modernity*, New York, Oxford University Press, 1968.

Curtis, Edward S., *The North American Indian*, vol. 17, Norwood, Mass., The Plimpton Press, 1926.

Cutts, James Madison, *The Conquest of California and New Mexico by the Forces of the United States in the Years 1846 and 1847*, Philadelphia, Carey and Hart, 1847, Albuquerque, Horn and Wallace, 1965.

Day, A. Grove, *Coronado's Quest: The Discovery of the Southwestern States*, Berkeley and Los Angeles, University of California Press, 1940.

Díaz, Albert James, *A Guide to the Microfilm of Papers relating to New Mexico Land Grants*, Albuquerque, University of New Mexico Press, 1960.

Documentos para la historia de Méjico, 21 vols., México, J. R. Navarro, 1853-1857.

Documentos para servir a la historia del Nuevo México, 1538-1778, Madrid, Ediciones José Porrúa Turanzas, 1962.

Domínguez. See Adams and Chavez.

Donohue, John Augustine, *After Kino, Jesuit Missions in Northwestern New Spain, 1711-1767*, Rome and St. Louis, Jesuit Historical Institute, 1969.

Dozier, Edward P., *The Pueblo Indians of North America*, New York, Holt, Rinehart, and Winston, 1970.

——————, "Spanish-Catholic Influences on Rio Grande Pueblo Religion," *American Anthropologist*, vol. 60 (1958), pp. 441-48.

Ellis, Florence Hawley, *A Reconstruction of the Basic Jemez Pattern of Social Organization, with Comparisons to Other Tanoan Social Structures*, Albuquerque, University of New Mexico Press, 1964.

Emory, W. H., *Notes of a Military Reconnaissance from Fort Leavenworth, in Missouri, to San Diego, in California, including part of the Arkansas, Del Norte, and Gila Rivers*, 30th Cong., 1st sess., House Ex. Doc. No. 41, Washington, D.C., Wendell and Van Benthuysen, 1848.

Espinosa, Isidro Félix de, *Crónica de los Colegios de Propaganda Fide de la Nueva España*, ed. Lino Gómez Canedo, Washington, D.C., Academy of American Franciscan History, 1964.

Espinosa, J. Manuel, *Crusaders of the Río Grande: The Story of Don Diego de Vargas and the Reconquest and Refounding of New Mexico*, Chicago, Institute of Jesuit History, 1942.

——————, ed., *First Expedition of Vargas into New Mexico, 1692*, Albuquerque, University of New Mexico Press, 1940.

——————, "Our Debt to the Franciscan Missionaries of New Mexico," *The Americas*, vol. 1 (1944), pp. 79-87.

Falconer, Thomas, *Letters and Notes on the Texan Santa Fe Expedition, 1841-1842*, ed. F. W. Hodge, New York, Dauber and Pine Bookshops, 1930.

Field. See Sunder.

Folmer, Henry, "Contraband Trade between Louisiana and New Mexico in the Eighteenth Century," *New Mexico Historical Review*, vol. 16 (1941), pp. 249-74.

——————, *Franco-Spanish Rivalry in North America, 1524-1763*, Glendale, Calif., Arthur H. Clark, 1953.

Forbes, Jack D., *Apache, Navaho, and Spaniard*, Norman, University of Oklahoma Press, 1960.

García Icazbalceta, Joaquín, ed., *Códice franciscano (Nueva colección de documentos para la historia de México)*, vol. 2, México, Editorial Salvador Chávez Hayhoe, 1941.

Gibson, Charles, *The Aztecs under Spanish Rule, A History of the Indians of the Valley of Mexico, 1519-1810*, Stanford, Stanford University Press, 1964.

——————, ed., *The Spanish Tradition in America*, New York, Harper and Row, 1968.

Gómez, Canedo, Lino, *Los archivos de la historia de América, período colonial español*, 2 vols., México, Instituto Panamericano de Geografía e Historia, 1961.

Greenleaf, Richard E., "Land and Water in Mexico and New Mexico 1700-1821," *New Mexico Historical Review*, vol. 47 (1972), pp. 85-112.

——————, "The Mexican Inquisition and the Enlightenment, 1763-1805," *New Mexico Historical Review*, vol. 41 (1966), pp. 181-96.

Gregg, Josiah, *Commerce of the Prairies*, ed. Max L. Moorhead, Norman, University of Oklahoma Press, 1954.

Gunnerson, Dolores A., *The Jicarilla Apaches: A Study in Survival*, DeKalb, Northern Illinois University Press, 1974.

——————, "The Southern Athabascans: Their Arrival in the Southwest," *El Palacio*, vol. 63 (1956), pp. 346-65.

Gunnerson, James H., and Dolores A. Gunnerson, "Evidence of Apaches at Pecos," *El Palacio*, vol. 76, no. 3 (1970), pp. 1-6.

Hackett, Charles Wilson, ed., *Historical Documents Relating to New Mexico, Nueva Vizcaya, and Approaches Thereto, to 1773, Collected by Adolph F. A. Bandelier and Fanny R. Bandelier*, 3 vols., Washington, D.C., Carnegie Institution, 1923-1937.

——————, ed., *Pichardo's Treatise on the Limits of Louisiana and Texas*, 4 vols., Austin, University of Texas Press, 1931-1946.

——————, ed., and Charmion Clair Shelby, trans., *Revolt of the Pueblo Indians of New Mexico and Otermín's Attempted Reconquest, 1680-1682*, 2 vols., Albuquerque, University of New Mexico Press, 1942, 1970.

Hall, Em, *A Study of Pecos Lands*, in progress.

Hammond, George P., ed., *A Guide to the Manuscript Collections of the Bancroft Library*, vol. 2 (Mexican and Central American Manuscripts), Berkeley and Los Angeles, University of California Press, 1972.

Hammond, George P., and Agapito Rey, *Don Juan de Oñate, Colonizer of New Mexico, 1595-1628,* 2 vols., Albuquerque, University of New Mexico Press, 1953.

——————— ———————, *Narratives of the Coronado Expedition 1540-1542,* Albuquerque, University of New Mexico Press, 1940.

——————— ———————, *Obregón's History of 16th Century Explorations in Western America,* Los Angeles, Wetzel Publishing Company, 1928.

——————— ———————, *The Rediscovery of New Mexico, 1580-1594,* Albuquerque, University of New Mexico, 1966.

Hanke, Lewis, *Aristotle and the American Indians: A Study in Race Prejudice in the Modern World,* Bloomington, Indiana University Press, 1959.

———————, *The Spanish Struggle for Justice in the Conquest of America,* Philadelphia, University of Pennsylvania Press, 1949.

Harrington, John Peabody, "The Ethnogeography of the Tewa Indians," *Twenty-Ninth Annual Report of the Bureau of American Ethnology,* Washington, D.C., Government Printing Office, 1916, pp. 29-636.

Hawley, Florence M., "The Role of Pueblo Social Organization in the Dissemination of Catholicism," *American Anthropologist,* vol. 48 (1946), pp. 407-15.

Hayes, Alden C., *The Four Churches of Pecos,* Albuquerque, University of New Mexico Press, 1974.

Hewett, Edgar L., "Studies on the Extinct Pueblo of Pecos," *American Anthropologist,* vol. 6 (1904), pp. 426-39. Extracted as "The Last Survivor of Pecos," *Records of the Past,* vol. 4 (1905), pp. 54-57.

Hewett, Edgar L., and Reginald G. Fisher, *Mission Monuments of New Mexico,* Albuquerque, University of New Mexico Press, 1943.

Hodge, Frederick Webb, ed., *Handbook of American Indians North of Mexico,* 2 parts, Bureau of American Ethnology, Bulletin 30, Washington, D.C., Government Printing Office, 1907-1910.

Holden, Jane, "A Preliminary Report on Arrowhead Ruin," *El Palacio,* vol. 62 (1955), pp. 102-19.

Hooton, Earnest A., *The Indians of Pecos Pueblo: A Study of Their Skeletal Remains,* New Haven, Yale University Press, 1930.

Icaza, Francisco A. de, *Conquistadores y pobladores de Nueva España: diccionario autobiográfico,* 2 vols., Madrid, Imprenta de "El Adelantado de Segovia," 1923.

James, Thomas, *Three Years Among the Indians and Mexicans,* Philadelphia and New York, J. B. Lippincott Co., 1962.

Jenkins, Myra Ellen, *Calendar of the Microfilm Edition of the Mexican Archives of New Mexico, 1821-1846,* Santa Fe, State of New Mexico Records Center, 1970.

———————, "Spanish Land Grants in the Tewa Area," *New Mexico Historical Review,* vol. 47 (1972), pp. 113-34.

———————, et al., *Calendar of the Spanish Archives of New*

Mexico, 1621-1821, Santa Fe, State of New Mexico Records Center, 1968.

——————, et al., *Guide to the Microfilm Edition of the Mexican Archives of New Mexico, 1821-1846,* Santa Fe, State of New Mexico Records Center, 1969.

——————, et al., *Guide to the Microfilm of the Spanish Archives of New Mexico, 1621-1821,* Santa Fe, State of New Mexico Records Center, 1967.

John, Elizabeth A. H., *Storms Brewed in Other Men's Worlds: The Confrontation of Indians, Spanish, and French in the Southwest,* 1540-1795, College Station, Texas A & M Press, 1975.

Jones, Oakah L., *Pueblo Warriors and Spanish Conquest,* Norman, University of Oklahoma Press, 1966.

Kelley, J. Charles, "Factors Involved in the Abandonment of Certain Peripheral Southwestern Settlements," *American Anthropologist,* vol. 54 (1952), pp. 356-87.

Kelly, Daniel T., *The Buffalo Head, A Century of Mercantile Pioneering in the Southwest,* Santa Fe, The Vergara Publishing Co., 1972.

Kelly, Henry W., *Franciscan Missions of New Mexico, 1740-1760,* Albuquerque, Historical Society of New Mexico, 1941.

Kendrick, T. D., *Mary of Agreda: The Life and Legend of a Spanish Nun,* London, Routledge and Kegan Paul, 1967.

Kenner, Charles L., *A History of New Mexican-Plains Indian Relations,* Norman, University of Oklahoma Press, 1969.

Kessell, John L., "Campaigning on the Upper Gila, 1756," *New Mexico Historical Review,* vol. 46 (1971), 133-60.

——————, "Diego Romero, the Plains Apaches, and the Inquisition," *The American West,* vol. 15, no. 3 (May-June 1978), pp. 12-16.

——————, *The Missions of New Mexico since 1776,* Albuquerque, University of New Mexico Press, in press.

Kidder, Alfred Vincent, *The Artifacts of Pecos,* New Haven, Yale University Press, 1932.

——————, "The Condition of the Main Pecos Ruin," *El Palacio,* vol. 4 (1917), pp. 18-21.

——————, "A Design Sequence from New Mexico," *Proceedings,* National Academy of Science, vol. 3 (1917), pp. 369-70.

——————, "Early Pecos Ruins on the Forked Lightning Ranch," *El Palacio,* vol. 21 (1926), pp. 275-83.

——————, *An Introduction to the Study of Southwestern Archaeology with a Preliminary Account of the Excavations at Pecos,* rev. ed., New Haven, Yale University Press, 1962.

——————, "The Old North Pueblo of Pecos," *El Palacio,* vol. 4 (1917), pp. 13-17.

——————, *Pecos, New Mexico: Archaeological Notes,* Andover, Phillips Academy, 1958.

——————, "Pecos Pueblo," *El Palacio,* vol. 58 (1951), pp. 83-89.

——————, "A Pipe of Unique Form from Pecos, New Mexico," Museum of the American Indian, Heye Foundation, *Indian Notes,* vol. 5 (1928), pp. 293-95.

——————, "The Pueblo of Pecos," *El Palacio,* vol. 3 (1916), pp. 43-49.

——————, "Southwestern Archeological Conference," *Science,* n.s., vol. 66 (1927), pp. 489-91.

Kidder, Alfred Vincent, and Charles A. Amsden, *The Pottery of Pecos,* vol. 1, Phillips Academy, Papers of the Southwest Expedition, vol. 5, 1931.

Kidder, Alfred Vincent, and Anna Shepard, *The Pottery of Pecos,* vol. 2, Phillips Academy, Papers of the Southwest Expedition, vol. 7, 1936.

Kidder, M. A., and Alfred Vincent Kidder, "Notes on the Pottery of Pecos," *American Anthropologist,* vol. 19, (1917), pp. 325-60.

Kubler, George, *The Rebuilding of San Miguel at Santa Fe in 1710,* Colorado Springs, The Taylor Museum, 1939.

——————, *The Religious Architecture of New Mexico in the Colonial Period and Since the American Occupation,* 4th ed., Albuquerque, University of New Mexico Press, 1972.

LaFora, Nicolás de, *Relación del viaje que hizo a los presidios internos situados en la frontera de la América Septentrional perteneciente al Rey de España,* ed. Vito Alessio Robles, México, Editorial Pedro Robredo, 1939. Translated and edited by Lawrence Kinnaird as *The Frontiers of New Spain: Nicolás de LaFora's Description, 1766-1768,* Berkeley, Quivira Society, 1958.

Lambert, Marjorie F., *Paa-ko, Archaeological Chronicle of an Indian Village in North Central New Mexico,* Santa Fe, School of American Research, 1954.

——————, "A Rare Stone Humpbacked Figurine from Pecos, New Mexico," *El Palacio,* vol. 64 (1957), pp. 93-108.

Lange, Charles H., *Cochití, A New Mexico Pueblo, Past and Present,* Carbondale, Southern Illinois University Press, 1968.

——————, "Plains-Southwestern Intercultural Relations during the Historic Period," *Ethnohistory,* vol. 4 (1957), pp. 150-73.

——————, "A Reappraisal of Evidence of Plains Influences among the Rio Grande Pueblos," *Southwestern Journal of Anthropology,* vol. 9 (1953), pp. 212-30.

Leonard, Irving A., *Baroque Times in Old Mexico: Seventeenth-Century Persons, Places, and Practices,* Ann Arbor, University of Michigan Press, 1966.

Libro de entradas y profesiones de novicios de este convento de Padre San Francisco de México, 1562-1680 (LEP), Bancroft Library, University of California, Berkeley, Mexican Manuscripts 216-218.

Loomis, Noel M., and Abraham P. Nasatir, *Pedro Vial and the Roads to Santa Fe,* Norman, University of Oklahoma Press, 1967.

Lowie, Robert H., *Indians of the Plains,* Garden City, N.Y., The Natural History Press, 1963.

Lummis, Charles Fletcher, *The Man Who Married the Moon and Other Pueblo Indian Folk-stories,* New York, The Century Co., 1894.

[Lummis, Charles Fletcher, ed.,] "Some Unpublished History: A New Mexican Episode in 1748," *Land of Sunshine,* vol. 8 (Jan. 1898), pp. 74-78, (Feb. 1898), pp. 126-30.

Maas, Otto, *Las órdenes religiosas de España y la colonización de América en la segunda parte del siglo XVIII: estadísticas y otros documentos,* 2 vols., Barcelona, 1918 and 1929.

Madoz, Pascual, *Diccionario geográfico-estadístico-histórico de España y sus posesiones de ultramar,* 16 vols., Madrid, 1845-1850.

McCarty, Kieran R., "Los franciscanos en la frontera chichimeca," *Historia Mexicana,* vol. 11 (1962), pp. 321-60.

McCloskey, Michael B., *The Formative Years of the Missionary College of Santa Cruz of Querétaro, 1683-1733,* Washington, D.C., Academy of American Franciscan History, 1955.

Mecham, J. Lloyd, *Francisco de Ibarra and Nueva Vizcaya,* Durham, N.C., Duke University Press, 1927.

Mendinueta, Pedro Fermín de, *Indian and Mission Affairs in New Mexico, 1773,* ed. Marc Simmons, Santa Fe, Stagecoach Press, 1965.

Meyer, Theodosius, *St. Francis and the Franciscans in New Mexico,* Santa Fe, Historical Society of New Mexico, 1926.

Miller, Robert Ryal, ed., "New Mexico in Mid-Eighteenth Century: A Report Based on Governor Vélez Cachupín's Inspection," *Southwestern Historical Quarterly,* vol. 79 (1975-1976), pp. 166-81.

Montgomery, Ross G., Watson Smith, and John O. Brew, *Franciscan Awatovi,* Cambridge, Mass., Peabody Museum, 1949.

Moorhead, Max L., *The Apache Frontier: Jacobo Ugarte and Spanish-Indian Relations in Northern New Spain, 1769-1791,* Norman, University of Oklahoma Press, 1968.

——————, *New Mexico's Royal Road: Trade and Travel on the Chihuahua Trail,* Norman, University of Oklahoma Press, 1958.

——————, *The Presidio: Bastion of the Spanish Borderlands,* Norman, University of Oklahoma Press, 1975.

Morfi, Juan Agustín de, *Diario y derrotero (1771-1781),* eds. Eugenio del Hoyo and Malcolm D. McLean, Monterrey, Instituto Tecnológico y de Estudios Superiores, 1967.

Nasatir, Abraham P., *Borderland in Retreat: From Spanish Louisiana to the Far Southwest,* Albuquerque, University of New Mexico Press, 1976.

Navarro García, Luis, *Don José de Gálvez y la Comandancia General de las Provincias Internas del Norte de Nueva España,* Sevilla, Escuela de Estudios Hispano-Americanos, 1964.

——————, *Las Provincias Internas en el siglo XIX,* Sevilla, Escuela de Estudios Hispano-Americanos, 1965.

Nelson, C. T., "The Teeth of the Indians of Pecos Pueblo," *American Journal of Physical Anthropology,* vol 23 (1938), pp. 261-94.

Ocaranza, Fernando, *Establecimientos franciscanos en el misterioso reino de Nuevo México,* México, 1934.

Opler, Morris E., Review of Gunnerson's *The Jicarilla Apaches* in *Plains Anthropologist,* vol. 20 (1975), pp. 150-57.

Ortiz, Alfonso, *The Tewa World: Space, Time, Being, and Becom-*

ing in *A Pueblo Society,* Chicago, The University of Chicago Press, 1969.

Parsons, Elsie Clews, *The Pueblo of Jemez,* New Haven, Yale University Press, 1925.

Paso y Troncoso, Francisco del, *Epistolario de Nueva España, 1505-1818,* 16 vols., México, Antigua Librería Robredo, 1939-1942.

Peabody, Charles, "A Prehistoric Wind Instrument from Pecos, New Mexico," *American Anthropologist,* vol. 19 (1917), pp. 30-33.

Pérez de Villagrá. See Villagrá.

Pike, Albert, *Prose Sketches and Poems Written in the Western Country,* ed. David J. Weber, Albuquerque, Calvin Horn Publisher, 1967.

Pino. See Carroll and Haggard.

Polzer, Charles W., "The Franciscan Entrada into Sonora, 1645-1652: A Jesuit Chronicle," *Arizona and the West,* vol. 14 (1972), pp. 253-78.

Poole, Stafford, " 'War by Fire and Blood,' The Church and the Chichimecas 1585," *The Americas,* vol. 22 (1965), pp. 115-37.

Powell, Philip Wayne, "Franciscans on the Silver Frontier of Old Mexico," *The Americas,* vol. 3 (1947), pp. 295-310.

——————, *Ponzoña en las nieves,* Madrid, Ediciones José Porrúa Turanzas, 1966.

——————, *Soldiers, Indians, and Silver: The Northward Advance of New Spain, 1550-1600,* Berkeley and Los Angeles, University of California Press, 1952.

Priestley, Herbert Ingram, *José de Gálvez: Visitor-General of New Spain, 1765-1771,* Berkeley, University of California Press, 1916.

——————, *Tristán de Luna, Conquistador of the Old South,* Glendale, Arthur H. Clark, 1936.

Prince, L. Bradford, *Spanish Mission Churches of New Mexico,* Cedar Rapids, The Torch Press, 1915.

Read, Benjamin M., "The Last Word on 'Montezuma,' " *New Mexico Historical Review,* vol. 1 (1926), pp. 350-58.

Reeve, Frank D., *History of New Mexico,* 2 vols., New York, Lewis Historical Publishing Co., 1961.

——————, "Navaho Foreign Affairs, 1795-1846: Part I, 1795-1815," *New Mexico Historical Review,* vol. 46 (1971), pp. 101-32.

Revillagigedo, Conde de, *Informe sobre las misiones, 1793, e instrucción reservada al Marqués de Branciforte, 1794,* ed. José Bravo Ugarte, México, Editorial Jus, 1966.

Rey, Agapito, "Missionary Aspects of the Founding of New Mexico," *New Mexico Historical Review,* vol. 23 (1948), pp. 22-31.

Ricard, Robert, *The Spiritual Conquest of Mexico: An Essay on the Apostolate and the Evangelizing Methods of the Mendicant Orders in New Spain: 1523-1572,* trans. Lesley Byrd Simpson, Berkeley and Los Angeles, University of California Press, 1966.

Rice, Josiah M., *A Cannoneer in Navajo Country: Journal of Private Josiah M. Rice, 1851,* ed. Richard H. Dillon, Denver, Old West Publishing Co., 1970.

Riley, Carroll L., "Early Spanish-Indian Communication in the Greater Southwest," *New Mexico Historical Review,* vol. 46 (1971), pp. 285-314.

Rittenhouse, Jack D., *The Santa Fe Trail: A Historical Bibliography,* Albuquerque, University of New Mexico Press, 1971.

Rivera, Pedro de, *Diario y derrotero de lo caminado, visto y observado en la visita que hizo a los presidios de la Nueva España septentrional,* ed. Vito Alessio Robles, México, Secretaría de la Defensa Nacional, 1946.

Rivera Cambas, Manuel, *Los gobernantes de México.* México, J. M. Aguilar Ortiz, 1872.

Roberts, Helen H., "The Reason for the Departure of the Pecos Indians for Jemez Pueblo," *American Anthropologist,* vol. 34 (1932), pp. 359-60.

Rosa Figueroa, Francisco Antonio de la, Becerro general menológico y cronológico de todos los religiosos que de las tres parcialidades conviene, a saber Padres de España, Hijos de Provincia, y Criollos, ha habido en esta Santa Provincia del Santo Evangelio desde su fundación hasta el presente año de 1764, Newberry Library, Chicago, Ayer Collection.

——————, Prontuario general y específico y colectivo de nomenclaturas de todos los religiosos que ha habido en esta Santa Provincia del Santo Evangelio desde su fundación, University of Texas Library, Austin, Latin American Manuscripts.

Santamaría, Francisco J., *Diccionario de Mejicanismos,* México, Editorial Porrúa, 1959.

Scholes, France V., *Church and State in New Mexico, 1610-1650,* Albuquerque, Historical Society of New Mexico, 1937.

——————, "Civil Government and Society in New Mexico in the Seventeenth Century," *New Mexico Historical Review,* vol. 10 (1935), pp. 71-111.

——————, "Correction," *New Mexico Historical Review,* vol. 19 (1944), pp. 243-46.

——————, "Documents for the History of the New Mexican Missions in the Seventeenth Century," *New Mexico Historical Review,* vol. 4 (1929), pp. 45-58, 195-201.

——————, "The First Decade of the Inquisition in New Mexico," *New Mexico Historical Review,* vol. 10 (1935), pp. 195-241.

——————, "Juan Martínez de Montoya, Settler and Conquistador of New Mexico," *New Mexico Historical Review,* vol. 19 (1944), pp. 337-42.

——————, "Notes on the Jemez Missions in the Seventeenth Century," *El Palacio,* vol. 44 (1938), pp. 61-71, 93-102.

——————, "Problems in the Early Ecclesiastical History of New Mexico," *New Mexico Historical Review,* vol. 7 (1932), pp. 32-74.

——————, "Royal Treasury Records Relating to the Province of New Mexico, 1596-1683," *New Mexico Historical Review,* vol. 50 (1975), pp. 5-23, 139-64.

——————, "The Supply Service of the New Mexican Missions in the Seventeenth Century," *New Mexico Historical Review,* vol. 5 (1930), pp. 93-115, 186-210, 386-404.

——————, *Troublous Times in New Mexico, 1659-1670,* Albuquerque, Historical Society of New Mexico, 1942.

Scholes, France V., and Lansing B. Bloom, "Friar Personnel and Mission Chronology, 1598-1629," *New Mexico Historical Review,* vol. 19 (1944), pp. 319-36, and vol. 20 (1945), pp. 58-82.

Scholes, France V., and H. P. Mera, "Some Aspects of the Jumano Problem," *Contributions to American Anthropology and History,* vol. 4, no. 34 (1940), Carnegie Institution Publications, no. 523, pp. 265-99.

Schroeder, Albert H., "An Ethnohistory of Pecos," article prepared for the forthcoming revision of *The Handbook of North American Indians.*

——————, "A Re-analysis of the Routes of Coronado and Oñate into the Plains in 1541 and 1601," *Plains Anthropologist,* vol. 7, no. 15 (Feb. 1962), pp. 2-23.

——————, "Shifting for Survival in the Spanish Southwest," *New Mexico Historical Review,* vol. 43 (1968), pp. 291-310.

——————, *A Study of the Apache Indians,* Parts I-III, New York, Garland Publishing, 1974.

Schroeder, Albert H., and Dan S. Matson, eds., *A Colony on the Move: Gaspar Castaño de Sosa's Journal, 1590-1591,* Santa Fe, School of American Research, 1965.

Seco Serrano, Carlos., ed., *Cartas de Sor María de Jesús de Ágreda y de Felipe IV,* in *Biblioteca de Autores Españoles,* vols. 108-09, Madrid, Ediciones Atlas, 1958.

Simmons, Marc, *Border Comanches: Seven Spanish Colonial Documents, 1785-1819,* Santa Fe, Stagecoach Press, 1967.

——————, ed., "Governor Anza, the Lipan Apaches and Pecos Pueblo," *El Palacio,* vol. 77, no. 1 (1970), pp. 35-40.

——————, "The Mysterious A Tribe of the Southern Plains," in *The Changing Ways of Southwestern Indians: A Historic Perspective,* ed. Albert H. Schroeder, Glorieta, N.M., Rio Grande Press, 1973.

——————, "New Mexico's Smallpox Epidemic of 1780-1781," *New Mexico Historical Review,* vol. 41 (1966), pp. 319-26.

——————, *Opening the Santa Fe Trail, One Hundred and Fifty Years, 1821-1971,* Cerrillos, N.M., Galisteo Press, 1971.

——————, *Spanish Government in New Mexico,* Albuquerque, University of New Mexico Press, 1968.

——————, *Witchcraft in the Southwest: Spanish and Indian Supernaturalism on the Rio Grande,* Flagstaff, Northland Press, 1974.

Simpson, James H., *Journal of a Military Reconnaissance from Santa Fé, New Mexico, to the Navajo Country,* Philadelphia, Lippincott, Grambo, and Co., 1852.

Spicer, Edward H., *Cycles of Conquest: The Impact of Spain, Mexico, and the United States on the Indians of the Southwest, 1533-1960,* Tucson, University of Arizona Press, 1962.

Spiess, Lincoln Bunce, "Church Music in Seventeenth-Century

New Mexico," *New Mexico Historical Review,* vol. 40 (1965), pp. 5-21.

Streit, Robert, *Bibliotheca Missionum,* vol. 3, Aachen, Aachener missionsdruckerei, 1927.

Stubbs, Stanley A., Bruce T. Ellis, and Alfred E. Dittert, Jr., " 'Lost' Pecos Church," *El Palacio,* vol. 64 (1957), pp. 67-92.

Sunder, John E., ed., *Matt Field on the Santa Fe Trail,* Norman, University of Oklahoma Press, 1960.

Tamarón y Romeral, Pedro, *Demostración del vastísimo obispado de la Nueva Vizcaya, 1765,* ed. Vito Alessio Robles, México, Antigua Librería Robredo, 1937.

——————, *Relación del atentado sacrilegio, cometido por tres indios de un pueblo de la provincia del Nuevo México; y de el severo castigo, que executó la divina justicia con el fautor principal de ellos,* México, Imprenta de la Bibliotheca Mexicana, 1763.

Thomas, Alfred Barnaby, *After Coronado, Spanish Exploration Northwest of New Mexico, 1696-1727,* 2nd ed., Norman, University of Oklahoma Press, 1966.

——————, "Antonio de Bonilla and Spanish Plans for the Defense of New Mexico 1772-1778" in *New Spain and the Anglo-American West: Historical Contributions Presented to Herbert Eugene Bolton,* 2 vols., Los Angeles, privately printed, 1932, II, pp. 183-209.

——————, ed., "Documents Bearing upon the Northern Frontier of New Mexico, 1818-1819," *New Mexico Historical Review,* vol. 4 (1929), pp. 146-64.

——————, *Forgotten Frontiers: A Study of the Spanish Indian Policy of Don Juan Bautista de Anza, Govenor of New Mexico, 1777-1787,* Norman, University of Oklahoma Press, 1932.

——————, *The Plains Indians and New Mexico, 1751-1778,* Albuquerque, University of New Mexico Press, 1940.

——————, "San Carlos, A Comanche Pueblo on the Arkansas River, 1787," *The Colorado Magazine,* vol. 6 (1929), pp. 79-91.

——————, *Teodoro de Croix and the Northern Frontier of New Spain, 1776-1783,* Norman, University of Oklahoma Press, 1941.

Twitchell, Ralph Emerson, "The Ancient Pueblo of Pecos," *Santa Fe Employes' Magazine,* vol. 4 (Oct. 1910), pp. 27-32.

——————, *The Leading Facts of New Mexican History,* vols. 1 and 2, Cedar Rapids, The Torch Press, 1911-1912, Albuquerque, Horn and Wallace, 1963.

——————, ed., "The Pueblo Revolt of 1696: Extracts from the Journal of General Don Diego de Vargas," *Old Santa Fe,* vol. 3 (1916), pp. 333-73.

——————, *The Spanish Archives of New Mexico,* 2 vols., Cedar Rapids, The Torch Press, 1914.

Tyler, S. Lyman, and H. Darrel Taylor, eds., "The Report of Fray Alonso de Posada in Relation to Quivira and Teguayo," *New Mexico Historical Review,* vol. 33 (1958), pp. 285-314.

U.S. Department of the Interior, National Park Service, *Draft*

Environmental Statement, Proposed Master Plan and Development Concept Plan, Pecos National Monument, New Mexico, Washington, D.C., Government Printing Office, 1975.

U.S. Indian Claims Commission, *Cases Decided by the Indian Claims Commission,* vols. 4 (August 26, 1955-January 18, 1957) and 8A (July 31, 1959-March 1, 1960).

Vélez de Escalante, Silvestre, Extracto de Noticias, Biblioteca Nacional, México, Archivo Franciscano, New Mexico Documents, legajo 3, no. 1.

Vetancurt, Agustín de, *Teatro Mexicano: descripción breve de los sucessos exemplares de la Nueva-España en el nuevo mundo occidental de las Indias* [1698], 4 vols., Madrid, José Porrúa Turanzas, 1960-1961.

Villagrá, Gaspar Pérez de, *History of New Mexico by Gaspar Pérez de Villagrá, Alcalá, 1610,* trans. Gilberto Espinosa, Los Angeles, The Quivira Society, 1933.

Vivian, Gordon, *Gran Quivira: Excavations in a 17th-Century Jumano Pueblo,* Washington, D.C., National Park Service, 1964.

Wagner, Henry R., *The Spanish Southwest, 1542-1794: An Annotated Bibliography,* Albuquerque, Quivira Society, 1937.

Wallace, Ernest and E. Adamson Hoebel, *The Comanches, Lords of the South Plains,* Norman, University of Oklahoma Press, 1952.

Warner, Ted J., "Don Félix Martínez and the Santa Fe Presidio, 1693-1730," *New Mexico Historical Review,* vol. 45 (1970), pp. 269-310.

Webb, James Josiah, *Adventures in the Santa Fé Trade, 1844-1847,* ed. Ralph P. Bieber, Glendale, Arthur H. Clark Co., 1931.

Weber, David J., *The Taos Trappers: The Fur Trade in the Far Southwest, 1540-1846,* Norman, University of Oklahoma Press, 1971.

——————————, "An Unforgettable Day: Facundo Melgares on Independence," *New Mexico Historical Review,* vol. 48 (1973), pp. 27-44.

Wedel, Waldo R., *An Introduction to Kansas Archeology,* Bureau of American Ethnology, Bulletin 174, Washington, D.C., Government Printing Office, 1959.

West, Robert C., *The Mining Community in Northern New Spain: The Parral Mining District, Ibero-Americana,* vol. 30, Berkeley and Los Angeles, University of California Press, 1949.

Whipple, A. W., *Report of Explorations for a Railway Route, near the Thirty-Fifth Parallel of North Latitude, from the Mississippi River to the Pacific Ocean,* in *Reports of Explorations and Surveys . . . 1853-4,* vol. 3, Washington, D.C., Beverley Tucker Printer, 1856.

Wilson, Richard L., *Short Ravelings from a Long Yarn, or Camp March Sketches of the Santa Fe Trail,* Santa Ana, Calif., Fine Arts Press, 1936.

Winship, George Parker, "The Coronado Expedition," *Fourteenth Annual Report,* Bureau of Ethnology, Smithsonian Institution, 1892-1893, Part I, Washington, D.C., Government Printing Office, 1896, pp. 329-613.

Woodbury, Richard B., *Alfred V. Kidder,* New York, Columbia University Press, 1973.

Zorita, Alonso de, *Life and Labor in Ancient Mexico: The "Brief and Summary Relation of the Lords of New Spain,"* ed. Benjamin Keen, New Brunswick, N.J., Rutgers University Press, 1963.

inòex